T0203043

Lecture Notes in Computer Science 14627

Formal Methods

Subline of Lecture Notes in Computer Science

More information about this series at https://link.springer.com/bookseries/558

Nathaniel Benz · Divya Gopinath ·
Nija Shi
Editors

NASA
Formal Methods

16th International Symposium, NFM 2024
Moffett Field, CA, USA, June 4–6, 2024
Proceedings

Editors
Nathaniel Benz
NASA Ames Research Center
Moffett Field, CA, USA

Divya Gopinath
NASA Ames Research Center
Moffett Field, CA, USA

Nija Shi
NASA Ames Research Center
Moffet Field, CA, USA

ISSN 0302-9743 ISSN 1611-3349 (electronic)
Lecture Notes in Computer Science
ISBN 978-3-031-60697-7 ISBN 978-3-031-60698-4 (eBook)
https://doi.org/10.1007/978-3-031-60698-4

This Springer imprint is published by the registered company Springer Nature Switzerland AG
The registered company address is: Gewerbestrasse 11, 6330 Cham, Switzerland

Preface

Recent years have seen a surge in the complexity of mission- and safety-critical systems widely used at NASA and in the aerospace industry. For instance, there is an increasing need for autonomous systems in deep space missions including NASA's Moon to Mars exploration plans. NASA and the aerospace industry are at the frontier of the effort to develop formal analysis approaches to ensure system safety and certification. However, new challenges have emerged for system specification, development, verification, and the need for system-wide fault detection, diagnosis, and prognostics.

The NASA Formal Methods (NFM) Symposium is a forum to foster collaboration between theoreticians and practitioners from NASA, other government agencies, academia, and industry, with the goal of identifying challenges and providing solutions towards achieving assurance for such critical systems. The focus of this symposium is on formal techniques for software and system assurance for applications in space, aviation, robotics, and other NASA-relevant safety-critical systems. NFM is an annual event organized by the NFM steering committee, comprised of researchers spanning several NASA centers. The series began in 1990 as the Langley Formal Methods Workshop (LFM) at NASA Langley and later became an annual NASA-wide event in 2009 when the inaugural NASA Formal Methods Symposium was held at the NASA Ames Research Center. The symposium is hosted by a different NASA center each year.

This year's symposium, the 16th NASA Formal Methods Symposium (NFM 2024), was held June 4–6, 2024 at the NASA Ames Research Center in Moffett Field, California, USA. This volume contains the proceedings for NFM 2024, which encouraged submissions in the topics of interest listed below. This year NFM extended its focus to also include safety assurance of machine learning enabled autonomous systems, formal methods for digital transformation, and accessibility for new industries.

– Advances in Formal Methods:

- Formal verification, model checking, and static analysis
- Interactive and automated theorem proving
- Program and specification synthesis, code transformation and generation
- Run-time verification and test case generation
- Techniques and algorithms for scaling formal methods
- Design for verification and correct-by-design techniques
- Requirements generation, specification, and validation

– Integration of Formal Methods:

- Use of machine learning techniques in formal methods
- Integration of formal methods and software engineering

- Integration of diverse formal methods techniques
- Combination of formal methods with simulation and analysis techniques

– Formal Methods in Practice:

- Experience reports of application of formal methods in industry
- Use of formal methods in education
- Applications of formal methods in; (i) concurrent and distributed systems, (ii) fault-detection, diagnostics, and prognostics systems, and (iii) human-machine interaction analysis
- Combination of formal methods with simulation and analysis techniques

– Safety Assurance of Autonomous Systems:

- Verification of machine learning (ML) enabled systems
- Runtime monitoring or model checking to ensure safe operation
- Formal specifications and modeling of ML enabled systems
- Case-studies/experience reports exploring the application of formal methods in autonomous safety-critical, cyber-physical and hybrid systems
- Using formal evidence for certification of ML enabled systems

– Formal Methods for Digital Transformation:

- Applications related to Digital Twin & Digital Thread
- Verification for integrated design and manufacturing
- AI digital assistants for system.design
- Runtime monitoring for Smart Campus and Smart Cities

– Accessibility of Formal Methods for New Industries:

- "New Space" markets
- Advanced Air Mobility and Startup Aviation
- Formal Methods as a Service

The main program contained two categories of papers: (1) regular papers, presenting fully developed work and complete results, and (2) short papers, presenting novel and publicly available tools, case studies detailing applications of formal methods, and new emerging ideas in the topics of interest.

We received 80 abstract submissions, which ultimately resulted in 68 paper submissions. The symposium accepted a total of 26 papers (20 regular, 6 short) to be presented, resulting in an overall acceptance rate of 38% (43% regular, 29% short). Amongst the short papers, there were three tool papers, two papers on new and emerging ideas, and one case study paper. The papers were reviewed by an international program committee of 59 members from a mix of academia, government, and industry. All submissions went through a rigorous single-blind reviewing process followed by a discussion period overseen by the program committee chairs. Each submission was reviewed by at least 3 reviewers and each PC member reviewed at least 3 papers. Submitting authors listed affiliations from 10 countries; USA (54), Germany (12), France (7), UK (7), Italy (4), China (3), India (1), Netherlands (1), Austria (1) and Japan (1).

The main program featured three invited talks with a common theme of safety for autonomous systems. The program began with a talk by Butler Hine, Project Manager for the HelioSwarm mission, who shed light on the challenges faced by future NASA Science and Exploration Missions in employing autonomy with little human control. Corina Păsăreanu presented a talk on Day 2 that covered formal verification and run-time monitoring to provide safety guarantees for autonomous systems that employ learning-enabled components such as deep neural networks (DNNs) for visual perception. She is an ACM Fellow and IEEE ASE Fellow, working at the NASA Ames Research Center. Day 3 featured Simon Burton, chair of Systems Safety at the University of York. He presented an in-depth look into emerging standards for AI safety for the automotive industry.

The paper presentations were categorized into the following sessions: *Advances in Solver Technology*, *Formal Methods for Program Analysis and Verification*, *SMT-Based Assurance of Behavioral Specifications*, *Formal Methods for Learning-Enabled Systems*, *Formal Methods for Automotive Systems*, *Formal Methods for Robotics*, and *Formal Methods for Software Engineering*. There was an equal distribution of papers under each category, with a combination of in-person and virtual presentations.

In addition to the main program, the symposium also featured a panel session on Trusted Autonomy, chaired by Guillaume Brat. The panel discussed challenges associated with the verification and validation (V&V) of machine learning components in critical systems in domains including aviation, automotive, space, and many others. Panelists represented prominent personalities in the field, including Huafeng Yu (Senior Scientist from US Department of Transport), Jean-Guillaume Durand (Applied Scientist from Xwing), Marco Pavone (Director of Autonomous Vehicle Research at NVIDIA), and Darren Cofer (Principal Fellow at Collins Aerospace).

The symposium also hosted a tool demonstration session where authors were given the opportunity to showcase their tools interactively with attendees. The session covered a wide range of software tools applying a range of formal techniques, including (i) testing (ii) requirement specification (iii) theorem proving (iv) constraint solving, and (v) SMT for multi-robot task allocation. These techniques were applied in a variety of different application domains, such as (i) urban automated driving (ii) hospitals (iii) robotic missions, and (iv) cyber-physical systems.

The organizers are grateful to the authors for submitting their work to NFM 2024 and to all invited speakers for sharing their insights. NFM 2024 would not have been possible without the work of the outstanding Program Committee and additional reviewers, the support of the Steering Committee, the support of the NASA Ames Research Center, and the general support of the NASA Formal Methods community. The NFM 2024 website can be found at: https://conf.researchr.org/home/nfm-2024.

June 2024

Nathan Benz
Divya Gopinath
Nija Shi

Organization

General and Program Committee Chairs

Nathan Benz	NASA Ames Research Center, USA
Divya Gopinath	KBR Inc./NASA Ames Research Center, USA
Nija Shi	NASA Ames Research Center, USA

Steering Committee

Julia Badger	NASA Johnson Space Center, USA
Aaron Dutle	NASA Langley Research Center, USA
Klaus Havelund	NASA Jet Propulsion Laboratory, USA
Michael R. Lowry	NASA Ames Research Center, USA
Kristin Y. Rozier	Iowa State University, USA
Johann Schumann	KBR Inc./NASA Ames Research Center, USA

Program Committee

Julia Badger	NASA Johnson Space Center, USA
Guillaume P. Brat	NASA Ames Research Center, USA
Tevfik Bultan	University of California at Santa Barbara, USA
Radu Calinescu	University of York, UK
Rafael C. Cardoso	University of Aberdeen, UK
Chih-Hong Cheng	Fraunhofer IKS/University of Hildesheim, Germany
Darren Cofer	Collins Aerospace, USA
Misty Davies	NASA Ames Research Center, USA
Ewen Denney	NASA Ames Research Center, USA
Clare Dixon	University of Manchester, UK
Jin Song Dong	National University of Singapore, Singapore
Aaron Dutle	NASA Langley Research Center, USA
Marie Farrell	The University of Manchester, UK
Angelo Ferrando	The University of Modena and Reggio Emilia, Italy
Antonio Filieri	AWS and Imperial College London, USA
Michael Fisher	University of Manchester, UK
Alwyn Goodloe	NASA Langley Research Center, USA
George Hagen	NASA Langley Research Center, USA
Klaus Havelund	NASA Jet Propulsion Laboratory, USA
Boyue Caroline Hu	University of Toronto, Canada
Calum Imrie	University of York, UK
Inigo Incer	Caltech, USA
Taylor T. Johnson	Vanderbilt University, USA
Andreas Katis	KBR Inc./NASA Ames Research Center, USA

Sarfraz Khurshid	University of Texas at Austin, USA
Edward Kim	University of California at Berkeley, USA
Joe Kiniry	Galois Inc., USA
Rory Lipkis	NASA Ames Research Center, USA
Alessio Lomuscio	Imperial College London, UK
Michael R. Lowry	NASA Ames Research Center, USA
Sandy Lozito	NASA Ames Research Center, USA
Matt Luckcuck	University of Nottingham, UK
Ravi Mangal	Carnegie Mellon University, USA
Lisa Marsso	University of Toronto, Canada
Anastasia Mavridou	KBR Inc./NASA Ames Research Center, USA
Sayan Mitra	University of Illinois at Urbana-Champaign, USA
Stefan Mitsch	DePaul University, USA
Cesar Munoz	NASA Langley Research Center, USA
Natasha Neogi	NASA Langley Research Center, USA
Corina S. Păsăreanu	Carnegie Mellon University at Silicon Valley/NASA Ames Research Center, USA
Ivan Perez	NASA Ames Research Center, USA
Lee Pike	Galois Inc., USA
Elvinia Riccobene	University of Milan, Italy
Kristin Yvonne Rozier	Iowa State University, USA
Sriram Sankaranarayanan	University of Colorado, USA
Johann Schumann	KBR Inc./NASA Ames Research Center, USA
Christel Seguin	ONERA, France
Chung-chieh Shah	Indiana University, USA
Satnam Singh	Groq, USA
Jun Sun	Singapore Management University, Singapore
Youcheng Sun	The University of Manchester, UK
Hazem Torfah	Chalmers University of Technology, Sweden
Martin Torngren	KTH, Sweden
Elena Troubitsyna	KTH, Sweden
Edwin Westbrook	Galois Inc., USA
Haoze Wu	Stanford University, USA
Mengwei Xu	University of Newcastle, UK
Sinem Getir Yaman	University of York, UK
Huafeng Yu	U.S. Department of Transportation, USA

Additional Reviewers

Lina Marsso
Kevin Cheang
Alejandro Luque Cerpa
Daniel Bethell
Gianfilippo Fornaro
Conor Reynolds
José Manuel Gaspar Sánchez
Kaige Tan
Laura Titolo
Gricel Vazquez
Laura Titolo
Lei Feng
Joseph Slagel
Richard Schmoetten
Louise Dennis
Gricel Vazquez Flores

Sponsors

Abstracts of Invited Talks

Autonomy Challenges for Future NASA Science and Exploration Missions

Butler Hine

HelioSwarm Project Manager
NASA Ames Research Center, USA
butler.p.hine@nasa.gov

Abstract

Future NASA Robotic Science and Exploration Missions are vastly enabled by high-level autonomy software capable of making critical decisions independently of human operators. Current missions are accomplished using a combination of direct human control and preprogrammed automatic responses. This approach has worked well in the past for certain classes of missions, but represents a limit on what we may accomplish in the future due to communications delays, mission complexity, or cost. Future missions need to operate in regimes in which direct human control is either impossible, impractical, or too expensive. Employing autonomy for these missions present formidable problems for mission designers, however, and will require robust implementation of software providing high levels of independent decision making to maintain vehicle health and safety, accomplish complex science and mission goals, and adapt to changing circumstances or opportunities.

Biography

Hine is an active space flight project manager at NASA Ames Research Center. He is currently the Project Manager for the HelioSwarm mission, which will lead to understanding the cascade and dissipation of energy in turbulent magnetized plasmas by using a novel swarm of spacecraft to investigate the physics of turbulence. He was previously the Project Manager for the LADEE mission, a Lunar science orbiter which launched in 2013 and successfully completed its mission in 2014. LADEE measured Lunar dust and examined the Lunar exosphere near its pristine state, prior to future significant human activity. LADEE also tested an optical communications payload from the Moon, which is an important technology enabling high-bandwidth communications links for future planetary missions. Prior to this, Hine managed the Small Spacecraft Division at NASA ARC, which developed ways to build low-cost, high-performance spacecraft to enable future NASA missions. He has also managed various NASA programs, such as the Robotic Lunar Exploration Program, the Computing, Information, and Communications Technology Program, and the Intelligent Systems Program. His earlier NASA career includes directing the Intelligent

Mechanisms Laboratory at NASA Ames Research Center, which pioneered the use of telepresence and virtual reality to control remote science exploration systems. Outside of NASA, Hine was President and CEO of a software start-up company which developed advanced visualization tools for managing large corporate networks. His background includes work in spacecraft design, flight software and avionics, information systems, radio and optical astronomy, optical instrumentation, machine vision, robotics, and information visualization. His research interests include low-cost spacecraft designs, avionics architectures, embedded systems, space telerobotics, image processing, machine vision, and 3D visualization.

Formal Verification and Run-time Monitoring for Learning-Enabled Autonomous Systems

Corina Păsăreanu

ACM Distinguished Scientist
NASA Ames, CMU, USA
corina.s.pasareanu@nasa.gov

Abstract

Providing safety guarantees for autonomous systems is difficult as these systems operate in complex environments that require the use of learning-Enabled components, such as deep neural networks (DNNs) for visual perception. DNNs are hard to analyze due to their size (they can have thousands or millions of parameters), lack of formal specifications (DNNs are typically learnt from labeled data, in the absence of any formal requirements), and sensitivity to small changes in the environment. We present compositional techniques for the formal verification of safety properties of such autonomous systems. The main idea is to abstract the hard-to-analyze components of the autonomous system, such as DNN-based perception and environmental dynamics, with either probabilistic or worst-case abstractions. This makes the system amenable to formal analysis using off-the-shelf model checking tools, enabling the derivation of specifications for the behavior of the abstracted components such that system safety is guaranteed. The derived specifications can be used as run-time monitors deployed on the DNN outputs. We illustrate the idea in a case study from the autonomous airplane domain.

Biography

Corina Pasareanu is an ACM Fellow and an IEEE ASE Fellow, working at NASA Ames. She is affiliated with KBR and Carnegie Mellon University's CyLab. Her research interests include model checking, symbolic execution, compositional verification, probabilistic software analysis, autonomy, and security. She is the recipient of several awards, including ETAPS Test of Time Award (2021), ASE Most Influential Paper Award (2018), ESEC/FSE Test of Time Award (2018), ISSTA Retrospective Impact Paper Award (2018), ACM Impact Paper Award (2010), and ICSE 2010 Most Influential Paper Award (2010). She has been serving as Program/General Chair for several conferences including: ICSE 2025, SEFM 2021, FM 2021, ICST 2020, ISSTA

2020, ESEC/FSE 2018, CAV 2015, ISSTA 2014, ASE 2011, and NFM 2009. She is on the steering committees for ICSE, ESEC/FSE and ISSTA conferences. She is currently an associate editor for IEEE TSE and for STTT, Springer Nature.

Safety Under Uncertainty: Automotive Standards for AI Safety and Research Perspectives

Simon Burton

Chair of Systems Safety at University of York
simon.burton@york.ac.uk

Abstract

This presentation describes the challenges related to the use of AI in safety-critical automotive applications (for example, automated driving). An overview of the upcoming standard ISO PAS 8800 Road Vehicles - Safety and AI will be provided, as well as the wider context of safety standards in this area (ISO 26262, ISO 21448, ISO TS 5083). The presentation will then motivate the structure and key concepts of ISO PAS 8800 and present how existing approaches to safety of automotive E/E systems are extended for AI and ML-based functions. This includes the consideration of AI-based functions within the wider system context, the derivation of AI safety requirements, data considerations, safety analysis and test.

The presentation will then focus on open research challenges. In particular, the need to address uncertainty in the assurance arguments for such systems and how this uncertainty can be evaluated and reduced. This includes determining the relevance of popular machine learning metrics and understanding their actual contribution to a rigorous safety assurance argument. The presentation is intended to provoke a dialogue between various application domains of safety-critical AI to compare and contrast the associated technical requirements, associated safety risks and assurance approaches.

Biography

Professor Simon Burton, PhD, holds the chair of Systems Safety at the University of York, UK. He graduated in computer science at the University of York in 1996, where he also achieved his PhD on the topic of the verification of safety-critical software in 2001. Professor Burton has worked in various safety-critical industries, including 20 years as a manager in automotive companies. During this time, Simon managed research and development projects, and led consulting, engineering services, product, and research organizations. More recently, he was Scientific Director for Safety Assurance at the Fraunhofer Institute for Cognitive Systems (Fraunhofer IKS) until December 2023. Professor Burton's personal research interests include the safety assurance of complex, autonomous systems and the safety of machine learning. He has published numerous academic articles covering a wide variety of perspectives within these fields, such as the application of formal methods to software testing, the joint consideration of safety and security in system analysis and design, as well as regulatory considerations and addressing gaps in the moral and legal responsibility of artificial intelligence (AI)-based systems. He is also an active member of the program committees of international safety conferences and workshops. Professor Burton is convener of the ISO working group ISO TC22/SC32/WG14 "Road Vehicles—Safety and AI" and currently leads the development of the standard ISO/AWI PAS 8800 "Safety and AI" scheduled for release in 2024.

Contents

Formal Methods for Learning-Enabled Systems

Formal Methods for Automotive Systems

Formal Methods for Robotics

Formal Methods for Software Engineering

Advances in Solver Technology

Structure-Guided Cube-and-Conquer for MaxSAT

Max Bannach[1(✉)] and Markus Hecher[2]

[1] European Space Agency, 2201 AZ Noordwijk, The Netherlands
max.bannach@esa.int
[2] Computer Science and Artificial Intelligence Lab, Massachusetts Institute of Technology, Cambridge, USA
hecher@mit.edu

Abstract. We present a black-box inprocessor for the partially weighted maximum satisfiability problem, which extends any given MaxSAT solver with inprocessing capabilities without modifying the core solver. Our approach combines the well-established *cube-and-conquer* technique with classical dynamic programming over a *tree decomposition* of the formula. While the first technique is limited in the size of the cubes it can handle, the second technique is limited by the treewidth of the input. By combining both paradigms, we cam handle significantly bigger cubes in instances with a treewidth of over a thousand, all without suffering performance losses on unstructured instances.

Through an extensive experimental study, we demonstrate the efficiency of our approach in enhancing established implementations of various standard algorithms for MaxSAT. Our results showcase that structure-guided cube-and-conquer can serve as a general black-box inprocessor for MaxSAT, making it a valuable addition to the MaxSAT toolbox.

Keywords: optimization · treewidth · cube-and-conquer · inprocessing

1 Introduction

The *partially weighted maximum satisfiability problem*, which we call MaxSAT, is the canonical problem of logic-based optimization that plays a crucial role in the theory of optimization and approximation algorithms [32]. Conceptually, it lies in the realm between SAT and optimization problems from operation research such as MILP. At this sweet spot, it combines the advantages of both fields by providing a powerful formalism that makes it convenient to express many problems, while being restricted enough to admit a rigorous proof system. This makes the problem interesting for practical applications, and the community is eager to develop ever faster MaxSAT solvers in an annual evaluation [7]. MaxSAT did become a valuable tool in the arsenal of formal methods, with

Authors are ordered alphabetically. For acknowledgements see the last page.

N. Benz et al. (Eds.): NFM 2024, LNCS 14627, pp. 3–20, 2024.
https://doi.org/10.1007/978-3-031-60698-4_1

applications in combinatorial testing [2], the detection of communities in complex networks [25], fault localization [27] and fault diagnosis [13], group testing [12], cost optimal planning [37], routing [28], scheduling [11], team formation [29], and data analysis [6]. Certified MaxSAT solvers capable of proof logging are available [5] and justify using this technology in mission-critical scenarios.

In contrast to SAT, where a single paradigm (namely CDCL [10, Chapter 4]) is used by all competitive solvers [17], the portfolio of MaxSAT is more diverse [7]. Such a portfolio comes with challenges, with the perhaps biggest one being that it is difficult to simultaneously make minor improvements to many of the available solvers. Recent research in improving MaxSAT solvers, therefore, focuses on techniques to improve a given solver Π to which only black-box access is given. Traditionally, this is done via *preprocessing*, i.e., an algorithm (called a preprocessor) maps a given formula φ to a solution equivalent formula φ' that then is solved with Π – see the top-left illustration in Fig. 1. However, preprocessing alone can only do so much. More generally, we would like to apply *inprocessing*, that is, a simplification of the formula during the solving process (see the bottom of Fig. 1). Inprocessing is widely used in SAT solving [9], but rarely adapted to MaxSAT. One reason is that inprocessing is tightly integrated into the solvers, which makes it difficult to implement for a heterogeneous portfolio.

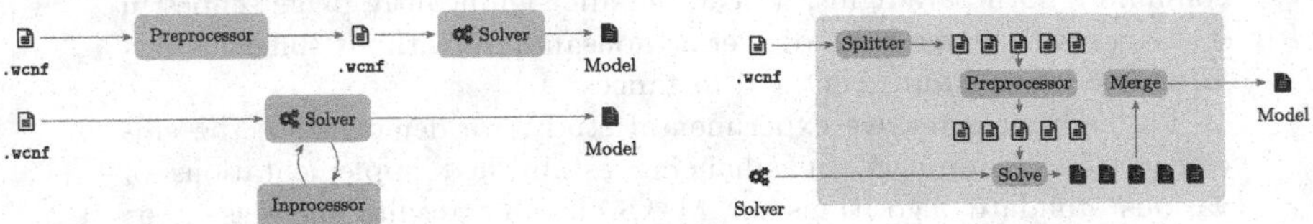

Fig. 1. Typical workflow of a preprocessor (top left picture) and of an inprocessor (bottom left picture). In contrast to a preprocessor, an inprocessor is tightly linked to the solver. A black-box inprocessor, as shown on the right, splits the input formula into multiple formulas, which are preprocessed and subsequently solved with the solver.

The solution for this dilemma is a *black-box inprocessor,* which is an algorithm that obtains as input an instance φ and a solver Π (via black-box access), and which solves φ using multiple calls to Π while applying preprocessing rules in between, see Fig. 1. A black-box inprocessor used in traditional SAT solving, originally designed to combine *conflict-driven clause learning* solvers (which are optimized for large industrial instances) and *lookahead* solvers (which focus on combinatorial challenging instances), is *cube-and-conquer* [22,23]. In this scheme, a lookahead solver explores partial assignments of a given formula φ in a binary search tree. The internal nodes of this tree correspond to variables, the edges to decisions, and the leaves are either already refuted assignments or subformulas that are solved using the CDCL solver – see the left side of Fig. 2. The assignments β_i from the root to the leaves ℓ_i are called *cubes* (hence the name), and the technique can be understood as a black-box inprocessor that splits the given formula φ into $\varphi \wedge \beta_1$, $\varphi \wedge \beta_2$, $\varphi \wedge \beta_3$, and so on. Whether the subformulas

$\varphi \wedge \beta_i$ are easier to solve than φ depends on the choice of the variables made by the lookahead solver. A *structural* explanation for *possible* improvements are cubes that separate the formula in a graph theoretic sense; see the right side of Fig. 2. However, such structural features are not utilized *explicitly* but just implicitly by the variable selection heuristics of the lookahead solver. A limitation of this approach is the depth of the search tree the lookahead solver explores, i.e., the size of the cubes. For a tree of depth k, we eventually have to solve 2^k subproblems, which quickly becomes infeasible.

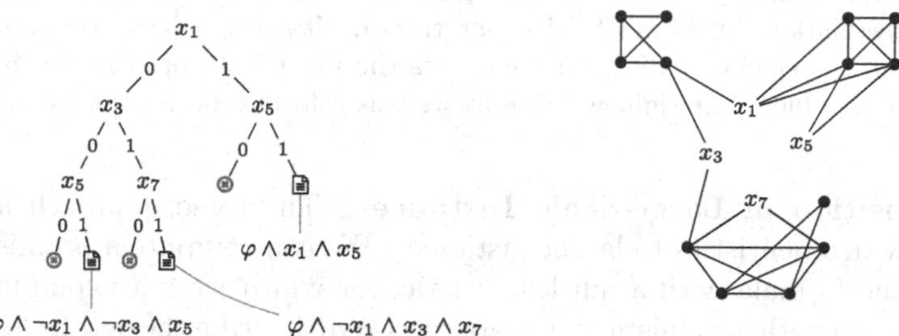

Fig. 2. Left: a search tree of a cube-and-conquer algorithm. Leaves with a red cross are refuted, and the others are labeled with the emerging subformula. Right: the *primal graph* of the formula, in which the vertices correspond to the variables of φ (variables appearing in the search tree are labeled x_i, others are shown as black dots). Assignments to $\{x_1, x_3, x_5, x_7\}$ will split the formula into up to three subformulas. (Color figure online)

A way of *explicitly* utilizing structure is dynamic programming over a *tree decomposition* of the formula. Early work in this direction was assumed to be of purely theoretical interest due to large hidden constants [10, Chapter 17]. One reason is that even computing a *heuristic* tree decomposition is often more expensive than testing satisfiability. Then, even if we can compute a tree decomposition, we can only utilize it to solve the problem via dynamic programming if it has a width of at most, say, 30. The distribution shown in Fig. 3 reveals that such an explicit use of structure is somewhat doomed in industrial applications.

1.1 Our Contributions

We combine cube-and-conquer and structure-guided dynamic programming to leverage the advantages of both. In *structure-guided cube-and-conquer,* we replace the first part of cube-and-conquer ("search cubes with a lookahead solver") with a dynamic program over a subformula of small treewidth, called the *torso* [16,19]. The leaves of a decomposition of the torso correspond to simplified subformulas (previously being the leaves of the search tree). By design, the torso can be large (compared to the size of cubes) since we do not have an exponential explosion in its size, but only in its treewidth. Conversely, the input can have large treewidth, as we only utilize the torso's structure.

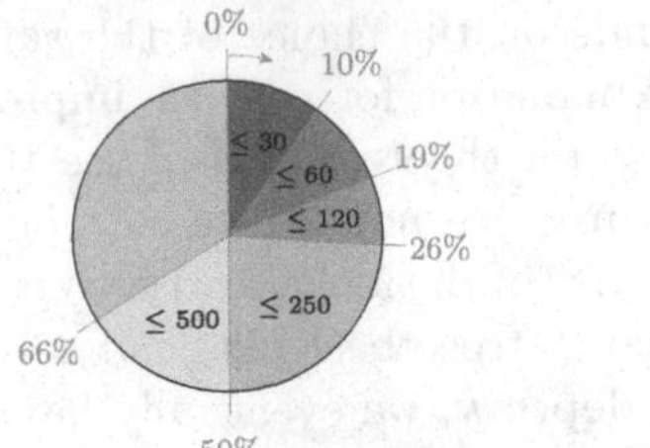

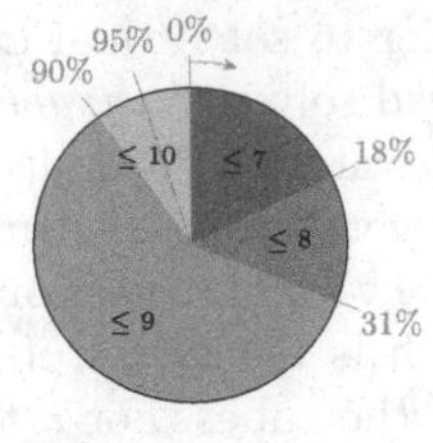

Fig. 3. The left wheel visualizes the treewidth distribution of the instances from the MaxSAT Evaluation 2023 (weighted exact track). Utilizing a heuristic approach for computation, the clockwise diagram illustrates the percentage of instances below specific threshold values. The right wheel mirrors this information for the torso width.

Decomposition of Large-Scale Instances. The torso approach allows to scale treewidth heuristics to larger instances: We can compute a promising subgraph of the formula with a quick heuristic, for which we later compute a tree decomposition with a sophisticated algorithm. We describe the details in Sect. 3.2 and demonstrate in Sect. 4.1 that we can compute torso decompositions of all instances of the recent MaxSAT evaluation in a few minutes, while classical treewidth heuristics cannot process some of these instances within an hour.

Existence of Torso Decompositions of Small Width. Some industrial instances do not have small treewidth, as we saw in Fig. 3. In contrast, *every* formula has a torso decomposition of small width (just take a very small torso), leaving us with the optimization problem of finding a large torso of small width. Hence, the structure-guided cube-and-conquer strategy can be applied to any formula and will utilize as much structure as possible. The right wheel of Fig. 3 shows the treewidth of the torsos we computed with the technique we will describe in Sect. 3.2. We analyze in Sect. 4.2 the size of these torsos, which may contain hundreds of variables while having treewidth at most 10.

Black-Box Inprocessing. We provide a publicly available [4] black-box inprocessor based on the structure-guided cube-and-conquer approach in Sect. 3.3. We then evaluate five MaxSAT solvers that implement various MaxSAT strategies on the benchmark set of the recent MaxSAT evaluation [7] in Sect. 4.2. All of the solvers obtain a partly significant performance boost on some instances; while no solver did become noticeably worse on any instance. Hence, the experiments suggest that structure-guided cube-and-conquer is a robust inprocessing technique that can safely be added to existing MaxSAT pipelines.

2 Preliminaries

A *weighted propositional formula in conjunctive normal* (a WCNF) is a conjunction of clauses (and-of-ors) together with a weight function on the clauses. We denote the sets of variables, literals, and clauses of φ as vars(φ), lits(φ), and clauses(φ); and refer to the weight function with $w_\varphi\colon \text{clauses}\{\varphi\} \to \mathbb{R} \cup \{\infty\}$. Clauses with a finite weight are called *soft*, while clauses with an infinite weight are *hard*. A *partial assignment* is a subset $\beta \subseteq \text{lits}(\psi)$ such that $|\{x, \neg x\} \cap \beta| \leq 1$ for all $x \in \text{vars}(\psi)$, that is, a set of literals that does not contain both polarities of any variable. For a set $X \subseteq \text{vars}(\varphi)$ we use $\beta \sqsubseteq X$ to denote partial assignments over X. An assignment β satisfies a clause $C \in \text{clauses}(\varphi)$ if $\beta \cap C \neq \emptyset$, and is called a *model* if it satisfies all hard clauses. The *fitness* of a model is the sum of the weights of the soft clauses it satisfies, and its *cost* is the sum of the weights of the remaining soft clauses. The *partially weighted maximum satisfiability problem*, which we call MaxSAT, asks, given a WCNF φ, to find a model of maximum fitness, or conclude that φ is unsatisfiable (i.e., has no model).

2.1 Structure of Propositional Formulas

The *primal graph* G_φ of a WCNF φ is the graph with vertex set $V(G_\varphi) = \text{vars}(\varphi)$ and edge set $E(G_\varphi) = \{\, \{x, y\} \mid x \text{ and } y \text{ occur together in a clause of } \varphi \,\}$. For a set $S \subseteq \text{vars}(\varphi)$ we denote with $\varphi \ominus S$ the set of formulas obtained by (i) computing the connected components C_i of $G_\varphi \setminus S$, and (ii) taking the subformulas ψ_i induced by $C_i \cup N(C_i)$, i.e., by the component and its neighborhood in S (the vertices in S connected to C_i via an edge). The formula ψ_i *induced* by a set X here means the subformula obtained from φ that contains only the clauses in which all variables appear in X.

Example 1. Consider the following formula (without weights):

$$\begin{aligned}\varphi = &(x_1 \vee \neg x_2 \vee x_3) \wedge (x_2 \vee x_3 \vee \neg x_4) \wedge (\neg x_4 \vee \neg x_5)\\ &\wedge (x_5 \vee \neg x_6 \vee \neg x_9) \wedge (\neg x_6 \vee x_7 \vee x_8) \wedge (x_9 \vee x_{10} \vee x_{11}).\end{aligned}$$

Its primal graph G_φ is illustrated in the following image, were we highlighted a set $S = \{x_4, x_5, x_6\} \subseteq \text{vars}(\varphi)$.

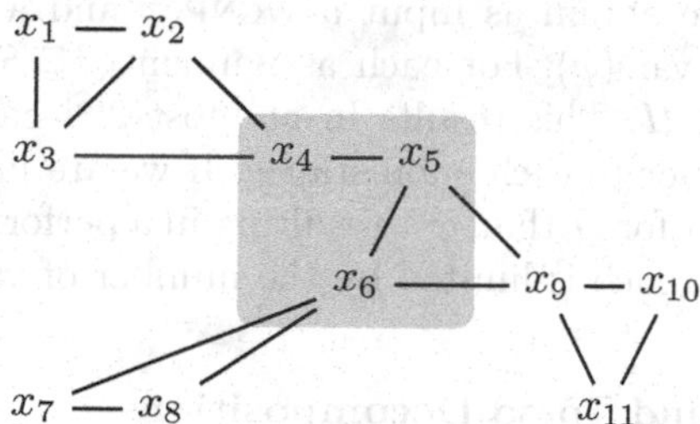

The connected components of $G_\varphi \setminus S$ are $C_1 = \{x_1, x_2, x_3\}$ with $N(C_1) = \{x_4\}$, $C_2 = \{x_7, x_8\}$ with $N(C_2) = \{x_6\}$, and lastly $C_3 = \{x_9, x_{10}, x_{11}\}$ with neighborhood $N(C_3) = \{x_5, x_6\}$. The formulas induced by $C_i \cup N(C_i)$ are the following:

1. $\psi_1 = (x_1 \vee \neg x_2 \vee x_3) \wedge (x_2 \vee x_3 \vee \neg x_4)$;
2. $\psi_2 = (\neg x_6 \vee x_7 \vee x_8)$;
3. $\psi_3 = (x_5 \vee \neg x_6 \vee \neg x_9) \wedge (x_9 \vee x_{10} \vee x_{11})$.

A *tree decomposition* of a graph G is a pair (T, bag), in which T is a tree and $\text{bag}\colon V(T) \to 2^{V(G)}$ maps nodes of T to subsets of vertices of G such that:

1. for all $v \in V(G)$ the set $\{\, t \mid v \in \text{bag}(t) \,\}$ is non-empty and connected in T;
2. for every $\{u, v\} \in E(G)$ there is a node $t \in V(T)$ with $\{u, v\} \subseteq \text{bag}(t)$.

The *width* of a tree decomposition is the maximum size of its bags minus one, i.e., $\max_{t \in V(T)} |\text{bag}(t)| - 1$. We do not enforce any further properties, but we assume that T is rooted at a $\text{root}(T) \in V(T)$ and, thus, that nodes $t \in V(T)$ have $\text{children}(t) \subseteq V(T)$. The *treewidth* $\text{tw}(G)$ of a graph G is the minimum width any tree decomposition of G must have, and the treewidth of a WCNF φ is the treewidth of its primal graph, that is, $\text{tw}(\varphi) := \text{tw}(G_\varphi)$. For a bag $t \in V(T)$ we denote with φ_t the set of clauses $c \in \text{clauses}(\varphi)$ with $\text{vars}(c) \subseteq \text{bag}(t)$.

Example 2. The treewidth of the Leo constellation (as graph shown on the left) is at most two, as proven by the tree decomposition on the right:

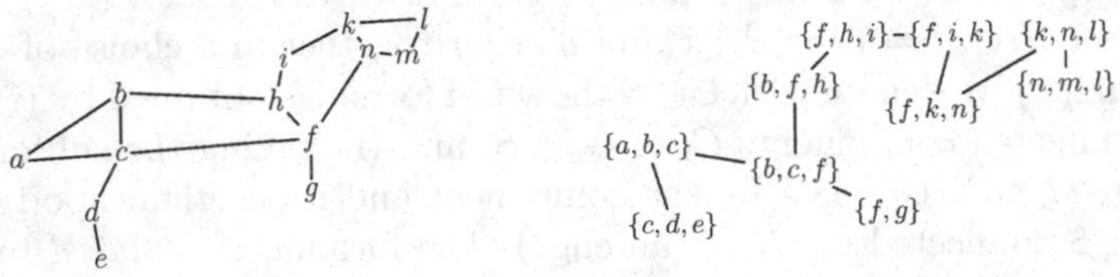

The Leo constellation is, for example, the primal graph of the following formula:

$$\varphi = (a \vee \neg b \vee c) \wedge (c \vee \neg d) \wedge (d \vee \neg e) \wedge (b \vee h) \wedge (h \vee f) \wedge (\neg h \vee \neg i) \wedge (c \vee \neg f) \\ \wedge\, (f \vee g) \wedge (i \vee k) \wedge (f \vee n) \wedge (k \vee n) \wedge (k \vee l) \wedge (\neg l \vee \neg m) \wedge (\neg n \vee \neg m).$$

For the bag t with $\text{bag}(t) = \{c, d, e\}$ we have $\varphi_t = \{(c \vee \neg d), (d \vee \neg e)\}$.

3 Inprocessing with Torso Decompositions

In cube-and-conquer we obtain as input a WCNF φ and a solver Π, and start by selecting a set $S \subseteq \text{vars}(\varphi)$. For each assignment $\beta \sqsubseteq S$ we find an optimal solution for[1] $\varphi|\beta$ using Π. This results in at most $2^{|S|}$ calls to Π, but allows us to apply a preprocessor to each subinstance. If we are lucky, the conditioned formulas are much easier for Π than φ – resulting in a performance improvement. Unfortunately, this approach is limited by the number of variables in S.

3.1 Graph Torsos and Torso Decompositions

The goal of the structure-guided approach is to increase the size of S without increasing the number of variables we have to brute-fore over. The insight is that we do *not* have to test all $2^{|S|}$ assignments, but only the ones that interface with

[1] The formula φ *conditioned* under β is obtained by removing all clauses that contain a literal $l \in \beta$ and by removing all literals l' with $\neg l' \in \beta$ from the remaining clauses.

the emerging subinstances. In particular, if G_S has small treewidth, we can get away brute-forcing locally while combining the found subsolutions via dynamic programming. Let G be a graph and $S \subseteq V(G)$. The *torso graph* $\text{torso}(G, S)$ is the subgraph with $V(\text{torso}(G, S)) = S$ that contains an edge $\{u, v\}$ iff there is an u-v-path in G whose internal vertices are not in S, see Fig. 4.

Definition 1. *A width-k* torso decomposition *of a* WCNF φ *and* $S \subseteq V(G_\varphi)$ *is a triple* (T, bag, π) *such that* (T, bag) *is a width-k tree decomposition of the graph* $\text{torso}(G_\varphi, S)$*; and* $\pi\colon V(T) \to 2^{\varphi \ominus S}$ *maps nodes t to formulas* $\psi \in \varphi \ominus S$ *with* $N(G_\psi \setminus S) \subseteq \text{bag}(t)$ *such that there is a unique* $t \in V(T)$ *with* $\psi \in \pi(t)$*.*

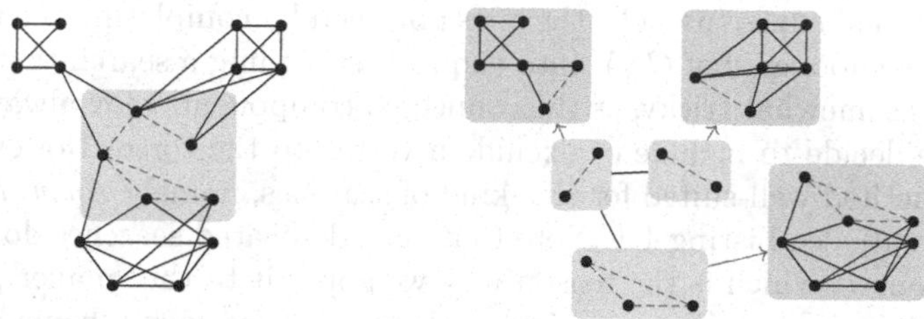

Fig. 4. Left: primal graph G_φ of a (not shown) WCNF φ with a green set $S \subseteq V(G_\varphi)$. The dashed edges are not in $E(G_\varphi)$, but in $\text{torso}(G_\varphi, S)$. The right image shows a torso decomposition with green bags and, in red, $\varphi \ominus S$. The red arrows illustrate π. (Color figure online)

3.2 Computing Torso Decompositions

As with most structural-based techniques, we first need to compute a torso decomposition in order to utilize it. In order to perform efficient dynamic programming on such decompositions, we cannot afford a width of more than roughly 10 (due to the underlying dynamic program, the running time of such tools is strictly of the form $2^k\text{poly}(|\varphi|)$ if the width is k), so the task at hand is: *Given a graph G, find a subset* $S \subseteq V(G)$ *as large as possible while maintaining* $\text{tw}(\text{torso}(G, S)) \leq 10$. This is an intriguing problem: estimating the treewidth alone is challenging, and we have to do it while maximizing a subgraph to which edges are added in a chaotic way. To the best of our knowledge, there are no tools available for that task, let alone tools that scale to instances with millions of edges (which frequently appear in industrial MaxSAT instances). We present a three phase heuristic, which computes a decent torso decomposition of such instances within a minute (we discuss experiments in the next section).

Phase I: Computing a Pre-torso. We start by computing a *pre-torso,* which is a torso that may not yet satisfy the width constraints. The pre-torso provides a search space for the "real" torso, which we find with the algorithm presented in the next section. The rational behind this approach is the following fact:

Fact 1 (Proposition 2.6 in [30]). *Let G be a graph and $X, Y \subseteq V(G)$ be two sets with $X \subseteq Y$. Then* $\text{torso}(\text{torso}(G, Y), X) = \text{torso}(G, X)$.

We compute the pre-torso with a degree-based heuristic: Initialize an empty set $Y = \emptyset$ and, repeatedly, add the vertex $v \in V(G) \setminus Y$ to Y that maximizes $|N(v) \cap V(G) \setminus Y| - |N(v) \cap Y|$, that is, a vertex that has many neighbors outside of Y while having few neighbors within Y. The first property makes it likely that the torso separates the graph, while the second ensures that the torso is sparse.

Phase II: Computing the Torso. In Phase I we looked for a sparse set Y that has good separation properties. However, we ignored the fact that $\text{torso}(G, Y)$ obtains additional edges (namely, the ones obtained by completing the neighborhoods of the components of $G \setminus Y$ into cliques). Designing a search that respects these edges is somewhat tricky, as the connected components may always change whenever we decide to include or exclude a vertex to the torso. However, there is a formal method well-suited for this kind of searches, namely *Answer Set Programming* (ASP), see Listing 1.1. Note that such dedicated searches do not scale to large instances, which is the reason why we apply it to the smaller pre-torso. Roughly, a logic program is a set of rule schemes, where each scheme uses first-order variables to generate rules similar to SAT implications [20]. Given a set of *facts*, we can generate the set of rules of the program by instantiating the rule schemes contained in the program. This step is typically referred to as *grounding*.

Listing 1.1. An ASP program that is given a graph in the form of a unary predicate node and a binary predicate edge. It computes a torso (as unary predicate torso) that is sparse, even if the neighborhoods of adjacent components are completed into cliques.

```
{ torso(X) : node(X) }.   edge(Y,X) :- edge(X,Y).
component(X,X) :- torso(X).
component(C,X) :- torso(C), not torso(X), edge(C,X).
component(C,Y) :- component(C,X), not torso(X), edge(X,Y).
:~ node(X), not torso(X). [10, X]
:~ X<Y, torso(X), torso(Y), edge(X,Y). [1,X,Y]  % induced edges
:~ X<Y, torso(Y), component(X,Y), not edge(X,Y). [1,X,Y]  % added edges
```

Example 3. A graph like is given via facts over the unary predicate node and the binary predicate edge: {node(1), node(2), node(3), node(4), edge(1,2), edge(1,3), edge(2,3), edge(3,4)}. These facts are used to instantiate the rule schemes of Listing 1.1. We obtain {torso(1) : node(1)}, ..., {torso(4) : node(4)}, component(1,1) :- torso(1), ..., component(4,4) :- torso(4); and so on.

The second step in evaluating ASP is *solving*. An *answer set* A is a set of variables set to true such that (i) *satisfaction*: every rule, treated as an implication from right to left, is satisfied; (ii) *justification*: there is an ordering ord over A such that for every claim $a \in A$ there is a rule with a in its consequence, where every variable v appearing positively in the rule's antecedent is in A and $\text{ord}(v) < \text{ord}(a)$, and none of the negatively appearing variables is in A.

Example 4. Intuitively, the definition of an answer set requires that it is built inductively from the facts, such that every rule is satisfied. In our example, we build the torso graph from the nodes and vertices of the given graph, where we derive additional facts whenever a rule body is satisfied. Suppose that in our example we selected torso(1) and torso(2). Then, by the rules generated with the rule scheme of Line 2, we also derive component(1, 1) and component(2, 2).

The semantic of Listing 1.1 is: First, Line 1 "guesses" a subset of the nodes as torso. Then, we compute components, where Line 2 ensures that every torso vertex is in its own component. Line 3 and 4 further ensure that vertices not contained in the torso but adjacent to a component get added to this component. Finally, Line 6 and 7 take care of the transitive closure, i.e., every component contains all adjacent non-torso vertices. We utilize the optimization capabilities of ASP in the form of weak constraints. Similar to MaxSAT, disobeying a weak constraint comes at a cost. In our case, we aim at (i) large torso graphs that are (ii) sparse. Line 5 ensures (i) by penalizing vertices that are not in the torso with a cost of 10. Lines 6 and 7 ensure that edges of the induced graph $G[T]$ and the edges that the torso graph adds to $G[T]$ impose a cost of 1, respectively.

Phase III: Estimating the Width. Once we have computed the torso, we compute a tree decomposition of it with a heuristics [1]. If the width exceeds a given threshold, we repeat the computation. Otherwise, we add the remaining connected components as special bags and return the obtained decomposition.

3.3 Structure-Guided Inprocessing

With the availability of decent torso decompositions, we are ready to present structure-guided cube-and-conquer for solving MaxSAT in Algorithm 1. The input is a WCNF φ and a torso decomposition $\mathcal{T} = (T, \text{bag}, \pi)$ of φ, on which a dynamic program is executed in post-order. Note that such algorithms usually use certain normal forms of the tree decompositions for simplicity. However, these come with an non-negligible overhead in practice and, hence, we explicitly work without such assumptions. For each node t, a table $\tau[t]$ is constructed, which is obtained via manipulating tables of child nodes and maintaining information restricted to the respective $\text{bag}(t)$ accordingly. For MaxSAT, the entries of these tables consist of an assignment J and a fitness value f, which refers to the best fitness value for any extension of the assignment below t.

The overall strategy of Algorithm 1 is as follows: First, we transform the content of the child tables to their parent nodes using *projections,* which remove information that is not needed anymore. Thereby, previously different assignments might collapse, for which we keep the largest fitness value. In case there is more than one child, the resulting tables are merged using *joins,* which ensure

Algorithm 1: $\mathsf{TorsoMaxSAT}(\varphi, \mathcal{T}, \Pi)$ for structure-guided inprocessing.

In: WCNF φ, Torso TD $\mathcal{T}=(T, \text{bag}, \pi)$ of φ, solver Π. **Out:** Maximal fitness of φ.

1 $\tau \leftarrow \{\}$ `/* Empty table mapping */`
2 **for** iterate t *in* post-order(T) `/* Bottom-up Dynamic Programming */` **do**
3 $\quad$ $\text{bag}' \leftarrow \emptyset$ `/* Union of child bags */` $\tau' \leftarrow \emptyset$ `/* Table initially empty */`
4 $\quad$ **for** t_i *in* children(T, t) `/* Project & join */` **do**
5 $\quad\quad$ $\text{bag}' \leftarrow \text{bag}' \cup \text{bag}(t_i)$
6 $\quad\quad$ $\tau[t_i] \leftarrow$ $\mathsf{DP}_{project}(\text{bag}(t_i) \setminus \text{bag}(t), \tau[t_i], \Pi)$ `/* Project tables to bag(t) */`
7 $\quad\quad$ **if** $i = 1$ `/* First child */` **then** $\tau' \leftarrow \tau[t_i]$
8 $\quad\quad$ **else** `/* Join with predecessor */` $\tau' \leftarrow \mathsf{DP}_{join}(\text{bag}(t) \cap \text{bag}', \{\tau', \tau[t_i]\}, \Pi)$
9 $\quad$ $\tau[t] \leftarrow \mathsf{DP}_{introduce}(\text{bag}(t) \setminus \text{bag}', \tau', \varphi_t, \pi(t), \Pi)$ `/* Introduce & solve */`
10 **return** $\Sigma_{(\cdot, f) \in \tau[\text{root}(T)]} f$ `/* Compute maximum fitness */`

that information among different tables is combined correctly. Our implementation uses binary joins, which are subsequently applied to incorporate several child tables one by one. When joining two tables, we keep only matching assignments and sum their fitness. Finally, we guess truth values for fresh variables not encountered below t, using an *introduce* operation. Here we ensure to fulfill φ_t, which are the clauses of φ using variables in bag(t), as well as the subinstances $\pi(t)$.

Example 5. Let φ be the following formula:

$$\varphi = (a \vee b) \wedge (a \vee c) \wedge (\neg b \vee e) \wedge (a \vee \neg e) \wedge (a \vee c \vee d) \\ \wedge (\neg c \vee \neg d) \wedge (a) \wedge (b) \wedge (c) \wedge (d) \wedge (e)$$

with $w_\varphi(a) = w_\varphi(c) = w_\varphi(d) = 2$, and $w_\varphi(b) = w_\varphi(e) = 1$; and with a torso decomposition $\{a,b,c\} \leftarrow \{a,b\} \overset{t_2}{-} \{a\} \overset{t_1}{-} \{a,c\} \overset{t_3}{\rightarrow} \{a,c,d\}$. We briefly sketch the workflow for $t = t_1$ in Line 2. First, we project on table $\tau[t_2]$ (Line 6), where $\{b\}$ is removed from the table, thereby adapting the fitness by $w_\varphi(b)$ for assignments setting $b \mapsto 1$, resulting in a table that is assigned to τ' (Line 7). Intuitively, since $\{b\}$ is removed from the bag, the properties of a tree decomposition ensure we already encountered every clause on b, i.e., we do not need to further track assignments over b. Then, we project on table $\tau[t_1]$, thereby removing $\{c\}$ and joining the result with τ' over $\{a\}$ (Line 8). The join operation merges assignments with the same truth assignment over $\{a\}$ (i.e., we enforce well-defined assignments) and takes the sum over the maximum fitness values per table, resulting in τ'. In this example bag(t_1) does not introduce new items and, hence, verifying φ_{t_1} does not provide new insights. Since also $\pi(t_1)=\emptyset$, Line 9 just assigns the join result τ' to $\tau[t_1]$. After the loop, Line 10 yields the maximum fitness value 6.

Specifications of the operations *project*, *introduce*, and *join* are given in Algorithm 2, where the set α depends on the operation type: For *projections*, α indicates those bag elements that will not be removed from the tables, see Line 3. For *joins* in Line 5, α is the set of common elements that are shared among two child tables. Line 7 covers the *introduce* type, where α indicates the set of bag elements subject to introduce. The introduce type for a node t also takes two additional parameters, one being φ_t and the other being the set π.

Algorithm 2: $\mathsf{DP}_{type}(\alpha, \tau, \varphi, \pi, \Pi)$ for *type* $\in \{project, join, introduce\}$.

In: Set α, child tables $\tau = \{\tau_1, \ldots\}$, φ, torso WCNFs π, solver Π. **Out:** Table τ.

1 **if** *type is project* `/* Project over variables not in` α `*/` **then**
2   `/* F(`I`) are the fitness values for assignments agreeing with` I `*/`
3    $\mathrm{F}(I) := \{f + \Sigma_{a \in J} w_\varphi(a) \mid \langle J, f \rangle \in \tau_1, I = J \setminus \{a \mapsto 0, a \mapsto 1 \mid a \in \alpha\}\}$
4   **return** $\{\langle I', \max_{f \in \mathrm{F}(I')} f \rangle \mid \langle I, \cdot \rangle \in \tau_1, I' = I \setminus \{a \mapsto 0, a \mapsto 1 \mid a \in \alpha\}\}$
5 **else if** *type is join* `/* Merge common assignments */` **then**
6   **return** $\{\langle I \cap I', f_1 + f_2 \rangle \mid \langle I, f_1 \rangle \in \tau_1, \langle I', f_2 \rangle \in \tau_2, I \cap \alpha = I' \cap \alpha\}$
7 **else if** *type is introduce* `/* Introduce and solve torso wcnfs */` **then**
8   **return** $\{\langle J, f{+}g \rangle \mid \langle I, f \rangle \in \tau_1, I' {\in} 2^\alpha, J{=}I{\cup}I', \varphi(J){=}\emptyset, g{=}\mathsf{MaxSAT}(\pi, J, \Pi), g{\neq}{-\infty}\}$

Every WCNF in π can be solved under assignment J independently, which is carried out by the function $\mathsf{MaxSAT}(\pi, J, \Pi)$ (not shown). This function iterates over all $\psi \in \pi$, shaves off weights for variables assigned in J (these are treated upon removal), preprocesses the formulas, and finally solves them using solver Π.

3.4 Soundness and Completeness

The space within this implementation-oriented paper is too limited for a thorough formal proof of the soundness and completeness of the algorithm. Nevertheless, we provide a short informal argument for its correctness. First, consider the two extreme cases of the algorithm, namely that the torso is *empty* or contains *all* vertices. In the first case, we inherit the correctness from the given solver; in the second case, the algorithm collapses to a dynamic program over a tree decomposition of the whole formula. The correctness of such dynamic programs is well understood [3,34]. In the general case, in which the torso contains only a subset of the formula, the dynamic program may reach the end of the torso. It then simply computes the next entry in its dynamic programming table with the given solver, which will handle the subformula correctly.

4 Experimental Evaluation

An implementation of the structure-guided cube-and-conquer approach is publicly available [4]. The experiments presented in this paper were carried out on an AMD EPYC 7702 64-bit processor with 256 cores, each operating with a maximum clock speed of 2.2 GHz. The system memory (RAM) was 528.1 GB.

4.1 Decomposing Large Formulas

We study the benchmarkset of the MaxSAT evaluation 2023 [7], which contains 558 instances from various domains. The first step in any structure-guided approach is to decompose the formula. We first computed tree decompositions of the benchmarkset using the three most popular libraries for that task: networkx [21], htd [1], and flowcutter [35]. The treewidth distribution of this data set is shown in the left wheel of Fig. 3 in the introduction, which reveals that a large portion of the instances actually has a rather high treewidth. In contrast, the right wheel in the same figure visualizes that we can find torso decompositions of width at most 10 of almost all instances (95%). Figure 5 presents the running times the libraries needed so solve these instances. Problematically, we can observe that even the best of the three is not able to compute *any* tree decomposition of around 20% of the instances within 15 min (in fact, most of the unsolved instances cannot be solved within an hour). In contrast, we can compute torso decompositions of all instances (shown in green) thanks to the three phase procedure described in Sect. 3.2.

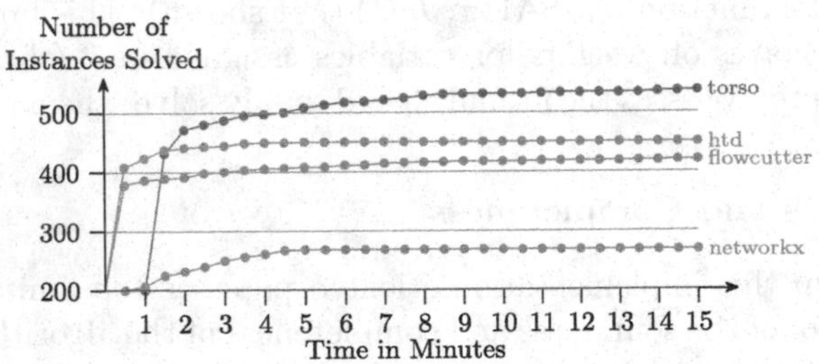

Fig. 5. A cumulative distribution function plot that shows the allowed time t on the x-axis, and the number of instances that the solver was able to solve within t minutes on the y-axis. The gray lines correspond to the three mentioned treewidth heuristics, while the green line corresponds to our implementation to compute a torso decomposition. (Color figure online)

4.2 Improving MaxSAT Solvers with Structure-Guided Inprocessing

We evaluated a prototype implementation [4] of structure-guided cube-and-conquer on the same 558 instances from the MaxSAT evaluation 2023 [7] in conjunction with five MaxSAT solvers that follow different algorithmic strategies. Tested where the award-winning RC2 implementation from PySAT [24], which implements the relaxable cardinality constraints algorithm. From the same library, we used the FM solver, a core-guided MaxSAT algorithm proposed by Fu and Malik [18]; as well as a simple implicit hitting set algorithm HS following the ideas of [14]. Furthermore, we used the open-source ILP solver scip [8] and Googles constraint solver ortools [33]. All solvers were run with a time limit of

15 min per instances. From the 558 instances of the benchmark set, we obtained an improvement on 77 instances for RC2 (14%), 59 for FM (10%), 28 for the implicit hitting set approach (5%), 112 for scip (20%), and 137 for ortools (25%). Scatter plots of three solvers are shown in Fig. 6 (the missing solvers look similar and are omitted due to lack of space).

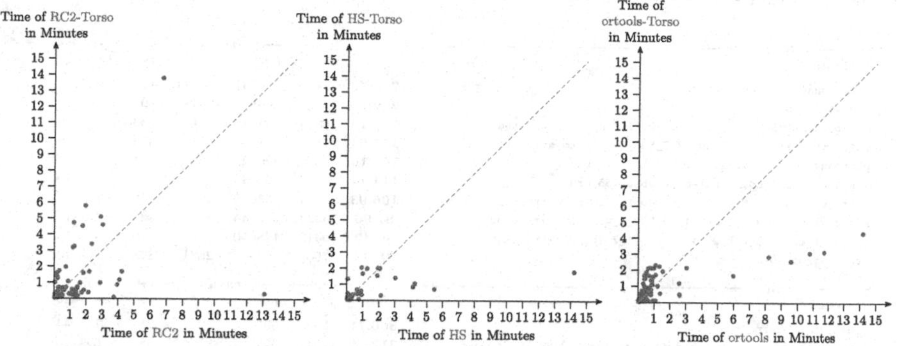

Fig. 6. From left to right: scatter plots for RC2, HS, and ortools. The x-axis shows the time the solver needed for an instance *without* using structure-guided cube-and-conquer; the y-axis shows the time using it. For each instance that the solver was able to solve in 15 min, there is a point visualizing both times. Green dots indicate instances on which the solver with cube-and-conquer is superior. (Color figure online)

We can observe that, with the exception of one instance for RC2, possible deteriorations are minor. Note that it is to be expected that an involved pre- or inprocessing technique is generally likely to reduce the performance of the solvers on "easy" instances as we add a lot of overhead (like computing the torso decomposition upfront). The increase in performance on the other instances is more interesting and, for all solvers, there are some instances for which we obtain significant improvements. Interestingly, these are different instances across the different solvers, as can be seen in Table 1, which shows the top ten instances per solver with respect to the improvement. We observe the best improvements for the solvers scip and ortools, whereby we can explain the former since it is an ILP solver that certainly profits from more MaxSAT reasoning in an inprocessing step. We are uncertain, however, why our approach improves ortools by such a margin. Perhaps, the solver is optimized to handle rather simple formulas very efficiently and, thus, is good in processing the emerging subproblems. Table 1 also reveals other interesting statistics. Most striking, many of the instances have a large treewidth in the hundreds to thousands. These are widths for which it is hopeless to apply a structure-based approach, like a dynamic program, directly. In that sense, structure-guided cube-and-conquer establishes a way to lift structure-based technologies to instances to which they were not applicable before. We can observe that most of our torsos have size 10, which is owed to the parameters we chose for the algorithm from Sect. 3.2: We computed a pre-torso

Table 1. An overview of the ten instances on which each of the solvers improved most when executed in structure-guided cube-and-conquer mode. For each of the solvers (RC2, FM, HS, scip, and ortools) the name of the ten instances is given together with the **improvement** in seconds (compared to running the solver directly). For each instance we also present the number of variables n, the number of hard and soft clauses, and the treewidth of the formula. The last two columns contain the treewidth and size of the used torso. We normalized the formulas with the usual reduction of making soft clauses *unit* (replace each soft clause C with a hard $C \vee \alpha$ and a unit soft-clause $\neg\alpha$).

RC2		Formula				Torso	
Instance	*Imp.*	*n*	*hard*	*soft*	*tw*	*tw*	*size*
relational-inference_wt-rc-2	**766.72**	594051	555637	553241	1154	6	9
frb_wt-frb15-9-1	**219.73**	2783	2648	2648	80	7	10
metro_wt-metro_9_8_7_30_10_6_500_1_7.lp.sm-extracted	**184.19**	94923	235026	161	233	5	10
metro_wt-metro_9_9_10_35_13_7_500_2_7.lp.sm-extracted	**174.64**	141635	639442	248	324	6	9
planning_wt-driverlog02c.wcsp	**152.16**	2866	22652	544	151	7	10
synplicate-BankLoan-run1-ms_0_28_0.955_erm	**114.14**	10226	29978	88	149	7	10
metro_wt-metro_9_8_7_30_10_6_500_1_3.lp.sm-extracted	**106.93**	98319	253612	163	268	7	10
metro_wt-metro_9_9_10_35_13_7_500_2_4.lp.sm-extracted	**81.96**	133237	666044	264	327	7	10
metro_wt-metro_8_8_5_20_10_6_500_1_7.lp.sm-extracted	**80.42**	59412	148650	128	179	5	10
frb_wt-frb15-9-3	**78.30**	2766	2631	2631	87	7	10

FM		Formula				Torso	
Instance	*Imp.*	*n*	*hard*	*soft*	*tw*	*tw*	*size*
spot5_wt-29.wcsp.log	**866.71**	183	692	82	25	7	44
pseudoBoolean_wt-normalized-factor-size=9-P=397-Q=449.opb	**312.45**	1151	3299	9	38	6	10
quantum-circuit-qaoa_4_16_ibmq-casablanca_7	**173.26**	8748	89004	1365	167	7	10
shiftdesign_wt-limits-10-10_data-1_inst-081_60m.sm-extracted	**143.14**	345988	685409	2220	831	8	10
haplotyping-pedigrees_wt-ped2.G.recomb10-0.01-5	**132.05**	227251	1706439	18980	3133	6	10
max-realizability_wt-power-distribution_9_6	**71.66**	7306	77980	15	488	4	7
haplotyping-pedigrees_wt-ped2.G.recomb5-0.01-4	**60.69**	227213	1768677	18980	2990	7	10
upgradeability_wt-mancoosi-test-i4000d0u98-80	**58.02**	36436	112632	18267	740	7	10
upgradeability_wt-mancoosi-test-i2000d0u98-37	**55.69**	36436	112632	18267	740	7	10
upgradeability_wt-mancoosi-test-i4000d0u98-81	**53.94**	36436	112632	18267	740	7	10

HS		Formula				Torso	
Instance	*Imp.*	*n*	*hard*	*soft*	*tw*	*tw*	*size*
metro_wt-metro_9_9_10_35_13_7_500_2_6.lp.sm-extracted	**744.69**	157748	706776	246	350	9	10
quantum-circuit-qaoa_4_16_ibmq-casablanca_7	**286.20**	8748	89004	1365	167	7	10
synplicate-AutoTaxi-run3-ms_0_47_0.96_erm	**198.79**	8889	25791	70	198	7	10
synplicate-TheoremProver-run3-ms_0_17_0.8771653543307086_erm	**192.19**	5576	16071	63	134	5	10
haplotyping-pedigrees_wt-ped3.F.recomb10-0.01-2	**109.90**	72867	463058	4960	876	7	9
frb_wt-frb30-15-3	**98.15**	18799	18349	18349	304	7	10
Security-CriticalCyber-PhysicalComponents_wt-test54-n-15000	**41.50**	33123	54065	9060	4	5	12
ParametricRBACMaintenance_mse20_wt-role_smallcomp_multiple_0.0_3	**35.91**	2870	7703	770	532	6	7
synplicate-AutoTaxi-run3-ms_0_71_0.92_erm	**21.21**	8890	25792	70	198	7	10
preference_planning_wt-WCNF_storage_p04	**18.82**	5129	36500	31	758	6	9

scip		Formula				Torso	
Instance	*Imp.*	*n*	*hard*	*soft*	*tw*	*tw*	*size*
dalculus_wt-f49-DC_TotalLoss.seq-A-3-2-EDCBAir	**782.82**	18220	59869	546	391	7	10
max-realizability_wt-power-distribution_3_5	**387.17**	3012	56126	6	244	4	7
haplotyping-pedigrees_wt-ped2.B.recomb1-0.10-6	**311.74**	173771	481698	2180	754	6	10
haplotyping-pedigrees_wt-ped2.B.recomb1-0.10-10	**191.69**	174042	448845	2180	857	6	10
dalculus_wt-f49-DC_TotalLoss.seq-B-2-2-irabcde	**114.85**	9850	24921	544	391	6	10
preference_planning_wt-WCNF_pathways_p11	**65.63**	6721	40521	25	743	5	9
css-refactoring_wt-openstreetmap.dimacs	**62.26**	9678	50705	3254	266	7	10
dalculus_wt-f49-DC_TotalLoss.seq-B-2-combined-abcdeir	**37.69**	10975	28671	544	412	7	10
Security-CriticalCyber-PhysicalComponents_wt-test68-n-20000	**34.40**	51957	75982	15977	4	6	13
synplicate-TheoremProver-run1-ms_0_100_0_erm	**31.45**	2477	7054	49	86	6	10

ortools		Formula				Torso	
Instance	*Imp.*	*n*	*hard*	*soft*	*tw*	*tw*	*size*
timetabling_wt-comp14	**589.19**	116436	677720	1756	2218	7	10
MaxSATQueriesinInterpretableClassifiers_wt-toms_test_3_CNF_1_20	**512.00**	9369	190004	3729	811	7	9
haplotyping-pedigrees_wt-ped3.F.recomb10-0.20-11	**460.02**	75443	862287	4960	2436	8	10
shiftdesign_wt-limits-10-10_data-1_inst-081_60m.sm-extracted	**420.05**	345988	685409	2220	831	8	10
haplotyping-pedigrees_wt-ped3.G.recomb10-0.01-3	**319.61**	90671	675374	10460	1564	6	10
metro_wt-metro_9_9_10_35_13_7_500_2_1.lp.sm-extracted	**256.94**	141272	801321	263	340	7	10
rna-alignment_wt-random-dif-9.rna.pre	**130.28**	1897	13649	272	191	7	10
synplicate-AutoTaxi-run4-ms_0_84_0.9015384615384615_erm	**126.34**	10658	31356	119	115	7	10
metro_wt-metro_9_9_10_35_13_7_500_2_6.lp.sm-extracted	**83.01**	157748	706776	246	350	9	10
Security-CriticalCyber-PhysicalComponents_wt-test68-n-20000	**58.98**	51957	75982	15977	4	6	13

Table 2. Ten selected instances in which we found a large torso (**size** in bold). We computed a pre-torso of fixed size 100, that is, the maximum possible torso size we could obtain is 100. Some of the instances have a very small treewidth and we could, in principle, compute larger torsos and solve the problem via dynamic programming. However, there are also instances, such as the last two, which have non-negligibly large treewidth, while we are still able to compute a torso of more than 50 elements.

Instance	Formula				Torso	
	n	*hard*	*soft*	*tw*	*tw*	*size*
`MaxSATQueriesinInterpretableClassifiers_wt-transfusion_test_7_DNF_3_5`	240	462	93	12	11	**100**
`MaxSATQueriesinInterpretableClassifiers_wt-compas_train_1_DNF_1_15`	15941	33472	6508	15	14	**100**
`mpe_wt-random-net-40-2_network-10.net`	758	693	658	11	10	**100**
`planning_wt-depot01c.wcsp.dir`	338	828	201	20	7	**100**
`spot5_wt-1502.wcsp.log`	520	534	209	12	7	**100**
`mpe_wt-random-net-30-2_network-4.net`	765	704	677	12	11	**88**
`mpe_wt-random-net-180-1_network-3.net`	1878	1578	1423	10	9	**79**
`mpe_wt-random-net-300-1_network-8.net`	3149	2641	2385	10	9	**69**
`spot5_wt-54.wcsp.log`	163	479	67	19	7	**50**
`spot5_wt-29.wcsp.log`	183	692	82	25	7	**44**

of size 100, in which we searched a torso with the ASP program for a period of two minuets while penalizing vertices that are not in the torso with a cost of 10 and edges within the torso with a cost of 1. In this way, apart from very sparse torsos, the ASP tends to pick torsos of roughly size 10. However, we can see that there are larger torsos, e.g., the peek in Table 1 is 44. In fact, there are instances in which we used even larger torsos. If the input formula has small treewidth (see the first 10% of the instances shown in Fig. 3), we can use the pre-torso directly, that is, in our setting we obtain torsos of size 100. However, there are also instances with a larger treewidth for which we obtain torsos of size 50 or larger, Table 2 showcases some of them. Note that a dynamic program over a tree decomposition *cannot* handle decompositions of high width since it needs to store tables of exponential size for every bag, and that the pure cube-and-conquer strategy brute-forces over the cubes and, thus, *cannot* handle sets of size 50. Hence, these are instances where the combination of the two techniques outperforms the individual techniques.

4.3 Limitations of Structure-Guided Cube-and-Conquer

Any pre- or inprocessing technique adds an overhead to the solver under consideration and, thus, bears the risk of decreasing its performance. Structure-guided cube-and-conquer is no exception and adds three points of overhead: (i) the computation of G_φ from φ, (ii) the computation of a torso decomposition of G_φ, and (iii) the dynamic program executed on that decomposition. Item (i) is expensive if φ contains large clauses (which become cliques in G_φ). The computation of the torso decomposition in (ii) is, in general, NP-hard and, in our implementation, realized with heuristics (see Sect. 3.2). While the results of Sect. 4.1 indicate that our implementation is decently fast and able to find large torsos of small width (see Table 2), it sometimes fails to do so and, hence, reduces the performance of the solver. Finally, the dynamic program (iii) is a memory-expensive operation that may add non-negligible overhead (both in time and memory) if the algorithm is executed on a torso decomposition of too large width.

5 Conclusion and Further Research

We presented a black-box inprocessor based on the structure-guided cube-and-conquer paradigm that can extend any MaxSAT solver with inprocessing techniques without modifying the solver. Extensive experiments have revealed that this approach improves the performance of many established MaxSAT solvers on the benchmark set of the recent MaxSAT evaluation.

We identify two sources for improvements of the current implementation, which open up new research directions: First, we found it remarkably challenging to compute good torso decompositions and believe that the approach presented in Sect. 3.2 can be improved noticeably. In particular, we encourage the development of dedicated solvers and heuristics for the computation of torso decompositions, perhaps in the light of a computational challenge such as the PACE [15]. In a similar spirit, we observed that state-of-the-art treewidth heuristics currently cannot handle the largest instances within the benchmark set of the MaxSAT evaluation 2023. That is not necessarily surprising, as the community that is developing these heuristics is, so far, mainly concerned with computing decompositions that are as *good* as possible. However, if the heuristics are used to guide an algorithm (rather than being the backbone for a dynamic program), a coarser decomposition would do, as long as we can obtain it very *quickly*.

The second issue we had was the lack of *incremental* MaxSAT solvers. When the algorithm from Sect. 3.3 handles a subproblem, it has to solve it for the assignments of the current bag. The corresponding problems are very similar and could be solved efficiently using *assumptions*. This is the standard procedure in the cube-and-conquer approach for SAT, where, nowadays, every solver is incremental. While the MaxSAT evaluation had an incremental track in 2022 and 2023, the track had to be canceled in 2023 due to a lack of participants [7]. We encourage the community to pursue the development of incremental solvers, as black-box inprocessing is an application for it.

Application-wise, the next natural step is to lift the prototype developed within this paper to be used in one of the many applications within verification and formal methods that rely on MaxSAT. A possible starting point could be the declarative specification language Alloy [26] or its recent extension Alloy^{max}, which can express and analyze problems with optimal solutions [36]. The latter is based on MaxSAT, and improvements of MaxSAT solvers have been successfully applied to it [31]. We also think that the structure-guided cube-and-conquer scheme can directly be applied to model-checking problems of first-order logic or logics with temporal properties. However, if this approach has an advantage over applying the techniques to the underlying low-level tools in propositional logic needs to be evaluated.

Acknowledgements. The work has been carried out while Hecher visited the Simons Institute at UC Berkeley. Research is supported by the Austrian Science Fund (FWF), grant J 4656, and the Society for Research Funding in Lower Austria (GFF) grant ExzF-0004.

References

1. Abseher, M., Musliu, N., Woltran, S.: htd - a free, open-source framework for (customized) tree decompositions and beyond. In: Salvagnin, D., Lombardi, M. (eds.) CPAIOR 2017. LNCS, vol. 10335, pp. 376–386. Springer, Cham (2017). https://doi.org/10.1007/978-3-319-59776-8_30
2. Ansótegui, C., Manyà, F., Ojeda, J., Salvia, J.M., Torres, E.: Incomplete MaxSAT approaches for combinatorial testing. J. Heuristics **28**, 377–431 (2022). https://doi.org/10.1007/s10732-022-09495-3
3. Bannach, M., Skambath, M., Tantau, T.: On the parallel parameterized complexity of MaxSAT variants. In: SAT (2022)
4. Bannach, M., Hecher, M.: Torsomaxsat. http://github.com/maxbannach/TorsoMaxSAT
5. Berg, J., Bogaerts, B., Nordström, J., Oertel, A., Vandesande, D.: Certified core-guided MaxSAT solving. In: Pientka, B., Tinelli, C. (eds.) CADE 2023. LNCS, vol. 14132, pp. 1–22. Springer, Cham (2023). https://doi.org/10.1007/978-3-031-38499-8_1
6. Berg, J., Hyttinen, A., Järvisalo, M.: Applications of MaxSAT in data analysis. In: SAT (2018)
7. Berg, J., Järvisalo, M., Martins, R., Niskanen, A. (eds.): MaxSAT Evaluation 2023: Solver and Benchmark Descriptions. University of Helsinki (2023)
8. Bestuzheva, K., et al.: Enabling research through the SCIP optimization suite 8.0. ACM Trans. Math. Softw. (2023)
9. Biere, A.: Preprocessing and inprocessing techniques in SAT. In: HVC (2011)
10. Biere, A., Heule, M., van Maaren, H., Walsh, T. (eds.): Handbook of Satisfiability, 2nd edn. IOS Press (2021)
11. Bofill, M., et al.: Constraint solving approaches to the business-to-business meeting scheduling problem. J. Artif. Intell. Res. (2022)
12. Ciampiconi, L., Ghosh, B., Scarlett, J., Meel, K.S.: A MaxSAT-based framework for group testing. In: IAAI (2020)
13. D'Almeida, D., Grégoire, É.: Model-based diagnosis with default information implemented through MaxSAT technology. In: IEEE (2012)
14. Davies, J.: Solving MaxSAT by decoupling optimization and satisfaction. Ph.D. thesis, University of Toronto (2014)
15. Dell, H., Husfeldt, T., Jansen, B.M.P., Kaski, P., Komusiewicz, C., Rosamond, F.A.: The first parameterized algorithms and computational experiments challenge. In: IPEC (2016)
16. Fichte, J.K., Hecher, M., Morak, M., Thier, P., Woltran, S.: Solving projected model counting by utilizing treewidth and its limits. Artif. Intell. **314**, 103810 (2023)
17. Froleyks, N., et al.: SAT competition 2020. Artif. Intell. (2021)
18. Fu, Z., Malik, S.: On solving the partial MaxSAT problem. In: SAT (2006)
19. Ganian, R., Ramanujan, M.S., Szeider, S.: Combining treewidth and backdoors for CSP. In: STACS. LIPIcs, vol. 66, pp. 36:1–36:17. Dagstuhl (2017)

20. Gebser, M., Kaminski, R., Kaufmann, B., Schaub, T.: Answer Set Solving in Practice. Morgan & Claypool (2012)
21. Hagberg, A., Swart, P.J., Schult, D.A.: Exploring Network Structure, Dynamics, and Function Using NetworkX (2008)
22. Heule, M.J.H., Kullmann, O., Wieringa, S., Biere, A.: Cube and conquer: guiding CDCL SAT solvers by lookaheads. In: Eder, K., Lourenco, J., Shehory, O. (eds.) HVC 2011. LNCS, vol. 7261, pp. 50–65. Springer, Heidelberg (2012). https://doi.org/10.1007/978-3-642-34188-5_8
23. Heule, M.J.H., Kullmann, O., Biere, A.: Cube-and-conquer for satisfiability. In: Hamadi, Y., Sais, L. (eds.) Handbook of Parallel Constraint Reasoning, pp. 31–59. Springer, Cham (2018). https://doi.org/10.1007/978-3-319-63516-3_2
24. Ignatiev, A., Morgado, A., Marques-Silva, J.: PySAT: a Python toolkit for prototyping with SAT oracles. In: Beyersdorff, O., Wintersteiger, C. (eds.) SAT 2018. LNCS, vol. 10929, pp. 428–437. Springer, Cham (2018). https://doi.org/10.1007/978-3-319-94144-8_26
25. Jabbour, S., Mhadhbi, N., Raddaoui, B., Sais, L.: A SAT-based framework for overlapping community detection in networks. In: Kim, J., Shim, K., Cao, L., Lee, J.G., Lin, X., Moon, Y.S. (eds.) PAKDD 2017. LNCS, vol. 10235, pp. 786–798. Springer, Cham (2017). https://doi.org/10.1007/978-3-319-57529-2_61
26. Jackson, D.: Software Abstractions - Logic, Language, and Analysis. MIT Press, Cambridge (2006)
27. Jose, M., Majumdar, R.: Cause clue clauses: error localization using maximum satisfiability. In: SIGPLAN (2011)
28. Li, Y., Lin, S., Nishizawa, S., Onodera, H.: MCell: multi-row cell layout synthesis with resource constrained MaxSAT based detailed routing. In: ICCAD (2020)
29. Manyà, F., Negrete, S., Roig, C., Soler, J.R.: Solving the team composition problem in a classroom. Fundam. Informaticae (2020)
30. Marx, D., O'Sullivan, B., Razgon, I.: Finding small separators in linear time via treewidth reduction. ACM Trans. Algorithms (2013)
31. Orvalho, P., Manquinho, V.M., Martins, R.: UpMax: user partitioning for MaxSAT. In: SAT (2023)
32. Papadimitriou, C.H.: Computational Complexity. Academic Internet Publ. (2007)
33. Perron, L., Furnon, V.: Or-tools. https://developers.google.com/optimization/
34. Samer, M., Szeider, S.: Constraint satisfaction with bounded treewidth revisited. In: Benhamou, F. (ed.) CP 2006. LNCS, vol. 4204, pp. 499–513. Springer, Heidelberg (2006). https://doi.org/10.1007/11889205_36
35. Strasser, B.: Computing Tree Decompositions with FlowCutter: PACE 2017 Submission. CoRR abs/1709.08949 (2017)
36. Zhang, C., et al.: AlloyMax: bringing maximum satisfaction to relational specifications. In: ESEC/FSE (2021)
37. Zhang, L., Bacchus, F.: MaxSAT heuristics for cost optimal planning. In: AAAI (2012)

Tackling the Polarity Initialization Problem in SAT Solving Using a Genetic Algorithm

Sabrine Saouli[1(✉)], Souheib Baarir[2], and Claude Dutheillet[1]

[1] Sorbonne Université, CNRS, LIP6, 75005 Paris, France
Sabrine.Saouli@lip6.fr
[2] EPITA, LRE, Le Kremlin-Bicêtre, France

Abstract. The Boolean satisfiability problem holds a significant place in computer science, finding applications across various domains. This problem consists of looking for a truth assignment to a given Boolean formula that either validates it or proves its impossibility.

An indispensable element influencing the efficacy of tools designed for tackling this challenge, known as SAT solvers, is the choice of an appropriate *initialization strategy*. This strategy encompasses the assignment of initial values, or polarities, to the variables before starting the search process. A well-crafted initialization strategy has the capability to curtail the search space and minimize the number of conflicts and backtracks by ensuring that variables are assigned values that are likely to satisfy the formula from the outset.

This paper introduces an innovative initialization approach founded on genetic algorithms, which are evolutionary algorithms inspired by the principles of natural selection and reproduction. Our approach executes a genetic algorithm on the given formula, persisting until it discovers a satisfying assignment or meets predetermined termination criteria.

Subsequently, it furnishes the satisfying assignment in case of success; otherwise, it employs the best assignment (that satisfies the highest number of clauses) to initialize the variables' polarities for the SAT solver.

Keywords: Boolean satisfiability · CDCL SAT solver · Initialization problem · Genetic algorithms · Evolutionary algorithms · Metaheuristic

1 Introduction

Boolean satisfiability is a decision problem that consists in determining whether a given Boolean formula is satisfiable (SAT) (*i.e.*, there exists an assignment of values to the Boolean variables that satisfies all the constraints) or unsatisfiable (UNSAT) (*i.e.*, there is no such assignment that satisfies all the constraints simultaneously). SAT solvers are used to determine the satisfiability of a formula and return SAT (with a model) when it is satisfiable and UNSAT when it is not.

One of the challenges in SAT solving is the *initialization problem*. It has been defined in [12] as follows: given a SAT formula ϕ, compute an initial order over

N. Benz et al. (Eds.): NFM 2024, LNCS 14627, pp. 21–36, 2024.
https://doi.org/10.1007/978-3-031-60698-4_2

the variables of the formula and values/polarities for them in order to reduce the Conflict Driven Clause Learning (CDCL) [26] solver's run-time.

The initialization problem arises in Boolean satisfiability because the solver's efficiency can be greatly affected by the initial assignment. An initial assignment that is close to a satisfying one can quickly lead the solver to a solution that satisfies all clauses while a distant one can slow down the solving process because the solver may need to make more deductions before finding a satisfying assignment or determining that none exists. Therefore, finding a good initialization strategy is critical to the performance of SAT solvers. Various methods have been developed to generate initial assignments for SAT solvers [8,10,12,19].

In this paper, we focus on one aspect of the initialization problem: the polarity initialization of the variables (we refer to this problem as IPP throughout the paper). IPP has been addressed by various heuristics, such as stochastic local search [29], or probabilistic methods, such as Bayesian Moment Matching (BMM) [12]. However, these methods have some limitations. Stochastic local search, for instance, may be trapped in local optima, as it only explores a single solution at a time and its immediate surroundings. Moreover, BMM may be computationally expensive, as it needs to update and sample from a distribution. On the other hand, the genetic algorithm can overcome these challenges. It can explore diverse regions of the search space by applying crossover and mutation operators to a population of candidate solutions (assignments). It can also exploit the quality and diversity of the population by using selection and elitism operators. Consequently, we introduce a new approach, Genetic Algorithm for SAT Polarity Initialization (GASPI), based on a genetic algorithm, that aims at tackling IPP. Our goal is to use a genetic algorithm to initialize the polarity of variables in a way that enhances the performance of SAT solvers.

We implemented this approach in three different state-of-the-art SAT solvers: KISSAT-MAB [24], GLUCOSE [2], and MAPLECOMSPS [21]. We evaluated our technique on the benchmark of SAT Competition 2022 [4] and compared it to the state of the art using two metrics: the number of solved instances and the PAR2 score (*Penalty Algorithm Runtime 2*). The results showed that our technique improve the performance of all three solvers. We also compared our approach to another initialization technique: BMM (Bayesian Moment Matching). The results showed that GASPI outperformed BMM on most of the instances.

The rest of this paper is organized as follows: In Sect. 2 we recall the basic definitions and the technical background related to SAT-solving and genetic algorithms. In Sect. 3, we review the related work on initialization techniques and genetic algorithms in SAT-solving. In Sect. 4, we present our novel approach for initializing the truth values of the variables in SAT solving using a genetic algorithm. Section 5, describes our experimental setup and results. Finally, in Sect. 6, we conclude and suggest some directions for future work.

2 Basic Definitions and Technical Background

2.1 Boolean Satisfiability

A Boolean satisfiability problem is often represented by a Boolean formula in a Conjunctive Normal Form (CNF) in order to be solved by SAT solvers. The CNF form expresses the formula F as a conjunction of clauses, such that $F = C_1 \wedge C_2 \wedge \ldots \wedge C_n$, where $n \geq 1$ and each C_i is a clause. Each clause is a disjunction of literals, such that $C = l_1 \vee l_2 \vee \ldots \vee l_k$, where $k \geq 1$. A literal is defined as either a Boolean variable or its negation where Boolean variables are the building blocks of SAT-solving. They are either true or false and represent the truth value of logical statements.

For a CNF formula F, an assignment α refers to a function that maps each Boolean variable to a truth value: true or false ($\top$ or $\bot$). If the assignment maps all the variables of the formula F, it is said to be *complete*, otherwise, it is *incomplete* or *partial*.

In SAT solving, the goal is to find at least one assignment that makes all the clauses in a CNF formula true. In this case, the satisfying assignment is called a *model* and the algorithm returns SAT. If no such assignment exists, the algorithm returns UNSAT. To achieve this goal, SAT solvers use a variety of algorithms and techniques. There are two main classes of algorithms for solving the satisfiability problem, namely *complete* and *incomplete* algorithms.

2.2 Complete and Incomplete Algorithms

Complete algorithms in SAT solving are those that guarantee a solution to the Boolean satisfiability problem, given enough time and memory. The most popular complete algorithm is the Davis-Putnam-Logemann-Loveland (DPLL) algorithm [11], which uses backtracking and unit propagation to search for a model. Another popular algorithm is the Conflict Driven Clause Learning (CDCL) algorithm [26], which extends DPLL with a conflict analysis mechanism that allows it to learn from conflicts encountered during the search process. This enables CDCL to quickly prune large portions of the search space and find solutions more efficiently than DPLL alone.

On the other hand, incomplete algorithms are based on a simpler approach known as stochastic local search (SLS) to solve the SAT problem. SLS algorithms rely on a series of heuristics and randomization techniques to guide the search toward a solution and require less memory compared to complete algorithms because they do not store any history of the previously explored assignments or learn any new clauses during the search. They only keep track of the current assignment and its fitness score and make local changes to improve it. The fitness here can be defined as a function that assigns a numerical value to each assignment based on its degree of compliance with the given formula, for example: the number of clauses satisfied by the assignment.

A typical SLS algorithm starts with a random initial assignment of variables and then iteratively modifies the assignment by randomly flipping the value of

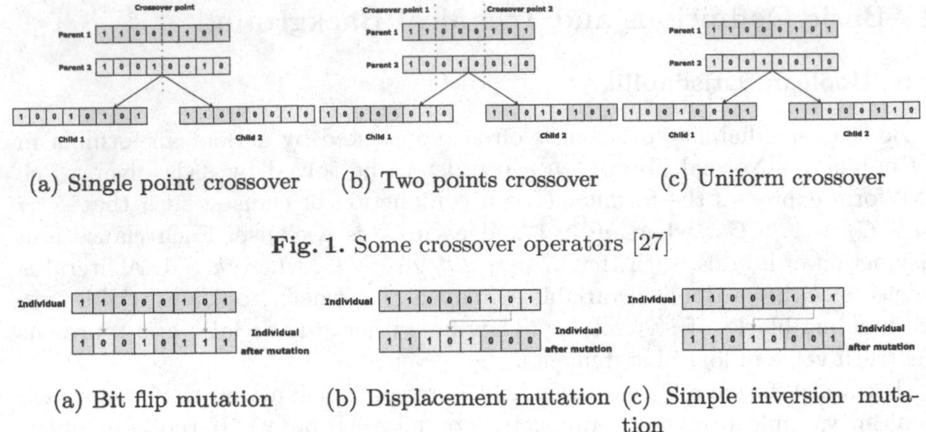

(a) Single point crossover (b) Two points crossover (c) Uniform crossover

Fig. 1. Some crossover operators [27]

(a) Bit flip mutation (b) Displacement mutation (c) Simple inversion mutation

Fig. 2. Some mutation techniques [28]

one variable. This is a simple and effective way to explore the search space, but it may also lead to stagnation. To overcome this problem, more recent SLS algorithms compute some scores for the variables to pick a variable to flip at each step. These scores are based on some heuristics that estimate the impact of flipping a variable on the overall fitness score of the assignment. For example, WALKSAT [25] algorithm uses the break-count heuristic, which counts the number of clauses that become unsatisfied after flipping a variable. CCANR [9] (Configuration Checking with Aspiration for Non-Random satisfiability) algorithm uses the configuration checking with aspiration heuristic, which measures the degree of satisfaction of each clause by an assignment. These heuristics help the SLS algorithms to avoid local optima and find better candidate solutions.

At each step, the SLS algorithms verify whether the new assignment satisfies the formula. If the current assignment is a model, the solver stops and returns SAT; otherwise, the process is repeated until a model is found or a termination condition is met. SLS solvers can be simple and fast since they do not exhaustively explore all possible combinations of variable assignments. However, they may not solve all problems, especially those that are UNSAT. Hence an incomplete algorithm returns SAT if it finds a model, otherwise, it returns UNKNOWN.

2.3 Genetic Algorithms

Genetic algorithms [16] are powerful meta-heuristics that mimic the process of natural selection and evolution to seek optimal or near-optimal solutions for complex problems. They are based on the idea that a population of candidate solutions can be improved over generations by applying operators such as *crossover, mutation, and selection* that are inspired by biological mechanisms. Due to their versatility and effectiveness, genetic algorithms have found extensive applications in artificial intelligence, computing, engineering, and optimization domains.

A genetic algorithm (GA) follows a systematic process to evolve and improve a population of "candidate solutions" (for simplicity, these will be referred to as "solutions" in the rest of the paper).

It begins with a set of random solutions generated to form the initial population. Then, each solution in the population is assigned a fitness score that measures how well it solves the problem. The fitness score is computed based on the objective function or constraints of the problem. During a *"Selection phase"*, a subset of solutions is chosen from the current population to produce offspring for the next generation. This process follows the principle of "survival of the fittest", favoring solutions with higher fitness scores. Various selection methods, such as roulette wheel, tournament, or rank-based, can be employed [18]. Afterward, a *"Crossover"* is performed by recombining pairs of selected solutions to create new offspring by exchanging parts of their encoding [27]. Inspired by biological chromosomal crossover (see Fig. 1), this step introduces genetic diversity and allows the exploration of new regions in the search space. A *"Mutation phase"* follows, where each solution in the offspring population undergoes a small random change in one or more parts of its encoding [28] (see Fig. 2). The crossover and mutation rates are parameters to be set. Then a subset of the solutions is selected to form the next generation. Different replacement strategies can be employed. For example, the entire current population can be replaced or only the worst solutions can be removed. The GA continues iterating through these previous phases until a stopping condition is met. Stopping conditions can be defined by a maximum number of generations, a minimum fitness score, a convergence criterion, or a combination of these.

3 Related Works

3.1 IPP Methods and Heuristics

Various techniques and heuristics have been explored in previous research for initializing the truth values of the variables in SAT solving. One of them is *default initialization*, which is used by most of the modern SAT solvers. This technique simply sets the polarity of all variables to *false*. Some examples of SAT solvers that use this technique are MiniSAT [13], Glucose [2], and MapleCOMSPS [21].

Another technique is to use an SLS SAT solver as a preprocessor. This technique is used in KISSAT-like[1] SAT solvers [24] and consists in running an SLS solver on the SAT problem at hand for a limited amount of time to either solve it or simply use the best complete assignment found to initialize the variables' polarity. This initialization strategy enhances the search effectiveness of CDCL solvers. It is adopted by some of the top-performing SAT solvers in the latest competitions [3,4,14].

Another sophisticated heuristic-based method that was explored is the online Bayesian Moment Matching (BMM) heuristic [12]. This technique is implemented

[1] KISSAT is a CDCL SAT solver originally developed by A. Biere [6] and subsequently improved over time by many others, giving rise to a family of KISSAT-like solvers.

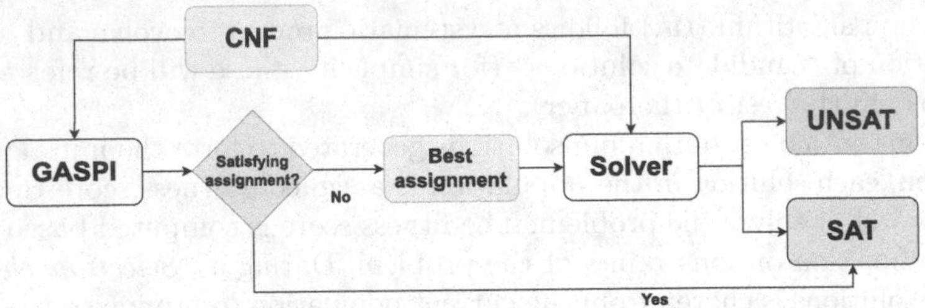

Fig. 3. Flowchart of GASPI

as a preprocessor that runs before the solver. It uses Bayesian inference to estimate the probability of each variable being true or false in a satisfiable formula. It then uses this information to initialize the values of the variables in a CDCL SAT solver. This technique was evaluated on a benchmark of real-world instances from various domains. It showed that it could improve the solver's performance in terms of the number of solved instances and average run-time.

3.2 Genetic Algorithms in SAT Solving

GAs are a type of evolutionary algorithm that can be applied to various optimization and search problems, including the SAT problem [20]. Many studies have investigated the use of GAs for solving SAT problems, especially 3-SAT problems [1,22], and proposed different variations and enhancements of the basic algorithm. For instance, some methods have introduced different crossover and mutation techniques [5], hybridized GAs with unit propagation [7], or incorporated greedy strategy and effective restart [15] to improve the performance and accuracy of GAs for SAT solving.

Despite the various enhancements of GAs for SAT solving, they still face some challenges, such as slow convergence rate, suboptimal solution quality, and parameter tuning [23,28] and have not been able to compete with the state-of-the-art CDCL solvers.

However, GAs can still be useful for SAT solving as a preprocessing tool for CDCL solvers. They can explore a larger portion of the search space than SLS, which tends to get trapped in local optima. By using GAs to initialize the polarity of the problem's variables, we can provide a good starting point for CDCL. This preprocessing approach can improve the efficiency and accuracy of CDCL and enhance its performance, without relying on GAs to find the optimal solution.

4 Tackling IPP with GA

In this section, we introduce the proposed approach for tackling the IPP, Genetic Algorithm for SAT Polarity Initialization (GASPI), which uses a GA to initialize the polarity of the variables for the SAT problem. We explain how GASPI works, how it interacts with the CDCL solver, and how it evaluates the quality of the assignments. We also describe the different genetic operators that we use and how they affect the performance and convergence of GASPI. Finally, we present the parameters configuration that we use and how we determined their values.

4.1 Description of Genetic Algorithm for SAT Polarity Initialization (GASPI)

GASPI is designed as a preprocessing algorithm that receives a SAT problem as input and attempts to find a model. If such an assignment is found, GASPI returns True; otherwise, the SAT solver starts with an initial assignment corresponding to the polarities of the variables for the best individual in the final generation (See Fig. 3).

Algorithm 1 shows how our initialization heuristic works. It follows the classical structure of a GA and takes as inputs the following parameters: `cnf`, the CNF formula representing the original problem, `numGen`, the maximum number of generations; `popSize`, the size of the population; `mutRate`, the mutation rate; `crossRate`, the crossover rate; and `occVars`, the set of variables that appear most frequently in the clauses of the treated problem. `crossOp`, `parentSelOp`, and `nextGenSelOp` represent the methods used for crossover, parent's selection, and selection of the individuals of the next generation respectively. Finally, `fitness`, that represents the fitness function used to measure the quality of the solutions.

```
Input: cnf, popSize, numGen, mutRate, crossRate, occVars, crossOp,
       parentSelOp, nextGenSelOp, fitness
Output: Complete assignment
Generate a random initial population;
for i ← 1 to numGen do
    evaluate the fitness of each individual in the population;
    if model found then
        return model;
    end
    Select parents for crossover using parentSelOp;
    Perform single-point crossover with probability crossRate using crossOp
      operator;
    Perform mutation with probability mutRate on occVars;
    Evaluate fitness of new individuals;
    Select individuals for the next generation using nextGenSelOp operator;
end
return best individual in final population;
```

Algorithm 1: GASPI Pseudocode

We then give some hints on the different steps of the GA algorithm and get into more details for some key operations: representation of the solutions, fitness evaluation, and mutation application.

4.1.1 Pseudocode The algorithm performs the following steps:

- It creates a random initial population of popSize individuals, where each individual represents a possible assignment for the SAT problem (line 1);
- It, then, evaluates the fitness of each individual in the population and keeps track of the best solution found so far (line 3);
- When an individual satisfies the CNF formula, it returns it as a model and declares the formula SAT (lines $4-6$);
- If no model is found, it selects half of the population as parents for reproduction using parentSelOp selection method. It then performs crossOp crossover with probability crossRate on pairs of parents to generate offspring (lines $7-8$);
- At this point, it performs mutation with probability mutRate on occVars to introduce diversity in the population. Mutation randomly flips some bits in a binary vector. occVars are the variables that have a higher impact on the fitness of the solutions, as they affect more clauses (line 9);
- It then evaluates the fitness of the new individuals created by crossover and mutation (line 10).
- Finally, individuals of the next generation are selected according to nextGenSelOp selection method (line 11).

4.1.2 Encoding Our approach uses the following encoding:

- **Individuals:** An individual is a candidate solution. It is represented by a binary vector (representing a complete assignment) where each bit corresponds to the polarity of a variable of the SAT problem.
- **Population:** The population at each generation is represented by a vector of individuals.

4.1.3 Fitness Function It is a crucial component of a GA, as it measures the quality of a candidate solution for a given problem. The fitness function used in this paper evaluates a candidate solution by counting the number of unsatisfied clauses under the given assignment. The lower the fitness value, the better the solution, as it means that more clauses are satisfied. The optimal fitness value is zero, which indicates that the solution is a model for the problem. Therefore, the fitness function guides the GA towards finding models or, at least, assignments that satisfy as many clauses as possible.

4.1.4 Mutation It can help introduce diversity and avoid premature convergence in the search process. However, mutation can also disrupt good solutions and reduce the quality of the population. Therefore, it is important to find the right balance when applying mutation. One way to do this is to mutate a limited number of variables and focus on the most influential ones in the problem.

In our context, we have to look for the variables that have the higher impact on the fitness of the solutions. Of course, this is not a trivial task but we can have some intuition about such variables with respect to their occurrence in the clauses of the treated problem. Indeed, we think that the variables that appear in the greatest number of clauses of the problem at hand are the more influential. Hence, by mutating these variables, we can explore more promising regions of the search space and increase the chances of finding satisfying assignments. However, we have to determine a threshold for the number of variables that we take into account. This is the aim of the `occVars` parameter introduced in Algorithm 1.

4.2 Configuration of GASPI Parameters

Configuration parameters, including population size, maximum number of generations, mutation and/or crossover rates, and specification of the genetic operators, are critical in the context of genetic algorithms because they profoundly influence the performance, behavior, and convergence characteristics of the algorithm. Here, convergence refers to the process of attaining a model or reaching a stable state in which the fitness ceases to progress significantly. The choice of each operator is crucial as it directly impacts which solutions are propagated to subsequent generations. Each method has its advantages and trade-offs in terms of maintaining diversity, preserving promising solutions, and enabling convergence toward optimal or near-optimal solutions.

The population size determines the number of potential solutions (chromosomes) considered in each generation. A larger population size searches a wider area but requires more memory and time while a smaller population size speeds up convergence but risks local optima. Therefore, it is a balance between exploration and exploitation. The number of generations also influences the algorithm's efficiency and effectiveness. Insufficient generations may cause the algorithm to stop before finding the optimal solution while too many generations can be computationally expensive without significant improvement in results. The number of generations is also related to the population size: Over a large number of generations, a small population size may negatively impact the diversity of the individuals, *i.e.*, all individuals in the population become very similar implying a premature convergence to a local minimum. Therefore, they should be considered together when designing a GA for a given problem.

Crossover and mutation probabilities represent the likelihood of genetic operators being applied to chromosomes. Crossover serves to transfer advantageous genetic traits to the succeeding generation, whereas mutation plays a vital role in introducing diversity within the population. For the crossover rate, the intuition is that a high value would mimic the living beings' nature of mating and reproduce novel and diverse solutions. So, we decided to fix its value to 0.95.

To preserve good genes in the next generation, we could use the elitist technique that selects the individuals of the current population with the best fitness values. This can improve the performance and convergence speed of the GA by preventing the loss of good solutions. However, elitist selection alone may also reduce the diversity of the population and cause premature convergence to a local optimum. To avoid this problem, we suggest introducing some randomness and diversity into the next population that will help the GA explore more regions of the search space and escape from local optima. The selection method for the next generation would be a combination of elitist and random selection where half of the best-fit individuals are selected for the next generation, and the other half is selected randomly from the remaining individuals

Starting from a blend of classical parameter settings, reflecting the state-of-the-art, and our insights tailored to the specific needs of our SAT problem, we fixed the definition domains of the different parameters as follows: `popSize` $\in$ {`20, 30`}, `numGen` $\in$ {`10, 20, 30, 40, 50`}, `mutRate` $\in$ {0.25, 0.50, 0.75, 0.88, 1}, `crossRate` $\in$ {0.95}, `occVars` $\in$ {10%}. `parentSelOp,nextGenSelOp` $\in$ {Elitist, Random, Tournament, Elitist+Random}, `crossOp` $\in$ {1-point, 2-points, 3-points}. As we can observe, the total number of possible configurations is 600, and testing all of them requires an excessively long computation time. Besides, there is no guarantee that the optimal values for one problem will be optimal for another. We decided then to select 5% of all these configurations that we thought promising and run a set of experiments using a random subset of 100 instances from the main track of the SAT Competition 2022 benchmark [4]. We conducted our experiments using a GASPI implementation, built upon the GLUCOSE solver. The results of our investigation revealed that specific parameter values had a notably more beneficial impact on our approach than others.

Accordingly, the parameter values we kept for the remaining experiments are as follows: `popSize:`20, `numGen:`40, `crossRate:0.95`, `mutRate:0.88`, `occVars:10% of the variables`, `parentSelOp:`Random, `nextGenSelOp:` `Elitist+`Random, `crossOp:1-point`.

5 Experimental Results

In this section, we report the results of our experiments to evaluate the performance of our proposed approach, GASPI, when compared with different existing initialization methods (default initialization, SLS, and BMM).

All experiments were conducted on a computer with an Intel(R) Xeon(R) Gold 6148 CPU @ 2.40 GHz and 1500 GB of memory. Each solver was run on each instance with a timeout of 7200 s (including the polarity initialization time if used).

5.1 Solvers

To evaluate the performance of our approach, we implemented GASPI on three different baseline solvers: KISSAT-MAB [24], GLUCOSE [2], and MAPLECOMSPS [21]. These solvers are among the top performers in the SAT competitions in the last decade and use various techniques to improve their efficiency and effectiveness. We evaluated the performance of GASPI against three existing initialization methods: (1) the default initialization that assigns false to all Boolean variables, as used by GLUCOSE and MAPLECOMSPS; (2) the stochastic local search (SLS) initialization as used by KISSAT-MAB; and (3) the Bayesian Moment Matching (BMM) initialization that estimates the probabilities of the variables and assigns them accordingly, as implemented on GLUCOSE and MAPLECOMSPS. We name the different versions of the solvers we will evaluate as follows:

1. SLS-KISSAT: This is KISSAT-MAB that uses stochastic local search (SLS) initialization.
2. GLUCOSE: This is the base solver GLUCOSE-Syrup that uses the default initialization.
3. BMM-GLUCOSE: This is GLUCOSE with BMM initialization.
4. MAPLECOMSPS: This is the base solver MAPLECOMSPS that uses the default initialization.
5. BMM-MAPLECOMSPS: This is the base solver MAPLECOMSPS with BMM initialization.
6. GASPI-SOLVER: This is a solver that uses GASPI for polarity initialization (instead of its original initialization technique) such as GASPI-GLUCOSE[2], GASPI-KISSAT[3] or GASPI-MAPLECOMSPS[4].

5.2 Benchmarks

To evaluate the performance of our approach, we randomly selected 350 instances (due to time constraints) from the main track of the SAT competition 2022 benchmark [4], which covers different categories and difficulty levels. However, we believe that this sample size is still large enough to provide meaningful results. These selected instances can be found here https://zenodo.org/records/10819491

5.3 Results

The experiments were run three times for both SLS-KISSAT and GASPI-KISSAT on each instance because of the non-deterministic and random nature of the GA and the SLS. Both GA and SLS generate the first population randomly which can lead to different results in each run. Therefore, running the experiments multiple times can reduce the effect of randomness and provide a more reliable and robust evaluation.

Table 1 summarizes the results of our experiment.

The sub-tables 1a, 1b, and 1c report the number of solved instances when we consider the minimum, maximum, and average run time for each instance, respectively.

The minimum and maximum run times can be intuitive and easy to understand, but they may not reflect the overall performance of the configuration. Therefore, we also use the average run time, which is computed as the mean run time of the three runs for each instance, where we consider an instance as solved if the average run time is less than 7200 s, and as unsolved otherwise.

The first column in each sub-table shows the name of the solver. The second, third, and fourth columns show the number of UNSAT, SAT, and total instances

[2] https://github.com/sabrinesaouli/GASPIGLUCOSE.

[3] https://github.com/sabrinesaouli/GASPIKISSAT.

[4] https://github.com/sabrinesaouli/GASPIMAPLE.

Table 1. Evaluation of GASPI-KISSAT and SLS-KISSAT

Solvers	UNSAT	SAT	Total (350)	PAR-2
VBS	129	141	270	1362534
SLS-KISSAT	127	133	260	1525795
GASPI-KISSAT	129	139	268	1405100

(a) Best run time

Solvers	UNSAT	SAT	Total (350)	PAR-2
VBS	126	126	252	1659595
SLS-KISSAT	124	122	246	1752335
GASPI-KISSAT	123	118	241	1816642

(b) Worst run time

Solvers	UNSAT	SAT	Total (350)	PAR-2
VBS	129	141	270	1453942
SLS-KISSAT	127	133	260	1594273
GASPI-KISSAT	129	139	268	1514151

(c) Average run time

solved by each solver, respectively. Finally, the fifth column represents the PAR-2 score of each solver, which is a metric, used in SAT competitions, that evaluates the effectiveness of the solver by penalizing timeouts and errors. PAR-2 stands for *Penalty Algorithm Runtime 2*, and it is calculated by multiplying the run time of each instance by a factor of 2 if the solver failed to solve it or reported an incorrect answer. The lower the PAR-2 score, the better the solver.

When we consider the best and average results, GASPI-KISSAT solves more instances than SLS-KISSAT (8 more instances). Moreover, GASPI shows higher effectiveness on SAT instances than on UNSAT instances, as it solves only 2 more UNSAT instances and 6 more SAT instances than SLS-KISSAT in both the best and average cases. This suggests that GASPI can find models more reliably than SLS, which may get trapped in local optima. These results were in line with our expectations, as GASPI is designed to find a satisfiable assignment for the SAT problem. When the problem is unsatisfiable, GASPI may waste time and resources trying to find a solution that does not exist, or it may reach a local optimum that satisfies most but not all of the clauses. Therefore, GASPI has higher performance on SAT instances than on UNSAT instances. Furthermore, GASPI-KISSAT has a lower PAR-2 score than SLS-KISSAT, which means that it is more efficient and this can also be observed on the scatter plots of Fig. 4.

Moreover, when evaluating the VBS (Virtual Best Solver) metric, which reflects the best performances combined, i.e. the number of instances that at least one solver can solve, we observe that it is always higher than the performance of each solver alone. In other words, GASPI-KISSAT solves instances that SLS-KISSAT didn't, and the other way around.

To go further in our study, we evaluated GASPI performance compared to the two other solvers: GLUCOSE and MAPLECOMSPS. We compared GASPI with the default initialization method of these solvers, which assigns false to all variables, as well as with the BMM initialization method. We used the same set of instances and ran GASPI-GLUCOSE and GASPI-MAPLECOMSPS only once (since the default initialization method and BMM initialization method are deterministic).

Table 2 presents the number of solved instances by GLUCOSE, MAPLECOMSPS, and their different initialization techniques. The results demonstrate that

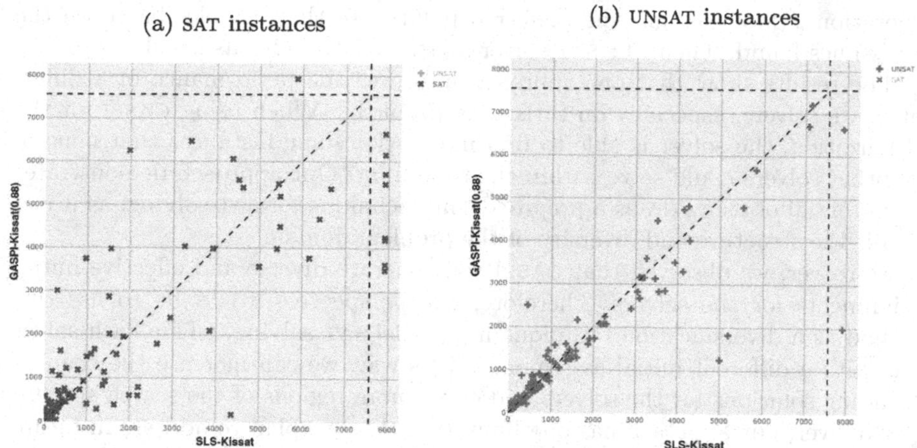

Fig. 4. Results of the comparison between SLS-KISSAT and GASPI-KISSAT(0.88) on the benchmark of 2022 when considering the average run time.

Table 2. Evaluation of GASPI-GLUCOSE and GASPI-MAPLECOMSPS

Solvers	UNSAT	SAT	Total (350)	PAR-2
GLUCOSE	99	72	171	2053133
BMM-GLUCOSE	99	75	174	2015878
GASPI-GLUCOSE	102	88	190	1920238
MAPLECOMSPS	107	101	208	2308575
BMM-MAPLECOMSPS	109	103	212	2295755
GASPI-MAPLECOMSPS	109	107	216	2259439

our approach improves the performance of both GLUCOSE and MAPLECOMSPS. Even though the improvements are more significant in SAT instances, GASPI still outperforms the default and BMM initialization methods on UNSAT instances as well. These results are consistent with the previous observations.

6 Conclusion and Future Works

One of the challenges in Boolean satisfiability (SAT) is the initialization problem, which involves determining the optimal initial configuration for the variables in a SAT solver for a given problem. The nature of the problem influences these values, and the closer they are to a satisfying assignment (for satisfiable problems), the faster the SAT solver converges.

This paper proposes a novel approach, called GASPI, that employs a Genetic Algorithm as a preprocessor for the solving process. Starting from a CNF formula, it attempts to find an optimal or near-optimal complete assignment that satisfies all or most of the clauses. If no model is found after a predefined number of generations, GASPI assigns the preferred polarity of the variables based on the best values found. Then, the SAT solver starts and operates as usual.

The results show that our approach improves the performance of 3 different CDCL solvers, especially on satisfiable problems. When using GASPI for the initialization, the solver is able to find models for some instances that none of the other solvers could solve within the time limit. Our approach demonstrates the potential of using GA as a preprocessing technique for SAT solving, as it can exploit the structure and diversity of the problem domain.

Moreover, we observed that GASPI can generate diverse and effective initial assignments for the solvers. Therefore, one perspective would be to use this method as a diversification technique in parallel SAT solving, where each solver runs with a different initial assignment. This way, we can increase the chances of finding solutions for the solvers and cover more regions of the search space.

However, our approach has one limitation that we plan to address in future work: the difficulty of finding the right configuration for each problem. The parameters affect the quality and speed of the GA, and they may vary depending on the characteristics of the CNF formula. We are aware that there are some tools, such as SMAC [17] (Sequential Model-based Algorithm Configuration) that can help automatically tune the parameters of algorithms. Nevertheless, we decided to perform manual tuning as a first step because it can provide us with some insights into the behavior and sensitivity of our method concerning different parameter settings. Furthermore, manual tuning can serve as a baseline for comparing the performance of automatic tuning methods in the future. Therefore, another perspective would be to use machine learning techniques to automatically tune the GA parameters based on some features of the problem.

References

1. Aiman, U., Asrar, N.: Genetic algorithm based solution to SAT-3 problem. J. Comput. Sci. Appl. **3**(2), 33–39 (2015)
2. Audemard, G., Simon, L.: Predicting learnt clauses quality in modern SAT solvers. In: Proceedings of the 21st International Joint Conference on Artificial Intelligence, IJCAI 2009, pp. 399–404 (2009)
3. Balyo, T., Heule, M., Iser, M., Järvisalo, M., Suda, M.: Proceedings of SAT competition 2023: solver, benchmark and proof checker descriptions (2023)
4. Balyo, T., Heule, M.J., Iser, M., Järvisalo, M., Suda, M.: SAT competition 2022 (2022)
5. Bhattacharjee, A., Chauhan, P.: Solving the SAT problem using genetic algorithm. Adv. Sci. Technol. Eng. Syst **2**(4), 115–120 (2017)
6. Biere, A., Fazekas, K., Fleury, M., Heisinger, M.: CaDiCaL, Kissat, Paracooba, Plingeling and Treengeling entering the SAT Competition 2020. In: Balyo, T., Froleyks, N., Heule, M., Iser, M., Järvisalo, M., Suda, M. (eds.) Proceedings of SAT Competition 2020 – Solver and Benchmark Descriptions. Department of Computer Science Report Series B, vol. B-2020-1, pp. 51–53. University of Helsinki (2020)
7. Boughaci, D., Drias, H., Benhamou, B., et al.: Combining a unit propagation with genetic algorithms to solve Max-SAT problems (2008)

8. Braunstein, A., Mézard, M., Zecchina, R.: Survey propagation: an algorithm for satisfiability. Random Struct. Algorithms **27**(2), 201–226 (2005)
9. Cai, S., Luo, C., Su, K.: CCAnr: a configuration checking based local search solver for non-random satisfiability. In: Heule, M., Weaver, S. (eds.) SAT 2015. LNCS, vol. 9340, pp. 1–8. Springer, Cham (2015). https://doi.org/10.1007/978-3-319-24318-4_1
10. Cai, S., Luo, C., Zhang, X., Zhang, J.: Improving local search for structured SAT formulas via unit propagation based construct and cut initialization (short paper). In: 27th International Conference on Principles and Practice of Constraint Programming (CP 2021) (2021)
11. Davis, M., Logemann, G., Loveland, D.: A machine program for theorem-proving. Commun. ACM **5**(7), 394–397 (1962)
12. Duan, H., Nejati, S., Trimponias, G., Poupart, P., Ganesh, V.: Online Bayesian moment matching based SAT solver heuristics. In: International Conference on Machine Learning, pp. 2710–2719. PMLR (2020)
13. Eén, N., Sörensson, N.: An extensible SAT-solver. In: International Conference on Theory and Applications of Satisfiability Testing (2003)
14. Froleyks, N., Heule, M., Iser, M., Järvisalo, M., Suda, M.: SAT competition 2020. Artif. Intell. **301**, 103572 (2021)
15. Fu, H., Xu, Y., Wu, G., Ning, X.: An improved genetic algorithm for solving 3-SAT problems based on effective restart and greedy strategy. In: 2017 12th International Conference on Intelligent Systems and Knowledge Engineering (ISKE), pp. 1–6. IEEE (2017)
16. Holland, J.H.: Adaptation in Natural and Artificial Systems: An Introductory Analysis with Applications to Biology, Control, and Artificial Intelligence. MIT Press, Cambridge (1992)
17. Hutter, F., Hoos, H.H., Leyton-Brown, K.: Sequential model-based optimization for general algorithm configuration. In: Coello, C.A.C. (ed.) LION 2011. LNCS, vol. 6683, pp. 507–523. Springer, Heidelberg (2011). https://doi.org/10.1007/978-3-642-25566-3_40
18. Jebari, K., Madiafi, M., et al.: Selection methods for genetic algorithms. Int. J. Emerg. Sci. **3**(4), 333–344 (2013)
19. Jeroslow, R.G., Wang, J.: Solving propositional satisfiability problems. Ann. Math. Artif. Intell. **1**(1–4), 167–187 (1990)
20. Katoch, S., Chauhan, S.S., Kumar, V.: A review on genetic algorithm: past, present, and future. Multimed. Tools Appl. **80**, 8091–8126 (2021)
21. Liang, J.H., Oh, C., Ganesh, V., Czarnecki, K., Poupart, P.: Maple-comsps, maple-comsps lrb, maplecomsps chb. In: Proceedings of SAT Competition 2016 (2016)
22. Marchiori, E., Rossi, C.: A flipping genetic algorithm for hard 3-SAT problems (1999)
23. Rana, S., Heckendorn, R.B., Whitley, D.: A tractable Walsh analysis of SAT and its implications for genetic algorithms. In: Proceedings of the AAAI Conference on Artificial Intelligence, vol. 15, pp. 392–397 (1998)
24. Sami Cherif, M., Habet, D., Terrioux, C.: Un bandit manchot pour combiner CHB et VSIDS. In: Actes des 16èmes Journées Francophones de Programmation par Contraintes (JFPC), Nice, France (2021)
25. Selman, B., Kautz, H.A.: An empirical study of greedy local search for satisfiability testing. In: AAAI, vol. 93, pp. 46–51 (1993)
26. Silva, J.P.M., Sakallah, K.A.: GRASP—a new search algorithm for satisfiability. In: Proceedings of the 16th IEEE/ACM International Conference on Computer-Aided Design (ICCAD), pp. 220–227. IEEE (1997)

27. Soon, G.K., Guan, T.T., On, C.K., Alfred, R., Anthony, P.: A comparison on the performance of crossover techniques in video game. In: 2013 IEEE International Conference on Control System, Computing and Engineering. IEEE (2013)
28. Springer, P., Katoch, S.: A review on genetic algorithm: past, present, and future. Multimed. Tools Appl. **79**, 44651–44681 (2020)
29. Zhang, X., Cai, S., Chen, Z.: Improving CDCL via local search. In: SAT Competition 2021, p. 42 (2021)

Formalization of Asymptotic Convergence for Stationary Iterative Methods

Mohit Tekriwal(✉), Joshua Miller, and Jean-Baptiste Jeannin

University of Michigan, Ann Arbor, MI 48109, USA
{tmohit,joshmi,jeannin}@umich.edu

Abstract. Solutions to differential equations, which are used to model physical systems, are computed numerically by solving a set of discretized equations. This set of discretized equations is reduced to a large linear system, whose solution is typically found using an iterative solver. We start with an initial guess, x_0, and iterate the algorithm to obtain a sequence of solution vectors, x_k, which are approximations to the exact solution of the linear system, x. The iterative algorithm is said to converge to x, in the field of reals, if and only if x_k converges to x in the limit of $k \to \infty$.

In this paper, we formally prove the asymptotic convergence of a particular class of iterative methods called the *stationary iterative methods*, in the Coq theorem prover. We formalize the necessary and sufficient conditions required for the *iterative convergence*, and extend this result to two classical iterative methods: the Gauss–Seidel method and the Jacobi method. For the Gauss–Seidel method, we also formalize a set of *easily testable conditions* for iterative convergence, called the *Reich theorem*, for a particular matrix structure, and apply this on a model problem of the one-dimensional heat equation. We also apply the main theorem of iterative convergence to prove convergence of the Jacobi method on the model problem.

Keywords: Stationary Iterative Methods · Iterative Convergence · Gauss–Seidel method · Jacobi method

1 Introduction

Solutions to differential equations are often obtained numerically, which involves solving a large linear system, $Ax = b$. This system is obtained after discretizing a differential equation in a finite computational domain to obtain a set of discretized equations. Direct methods to solve this linear system, such as Gaussian elimination, usually involve matrix inversion, which is computationally expensive with computational complexity of $\mathcal{O}(N^3)$, where N is the dimension of the linear system. Therefore, low-cost methods such as *iterative methods* [21], which have

M. Tekriwal—Currently affiliated with the Lawrence Livermore National Laboratory, USA.

N. Benz et al. (Eds.): NFM 2024, LNCS 14627, pp. 37–56, 2024.
https://doi.org/10.1007/978-3-031-60698-4_3

an average complexity of $\mathcal{O}(N^2)$, are used to obtain an *approximate* solution of the linear system.

The goal of an iterative method is to build a sequence of approximations of the *true numerical solution*, which is defined as $x \triangleq A^{-1}b$. One starts with an initial guess vector x_0, and builds a sequence of approximate solutions: $\{x_1, x_2, \ldots, x_{k-1}, x_k\}$ for k iterations, with the hope that x_k is close to x. The distance between x_k and x is called the *iterative convergence error*. To ensure the asymptotic convergence of these approximate solutions to the true numerical solution, we need to bound the iterative convergence error, and further show that this error decreases as we increase the number of iterations.

Many general purpose ordinary differential equation (ODE) solvers use some kind of iterative method to solve linear systems. For instance, ODEPACK [10], which is a collection of FORTRAN solvers for initial value problems for ODEs, uses iterative (preconditioned Krylov) methods instead of direct methods for solving linear systems. Another widely used suite of ODE solvers is SUNDIALS [11]. SUNDIALS has support for a variety of direct and Krylov iterative methods for solving systems of linear equations. SUNDIALS solvers are used by the mixed finite element (MFEM) package for solving nonlinear algebraic systems and by NASA for spacecraft trajectory simulation [11]. Because those iterative methods are widely used, it is important to obtain formal guarantees for the convergence of iterative solutions to the "true" solution of differential equations. In this work we use the Coq theorem prover to formalize the convergence guarantees for a class of iterative methods called the *Stationary iterative methods.* The choice of stationary iterative methods for formalization is motivated by the fact that this class of methods is used as building blocks for more complicated iterative solvers like Krylov subspace and conjugate gradient methods [21].

Contributions: We provide an overview of the *stationary iterative methods* in Sect. 2, followed by a formalization of a generalized iterative convergence theorem in Coq, and its specialization to two classical iterative methods. Overall, this work[1] makes the following contributions:

- we provide a formalization of the necessary and sufficient conditions for iterative convergence in Coq in Sect. 4;
- we formalize a set of easily testable conditions for convergence of the Gauss–Seidel classical iterative method for a specific matrix structure in Sect. 5 and prove convergence on a model problem in Sect. 6.1;
- we then apply the generalized iterative convergence theorem to an example of the Jacobi iteration, another classical iterative method, to prove its convergence in Sect. 6.2;
- we develop libraries for dealing with complex matrices and vectors, and formalize ℓ^2 norm of a matrix and its spectral properties.

All of the above formalization has been done in the field of real numbers.

[1] Our Coq formalization is available at https://github.com/mohittkr/iterative_convergence.git.

2 Overview of Stationary Iterative Methods

In this section, we provide an overview of the stationary iterative methods adapted from the textbook [21].

Let x be the true numerical solution, or the direct solution obtained by inverting the linear system $Ax = b$ as

$$x \triangleq A^{-1}b \tag{1}$$

Here, the *coefficient* matrix $A \in \mathbb{R}^{n \times n}$ and the *right hand side* vector $b \in \mathbb{R}^n$ are known to us and we are computing the unknown vector $x \in \mathbb{R}^n$. We assume that the matrix A is non-singular. Thus, there exists a unique solution x of the linear system $Ax = b$. For any iterative algorithm, we start with an initial guess vector x_0 and obtain a sequence of numerical solutions which are an approximation of the solution x. Let x_k be the iterative solution obtained after k iterations obtained by solving the iterative system

$$Mx_k + Nx_{k-1} = b \tag{2}$$

for some choice of initial solution vector x_0. The vector x_{k-1} is the iterative solution obtained after $k-1$ iterations. At the kth iteration step, x_{k-1} is known to us. The matrices M and N are obtained by splitting (*regular splitting* [21]) the original coefficient matrix A such that M is easily invertible. Therefore,

$$A = M + N. \tag{3}$$

The choice of matrices M and N define the choice of an iterative method. For instance, if we choose M to be the lower triangular entries of A and N to be the strictly upper triangular entries of A, we get the Gauss–Seidel iterative method [21]. Thus, for the Gauss–Seidel method, $M = L + D$, and $N = U$, where L, D, and U are illustrated in Fig. 1. If we choose M to be the diagonal entries of matrix A and N to be the strictly lower and upper triangular entries of A, we obtain the Jacobi method [21]. Thus, for the Jacobi method, $M = D$, and $N = L + U$. Therefore, the matrices M and N are also known to us based on the choice of an iterative method. The right hand vector b is also known to us. Thus, the unknown solution vector x_k at k^{th} step is obtained by rearranging terms in the iterative system (2) as

$$x_k = (-M^{-1}N)x_{k-1} + M^{-1}b \tag{4}$$

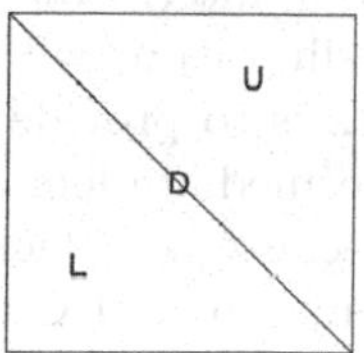

Fig. 1. Initial partitioning of matrix $A = L + D + U$. L is the strictly lower triangular matrix. D is the diagonal matrix. U is the strictly upper triangular matrix.

The quantity $(-M^{-1}N)$ in Eq. (4) is called an *iterative matrix* and we will denote it as S. Therefore,

$$S \triangleq -M^{-1}N \tag{5}$$

The iterative convergence error after k iterations is defined as

$$e_k^{iterative} \triangleq x_k - x = S^k e_0; \quad e_o \triangleq x_o - x \tag{6}$$

The iterative solution x_k is said to converge to x in the field of reals if and only if

$$\lim_{k\to\infty} ||e_k^{iterative}|| = \lim_{k\to\infty} ||x_k - x|| = 0 \tag{7}$$

where $||.||$ denotes a vector norm. In this paper, we will be using the ℓ^2 vector norm defined as $||x||_2 = \sqrt{\sum_{j=1}^{n} |x_{\{i\}}|^2}$.

In this work, we consider two concrete instances of stationary iterative methods: the Gauss–Seidel method [21], for which the iterative matrix $S_G \triangleq -M^{-1}N = -(L+D)^{-1}U$, and the Jacobi method [21], for which the iterative matrix $S_J \triangleq -M^{-1}N = -D^{-1}(A-D) = I - D^{-1}A$.

3 Generic Iterative Convergence Theorem in the Field of Reals

The following theorem provides necessary and sufficient conditions for iterative convergence in the field of reals.

Theorem 1. *[21] Let an iterative matrix be defined as (5) for the iterative system (2). The sequence of iterative solutions $\{x_k\}$ converges to the direct solution x for all initial values x_0, if and only if the spectral radius of the iterative matrix $S = -M^{-1}N$ is less than 1, i.e.,*

$$(\forall\ x_o, \lim_{k\to\infty} ||x_k - x|| = 0) \iff \rho(-M^{-1}N) < 1.$$

The spectral radius ρ of a matrix is defined as the maximum eigenvalue in magnitude. We next discuss the proof of Theorem 1 followed by its formalization in the Coq proof assistant. It is noteworthy that while such proofs have been discussed in numerical analysis literature, we found several missing pieces during the formalization. Most facts about intermediate steps in the proof were just stated in the numerical analysis literature without a rigorous proof. In that regard, a contribution of this work is to provide a clean machine-checked proof of the main theorem and any intermediate lemma or fact that was required to close the proof of Theorem 1. Because of a lack of space, we provide most of the informal proofs in the Appendix A and C in the extended version of this paper [24].

To prove Theorem 1, we first need to obtain a recurrence relation for the iterative convergence error at k^{th} step in terms of the initial iteration error $(x_0 - x)$. Therefore,

Proof (Proof of Theorem 1).

$$\begin{aligned} x_k - x &= -M^{-1}Nx_{k-1} + M^{-1}b - x \\ &= -M^{-1}Nx_{k-1} + M^{-1}(Ax) - x \quad [\text{Since, } Ax \triangleq b] \\ &= -M^{-1}Nx_{k-1} + M^{-1}(M+N)x - x \; [\text{Since, } M+N = A] \\ &= -M^{-1}Nx_{k-1} + M^{-1}Mx + M^{-1}Nx - x \\ &= -M^{-1}N(x_{k-1} - x) \quad [\text{Since, } M^{-1}M \triangleq I] \end{aligned}$$

Taking the norm of the vector on both sides, the iterative convergence error at the kth step can be written in terms of the iterative convergence error at $(k-1)$ step as

$$||x_k - x|| = ||(-M^{-1}N)(x_{k-1} - x)|| \tag{8}$$

Since, the system is linear, Eq. (8) can be written in terms of the initial iteration error as

$$||x_k - x|| = ||(-M^{-1}N)^k(x_0 - x)|| \tag{9}$$

Taking limits of the vector norms on both sides of Eq. (9),

$$\lim_{k\to\infty} ||x_k - x|| = \lim_{k\to\infty} ||(-M^{-1}N)^k(x_0 - x)|| \tag{10}$$

If $x_0 = x$, the iterative convergence error is zero trivially. The case $x_0 \neq x$ is interesting and we can prove Theorem 1 by splitting it into two lemmas

Lemma 1. *For given matrices $M \in \mathbb{R}^{n\times n}$ and $N \in \mathbb{R}^{n\times n}$ respecting the regular splitting, i.e., $A = M + N$, the sequence of iterative solutions $\{x_k\}$ converges to x for any given initial vector x_0 if and only if the ℓ^2 matrix norm of the iterated product of the iteration matrix, $(-M^{-1}N)^k$ approaches zero as $k \to \infty$, i.e.,*

$$(\forall x_0, \lim_{k\to\infty} ||(-M^{-1}N)^k(x_0 - x)|| = 0) \iff \lim_{k\to\infty} ||(-M^{-1}N)^k|| = 0 \tag{11}$$

Lemma 2. *For given matrices $M \in \mathbb{R}^{n\times n}$ and $N \in \mathbb{R}^{n\times n}$ respecting the regular splitting, i.e., $A = M + N$, the ℓ^2 matrix norm of the iterated product of the iteration matrix, $(-M^{-1}N)^k$ approaches zero as $k \to \infty$ if and only if the spectral radius of the iteration matrix is less than 1, i.e.,*

$$\lim_{k\to\infty} ||(-M^{-1}N)^k|| = 0 \iff \rho(-M^{-1}N) < 1 \tag{12}$$

Therefore, by composing proofs of the Lemma 1 (see Appendix A in the extended version [24]) and the Lemma 2 (see Appendix C in the extended version [24]), we close the proof of the Theorem 1.

4 Formalization of the the Generalized Iterative Convergence Theorem (Theorem 1) in Coq

One of the main challenges that we encountered during our formalization was the lack of theories for matrix and vector norm and generic properties about complex vectors and matrices. We will first discuss the formalization of these properties in Coq, followed by their adoption in our formalization on iterative convergence.

4.1 Formalizing Properties of Complex Matrices and Vectors

The `complex` theory in the `real_closed` [7] library in MathComp defines complex numbers and basic operations on them. They define complex numbers as a real closed field, thereby allowing us to instantiate a generic field with a complex field. This was useful when we used the `eigenvalue` definition from MathComp matrix algebra library and the canonical forms library by Cano et al. [6]. However, since the basic properties like modulus of a complex number, conjugates, properties of complex matrices and vectors were lacking, we added them in our formalization[2]. We define the modulus of a complex number as

```
Definition C_mod (x: complex R):= sqrt ( (Re x)^+2 + (Im x)^+2).
```

`Re x` and `Im x` denote the real and imaginary part of `x`, respectively. We proved some basic properties of the modulus, which we enumerate in Table 1. We also found that some theory on complex conjugates were missing in the MathComp library. The Table 2 lists the missing formalization of complex conjugates that we added for this formalization. We also formalize the properties of a conjugate matrix like idempotent property, scaling of a complex matrix, conjugate transpose of matrix multiplication, etc., which we do not list here for brevity.

4.2 Formalization of Vector and Matrix Norms

Another missing piece in the existing linear algebra theory in MathComp was the norm of a vector and a matrix. In this work, we formalize the ℓ^2-norm of a vector and its induced matrix norm. In Coq, we define the ℓ^2-norm of a matrix as

```
Definition matrix_norm (n:nat) (A: 'M[complex R]_n.+1) := Lub_Rbar (fun x ⇒
    ∃v: 'cV[complex R]_n.+1, v != 0 ∧ x = (vec_norm_C (A *m v))/ (vec_norm_C v)).
```

where `vec_norm_C` is the ℓ^2-norm of a complex vector, which we define in Coq as

```
Definition vec_norm_C (n:nat) (x: 'cV[complex R]_n.+1):= sqrt (∑_l (C_mod x l 0)^2)
```

[2] The theory about complex modulus and norms has been added in most recent developments of MathComp after our discussion with the developers. We were pointed to the development of matrix norms in the CoqQ project (https://github.com/coq-quantum/CoqQ/blob/main/src/mxnorm.v), which was done concurrently with our development.

Table 1. Formalization of properties of complex modulus in Coq

Mathematical properties	Formalization in Coq
$\|\|0\|\| = 0$	**Lemma** C_mod_0: C_mod 0 = 0%Re.
$0 \leq \|\|x\|\|$	**Lemma** C_mod_ge_0: ∀(x: complex R), (0<= C_mod x)%Re.
$\|\|xy\|\| = \|\|x\|\| \; \|\|y\|\|$	**Lemma** C_mod_prod: ∀(x y: complex R), C_mod (x * y) = C_mod x * C_mod y.
$\|\|\frac{x}{y}\|\| = \frac{\|\|x\|\|}{\|\|y\|\|}, y \neq 0$	**Lemma** C_mod_div: ∀(x y: complex R), y <> 0 → C_mod (x / y) = (C_mod x) / (C_mod y).
$\|\|x\|\| \neq 0, \quad \text{if. } x \neq 0$	**Lemma** C_mod_not_zero: ∀(x: complex R), x <> 0 → C_mod x <> 0.
$\|\|1\|\| = 1$	**Lemma** C_mod_1: C_mod 1 = 1.
$\|\|x^n\|\| = \|\|x\|\|^n$	**Lemma** C_mod_pow: ∀(x: complex R) (n:nat), C_mod (x^+ n) = (C_mod x)^+n.
$\|\|x + y\|\| \leq \|\|x\|\| + \|\|y\|\|$	**Lemma** C_mod_add_leq : ∀(a b: complex R), C_mod (a + b) <= C_mod a + C_mod b.
$\|\|\frac{1}{x}\|\| = \frac{1}{\|\|x\|\|}, \quad \text{if } x \neq 0$	**Lemma** C_mod_inv : ∀x : complex R, x <> 0 → C_mod (invc x) = Rinv (C_mod x).
$\|\|xy\|\|^2 = \|\|x\|\|^2 \|\|y\|\|^2$	**Lemma** C_mod_sqr: ∀(x y : complex R), Rsqr (C_mod (x * y)) = (Rsqr (C_mod x)) * (Rsqr (C_mod y)).
$\|\| - x\|\| = \|\|x\|\|$	**Lemma** C_mod_minus_x: ∀(x: complex R), C_mod (−x) = C_mod x.
$\|\| \sum_{j=0}^{n} u(j)\|\| \leq \sum_{j=0}^{n} \|\|u(j)\|\|$	**Lemma** C_mod_sum_rel: ∀(n:nat) (u : 'I_n.+1 → (complex R)), (C_mod ($\sum_j$ (u j))) <= $\sum_j$ ((C_mod (u j))).

Table 2. Formalization of properties of complex conjugates in Coq. [1]Here, RtoC is a coercion from reals to complex.

Mathematical properties	Formalization in Coq
$\overline{xy} = \bar{x}\,\bar{y}$	**Lemma** Cconj_prod: ∀(x y: complex R), conjc (x*y)%C = (conjc x * conjc y)%C.
$\overline{x + y} = \bar{x} + \bar{y}$	**Lemma** Cconj_add: ∀(x y: complex R), conjc (x+y) = conjc x + conjc y.
$\|\|x\|\| = \|\|\bar{x}\|\|$	**Lemma** Cconjc_mod: ∀(a: complex R), C_mod a = C_mod (conjc a).
$x = \bar{\bar{x}}$	**Lemma** conj_of_conj_C: ∀(x: complex R), x = conjc (conjc x).
$\bar{x}x = \|\|x\|\|^2$	**Lemma** conj_prod: ∀(x:complex R), ((conjc x)*x)%C = RtoC (Rsqr (C_mod x)). [1]
$Re[x] + Re[\bar{x}] = 2Re[x]$	**Lemma** Re_conjc_add: ∀(x: complex R), Re x + Re (conjc x) = 2 * (Re x).
$\overline{\sum_{j=0}^{n} f(i)} = \sum_{j=0}^{n} \overline{f(i)}$	**Lemma** Cconj_sum: ∀(p:nat) (x: 'I_p → complex R), conjc ($\sum_{j<p}$ x j)= $\sum_{j<p}$ conjc (x j).

The definition `Lub_Rbar` is the least upper bound and is already defined in the `Coquelicot` [5] library. Mathematically, `matrix_norm` formalizes the following definition of a matrix norm $||A||_i = \sup_{x \neq 0} \frac{||Ax||}{||x||}$, for a given vector norm $||.||$, which in this case is the ℓ^2 vector norm. In Table 3 and Table 4 we enumerate the properties of vector and matrix norms that we formalized.

Table 3. Formalization of properties of vector norm in Coq. [1] vec_not_zero is Coq's definition of $v \neq 0$.

Mathematical properties	Formalization in Coq
$0 \leq \|\|v\|\|$	**Lemma** vec_norm_C_ge_0: ∀(n:nat) (v: 'cV[complex R]_n.+1), 0<= vec_norm_C v.
$\|\|av\|\| = \|a\| \; \|\|v\|\|, \quad a$ is scalar	**Lemma** ei_vec_ei_compat: ∀(n:nat) (x:complex R) (v: 'cV[complex R]_n.+1), vec_norm_C (scal_vec_C x v) = C_mod x ∗ vec_norm_C v.
$\|\|v_1 + v_2\|\| \leq \|\|v_1\|\| + \|\|v_2\|\|$	**Lemma** vec_norm_add_le: ∀(n:nat) (v1 v2 : 'cV[complex R]_n.+1), vec_norm_C (v1 + v2) <= vec_norm_C v1 + vec_norm_C v2.
$v \neq 0 \implies \|\|v\|\| \neq 0$[1]	**Lemma** non_zero_vec_norm: ∀(n:nat) (v: 'cV[complex R]_n.+1), vec_not_zero v → vec_norm_C v <> 0.

An important point to note here is that since we are using the `Coquelicot` definition of an extended real line, `Rbar`, coercion of a quantity of type `Rbar` to real requires us to prove finiteness of that quantity. We therefore have to prove that the matrix norm is finite, which we state as the following lemma in Coq

Lemma matrix_norm_is_finite: ∀(n:nat) (A: 'M[complex R]_n.+1), is_finite (matrix_norm A).

Since we prove asymptotic convergence of component-wise limit of the elements of a Jordan matrix, we have to work with the Frobenius norm of a matrix, which we define in Coq as

Definition mat_norm (n:nat) (A: 'M[complex R]_n.+1) : R := sqrt ($\sum_i \sum_j$ (C_mod (A i j))^2)

We will next discuss the formalization of the Theorem 1.

4.3 Formalization of the Theorem 1 in Coq

We state Theorem 1 in Coq as follows:

Theorem iter_convergence: ∀(n:nat) (A: 'M[R]_n.+1) (b: 'cV[R]_n.+1) (M N : 'M[R]_n.+1),
A \in unitmx → M \in unitmx → A = M + N →
let x := (A^−1) ∗m b **in**
(**let** S_mat := RtoC_mat (− (M^−1 ∗m N)) **in**
(∀ (i: 'I_n.+1), (C_mod (lambda S_mat i) < 1))) ↔
(∀ x0: 'cV[R]_n.+1, is_lim_seq (fun k:nat ⇒ vec_norm ((X_m k.+1 x0 b M N) − x)) 0).

Table 4. Formalization of properties of matrix norm in Coq. [1]Here, x is a vector and the relation proves compatibilty relation between a matrix norm and its induced vector norm. [2]Here, $||A||_F$ is the Frobenius norm and we prove that the 2-norm of a matrix is bounded above by the Frobenius matrix norm. The Frobenius norm of a matrix is defined as $||A||_F = \sqrt{\sum_{j=1}^{n}\sum_{j=1}^{n}|A_{ij}|^2}$

Mathematical properties	Formalization in Coq
$0 \leq \|\|A\|\|_i$	**Lemma** matrix_norm_ge_0: ∀(n:nat) (A: 'M[complex R]_n.+1), 0 <= matrix_norm A.
$\|\|Ax\|\| \leq \|\|A\|\|_i \|\|x\|\|, \quad x \neq 0$[1]	**Lemma** matrix_norm_compat: ∀(n:nat) (x: 'cV[complex R]_n.+1) (A: 'M[complex R]_n.+1), x != 0 → vec_norm_C (mulmx A x) <= (matrix_norm A) * vec_norm_C x.
$\|\|AB\|\|_i \leq \|\|A\|\|_i \|\|B\|\|_i$	**Lemma** matrix_norm_prod: ∀(n:nat) (A B: 'M[complex R]_n.+1), matrix_norm (A *m B) <= (matrix_norm A) * (matrix_norm B).
$0 \leq \|\|A\|\|_i \leq \|\|A\|\|_F$[2]	**Lemma** mat_2_norm_F_norm_compat: ∀(n:nat) (A: 'M[complex R]_n.+1), 0 <= matrix_norm A <= mat_norm A.

The theorem iter_convergence states that if the square matrix $A \in \mathbb{R}^{n+1 \times n+1}$ is invertible, which is formalized by the condition A \in unitmx and if the sub-matrices $M, N \in \mathbb{R}^{n+1 \times n+1}$ respect the regular splitting property, which is formalized by $A = M + N$, and if M is invertible, which is formalized by M \in unitmx, then $\lim_{k \to \infty} ||x_{k+1} - x|| = 0$ if and only if $\forall\ i, |\lambda_i(S)| < 1$. Here, $|.|$ is the complex modulus of the eigenvalues of the iteration matrix S (S_mat as defined in the let statement of the theorem iter_convergence), which is defined as in Eq. (5). The is_lim_seq predicate from the Coquelicot library [5] defines limit of a sequence. The reason for having the dimension of A as $(n+1) \times (n+1)$ is that the natural numbers start from 0 in Coq and a square matrix of size 0 does not type check. Thus, instead of having $0 < n$ as pre-condition in the theorem explicitly, we specify this implicitly in the dimension of A. This change also makes our development compatible with the Jordan canonical formalization by Cano et al. [6], who need this constraint on the dimension to define and work with block matrix.

Since we deal with a generic case where a real matrix is allowed to have complex eigenvalues and eigenvectors, we need to transform the real iteration matrix S to a complex matrix, so as to be consistent with types. Thus, given a real matrix A, RtoC_mat transforms a real entry $A_{ij} : \mathbb{R}$ to a complex number $\tilde{A}_{ij} : \mathbb{C} := (A_{ij} + i * 0)$. An important point to note here is that we do not compute the *true numerical solution* x explicitly, but define it as $x \triangleq A^{-1}b$ in the let binding of the theorem statement – **let** x := (A^−1) *m b. We define the iterative solution after k steps, x_k from the iterative system (2) using the **Fixpoint** operator in Coq, which lets us define the recurrence relation (4)

```
Fixpoint X_m (k n:nat) (x0 b: 'cV[R]_n.+1) (M N: 'M[R]_n.+1) : 'cV[R]_n.+1:=
match k with
| O ⇒ x0
| S p ⇒ ((− ((M^−1) *m N)) *m (X_m p x0 b M N)) + ((M^−1) *m b)
end.
```

Formalization of Eigenvalues. One of the main issues we faced was coming up with a scalar definition of eigenvalues, which satisfies the characteristic definition $Av = \lambda v$. The MathComp library defines a non-computable definition of eigenvalues, eigenvalue, which is a predicate stating that λ is an eigenvalue of a matrix A, if the eigenspace corresponding to λ is non-zero. For the scalar definition of eigenvalue, we took an inspiration from the Jordan canonical forms formalization by Guillaume Cano and Maxime Dénès [6]. They define a Jordan form, whose diagonal elements are the characteristic polynomials of the Smith Normal form of a matrix A. Since the diagonal elements of a Jordan form are the eigenvalues of that matrix, we then define a sequence of eigenvalues from these diagonal entries of the Jordan matrix as

```
Definition lambda_seq (n: nat) (A: 'M[complex R]_n.+1) :=
let sizes:= size_sum [seq x.2.−1 | x <− root_seq_poly (invariant_factors A)] in
[seq (Jordan_form A) i i | i <− enum 'I_sizes.+1].
```

where root_seq_poly p returns a sequence of pair of roots and its multiplicity, of the polynomial p. The invariant_factors are the polynomials in the diagonal of the Smith Normal form of a matrix. In this case, the sequence contains the pair of eigenvalues of matrix A and its multiplicity. The ith eigenvalue of A is then defined as the ith component of the sequence of eigenvalues lambda_seq.

```
Definition lambda (n: nat) (A: 'M[complex R]_n.+1) (i: 'I_n.+1) :=
    (@nth _ 0%C (lambda_seq A) i).
```

To take full advantage of the lemmas describing eigenvalues and eigenvectors as defined in MathComp, we had to relate the definition of eigenvalue, `lambda`, and the one defined in MathComp. The lemma Jordan_ii_is_eigen asserts that lambda satisfies the predicate eigenvalue, and is indeed an eigenvalue of a matrix A.

```
Lemma Jordan_ii_is_eigen: ∀(n: nat) (A: 'M[complex R]_n.+1),
  ∀(i: 'I_n.+1), @eigenvalue (complex_fieldType _) n.+1 A (@nth _
0%C (lambda_seq A) i).
```

Here, `size_sum` is the sum of the algebraic multiplicities of the eigenvalues and equals the total size of the matrix n. We prove this fact using the following lemma statement in Coq

```
Lemma total_eigen_val: ∀(n:nat) (A: 'M[complex R]_n.+1),
(size_sum [seq x.2.−1 | x <− root_seq_poly (invariant_factors A)]).+1 = n.+1.
```

The lemma `total_eigen_val` helps us get around the dimension constraint imposed by the design of the Jordan form of a matrix A.

Formalization of the Ratio Test. As discussed in the informal proof in Appendix C to prove sufficiency condition for iterative convergence, we had to formalize the ratio test for convergence of sequences which was missing in the existing Coq libraries. In Coq, we state the ratio test (Lemma 3 in Appendix C in the extended version [24]) as:

```
Lemma ratio_test: ∀(a: nat → R) (L:R), (0 < L ∧ L < 1) →
(∀ n:nat, (0 < a n)) →
(is_lim_seq ( fun n:nat ⇒ ((a (n.+1))/(a n))) L) →
is_lim_seq (fun n: nat ⇒ a n) 0.
```

Proving Convergence of the Jordan Block Matrix. To prove that each element of the Jordan block matrix J^k (see Appendix C in the extended version [24] for more details) converges to zero, i.e.,

$$\forall i\ j, \lim_{k\to\infty} |(J^k)_{(i,j)}|^2 = 0$$

where

$$J^k = \begin{bmatrix} J^k_{m_1}(\lambda_1) & 0 & 0 & \dots & 0 \\ 0 & J^k_{m_2}(\lambda_2) & 0 & \dots & 0 \\ \vdots & \dots & \ddots & \dots & \vdots \\ 0 & \dots & 0 & J^k_{m_{s-1}}(\lambda_{s-1}) & 0 \\ 0 & \dots & \dots & 0 & J^k_{m_s}(\lambda_s) \end{bmatrix}$$

and

$$J^k_{m_i}(\lambda_i) = \begin{bmatrix} \lambda_i^k & \binom{k}{1}\lambda_i^{k-1} & \binom{k}{2}\lambda_i^{k-2} & \dots & \binom{k}{m_i-1}\lambda_i^{k-m_i+1} \\ 0 & \lambda_i^k & \binom{k}{1}\lambda_i^{k-1} & \dots & \binom{k}{m_i-2}\lambda_i^{k-m_i+2} \\ \vdots & \vdots & \ddots & \ddots & \vdots \\ 0 & 0 & \dots & \lambda_i^k & \binom{k}{1}\lambda_i^{k-1} \\ 0 & 0 & \dots & 0 & \lambda_i^k \end{bmatrix},$$

we prove the following lemma.

```
Lemma each_entry_zero_lim: ∀(n:nat) (A: 'M[complex R]_n.+1), (i j: 'I_(size_sum sizes).+1),
let sp := root_seq_poly (invariant_factors A) in
let sizes := [seq x0.2.−1 | x0 <− sp] in
(∀ i: 'I_(size_sum sizes).+1 , (C_mod (nth 0%C (lambda_seq A) i) < 1) ) →
is_lim_seq (fun m: nat ⇒
let block := (fun n0 i1 : nat ⇒ let lambda := (nth (0, 0%N) sp i1).1 in
        \matrix_(i2, j0) (('C(m.+1, j0−i2)) * (lambda ^ (m.+1 − (j0 − i2))) *+ (i2 <= j0)) in
    (C_mod ((diag_block_mx sizes block) i j))^2) 0.
```

The lemma each_entry_zero_lim states that if the magnitude of each eigenvalue of a matrix A is less than 1, i.e., $|\lambda_i(A)| < 1,\ \forall i,\ 0 \leq i < N$, then the limit of each term in the expanded Jordan matrix is zero as $k \to \infty$. Here, the block diagonal matrix diag_block_mx takes an expanded Jordan block $J^k_{m_i}(\lambda_i), \forall i, 0 \leq i < N$ and constructs the Jordan matrix J^k. We then take a modulus of each entry of J^k and prove that its limit is zero as $k \to \infty$. A key challenge we faced when proving the lemma each_entry_zero_lim was extracting each Jordan block of the diagonal block matrix. The diagonal block matrix is defined recursively over a function which takes a block matrix of size μ_i denoting the algebraic multiplicity of each eigenvalues λ_i. We had to carefully destruct this definition of diagonal block matrix and extract the Jordan block and the zeros on the off-diagonal entries, which we formalize using the lemma diag_destruct in Coq. We can then prove the limit on this Jordan block by exploiting its upper triangular structure.

Limits of the off-diagonal elements can then be trivially proven to be zero since each of those elements are zero. This completes the proof of sufficiency condition for convergence of iterative convergence error.

5 Proof of Convergence for the Gauss–Seidel Method

To prove the convergence of a Gauss–Seidel method, we need to prove that the spectral radius of S_G is less than 1. But computing the eigenvalues of S_G explicitly is almost impossible for a generic matrix. Therefore, we need an easier check to assert that the spectral radius of S_G is indeed less than 1. The *Reich theorem* [20] provides a sufficient condition for the spectral radius of S_G to be less than 1, for a real and symmetric coefficient matrix A, with all of the elements in its main diagonal positive. This condition provides a much easier check, which is linear in time, and when layered with the Theorem 1, provides a sufficient condition for convergence of the Gauss–Seidel iteration for a real and symmetric coefficient matrix A, with all of the elements in its main diagonal positive.

We next discuss the formalization of the *Reich theorem*, followed by the main convergence theorem for the Gauss–Seidel iteration.

5.1 Formalization of Easily Checkable Conditions

Theorem 2 (Reich theorem). *[20] If A is real, symmetric nth-order matrix with all terms on its main diagonal positive, then a sufficient condition for all the n characteristic roots of $(-M^{-1}N)$ to be smaller than unity in magnitude is that A is positive definite.*

From an application point of view, only the sufficiency condition is important. This is because to apply Theorem 1, we only need to know that the magnitude of the eigenvalues are less than 1. Thus, to prove the convergence of Gauss–Seidel iteration, we first apply Theorem 1 to get the eigenvalue condition in the goal and then apply Theorem 2 to complete the proof. Since computing eigenvalues are not very trivial in most cases, the positive definite property of the matrix A provides an easy test for $|\lambda| < 1$ for Gauss–Seidel iteration matrix.

We next present an informal proof of the Reich Theorem followed by its formalization in Coq

Proof. Let z_i be the ith characteristic vector of $-(A_1^{-1}A_2)$ corresponding to the characteristic root μ_i. Then

$$-(A_1^{-1}A_2)z_i = \mu_i z_i \tag{13}$$

Multiplying by $-(\bar{z_i}'A_1)$ on both sides,

$$(-\bar{z_i}'A_1)(-A_1^{-1}A_2)z_i = -\mu_i\bar{z_i}'A_1z_i \tag{14}$$

where $\bar{z_i}'$ is the conjugate transpose of z_i obtained by taking the conjugate of each element of z_i followed by transpose of the vector. Equation (14) then simplifies to:

$$\bar{z_i}'A_2z_i = -\mu_i\bar{z_i}'A_1z_i; \quad [A_1A_1^{-1} = I] \tag{15}$$

Consider the bi-linear form, $\bar{z_i}'Az_i$,

$$\begin{aligned}\bar{z_i}'Az_i = \bar{z_i}'(A_1 + A_2)z_i &= \bar{z_i}'A_1z_i + \bar{z_i}'A_2z_i \\ &= \bar{z_i}'A_1z_i - \mu_i\bar{z_i}'A_1z_i \\ &= (1-\mu_i)\bar{z_i}'A_1z_i\end{aligned} \tag{16}$$

Taking conjugate transpose of Eq. (16) on both sides,

$$\bar{z_i}'Az_i = (1-\bar{\mu_i})\bar{z_i}'A_1'z_i \tag{17}$$

Let D be the diagonal matrix defined as:

$$D_{ij} = \begin{cases} A_{ij} & \text{if } i = j \\ 0 & \text{if } i \neq j \end{cases} \tag{18}$$

It can be shown that

$$A_1' = D + A_2 \tag{19}$$

Substituting Eq. (19) in Eq. (17),

$$\begin{aligned}\bar{z_i}'Az_i &= (1-\bar{\mu_i})\bar{z_i}'(D + A_2)z_i \\ &= (1-\bar{\mu_i})\bar{z_i}'Dz_i + (1-\bar{\mu_i})\bar{z_i}'A_2z_i \\ &= (1-\bar{\mu_i})\bar{z_i}'Dz_i + \frac{(1-\bar{\mu_i})}{1-\mu_i}\bar{z_i}'Az_i\end{aligned} \tag{20}$$

Simplifying Eq. (20),

$$(1-\bar{\mu_i}\mu_i)\bar{z_i}'Az_i = (1-\bar{\mu_i})(1-\mu_i)\bar{z_i}'Dz_i \tag{21}$$

But, $\bar{\mu_i}\mu_i = |\mu_i|^2$ and $(1-\bar{\mu_i})(1-\mu_i) = |1-\mu_i|^2$ Hence, Eq. (21) simplifies to,

$$(1-|\mu_i|^2)\bar{z_i}'Az_i = (|1-\mu_i|^2)\bar{z_i}'Dz_i \tag{22}$$

Since, the diagonal elements of A is positive, i.e., $A_{ii} > 0$, $\bar{z_i}'Dz_i$ is positive definite, i.e., $\bar{z_i}'Dz_i > 0$. Since $\bar{z_i}'Dz_i > 0$ and $\bar{z_i}'Az_i > 0$, $|\mu_i| < 1$.

Formalization in Coq: We formalize the Theorem 2 in Coq as follows:

```
Theorem Reich_sufficiency: ∀(n:nat) (A: 'M[R]_n.+1),
(∀ i:'I_n.+1, A i i > 0) →
(∀ i j:'I_n.+1, A i j = A j i) →
is_positive_definite A →
(let S_G := − ( (RtoC_mat (M_G A)^−1) *m (RtoC_mat (N_G A))) in
    (∀ i: 'I_n.+1, C_mod (lambda S_G i) < 1)).
```

where positive definiteness of a complex matrix A is defined as: $\forall x \in \mathbb{C}^{n\times 1}, Re\ [x^* Ax] > 0$. x^* is the complex conjugate transpose of vector x and $Re\ [x^* Ax]$ is the real part of the complex scalar $x^* Ax$. The hypothesis ∀i:'I_n.+1, A i i > 0 states that all terms in the main diagonal of A are positive. The hypothesis ∀i j:'I_n.+1, A i j = A j i states that the matrix A is symmetric.

5.2 Proof of Convergence for the Gauss–Seidel Method

We then apply the theorem iter_convergence with Reich_sufficiency to prove convergence of the Gauss–Seidel iteration method. We formalize the convergence of the Gauss–Seidel iteration method in Coq as

```
Theorem Gauss_Seidel_converges: ∀(n:nat) (A: 'M[R]_n.+1) (b: 'cV[R]_n.+1),
let x := (A^−1) *m b in
A \in unitmx →
(∀ i : 'I_n.+1, 0 < A i i) →
(∀ i j : 'I_n.+1, A i j = A j i) →
is_positive_definite A →
(∀ x0: 'cV[R]_n.+1, is_lim_seq (fun k:nat ⇒
        vec_norm ((X_m k.+1 x0 b (M_G A) (N_G A)) − x)) 0).
```

Thus, to prove convergence of the Gauss–Seidel method for a real, symmetric matrix with all of its diagonal elements positive, we just need positive-definiteness of A, which can be proved by showing positivity of determinants of all upper-left sub-matrices (principal minors) [19]. We illustrate this approach using the following example.

Example 1. To show that the following matrix is positive definite,

$$A_{example} = \begin{bmatrix} 2 & -1 & 0 \\ -1 & 2 & -1 \\ 0 & -1 & 2 \end{bmatrix}$$

we compute the determinants of all possible $k \times k$ upper sub-matrices, i.e.,

$$|2| = 2; \quad \begin{vmatrix} 2 & -1 \\ -1 & 2 \end{vmatrix} = 3; \quad \begin{vmatrix} 2 & -1 & 0 \\ -1 & 2 & -1 \\ 0 & -1 & 2 \end{vmatrix} = 4.$$

Since the determinant of all $k \times k$ upper sub-matrices are positive, the matrix $A_{example}$ is positive definite. We will be using this approach to show positive definiteness in Sect. 6.1. Note that this approach did not involve computing the eigenvalues of S_G and only relies on the structure of matrix $A_{example}$, thereby making it easy to check for positive definiteness and hence convergence of Gauss–Seidel method, by virtue of the Reich theorem (Theorem 2).

Note on Sufficient Conditions for Convergence of the Jacobi Method. The Reich theorem, which we formalized in Coq, provides sufficient conditions for convergence of the Gauss–Seidel method for a symmetric and positive definite matrix. Similar sufficient conditions also exist for convergence of the Jacobi method, which relies on showing *strict row diagonal dominance of the matrix*, or *diagonal dominance and irreducibility of the matrix* [1]. A matrix A is said to be strictly diagonally dominant if $|A_{ii}| > \sum_{j \neq i} |A_{ij}|$. This is a much easier check for convergence than computing the eigenvalues of the iterative matrix explicitly. However, we do not formalize this check in this work because the proof of this fact uses the proof of the *Gersǵorin-type theorems* [16]. The Gersǵorin-type theorems have not been formalized in Coq, and therefore their adoption in our work would require a separate proof effort for this theorem.

6 Model Problem

We apply our convergence theorems on a concrete linear differential equation $\frac{d^2u}{dx^2} = 1$ for $x \in (0, 1)$, with boundary conditions: $u(0) = u(1) = 0$, as a proof of concept. This differential equation is used to model the heat diffusion in a rod, i.e., 1-D domain. We chose a uniform grid with P points in the interior of the 1–D domain. The grid has a uniform spacing h. We will be using a centered difference scheme [23] for discretizing the differential equation. Therefore, the difference equation at point x_i in the interior of the 1–D domain is given by

$$\frac{-u(x_{i+1}) + 2u(x_i) - u(x_{i-1})}{h^2} = -1; \quad h = x_{i+1} - x_i = \frac{1}{P+1} \tag{23}$$

When we stack the Eq. (23) for all points in the interior of the 1–D domain, we get a linear matrix system

$$\underbrace{\frac{1}{h^2}\begin{bmatrix} 2 & -1 & 0 & 0 & 0 & \dots & 0 \\ -1 & 2 & -1 & 0 & 0 & \dots & 0 \\ \vdots & & \ddots & \ddots & \ddots & & \vdots \\ 0 & \dots & 0 & 0 & -1 & 2 & -1 \\ 0 & \dots & 0 & 0 & 0 & -1 & 2 \end{bmatrix}}_{A} \underbrace{\begin{bmatrix} u_1 \\ u_2 \\ \vdots \\ u_N - 1 \\ u_N \end{bmatrix}}_{x} = \underbrace{\begin{bmatrix} -1 \\ -1 \\ \vdots \\ -1 \\ -1 \end{bmatrix}}_{b} \tag{24}$$

Here, A is the coefficient matrix, b is the right hand side vector and x is the unknown solution vector, which can be exactly obtained by inverting the matrix A, i.e., $x = A^{-1}b$. But, we will obtain an approximation of x using iterative algorithms. We will instantiate two classical iterative algorithms: Gauss–Seidel and Jacobi, with this example problem and apply Theorem 1 to prove convergence of the approximate solutions, obtained using these algorithms, to the exact solution.

6.1 Gauss–Seidel Method

We next demonstrate the convergence of the Gauss–Seidel iteration on the example (24). We choose $P = 1$. Thus, we have a symmetric tri-diagonal coefficient matrix of size 3×3, which we will denote as A_{GS}. To show that iterative system for the system $A_{GS}x = b$ converges, we need to show that A_{GS} is positive definite by application of the theorem Gauss_Seidel_converges, which we proved in Sect. 5.2. In Coq, we prove that A_{GS} is positive definite (by proving positivity of determinant of the principal minors of A_{GS}, as illustrated in Example 1) the following lemma statement

```
Lemma Ah_pd: ∀(h:R), (0<h) → is_positive_definite (Ah 2%N h).
```

Proving that A_{GS} is positive definite using the approach illustrated in Example 1 for a generic N is tedious and does not add much to our line of argument. Hence, we chose to do it for A_{GS} of size 3×3. One can perform this exercise for any choice of N by defining an algorithm for computing the determinant of principal minors of a matrix and get the same result. The statement of convergence of Gauss–Seidel iteration method for the 3×3 matrix is stated in Coq as

```
Theorem Gauss_seidel_Ah_converges: ∀(b: 'cV[R]_3) (h:R), (0 < h) →
let A := (Ah 2%N h) in
let x:= (A^-1) *m b in
∀x0: 'cV[R]_3, is_lim_seq (fun k:nat ⇒ vec_norm ((X_m k.+1 x0 b (M_G A) (N_G A)) –
x)) 0.
```

This closes the proof of the convergence of the Gauss–Seidel iteration for the model problem.

6.2 Jacobi Method

We next apply the Theorem 1 to prove convergence of the Jacobi iteration on the model problem (24). As discussed earlier, the iteration matrix for a Jacobi iteration method is $S_J = I - D^{-1}A_J$. We choose $P = 1$, thereby obtaining a 3×3 matrix system, like we did for the Gauss–Seidel iteration.

Formalization in Coq: We prove the following theorem in Coq for convergence of the Jacobi method for the model problem

```
Theorem Jacobi_converges: ∀(b: 'cV[R]_3) (h:R), (0 < h) →
let A := (Ah 2h) in
let x := (A^-1) *m b in
∀x0: 'cV[R]_3, is_lim_seq (fun k:nat ⇒ vec_norm ((X_m k.+1 x0 b (M_J 2 h) (N_J 2 h)) – x)) 0.
```

To prove jacobi_converges using the Theorem 1, we need to prove that the modulus of each of the eigenvalues of S_J is less than 1. We prove this using the following lemma statement in Coq

```
Theorem eig_less_than_1: ∀(n:nat) (i: 'I_n.+1) (h:R),
  (0 < h) → (0 < n) → (C_mod (lambda_J i n h) < 1).
```

Since the iteration matrix S_J is tri-diagonal, we can define a closed form expression for lambda_J using the formula

$$|\lambda_i(S_J)| = \left|1 + \frac{h^2}{2}\lambda_i(A_J)\right| = \left|\cos\left(\frac{m\pi}{P+1}\right)\right| \tag{25}$$

A caveat in using lambda_J explicitly is that the definition of eigenvalue, lambda in Theorem 1 is based on the roots of the polynomials in the diagonal of the Smith Normal form of a matrix. However, we use the closed form expression for eigenvalue of the tridiagonal iteration matrix S_J for our model problem. Ideally, we would like to prove that lambda_J equals lambda. Since the proof of this relation is a tangent to the line of argument we are making in this work, we assume that this relation holds in this work, which we state formally in Coq as the following hypothesis

```
Hypothesis Lambda_eq: ∀(n:nat) (h:R) (i: 'I_n.+1),
  let S_mat := RtoC_mat (− ( (M_J n h)^−1 *m (N_J n h) )) in
  lambda S_mat i = lambda_J i n h.
```

This closes the proof of iterative convergence for Jacobi iteration on the model problem.

7 Related Work

A number of works have recently emerged in the area of formalization of numerical analysis. This has been facilitated by advancements in automatic and interactive theorem proving [5,9]. Some notable works in the formalization of numerical analysis include the formalization of the Kantorovich theorem for convergence of Newton methods [18], the formalization of the matrix canonical forms [6], and the formalization of the Perron-Frobenius theorem in Isabelle/HOL [25] for determining the growth rate of A^n for small matrices A. Boldo et al. [2–4] prove consistency, stability and convergence of a second-order centered scheme for the wave equation. Tekriwal et al. [23] formalize the Lax equivalence theorem to guarantee convergence of a generic class of finite difference schemes. Besides Coq, numerical analysis of ordinary differential equations (ODEs) has also been done in Isabelle/ HOL [13]. Immler et al. [14,15] formalize flows, Poincaré map of dynamical systems, and verified rigorous bounds on numerical algorithms in Isabelle/HOL. In [12], Immler formalized a functional algorithm that computes enclosures of solutions of ODEs in Isabelle/HOL. Deniz et al. [8] formally analyze the problem of heat conduction in Isabelle/HOL, which assumes a closed form solution in a 1-D domain and is thus specific to the problem.

Since most of the existing formalizations on differential equations assume either a closed form solution or use integration schemes which are problem specific, these works do not provide a generalized framework for solving differential equations numerically. Our work however addresses the issue of generalizability by formalizing a framework for solving a linear system iteratively, which is the approach followed by most general purpose linear solvers like ODEPACK [10] and SUNDIALS [11].

8 Conclusion and Future Work

In this work we formalized a *generalized theorem* about convergence of the solutions of an iterative algorithm to the *true numerical solution (direct solution)*. In this process, we clarify various details in the proof of convergence, which are missing in the classical numerical analysis literature. We then instantiate this *generalized* theorem to two classical iterative methods – the Gauss-Seidel method, and the Jacobi method on a model problem. Since it is cumbersome to compute the eigenvalues of a generic matrix system, and verify that its magnitude is less than 1, we provide a much easier check for convergence, especially for the Gauss–Seidel method, called the *Reich theorem* [20], which relies on the structure of matrix A. By composing the proof of the Reich theorem with the main iterative convergence theorem, we show convergence of the Gauss–Seidel method for this matrix A. Thus, our approach is *modular*, and can be extended to prove convergence of the Gauss–Seidel method on any desired matrix structure for which one can formalize conditions similar to the Reich theorem. During our fomalization, we develop a library in Coq to deal with complex vectors and matrices. We define absolute values of complex numbers, common properties of complex conjugates and operations on conjugate matrices and vectors. This development leverages the existing formalization [7,17] of complex numbers and matrices in MathComp. The overall length of the Coq code and proofs is about 8.5k lines of code. It took us about 8 person-months of full time work for the entire formalization.

This work could be extended to develop a generalized end-to-end framework for verification of stationary iterative methods, which includes floating-point error analysis for a concrete implementation of the algorithm in C. In a related work by Tekriwal et al. [22], the authors provide an end-to-end correctness proof for a concrete implementation of the Jacobi iteration, which is an instance of stationary iterative methods. They use a bound on the real iterative solution for the Jacobi method, which relies on a proof of convergence of this real iterative solution to the "true" numerical solution. Thus, a crucial step in extending this result to a generic stationary iterative method, would be to use a *generalized* proof of convergence for a stationary iterative method. The results from this paper can thus be directly used in extending the results from [22] to a concrete implementation of a generic stationary iterative method.

This work could also be extended to verify solutions of non-linear systems. Most physical systems behave non-linearly, and the analysis of these non-linear systems is usually done by linearlizing it around an optimal trajectory. We also plan on extending this work to analyze more practical class of iterative methods called the *Krylov subspace methods* [21], which use stationary iterative methods like Jacobi methods as preconditioners. Thus, our work is foundational in the analysis of these complicated and practical iterative solvers.

References

1. Bagnara, R.: A unified proof for the convergence of Jacobi and Gauss-Seidel methods. SIAM Rev. **37**(1), 93–97 (1995)
2. Boldo, S., Clément, F., Filliâtre, J.-C., Mayero, M., Melquiond, G., Weis, P.: Formal proof of a wave equation resolution scheme: the method error. In: Kaufmann, M., Paulson, L.C. (eds.) ITP 2010. LNCS, vol. 6172, pp. 147–162. Springer, Heidelberg (2010). https://doi.org/10.1007/978-3-642-14052-5_12
3. Boldo, S., Clément, F., Filliâtre, J.C., Mayero, M., Melquiond, G., Weis, P.: Wave equation numerical resolution: a comprehensive mechanized proof of a C program. J. Autom. Reason. **50**(4), 423–456 (2013)
4. Boldo, S., Clément, F., Filliâtre, J.C., Mayero, M., Melquiond, G., Weis, P.: Trusting computations: a mechanized proof from partial differential equations to actual program. Comput. Math. Appl. **68**(3), 325–352 (2014)
5. Boldo, S., Lelay, C., Melquiond, G.: Coquelicot: a user-friendly library of real analysis for Coq. Math. Comput. Sci. **9**(1), 41–62 (2015)
6. Cano, G., Dénès, M.: Matrices à blocs et en forme canonique. In: JFLA – Journées francophones des langages applicatifs (2013). https://hal.inria.fr/hal-00779376
7. Cohen, C.: Construction of real algebraic numbers in Coq. In: Interactive Theorem Proving (2012). https://hal.inria.fr/hal-00671809
8. Deniz, E., Rashid, A., Hasan, O., Tahar, S.: On the formalization of the heat conduction problem in HOL. In: Buzzard, K., Kutsia, T. (eds.) CICM 2022. LNCS, vol. 13467, pp. 21–37. Springer, Cham (2022). https://doi.org/10.1007/978-3-031-16681-5_2
9. Garillot, F., Gonthier, G., Mahboubi, A., Rideau, L.: Packaging mathematical structures. In: Berghofer, S., Nipkow, T., Urban, C., Wenzel, M. (eds.) TPHOLs 2009. LNCS, vol. 5674, pp. 327–342. Springer, Heidelberg (2009). https://doi.org/10.1007/978-3-642-03359-9_23
10. Hindmarsh, A.C.: Odepack, a systematized collection of ode solvers. Sci. Comput. 55–64 (1983)
11. Hindmarsh, A.C., et al.: SUNDIALS: suite of nonlinear and differential/algebraic equation solvers. ACM Trans. Math. Softw. (TOMS) **31**(3), 363–396 (2005)
12. Immler, F.: Formally verified computation of enclosures of solutions of ordinary differential equations. In: Badger, J.M., Rozier, K.Y. (eds.) NFM 2014. LNCS, vol. 8430, pp. 113–127. Springer, Cham (2014). https://doi.org/10.1007/978-3-319-06200-6_9
13. Immler, F., Hölzl, J.: Numerical analysis of ordinary differential equations in Isabelle/HOL. In: Beringer, L., Felty, A. (eds.) ITP 2012. LNCS, vol. 7406, pp. 377–392. Springer, Heidelberg (2012). https://doi.org/10.1007/978-3-642-32347-8_26
14. Immler, F., Traut, C.: The flow of ODEs. In: Blanchette, J.C., Merz, S. (eds.) ITP 2016. LNCS, vol. 9807, pp. 184–199. Springer, Cham (2016). https://doi.org/10.1007/978-3-319-43144-4_12
15. Immler, F., Traut, C.: The flow of ODEs: formalization of variational equation and Poincaré map. J. Autom. Reason. **62**(2), 215–236 (2019)
16. Lancaster, P., Tismenetsky, M.: The Theory of Matrices: With Applications. Elsevier (1985)
17. Mahboubi, A., Cohen, C.: Formal proofs in real algebraic geometry: from ordered fields to quantifier elimination. Logical Methods Comput. Sci. **8** (2012)

18. Pasca, I.: Formal verification for numerical methods. Ph.D. thesis, Université Nice Sophia Antipolis (2010)
19. Prussing, J.E.: The principal minor test for semidefinite matrices. J. Guid. Control. Dyn. **9**(1), 121–122 (1986)
20. Reich, E.: On the convergence of the classical iterative method of solving linear simultaneous equations. Ann. Math. Stat. **20**(3), 448–451 (1949)
21. Saad, Y.: Iterative Methods for Sparse Linear Systems, 2nd edn. Society for Industrial and Applied Mathematics (SIAM), Philadelphia (2003)
22. Tekriwal, M., Appel, A.W., Kellison, A.E., Bindel, D., Jeannin, J.B.: Verified correctness, accuracy, and convergence of a stationary iterative linear solver: Jacobi method. In: Dubois, C., Kerber, M. (eds.) CICM 2023. LNCS, vol. 14101, pp. 206–221. Springer, Cham (2023). https://doi.org/10.1007/978-3-031-42753-4_14
23. Tekriwal, M., Duraisamy, K., Jeannin, J.-B.: A formal proof of the lax equivalence theorem for finite difference schemes. In: Dutle, A., Moscato, M.M., Titolo, L., Muñoz, C.A., Perez, I. (eds.) NFM 2021. LNCS, vol. 12673, pp. 322–339. Springer, Cham (2021). https://doi.org/10.1007/978-3-030-76384-8_20
24. Tekriwal, M., Miller, J., Jeannin, J.B.: Formalization of asymptotic convergence for stationary iterative methods (extended version) (2022). https://arxiv.org/abs/2202.05587
25. Thiemann, R.: A Perron-Frobenius theorem for deciding matrix growth. J. Logical Algebraic Methods Program. **123**, 100699 (2021)

Distributional Probabilistic Model Checking

Ingy Elsayed-Aly[1(✉)], David Parker[2], and Lu Feng[1]

[1] University of Virginia, Charlottesville, VA 22904, USA
{ie3ne,lu.feng}@virginia.edu
[2] University of Oxford, Oxford, UK
david.parker@cs.ox.ac.uk

Abstract. Probabilistic model checking provides formal guarantees for stochastic models relating to a wide range of quantitative properties, such as runtime, energy consumption or cost. But this is typically with respect to the *expected* value of these quantities, which can mask important aspects of the full probability distribution, such as the possibility of high-risk, low-probability events or multimodalities. We propose a *distributional* extension of probabilistic model checking, for discrete-time Markov chains (DTMCs) and Markov decision processes (MDPs). We formulate distributional queries, which can reason about a variety of distributional measures, such as variance, value-at-risk or conditional value-at-risk, for the accumulation of reward or cost until a co-safe linear temporal logic formula is satisfied. For DTMCs, we propose a method to compute the full distribution to an arbitrary level of precision, based on a graph analysis and forward analysis of the model. For MDPs, we approximate the optimal policy using distributional value iteration. We implement our techniques and investigate their performance and scalability across a range of large benchmark models.

1 Introduction

Computer systems are increasingly being integrated seamlessly with sensing, control and actuation of the physical world. Many of these systems (e.g., robotics) exhibit probabilistic and non-deterministic behavior due to inherent uncertainty (e.g., sensor noise, human interactions), which pose significant challenges for ensuring their safe, reliable, timely and resource-efficient execution.

Probabilistic model checking offers a collection of techniques for modelling systems that exhibit probabilistic and non-deterministic behavior. It supports not only their verification against specifications in temporal logic, but also synthesis of optimal controllers (policies). Commonly used models include discrete-time Markov chains (DTMCs) and Markov decision processes (MDPs). A range of verification techniques for these, and other models, are supported by widely used probabilistic model checkers such as PRISM [22] and Storm [11].

To capture the range of quantitative correctness specifications needed in practice, it is common to reason about *rewards* (or, conversely, *costs*). Examples

N. Benz et al. (Eds.): NFM 2024, LNCS 14627, pp. 57–75, 2024.
https://doi.org/10.1007/978-3-031-60698-4_4

include checking the worst-case execution time of a distributed coordination algorithm, or synthesizing a controller that guarantees the minimal energy consumption for a robot to complete a sequence of tasks. Typically the *expected* value of these quantities is computed, but in some situations it is necessary to consider the full probability distribution. Notably, in safety-critical applications, it can be important to synthesize *risk-sensitive* policies, that avoid high-cost, low-probability events, which can still arise when minimizing expected cost. Risk-aware distributional measures such as *conditional value-at-risk* (CVaR) [25] address this by minimizing the costs that occur above a specified point in the tail of the distribution. Within probabilistic model checking, the use of *quantiles* has been proposed [16,18,28,32] to reason about cost or reward distributions.

In this paper, we develop a *distributional probabilistic model checking* approach, which computes and reasons about the full distribution over the reward associated with a DTMC or MDP. More precisely, we consider the reward accumulated until a specification in co-safe LTL is satisfied, the latter providing an expressive means to specify, for example, a multi-step task to be executed by a robot [19], or a sequence of events leading to a system failure. We propose a temporal logic based specification for such distributional queries.

For a DTMC, we perform model checking of these queries by generating a precise representation of the distribution, up to an arbitrary, pre-specified level of accuracy (the distribution is discrete, but often has countably infinite support, so at least some level of truncation is typically required). This is based on a graph analysis followed by a forward numerical computation. From this, we can precisely compute a wide range of useful properties, such as the mean, variance, mode or various risk-based measures.

For an MDP, we instead aim to optimize such properties over all policies. In this paper, we focus on optimizing the expected value or CVaR, whilst generating the full reward distribution for each state of the MDP. This is done using *distributional value iteration* (DVI) [3], which can be seen as a generalization of classical value iteration. Rather than computing a single scalar value (e.g., representing the optimal expected reward) for each MDP state, DVI associates a full distribution with each state, replacing the standard Bellman equation with a distributional Bellman equation.

We consider two types of DVI algorithms, namely *risk-neutral* DVI for optimizing the expected value and *risk-sensitive* DVI for optimizing CVaR. Risk-neutral DVI can be shown to converge to a deterministic, memoryless optimal policy, if a unique one exists [3]. For CVaR, memoryless policies do not suffice for optimality, but risk-sensitive DVI does converge for a product MDP that incorporates a (continuous) slack variable representing a cost/reward budget [2]. For computational tractability, we present a risk-sensitive DVI algorithm based on a discretization of the slack variable, and show that the algorithm converges to a CVaR optimal policy for increasingly precise discretizations.

For both DVI algorithms, in practice it is necessary to use approximate distributional representations. We consider the use of categorical and quantile representations. This can impact both optimality and the precision of computed distributions but, for the latter, we can construct the DTMC induced by generated

MDP policies and use our precise approach to generate the correct distribution. Finally, we implement our distributional probabilistic model checking framework as an extension of the PRISM model checker [22] and explore the feasibility and performance of the techniques on a range of benchmarks.

An extended version of this paper, with proofs, is available as [12].

1.1 Related Work

Distributional Properties. Some existing probabilistic model checking methods consider distributional properties beyond expected values, notably *quantiles* [16,18,28,32], i.e., optimal reward thresholds which guarantee that the maximal or minimal probability of a reward-bounded reachability formula meets a certain threshold. While [32] and [28] focus on complexity results, [18] and [16] consider practical implementations to compute quantiles, for single- and multi-objective variants, respectively, using model unfoldings over "cost epochs"; [16] also proposes the use of interval iteration to provide error bounds. By contrast, our methods derive the full distribution, rather than targeting quantiles specifically, and our DTMC approach derives error bounds from a forward computation. We also mention [7], which computes probability distributions in a forwards manner, but for infinite-state probabilistic programs and using generating functions, and [6], which proposes an algorithm (but not implementation) to compute policies that trade off expected mean payoff and variance.

Risk-Aware Objectives. For MDPs, we focus in particular on *conditional value-at-risk* (CVaR). There are alternatives, such as mean-variance [31] and value-at-risk [14] but, as discussed in [25], these are not *coherent risk metrics*, which may make them unsuitable for rational decision-making. Other work on the CVaR objective includes: [20], which studies decision problem complexity, but for mean-payoff rewards and without implementations; [9], which repeatedly solves piecewise-linear maximization problems, but has limited scalability, taking over 2 h to solve an MDP with about 3,000 states; and [26], which proposes both linear programming and value iteration methods to solve CVaR for MDPs and DTMCs. Other, not directly applicable, approaches tackle constrained problems that incorporate the CVaR objective [5,8,29]. Again, our approach differs from all these in that it computes the full distribution, allowing multiple distributional properties to be considered. We also work with temporal logic specifications. Alternative temporal logic based approaches to risk-aware control include [10], which proposes risk-aware verification of MDPs using cumulative prospect theory, and [17] which proposes chance constrained temporal logic for control of deterministic dynamical systems.

Distributional Reinforcement Learning. Our work is based on probabilistic model checking, which fully explores known models, but our use of DVI is inspired by *distributional reinforcement learning* [3], which can be used to learn risk-sensitive policies and improve sample efficiency (see [24] for a comparison of expected and distributional methods). We take a formal verification approach and use numerical solution, not learning, but adopt existing categorical and quantile distributional approximations and our risk-neutral DVI algorithm is a minimization variant adapted from [3]. Risk-sensitive DVI is also sketched in [3], based on [2], but only a theoretical analysis of the method is given, without considering practical implementation aspects, such as how to discretize slack variables for computational efficiency, and how such approximations would affect the correctness of model checking. We extend risk-sensitive DVI with a discretized slack variable and show its effects theoretically in Sect. 4.3 and empirically via computational experiments in Sect. 5.

2 Background

We begin with some background on random variables, probability distributions, and the probabilistic models used in this paper. We let $\mathbb{N}$, $\mathbb{R}$, and $\mathbb{Q}$ denote the sets of naturals, reals and rationals, respectively, and write $\mathbb{N}_\infty = \mathbb{N} \cup \{\infty\}$.

2.1 Random Variables and Probability Distributions

Let $X : \Omega \to \mathbb{R}$ be a random variable over a probability space $(\Omega, \mathcal{F}, \Pr)$. The *cumulative distribution function* (CDF) of X is denoted by $\mathcal{F}_X(x) := \Pr(X \leq x)$, and the inverse CDF is $\mathcal{F}_X^{-1}(\tau) := \inf\{x \in \mathbb{R} : \mathcal{F}_X(x) \geq \tau\}$. Common properties of interest for X include, e.g., the *expected value* $\mathbb{E}(X)$, the *variance* $\mathrm{Var}(X)$ which is the square of the *standard deviation* (s.d.), or the *mode*.

In this paper, we also consider several *risk*-related measures. The *value-at-risk* of X at level $\alpha \in (0,1)$ is defined by $\mathsf{VaR}_\alpha(X) := \mathcal{F}_X^{-1}(\alpha)$, which measures risk as the minimum value encountered in the tail of the distribution with respect to a risk level α. The *conditional value-at-risk* of X at level $\alpha \in (0,1)$ is given by $\mathsf{CVaR}_\alpha(X) := \frac{1}{1-\alpha}\int_\alpha^1 \mathsf{VaR}_\nu(X)d\nu$, representing the expected loss given that the loss is greater or equal to VaR_α. Figure 1a illustrates an example probability distribution of a random variable X, annotated with its expected value $\mathbb{E}(X)$, value-at-risk $\mathsf{VaR}_{0.9}(X)$ and conditional value-at-risk $\mathsf{CVaR}_{0.9}(X)$.

When working with the probability distributions for random variables, we write distributional equations as $X_1 \stackrel{D}{:=} X_2$, denoting equality of probability laws (i.e., the random variable X_1 is distributed according to the same law as X_2). We use δ_θ to denote the Dirac delta distribution that assigns probability 1 to outcome $\theta \in \mathbb{R}$. In practice, even when distributions are discrete, we require approximate, finite representations for them. In this paper, we consider *categorical* and *quantile* distributional representations, both of which provide desirable characteristics such as tractability and expressiveness [3].

Definition 1 (Categorical representation). *A* categorical representation *parameterizes the probability of* m *atoms as a collection of evenly-spaced locations* $\theta_1 < \cdots < \theta_m \in \mathbb{R}$. *Its distributions are of the form* $\sum_{i=1}^m p_i \delta_{\theta_i}$ *where* $p_i \geq 0$ *and* $\sum_{i=1}^m p_i = 1$. *We define the* stride *between successive atoms as* $\varsigma_m = \frac{\theta_m - \theta_1}{m-1}$.

Definition 2 (Quantile representation). *A* quantile representation *parameterizes the location of* m *equally-weighted atoms. Its distributions are of the form* $\frac{1}{m}\sum_{i=1}^m \delta_{\theta_i}$ *for* $\theta_i \in \mathbb{R}$. *Multiple atoms may share the same value.*

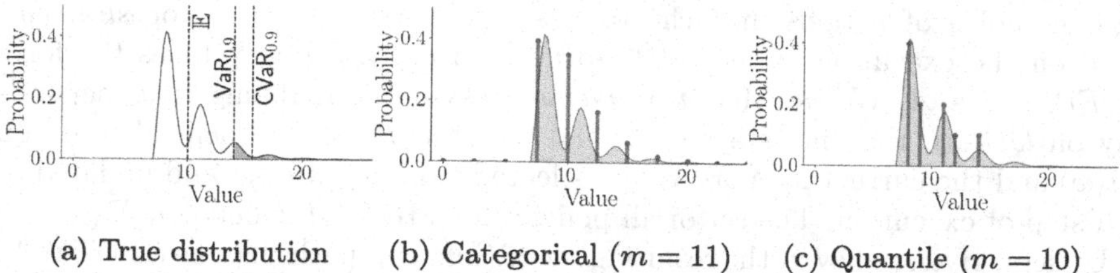

(a) True distribution (b) Categorical ($m = 11$) (c) Quantile ($m = 10$)

Fig. 1. An example distribution with its categorical and quantile representations.

Figures 1b and 1c show categorical and quantile representations, respectively, approximating the distribution shown in Fig. 1a. When performing operations on distributions (e.g., during DVI), the intermediate result might not match the chosen representation parameters. In that case, the result is *projected* back onto the chosen representation as described in [3].

2.2 Markov Chains and Markov Decision Processes

In this paper, we work with both discrete-time Markov chains (DTMCs) and Markov decision processes (MDPs).

Definition 3 (DTMC). *A* discrete-time Markov chain *(DTMC) is a tuple* $\mathcal{D} = (S, s_0, P, AP, L)$*, where* S *is a set of states,* $s_0 \in S$ *is an initial state,* $P : S \times S \rightarrow [0, 1]$ *is a probabilistic transition matrix satisfying* $\forall s \in S : \sum_{s' \in S} P(s, s') = 1$*,* AP *is a set of atomic propositions and* $L : S \rightarrow 2^{AP}$ *is a labelling function.*

A DTMC $\mathcal{D}$ evolves between states, starting in s_0, and the probability of taking a transition from s to s' is $P(s, s')$. An (infinite) *path* through $\mathcal{D}$ is a sequence of states $s_0 s_1 s_2 \ldots$ such that $s_i \in S$ and $P(s_i, s_{i+1}) > 0$ for all $i \geq 0$, and a finite path is a prefix of an infinite path. The sets of all infinite and finite paths in $\mathcal{D}$ are denoted $IPaths_{\mathcal{D}}$ and $FPaths_{\mathcal{D}}$, respectively. We define a probability measure $Pr_{\mathcal{D}}$ over the set of paths $IPaths_{\mathcal{D}}$.

Definition 4 (MDP). *A* Markov decision process *(MDP) is a tuple* $\mathcal{M} = (S, s_0, A, P, AP, L)$*, where states* S*, initial state* s_0*, atomic propositions* AP *and labelling* L *are as for a DTMC,* A *is a finite set of* actions, *and* $P : S \times A \times S \rightarrow [0, 1]$ *is a probabilistic transition function satisfying* $\forall s \in S, \forall a \in A : \sum_{s' \in S} P(s, a, s') \in \{0, 1\}$.

In each state s of an MDP $\mathcal{M}$, there are one or more *available* actions which can be taken, denoted $A(s) = \{a \in A \mid P(s, a, s') > 0 \text{ for some } s'\}$. If action a is taken in s, the probability of taking a transition from s to s' is $P(s, a, s')$, also denoted $P(s'|s, a)$. Paths are defined in similar fashion to DTMCs but are now alternating sequences of states and actions $s_0 a_0 s_1 a_1 s_2 \ldots$ where $a_i \in A(s_i)$ and $P(s_i, a_i, s_{i+1}) > 0$ for all $i \geq 0$, and the sets of all infinite and finite paths are $IPaths_{\mathcal{M}}$ and $FPaths_{\mathcal{M}}$, respectively.

The choice of actions in each state is resolved by a *policy* (or *strategy*), based on the execution of the MDP so far. Formally, a policy takes the form $\pi : FPaths \rightarrow A$. We say that π is *memoryless* if the mapping $\pi(\omega)$ depends only on $last(\omega)$, the final state of ω, and *finite-memory* if it depends only on $last(\omega)$ and the current memory value, selected from a finite set and updated at each step of execution. The set of all policies for MDP $\mathcal{M}$ is denoted $\Sigma_{\mathcal{M}}$.

Under a given policy π, the resulting set of (infinite) paths has, as for DTMCs, an associated probability measure, which we denote $\mathrm{Pr}^{\pi}_{\mathcal{M}}$. Furthermore, for both memoryless and finite-memory policies, we can build a (finite) *induced DTMC* which is equivalent to $\mathcal{M}$ acting under π.

Definition 5 (Reward structure). *A* reward structure *is, for a DTMC $\mathcal{D}$, a function $r : S \rightarrow \mathbb{N}$ and, for an MDP $\mathcal{M}$, a function $r : S \times A \rightarrow \mathbb{N}$.*

For consistency with the literature on probabilistic model checking and temporal logics, we use the terminology *rewards* although in practice these can (and often do) represent *costs*, such as time elapsed or energy consumed. For the purposes of our algorithms, we assume that rewards are integer-valued, but we note that these could be defined as rationals, using appropriate scaling. For an infinite path ω, we also write $r(\omega, k)$ for the sum of the reward values over the first k steps of the path, i.e., $r(s_0 s_1 s_2 \ldots, k) = \sum_{i=0}^{k-1} r(s_i)$ for a DTMC and $r(s_0 a_0 s_1 a_1 s_2 \ldots, k) = \sum_{i=0}^{k-1} r(s_i, a_i)$ for an MDP.

To reason about rewards, we define random variables over the executions (infinite paths) of a model, typically defined as the total reward accumulated along a path, up until some event occurs. Formally, for a DTMC $\mathcal{D}$, such a random variable is defined as a function of the form $X : IPaths_{\mathcal{D}} \rightarrow \mathbb{R}$, with respect to the probability measure $\mathrm{Pr}_{\mathcal{D}}$ over $IPaths_{\mathcal{D}}$. For an MDP $\mathcal{M}$ and policy $\pi \in \Sigma_{\mathcal{M}}$, a random variable is defined as a function $X : IPaths_{\mathcal{M}} \rightarrow \mathbb{R}$, with respect to the probability measure $\mathrm{Pr}^{\pi}_{\mathcal{M}}$.

3 Distributional Probabilistic Model Checking

We formulate our approach as a *distributional* extension of probabilistic model checking, which is a widely used framework for formally specifying and verifying quantitative properties of probabilistic models. In particular, we build upon existing temporal logics in common use. The core property we consider is the probability distribution over the amount of reward (or cost) that has been accumulated until some specified sequence of events occurs (which could constitute, for example, the successful completion of a task by a robot).

To represent events, we use the co-safe fragment [21] of linear temporal logic (LTL) [27]. LTL formulae are evaluated over infinite paths of a model labelled with atomic propositions from the set AP but, for use with cumulative reward, we restrict our attention to the *co-safe* fragment, containing formulae which are satisfied in finite time. Formally, this means any satisfying path ($\omega \models \psi$) has a *good prefix*, i.e., a finite path prefix ω' such that $\omega' \omega'' \models \psi$ for any suffix ω''.

The key ingredient of our temporal logic specifications is a *distributional query*, which gives a property (such as the expected value, or variance) of the distribution over the accumulated reward until an event's occurrence.

Definition 6 (Distributional query). *For a DTMC, a* distributional query *takes the form* $\mathtt{R}^{\mathsf{f}(r)}_{=?}[\,\psi\,]$*, where* r *is a reward structure,* f *is a random variable property (e.g.,* $\mathbb{E}$, Var, s.d., mode, VaR, CVaR*), and* ψ *is a formula in co-safe LTL.*

Examples of distributional queries for a DTMC are:

- $\mathtt{R}^{\mathrm{Var}(r_{energy})}_{=?}[\,\mathtt{F}\ (goal_1 \wedge \mathtt{F}\ goal_2)\,]$ – the variance in energy consumption until a robot visits location $goal_1$ followed by location $goal_2$;
- $\mathtt{R}^{\mathrm{mode}(r_{coll})}_{=?}[\,\mathtt{F}\ sent_1 \vee \mathtt{F}\ sent_2\,]$ - the most likely number of packet collisions before a communication protocol successfully sends one of two messages.

For an MDP, the goal is to optimize a random variable property f over its policies, which we call *distributional optimization queries.* In this paper, we focus on two particular cases, expected value ($\mathbb{E}$) and conditional value-at-risk (CVaR),

Definition 7 (Distributional optimization query). *For an MDP, a* distributional optimization query *takes the form* $\mathtt{R}^{\mathsf{f}(r)}_{\mathrm{opt}=?}[\,\psi\,]$*, where* r *is a reward structure,* $\mathsf{f} \in \{\mathbb{E}, \mathsf{CVaR}\}$*,* $\mathrm{opt} \in \{\min, \max\}$ *and* ψ *is a formula in co-safe LTL. For the resulting policy, we can perform* policy evaluation *on the induced DTMC using one or more other distributional queries* $\mathtt{R}^{\mathsf{f}'(r')}_{=?}[\,\psi'\,]$.

An example optimization query is $\mathtt{R}^{\mathsf{CVaR}_{0.9}(r_{time})}_{\min=?}[\,\mathtt{F}\ goal\,]$, which minimizes the conditional value-at-risk with respect to the time for a robot to reach its goal.

Semantics. A distributional query $\mathtt{R}^{\mathsf{f}(r)}_{=?}[\,\psi\,]$ is evaluated on a DTMC $\mathcal{D}$, and a distributional optimization query $\mathtt{R}^{\mathsf{f}(r)}_{\mathrm{opt}=?}[\,\psi\,]$ on an MDP $\mathcal{M}$, in each case via a random variable for the reward accumulated from its initial state:

$$\mathtt{R}^{\mathsf{f}(r)}_{=?}[\,\psi\,] = \mathsf{f}(X^{r,\psi}_{\mathcal{D}})$$

$$\mathtt{R}^{\mathsf{f}(r)}_{\min=?}[\,\psi\,] = \inf_{\pi \in \Sigma_{\mathcal{M}}} \mathsf{f}(X^{r,\psi}_{\mathcal{M},\pi}) \ \text{ or } \ \mathtt{R}^{\mathsf{f}(r)}_{\max=?}[\,\psi\,] = \sup_{\pi \in \Sigma_{\mathcal{M}}} \mathsf{f}(X^{r,\psi}_{\mathcal{M},\pi})\ .$$

where the random variables $X^{r,\psi}_{\mathcal{D}} : IPaths_{\mathcal{D}} \to \mathbb{R}$, $X^{r,\psi}_{\mathcal{M},\pi} : IPaths_{\mathcal{M}} \to \mathbb{R}$ are:

$$X^{r,\psi}_{\mathcal{D}}(\omega) \ = \ X^{r,\psi}_{\mathcal{M},\pi}(\omega) \ = \ \{r(\omega, k_\psi - 1) \text{ if } \omega \models \psi;\ \infty \text{ otherwise}\}$$

and $k_\psi = \min\{k \mid (\omega, k) \models \psi\}$ is the length of the shortest good prefix for ψ.

Example 1. We illustrate our framework with an example of an autonomous robot navigating within a risky environment modelled as an MDP (Fig. 2). The robot starts in the leftmost location (blue circle), and may pass through two types of terrain, mud (orange zigzag) and ground littered with nails (purple hatching). The default cost of navigation is 1 per step, obstacles (gray) incurring a cost of 35. In the "nails" terrain, there is a probability of 0.2 incurring a cost of 5; the

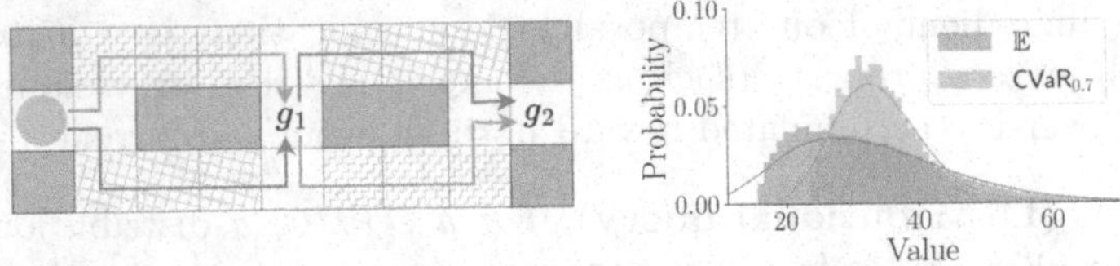

Fig. 2. The "mud & nails" example. Left: Map of the terrain to navigate, with two policies that minimize expected cost and conditional value-at-risk to visit g_1 and then g_2. Right: The corresponding distributions over cost.

"mud" terrain is safer but slower: a fixed cost of 3 per step. Consider the total cost to visit g_1 and then g_2. Given a reward structure *cost* encoding the costs as above, we can aim to minimize either the expected cost or the conditional value-at-risk, using queries $\mathtt{R}^{\mathbb{E}(cost)}_{\min=?}[\,\mathtt{F}\ (g_1 \wedge \mathtt{F}\ g_2)\,]$ or $\mathtt{R}^{\mathsf{CVaR}_{0.7}(cost)}_{\min=?}[\,\mathtt{F}\ (g_1 \wedge \mathtt{F}\ g_2)\,]$. Figure 2 also shows the resulting policies, plotted on the map in purple and orange, respectively, and the corresponding probability distributions over cost. We can analyze each policy with further distributional queries, e.g., $\mathtt{R}^{\mathsf{f}(cost)}_{=?}[\,\mathtt{F}\ g_1\,]$ for $\mathsf{f} = \{\mathbb{E}, \mathsf{Var}\}$ to evaluate the mean and variance of the cost to reach g_1. ■

4 Distributional Model Checking Algorithms

We now describe algorithms for distributional probabilistic model checking, i.e., to evaluate distributional queries of the form $\mathtt{R}^{\mathsf{f}(r)}_{=?}[\,\psi\,]$ for a DTMC or $\mathtt{R}^{\mathsf{f}(r)}_{\mathrm{opt}=?}[\,\psi\,]$ for an MDP. Following the semantics given in Sect. 3, for a DTMC $\mathcal{D}$, this necessitates generating the probability distribution of the random variable $X^{r,\psi}_{\mathcal{D}}$, corresponding to reward structure r and LTL formula ψ, on $\mathcal{D}$. The value $\mathsf{f}(X^{r,\psi}_{\mathcal{D}})$ can then be evaluated on the distribution for any f. For an MDP $\mathcal{M}$, we aim to find a policy π^* which optimizes the value $\mathsf{f}(X^{r,\psi}_{\mathcal{M},\pi})$ over policies π.

For both classes of model, in standard fashion, we reduce the problem to the simpler case where ψ is a *reachability* formula by constructing an automaton product. More precisely, we build a deterministic finite automaton (DFA) $\mathcal{A}_\psi$ representing the "good" prefixes of co-safe LTL formula ψ, and then construct a DTMC-DFA product $\mathcal{D} \otimes \mathcal{A}_\psi$ or MDP-DFA product $\mathcal{M} \otimes \mathcal{A}_\psi$ with state space $S \times Q$, where S is the state space of the original model and Q the states of the DFA. There is a one-to-one correspondence between paths (and, for MDPs, policies) in the original model and the product model [1].

Hence, in what follows, we restrict our attention to computing the probability distributions for random variables defined as the reward to reach a target set of states $T \subseteq S$, describing first the case for a DTMC and then the cases for risk-neutral ($\mathsf{f} = \mathbb{E}$) and risk-sensitive ($\mathsf{f} = \mathsf{CVaR}$) optimization for an MDP. For the latter two, for presentational simplicity, we focus on the case of minimization, but it is straightforward to adapt the algorithms to the maximizing case.

Algorithm 1: Forward distribution generation for DTMCs

Input : DTMC $\mathcal{D} = (S, s_0, P, AP, L)$, rewards r, target $T \subseteq S$, accuracy $\varepsilon \in \mathbb{R}_{>0}$
Output: The discrete probability distribution μ for $X_{\mathcal{D}}^{r,\mathtt{F}\,T}$.

$S_\infty \leftarrow \{s \in S \mid s \in \text{BSCC } C \subseteq S \text{ with } C \cap T = \emptyset\}$; $\mu_\times \leftarrow \delta_{(s_0,0)}$; $p_{\overline{T}} = 1$; $p_\infty = 0$
while $p_{\overline{T}} - p_\infty > \varepsilon$ **do**
    $\mu'_\times \leftarrow \{\}$; $p_{\overline{T}} \leftarrow 0$
    for $((s,i) \mapsto p_{s,i}) \in \mu_\times$ **do**
        if $s \in T$ **then**
            $\mu'_\times(s,i) \leftarrow \mu'_\times(s,i) + p_{s,i}$
        else
            for $(s' \mapsto p_{s'}) \in P(s,\cdot)$ **do**
                if $s' \notin T$ **then**
                    $p_{\overline{T}} \leftarrow p_{\overline{T}} + p_{s,i} \cdot p_{s'}$
                if $s' \notin S_\infty$ **then**
                    $\mu'_\times(s', i + r(s)) \leftarrow \mu'_\times(s', i + r(s)) + p_{s,i} \cdot p_{s'}$
                else
                    $p_\infty \leftarrow p_\infty + \mu_\times(s,i) \cdot p_{s'}$
    $\mu_\times \leftarrow \mu'_\times$
return $\{i \mapsto p_i \mid p_i = \sum_s \mu_\times(s,i)\} \cup \{\infty \mapsto p_\infty\}$

4.1 Forward Distribution Generation for DTMCs

We fix a DTMC $\mathcal{D}$, reward structure r and set of target states T. In this section, we describe how to compute the probability distribution for the reward r accumulated in $\mathcal{D}$ until T is reached, i.e., for the random variable $X_{\mathcal{D}}^{r,\mathtt{F}\,T}$. We denote this distribution by μ. Note that, since individual rewards are integer-valued, and are summed along paths, μ is a discrete distribution.

We compute the distribution in a forward manner, up to a pre-specified accuracy ε, using Algorithm 1. First, note that the reward accumulated along a path that never reaches the target T is defined to be ∞ (see Sect. 3). Probabilistic model checking algorithms typically compute the *expected* reward to reach a target T from a state s, which is therefore infinite if s has a non-zero probability of not reaching T. Here, we have to take slightly more care since there may be states from which there is a non-zero probability of both accumulating finite and infinite reward. This means that μ is a distribution over $\mathbb{N}_\infty$.

Algorithm 1 first identifies the states S_∞ of $\mathcal{D}$ from which the probability of accumulating infinite reward is 1, which are those in bottom strongly connected components (BSCCs) of $\mathcal{D}$ that do not intersect with T. It then computes a discrete distribution $\mu_\times$ over $S \times \mathbb{N}_\infty$ where, at the kth iteration, $\mu_\times(s,i)$ is the probability of being in state s and having accumulated reward i after k steps. A new version $\mu'_\times$ is computed at each step. Abusing notation, we write distributions as lists $\{x_1 \mapsto p_1, \dots\}$ of the elements x_j of their support and their probabilities p_j. We also keep track of the probabilities $p_{\overline{T}}$ and p_∞ of, by the

Algorithm 2: Risk-Neutral Distributional Value Iteration

Input : MDP $\mathcal{M} = (S, s_0, A, P, AP, L)$, rewards r, target $T \subseteq S$, and $\epsilon \in \mathbb{R}_{>0}$
Output: optimal policy π^* for query $\mathtt{R}^{\mathbb{E}(r)}_{\min=?}[\,\mathtt{F}\,T\,]$, distribution μ_{s_0} under π^*

1 $e = \infty$; $\mu_s \leftarrow \delta_0, \forall s \in S$
2 **while** $e > \epsilon$ **do**
3   **foreach** $s \in S \setminus T$ **do**
4   **foreach** $a \in A(s)$ **do**
5       $\eta(s,a) \stackrel{D}{:=} \mathtt{proj}\,(r(s,a) + \sum_{s' \in S} P(s,a,s') \cdot \mu_{s'})$
6     $\pi^*(s) \leftarrow \arg\min_{a \in A(s)} \mathbb{E}(X|X \sim \eta(s,a))$; $\mu'_s \leftarrow \eta(s, \pi^*(s))$
7   $e \leftarrow \sup_{s \in S \setminus T} d(\mu_s, \mu'_s)$
8   $\mu_s \leftarrow \mu'_s, \forall s \in S$
9 **return** π^* and μ_{s_0}

kth iteration, *not* having reached the target set T and being in S_∞, respectively. The distribution μ is finally computed by summing $\mu_\times(s,i)$ values over all states and can be analyzed with additional distributional properties.

Correctness and Convergence. Let μ be the exact distribution for $X_{\mathcal{D}}^{r,\mathtt{F}\,T}$ and $\hat{\mu}$ be the one returned by Algorithm 1, using accuracy $\varepsilon > 0$. We have:

$$\mu(i) \leq \hat{\mu}(i) \leq \mu(i) + \varepsilon \quad \text{for all } i \in \mathbb{N}_\infty \tag{1}$$

Note that the support of μ may be (countably) infinite, but $\hat{\mu}$ is finite by construction. In this case, the total truncation error is also bounded by ε: if $\hat{k} \in \mathbb{N}$ is the maximum finite value in the support of $\hat{\mu}$, then $\sum_{\hat{k}<i<\infty} \mu(i) \leq \varepsilon$.

To see the correctness of Eq. (1), observe that $\hat{\mu}(i)$ is ultimately computed from the sum of the values $\sum_s \mu_\times(s,i)$ in Algorithm 1, the total value of which is non-decreasing since rewards are non-negative. In any iteration, at most $p_{\overline{T}} - p_\infty$ will be added to any value $\mu_\times(s,i)$ and, on termination, $p_{\overline{T}} - p_\infty \leq \varepsilon$. Convergence is guaranteed for any $\varepsilon > 0$: since we separate the states S_∞ in non-target BSCCs, within k iterations, the combined probability of having reached T (i.e., $1 - p_{\overline{T}}$) or reaching S_∞ (i.e., p_∞) tends to 1 as $k \to \infty$.

4.2 Risk-Neutral Distributional Value Iteration for MDPs

In this section, we present a *risk-neutral* DVI method, for computing value distributions of states of an MDP $\mathcal{M}$ under an optimal policy that minimizes the *expected* cumulative reward to reach a target set $T \subseteq S$, i.e., minimizes $\mathbb{E}(X_{\mathcal{M},\pi}^{r,\mathtt{F}\,T})$ for random variables $X_{\mathcal{M},\pi}^{r,\mathtt{F}\,T}$ of MDP policies π. In contrast to the case for DTMCs, we now assume that there exists an optimal policy with finite expected reward, i.e., which reaches the target set T with probability 1. This can be checked efficiently with an analysis of the underlying graph of the MDP [4].

The risk-neutral DVI method is shown in Algorithm 2. For each MDP state $s \in S$, it initializes its value distribution μ_s to Dirac distribution δ_0. The algorithm loops through lines 2–8 to update value distributions of any non-target state $s \in S \backslash T$ as follows. For each available action $a \in A(s)$ in state s, a value distribution is obtained via the distributional Bellman equation shown in line 5 then projected to $\eta(s, a)$ to match the chosen representation (see Sect. 2.1). The optimal action $\pi^*(s)$ in state s is the one that achieves the minimal expected value of $\eta(s, a)$. The updated value distribution μ'_s of state s is given by $\eta(s, \pi^*(s))$. The algorithm terminates when the supremum of distributional distance $d(\mu_s, \mu'_s)$ across all states (the choice of metrics is discussed below) is less than the convergence threshold ϵ. Unlike the accuracy ε for Algorithm 1, this threshold ϵ does *not* provide a guarantee on the precision of the result after convergence (similar issues occur in classical value iteration for MDPs [15]).

Distributional Approximation. To enable a practical implementation of the algorithm, we need a probability distribution representation with finitely many parameters to store value distributions in memory. Here, we can adopt the categorical (see Definition 1) or quantile (see Definition 2) representations. Specifically, we need to apply the categorical or quantile projection (see [3]) after each update of the distributional Bellman equation (line 5). We use the supremum Cramér distance $\overline{\ell}_2$ for categorical representations and the supremum Wasserstein distance $\overline{w}_1$ for quantile representations as the distance metric in line 7 (see [3] for distributional distance definitions).

Policy Convergence. When there exists a unique risk-neutral optimal policy, Algorithm 2 is guaranteed to converge to it (following [3, Theorem 7.9]). However, when there are multiple optimal policies, risk-neutral DVI may fail to converge (see [3, Section 7.5]). Furthermore, inaccuracies due the use of distributional approximations could potentially lead to a sub-optimal policy being chosen. To mitigate this, for either categorical or quantile representations, increasing the number m of atoms used yields tighter approximation error bounds [3].

4.3 Risk-Sensitive Distributional Value Iteration for MDPs

By contrast to risk-neutral policies that seek to minimize the expected reward, *risk-sensitive* policies make decisions accounting for risk properties. In this section, we present a risk-sensitive DVI method for minimizing the *conditional value-at-risk* of reaching a target set in an MDP $\mathcal{M}$, i.e., minimizing $\mathsf{CVaR}_\alpha(X^{r,\mathrm{F}\,T}_{\mathcal{M},\pi})$ for random variables $X^{r,\mathrm{F}\,T}_{\mathcal{M},\pi}$ of MDP policies π. Our method follows a key insight from [2,30] that conditional value-at-risk can be represented as the solution of a convex optimization problem.

Lemma 1 (Dual Representation of CVaR **[2,30]).** *Let* $[x]^+$ *denote the function that is 0 if* $x < 0$*, and* x *otherwise. Given a random variable* X *over the probability space* $(\Omega, \mathcal{F}, \Pr)$*, it holds that:*

$$\mathsf{CVaR}_\alpha(X) = \min_{b \in \mathbb{R}} \left\{ b + \frac{1}{1-\alpha} \mathbb{E}\big([X - b]^+ \big) \right\}, \tag{2}$$

and the minimum-point is given by $b^* = \mathsf{VaR}_\alpha(X)$. □

Algorithm 3: Risk-Sensitive Distributional Value Iteration

Input : MDP $\mathcal{M} = (S, s_0, A, P, AP, L)$, reward structure r, target set $T \subseteq S$, risk level α, slack variable set B, convergence threshold $\epsilon \in \mathbb{R}_{>0}$

Output: optimal policy π^* for query $\mathtt{R}^{\mathsf{CVaR}_\alpha(r)}_{\min=?}[\mathtt{F}\,T]$, distribution μ_{s_0} under π^*

1 Construct product MDP $\mathcal{M}^{\mathsf{b}} = (S \times B, \{s_0\} \times B, A, P^{\mathsf{b}}, AP, L^{\mathsf{b}})$
2 $\mu_{\langle s,b\rangle} \leftarrow \delta_0, \forall \langle s,b\rangle \in S \times B$
3 **while** $e > \epsilon$ **do**
4   **foreach** $\langle s,b\rangle \in (S \setminus T) \times B$ **do**
5   **foreach** $a \in A(s)$ **do**
6             $\eta(\langle s,b\rangle, a) \stackrel{D}{:=}$ $\mathtt{proj}(r(s,a) + \sum_{\langle s',b'\rangle \in S \times B} P^{\mathsf{b}}(\langle s,b\rangle, a, \langle s',b'\rangle) \cdot \mu_{\langle s',b'\rangle})$
7         $\pi^{\mathsf{b}}(\langle s,b\rangle) \leftarrow \arg\min_{a \in A(s)} \mathbb{E}(\,[X - b]^+ \,|X \sim \eta(\langle s,b\rangle, a))$
8         $\mu'_{\langle s,b\rangle} \leftarrow \eta(\langle s,b\rangle, \pi^{\mathsf{b}}(\langle s,b\rangle))$
9     $e \leftarrow \sup_{\langle s,b\rangle \in (S\setminus T)\times B} d(\mu_{\langle s,b\rangle}, \mu'_{\langle s,b\rangle})$
10     $\mu_{\langle s,b\rangle} \leftarrow \mu'_{\langle s,b\rangle}, \forall \langle s,b\rangle \in (S \setminus T) \times B$
11 $\bar{b}^* \leftarrow \arg\min_{\bar{b}\in B} \mathsf{CVaR}_\alpha(X|X \sim \mu_{\langle s_0,\bar{b}\rangle}), \forall \bar{b} \in B$
12 $\pi^* \leftarrow$ policy π^{b} of the product MDP $\mathcal{M}^{\mathsf{b}}$ with initial state fixed to $\langle s_0, \bar{b}^*\rangle$
13 **return** π^* and $\mu_{\langle s_0,\bar{b}^*\rangle}$

Intuitively, the *slack variable* $b \in [V_{\min}, V_{\max}]$ encodes the risk budget and possible $\mathsf{VaR}_\alpha(X)$ values. Since $\mathsf{VaR}_\alpha(X) \in [V_{\min}, V_{\max}]$, the slack variable is similarly bounded by the minimum and maximum possible accumulated reward within the MDP, respectively. We assume that the reward values are bounded and the probability of reaching the target states is 1, therefore $V_{\min}$ and $V_{\max}$ are also bounded. To enable efficient computation, we consider a discrete number of values for b. More precisely, we define a set B with n evenly-spaced atoms $b_1 < \cdots < b_n$ such that $b_1 = V_{\min}$, $b_n = V_{\max}$, and the stride between two successive atoms is $\varsigma_n = \frac{V_{\max} - V_{\min}}{n-1}$. Based on Lemma 1, determining the optimal slack variable value b^* requires computation of VaR_α for the distribution, which cannot be obtained *a priori*. Thus, we consider all possible risk budgets.

Algorithm 3 illustrates the proposed method. We construct a product MDP model $\mathcal{M}^{\mathsf{b}} = (S \times B, \{s_0\} \times B, A, P^{\mathsf{b}}, AP, L^{\mathsf{b}})$. Unlike the product MDP defined in Sect. 3, this MDP has multiple initial states, one state $\langle s_0, \bar{b}\rangle$ for each risk budget $\bar{b} \in B$, where s_0 is the initial state of the MDP $\mathcal{M}$. For each transition $s \xrightarrow{a} s'$ in $\mathcal{M}$ with $P(s,a,s') > 0$, there is a corresponding transition $\langle s,b\rangle \xrightarrow{a} \langle s',b'\rangle$ in $\mathcal{M}^{\mathsf{b}}$, where b' is obtained by rounding down the value of $b - r(s,a)$ to the nearest smaller atom in B and $P^{\mathsf{b}}(\langle s,b\rangle, a, \langle s',b'\rangle) = P(s,a,s')$. The labelling function is given by $L^{\mathsf{b}}(\langle s,b\rangle) = L(s)$. Next, in lines 2–12, Algorithm 3 initializes and updates the value distribution of each augmented state $\langle s,b\rangle \in S \times B$ in the product MDP $\mathcal{M}^{\mathsf{b}}$ in a similar fashion to the risk-neutral DVI described in Sect. 4.2. However, when choosing the optimal action (line 8), Algorithm 3 adopts a different criterion that minimizes $\mathbb{E}([X - b]^+)$ based on the dual representation of CVaR (see Eq. 2).

Different choices of the initial risk budget $\bar{b}$ lead to various value distributions. Once DVI on the product MDP $\mathcal{M}^{\mathsf{b}}$ converges, the algorithm selects the optimal risk budget, denoted by $\bar{b}^*$, that yields the minimum CVaR of all possible initial value distributions $\mu_{\langle s_0,\bar{b}\rangle}$. Finally, the algorithm returns the optimal policy π^* resulting from the risk-sensitive DVI on the product MDP $\mathcal{M}^{\mathsf{b}}$ with initial state $\langle s_0,\bar{b}^*\rangle$, and returns the distribution $\mu_{\langle s_0,\bar{b}^*\rangle}$.

Correctness and Convergence. Following [2, Theorem 3.6], when the slack variable b is continuous (i.e., $B=\mathbb{R}$), there exists a solution b^* of Eq. 2 and the optimal policy π^{b} of product MDP $\mathcal{M}^{\mathsf{b}}$ with initial state fixed to $\langle s_0,b^*\rangle$ is the CVaR optimal policy of MDP $\mathcal{M}$. Algorithm 3, which uses a discretized slack variable (i.e., the set of atoms B is finite), converges to the same optimal policy π^{b} as $|B|$ increases, which is formalised below (and a proof can be found in the extended version of this paper [12]).

Lemma 2. *Let π_1 denote the optimal policy for minimizing $\mathsf{CVaR}_\alpha(X^{r,\mathtt{F}\,T}_{\mathcal{M},\pi})$, which is obtained with a continuous slack variable. Let π_2 denote the optimal policy returned by Algorithm 3 where B is a finite set of n evenly-spaced atoms with stride ς_n. It holds that $\mathsf{CVaR}_\alpha(X^{r,\mathtt{F}\,T}_{\mathcal{M},\pi_2})-\mathsf{CVaR}_\alpha(X^{r,\mathtt{F}\,T}_{\mathcal{M},\pi_1})=\mathcal{O}(\varsigma_n)$. As ς_n tends to 0 (i.e., $|B|$ increases), π_2 converges to the CVaR optimal policy.* □

5 Experiments

We built and evaluated a prototype implementation[1] of our distributional probabilistic model checking approach based on PRISM [22], extending its Java explicit-state engine. Our evaluation focuses initially on solving MDPs using the DVI methods (of Sects. 4.2 and 4.3), then on solving the resulting policies using the DTMC method (of Sect. 4.1). All experiments were run on a machine with an AMD Ryzen 7 CPU and 14 GB of RAM allocated to the JVM. We set $V_{\min}=0$ for all case studies; $V_{\max}$ varies, as detailed below.

5.1 Case Studies

Betting Game. This case study is taken from [29]. The MDP models an agent with an amount of money, initially set to 5, which can repeatedly place a bet of amount $0\le\lambda\le5$. The probability of winning is 0.7, the probability of losing is 0.25, and the probability of hitting a jackpot (winning 10λ) is 0.05. The game ends after 10 stages. The reward function is given by the maximal allowance (e.g., 100) minus the final amount of money that the agent owns. We use $V_{\max}=100$.

Deep Sea Treasure. This case study is also taken from [29]. The model represents a submarine exploring an area to collect one of several treasures. At each time step, the agent chooses to move to a neighbouring location; it succeeds with probability 0.6, otherwise moves to another adjacent location with probability

[1] Code and models are at https://www.prismmodelchecker.org/files/nfm24dpmc.

Table 1. Experimental results: Timing and accuracy of each method.

Model	Method	MDP	Time (s)	$\mathbb{E}$	CVaR_α	$\text{Time}_{\text{dtmc}}$ (s)	$\Delta^{\%}_{\mathbb{E}}$	$\Delta^{\%}_{\mathsf{CVaR}}$
Betting Game	risk-neut. VI	$8.9 \cdot 10^2$	<1	**61.9**	–	<1	–	–
	risk-neut. DVI	$8.9 \cdot 10^2$	<1	**61.9**	98.0	<1	0.0	0.0
	risk-sens. DVI	$9.0 \cdot 10^4$	36	85.3	**92.2**	<1	0.0	0.0
DS Treasure	risk-neut. VI	$1.2 \cdot 10^3$	<1	**359.3**	–	<1	–	–
	risk-neut. DVI	$1.2 \cdot 10^3$	<1	**359.3**	474.6	<1	0.0	0.33
	risk-sens. DVI	$1.2 \cdot 10^5$	72	370.1	**458.6**	<1	0.0	0.32
Obstacle ($N = 150$)	risk-neut. VI	$2.3 \cdot 10^4$	<1	**402.8**	–	1,838	–	–
	risk-neut. DVI	$2.3 \cdot 10^4$	97	**402.7**	479.2	1,838	0.01	1.95
	risk-sens. DVI	$2.3 \cdot 10^6$	15,051	402.9	**478.4**	1,673	0.01	2.00
UAV	risk-neut. VI	$1.7 \cdot 10^4$	<1	**124.1**	–	<1	–	–
	risk-neut. DVI	$1.7 \cdot 10^4$	4	**123.8**	168.8	<1	0.2	0.47
	risk-sens. DVI	$1.7 \cdot 10^6$	2,366	134.9	**169.1**	<1	0.0	0.01
Energy ($N = 15$)	risk-neut. VI	$2.6 \cdot 10^4$	10	**184.3**	–	251	–	–
	risk-neut. DVI	$2.6 \cdot 10^4$	108	**184.0**	382.0	234	0.17	0.47
	risk-sens. DVI	$1.3 \cdot 10^6$	9,384	184.6	**380.9**	122	0.16	0.33

0.2. The agent stops when it finds a treasure or has explored for 15 steps. The reward function is defined based on the travel cost (5 per step) and opportunity cost (i.e., maximal treasure minus collected treasure value). We set $V_{\max} = 800$.

Obstacle. This case study is inspired by the navigation example in [9]. We consider an MDP model of an $N \times N$ gridworld with a set of scattered obstacles. The agent's goal is to navigate to a destination, while avoiding obstacles which cause a delay. At each time step, the agent moves in a selected direction with probability 0.9 and an unintended direction with probability 0.1. The reward function is given by the time spent to reach the destination. We use $V_{\max} = 600$.

UAV. This case study is adapted from the MDP model of the interaction between a human and an unmanned aerial vehicle (UAV) from [13]. A UAV performs road network surveillance missions with the assistance of a human operator, and is given a mission specified with LTL formula $\psi = (\mathtt{F}\ w_2) \wedge (\mathtt{F}\ w_5) \wedge (\mathtt{F}\ w_6)$, which translates into covering waypoints w_2, w_5 and w_6 in any order. The reward function is given by the mission completion time. We pick $V_{\max} = 500$.

Energy. This case study considers a robot navigating an $N \times N$ gridworld with energy constraints. At each time step, the robot moves to an adjacent grid location with probability 0.7, or to an unintended adjacent location otherwise. It starts with a fixed amount of energy and consumes 1 unit per step. The robot can only recharge its battery in the charging station. When the energy is depleted, the robot is transported with a delay to the charging station. The robot is asked to complete a mission specified with LTL formula $\psi = (\mathtt{F}\ w_1) \wedge (\mathtt{F}\ w_2) \wedge (\mathtt{F}\ w_3)$. The reward function represents the mission completion time. We use $V_{\max} = 500$.

5.2 Results Analysis

Method Comparison. Table 1 summarizes our experimental results across the benchmarks described above. For each MDP, we run both the risk-neutral and risk-sensitive variants of distributional value iteration (DVI), optimizing expected value and CVaR, as described in Sect. 4.2 and Sect. 4.3, respectively. For the risk neutral case we also run standard value iteration (VI), as implemented in PRISM. For all three methods, we then evaluate the resulting policy, computing the full reward distribution using the forward distribution generation method described in Sect. 4.1, allowing us to compute more precise results for the expected value and CVaR on those policies.

The table shows the time to run each algorithm and the values computed during optimization (the value for the objective being optimized is shown in bold). Additionally, the table shows the time to run the forward distribution method on the induced DTMC, and the (percentage) relative error when comparing the VI/DVI results with the forward distribution outcomes.

For each case study, we also report the number of states in the (product) MDP that is solved. The UAV and Energy benchmarks use non-trivial co-safe LTL formulae for the mission specification (the others are reachability specifications) and so the MDP is a MDP-DFA product. For risk-sensitive DVI, the state space is also augmented with a slack variable resulting in larger product MDPs. We set the slack variable size to $|B| = 51$ for the Energy model, and $|B| = 101$ for the rest. We use the categorical representation with $m = 201$ for DVI, with $\epsilon = 0.01$ for the convergence metric. For policy evaluation, we use precision $\varepsilon = 10^{-3}$ for the Obstacle and Energy case studies and $\varepsilon = 10^{-5}$ for the others.

Our DVI methods successfully optimize their respective objectives on a range of large MDPs Generally, the policy resulting from the risk-neutral method has a lower expected value, while the policy from the risk-sensitive method has a lower CVaR_α, and the risk-neutral method yields the same optimal policy as baseline VI. As expected, DVI methods are more expensive than VI, since they work with distributions, but the DVI methods are successfully applied to MDPs with several million states. Additionally, the baseline VI method can only provide expected reward values, while the distribution returned by our methods can be used to compute additional distributional properties (variance, VaR, etc.). Comparing the two variants of DVI, the risk-sensitive version takes considerably longer to run. This is primarily due to the use of a larger product model, incorporating a slack variable, rather than the computation required for DVI itself. For the same reason, risk-neutral DVI scales to larger models, but for clarity Table 1 only includes models that all methods can solve.

The DTMC forward computation also works on all models. It is often very fast (under a second in 3 cases), but grows expensive on models where the support of the distribution is large. From its results, we see that both DVI methods produce approximate distributions that are close to the true distribution.

Note that in the last three case studies, the $V_{\max}$ value is higher, resulting in a larger stride and thus more coarse representations for both the value distributions and the slack variable (for risk-sensitive DVI). This results in more

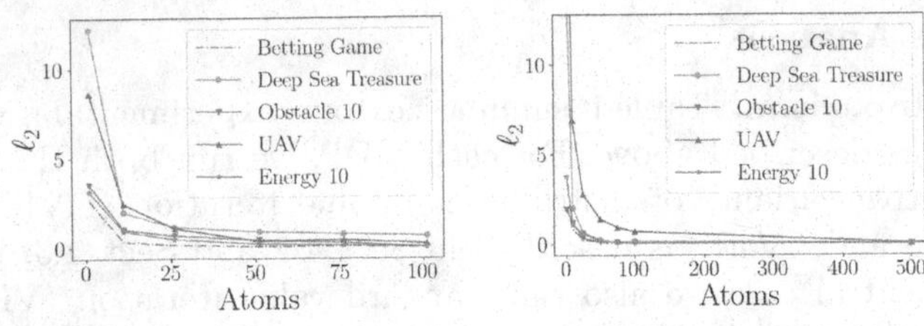

(a) Categorical representation (b) Quantile representation

Fig. 3. Varying the numbers of atoms for distributional representations.

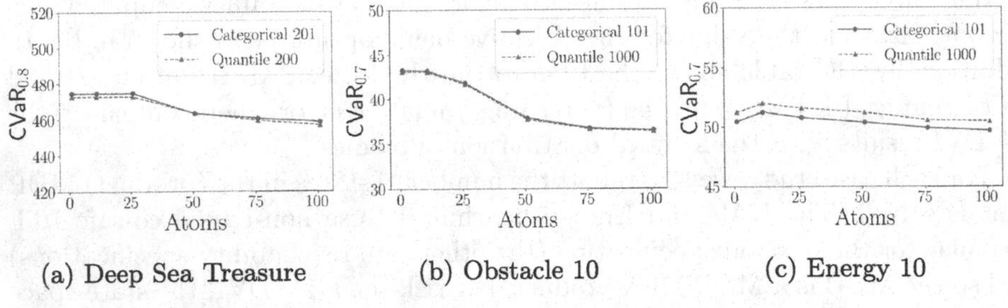

(a) Deep Sea Treasure (b) Obstacle 10 (c) Energy 10

Fig. 4. Results for varying the numbers of atoms in risk-sensitive DVI.

approximation errors when computing metrics from the value distributions generated using DVI. This can be seen in the case of the UAV model where the risk-neutral method underestimates CVaR_α (168.8 compared to 169.6 from the true distribution generated by the DTMC method for the same policy). The following experiments aim to evaluate how the parameters of the distributional representation affect the resulting approximate distributions generated by DVI.

Effects on Distributional Approximation. Figure 3 plots the effects of varying the number of atoms used for categorical and quantile representations for distributions, in terms of the ℓ_2 distance between the approximate distribution resulting from risk-neutral DVI and the ground truth (obtained via applying the DTMC forward distribution generation method with $\varepsilon = 10^{-5}$ on the resulting optimal policy). *For both representations, the ℓ_2 distance approaches 0 as the number of atoms increases, indicating that the approximate distributions become very close to the ground truth.* We observe similar effects with the risk-sensitive method and thus omit the resulting plot. Note that the Deep Sea Treasure model has a larger $V_{\max}$ and thus the resulting ℓ_2 is higher than other models when using a maximum of 101 atoms in the categorical representation.

A larger number of atoms (m value) leads to a higher computational cost, thus we consider smaller models for the Obstacle and Energy case studies with $N = 10$ for plotting. As an illustration of accuracy/cost trade-off, for Energy 10, the runtime using categorical representations with 11 atoms (resp. 101 atoms) is 0.3 s (resp. 0.63 s), while the runtime when using quantile representations with

Table 2. Performance comparison for DTMC forward computation

Model	Param.s	States	Transitions	$V_{\max}$	DVI(s)	DTMC(s)	$\Delta^{\%}_{\mathbb{E}}$	$\Delta^{\%}_{\mathsf{CVaR}}$
EGL	N=8,L=3	$5.4 \cdot 10^6$	$5.5 \cdot 10^6$	40	439	1	0.4	0.5
	N=8,L=4	$7.5 \cdot 10^6$	$7.6 \cdot 10^6$	40	897	1	0.4	0.4
	N=8,L=5	$9.6 \cdot 10^6$	$9.7 \cdot 10^6$	50	4,345	1	0.3	0.4
Leader	N=8,K=5	$2.7 \cdot 10^6$	$3.1 \cdot 10^6$	20	41	2	0.0	0.0
	N=10,K=4	$9.4 \cdot 10^6$	$1.0 \cdot 10^7$	30	577	15	0.3	0.6
	N=8,K=6	$1.2 \cdot 10^7$	$1.3 \cdot 10^7$	20	163	9	0.0	0.1
Herman	N=13	$8.2 \cdot 10^3$	$1.6 \cdot 10^6$	100	4	14	0.6	0.9
	N=15	$3.3 \cdot 10^4$	$1.4 \cdot 10^7$	120	57	190	0.5	0.9
	N=17	$1.3 \cdot 10^5$	$1.3 \cdot 10^8$	140	1,234	2,369	0.8	1.2

10 atoms (resp. 100 atoms) is 0.9 s (resp. 5 s). The quantile projection is more expensive than the categorical projection, resulting in higher runtimes.

Effects of Slack Variable Atoms. Figure 4 illustrates the effects of varying the number of atoms used for the slack variables ($|B|$) in risk-sensitive DVI. *The results show that increasing $|B|$ generally leads to better policies with smaller* CVaR *values.* This is in part because the algorithm would check a larger set of initial risk budgets $\bar{b} \in B$. But there is a trade-off since the computational cost grows with an increasing $|B|$. For example, in the Energy 10 model, the runtime using the categorical representation with 101 atoms for $|B| = 11$ (resp. $|B| = 101$) is 7.8 s (resp. 78.6 s), whereas the runtime of using the quantile representation with 1,000 atoms for $|B| = 11$ (resp. $|B| = 101$) is 477 s (resp. 5,163 s).

DTMC Forward Computation. Finally, we further evaluate the forward computation method for DTMCs from Sect. 4.1 on a range of common DTMC benchmarks from the PRISM benchmark suite [23]. In particular, we compare to an alternative computation using the risk-neutral DVI method of Sect. 4.2, treating DTMCs as a special case of MDPs. Table 2 shows the performance of the two methods. For each model, we indicate the parameters used for the benchmark and the DTMC size (states and transitions). For the DVI method, we use the categorical representation with a stride of 1 and a value of $V_{\max}$ large enough to represent the distribution (also shown in the table).

In Two of the Three Models, the DTMC Computation is Much Faster. This is because the DVI method calculates a reward distribution for every state. For the third model, where $V_{\max}$ is significantly higher, DVI is actually faster (the same can be seen for the Obstacle and Energy models in Table 1). The DTMC method computes distribution to a pre-specified accuracy, but DVI may incur approximation errors, primarily due to convergence. Table 2 also shows (relative) errors for the expected value and CVaR metrics for each benchmark.

6 Conclusion

This paper presents a distributional approach to probabilistic model checking, which supports a rich set of distributional queries for DTMCs and MDPs. Experiments on a range of benchmark case studies demonstrate that our approach can be successfully applied to check various distributional properties (e.g., CVaR, VaR, variances) of large MDP and DTMC models. We believe that this work paves the way for applying distributional probabilistic model checking in many safety-critical and risk-averse domains. For future work, we will explore distributional queries with multiple objectives and under multi-agent environments.

Acknowledgements. This work was supported in part by NSF grant CCF-1942836 and the ERC under the European Union's Horizon 2020 research and innovation programme (FUN2MODEL, grant agreement No. 834115).

References

1. Baier, C., Katoen, J.P.: Principles of Model Checking. MIT Press, Cambridge (2008)
2. Bäuerle, N., Ott, J.: Markov decision processes with average-value-at-risk criteria. Math. Methods Oper. Res. **74**(3), 361–379 (2011)
3. Bellemare, M.G., Dabney, W., Rowland, M.: Distributional Reinforcement Learning. MIT Press (2023). http://www.distributional-rl.org
4. Bianco, A., de Alfaro, L.: Model checking of probabilistic and nondeterministic systems. In: Thiagarajan, P.S. (ed.) FSTTCS 1995. LNCS, vol. 1026, pp. 499–513. Springer, Heidelberg (1995). https://doi.org/10.1007/3-540-60692-0_70
5. Borkar, V., Jain, R.: Risk-constrained Markov decision processes. IEEE Trans. Autom. Control **59**(9), 2574–2579 (2014)
6. Brazdil, T., Chatterjee, K., Forejt, V., Kucera, A.: Trading performance for stability in Markov decision processes. J. Comput. Syst. Sci. **84**, 144–170 (2017)
7. Chen, M., Katoen, J.P., Klinkenberg, L., Winkler, T.: Does a program yield the right distribution? In: Shoham, S., Vizel, Y. (eds.) CAV 2022. LNCS, vol. 13371, pp. 79–101. Springer, Cham (2022). https://doi.org/10.1007/978-3-031-13185-1_5
8. Chow, Y., Ghavamzadeh, M.: Algorithms for CVaR optimization in MDPs. In: Advances in Neural Information Processing Systems, vol. 27 (2014)
9. Chow, Y., Tamar, A., Mannor, S., Pavone, M.: Risk-sensitive and robust decision-making: a CVaR optimization approach. In: Advances in Neural Information Processing Systems, vol. 28 (2015)
10. Cubuktepe, M., Topcu, U.: Verification of Markov decision processes with risk-sensitive measures. In: Proceedings of the Annual American Control Conference (ACC 2018), pp. 2371–2377. IEEE (2018)
11. Dehnert, C., Junges, S., Katoen, J.P., Volk, M.: A storm is coming: a modern probabilistic model checker. In: Proceedings of the 29th International Conference on Computer Aided Verification (CAV 2017) (2017)
12. Elsayed-Aly, I., Parker, D., Feng, L.: Distributional probabilistic model checking. arXiv preprint arXiv:2309.05584 (2023)
13. Feng, L., Wiltsche, C., Humphrey, L., Topcu, U.: Synthesis of human-in-the-loop control protocols for autonomous systems. IEEE Trans. Autom. Sci. Eng. **13**(2), 450–462 (2016)

14. Filar, J.A., Krass, D., Ross, K.W.: Percentile performance criteria for limiting average Markov decision processes. IEEE Trans. Autom. Control **40**(1), 2–10 (1995)
15. Haddad, S., Monmege, B.: Reachability in MDPs: refining convergence of value iteration. In: Ouaknine, J., Potapov, I., Worrell, J. (eds.) RP 2014. LNCS, vol. 8762, pp. 125–137. Springer, Cham (2014). https://doi.org/10.1007/978-3-319-11439-2_10
16. Hartmanns, A., Junges, S., Katoen, J.P., Quatmann, T.: Multi-cost bounded tradeoff analysis in MDP. J. Autom. Reason. **64**(7), 1483–1522 (2020)
17. Jha, S., Raman, V., Sadigh, D., Seshia, S.A.: Safe autonomy under perception uncertainty using chance-constrained temporal logic. J. Autom. Reason. **60**(1), 43–62 (2018)
18. Klein, J., et al.: Advances in probabilistic model checking with PRISM: variable reordering, quantiles and weak deterministic Büchi automata. Int. J. Softw. Tools Technol. Transfer **20**(2), 179–194 (2018)
19. Kress-Gazit, H., Fainekos, G.E., Pappas, G.J.: Temporal logic-based reactive mission and motion planning. IEEE Trans. Rob. **25**(6), 1370–1381 (2009)
20. Křetínský, J., Meggendorfer, T.: Conditional value-at-risk for reachability and mean payoff in Markov decision processes. In: Proceedings of the 33rd Annual ACM/IEEE Symposium on Logic in Computer Science, pp. 609–618 (2018)
21. Kupferman, O., Vardi, M.Y.: Model checking of safety properties. Formal Methods Syst. Des. **19**(3), 291–314 (2001)
22. Kwiatkowska, M., Norman, G., Parker, D.: PRISM 4.0: verification of probabilistic real-time systems. In: Gopalakrishnan, G., Qadeer, S. (eds.) CAV 2011. LNCS, vol. 6806, pp. 585–591. Springer, Heidelberg (2011). https://doi.org/10.1007/978-3-642-22110-1_47
23. Kwiatkowska, M., Norman, G., Parker, D.: The PRISM benchmark suite. In: Proceedings of the 9th International Conference on Quantitative Evaluation of SysTems (QEST 2012), pp. 203–204. IEEE CS Press (2012)
24. Lyle, C., Bellemare, M.G., Castro, P.S.: A comparative analysis of expected and distributional reinforcement learning. In: Proceedings of the AAAI Conference on Artificial Intelligence, vol. 33, pp. 4504–4511 (2019)
25. Majumdar, A., Pavone, M.: How should a robot assess risk? Towards an axiomatic theory of risk in robotics. In: Amato, N.M., Hager, G., Thomas, S., Torres-Torriti, M. (eds.) Robotics Research. SPAR, vol. 10, pp. 75–84. Springer, Cham (2020). https://doi.org/10.1007/978-3-030-28619-4_10
26. Meggendorfer, T.: Risk-aware stochastic shortest path. In: Proceedings of the AAAI Conference on Artificial Intelligence, vol. 36, pp. 9858–9867 (2022)
27. Pnueli, A.: The temporal semantics of concurrent programs. Theor. Comput. Sci. **13**, 45–60 (1981)
28. Randour, M., Raskin, J.F., Sankur, O.: Percentile queries in multi-dimensional Markov decision processes. Formal Methods Syst. Des. **50**, 207–248 (2017)
29. Rigter, M., Duckworth, P., Lacerda, B., Hawes, N.: Planning for risk-aversion and expected value in MDPs. In: Proceedings of the International Conference on Automated Planning and Scheduling, vol. 32, pp. 307–315 (2022)
30. Rockafellar, R.T., Uryasev, S.: Conditional value-at-risk for general loss distributions. J. Banking Financ. **26**(7), 1443–1471 (2002)
31. Sobel, M.J.: The variance of discounted Markov decision processes. J. Appl. Probab. **19**(4), 794–802 (1982)
32. Ummels, M., Baier, C.: Computing quantiles in Markov reward models. In: Pfenning, F. (ed.) FoSSaCS 2013. LNCS, vol. 7794, pp. 353–368. Springer, Heidelberg (2013). https://doi.org/10.1007/978-3-642-37075-5_23

14. [illegible]
18. [illegible]

Formal Methods for Program Analysis and Verification

Quantitative Input Usage Static Analysis

Denis Mazzucato(✉), Marco Campion, and Caterina Urban

INRIA & ENS | PSL, Paris, France
{denis.mazzucato,marco.campion,caterina.urban}@inria.fr

Abstract. Programming errors in software applications may produce plausible yet erroneous results, without providing a clear indication of failure. This happens, for instance, when certain inputs have a disproportionate impact on the program result. To address this issue, we propose a novel quantitative static analysis for determining the impact of inputs on the program computations, parametrized in the definition of impact. This static analysis employs an underlying abstract backward analyzer and computes a sound over-approximation of the impact of program inputs, providing valuable insights into how the analyzed program handles them. We implement a proof-of-concept static analyzer to demonstrate potential applications.

1 Introduction

Disastrous outcomes may result from programming errors in safety-critical settings, especially when they do not result in software failures but instead produce a plausible yet erroneous outcome. Such bugs are hard to spot since they provide no indication that something went wrong. A potential source of such errors is when an input variable has disproportionate impact on the program computations compared to the developers' expectations. A notable example is the Reinhart and Rogoff article "Growth in a Time of Debt" [19], which was heavily cited to justify austerity measures around the world in the following years, and was later discovered to be flawed [12]. Notably, one of the several programming and methodological errors discovered in the article is the incorrect usage of the input value relative to Norway's economic growth in 1964, compromising the authors' conclusion. Hence, it is important to employ techniques that enhance the confidence in the usage of input variables.

In this direction, Barowy et al. [2] proposed a stochastic approach specific for spreadsheet applications. Such approach is able to estimate the impact of input cells. However, the lack of mathematical guarantees precludes the employment of such technique in safety-critical contexts. On the other hand, existing formal methods-based approached only target qualitative properties about input data usage, e.g., only addressing whether an input variable is used or not [22,23].

In this work, we present a novel quantitative input usage framework to discriminate between input variables with different impact on the outcome of a program. Such knowledge could either certify intended behavior or reveal potential flaws, by matching the developers' intuition on the expected impact of their

N. Benz et al. (Eds.): NFM 2024, LNCS 14627, pp. 79–98, 2024.
https://doi.org/10.1007/978-3-031-60698-4_5

input with the actual result of the quantitative study. We characterize the impact of an input variable with a notion of dependency between variables and outputs. Compared to other quantitative notions of dependency, e.g., quantitative information flow [10,11], there are some key differences as the information we measure or the granularity of input contributions. Our framework is parametric in the choice of impact definition to better fit several factors, such as the program structure, the environment, the expertise of the developer, and the intuition of the researcher.

We propose a sound static analysis leveraging a backward analyzer to compute an over-approximation of the program semantics. In particular, this last component takes as input sets of program outputs, called output buckets, and computes an over-approximation of the input states leading to these buckets. Then, the end-user chooses the impact definition that best fits their needs, and our analysis applies such definition on the result of the previous phase. This approach, parametrized on the impact definition, ensures a more targeted and customizable analysis. We demonstrate the potential applications of our approach, by evaluating an automatic proof-of-concept tool of our static analysis against a set of use cases.

Contributions. We make the following contributions:

1. In Sect. 3, we develop a theoretical framework by abstract interpretation [9] to quantify the impact of input variables by considering two instances of impact: OUTCOMES and RANGE. Section 6 discusses the origins of our impact definitions in comparison with related metrics found in the literature.
2. In Sect. 4, we present our static analysis and a possible abstract implementation of the impact instances.
3. Finally, Sect. 5 evaluates our proof-of-concept against four use cases: a simplified program from the Reinhart and Rogoff article, a program extracted from the recent OpenAI keynote, one from termination analysis, and the example presented in the overview. More use cases can be found in our online supplementary material [16, Appendix B].

2 Overview

In this section, we present an overview of our quantitative analysis using the simple Program 1, referred to as L, which is a prototype of an aircraft landing alarm system. The goal of program L is to inform the pilot about the level of risk associated with the landing approach. It takes two input variables, denoted as `angle` and `speed`, for the aircraft-airstrip alignment angle and the aircraft speed, respectively. A value of 1 represents a good alignment while -4 a non-aligned angle, whereas 1, 2, 3 denote low, medium, and high speed[1]. A safer approach is indicated by lower speed. The landing risk coefficient combines the

[1] We initially focus on discrete values to simplify the example and convey the concept. We expand to continuous inputs in Sect. 5.

Input preconditions:

$$\texttt{angle} \in \{-4, 1\}$$
$$\texttt{speed} \in \{1, 2, 3\}$$

```
landing_coeff = abs(angle) + speed
if landing_coeff < 2 then
  risk = 0
else if landing_coeff > 5 then
  risk = 3
else
  risk = floor(landing_coeff) - 2
```

Program 1. Aircraft landing alarm system.

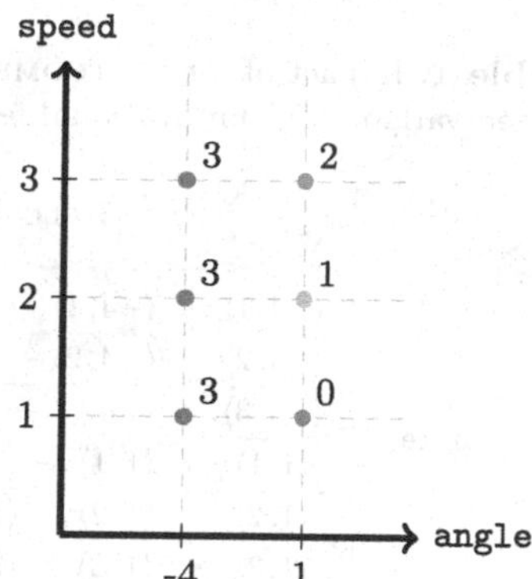

Fig. 1. Input space.

absolute landing angle and speed. The output variable `risk` is the danger level with possible values $\{0, 1, 2, 3\}$, where 0 represents low danger and 3 high danger. Figure 1 shows the input space composition of this system, where the label near each input represents the degree of risk assigned to the corresponding input configuration. It is easy to note that a nonaligned angle of approach corresponds to a considerably higher level of risk, whereas the risk with a correct angle depends mostly on the aircraft speed. Our goal is to develop a static analysis capable of quantifying the contribution of each input variable to the computation of the output variable `risk`.

Impact Analysis. We propose two impact definitions which, from value variations of the input variable under consideration, respectively focus on *the number of* resulting reachable outputs, and *the distance of* extreme reachable outputs.

The column INPUT$_L$ in Table 1 shows all the possible input configurations $\langle angle, speed \rangle$ for the program L. For each input configuration, column RELEVANT TRACES groups together the program traces resulting from value variation of the input variable of interest (in column VARIABLE), and column OUTPUTS collects the set of all reachable outputs.

First Impact Definition (OUTCOMES). The first impact definition that we consider is OUTCOMES$_i$(P), where i is the input variable of interest and P the program under analysis. Intuitively (the formal definition is given in Sect. 3), OUTCOMES$_i$ returns the maximum number of outputs that are reachable from value variations of the input variable i. For the program L, the result is shown in column OUTCOMES(L) of Table 1: we obtain OUTCOMES$_{\texttt{angle}}$(L) $= 2$ and OUTCOMES$_{\texttt{speed}}$(L) $= 3$. The conclusion is that **speed** has a greater influence than **angle** on the output of the program.

Second Impact Definition (RANGE). The second impact definition is RANGE$_i$, which yields the maximum difference between the maximum and the minimum outputs that are reachable from value variations of the input variable i. The result for program L is shown in column RANGE(L) of Table 1: the range of reach-

Table 1. Impact of for OUTCOMES(L) and RANGE(L) definitions for both `angle` and `speed` variables. Computational features are highlighted in blue.

VARIABLE	INPUTL	RELEVANT TRACES	OUTPUTS	OUTCOMES	RANGE
angle	⟨−4, 1⟩	⟨−4, 1⟩ → ⟨3⟩, ⟨1, 1⟩ → ⟨0⟩	{3, 0}	2	3
	⟨−4, 2⟩	⟨−4, 2⟩ → ⟨3⟩, ⟨1, 2⟩ → ⟨1⟩	{3, 1}		
	⟨−4, 3⟩	⟨−4, 3⟩ → ⟨3⟩, ⟨1, 3⟩ → ⟨2⟩	{3, 2}		
	⟨1, 1⟩	⟨1, 1⟩ → ⟨0⟩, ⟨−4, 1⟩ → ⟨3⟩	{0, 3}		
	⟨1, 2⟩	⟨1, 2⟩ → ⟨1⟩, ⟨−4, 2⟩ → ⟨3⟩	{1, 3}		
	⟨1, 3⟩	⟨1, 3⟩ → ⟨2⟩, ⟨−4, 3⟩ → ⟨3⟩	{2, 3}		
speed	⟨−4, 1⟩	⟨−4, 1⟩ → ⟨3⟩, ⟨−4, 2⟩ → ⟨3⟩, ⟨−4, 3⟩ → ⟨3⟩	{3}	3	2
	⟨−4, 2⟩	⟨−4, 1⟩ → ⟨3⟩, ⟨−4, 2⟩ → ⟨3⟩, ⟨−4, 3⟩ → ⟨3⟩	{3}		
	⟨−4, 3⟩	⟨−4, 1⟩ → ⟨3⟩, ⟨−4, 2⟩ → ⟨3⟩, ⟨−4, 3⟩ → ⟨3⟩	{3}		
	⟨1, 1⟩	⟨1, 1⟩ → ⟨0⟩, ⟨1, 2⟩ → ⟨1⟩, ⟨1, 3⟩ → ⟨2⟩	{0, 1, 2}		
	⟨1, 2⟩	⟨1, 1⟩ → ⟨0⟩, ⟨1, 2⟩ → ⟨1⟩, ⟨1, 3⟩ → ⟨2⟩	{0, 1, 2}		
	⟨1, 3⟩	⟨1, 1⟩ → ⟨0⟩, ⟨1, 2⟩ → ⟨1⟩, ⟨1, 3⟩ → ⟨2⟩	{0, 1, 2}		

able outputs from variations of `angle` is, at most, the interval $[0, 3]$, with a length of 3. Instead, the range of reachable outputs from variations of `speed` is, at most, the interval $[0, 2]$, with a length of 2. Therefore, we obtain $\text{RANGE}_{\texttt{angle}}(\text{L}) = 3$ and $\text{RANGE}_{\texttt{speed}}(\text{L}) = 2$. In other words, varying the angle of approach might drastically alter the landing risk, whereas the speed has less influence. This is in contrast to the conclusion of OUTCOMES where `speed` has a greater impact than `angle`. Although it may seem counterintuitive at first, the difference between the two impact instances is due to the different program traits they explore. RANGE quantifies over the variance in the extreme values of the set of output values, while OUTCOMES quantifies over the variance in the number of unique output values. Consequently, changes in `angle` yield a bigger variation in the degree of risk compared to `speed`, while changes in `speed` reach far more risk levels compared to `angle`. Note that, the impact definitions presented above are not computationally practical as they rely on a complete enumeration of all possible input configurations. Specifically, when dealing with more complex input space compositions, this approach is highly inefficient or even infeasible (as in the case of continuous input spaces). As a consequence, our approach is based on an abstraction of input-output relations, which allows us to automatically infer a sound upper bound on the program's impact.

Abstract Analysis. The analysis starts with a set of output abstractions called *output buckets.* A bucket is an abstract element representing a set of output states. While this abstraction may limit the ability to precisely reason about the impact of output values within the same bucket, it permits automatic reasoning across different buckets. Afterwards, an abstract interpretation-based static analyzer propagates each output bucket backward through the program under consideration. The analyzer returns an abstract element for each output bucket, representing an over-approximation of the set of input configurations that lead to the output values inside the starting bucket. This result contains also spurious input configurations that may not lead to a value inside the output bucket. Based on the chosen impact definition IMPACT (e.g., RANGE or OUTCOMES), we perform computations and comparisons on the abstract elements returned by the analysis to obtain an upper bound k'. This upper bound is sound by construction of the theoretical framework, meaning that if k is the real (concrete) impact quantity obtained by IMPACT, then $k \leq k'$. The precision of our analysis is mostly affected by the choice of output buckets and the approximation induced by the backward analysis (as outlined by the use cases shown in Sect. 5 and in the supplementary material [16, Appendix B]).

3 Quantitative Input Data Usage

In this section we present some preliminaries on program computations, then we introduce our quantitative framework with the formal definitions of RANGE and OUTCOMES.

Program Semantics. The *semantics* of a program is a mathematical characterization of its behavior for all possible input data. We model the operational semantics of a program as a *transition system* $\langle \Sigma, \tau \rangle$ where Σ is a (potentially infinite) set of program states and the transition relation $\tau \subseteq \Sigma \times \Sigma$ describes the feasible transitions between states [8,9]. The set $\Omega \stackrel{\text{def}}{=} \{s \in \Sigma \mid \forall s' \in \Sigma.\ \langle s, s' \rangle \notin \tau\}$ represents the *final states* of the program.

Let $\Sigma^n \stackrel{\text{def}}{=} \{s_0 \dots s_{n-1} \mid \forall i < n.\ s_i \in \Sigma\}$ be the set of all sequences of exactly n program states. We write ϵ to denote the empty sequence, i.e., $\Sigma^0 \stackrel{\text{def}}{=} \{\epsilon\}$. We define $\Sigma^\star \stackrel{\text{def}}{=} \bigcup_{n \in \mathbb{N}} \Sigma^n$ as the set of all finite sequences, $\Sigma^+ \stackrel{\text{def}}{=} \Sigma^\star \setminus \Sigma^0$ as the set of all non-empty finite sequences, $\Sigma^\infty \stackrel{\text{def}}{=} \{s_0 \dots \mid \forall i \in \mathbb{N}.\ s_i \in \Sigma\}$ as the set of all infinite sequences, and $\Sigma^{+\infty} \stackrel{\text{def}}{=} \Sigma^+ \cup \Sigma^\infty$ as the set of all non-empty finite or infinite sequences. Additionally, let $\Sigma^\perp \stackrel{\text{def}}{=} \Sigma \cup \{\perp\}$. Given a sequence $\sigma \in \Sigma^{+\infty}$, we write $\sigma_0 \in \Sigma$ to denote the initial state of σ and $\sigma_\omega \in \Sigma^\perp$ to denote the final state of σ when $\sigma \in \Sigma^+$, otherwise $\sigma_\omega = \perp$ when $\sigma \in \Sigma^\infty$. To concatenate two sequences of states $\sigma, \sigma' \in \Sigma^{+\infty}$, we write $\sigma \cdot \sigma'$. It holds that $\sigma \cdot \epsilon = \epsilon \cdot \sigma = \sigma$ and $\sigma \cdot \sigma' = \sigma$ whenever $\sigma \in \Sigma^\infty$. To merge two sets of sequences $T \subseteq \Sigma^+$ and $T' \subseteq \Sigma^{+\infty}$, we write $T \,;\, T' \stackrel{\text{def}}{=} \{\sigma \cdot s \cdot \sigma' \mid s \in \Sigma \wedge \sigma \cdot s \in T \wedge s \cdot \sigma' \in T'\}$ when a finite sequence in T terminates with the initial state of a sequence in T'.

In the rest of the paper, $\mathbb{I} \in \{\mathbb{N}, \mathbb{Z}, \mathbb{R}\}$ represents a set of numerical values. We write $\mathbb{I}^{\pm\infty}$ to denote $\mathbb{I}$ extended with the symbols $+\infty$ and $-\infty$. The set

$\mathbb{I}_{\geq 0} \stackrel{\text{def}}{=} \{n \in \mathbb{I} \mid n \geq 0\}$ denotes non-negative numbers. Similarly, we can use other predicates, for instance, $\mathbb{I}_{\leq m} \stackrel{\text{def}}{=} \{n \in \mathbb{I} \mid n \leq m\}$ denotes the set of numbers below or equal $m \in \mathbb{I}$.

Given a transition system $\langle \Sigma, \tau \rangle$, a *trace* is a non-empty sequence of program states that respects the transition relation τ, i.e., for every pair of consecutive states $s, s' \in \Sigma$ in the trace, it holds that $\langle s, s' \rangle \in \tau$. The *trace semantics* $\Lambda \in \wp(\Sigma^{+\infty})$ generated by a transition system $\langle \Sigma, \tau \rangle$ is the union between all finite traces that are terminating in a final state in Ω, and all non-terminating infinite traces [8]:

$$\Lambda \stackrel{\text{def}}{=} \bigcup_{n \in \mathbb{N}_{\geq 0}} \{s_0 \dots s_{n-1} \in \Sigma^n \mid \forall i < n-1.\ \langle s_i, s_{i+1} \rangle \in \tau \wedge s_{n-1} \in \Omega\}$$
$$\cup \{s_0 \ldots \in \Sigma^\infty \mid \forall i \in \mathbb{N}.\ \langle s_i, s_{i+1} \rangle \in \tau\}$$

We write $\Lambda[\![\mathrm{P}]\!]$ to denote the trace semantics of a particular program P. The same applies for other semantics defined in the rest of paper.

The trace semantics fully describes the behavior of a program. However, reasoning about a particular property of a program is facilitated by the design of a semantics that abstracts away from irrelevant details about program executions. In our work, we focus on *extensional* properties, namely, properties based on the observation of input-output relations of $\Lambda[\![\mathrm{P}]\!]$. Therefore, we employ the dependency semantics $\Lambda^{\rightsquigarrow} \in \wp(\Sigma \times \Sigma^{\perp})$ [22] as an abstraction of the trace semantics removing intermediate steps, i.e., $\Lambda^{\rightsquigarrow} \stackrel{\text{def}}{=} \{\langle \sigma_0, \sigma_\omega \rangle \mid \sigma \in \Lambda[\![\mathrm{P}]\!]\}$. Starting from the dependency semantics, we define our property of interest – quantitative input data usage – and use abstract interpretation to systematically derive a semantics tailored to reason about this property.

Property. A *property* is specified by its extension, that is, the set of elements that manifest such a property [9]. We consider properties of programs, with dependency semantics in $\wp(\Sigma \times \Sigma^{\perp})$, which are sets of sets of dependencies in $\wp(\wp(\Sigma \times \Sigma^{\perp}))$. The strongest property of the dependency semantics $\Lambda^{\rightsquigarrow}$ is the standard *collecting semantics* $\Lambda^c \in \wp(\wp(\Sigma \times \Sigma^{\perp}))$, defined as $\Lambda^c \stackrel{\text{def}}{=} \{\ \Lambda^{\rightsquigarrow}\ \}$, which is satisfied only and exactly by $\Lambda^{\rightsquigarrow}$. Therefore, a program P satisfies a given property $F \in \wp(\wp(\Sigma \times \Sigma^{\perp}))$, written $\mathrm{P} \models F$, if and only if P belongs to F, or equivalently, its collecting semantics Λ^c is a subset of F, formally

$$\mathrm{P} \models F \Leftrightarrow \Lambda^c[\![\mathrm{P}]\!] \subseteq F$$

Our goal is to quantify the impact of a specific input variable on the computation of the program. To this end, we introduce the notion of impact, denoted by the function $\textsc{Impact}_i \in \wp(\Sigma \times \Sigma^{\perp}) \rightarrow \mathbb{I}^{+\infty}_{\geq 0}$, which maps program semantics to a non-negative domain of quantities, where i represents the input variable of interest in the program under analysis. We implicitly assume the use of an *output descriptor* $\phi \in \Sigma^{\perp} \rightarrow \mathbb{I}^{\pm\infty}$ to determine the desired output of a program by observations on program states[2]. The output descriptor ϕ is generic enough

[2] The option of returning $\pm\infty$ from the output descriptor is to deal with infinite traces, which do not have a final state ($\sigma_\omega = \perp$ for any $\sigma \in \Sigma^\infty$).

to cover plenty of use cases, providing the end-user the flexibility to choose the interpretation and meaning of program outputs.

Example 1. Consider the Program 1 for the landing alarm system with program states $\Sigma = \{\langle a, b, c, d\rangle \mid a \in \{-4, 1\} \wedge b \in \{1, 2, 3\} \wedge c \in \mathbb{N} \wedge d \in \{0, 1, 2, 3\}\}$, where a is the value of `angle`, b of `speed`, c of `landing_coeff`, and d of `risk`. Here, we abuse the notation and use Σ as set of tuples instead of a map between variables and values, the two views are equivalent. The output descriptor is instantiated with

$$\phi(x) \stackrel{\text{def}}{=} \begin{cases} d & \text{if } x = \langle a, b, c, d\rangle \\ +\infty & \text{otherwise} \end{cases}$$

In other words, we are interested in the value of `risk` for terminating traces.

Given an impact definition of interest, we define the *k-bounded impact property* $\mathscr{B}_i^{\leq k} \in \wp(\wp(\Sigma \times \Sigma^{\perp}))$ as the set of dependency semantics with impact with respect to the input variable i below the threshold $k \in \mathbb{I}_{\geq 0}^{+\infty}$. Formally,

$$\mathscr{B}_i^{\leq k} \stackrel{\text{def}}{=} \{\Lambda^{\rightsquigarrow} \in \wp(\Sigma \times \Sigma^{\perp}) \mid \text{IMPACT}_i(\Lambda^{\rightsquigarrow}) \leq k\}$$

We require IMPACT_i to be monotonic, i.e., for any $S, S' \in \wp(\Sigma \times \Sigma^{\perp})$, it holds that:

$$S \subseteq S' \Rightarrow \text{IMPACT}_i(S) \leq \text{IMPACT}_i(S')$$

Intuitively, this ensures that an impact applied to an over-approximation of the program semantics can only produce a higher quantity, allowing for a sound k-bounded impact verification.

Next, we formalize the already introduced impact metrics OUTCOMES and RANGE. Given a program P and its variables $\mathbb{V}$, we assume program states are maps from variables to a numerical domain, i.e., $\Sigma = \mathbb{V} \to \mathbb{I}$. The set $\Delta \subseteq \mathbb{V}$ is the set of input variables. We write $\Sigma|_K = K \to \mathbb{I}$ for the program states reduced to the subset of variables $K \subseteq \mathbb{V}$. For instance $\Sigma|_\Delta$ is the set of states restricted to the input variables. The predicate $s =_K s'$ indicates that the two states $s, s' \in \Sigma^{\perp}|_K$, agree on the values of the variables in $K \subseteq \mathbb{V}$, or they are both $\perp$, formally

$$s =_K s' \Leftrightarrow (s \neq \perp \wedge s' \neq \perp \wedge \forall v \in K.\ s(v) = s'(v)) \vee (s = \perp \wedge s' = \perp)$$

OUTCOMES. Formally $\text{OUTCOMES}_i \in \wp(\Sigma \times \Sigma^{\perp}) \to \mathbb{N}^{+\infty}$ counts the number of different output values reachable by varying the input variable $i \in \Delta$. Intuitively, for any possible input configuration $s \in \Sigma|_\Delta$, we gather the set $S \in \wp(\Sigma \times \Sigma^{\perp})$ of all input-output state dependencies with an input configuration that is a variation of s on the input variable i, i.e., $\{\langle s_0, s_\omega\rangle \in S \mid s_0 =_{\Delta\setminus\{i\}} s\}$. Then, OUTCOMES_i is the maximal cardinality of the output values $\{\phi(s_\omega) \mid \langle s_0, s_\omega\rangle \in S \wedge s_0 =_{\Delta\setminus\{i\}} s\}$. Formally,

$$\text{OUTCOMES}_i(S) \stackrel{\text{def}}{=} \sup_{s \in \Sigma|_\Delta} |\ \{\phi(s_\omega) \mid \langle s_0, s_\omega\rangle \in S \wedge s_0 =_{\Delta\setminus\{i\}} s\}\ | \qquad (1)$$

where $|\cdot|$ is the cardinality operator, and $\sup(X)$ is the supremum operator, i.e., the smallest q such that $q \geq x$ for all $x \in X$. From the definition above, it is easy to note that $\text{OUTCOMES}_i(S)$ is monotone in the amount of dependencies S. That is, the more dependencies in input, the higher the impact as only more dependencies can satisfy the condition of Eq. (1), cf. $s_0 =_{\Delta\setminus\{i\}} s$, and hence increase the number of outcomes.

RANGE. The quantity $\text{RANGE}_i \in \wp(\Sigma \times \Sigma^\perp) \rightarrow \mathbb{R}^{+\infty}_{\geq 0}$ determines the length of the range of output values from all the possible variations in the input variable $i \in \Delta$. This definition employs the auxiliary function $\text{LENGTH} \in \wp(\mathbb{I}^{\pm\infty}) \rightarrow \mathbb{I}^{+\infty}_{\geq 0}$, defined as follows: $\text{LENGTH}(X) \stackrel{\text{def}}{=} \sup\ X - \inf\ X$ if $X \neq \emptyset$, where sup and inf are the supremum and infimum operators, while $\text{LENGTH}(X) \stackrel{\text{def}}{=} 0$ otherwise. Formally,

$$\text{RANGE}_i(S) \stackrel{\text{def}}{=} \sup_{s \in \Sigma|_\Delta} \text{LENGTH}(\{\phi(s_\omega) \mid \langle s_0, s_\omega \rangle \in S \wedge s_0 =_{\Delta\setminus\{i\}} s\})$$

Similarly to OUTCOMES, RANGE is monotone in the amount of dependencies S.

4 A Static Analysis for Quantitative Input Data Usage

In this section, we introduce a sound computable static analysis to determine an upper bound on the impact of an input variable i. The soundness of the approach leverages two elements: (1) an underlying abstract semantics $\Lambda^{\leftarrow}$ to compute an over-approximation of the dependency semantics $\Lambda^{\rightsquigarrow}$; and (2) a sound computable implementation of IMPACT_i, written $\texttt{Impact}^\natural_i$, used in the property $\mathscr{B}^{\leq k}_i$. All proofs can be found in the supplementary material [16, Appendix A].

To quantify the usage of an input variable, we need to determine the input configurations leading to specific output values. As our impact definitions OUTCOMES_i and RANGE_i measure over the different output values (i.e., $\phi(s_\omega)$) our underlying abstract semantics will be a *backward* (co-)reachability semantics starting from *disjoint* abstract post-conditions, over-approximating the (concrete) output values of the dependency semantics. Specifically, we abstract the concrete output values with an indexed set $B^\natural \in \mathbb{D}^{\natural n}$ of n disjoint *output buckets*, where $\langle \mathbb{D}^\natural, \sqsubseteq, \perp^\natural, \top^\natural, \sqcup, \sqcap \rangle$ is an abstract state domain with concretization function $\gamma^\natural \in \mathbb{D}^\natural \rightarrow \wp(\Sigma^\perp)$. The choice of these output buckets is essential for obtaining a precise and meaningful analysis result.

For each output bucket $B^\natural_j \in \mathbb{D}^\natural$, our analysis computes an over-approximation of the dependency semantics restricted to the input configurations leading to $\gamma^\natural(B^\natural_j)$. More formally, let $\Lambda^{\rightsquigarrow}|_X \stackrel{\text{def}}{=} \{\langle s_0, s_\omega \rangle \in \Lambda^{\rightsquigarrow} \mid s_\omega \in X\}$ be the reduction of the dependency semantics $\Lambda^{\rightsquigarrow}$ to the dependencies with final states in X. Our static analysis is parametrized by an underlying backward abstract family[3] of semantics $\Lambda^{\leftarrow}[\![P]\!] \in \mathbb{D}^\natural \rightarrow \mathbb{D}^\natural$ which computes the backward semantics $\Lambda^{\leftarrow}[\![P]\!] B^\natural_j$ from a given output bucket $B^\natural_j \in \mathbb{D}^\natural$. The concretization function

[3] A family of semantics is a set of program semantics parametrized by an initialization.

$\gamma^{\leftarrow} \in (\mathbb{D}^{\natural} \to \mathbb{D}^{\natural}) \to \mathbb{D}^{\natural} \to \wp(\Sigma \times \Sigma^{\perp})$ employs $\gamma^{\natural}$ to restore all possible input-output dependencies, i.e., $\gamma^{\leftarrow}(\Lambda^{\leftarrow}[\![\mathrm{P}]\!])B_j^{\natural} \stackrel{\text{def}}{=} \{\langle s_0, s_\omega\rangle \mid s_0 \in \gamma^{\natural}(\Lambda^{\leftarrow}[\![\mathrm{P}]\!]B_j^{\natural}) \wedge s_\omega \in \gamma^{\natural}(B_j^{\natural})\}$. We can thus define the soundness condition for the backward semantics with respect to the reduction of the dependency semantics.

Definition 1 (Sound Over-Approximation for $\Lambda^{\leftarrow}$). *For all programs* P, *and output bucket $B_j^{\natural} \in \mathbb{D}^{\natural}$, the family of semantics $\Lambda^{\leftarrow}$ is a* sound over-approximation *of the dependency semantics $\Lambda^{\rightsquigarrow}$ reduced with $\gamma^{\natural}(B_j^{\natural})$, when it holds that:*

$$\Lambda^{\rightsquigarrow}[\![\mathrm{P}]\!]|_{\gamma^{\natural}(B_j^{\natural})} \subseteq \gamma^{\leftarrow}(\Lambda^{\leftarrow}[\![\mathrm{P}]\!])B_j^{\natural}$$

We define $\Lambda^{\times} \in \mathbb{D}^{\natural n} \to \mathbb{D}^{\natural n}$ as the backward semantics repeated on a set of output buckets $B^{\natural} \in \mathbb{D}^{\natural n}$, that is, $\Lambda^{\times}[\![\mathrm{P}]\!]B^{\natural} \stackrel{\text{def}}{=} (\Lambda^{\leftarrow}[\![\mathrm{P}]\!]B_j^{\natural})_{j \leq n}$. Again, the concretization function $\gamma^{\times} \in (\mathbb{D}^{\natural n} \to \mathbb{D}^{\natural n}) \to \mathbb{D}^{\natural n} \to \wp(\Sigma \times \Sigma^{\perp})$ employs the abstract concretization $\gamma^{\natural}$ to restore all possible input-output dependencies over all the output buckets, i.e., $\gamma^{\times}(\Lambda^{\times}[\![\mathrm{P}]\!])B^{\natural} \stackrel{\text{def}}{=} \bigcup_{j \leq n}\{\langle s_0, s_\omega\rangle \mid s_0 \in \gamma^{\natural}((\Lambda^{\times}[\![\mathrm{P}]\!]B^{\natural})_j) \wedge s_\omega \in \gamma^{\natural}(B_j^{\natural})\}$.

Lemma 1 (Sound Over-Approximation for $\Lambda^{\times}$). *For all programs* P, *output buckets $B^{\natural} \in \mathbb{D}^{\natural n}$, and a family of semantics $\Lambda^{\leftarrow}$, the semantics $\Lambda^{\times}$ is a* sound over-approximation *of the dependency semantics $\Lambda^{\rightsquigarrow}$ when reduced to $\bigcup_{j \leq n} \gamma^{\natural}(B_j^{\natural})$:*

$$\Lambda^{\rightsquigarrow}[\![\mathrm{P}]\!]|_{\bigcup_{j \leq n} \gamma^{\natural}(B_j^{\natural})} \subseteq \gamma^{\times}(\Lambda^{\times}[\![\mathrm{P}]\!])B^{\natural}$$

Whenever the output buckets *cover* the whole output space, $\Lambda^{\times}$ is a sound over-approximation of $\Lambda^{\rightsquigarrow}$. The concept of covering for output buckets ensures that no final states of the dependency semantics, i.e. $\Omega^{\rightsquigarrow} \stackrel{\text{def}}{=} \{s_\omega \mid \langle s_0, s_\omega\rangle \in \Lambda^{\rightsquigarrow}\}$, are missed from the analysis.

Definition 2 (Covering). *We say that the output buckets $B^{\natural} \in \mathbb{D}^{\natural n}$ cover the whole output space whenever $\Omega^{\rightsquigarrow} \subseteq \bigcup_{j \leq n} \gamma^{\natural}(B_j^{\natural})$.*

Next, we expect a sound implementation $\mathtt{Impact}_i^{\natural} \in \mathbb{D}^{\natural n} \times \mathbb{D}^{\natural n} \to \mathbb{I}^{\pm\infty}$ to return a bound on the impact which is always higher than the concrete counterpart $\textsc{Impact}_i$.

Definition 3 (Sound Implementation). *For all output buckets $B^{\natural}$ and family of semantics $\Lambda^{\leftarrow}$, $\mathtt{Impact}_i^{\natural}$ is a* sound implementation *of* $\textsc{Impact}$, *whenever*

$$\textsc{Impact}_i(\gamma^{\times}(\Lambda^{\times}[\![\mathrm{P}]\!])B^{\natural}) \leq \mathtt{Impact}_i^{\natural}(\Lambda^{\times}[\![\mathrm{P}]\!]B^{\natural}, B^{\natural})$$

The next result shows that our static analysis is sound when employed to verify the property of interest $\mathscr{B}_i^{\leq k}$ for the program P. That is, if $\mathtt{Impact}_i^{\natural}$ returns the bound k', and $k' \leq k$, then the program P satisfies the property $\mathscr{B}_i^{\leq k}$, cf. $\mathrm{P} \models \mathscr{B}_i^{\leq k}$.

Theorem 1 (Soundness). *Let $\mathscr{B}_i^{\leq k}$ be the property of interest we want to verify for the program* P *and the input variable $i \in \Delta$. Whenever,*

(i) $\Lambda^{\leftarrow}$ *is sound with respect to* $\Lambda^{\leadsto}$*, cf. Definition (1), and*
(ii) $B^{\natural}$ *covers the whole output space, cf. Definition (2), and*
(iii) $\texttt{Impact}_i^{\natural}$ *is a sound implementation of* $\textsc{Impact}_i$*, cf. Definition (3),*

the following implication holds:

$$\texttt{Impact}_i^{\natural}(\Lambda^{\times}[\![\mathrm{P}]\!]B^{\natural}, B^{\natural}) = k' \ \wedge\ k' \leq k \ \Rightarrow\ \mathrm{P} \models \mathscr{B}_i^{\leq k}$$

Finally, we define $\texttt{Range}_i^{\natural}$ and $\texttt{Outcomes}_i^{\natural}$ as possible implementations for $\textsc{Range}_i$ and $\textsc{Outcomes}_i$, respectively. We assume the underlying abstract state domain $\mathbb{D}^{\natural}$ is equipped with an operator $\texttt{Project}_i^{\natural} \in \mathbb{D}^{\natural} \to \mathbb{D}^{\natural}$ to project away the input variable i. For example, in the context of the interval domain, where each input variable is related to a possibly unbounded lower and upper bound, $\texttt{Project}_i^{\natural}(\langle i \mapsto [1,3], j \mapsto [2,4]\rangle) = \langle i \mapsto [-\infty,\infty], j \mapsto [2,4]\rangle$ removes the constraints related to i.

The definition of $\texttt{Outcomes}_i^{\natural}$ first projects away the input variable i from all the given abstract values, then it collects all intersecting abstract values via the meet operator $\sqcap$. These intersections represent potential concrete input configurations where variations on the value of i lead to changes of program outcome, from a bucket to another. We return the maximum number of abstract values that intersects after projections:

$$\texttt{Outcomes}_i^{\natural}(X^{\natural}, B^{\natural}) \stackrel{\text{def}}{=} \max\ \{|J| \mid J \in \texttt{IntersectAll}((\texttt{Project}_i^{\natural}(X_j^{\natural}))_{j \leq n})\}$$

Note the use of max instead of sup as in the concrete counterpart (Eq. (1)) since the number of intersecting abstract values is bounded by n, i.e., the number of output buckets. The function `IntersectAll` takes as input an indexed set of abstract values and returns the set of indices of abstract values that intersect together, defined as follows:

$$\texttt{IntersectAll}(X^{\natural} \in \mathbb{D}^{\natural n}) \stackrel{\text{def}}{=} \{J \mid J \subseteq \mathbb{N} \wedge \forall j \leq n, p \leq n.\ j \in J \wedge p \in J \ \wedge\ X_j^{\natural} \sqcap X_p^{\natural}\}$$

Finding all the indices of intersecting abstract values is equivalent to find cliques in a graph, where each node represents an abstract value and an edge exists between two nodes if and only if the corresponding abstract values intersect. Therefore, `IntersectAll` can be efficiently implemented based on the graph algorithm by Bron and Kerbosch [3].

Similarly, we define $\texttt{Range}_i^{\natural}$ as the maximum length of the range of the extreme values of the buckets represented by intersecting abstract values after projections. In such case, we assume $\mathbb{D}^{\natural}$ is equipped with an additional abstract operator $\texttt{Length}^{\natural} \in \mathbb{D}^{\natural} \to \mathbb{I}_{\geq 0}^{+\infty}$, which returns the length of the given abstract element, otherwise $+\infty$ if the abstract element is unbounded or represents multiple variables.

$$\begin{aligned} \texttt{Range}^\natural_i(X^\natural, B^\natural) &\stackrel{\text{def}}{=} \max \{\texttt{Length}^\natural(K) \mid K \in I\} \\ \text{where } I &= \{\sqcup\{B^\natural_j \mid j \in J\} \mid J \in \texttt{IntersectAll}((\texttt{Project}^\natural_i(X^\natural_j))_{j \leq n})\} \end{aligned}$$

In the supplementary material [16, Appendix A], we prove that the abstract counterparts $\texttt{Range}^\natural_i$ and $\texttt{Outcomes}^\natural_i$ are sound over-approximations of the concrete counterparts RANGE_i and OUTCOMES_i.

5 Experimental Results

The goal of this section is to highlight the potential of our static analysis for quantitative input data usage. We implemented a proof-of-concept tool[4] in Python 3 that employs the `Interproc`[5] abstract interpreter to perform the backward analysis. Then, we exploited this tool to automatically derive a sound input data usage of three different scenarios. More use cases are shown in the supplementary material [16, Appendix B]. As each impact result must be interpreted with respect to what the program computes, we analyze each scenario separately.

Growth in a Time of Debt. Reinhart and Rogoff article "Growth in a Time of Debt" [19] proposed a correlation between high levels of public debt and low economic growth, and was heavily cited to justify austerity measures around the world. One of the several errors discovered in the article is the incorrect usage of the input value relative to Norway's economic growth in 1964. The data used in the article is publicly available but not the spreadsheet file. We reconstructed this simplified example based on the technical critique by Herndon et al. [12], and an online discussion[6]. The Program 2 computes the cross-country mean growth for the public debt-to-GDP 60–90% category, key point to the article's conclusions. The input data is the average growth rate for each country within this public dept-to-GDP category. The problem with this computation is that Norway has only one observation in such category, which alone could disrupt the mean computation among all the countries. Indeed, the year that Norway appears in the 60–90% category achieved a growth rate of 10.2%, while the average growth rate for the other countries is 2.7%. With such high rate, the mean growth rate raised to 3.4%, altering the article's conclusions. We assume growth rate values between −20% and 20% for all countries, consequentially, the output ranges are between these bounds as well. We instrumented the output buckets to cover the full output space in buckets of size 1, i.e., $\{t \leq \texttt{avg} < t+1 \mid -20 \leq t \leq 20\}$. Results for both OUTCOMES and RANGE are shown in Table 2. The analysis discovers that the Norway's only observation for this category `norway1` has the biggest impact on the output, as perturbations on its

4 https://github.com/denismazzucato/impatto.
5 https://github.com/jogiet/interproc.
6 https://economics.stackexchange.com/q/18553.

Table 2. Quantitative input usage for Program 2 from the Reinhart and Rogoff's article.

IMPACT	portugal1	portugal2	portugal3	norway1	uk1	uk2	uk3	uk4	us1	us2	us3
OUTCOMES	5	5	5	10	2	2	2	2	3	3	3
RANGE	5	5	5	10	2	2	2	2	3	3	3

value are capable of reaching 10 different outcomes (cf. column `norway1`), while the other countries only have 5, 2, and 3, respectively for Portugal, UK, and US. The same applies to RANGE as the output buckets have size 1 and all the input perturbations are only capable of reaching contiguous buckets. Hence, we obtain the same exact results.

```
def mean_growth_rate_60_90(
      portugal1, portugal2, portugal3,
      norway1,
      uk1, uk2, uk3, uk4,
      us1, us2, us3):
   portugal_avg = (portugal1 + portugal2 + portugal3) / 3
   norway_avg = norway1
   uk_avg = (uk1 + uk2 + uk3 + uk4) / 4
   us_avg = (us1 + us2 + us3) / 3
   avg = (portugal_avg + norway_avg + uk_avg + us_avg) / 4
```

Program 2. Program computing the mean growth rate in the 60–90% category.

Our analysis is able to discover the disproportionate impact of Norway's only observation in the mean computation, which would have prevented one of the several programming errors found in the article. From a review of Program 2, it is clear that Norway's only observation has a greater contribution to the computation, as it does not need to be averaged with other observations first. However, such methodological error is less evident when dealing with a higher number of input observations (1175 observations in the original work) and the computation is hidden behind a spreadsheet.

GPT-4 Turbo. The second use case we present is drawn from Sam Altman's recent OpenAI keynote in September 2023[7], where he presented the GPT-4 Turbo. This new version of the GPT-4 language model brings the ability to write and interpret code directly without the need of human interaction. Hence, as showcased in the keynote, the user could prompt multiple information to the model, such as related to the organization of a holiday trip with friends in Paris, and the model automatically generates the code to compute the share of the total cost of the trip and run it in background. In this environment, users are unable to directly view the code unless they access the backend console. This

7 https://www.youtube.com/live/U9mJuUkhUzk?si=HOzuH3-gr_kTdhCt&t=2330.

Table 3. Results of the quantitative analysis for Program 3 and Program 4.

IMPACT	airbnb_total_cost_eur	flight_cost_usd	number_of_friends	x	y
OUTCOMES	10	17	9	50	10
RANGE	1099	1709	999	499	99

(a) Program 3 computing the share division among friends. (b) Program 4.

```
def share_division(
        airbnb_total_cost_eur,
        flight_cost_usd,
        number_of_friends):
    share_airbnb = airbnb_total_cost_eur / number_of_friends
    usd_to_eur = 0.92
    flight_cost_eur = flight_cost_usd * usd_to_eur
    total_cost_eur = share_airbnb + flight_cost_eur
```

Program 3. Program computing share division for holiday planning among friends.

limitation makes it challenging for them to evaluate whether the function has been implemented correctly or not, assuming users have the capability to do so. From the keynote, we extracted the Program 3 which computes the user's share of the total cost of a holiday trip to Paris, given the total cost of the Airbnb, the flight cost, and the number of friends going on the trip. Regarding the input bounds, users are willing to spend between 500 and 2000 for the Airbnb, between 50 and 1000 for the flight, and travel with between 2 and 10 friends. As a result, they expect their share, variable `total_cost_eur`, to be between 90 and 1900. To compute the impact of the input variables we choose the output buckets to cover the expected output space in buckets of size 100, i.e., $\{100t + 90 \leq$ `total_cost_eur` $< \min\{100(t+1) + 90, 1900\} \mid 0 \leq t \leq 19\}$. The findings are similar for both the OUTCOMES and RANGE analysis, see Table 3a. The input variable `flight_cost_usd` has the biggest impact on the output, as perturbations on its value are capable of reaching 17 different output buckets (resp. a range of 1709 output values), while the other two, `airbnb_total_cost_eur` and `number_of_friends`, only reach 10 and 9 output buckets (resp. have ranges of size 1099 and 999), respectively.

These results confirm the user expectations about the proposed program from ChatGPT: the flight cost yields the biggest impact as it cannot be shared among friends.

```
def example(x, y):
  counter = 0
  while x >= 0:
    if y <= 50:
      x += 1
    else
      x -= 1
    y += 1
    counter += 1
```

Program 4. Timing analysis.

Termination Analysis. Program 4 is adapted from the termination category of the software verification competition SV-COMP[8]. Assuming both input positives, $\texttt{x}, \texttt{y} \geq 0$, this program terminates in $\texttt{x} + 1$ iterations if $\texttt{y} > 50$, otherwise it terminates in $\texttt{x} - 2\texttt{y} + 103$ iterations. We define `counter` as the output variable, with output buckets defined as $\{10k \leq \texttt{counter} < 10(k+1) \mid 0 \leq k < 50\}$ and $\{\texttt{counter} \geq 500\}$. These output buckets represent cumulative ranges of iterations required for termination. The analysis results are illustrated in Table 3b, they show that the input variable x has the biggest impact. Modifying the value of x can result in the program terminating within any of the other 50 iteration ranges. On the other hand, perturbations on y can only result in the program terminating within 10 different iteration ranges. Such difference is motivated by the fact that y is only used to determine the number of iterations in the case where y is greater than 50, otherwise it is not used at all. Therefore, two values of y, e.g., y_0 and y_1, only result in two different ranges of iterations required to make the program terminate if either both of them are below 50 or $y_0 < 50 \wedge y_1 \geq 50$ or $y_0 \geq 50 \wedge y_1 < 50$, not in all the cases.

The given results can be interpreted as follows: the speed of termination of this loop is highly dependent on the value of x, while y has a much smaller impact.

Landing Risk System. We apply our quantitative analysis to Program 1 for the landing alarm system extended with the continuous input space for the aircraft angle of approach, where $(-4 \leq \texttt{angle} \leq 4) \wedge (1 \leq \texttt{speed} \leq 3)$, see Fig. 2. In this instance, the precision of the abstraction drastically drops as convex abstract domains are not able to capture the symmetric features of the input space around 0. Indeed, the analysis result, first row of Fig. 3, is unable to reveal any difference in the input usage of input variables as all the abstract preconditions result of the backward analysis intersect together. As a consequence, OUTCOMES and RANGE are unable to provide any meaningful information, first row of Table 4.

A possible approach to overcome the non-convexity of the input space is to split the input space into two subspaces (as a bounded set of disjunctive

[8] https://sv-comp.sosy-lab.org/.

Table 4. Quantitative input usage for Program 1.

Input Bounds		OUTCOMES		RANGE	
		angle	speed	angle	speed
$-4 \leq$ angle ≤ 4	$\wedge\, 1 \leq$ speed ≤ 3	3	3	3	3
$-4 \leq$ angle ≤ 0		3	2	3	2
$0 \leq$ angle ≤ 4		3	2	3	2

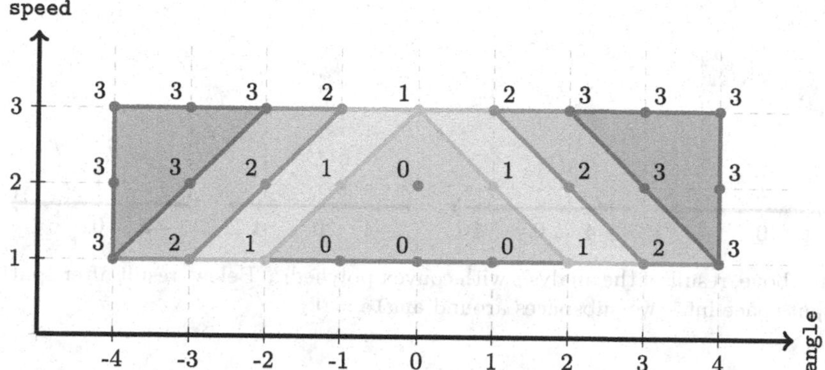

Fig. 2. Input space composition with continuous input values.

polyhedra), $-4 \leq$ **angle** ≤ 0 and $0 \leq$ **angle** ≤ 4, second and third row of Table 4. In the first subset $-4 \leq$ **angle** ≤ 0, we are able to perfectly captures the input regions that lead to each output bucket with our abstract analysis, second row of Fig. 3. Therefore, we are able to recover the information that the input configurations from the bucket $\{$**risk** $= 3\}$ do not intersect with the ones from the bucket $\{$**risk** $= 0\}$ after projecting away the axis **speed**. As the end, our analysis notices that variations in the value of the input **angle** results in three possible output values, while variations in the **speed** input lead to two. Similarly, regarding the range of values, variations in the **angle** input cover the entire spectrum of output values, whereas to the **speed** input only span a range of 2 since it exists no input value such that modifications in the **speed** value could obtain a range of output values bigger than 2. The same reasoning applies to the other subspace with $0 \leq$ **angle** ≤ 4.

6 Related Work

Given the connection between *qualitative* input usage and information flow analyses [22], to design a quantitative input usage analysis that fits our purposes, it may come natural to use *quantitative* information flow [10,11]. Such analyses measure information leakage about a secret through the concept of entropy, based on observations of the program's output values. Remarkably, this similarity between entropy and our notion of impact is even more evident in the work

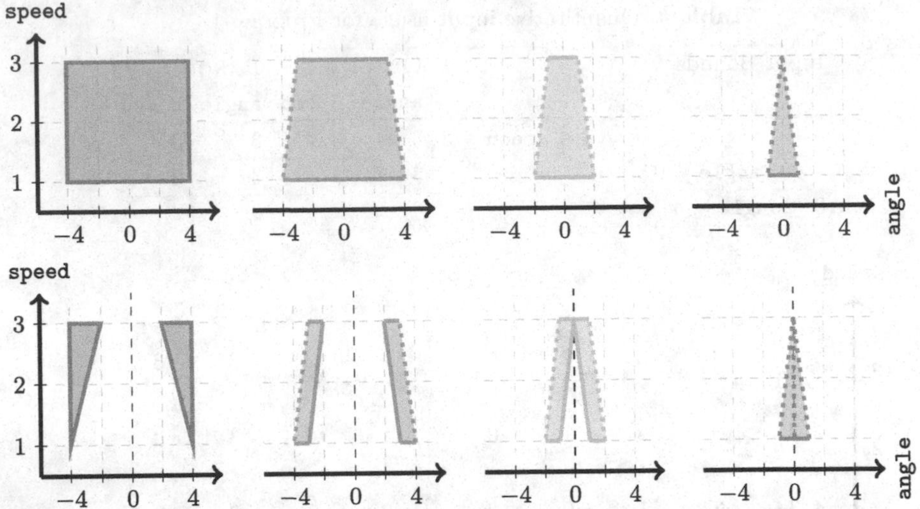

Fig. 3. Above, result of the analysis with convex polyhedra. Below, result after splitting the input space into two subspaces around **angle** = 0.

proposed by Köpf and Rybalchenko [13] which quantifies an upper bound of the entropy of a program's input variables by computing an over-approximation of the set of input-output observations, sometimes called equivalence classes. They employ Shannon entropy, min-entropy, and other entropies through the enumeration of these equivalence classes and their respective sizes. The equivalence classes are partitions of the input space in which two input assignments belong to the same class whenever the program produces an equivalent output. For example, the equivalence classes of the program L are $\Pi(\mathrm{L}) = \{\{\langle x, y\rangle \mid \mathrm{L}(x, y) = z\} \mid z \in \{0, 1, 2, 3\}\} = \{\{\langle 1, 1\rangle\}, \{\langle 1, 2\rangle\}, \{\langle 1, 3\rangle\}, \{\langle -4, 1\rangle, \langle -4, 2\rangle, \langle -4, 3\rangle\}\}$. We developed our impact definitions by adapting entropy measures to our needs in three successive attempts.

Initially, we notice that Shannon-entropy computes the average uncertainty of input values based on observations of the program's outcomes, while min-entropy, defined as:

$$H_\infty(\mathrm{P}) \stackrel{\text{def}}{=} \log_2 \frac{|\textsc{Input}_\mathrm{P}|}{|\Pi(\mathrm{P})|}$$

computes the worst-case uncertainty, where $\textsc{Input}_\mathrm{P}$ is the set of all input values of a given program P. As a first attempt, we consider min-entropy as closer to our needs since our aim is to discover the worst-case impact, i.e., the case in which a variable contributes the most. By computing min-entropy on the program L, we obtain $H_\infty(\mathrm{L}) = 0.58$, indicating that the input is highly guessable. Indeed, when the risk level is 3, the potential values of input variables are `angle` $= -4$ and `speed` $\in 1, 2, 3$; for all other output values, the input values are completely determined. Unfortunately, min-entropy lacks granularity and measures the uncertainty of the input variables collectively. Instead, our aim is to quantify the individual contributions.

To address the previous issue, as a second attempt we exploit low and high labels for input variables, where the former are considered as public, available to the attacker, and the latter as secret. To assess the impact of each input variable, we prioritize one high variable at a time, considering all others as low variables. Subsequently, we compute the min-entropy of the labelled program to quantify the extent of the impact. We define $\mathrm{L}^{\mathtt{angle}}(x) \stackrel{\text{def}}{=} \langle \mathrm{L}(x,1), \mathrm{L}(x,2), \mathrm{L}(x,3) \rangle$ which represents the sequence of programs where `angle` is high and `speed` is low. Similarly, $\mathrm{L}^{\mathtt{speed}}(y) \stackrel{\text{def}}{=} \langle \mathrm{L}(-4,y), \mathrm{L}(1,y) \rangle$ where `speed` is high and `angle` is low. Computing $H_\infty(\mathrm{L}^{\mathtt{angle}})$ and $H_\infty(\mathrm{L}^{\mathtt{speed}})$ yields 0 on both because all equivalence classes consist of singletons, meaning the number of inputs equals the number of outputs. Thus, there's no uncertainty in the value of `angle` given outputs of $\mathrm{L}^{\mathtt{angle}}$, or in the value of `speed` given outputs of $\mathrm{L}^{\mathtt{speed}}$. Indeed, observing the output $\langle 3,3,3 \rangle$ from the program $\mathrm{L}^{\mathtt{angle}}$ implies that `angle` is -4, while observing $\langle 0,1,2 \rangle$ implies that `angle` is 1. The same applies to $\mathrm{L}^{\mathtt{speed}}$ where observing $\langle 3,0 \rangle$ implies `speed` $= 1$, $\langle 3,1 \rangle$ implies `speed` $= 2$, and $\langle 3,2 \rangle$ implies `speed` $= 3$. However, this approach does not isolate the contributions of high variables; these outcomes are combined into a tuple of values through the return statement and thus evaluated together. Consequently, min-entropy cannot distinguish the contribution of each input variable independently.

An immediate solution is to develop a similar approach to the one used for the high-low variables, but instead of using min-entropy for the derived programs ($\mathrm{L}^{\mathtt{angle}}$ and $\mathrm{L}^{\mathtt{speed}}$), we count the number of outcomes of the partially-applied programs, cf. programs $\mathrm{L}(x,1), \mathrm{L}(x,2)$, and $\mathrm{L}(x,3)$ for $\mathrm{L}^{\mathtt{angle}}$; $\mathrm{L}(-4,y)$ and $\mathrm{L}(1,y)$ for $\mathrm{L}^{\mathtt{speed}}$. These programs are referred to as $\mathrm{L}_y^{\mathtt{angle}}$ and $\mathrm{L}_x^{\mathtt{speed}}$ respectively. Therefore, the third attempt defines $H_{\mathrm{O}}(\mathrm{L}^{\mathtt{angle}}) \stackrel{\text{def}}{=} \max\{|\Pi(\mathrm{L}_y^{\mathtt{angle}})| \mid y \in \{1,2,3\}\}$ and $H_{\mathrm{O}}(\mathrm{L}^{\mathtt{speed}}) \stackrel{\text{def}}{=} \max\{|\Pi(\mathrm{L}_x^{\mathtt{speed}})| \mid x \in \{-4,1\}\}$ retaining the maximum to obtain the worst-case scenario. As a result, $H_{\mathrm{O}}(\mathrm{L}^{\mathtt{angle}}) = 2$ and $H_{\mathrm{O}}(\mathrm{L}^{\mathtt{speed}}) = 3$. This means that variations of the value of `angle` result in at most 2 different outputs, while variations of the value of `speed` result in at most 3. Effectively, this is the first notion of impact derived from min-entropy capable of discriminating the contribution of each input variable on the program computation, exploiting the number of reachable outcomes from variations of the value of the input variable under consideration. Indeed, $H_{\mathrm{O}}(\mathrm{P}^i) = \textsc{Outcomes}_i(\mathrm{P})$ holds for a generic program P.

Overall, entropy measures and the approach proposed by Köpf and Rybalchenko [13] can be adapted to our needs. Nevertheless, their analysis grows exponentially with the number of low variables, which in our adaptation corresponds to the number of inputs, minus one. To address this limitation, we leverage an over-approximation of input-output observations of the program, focusing solely on the low variables. By doing so, we obtain the set of input configurations that lead to the same output value by variation on the value of high variables. As a result, our approach performs the backward analysis only one time per output bucket, independently of the number of low variables. A similar technique could also be used to mitigate such explosion in their work.

Other works include Chothia et al. [6], which proposed a statistical approach to quantify information leakage for Java programs. Phan et al. [18] and Saha et al. [20] employed symbolic execution techniques and model counting to obtain sound bounds on the entropy of programs. Other static analyses, e.g., Assaf et al. [1] and Clark et al. [7], are based on abstract interpretation. The key difference among our framework and their work is the information we measure. Our analysis quantifies the effect of each of the input variables on the program outcome, focusing on numerical properties, while quantitative information flow usually measures quantities in terms of bits of information transferred from the input variables to the program outcome, more specific to security properties. For example, Assaf et al. [1] counts how many bits of information of input variables are used to compute the result; Smith [21] computes the probability of guessing the value of a private variable from the value of input variables; and McCamant and Ernst [17] retrieves the channel capability, which is the worst-case possible for information leakages. Most of these approaches are based on the concept of entropy measures, which are orthogonal to our approach. Instead, we present a more fine-grained analysis, which discovers the impact of each input variable separately.

7 Conclusion

In this work, we presented an automated and sound analysis to statically quantify the usage of input variables based on a given impact definition. Our static analysis employs a backward analysis to compute an over-approximation of the precondition of the program, starting from the set of output buckets. While a forward approach based on input space partitioning seems plausible it is not practical due to the necessity of guessing the correct input partitions to obtain a meaningful result. On the other hand, the backward analysis directly starts from output values, thus avoiding the necessity of guessing the correct input partitions. Additionally, the input space partitions of the forward analysis need to not limit the axis of the input variable under consideration, otherwise the impact computed on two different partitions cannot be summed together, thus limiting the expressiveness of possible input partitions. This limitation is not present in the backward analysis as the expressiveness of the input invariant computed by the backward analysis is limited only by the chosen abstraction.

As a future work, we plan to develop a modular tool to support the analysis in a solid and extensible way. We also plan to introduce heuristics able to automatically (or iteratively) infer the output buckets, since the choice of the starting buckets is essential to our quantitative analysis. Future directions could extend fairness certification studies on neural network models [15,23]. Our quantitative notion introduces a quantitative fairness measure. Another promising direction is the exploration of new impact definitions for cyber-physical systems [14]. It could also be interesting to exploit an impact definition to analyze the impact of abstract domains in static program analyzers, e.g., by using pre-metrics as defined in [4,5]. Developing new relational abstract domains to discover specific non-linear variable relations could drastically improve the analysis precision, additionally taking into account input distributions. Further investigations of our analysis could also reveal new perspectives in the context of timing side-channel attacks [24], broadening the practical applications of our research.

Acknowledgements. We thank Michele Pasqua for suggestions on related work, Jérôme Boillot for his thorough review, and the anonymous reviewer for valuable feedback. This work was partially supported by the SAIF project, funded by the "France 2030" government investment plan managed by the French National Research Agency, under the reference ANR-23-PEIA-0006.

References

1. Assaf, M., Naumann, D.A., Signoles, J., Totel, É., Tronel, F.: Hypercollecting semantics and its application to static analysis of information flow (2017). https://doi.org/10.1145/3009837.3009889
2. Barowy, D.W., Gochev, D., Berger, E.D.: Checkcell: data debugging for spreadsheets. In: OOPSLA (2014). https://doi.org/10.1145/2660193.2660207
3. Bron, C., Kerbosch, J.: Finding all cliques of an undirected graph (algorithm 457). ACM Commun. (1973)
4. Campion, M., Dalla Preda, M., Giacobazzi, R.: Partial (in)completeness in abstract interpretation: limiting the imprecision in program analysis. In: POPL (2022). https://doi.org/10.1145/3498721
5. Campion, M., Urban, C., Dalla Preda, M., Giacobazzi, R.: A formal framework to measure the incompleteness of abstract interpretations. In: Hermenegildo, M.V., Morales, J.F. (eds.) SAS 2023. LNCS, vol. 14284, pp. 114–138. Springer, Cham (2023). https://doi.org/10.1007/978-3-031-44245-2_7
6. Chothia, T., Kawamoto, Y., Novakovic, C.: LeakWatch: estimating information leakage from Java programs. In: Kutyłowski, M., Vaidya, J. (eds.) ESORICS 2014. LNCS, vol. 8713, pp. 219–236. Springer, Cham (2014). https://doi.org/10.1007/978-3-319-11212-1_13
7. Clark, D., Hunt, S., Malacaria, P.: A static analysis for quantifying information flow in a simple imperative language. J. Comput. Secur. (2007). https://doi.org/10.3233/JCS-2007-15302
8. Cousot, P.: Constructive design of a hierarchy of semantics of a transition system by abstract interpretation. Theor. Comput. Sci. (2002). https://doi.org/10.1016/S0304-3975(00)00313-3
9. Cousot, P., Cousot, R.: Abstract interpretation: a unified lattice model for static analysis of programs by construction or approximation of fixpoints. In: POPL (1977). https://doi.org/10.1145/512950.512973
10. Denning, D.E.: Cryptography and Data Security. Addison-Wesley (1982)
11. Gray, J.W.: Toward a mathematical foundation for information flow security. IEEE Computer Society (1991). https://doi.org/10.1109/RISP.1991.130769
12. Herndon, T., Ash, M., Pollin, R.: Does high public debt consistently stifle economic growth? A critique of Reinhart and Rogoff. Camb. J. Econ. (2014). https://doi.org/10.1093/cje/bet075

13. Köpf, B., Rybalchenko, A.: Automation of quantitative information-flow analysis. In: Bernardo, M., de Vink, E., Di Pierro, A., Wiklicky, H. (eds.) SFM 2013. LNCS, vol. 7938, pp. 1–28. Springer, Heidelberg (2013). https://doi.org/10.1007/978-3-642-38874-3_1
14. Kwiatkowska, M.: Advances and challenges of quantitative verification and synthesis for cyber-physical systems. In: 2016 Science of Security for Cyber-Physical Systems Workshop (SOSCYPS) (2016). https://doi.org/10.1109/SOSCYPS.2016.7579999
15. Mazzucato, D., Urban, C.: Reduced products of abstract domains for fairness certification of neural networks. In: Drăgoi, C., Mukherjee, S., Namjoshi, K. (eds.) SAS 2021. LNCS, vol. 12913, pp. 308–322. Springer, Cham (2021). https://doi.org/10.1007/978-3-030-88806-0_15
16. Mazzucato, D., Campion, M., Urban, C.: Quantitative Input Usage Static Analysis (2023). https://hal.science/hal-04339001. Supplementary material
17. McCamant, S., Ernst, M.D.: Quantitative information flow as network flow capacity. In: Proceedings of the ACM SIGPLAN Conference on Programming Language Design and Implementation (PLDI) (2008). https://doi.org/10.1145/1375581.1375606
18. Phan, Q.-S., Malacaria, P., Tkachuk, O., Păsăreanu, C.S.: Symbolic quantitative information flow. ACM SIGSOFT Softw. Eng. Notes (2012). https://doi.org/10.1145/2382756.2382791
19. Reinhart, C.M., Rogoff, K.S.: Growth in a time of debt. Am. Econ. Rev. (2010). https://doi.org/10.1257/AER.100.2.573
20. Saha, S., Barbara, U.S., Ghentiyala, U.S., Shihua, U.L.: Obtaining information leakage bounds via approximate model counting (2023). https://doi.org/10.1145/3591281
21. Smith, G.: On the foundations of quantitative information flow. In: de Alfaro, L. (ed.) FoSSaCS 2009. LNCS, vol. 5504, pp. 288–302. Springer, Heidelberg (2009). https://doi.org/10.1007/978-3-642-00596-1_21
22. Urban, C., Müller, P.: An abstract interpretation framework for input data usage. In: Ahmed, A. (ed.) ESOP 2018. LNCS, vol. 10801, pp. 683–710. Springer, Cham (2018). https://doi.org/10.1007/978-3-319-89884-1_24
23. Urban, C., Christakis, M., Wüstholz, V., Zhang, F.: Perfectly parallel fairness certification of neural networks. In: OOPSLA (2020). https://doi.org/10.1145/3428253
24. Wong, W.H.: Timing attacks on RSA: revealing your secrets through the fourth dimension. ACM Crossroads (2005). https://doi.org/10.1145/1144396.1144401

Verifying a C Implementation of Derecho's Coordination Mechanism Using VST and Coq

Ramana Nagasamudram[1(✉)], Lennart Beringer[2], Ken Birman[3], Mae Milano[2], and David A. Naumann[1]

[1] Stevens Institute of Technology, Hoboken, USA
rnagasam@stevens.edu
[2] Princeton University, Princeton, USA
[3] Cornell University, Ithaca, USA

Abstract. Derecho is a C++ framework for distributed programming leveraging high performance communication primitives such as RDMA. At its core is the shared state table (SST), a replicated data structure that supports efficient protocols for consensus and group membership. Our aim is to formalize the reasoning principles articulated by the designers, which focus on knowledge and monotonicity, as basis for highly assured high performance distributed applications. To this end we develop a high level model that exposes the SST principles in an application-friendly way. We use the model to specify and verify a re-implementation in C of the SST API. We validate the specifications by verifying simple applications that embody key parts of the Derecho protocols. The development is carried out using VST and Coq. This lays groundwork for verification of the full Derecho protocols and applications built on them.

1 Introduction

Distributed systems occur ubiquitously in modern computational infrastructures, ranging from sensor networks or communicating embedded systems in the automotive domain to the datacenter and the global communication infrastructure. As application domains differ in their requirements concerning the performance and the applicable notion of consensus, numerous protocols have been developed.

In the domain of datacenter networks, latency and throughput requirements have recently led to the emergence of protocols that exploit monotonicity [14] to reduce communication overhead while facilitating strong notions of consensus [17]. At the same time, the reliance of everyday life on cloud computing necessitates that the expected efficiency and functionality guarantees of these protocols ought to be substantiated by verified implementations. But research that connects formal analyses of protocol-level properties [2,35,44] to implementation-level verification frameworks is only emerging now [13,16,37,39]. Ultimately, assurance of such *comprehensively verified* systems should encompass implementation correctness (down to instructions and hardware), protocol properties,

N. Benz et al. (Eds.): NFM 2024, LNCS 14627, pp. 99–117, 2024.
https://doi.org/10.1007/978-3-031-60698-4_6

and application-level guarantees, in a provably gap-free manner, with machine-checkable proofs.

To explore this challenge in a concrete setting, this paper reports on a comprehensive verification effort for the key data structure of Derecho [17], a distributed system platform implemented in C++ that combines protocol efficiency with low-latency communication, as facilitated through CPU-bypass technologies such as RDMA (remote direct memory access) [32]. Our approach is to:

- isolate the data structure, *shared state table* (SST), as a separate code unit in C, with a simplified API that supports the key functionality but can potentially be retrofitted into Derecho;
- equip the API with an expressive specification that connects functional code correctness to an abstract model of local data structure operations and global synchronization events but does not unduly constrain concurrency (Sect. 3);
- formulate the designer's intuitions concerning monotonicity and knowledge-based consensus as abstract trace (hyper-)properties over the operations and events (Sect. 3);
- confirm applicability of the resulting programming model by verifying two applications, exploiting only the API-level specifications and the trace properties to establish application-level correctness guarantees (Sect. 4 and 6);
- verify the isolated SST implementation and connect all verification components to a comprehensive verification artifact (Sect. 5).

Our verification is carried out in Coq and utilizes the Verified Software Toolchain (VST [5]) to verify implementation correctness. Our choice of a (dependently-typed) higher-order logic is motivated by the need to integrate multiple abstraction levels in a common logical framework and the need to support the formulation of monotonicity, epistemic principles, and trace-based models. Indeed, prior attempts by Derecho's developers to verify the monotonicity principles in Ivy [27] were unsatisfactory, in part due to a lack of expressiveness. Our choice to use VST is motivated by its foundational connection to a verified compiler [23], its demonstrated robustness and suitability for abstraction-bridging verification, and the fact that it targets an established systems programming language, providing an avenue for future work to gradually integrate treatments of more advanced aspects of Derecho and its applications.

We begin with background on Derecho, Coq, and VST (Sect. 2). Section 7 discusses related and future work. A current snapshot of our development, including C code and Coq proof scripts can be found at https://zenodo.org/records/10819602.

2 Background on Derecho, Coq, and VST

Derecho. The Derecho system is an open-source library for leveraging high-speed networking in modern cloud computing platforms such as file systems, key-value stores, coordination and pub-sub [17]. The central feature is the support for a strong consistency model: state machine replication (atomic multicast and Paxos, integrated with a "virtual synchrony" layer for self-managed and self-repairing membership). Derecho supports replication and state-machine actions in a manner that maps cleanly to modern communications hardware, as supported by the LibFabric library [12] such as RDMA, DPDK, and other forms of high-speed networking. Even on standard TCP, Derecho is said to be faster than any prior Paxos-like technology [4,38]. In part this speed reflects modern engineering: The system is coded in C++ 17, entirely zero-copy, lock-free, and all data paths are opportunistically batched. The mapping to RDMA is particularly efficient and enables continuous data transmission so that the RDMA transport can run non-stop at its peak speed. Another important aspect of performance is the way that the Derecho protocols are implemented using the *shared state table*, SST. Owing to monotonic operations that can be understood in terms of knowledge, Derecho has a control plane that is especially well-suited to shared memory implemented using one-sided RDMA.

Several industrial applications of Derecho are in deployment or development, for safety- and security-critical applications, which motivates the need for high assurance [38]. It becomes important to formally specify the system itself, to verify that the protocols as implemented are correct solutions with respect to these specifications, to fully quantify their assumptions about the environment and the types of failures that might occur at runtime, and to formally characterize the conditions under which progress can be guaranteed. An initial attempt to prove the Derecho protocols using Ivy [27] was a mixed success [4]. With the help of the Ivy developers, the Derecho team was successful in translating the Derecho specification into a solvable fragment of first order logic and then verifying the protocols using Ivy's prover. But such first-order invariants are not adequate to express the monotonicity and epistemic properties that are key to Derecho and to applications built on it. There has been much other work on verifying Paxos protocols (e.g. [31]) or implementations of Paxos (e.g. [13]) but not on leveraging monotonicity or explicating the role of knowledge. There have been no prior efforts to verify Derecho at the implementation level.

The Coq Proof Assistant. Coq is a system for interactive development of formal proofs in a powerful higher order logic. The system home page (coq.inria.fr) includes information on the user community and teaching materials including the Software Foundations textbook series (softwarefoundations.cis.upenn.edu). The Coq system may have been renamed to "The Rocq Prover" by the time the conference takes place.

Verified Software Toolchain. The Verified Software Toolchain (VST) [5] implements a concurrent separation logic for C in Coq and is justified by a machine-checked proof of soundness with respect to the C semantics as formalized by the CompCert compiler [23]. Verification using VST provides higher assurance than SMT-based tools, which rely on trusted axiomatizations of program semantics. Being embedded in Coq, VST specifications can exploit whatever mathematics is convenient for the application domain – including high level distributed system properties.

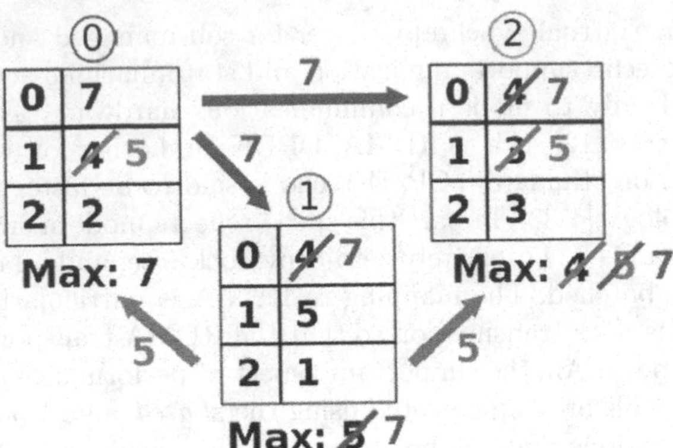

Fig. 1. Distributed system with three nodes, each holding an SST replica and maintaining local state, *Max*. The first column of the SST represents the *myrow* index. Values in the second (data) column monotonically increase over time. When replica 1's row is synchronized with the SSTs of replicas 0 and 2, the local state of replica 2 is updated to value 5. Replica 0's local state is unaffected as the received value does not dominate the current local state. Subsequent synchronization of replica 0's row triggers updates to the local states of replicas 1 and 2, yielding agreement between the local states. A final synchronization of replica 2's row (not shown) would affect the SSTs in replicas 0 and 1 but not the local states.

Similar to auto-active tools like Dafny, the proof engineer using VST must write specs, provide loop invariants, and sometimes guide other reasoning (using the Coq IDE). The VST tactics automate forward symbolic execution. Any code verified in VST is proved to be safe and free of undefined behavior, assuring the absence of numeric overflows, memory errors, etc. VST supports refinement ("subsumption") between specifications, so a component can be verified with respect to detailed low-level specs that are in turn connected to more abstract or client-friendly specs, such as a distributed system model.

3 The SST Interfaces: Code API and Trace-Based Specs

Here is a sketch of the Derecho programming model. A system is comprised of a collection of replicas, as shown in Fig. 1. The replicas all run the same program. A replica's state has its private state and its copy of the *shared state table* (SST). Replicas are numbered $0..N-1$ and the SST has N rows. During an *epoch* between failures, there is a fixed group with N members. The shared state of replica i comprises row i, called its *own row*; this is the only row that a replica can write in its SST. The framework asynchronously copies row i from its owner to the SST's of all other replicas. This is called a *sync*. In this way the SST provides replica i with a possibly stale snapshot of the rows for all other replicas j, $j \neq i$.

Figure 2 shows excerpts from the SST API in C. Function new_system initializes the system, specifying the number nrows of replicas and an application

```
typedef struct sst sst_t;
int getMyrow(sst_t *sst);
int getCell(sst_t *sst, int r, int c);
void setCell(sst_t *sst, int c, int z); /* set column c of sst's own row to z */

typedef struct priv_state priv_state_t; /* kept abstract: struct priv_state defined by client */
typedef bool (*predicate_t) (priv_state_t *, sst_t *); /* guard of an action */
typedef void (*trigger_t) (priv_state_t *, sst_t *); /* effect of an action */

typedef struct action action_t;
action_t *mkAction(predicate_t p, trigger_t t, priv_state_t *s);

typedef struct sys_state sys_state_t;
sys_state_t *new_system(int nrows, int nappcols, int *iniRow);
void install_action(sys_state_t *reps, int repId, action_t *act);

void run(sys_state_t *reps, int rounds);
```

Fig. 2. SST interface in C; excerpts.

specific number nappcols of columns in the SST of each replica. A fixed initial row value iniRow is used to populate all rows of all replicas. The SST is a matrix of **int**'s, but the API can easily be extended to cater for other base types. Finally, in addition to application specific columns, the SST has columns used to store framework specific data. These keep track of whether a replica has been suspected to have failed, or whether a replica is no longer actively participating. Derecho's treatment of failure is important and leverages monotonicity in interesting ways, but for lack of space we do not elaborate on it here.

Application code is organized as a collection of *actions*, where each action comprises a *predicate* and *trigger* in addition to auxiliary private state. (We use the Derecho [17] terms for the guard and effect, respectively, of an action.) The typedefs predicate_t and trigger_t define the type of these as function pointers. A replica's actions can read the SST, and the trigger of an action can write the replica's own row of its SST (function getMyrow returns the index to its own row). The application defines a struct type priv_state_t which is left abstract in the interface. This is meant for the private state used by an action. Each action has its own private state. At a minimum, this can be used to communicate from a predicate (which checks some condition) to its trigger, which gets executed only if the predicate returns true. Private state persists between invocations of an action. Actions are installed during initialization; the client calls install_action for this purpose: the parameter repId is the index of the replica in the system.

In general, application code is structured to include definitions of nrows and nappcols; a definition of priv_state_t; one or more actions, each comprising a predicate and a trigger; and a main function. The main function:

- creates the application-specific data of the initial row,
- calls new_system to construct and initialize the replicas' SSTs
- allocates private states for the actions,

```
Class ClientParams := { NROWS: Z; NAPPCOLS: Z; privSt: Type; ... }.

Definition repId := {n: Z | 0 ≤ n < NROWS}. (* replica identifier *)
Definition NCOLS := NAPPCOLS + ... (* framework specific columns *)
Definition SSTrow := {xs: list Z | length xs = NCOLS}.
Record SST_Tp := {the_tbl: {xs: list SSTrow | length xs = NROWS}; the_id: repId }.

Definition PredicateTp := SST_Tp → privSt → bool * privSt.
Definition TriggerTp := SST_Tp → privSt → SSTrow * privSt.
Definition ActionTp := PredicateTp * TriggerTp * privSt.

Record replica := {the_sst: SST_Tp; actions: list ActionTp}.
Definition sys_state := {reps: list replica | length reps = NROWS}.
```

Fig. 3. SST model in Coq; excerpts.

- calls install_action to install the actions,
- calls run, which runs the main computation,
- and finally deallocates everything, using API functions like teardown.

The main computation is carried out by the function run. Derecho arranges that all the actions of all the replicas are repeatedly invoked. Each invocation first calls the predicate and then, if the predicate returns true, calls the trigger. Function run is called with a bound, rounds, which is the number of rounds to be executed, meaning the number of times a given action is invoked on a given replica.

Coq Model and C Specifications. Figure 3 shows types in Coq used to model the SST and replica data structures. A sys_state in Coq is a list of replicas where each replica contains an SST and a list of actions. SSTs are modeled using the type SST_Tp which, essentially, is a matrix of a fixed dimension. The field the_id keeps track of the index of the SSTs own row. Clients specify SST dimensions by creating an instance of the ClientParams typeclass; they also provide the type for private states, provide an initial condition on private states and prove that NROWS and NAPPCOLS fall within implementable bounds (these details are elided in Fig. 3). The types PredicateTp and TriggerTp model predicates and triggers respectively. Note that these types model monadic computations in the state monad for privSt. A trigger returns the updated value for the replica's own row.

The Coq model includes definitions corresponding to each C function in the SST API (Fig. 2). Specifications defined in VSTs separation logic tie C code to model programs. They posit that C implementations have the same effect on concrete structures as model programs have on abstract ones; a connection made precise using representation predicates which relate data structures laid out in the heap in C to structures in Coq. For example, here is the spec for install_action written in stylized notation and using $*$ for separating conjunction.

```
{ Replicas_rep sys reps ∗ Action_rep act a }
install_action(reps, n, a)
{ Replicas_rep (model_install_action sys n act) reps }
```

The precondition says the heap contains Replicas_rep sys reps and Action_rep act a. The first conjunct says that pointer reps points to a data structure that represents the abstract system state sys of Coq type sys_state. The second says that pointer a points to a data structure that represents the abstract action act of Coq type ActionTp. Calling install_action then ensures that reps represents an abstract state consistent with applying the model level function model_install_action on the initial abstract state. The postcondition also expresses a transfer of resources: the Action_rep is no longer available to the caller.

Specifications for other API functions are given in a similar style. For predicates and triggers, we define generic specifications. These are used, for instance, by Action_rep act a above which asserts that a's predicate satisfies predicate_spec for the abstract predicate for act (resp. for a's trigger). Here is the generic predicate spec for predicate pred in C with respect to the model predicate model_pred.

{ SST_rep SST sst * privSt_rep pst p }
pred(sst, p)
{ **let** (b, pst') := model_pred SST pst **in** SST_rep SST sst * privSt_rep pst' p ∧
RET b }

The precondition expresses that pointers sst and p represent the abstract SST and the abstract private state pst, respectively. Note that privSt_rep is application-specific and provided to the framework by the client. The postcondition then asserts that the SST is left unmodified and that the effect on the private state is in accord with the function model_pred. Expression RET b denotes the return value, which must also be in accord with model_pred.

The generic trigger spec is similar. Its precondition requires the corresponding predicate to be true and its postcondition ensures that the SST's own row is updated in accord with the given model trigger. Predicates and triggers defined by client applications are required to satisfy these generic specs.

Schedules, Traces, and Run Spec. In order to capture distributed computation and its inherent nondeterminism, we depart from the above style of specification when it comes to run. The spec for run is formulated in terms of global traces which in turn are based on schedules. A schedule is a list of events that serves to record a linear order in which actions have taken place at particular replicas, and syncs have happened between replicas.

In the model, a sched_item (intuitively, an *event*) is either of the form sch_act r n t which indicates that replica r has performed its nth action at timestamp t, or sch_sync from to t for from≠to which indicates that replica from has sync'd its own row at timestamp t to replica to.[1] Syncs in Derecho are based on totally ordered point-to-point channels (e.g., as implemented in one-sided RDMA) and the timestamps associated with events help model this behavior. The timestamp in a sch_sync event connects the sync with the state of its "from" replica following a designated action instance. This is needed because at the time

[1] In our formal development events are also used to keep track of Derecho-style failures where one replica can suspect another of failing if it hasn't received a sync for some amount of time. We omit discussion since failures are not the focus of this article.

the “to” replica’s SST gets updated by the sync, the “from” replica may have changed its state.

We say a list of sched_item’s is a schedule if it satisfies certain well-formed constraints on the order of timestamps: (a) action timestamps are unique and increasing, and (b) syncs to a given replica are for actions in increasing timestamp order. This is meant to capture an accurate minimal model of what Derecho provides. Our library defines some additional constraints on schedules, such as bounds on relative progress between actions at different replicas. Such bounds may need to be assumed in order to prove progress properties of applications.

A *trace* is a list of system states generated from an initial system state and a schedule. Traces are defined by the predicate traceOf which goes by induction on the schedule sch, performing state updates in accord with sched_item’s in sch. The event sch_act r n t updates replica r’s own row in accord to it’s nth action. The event sch_sync from to t updates row from in replica to. The updated value is the own row of from at some point earlier in the execution, determined by timestamp t. The model works with finite traces. Although Derecho is a nonterminating system, a trace models execution up to some arbitrary point. The schedule predicate is prefix-closed and likewise the prefix of a trace is itself a trace.

The run API function (Fig. 2) runs a system once its actions have been installed. It acts on a single system state, running actions on all replicas, to simulate a distributed system in which each replica runs concurrently on its own node. In principle, the system runs forever. To reason about partial executions, our prototype parameterizes run on the number of rounds of execution to perform, rounds. The specification for run is given as follows.

{ Replicas_rep sys reps $\wedge$ initial sys $\wedge$ Forall (**fun** r $\Rightarrow$ length r.(actions) $>$ 0) sys }
run(reps, rounds)
{ $\exists$sch tr, schedule sch $\wedge$ traceOf sys sch tr $\wedge$ nActions sch sys rounds
  $\wedge$ Replicas_rep (lastState tr) reps }

The spec is formulated in terms of the abstract state sys which is required to satisfy an initial condition – this is given by initial sys and includes an application-specific condition provided by clients. The precondition also requires every replica in sys to have at least one action installed. The postcondition says that there is some schedule sch and trace tr of that schedule from initial state sys. Moreover, every action of every replica has been invoked rounds many times as expressed by nActions sch sys rounds. The final conjunct says that the concrete state pointed to by reps represents the final state of the trace.

For invariance-based reasoning about safety properties, this postcondition is directly applicable as we will seen in the example of Sect. 4. Progress-based reasoning is less direct, as it must be in a partial correctness logic like VST. The spec caters for application-specific postconditions of this form: “if sufficiently many action invocations have occurred then [something interesting about the final state]”. The antecedent might be expressed by a numerical lower bound on rounds. For an application intended to converge to a result, an alternative to bounding rounds is for the antecedent to say a fixed point has been reached, i.e., the actions no longer change the state. An example of this kind is in Sect. 6.

Monotonicity, System Invariants and Knowledge. Invariants on system states are needed in order to prove top-level safety properties of interest. A predicate on system states P is invariant provided it holds initially and is preserved by all transitions of the system. Here, a transition is either a sync from a replica to another, or the invocation of an action on a replica. Showing that P is preserved by syncs may be harder than showing that it is preserved by actions.

An invariance proof is made easier when P is restricted to be of certain special forms. For example, suppose P is of the form "all rows of all replicas satisfy Q", where Q is a predicate on SST rows. To show P is invariant, it suffices to show it holds initially and is preserved by all actions; syncs don't have to be considered at all. This is because such a P is always preserved by syncs. Consider a sync between replica from and to. Preceding the sync, all rows of both replicas satisfy Q. The sync updates row from of replica to. This new row also satisfies Q, and hence Q continues to hold for all rows of both replicas. Our library includes reasoning principles for invariants expressed in these special forms.

Even when P is a predicate on the whole SST or the whole system, one can often reason only in terms of the actions. This can be done when P is monotonic and the actions are *inflationary*, i.e., each action increases the own row of a replica with respect to the pointwise (cell-wise) ordering. In such cases, all traces are non-decreasing. Reasoning based on monotonicity is conceivable for any ordering. However, for our purposes, it suffices to use the magnitude ordering on integers and its pointwise liftings to SST rows, SSTs and system states (all written $\geq$).

Now suppose a sys_state predicate P is monotonic: if P holds for sys, then it holds for any sys' with sys' $\geq$ sys. Then P is stable, provided the actions are inflationary *Stability* of a predicate means that once it holds, it continues to hold. Further, if P is stable and holds in the initial state, then P is invariant. Thus, in a system with inflationary actions, all the monotonic predicates are invariants.

This reasoning is captured by the following two results in our library. File sst_theory.v defines the pointwise ordering on rows, non-decreasingness of traces, etc., and proves this key result.

```
Theorem mono_act_non_dec_trace: ∀(init: sys_state) sch tr,
  allReplicasSame init ∧ inflaActions init ∧ schedule sch ∧ traceOf init sch tr →
  non_dec_trace tr.
```

It says that any trace is non-decreasing provided that the system's actions are inflationary. Traces are based on schedules, so the theorem quantifies over all schedules. It also assumes all replicas have the same own row value initially. This simplification is in accord with our prototype implementation.[2]

[2] It loses no generality since one of the actions might serve as an actual initializer. Action predicates can be used to arrange that no other actions are enabled until the initializer has run, and that the initializer becomes effectively disabled thereafter.

The connection with monotonic predicates is made precise by the following theorem: it says that if actions are inflationary and pred is a monotonic predicate on SSTs, then if it holds in replica r in the final state of a trace tr', it holds in r at any later final state. (This result can be extended to monotonic predicates on system states.)

Theorem monoPred_stable_trace: ∀ (pred: SST_Tp → Prop) sch ini tr st r,
initial ini ∧ inflaActions ini ∧ monotonic pred ∧ schedule sch ∧ traceOf ini sch tr →
∀ tr', tr' ≲ tr ∧ pred (lastState tr').[r] → pred (lastState tr).[r].

Here ≲ is the temporal (prefix) order on traces with which we express that trace tr' extends to trace tr. We use notation sys.[r] to refer to replica r in state sys.

These results are used to prove general facts about the SST framework. For example, it's a general invariant in any system with inflationary actions that any row of an SST is less than or equal to the corresponding replica's own row. In this sense, an SST approximates the "ideal SST" comprised of all the own rows. Our library provides general rules for proving invariants of several forms, including those that aren't monotonic.

Prior work on Derecho emphasizes epistemic reasoning [4]. Our library adapts the standard semantics of epistemic logic to our setting. Rather than formalizing the syntax of epistemic logic [10], we define the "knows" operator semantically and prove various useful properties. Here we just sketch the ideas. We consider what a given replica knows, in the final state of a trace, based on what it has observed. The replica observes the sequence of updates to its SST. So two traces are indistinguishable for r if projecting them to the list of r's SSTs, and removing stuttering steps, results in the same list of SSTs. In other words, r can distinguish between two traces only if its SST differs at some step. So r *knows* system predicate P in the final state of tr just if P is true in the final state of all traces r-indistinguishable from tr. This is written Know tr r P. Our library includes a collection of standard theorems about knowledge, as well as connections between knowledge, invariants, and monotonic predicates.

4 Example: Stability Detection

Our first example, stability_detection, illustrates message streaming. Each replica is equipped with two actions. The first, multicast, sends a message to all replicas in the system. The second, receive, acknowledges receipt of a message. Message sends and receives are modeled using counters, which are kept track of in the SST of each replica.

In the model, sys.[r] is the SST of replica r in state sys, and sys.[r].[i,k] is cell k of row i of replica r. Cell sys.[r].[r,r] stores the number of messages r has sent and sys.[r].[r,k], the number of messages sent by replica k that r has acknowledged. In our setup, r acknowledges a message sent by k simply by incrementing the cell sys.[r].[r,k].

On replica r, the multicast action increments sys.[r].[r,r]. It is guarded by the predicate true, modeling the scenario where message sends are always possible.

Other replicas learn about messages from r through syncs of r's own row. The receive action scans r's SST and checks whether there is a pending message from a replica, say k, that hasn't been acknowledged yet. If so, it increments sys.[r].[r,k].

Our model-level implementation of the application first creates an instance of the ClientParams type class, specifying the number of application columns in each SST to be NUM_REPLICAS in accord with the layout described above. Private state in stability_detection is only used by the receive predicate to communicate to its following trigger invocation; it does not rely on the private state persisting between action invocations. (See Sect. 6 for an example using persistence.)

The initial condition asserts that no replica has sent or acknowledged any messages. The implementations of triggers and predicates then use the generic functions from the SST model library to create system states and simulate runs. The model-level application specification is knowledge-oriented:

```
Definition stabDet (tr: list sys_state) : Prop :=
  (∀ (r k:repId), Know tr r (fun sys ⇒ sys.[r].[k,r] ≤ sys.[k].[k,r])) ∧
  (∀ (r k:repId), Know tr r (fun sys ⇒ sys.[r].[k,k] ≤ sys.[k].[k,k])) ∧
  (∀ (i k:repId), everyoneKnows tr (fun sys ⇒
     ForallReplica (fun (r: replica) ⇒ Min_of_col r i ≤ sys.[k].[k,i]) sys)).
```

The first conjunct says any replica r knows it has received no more acknowledgements from k than have been sent by k. The second says any r knows it has acknowledged no more messages from k than have been sent. The third says everyone knows (the $K1$ operator of epistemic logic) for each sender i, receiver k, and every replica r, that k has acknowledged at least Min_of_col r i many messages from i. Thus by computing, on its own SST, the value of Min_of_col r i, replica r can determine which messages from i are committed. All of these properties are relative to a trace tr. The top-level specification, described below, relies on proof that stabDet holds for all traces of an initial system in which the send and receive actions are installed in all replicas.

At the C level, we define predicates and triggers, relying on generic functions provided in simple_sst.h. We prove that each C predicate/trigger pair conforms to corresponding model-level functions, in accord with generic specifications for SST actions defined in our library. For example, we prove the multicast trigger satisfies the generic triggerSpec with its parameters P and T instantiated with predicate **fun** SST st ⇒ (true, st) and the increment of sys.[r].[r,r] respectively.

The top-level program, unittest, calls run for some number of rounds and is structured as a generic application of the SST API (described in Sect. 3). Its specification is as follows.

```
{ Replicas_rep ini reps ∧ initial ini ∧ sys_with_actions ini stabilityActions }
unittest(reps,N)
{ ∃sch tr, Replicas_rep (lastState tr) reps ∧ schedule sch ∧ traceOf ini sch tr ∧
stabDet tr }
```

By formulating this for arbitrary number N of rounds, we show that stabDet holds at any point of any execution.

The code of unittest just calls run, the spec of which provides all but the last conjunct of the postcondition. To prove stabDet tr we reason entirely at the model level: we have a trace in which the multicast and receive actions take place, interleaved with syncs. General results about monotonicity in connection with invariants reduce our proof obligation to reasoning about the two actions.

5 The SST Implementation and Its Verification

Our C implementation represents replicas as an SST table whose main component is row-oriented matrix, and a linked list of actions. Each action contains function pointers for a predicate and a trigger, and some action-private state.

```
struct sst{
  int numrows;
  int numcols;
  int my_row;
  row_t rows[];};

struct action{
  predicate_t predicate;
  trigger_t trigger;
  priv_state_t *act_state;
  action_t *next;};

typedef struct replica{
  action_t* actions;
  sst_t sst;} replica_t;
struct replicas {
  replica_t **collection; };
```

We omit descriptions of the administrative functions that construct or deallocate replicas and install or uninstall actions. The main execution loop is the function run, which carries out a client-specifiable number of rounds, each round invoking the following (non-API-exposed) do_actions_sync_all function on all replicas.

```
void do_actions_sync_all(replicas_t* reps, int r)
{ replica_t *rep = reps→collection[r];
  action_t *act = rep→actions;
  while (act)
  { run_action(rep, act);
    for (int to = 0; to < getNumreplicas(reps); to++)
    { if (to != r) sync_sst(&rep→sst, getSST(reps, to)); }
    act = act→next; }}
```

The function traverses the replica's actions by executing run_action on each element – which is non-trivial only in case the action's predicate fires – and immediately invoking sync_sst afterwards to communicate any update to its local SST matrix to all other replicas. We currently implement sync_sst as a memcpy instruction, which suffices for our sequential 'run' function. Future refinements will realize concurrent execution with fine-grained communication primitives (ultimately, RDMA as in Derecho). In anticipation, our specifications – and the model of schedules, traces, etc. – do not expose the sequential nature of our implementation.

The VST specification of do_actions_sync_all asserts adherence to the following Coq expression, where sync_sst_all models the communication and do_action_sys models the execution of a single action:

```
Definition do_actions_sync_all (n:Z) (i:repId) (sys:sys_state) : sys_state :=
let f sys actnum := sync_sst_all NROWS (do_action_sys i actnum sys) i in
fold_left f (upto (Z.to_nat n)) sys.
```

We embed this Coq expression in VST as shown in earlier sections and then verify the C code; we then verify run against the specification from Sect. 3.

6 Example: Distributed Transitive Closure

In our second application, replicas collectively compute the transitive closure of a given graph with N vertices. Each row of the SST is divided into two portions. The first N^2 columns, the edge matrix, stores a copy of the adjacency matrix of the input graph as a one-dimensional array. The second N^2 columns, the path matrix, stores the transitive closure of the graph. The replica is equipped with two actions that update the path matrix. The first, Find, computes new paths in the transitive closure. The second, Copy, learns new paths by copying those that other replicas may have already found. Find suffices to ensure the transitive closure is eventually computed by every replica. Copy improves performance by allowing replicas that are "lagging behind" to catch up.

```
Definition Find_aux : (Z * Z * Z) → PredicateTp := Fix (well_founded_ltof _ lexSize) ...
Lemma Find_aux_def : ∀(i s e: Z) (SST: SST_Tp) (p: privSt),
  Find_aux (i, s, e) SST p = (* i: intermediate vertex, s: start vertex, e: end vertex *)
    if inBounds (i, s, e)
    then if hasPath SST s i && hasPath SST i e && negb (hasPath SST s e)
         then (true, (i, s, e)) else Find_aux (incr (i, s, e)) SST p
    else (false, (i, s, e)).
Definition Find_pred : PredicateTp := '(i,s,e) ← st_get ;; Find_aux (i,s,e).
Definition Find_trig : TriggerTp :=
  '(i,s,e) ← st_get ;; markPath SST s e ;; st_put (incr (i,s,e)) ;; ret SST.[the_id SST].
```

Fig. 4. The Find action for the distributed transitive closure client.

Implementation of Predicates and Triggers. The implementation of the Find action at the model level is shown in Fig. 4. It is a rendering of the usual Floyd-Warshall algorithm with two key changes. The first is that it recurses over lexicographically ordered triples of graph vertices; this departs from the usual presentation of the algorithm as three nested loops. This is done by the function Find_aux, elided in Fig. 4. For reasoning, the lemma Find_aux_def provides a convenient unfolding of the definition. This change facilitates the second.

The second change is that the predicate/trigger pair follow a "resumption" style of computation in order to fit with our general framework of SST actions, wherein the trigger is used to update the SST and communication between predicate and trigger is facilitated by private state. The private state for this application stores a triple of graph vertices.[3]

Function Find_pred first checks whether a new path exists via intermediate vertex i between start and end vertices s and e. If so, it updates the private state to (i,s,e). The corresponding path is then marked in the SST by the trigger Find_trig. In addition, the trigger increments the private state so that in a subsequent invocation, the predicate starts searching for paths from the next

[3] This is a simplification for expository purposes. In our implementation, the private state contains an additional component used by the Copy action.

lexically ordered triple of graph vertices. In the case where a path hasn't been found, the predicate doesn't update the private state and recursively tries the next lexically ordered triple. In Fig. 4, the functions st_get and st_put operate on the state monad. We use standard notations for monads.

The Copy action is implemented similarly. It continuously polls each row of the SST and marks any path not already recorded in the own row. Both actions monotonically increase the path matrix.

We verify C implementations of the Find and Copy actions using the generic predicate and trigger specs.

Application Specifications. Like unittest in Sect. 4, the main program, tc_main, calls run for some number of rounds (here, N^3). Its specification is as follows.

{ Replicas_rep ini reps ∧ initial_TC_sys ini gph }
  tc_main(reps)
{ ∃sch tr, **let** fin := lastState tr **in**
  Replicas_rep fin reps ∧ schedule sch ∧ traceOf ini sch tr ∧ computedTC fin }

In the precondition, initial_TC_sys ini expresses that ini is a system that is initialized with the graph gph and each replica is equipped with the Find and Copy actions. The postcondition says that there is a schedule and a trace and moreover, that each replica has computed the transitive closure of the graph provided it has reached a fixpoint. Since the Find action is sufficient for correctness, we define fixpoint to mean that the Find predicate returns false: there are no more paths to be found in the transitive closure. In the definition below, Find_privSt refers to the private state of the Find action. The antecedent expresses "reached a fixpoint" and the consequent says that the path matrix of sys.[r] is equal to the transitive closure of the edge matrix of sys.[r]. Recall the sys.[r,r] notation refers to the own row (which is at index r) of sys.[r].

Definition computedTC sys := ∀r, fst (Find sys.[r] (Find_privSt sys.[r])) = false →
  clos_trans (hasEdge sys.[r,r]) = hasPath sys.[r,r].

We verify the final conjunct of tc_main entirely at the model level. We start by proving two invariants of any trace of the application. The first, TC_row_inv, is a predicate on rows and says that the edge matrix of replica sys.[r] is contained in its path matrix, which in turn is contained in the transitive closure of its edge matrix. We prove this using generic lemmas about invariants provided by the SST model library. The second invariant path_via_inv is a predicate on a replica and the private states of its actions. Given sys.[r] and a private state (i,s,e), it says that all paths that go via intermediate vertices {0,...,i} are marked in the path matrix of sys.[r]. This is again proved using library support for reasoning about invariants. Together, these invariants suffice to prove computedTC (lastState tr) holds for any trace tr of the application.

7 Related and Future Work

TLA+ has been used to verify versions of the Paxos protocol [7]. Padon et al. [31] used first-order provers for fully automated verification of several Paxos variants. Ivy [27] has been used to verify single instances of a Paxos interaction [30].

Auto-active verification tools based on SMT typically structure proofs in terms of program annotations (e.g., Dafny, Frama-C, Verifast). IronFleet [13] uses a methodology in which behaviors described in the TLA logic are expressed as Dafny specifications; a version of Paxos, and a sharded key-value store application are verified, and there is an (un-verified) compiler from Dafny to C#.

Like VST, RefinedC [34], Bedrock2 [9], and Autocorres [11] are embedded in higher order proof assistants whose expressive logics enable the integration of code verification and model level reasoning. RefinedC builds on Iris [18] and provides a higher degree of automation thanks to the use of refinement types and backtracking-free proof search. It is based on an adhoc semantics of C rather than an established semantics such as CompCert. Bedrock2 is a C-like language and Coq-verified compiler under active development at MIT. Rather than supporting the entire C language, its language features and compilation strategy are limited, motivated by its intended application domain of embedded systems.

VST's concurrent separation logic enables thread-modular verification of shared-memory concurrent code [24,29] and programs with I/O [45]. The latter work concerns a rudimentary web server in C – one node in a distributed system, whose external behavior is specified using *interaction trees* [43]. The server contains a KV store and communicates using a socket API spec compatible with the implementation-side view of the CertiKOS operating system kernel [26]. Recent work [25] further enhances VST's concurrency capabilities by incorporating the Iris theory and proof mode, atomic specifications [33], higher-order ghost state and invariants, and persistent state. These developments will be relevant for verifying a multi-threaded implementation of our system.

Modeling and reasoning about about state machine replication, failure handling, chain replication, two-phase-commit, and variations of Paxos or Raft protocols in Coq is a topic of substantial current interest (e.g. [6,16,35,40,41]). Most of these works present clean-slate formalizations, proposing novel models or domain-specific proof libraries. Typically, they achieve executability only by extraction to OCaml code (with performance limitations) or handle client-side applications only at the model level.

ADO [15] and Adore [16] are recent Coq theories for justifying state machine replication abstractions, focusing on failures and reconfiguration, respectively. ADO takes inspiration from the push/pull model developed for shared-memory concurrency in CertiKOS and involves an event log trace. It includes an implementation of multiPaxos and Chain Replication, but its execution employs unverified send/recv system calls and applications are directly written inside the Coq prover. Adore enables derivation of ADO's mechanism using a slightly more refined state/event model, but its implementation is only extracted to OCaml and has hence not been subjected to realistic performance evaluation. Likewise for execution in Aneris [19] and Verdi [40] (including its application to Raft [41]) and Disel [35].

Monotonicity-exploiting programming models are increasingly popular, in the context of databases [8], logic programming [1], distributed programming languages [28], and parallel programming [20].

Much recent excitement has centered around monotonic uses of Conflict-Free Replicated Datatypes (CRDTs) [36]. These datatypes feature the ability to merge uncoordinated, concurrent updates across weakly-synchronized replicas, without risking replica divergence. This in turn allows development of software which does not rely on consistent or immediate replication, enabling new trends in everything from local-first software [3] (where a user's machine is not expected to wait for synchronization) to high-speed datacenter settings [42] (where a replica should not need to wait for coordination to make progress).

Recent work has made CRDTs far more tractable as a programming model. Some recent work makes CRDTs easier for programmers to use; in particular, monotonic observations (as proposed in [21]) provide the ability to consistently observe projections of an inconsistently-replicated CRDT. Other work has made CRDTs easier to build; in particular, Katara [22] provides the ability to synthesize CRDTs automatically from programmer-provided specifications.

Future Work. We have completed the verification of Derecho's core coordination mechanism together with small applications that embody features of the full replication/consensus protocols. VST ensures only partial correctness but our high level model features partial traces and considers arbitrary finite executions whereby we specify nonterminating computations. We formulate a standard semantics of knowledge, but leave to future work the extension of the model to temporal properties, and its use in verification of the full protocols.

While VST has no intrinsic notion of distributed computation, its separation logic lets us specify a system as a collection of replicas acting in disjoint state spaces, modeling RDMA by `memcpy`. One of our next steps will exploit VST's concurrency principles to verify a more faithful (non-sequential) implementation of Derecho in which each replica executes in a separate thread, with lock-free syncs that exploit monotonicity and the fact that rows are single-writer. Towards verifying the core Derecho group membership and view change protocols, a next step will be to verify a 2-phase commit implementation, building on stability detection. Once the core protocols have been implemented and verified, existing applications built on top of Derecho can be formalized.

Acknowledgement. The authors gratefully acknowledge support from Siemens Corporation for this project, initiated and coordinated by Charif Mahmoudi. First author Ramana Nagasamudram is the beneficiary of a graduate fellowship grant from Siemens called the #FutureMakers Fellowship.

References

1. Arntzenius, M., Krishnaswami, N.: Seminaïve evaluation for a higher-order functional language. Proc. ACM Program. Lang. **4**(POPL), 22:1–22:28 (2020). https://doi.org/10.1145/3371090
2. Azmy, N., Merz, S., Weidenbach, C.: A machine-checked correctness proof for Pastry. Sci. Comput. Program. **158**, 64–80 (2018)
3. Bieniusa, A., Haas, J., Kleppmann, M., Mogk, R. (eds.): Programming Local-First Software (ECOOP Workshop). European Conference on Object-Oriented Programming (2022). https://2022.ecoop.org/home/plf-2022
4. Birman, K., Jha, S., Milano, M., Rosa, L., Song, W., Tremel, E.: Monotonicity and opportunistically-batched actions in Derecho. In: Dolev, S., Schieber, B. (eds.) SSS 2023. LNCS, vol. 14310, pp. 172–190. Springer, Cham (2023). https://doi.org/10.1007/978-3-031-44274-2_14
5. Cao, Q., Beringer, L., Gruetter, S., Dodds, J., Appel, A.W.: VST-Floyd: a separation logic tool to verify correctness of C programs. J. Autom. Reason. **61**, 367–422 (2018)
6. Chajed, T., Tassarotti, J., Theng, M., Kaashoek, M.F., Zeldovich, N.: Verifying the DaisyNFS concurrent and crash-safe file system with sequential reasoning. In: OSDI (2022)
7. Chand, S., Liu, Y.A., Stoller, S.D.: Formal verification of Multi-paxos for distributed consensus. ArXiv abs/1606.01387 (2016)
8. Cheung, A., Crooks, N., Hellerstein, J.M., Milano, M.: New directions in cloud programming. In: Conference on Innovative Data Systems Research (CIDR) (2021). http://cidrdb.org/cidr2021/papers/cidr2021_paper16.pdf
9. Erbsen, A., Gruetter, S., Choi, J., Wood, C., Chlipala, A.: Integration verification across software and hardware for a simple embedded system. In: PLDI (2021)
10. Fagin, R., Halpern, J.Y., Moses, Y., Vardi, M.Y.: Reasoning About Knowledge. MIT Press, Cambridge (1995)
11. Greenaway, D., Lim, J., Andronick, J., Klein, G.: Don't sweat the small stuff: formal verification of C code without the pain. In: PLDI (2014)
12. Grun, P., et al.: A brief introduction to the OpenFabrics interfaces - a new network API for maximizing high performance application efficiency. In: IEEE Annual Symposium on High-Performance Interconnects, pp. 34–39 (2015). https://doi.org/10.1109/HOTI.2015.19
13. Hawblitzel, C., et al.: IronFleet: proving safety and liveness of practical distributed systems. Commun. ACM **60**(7), 83–92 (2017)
14. Hellerstein, J.M., Alvaro, P.: Keeping CALM: when distributed consistency is easy. Commun. ACM **63**, 72–81 (2020)
15. Honoré, W., Kim, J., Shin, J., Shao, Z.: Much ADO about failures: a fault-aware model for compositional verification of strongly consistent distributed systems. Proc. ACM Program. Lang. **5**(OOPSLA), 1–31 (2021). https://doi.org/10.1145/3485474
16. Honoré, W., Shin, J., Kim, J., Shao, Z.: Adore: atomic distributed objects with certified reconfiguration. In: Jhala, R., Dillig, I. (eds.) PLDI (2022)
17. Jha, S., et al.: Derecho: fast state machine replication for cloud services. ACM Trans. Comput. Syst. **36**, 1–49 (2019)
18. Jung, R., Krebbers, R., Jourdan, J., Bizjak, A., Birkedal, L., Dreyer, D.: Iris from the ground up: a modular foundation for higher-order concurrent separation logic. J. Funct. Program. **28**, e20 (2018)

19. Krogh-Jespersen, M., Timany, A., Ohlenbusch, M.E., Gregersen, S.O., Birkedal, L.: Aneris: a mechanised logic for modular reasoning about distributed systems. In: ESOP 2020. LNCS, vol. 12075, pp. 336–365. Springer, Cham (2020). https://doi.org/10.1007/978-3-030-44914-8_13
20. Kuper, L., Turon, A., Krishnaswami, N.R., Newton, R.R.: Freeze after writing: quasi-deterministic parallel programming with LVars. In: POPL, pp. 257–270 (2014). https://doi.org/10.1145/2535838.2535842
21. Laddad, S., Power, C., Milano, M., Cheung, A., Crooks, N., Hellerstein, J.M.: Keep CALM and CRDT on. Proc. VLDB Endow. **16**(4), 856–863 (2022). https://doi.org/10.14778/3574245.3574268
22. Laddad, S., Power, C., Milano, M., Cheung, A., Hellerstein, J.M.: Katara: Synthesizing CRDTs with verified lifting. Proc. ACM Program. Lang. **6**(OOPSLA2), 1349–1377 (2022). https://doi.org/10.1145/3563336
23. Leroy, X.: Formal verification of a realistic compiler. CACM **52**(7), 107–115 (2009)
24. Mansky, W., Appel, A.W., Nogin, A.: A verified messaging system. In: OOPSLA (2017)
25. Mansky, W., Du, K.: An Iris instance for verifying CompCert C programs. Proc. ACM Program. Lang. **8**(POPL), 148–174 (2024)
26. Mansky, W., Honoré, W., Appel, A.W.: Connecting higher-order separation logic to a first-order outside world. In: ESOP (2020)
27. McMillan, K.L., Padon, O.: Ivy: a multi-modal verification tool for distributed algorithms. In: Lahiri, S.K., Wang, C. (eds.) CAV 2020. LNCS, vol. 12225, pp. 190–202. Springer, Cham (2020). https://doi.org/10.1007/978-3-030-53291-8_12
28. Milano, M., Recto, R., Magrino, T., Myers, A.: A tour of Gallifrey, a language for geodistributed programming. In: Lerner, B.S., Bodík, R., Krishnamurthi, S. (eds.) 3rd Summit on Advances in Programming Languages (SNAPL 2019). Leibniz International Proceedings in Informatics (LIPIcs), vol. 136, pp. 11:1–11:19. Schloss Dagstuhl–Leibniz-Zentrum fuer Informatik, Dagstuhl (2019). https://doi.org/10.4230/LIPIcs.SNAPL.2019.11
29. Nguyen, D.T., Beringer, L., Mansky, W., Wang, S.: Compositional verification of concurrent C programs with search structure templates. In: CPP (2024)
30. Padon, O.: Deductive verification of distributed protocols in first-order logic. In: FMCAD (2018)
31. Padon, O., Losa, G., Sagiv, M., Shoham, S.: Paxos made EPR: Decidable reasoning about distributed protocols. Proc. ACM Program. Lang. **1**(OOPSLA), 1–31 (2017)
32. Recio, R.J., Culley, P.R., Garcia, D., Metzler, B., Hilland, J.: A remote direct memory access protocol specification. RFC 5040 (2007). https://doi.org/10.17487/RFC5040, https://www.rfc-editor.org/info/rfc5040
33. da Rocha Pinto, P., Dinsdale-Young, T., Gardner, P.: TaDA: a logic for time and data abstraction. In: Jones, R. (ed.) ECOOP 2014. LNCS, vol. 8586, pp. 207–231. Springer, Heidelberg (2014). https://doi.org/10.1007/978-3-662-44202-9_9
34. Sammler, M., Lepigre, R., Krebbers, R., Memarian, K., Dreyer, D., Garg, D.: RefinedC: automating the foundational verification of C code with refined ownership types. In: PLDI (2021)
35. Sergey, I., Wilcox, J.R., Tatlock, Z.: Programming and proving with distributed protocols. Proc. ACM Program. Lang. **2**(POPL), 1–30 (2017)
36. Shapiro, M., Preguiça, N., Baquero, C., Zawirski, M.: Conflict-free replicated data types. In: Défago, X., Petit, F., Villain, V. (eds.) SSS 2011. LNCS, vol. 6976, pp. 386–400. Springer, Heidelberg (2011). https://doi.org/10.1007/978-3-642-24550-3_29

37. Sharma, U., Jung, R., Tassarotti, J., Kaashoek, M.F., Zeldovich, N.: Grove: a separation-logic library for verifying distributed systems. In: SOSP (2023)
38. Song, W., et al.: Cascade: an edge computing platform for real-time machine intelligence. In: ApPLIED 2022 (2022)
39. Timany, A., et al.: Trillium: higher-order concurrent and distributed separation logic for intensional refinement. Proc. ACM Program. Lang. **8**(POPL), 241–272 (2024)
40. Wilcox, J.R., et al.: Verdi: a framework for implementing and formally verifying distributed systems. In: PLDI (2015)
41. Woos, D., Wilcox, J.R., Anton, S., Tatlock, Z., Ernst, M.D., Anderson, T.E.: Planning for change in a formal verification of the raft consensus protocol. In: CPP (2016)
42. Wu, C., Faleiro, J.M., Lin, Y., Hellerstein, J.M.: Anna: a KVS for any scale. IEEE Trans. Knowl. Data Eng. **33**(2), 344–358 (2021). https://doi.org/10.1109/TKDE.2019.2898401
43. Xia, L., et al.: Interaction trees: representing recursive and impure programs in Coq. Proc. ACM Program. Lang. **4**(POPL), 1–32 (2020)
44. Zave, P.: Reasoning about identifier spaces: How to make Chord correct. IEEE Trans. Software Eng. **43**(12), 1144–1156 (2017)
45. Zhang, H., et al.: Verifying an HTTP Key-Value Server with Interaction Trees and VST. In: ITP (2021)

Verification of Scapegoat Trees Using Dafny

Jiapeng Wang, Sini Chen, and Huibiao Zhu(✉)

East China Normal University, Shanghai, China
{51255902102,52265902002}@stu.ecnu.edu.cn, hbzhu@sei.ecnu.edu.cn

Abstract. Self-balancing binary search trees are essential in Computer Science for their versatility and efficient management of ordered data. While a clear definition might exist for a specific kind of balanced tree, multiple implementations can exist. This diversity highlights the critical importance of verifying the correctness of a specific implementation. With this perspective, this paper shifts focus to the scapegoat tree, a type of self-balancing tree, prized for its operational simplicity. Utilizing the formal verification tool, Dafny, we undertake a rigorous examination of a scapegoat tree implementation. Through Dafny's powerful specification and verification techniques, we prove the correctness of its core operations within our chosen implementation. We also summarized our user experience with Dafny, presenting several techniques that can enhance the efficiency of the proof process.

Keywords: Verification · Formal Methods · Scapegoat Trees · Dafny

1 Introduction

The Binary search tree (BST) is a cornerstone data structure in Computer Science that facilitates fast data retrieval, insertion, and deletion operations. Although BST excels in terms of average-case performance, it suffers from performance degradation in worst-case scenarios. In order to address limitations of regular BSTs, the notion of balanced trees was introduced. Balanced trees, such as AVL trees and Red-Black trees, are specialized versions of BSTs designed to maintain a low tree height, thereby ensuring that the tree remains approximately balanced. The balancing is enforced by applying specific rotations and color changes in the tree upon every insertion or deletion operation. This innovation has made a great progress towards taking the performance of tree-based data structures away from worst-case, making them a standard tool in a variety of applications ranging from databases to computer graphics. For example, in JAVA, a *hashmap* is implemented based on a red-black tree. Over time, red-black trees have also spawned many variants, such as AA trees, LLRB trees, and so on.

However, a new question arises: how can we ensure that these trees behave as expected when used? Although each type of tree is accompanied by detailed and rigorous mathematical proofs when invented, correctness may not be necessarily

N. Benz et al. (Eds.): NFM 2024, LNCS 14627, pp. 118–135, 2024.
https://doi.org/10.1007/978-3-031-60698-4_7

preserved when it comes to the level of concrete code implementation. Since formal methods are based on strict math principles, we would consider using formal methods to prove their correctness of these implementations.

Currently, there are several well-established theorem provers and related tools like Z3, Isabelle and Why3. Many researchers have proven the correctness of various trees using these tools. [14] used Auto2 [13] to verify six data structures and algorithms. In [10], the correctness of various root-balanced trees was established through theorem proving in Isabelle. It is worth noting, however, that both of these two proof assistants employ languages that may entail a certain learning curve. Given this, [12] and [6] independently conducted verification of their respective tree structures using the KIV [2] and Why3 verification tools. While the programming languages utilized in both cases are relatively close in syntax to commonly used development languages, they still fall short in terms of ease of use when compared to Dafny [9]. In addition, [1] employed the VERCORS [3] tool to verify red-black trees and their merge operations. Although VERCORS supports concurrent program verification, unfortunately, it is currently limited in its versatility as it supports verification for only a handful of languages and platforms such as JAVA, C, CUDA.

Based on the aforementioned comparisons, we choose Dafny [9] as our verification tool. Its syntax closely resembles that of commonly used high-level languages, making it easy to learn and master. Moreover, Dafny provides many built-in container types and excellent support for object-oriented programming. Based on Dafny, the correctness of Red-Black Trees, LLRB Trees, and Incremental Merkle Trees, are proven by previous work [4,5,11]. But the Dafny versions referenced in these papers were outdated, including several deprecated syntax elements. Hence, we made improvements and optimizations to their code base and conducted validation on the scapegoat tree.

The remaining parts of this paper are organized as follows: In Sect. 2, we provide a brief introduction to the Scapegoat Tree and verification tool Dafny. In Sect. 3, we give some code outlines of core functions, along with verification result of our full codes. In Sect. 4, we offer discussions about issues encountered during the proofs, and present techniques to accelerate proving process when using Dafny. Based on this, a proof example is provided in Sect. 5, employing the optimization techniques introduced in Sect. 4. Finally, Sect. 6 presents a summarizing statement and outlines some prospects for future work.

2 Background

2.1 Scapegoat Trees

Scapegoat trees are binary search trees with specific insertion and deletion logic. They employ specialized mechanisms for balancing, which ensures tree balance properties, while reducing memory consumption and operational complexity. Our purpose is to demonstrate that the insertion and deletion operations can

Table 1. Useful notations

Notation	Meaning	Explanation
$h(T)$	Tree height	Height of a tree T
$size(T)$	Tree size	Size of a tree T
$max\_size(T)$	Tree max size	Maximal value of $size(T)$ since last complete tree rebuilding
$h_\alpha(n)$	h_α function	For some α in $[0.5, 1)$, define $h_\alpha(n) = \lfloor \log_{\frac{1}{\alpha}} n \rfloor$

maintain balance properties. Therefore, in Sect. 2.2 and 2.3, we provide a brief introduction to several balance properties and rebuild/rebalance operations.

2.2 Balance Properties

As a self-balancing binary tree, the scapegoat tree is associated with three balance properties, denoted as *α-weight-balanced, α-height-balanced,* and *loose-α-height-balanced.* According to [7], the scapegoat tree ensures the preservation of *loose-α-height-balanced* after any complete operation (insertion or deletion). For convenience of discussion, we propose notations in Table 1.

α-Weight-Balanced. A node x is called *α-weight-balanced* for some α in $[0.5, 1)$ if both of the following inequations hold

$$size(x.left) \leq \alpha * size(x) \tag{1}$$

$$size(x.right) \leq \alpha * size(x) \tag{2}$$

If x is α-weight-balanced, the heavier child of x has no more than $\alpha * size(x)$ nodes. Intuitively, a tree T is α-weight-balanced if for every node x in T, x is always α-weight-balanced. In terms of weight, this ensures that no node is too "heavy" compared to its sibling, preventing the tree from becoming too skewed.

α-Height-Balanced. A tree T is called *α-height-balanced* for some α in $[0.5, 1)$ if

$$h(T) \leq h_\alpha(size(T)) \tag{3}$$

holds. If a tree is α-height-balanced, that means the tree height is restricted to some "ceiling", in case of degenerating to tree-style linked list. In terms of height, this property ensures that the tree is relatively shallow, promoting faster search times.

Loose-α-Height-Balanced. A tree T is called *loose-α-height-balanced* for some α in $[0.5, 1)$ if

$$h(T) \leq h_\alpha(size(T)) + 1 \tag{4}$$

holds. This is a more relaxed version of the *α-height-balanced* definition. It allows for more flexibility in the tree's structure while still maintaining a reasonable balance.

All three definitions above aim to maintain the balance of a scapegoat tree, but in slightly different ways. *α-weight-balanced* places constraints on the number of nodes in sub-trees. It also indirectly influences the tree's height since we know there is an inequality constraint relationship between tree height and tree size. As to *α-height-balanced* and *loose-α-height-balanced*, they only limit the whole tree height without any other constraints about sub-trees.

2.3 Rebuild and Rebalance

For pure insertion and deletion operations, there is no difference between a scapegoat tree and a regular binary search tree. The key feature of a scapegoat tree lies in its **balancing mechanism**. The rebalance operation aims to restore the *loose-α-height-balanced* property after modifying the tree by either reorganizing some sub-trees or, in extreme cases, rebuilding the whole tree entirely. For insertion, the algorithm checks for an imbalance in the tree's structure. If an imbalance is detected, a rebalance operation is triggered. As for deletion, the operation itself does not affect balance property (tree size does not decrease since scapegoat trees use lazy deletion). A complete rebuild operation is needed only when too many lazy-deleted nodes are there.

In fact, the rebalance operation is essentially a rebuild operation for unbalanced subtrees. So now we focus on how the rebuild operation works. In contrast to other balanced binary trees that employ complex rotation mechanisms, the scapegoat tree utilizes a remarkably simple reconstruction mechanism: it first "flattens" the unbalanced sub-tree into a sequence, and then lifts it from the middle of the sequence to form a tree. This special mechanism offers two advantages: firstly, it is a straightforward and easily implementable procedure, always done by a recursive method. And secondly, it is evident that it guarantees the new tree to be 0.5-weight-balanced, thereby ensuring the strictest form of balance. Figure 1 shows how this reconstruction works. After the insertion of new key 51, the subtree with a root node of 35 becomes the **scapegoat**. All nodes on this subtree are flattened into an ordered list, then lifted from the middle to progressively form a balanced new subtree.

2.4 Dafny

Dafny is a modern verification tool based on Hoare logic [8], developed by Microsoft Research [9].[1] The word "Dafny" can refer to both the tool and the language used by the tool. It can establish the complete correctness of a program by leveraging automated theorem provers like Z3.

In syntax, apart from various specifications, it combines ideas from the functional and imperative paradigms. Also, it includes support for object-oriented programming. Here is an example:

[1] Dafny was originally developed by Microsoft Research, but Amazon are now doing most of the current development.

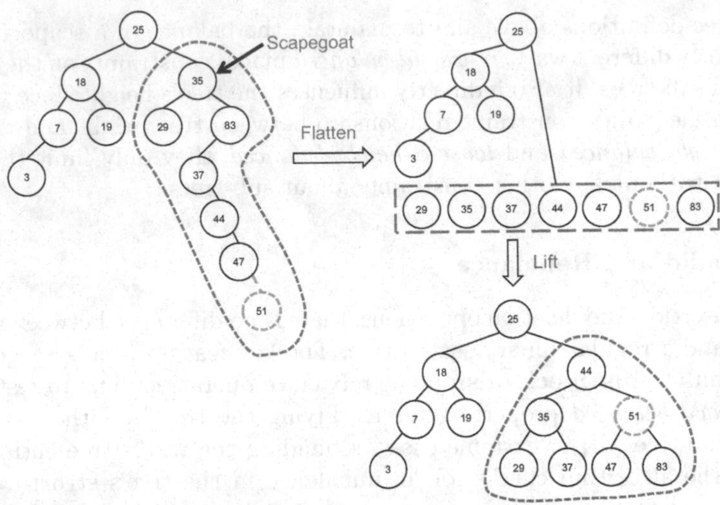

Fig. 1. Insert a new key 51 and rebalance the tree ($\alpha = 0.6$)

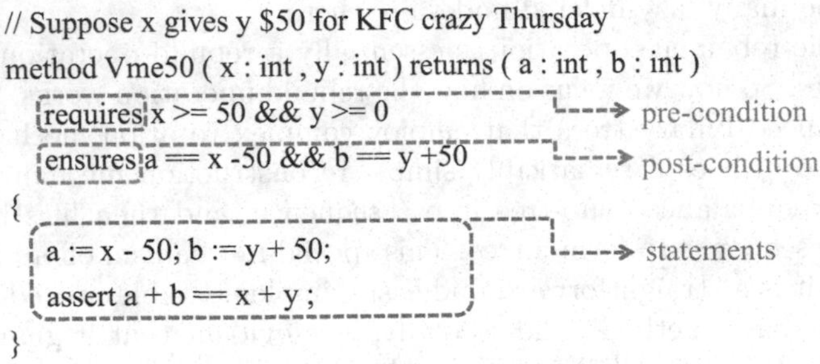

```
// Suppose x gives y $50 for KFC crazy Thursday
method Vme50 ( x : int , y : int ) returns ( a : int , b : int )
  requires x >= 50 && y >= 0                  ----> pre-condition
  ensures a == x -50 && b == y +50            ----> post-condition
{
  a := x - 50; b := y + 50;                   ----> statements
  assert a + b == x + y ;
}
```

Fig. 2. A method example (Color figure online)

In Fig. 2, the green and red portions are **specifications**, they can intuitively express requirements on the function's behavior and output constraints, while the blue portion represents statements, which share many similarities with those in traditional programming languages. Here, $\mathbf{x \geq 50}$ **&&** $\mathbf{y \geq 0}$ is specified because we don't allow overdrawn bank balance (maybe they use debit cards). **a == x-50 && b == y+50** is specified to ensure that x can smoothly transfer $50 to y. Furthermore, we use an `assert` statement to test whether the sum of the balances remains the same before and after the transaction.

This section provides an introductory understanding of Dafny and highlights its key features. For more detailed and full version of documentation, see[2].

[2] http://dafny.org/dafny/DafnyRef/DafnyRef.

3 Implementation

3.1 Basics

In this section, we provide the code implementation of a binary search tree along with definitions related to balance properties mentioned in Sect. 2.1. Due to space limitations, the Dafny code snippets in this article may not be executable. Complete code is provided on[3].

Binary Search Trees. Scapegoat trees are binary search trees. So we first build a binary tree:

```
datatype Tree = Empty | Node(key: int, left: Tree, right:
    Tree, exist: bool)
```

Here we first define two types: `Empty` and `Node`. `Empty` can be treated as a null pointer, representing that there is no node in the position. `Node` has an additional field called `exist`, used for the rebuild operation and lazy deletion.

Following that, we apply constraints to the ordering of keys contained within the nodes of the binary tree:

```
1 // Recursive definition of BST(Binary-Search-Tree)
2 predicate BST(t: Tree)
3 {
4   match t
5   case Empty => true
6   case Node(k, l, r, _) => BST(l) && BST(r)
7       && (forall e :: e in tree_elements(l) ==> e < k)
8       && (forall e :: e in tree_elements(r) ==> e > k)
9 }
```

Above is a predicate to determine if a tree is a BST. The keyword `predicate` is an alternative syntax for a `function` that returns a bool value. For any non-empty tree `t`, the predicate checks if the left and right sub-trees satisfy the BST property (Line 6), and if all keys are in order (Line 7 & 8). Here, the `tree_elements` is a function to get all the keys stored in a tree as a set. Naturally, as a binary search tree, nodes within the tree are not permitted to have duplicate keys. Therefore, the effect of `e < k` (`e > k`) and `e <= k` (`e >= k`) in Line 7 (Line 8) is the same.

h_α Function. In Sect. 2.1, we define the h_α function. But there are some problems here: Dafny indeed provides a range of commonly utilized mathematical libraries. However, the majority of these computational operations are confined to integers, or at least some of their parameters are integers. There is not substantial support offered for computations among real numbers. To implement

[3] https://github.com/ppooii12009/Scapegoat-tree.

some elementary functions, a common approach is to simulate them using arithmetic operations. In [4], they simulate 2^n by multiplication. However, since in the logarithmic function, both parameters and return value are of `real` type, it is impossible to simulate them using simple arithmetic operations. In a majority of commonly used high-level programming languages such as Java, C++, C, Python, etc., *Taylor Series Expansion, Polynomial or Rational Approximations, CORDIC Algorithm, Table Lookup and Interpolation*, and so forth are regular methods for implementing arithmetic functions. All these methods are approximations rather than precise calculations. The reasoning is straightforward: we can simulate 2^5 as $2 \times 2 \times 2 \times 2 \times 2$, but for $3^{2.73} \rightarrow 3 \times 3 \times 3^{0.73}$, we are unable to calculate what $3^{0.73}$ is. Furthermore, the exponential function can be simulated using simple multiplication, whereas the logarithmic function cannot be easily simulated with division, which further increases the difficulty of calculating its value. So we leverage a feature in Dafny: functions (or methods, lemmas) can be declared without implementation.

```
function h_alpha(n: real, alpha: real): (r: real)
  requires 0.5 <= alpha < 1.0
  requires n > 0.0
  ensures n == 1.0 ==> h_alpha(n,alpha) == 0.0
  ensures n == alpha ==> h_alpha(n, alpha) == -1.0
  // no curly braces here
```

When no implementation is offered, all of the post-conditions are set to true. We also use this feature to describe three basic properties of h_α function in `h_alpha_properties`.

In general, our goal is to prove the correctness of the operation, rather than the correctness of one or some cases with specific numerical values. Therefore, we do not actually need the logarithm function to calculate specific values. What we need are merely some properties (such as monotonicity, zeros)[4] of the logarithm function to assist us in completing the proof. Thus, although using Dafny's features to omit the implementation of the logarithm function carries a sense of incompleteness, it is acceptable from the perspective of the overall proof objective.

Balance Properties. Next, we will describe three different balance properties through Dafny codes.

```
predicate alpha_weight_balanced(t: Tree, alpha: real)
  requires 0.5 <= alpha < 1.0
{
  match t
  case Empty => true
  case Node(_, l, r, _) =>
```

[4] Apart from the two `ensures` in `h_alpha`, other properties are described under the `h_alpha_properties` lemma in the code.

```
    size(l) as real <= multiply(alpha, (size(t) as real))
    && size(r) as real <= multiply(alpha, (size(t) as real))
    && alpha_weight_balanced(l,alpha)
    && alpha_weight_balanced(r,alpha)
}

predicate alpha_height_balanced(t: Tree, alpha: real)
  requires 0.5 <= alpha < 1.0
{
  match t
  case Empty => true
  case Node(_, l, r, _) =>
    tree_height(t) as real <= h_alpha(size(t) as real, alpha)
}

// loose_alpha_height_balanced is omitted here
```

The code for `loose-α-weight-balanced` and `α-weight-balanced` is nearly identical, with the sole difference being the replacement of `h_alpha(size(t) as real, alpha)` with `h_alpha(size(t) as real, alpha) + 1.0`.

The structure for implementing these three properties is entirely consistent: using a `match` statement to check if the tree is empty, and when it's not, further verifying whether the specific conditions are met. Additionally, we do not round the result of `h_alpha`. Considering that the return value of `tree_height` is always an integer, whether we round the result does not affect the comparison of numerical values. Furthermore, You may notice in predicate `alpha_weight_balanced`, we use a function called `multiply`. The effect is the same as directly using `*`, the reason will be explained later in Sect. 4.1.

3.2 Insert

The insert operation contains two main parts. First we find the proper position and insert the new key. Then balance the tree if the balance property was broken. We split the insertion operation into two functions because using a single function for the entire insertion would demand each recursive step to meet all pre-conditions and post-conditions, often an unnecessary requirement. Hence, we strive to decompose the original insertion function into multiple sub-steps, with each sub-step focusing only on the minimal set of pre-conditions and post-conditions required for its specific scope. This approach not only reduces the complexity and difficulty of proofs but also makes the code more adaptable to future modifications, enhancing code reusability.

```
function insert(t: Tree, x: int) : (t': Tree)
/*
  some requires and ensures statements are omitted,
  the same applies below
*/
{
  match t
```

```
8      case Empty => Node(x, Empty, Empty, true)
9      case Node(k, l, r, e) =>
10       var t' := insert_key(t, x);
11       if loose_alpha_height_balanced(t', ALPHA) then t'
12       else balance_tree(t')
13   }
```

The code shown above is the framework of the `insert` function. If the initial tree `t` is an empty tree, we directly create a new one (Line 6), which is of course balanced. Otherwise, we use `insert_key` to insert the key without consideration of balance (Line 8). Then we check it recursively: If it is not balanced, we adjust the tree with the `balance_tree` function (Line 10).

Insert_key. The `insert_key` function is solely responsible for inserting the specified key into the tree without considering the balance property. The implementation of this function is also quite apparent.

```
function insert_key(t: Tree, x: int) : (t': Tree)
  ensures tree_elements(t') == tree_elements(t) + {x}
{
  match t
  case Empty => Node(x, Empty, Empty, true)
  case Node(k, l, r, e) =>
    if x < k then Node(k, insert_key(l, x), r, e)
    else if x > k then Node(k, l, insert_key(r, x), e)
    else
      if e then t else Node(k, l, r, true)
}
```

build_tree. `build_tree` is the most frequently used function in the scapegoat tree. Another core function, `balance_tree`, is also implemented based on `build_tree`. This function is responsible for constructing a binary search tree with an increasing order of keys based on the given sorted key sequence, resulting in an in-order traversal sequence. In our version of the implementation, to enhance code reusability, the tree built by the `build_tree` function will treat all of the given elements as not lazy-deleted. This design allows us to avoid rewriting a new "build" function when rebuilding the entire tree during the delete operation. We can directly utilize this existing function because rebuilding the entire tree will permanently remove all the lazy-deleted nodes.

```
function build_tree(s: seq<int>) : (t: Tree)
  ensures alpha_weight_balanced(t, 0.5)
{
  if s == [] then Empty
  else
    var mid := |s| / 2; var key := s[mid];
```

```
    var lseq := s[..mid]; var rseq := s[mid+1..];
    var l := build_tree(lseq); var r := build_tree(rseq);
    Node(key, l, r, true)
}
```

In fact, this function is the most complex operation to prove among the main operations. We employ over 60 **assert** statements and refer to a few other lemmas multiple times. Furthermore, as it involves conversions between different container structures (sequence, set and multiset), we have provided several lemmas and proofs specifically for these data structure conversions. Through this, we have also identified certain weaknesses in the proof verifier, which will be discussed in Sect. 4.1.

3.3 Delete

The delete operation is much simpler compared to the insert operation. Because we use a lazy deletion mechanism, the delete operation does not affect the height or size of the tree, ensuring that the tree's balance properties remain intact. Only when there are too many lazy-deleted nodes, rebuilding of the entire tree is needed.

Here, we provide the implementation only for `delete`. As before, we first implement the lazy deletion marking functionality for the given key using `delete_key` (Line 7). Then, we check if there are too many lazy-deleted nodes. If there are, we use `whole_rebuild` to rebuild the entire tree (Line 8).

```
1  function delete(t: Tree, x: int) : (t': Tree)
2    ensures loose_alpha_height_balanced(t, ALPHA)
3  {
4    match t
5    case Empty => Empty
6    case Node(_, _, _, _) =>
7      var tmp := delete_key(t, x);
8      if real_size(tmp) as real < ALPHA*(size(tmp) as real) then
         whole_rebuild(tmp)
9      else tmp
10 }
```

3.4 Verification Result

We executed our verification code on a machine equipped with an Intel i9-13900HX CPU and 16 GB of RAM, and the results were accurate without any errors. A total of **54** proof obligations were generated, including **22 functions**, **20 lemmas**, and **11 predicates**. The total proof time was **32.4** s. **39%** of the proof obligations were completed within **10** s, **59%** within **20** s, and there was one relatively complex proof obligation that took **23.3** s to complete. The average time spent on each proof obligation was **10.2** s. We selected 19 obligations that are closely related to the proof, with their execution times illustrated in Fig. 3.

Among these 19 proof obligations, the two most crucial ones are `insert` and `delete`. Our ultimate goal is to prove that both operations can both correctly modify the nodes in the tree and always maintain balance properties. Below are the `ensures` specifications for these two operations. For the `insert` function, Line 2 and Line 5 guarantee that the new tree is a balanced BST. Line 3 and Line 4 ensure that the new tree definitely contains the inserted key. For the delete operation, it is necessary to ensure through Line 9–11 that the key to be deleted is marked for lazy deletion and cannot be searched.

```
1  function insert(t: Tree, x: int) : (t': Tree)
2    ensures BST(t')
3    ensures tree_elements(t') == tree_elements(t) + {x}
4    ensures real_tree_elements(t') == real_tree_elements(t) + {x}
5    ensures loose_alpha_height_balanced(t', ALPHA)
6
7  function delete(t: Tree, x: int) : (t': Tree)
8    ensures BST(t')
9    ensures real_tree_elements(t) - {x} == real_tree_elements(t')
10   ensures search(t, x) <==> real_tree_elements(t) ==
         real_tree_elements(t') + {x}
11   ensures x !in real_tree_elements(t')
12   ensures loose_alpha_height_balanced(t, ALPHA)
```

Despite these being the test results obtained after employing the optimization techniques discussed in Sect. 4.2, there remains a particularly complex lemma, `balanced_properties`, which took over 20 s to prove. We identify three main reasons for this: firstly, the lemma includes five `ensures` statements, all related to balance properties, making the proof rather cumbersome. Secondly, the proof process involves separately proving aspects related to the left and right subtrees, resulting in a significant amount of structural repetition. Lastly, the proof process involves several other auxiliary lemmas and frequently employs mathematical induction, increasing its complexity. An obvious solution is to split these five `ensures` specifications into five separate lemmas for proof, which we have tried and indeed significantly speeds up the proof process. However, considering the need to individually name these five lemmas and taking into account the overall readability of the code, we still choose to put them together under the single lemma `balanced_properties`.

4 Discussions

In this section, we will delve into a detailed discussion of the proof process, including proof techniques that can enhance efficiency and some issues encountered during the proof process.

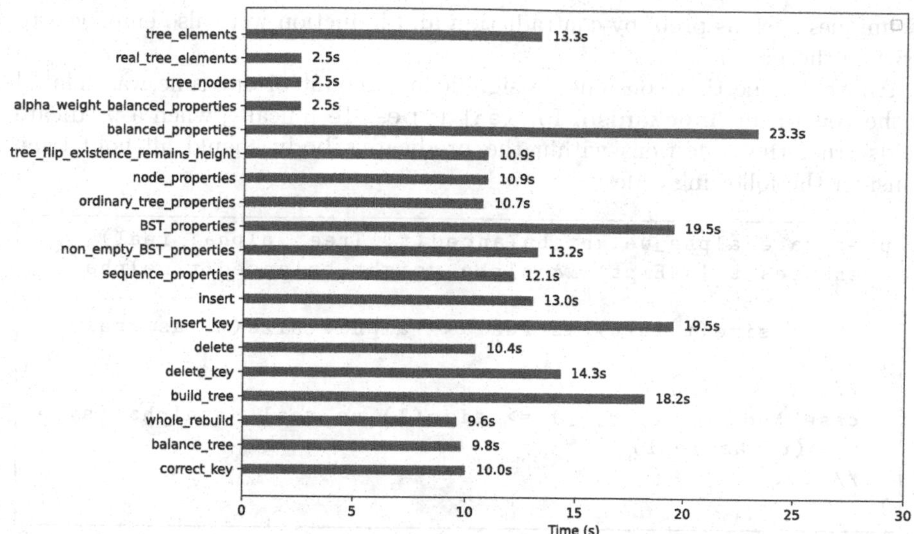

Fig. 3. Time cost of 19 proof obligations

4.1 Issues

One of the main issues we encountered is the **relatively weak reasoning ability when dealing with conversions between containers**. For example, using `multiset()` allows user to convert a set or sequence into a multiset. However, many properties cannot be naturally proven using these conversion functions. Here we give an example:

```
1  predicate unique_elements(s: seq<int>)
2  {
3    forall i,j :: 0 <= i < j < |s| ==> s[i] != s[j]
4  }
5
6  lemma sequence_properties(s: seq<int>, r: seq<int>)
7    requires unique_elements(s)
8    requires multiset(s) == multiset(r)
9    ensures unique_elements(r)
10 {}
```

The predicate checks if there exists two same elements in sequence `s`. This lemma aims to illustrate that if the multisets of two sequences are the same (Line 8), and one of the sequences does not contain duplicate elements (Line 7), then the other sequence also does not contain duplicate elements (Line 9). Mathematically, this lemma is quite obvious. However, in practical operations, we used three additional lemmas to prove it. The full proof is presented in Sect. 5.

Techniques such as proof by contradiction and induction were also employed to assist in the proof.

Another issue that consumed a significant amount of our time was related to the **reasoning mechanism for real types**. Technically, when a predicate yields true, the conditions within the predicate's body should all hold true. Consider the following codes:

```
1 predicate alpha_weight_balanced(t: Tree, alpha: real)
2   ensures t != Empty && alpha_weight_balanced(t, alpha)
      ==>
3         size(t.left) as real <= alpha*(size(t) as real)
4 {
5   // ...
6   case Node(_, l, r, _) => size(l) as real <= alpha*(size
      (t) as real)
7   // ...
8 }
```

Since the condition size(l) as real ≤ alpha*(size(t) as real) is declared in the predicate body (Line 6), it is very reasonable that when this predicate holds, the post-condition also holds. But actually, Dafny cannot prove this. It will immediately tell you "a post-condition could not be proved on this return path". However, if we introduce some encapsulation, replacing * with multiply() and implement alpha_weight_balanced() as outlined in Sect. 3.1, then the proof process can be completed smoothly right away.

```
function multiply(a: real, b: real): (r: real)
  ensures r == a*b
{
  a * b
}
```

The reason for this issue is that the theorem prover Z3 which Dafny uses, can encounter non-linear logical reasoning when it is used for proof of real numbers. By introducing encapsulation through the multiply method, we can avoid the use of non-linear logic.[5]

4.2 Proof Techniques

This section will introduce some techniques that can help expedite the proof process. While automated provers can intelligently deduce many properties to some extent, they are still limited when it comes to more complex or numerous properties. In other words, theorem provers often struggle with such tasks.

[5] We discovered an attribute, {:disableNonlinearArithmetic}, within a certain official Dafny library that is not mentioned on the official user manual page. From its literal meaning, it seems it could avoid nonlinear operations. But after testing, we found that it did not solve the problem.

Split Complex Functions or Lemmas. Since our goal is to prove the correctness of the code, as long as our implementation is equivalent to the original version, when our code is proven correct, the original version is also mathematically correct. Indeed, proving the correctness of smaller pieces of code is generally easier than proving the correctness of larger-scale code. Hence, we highly recommend to break down a larger-scale function into several sub-functions.

Improve Assert Statements. The `assert` statement is a fundamental feature in the proof mechanism. The efficiency of `assert` statements largely determines the speed of the entire proof process. When we attempt to prove property `P` using simple assert statements, Dafny will automatically try to reason based on known conditions. However, if there are too many existing conditions, the automated proof may have problem in finding the correct proof path. Therefore, we can optimize this process using `assert ... by {}`, which will directly specify priority conditions for the proof, thus speeding up the proof process.

Use Attributes. Dafny allows many of its entities to be annotated with *attributes*. Attributes can be parameterless, or can have one or more parameters, depending on the specific attribute. They are declared between **{:** and **}** like this

```
{:axiom} {:extern s1, s2}
```

In Dafny, assert statements are verified in *batches*, with multiple asserts grouped into a single batch for the prover. By default, asserts within a function form one *batch* and are verified sequentially. If an earlier assert is unprovable or time-consuming, later asserts may exceed time limits. To address this, attributes like {:focus}, {:split_here} or {:vcs_split_on_every_assert} can be used to divide a batch into several smaller ones, allowing parallel verification and enhancing efficiency.

5 Proof Example: Sequence_Properties

In this section, we will utilize various optimization techniques introduced in the previous section to prove the lemma `sequence_properties` presented in Sect. 4.1.

Before formally presenting the proof code, let's briefly outline the strategy. Two data structures are involved here: `seq` and `multiset`. Therefore, we can consider leveraging the properties of `multiset` as a bridge to advance the proof steps. For example, if when a sequence has the property `unique_elements`, its corresponding multiset has a certain property `P`, and this derivation relationship is bidirectional, then by utilizing the fact that the multisets of `s` and `r` are equal, we can quickly complete the proof. So the code should somehow look like this:

```
// Suppose P() <==> unique_elements()
assert unique_elements(s);
assert P(multiset(s));
assert P(multiset(r));
assert unique_elements(r);
```

The next key step is to determine how to find a property P that meets the conditions. It's worth noting that **unique_elements** is related to the number of elements, and in a multiset, the concept of **multiplicity** is also related to the number of elements. For any multiset ms, ms[e] returns the number of times the element e appears in ms. Hence, we can quickly come up with property P:

```
forall k :: k in multiset(s) ==> multiset(s)[k] == 1
```

Next, it is only necessary to prove that property P and unique_elements can be mutually derived. Now, we provide the complete proof process:

```
lemma sequence_properties(s: seq<int>, r: seq<int>)
  requires unique_elements(s)
  requires multiset(s) == multiset(r)
  ensures unique_elements(r)
{
  unique_elements_equivalence(s);
  unique_elements_equivalence(r);
}

lemma unique_elements_equivalence(s: seq<int>)
  ensures unique_elements(s) <==>
    forall k :: k in multiset(s) ==> multiset(s)[k] == 1
{
  if(unique_elements(s))
  {
    unique_elements_implies_multiplicity_equals_1(s);
  }
  if(forall k :: k in multiset(s) ==> multiset(s)[k] == 1)
  {
    multiplicity_equals_1_implies_unique_elements(s);
  }
}

lemma unique_elements_implies_multiplicity_equals_1(s: seq<int
    >)
  requires unique_elements(s)
  ensures forall k::k in multiset(s) ==> multiset(s)[k]==1
{
  var ms := multiset(s);
  if !(forall k :: k in ms ==> ms[k] == 1)
  {
    var k :| k in ms && ms[k] > 1;
    var i :| 0 < i < |s|;
```

```
33      var left := s[..i];
34      var right := s[i..];
35      assert s == left+right;
36      if k in left && k in right
37      {
38        assert !unique_elements(s);
39      } else if k in left && k !in right
40      {
41        unique_elements_implies_multiplicity_equals_1(left);
42      } else if k !in left && k in right
43      {
44        unique_elements_implies_multiplicity_equals_1(right);
45      }else
46      {
47        assert k !in multiset(s);
48      }
49    }
50  }
51
52  lemma multiplicity_equals_1_implies_unique_elements(s: seq<int
    >)
53    requires forall k::k in multiset(s) ==> multiset(s)[k]==1
54    ensures unique_elements(s)
55  {
56    if(!unique_elements(s))
57    {
58      var i, j, k :| 0 <= i < j < |s| && s[i] == s[j] == k;
59      var left := s[..i+1];
60      var right := s[i+1..];
61      assert s == left + right;
62      assert j >= i+1;
63      assert k in left && k in right;
64      assert multiset(s)[k] >= 2;
65    }
66  }
```

Here, we use contradiction and induction in the proofs of the last two lemmas. In `unique_elements_implies_multiplicity_equals_1`, we begin by assuming that the post-condition is false (Line 29), i.e., there exists an element `k` that appears more than once in `multiset(s)` (Line 31). Then, we arbitrarily divide `s` into two parts and proceed to discuss the occurrences of `k` (Line 32–35). There are a total of four possible scenarios. When `k` appears in both the left and right parts of `s` (Line 36), we can immediately deduce a contradiction: this conflicts with the `unique_elements` property. When `k` does not appear in either the left or right parts of `s` (Line 45), the contradiction is also evident. Finally, when `k` appears only in the left or right part (Line 39 & 42), we recursively invoke this lemma on the corresponding left or right part until a contradiction is reached. The process of recursive invocation is essentially assuming that this lemma holds on a subset of `s` and attempting to prove that its validity on the subset implies its validity on `s` as a whole, which is the essence of mathematical induction. Certainly, in practice, we also use the pigeonhole principle to complete the proof. However, such methods require clever constructions and may not be straightforward to devise, so we omit this approach here.

6 Conclusion

In this article, we conducted verification of the scapegoat tree using the formal verification tool Dafny, and our proof code ran successfully. We have successfully proven that the insertion and deletion operations of the scapegoat tree can maintain the *loose-α-height-balanced* property. During the proof process, we identified certain issues with Dafny and proposed corresponding solutions to address these issues. Additionally, we discovered several techniques that can enhance the efficiency of the proof process. Finally, a concrete proof example is provided to apply the aforementioned proof techniques.

Future Work. Certainly, we must acknowledge that the implementation of the scapegoat tree presented in this paper is a simplified version, and there remains room for optimization in details such as finding the scapegoat. At the same time, for a data structure, its correctness and complexity are of equal importance. We have completed its correctness proof, but there are some operational difficulties in proving complexity using theorem provers. For manual proofs, we can complete the proof by observation and analysis, combined with relevant lemmas and theorems on time complexity calculation. However, for a machine, we first need to define what "time complexity" means. In the majority of contexts, **Big O notation** is utilized to denote time complexity. Let's revisit its definition: For a given function $f(n)$, where n represents the input size, we write $f(n) = O(g(n))$ if there exist positive constants c and n_0 such that for all $n \geq n_0$, $f(n)$ is bounded above by $c \times g(n)$. Typically, $f(n)$ represents the number of operations we are concerned with, which can be easily obtained using a counter. But how to determine the values of c and n_0 still remains an issue that needs to be considered.

Furthermore, the scapegoat tree is one of the simpler variations of binary search trees. We aim to leverage the existing codebase to verify more complex multiway trees (like B+ trees, B*trees) and their operations in the future. We also hope that there will be a way to handle the computation of elementary functions involving real numbers within Dafny.

References

1. Armborst, L., Huisman, M.: Permission-based verification of red-black trees and their merging. In: 2021 IEEE/ACM 9th International Conference on Formal Methods in Software Engineering (FormaliSE), pp. 111–123 (2021). https://doi.org/10.1109/FormaliSE52586.2021.00017
2. Balser, M., Reif, W., Schellhorn, G., Stenzel, K., Thums, A.: Formal system development with KIV. In: Maibaum, T. (ed.) FASE 2000. LNCS, vol. 1783, pp. 363–366. Springer, Heidelberg (2000). https://doi.org/10.1007/3-540-46428-X_25

3. Blom, S., Darabi, S., Huisman, M., Oortwijn, W.: The VerCors tool set: verification of parallel and concurrent software. In: Polikarpova, N., Schneider, S. (eds.) IFM 2017. LNCS, vol. 10510, pp. 102–110. Springer, Cham (2017). https://doi.org/10.1007/978-3-319-66845-1_7
4. Cassez, F.: Verification of the incremental Merkle tree algorithm with Dafny. In: Huisman, M., Păsăreanu, C., Zhan, N. (eds.) FM 2021. LNCS, vol. 13047, pp. 445–462. Springer, Cham (2021). https://doi.org/10.1007/978-3-030-90870-6_24
5. Cassez, F., Fuller, J., Quiles, H.M.A.: Deductive verification of smart contracts with Dafny. In: Groote, J.F., Huisman, M. (eds.) FMICS 2022. LNCS, vol. 13487, pp. 50–66. Springer, Cham (2022). https://doi.org/10.1007/978-3-031-15008-1_5
6. Clochard, M.: Automatically verified implementation of data structures based on AVL trees. In: Giannakopoulou, D., Kroening, D. (eds.) VSTTE 2014. LNCS, vol. 8471, pp. 167–180. Springer, Cham (2014). https://doi.org/10.1007/978-3-319-12154-3_11
7. Galperin, I., Rivest, R.L.: Scapegoat trees. In: Proceedings of the Fourth Annual ACM-SIAM Symposium on Discrete Algorithms, SODA 1993, pp. 165–174. Society for Industrial and Applied Mathematics, USA (1993). https://doi.org/10.5555/313559.313676
8. Hoare, C.A.R.: An axiomatic basis for computer programming. Commun. ACM **12**(10), 576–580 (1969). https://doi.org/10.1145/363235.363259
9. Leino, K.R.M.: Dafny: an automatic program verifier for functional correctness. In: Clarke, E.M., Voronkov, A. (eds.) LPAR 2010. LNCS (LNAI), vol. 6355, pp. 348–370. Springer, Heidelberg (2010). https://doi.org/10.1007/978-3-642-17511-4_20
10. Nipkow, T.: Verified root-balanced trees. In: Chang, B.-Y.E. (ed.) APLAS 2017. LNCS, vol. 10695, pp. 255–272. Springer, Cham (2017). https://doi.org/10.1007/978-3-319-71237-6_13
11. Peña, R.: An assertional proof of red-black trees using Dafny. J. Autom. Reason. **64**(4), 767–791 (2020). https://doi.org/10.1007/s10817-019-09534-y
12. Schellhorn, G., Bodenmüller, S., Bitterlich, M., Reif, W.: Separating separation logic-modular verification of red-black trees. In: Lal, A., Tonetta, S. (eds.) VSTTE 2022. LNCS, vol. 13800, pp. 129–147. Springer, Cham (2022). https://doi.org/10.1007/978-3-031-25803-9_8
13. Zhan, B.: AUTO2, a saturation-based heuristic prover for higher-order logic. In: Blanchette, J.C., Merz, S. (eds.) ITP 2016. LNCS, vol. 9807, pp. 441–456. Springer, Cham (2016). https://doi.org/10.1007/978-3-319-43144-4_27
14. Zhan, B.: Efficient verification of imperative programs using Auto2. In: Beyer, D., Huisman, M. (eds.) TACAS 2018, Part I. LNCS, vol. 10805, pp. 23–40. Springer, Cham (2018). https://doi.org/10.1007/978-3-319-89960-2_2

Real Arithmetic in TLAPM

Ovini V. W. Gunasekera(✉), Andrew Sogokon, Antonios Gouglidis, and Neeraj Suri

School of Computing and Communications, Lancaster University, Lancaster, UK
{o.gunasekera,a.sogokon,a.gouglidis,neeraj.suri}@lancaster.ac.uk

Abstract. TLA$^+$ is a formal specification language for modelling systems and programs. While TLA$^+$ allows writing specifications involving real numbers, its existing tool support does not currently extend to automating real arithmetic proofs. This functionality is crucial for proving properties of hybrid systems, which may exhibit both continuous and discrete behaviours. In this paper, we address this limitation by enabling support for deciding first-order real arithmetic formulas (involving only polynomials). Specifically, we update the TLA$^+$ Proof System (TLAPS) to support reals and basic real arithmetic operations and implement them in the TLA$^+$ Proof Manager. The latter generates assertions in SMT-LIB and directs them to a selected backend (currently the Z3 SMT solver, which supports the theory of nonlinear real arithmetic). We motivate this functionality with problems arising in safety verification.

Keywords: formal verification · real arithmetic · hybrid systems · TLA$^+$

1 Introduction

TLA$^+$ is a general-purpose formal language based on the Zermelo-Fraenkel set theory for specifying digital systems and is supported by industrial strength tools. Over the years, TLA$^+$ gained considerable attention from both the academic community and industry [8], where it was used by major companies such as Amazon, Intel and Microsoft in applications ranging from concurrent to distributed systems. Indeed, TLA$^+$ is so expressive that it can even be applied to model *hybrid systems* [6] (and therefore *cyber-physical systems* in which the state may evolve in discrete time steps or *continuously*). Modelling and reasoning about continuous state evolution in these systems fundamentally requires real numbers. TLA$^+$ allows one to work with variables ranging over the set of real numbers (see [7, §18.4]) and was designed anticipating the use of decision procedures that could work with the structures defined in its standard arithmetic modules [7, Ch. 18][1]. Work by Merz et al. [9] created the necessary infrastructure

[1] *"If you want to prove something about a specification, you can reason about numbers however you want. Tools like model checkers and theorem provers that care about these operators will have their own ways of handling them."* – *L. Lamport* [7, §18.4].

Research supported by the UKRI Trustworthy Autonomous Systems (TAS) Node in Security. EPSRC Grant EP/V026763/1.

N. Benz et al. (Eds.): NFM 2024, LNCS 14627, pp. 136–143, 2024.
https://doi.org/10.1007/978-3-031-60698-4_8

to handle arithmetic problems involving integers and created an interface to SMT solvers. However, support for real arithmetic has, up to now, been notably absent, which represents a fundamental limitation that must be addressed before hybrid system verification in TLA^+ can become a practical endeavour.

Contributions. We extend TLAPM (the TLA^+ Proof Manager) to support real arithmetic, enabling automatic proofs using the Z3 SMT solver. In this work, we are concerned solely with decidable first-order real arithmetic conjectures.

Related Work. Our work is very close in spirit to that of Denman and Muñoz [2], who enabled automatic handling of real arithmetic conjectures in PVS [12] using an external oracle (MetiTarski [13]). Our work builds on an earlier effort by Merz et al. [11], who developed the TLA^+ Proof System (TLAPS), i.e., a proof manager for TLA^+ (TLAPM) and the infrastructure necessary for interfacing with SMT solvers (and who indeed commented that support for real numbers should be facilitated, which we carry through in this work). There exist a number of purpose-built theorem proving systems for reasoning about cyber-physical systems, such as KeYmaera X [3] and the HHL Prover [14], which likewise treat real arithmetic backends (e.g., Mathematica) as trusted external oracles.

2 Enabling Real Arithmetic in the TLA^+ Proof Manager

The TLA^+ Proof System (TLAPS) includes a proof manager which interfaces with backend verifiers. This enables the proof system to perform deductive verification of safety properties of TLA^+ specifications. The proof manager interprets the proofs, generates a set of proof obligations and directs them to a solver (trusted external oracle) such as Z3, Yices, etc. *Figure* 1 provides a partial representation of the TLAPS architecture in [1,9, §1], with an emphasis on

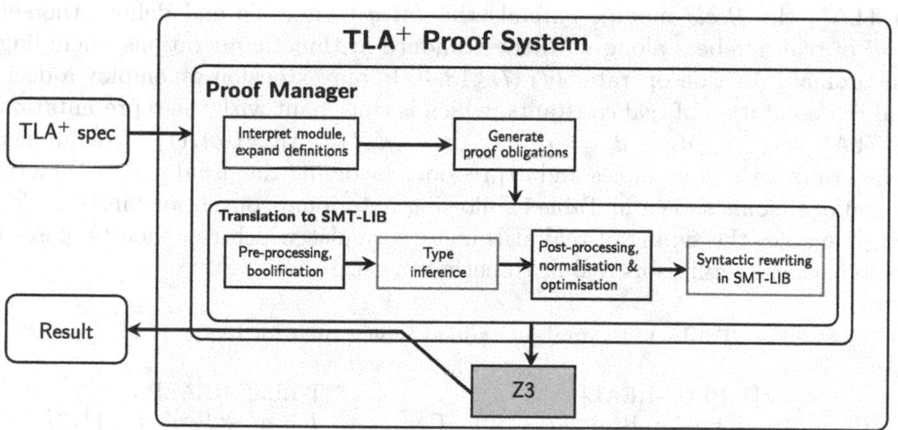

Fig. 1. TLAPS architecture with the Z3 backend

the components we updated in this work. The basic operations including pre-processing, boolification, post-processing, normalisation and optimisation performed by the proof manager are described in detail in [9–11]. The components with a red outline in *Fig.* 1 depict the changes to the *SMT translation* process that we made in order to support the proving of real arithmetic conjectures using Z3. TLAPS features a *type inference* algorithm that assigns types to the untyped TLA$^+$ variables and values; this is updated to interpret reals (see *Sect.* 2.1). During the *syntactic rewriting* stage, TLA$^+$ expressions are encoded in the SMT-LIB language, at which point they are ready to be passed to a backend verifier. In the latter stage, an alternative *untyped encoding* process can be employed to instead delegate type inference to the SMT-solvers. This process requires new lifting axioms to assert that TLA$^+$ arithmetic coincides with the SMT arithmetic over reals (described in *Sect.* 2.2). The implementation of the extended TLAPM supporting real arithmetic can be found in [5].

2.1 Typed Encodings

TLA$^+$ is an untyped language. Hence, type encoding is required to assign types to the untyped variables and values. Assigning types enforces restrictions on admissible formulas that can be directed to the backend verifiers. This operation is performed by a type inference algorithm consisting of a constraint generation and solving phase. The result of the constraint generation phase is a set of constraints based on the type environment, a TLA$^+$ expression and a type variable. The constraint generation rules are derived from the corresponding typing rules, and the constraint solving phase solves the equality and subtyping constraints and proves some residual subtype checking constraints [10].

To enable the interpretation of TLA$^+$ expressions containing reals, we extend the type system and type inference algorithm developed by Merz et al. in [10] by introducing a new type *Real*, i.e., $\tau ::= Real$ to the existing grammar that describes the supported types and introducing a set of additional typing rules. In TLA$^+$, the *Reals* module extends the *Integers* module and defines the set *Real* of real numbers along with the standard arithmetic operations, including the ordinary division operator (/) [7, §18.4]. In our extension we employ a decimal representation of real constants, which is consonant with the representation in TLA$^+$ ($c_1 \dots c_m.d_1 \dots d_n \triangleq c_1 \dots c_m d_1 \dots d_n / 10^n$ [7, §16.1.11]). We further define rules for real variables and expressions involving the usual real arithmetic operations (some shown in Table 1 following notational conventions in [10, §3]), which enables the typing of real arithmetic formulas which can then be passed on to backend verifiers as real arithmetic conjectures.

Table 1. Examples of added typing rules for Reals

[T-PLUS-REAL]	[T-LESS-REAL]
$\dfrac{\Gamma \vdash e_i : a_i \quad \Gamma \vdash a_i \prec: \text{Real} \quad i \in \{1,2\}}{\Gamma \vdash e_1 + e_2 : \{x : \text{Real} \mid x = e_1 + e_2\}}$	$\dfrac{\Gamma \vdash e_i : a_i \quad \Gamma \vdash a_i \prec: \text{Real} \quad i \in \{1,2\}}{\Gamma \vdash e_1 < e_2 : \text{Bool}}$

2.2 Untyped Encodings

Untyped encodings for TLA$^+$ formulas are an alternative encoding method implemented in TLAPS, where type inference is delegated to the SMT solver. The reader may find a helpful discussion of some of the advantages afforded by using this kind of encoding in [9,10], along with some of the disadvantages which may carry a performance penalty.

With untyped encoding, a single SMT sort U is used to represent TLA$^+$ values and its operators are represented as uninterpreted functions having sort U as their arguments [9]. In order to encode real arithmetic formulas, we declare uninterpreted functions that embed SMT reals into the sort U representing TLA$^+$ values, i.e., $real2u : \mathsf{Real} \rightarrow \mathsf{U}$ and $u2real : \mathsf{U} \rightarrow \mathsf{Real}$. Real represents SMT reals, *real2u* embeds SMT reals into a sort U representing TLA$^+$ values and *u2real* performs the reverse. This is supported by the axiom $\forall m \in \mathsf{Real} : u2real(real2u(m)) = m$ to ensure the consistency and soundness of translating SMT reals into the sort U. Real arithmetic operations over TLA$^+$ values are homomorphically defined over the image of *real2u* using axioms. In the axiom $\forall m, n \in \mathsf{Real} : plus(real2u(m), real2u(n)) = real2u(m + n)$, the $+$ operation on the right-hand side denotes the built-in addition operation over SMT reals, while *plus* has function type $\mathsf{U} \times \mathsf{U} \rightarrow \mathsf{U}$. Similar axioms are defined for other real arithmetic operations and utilise the existing uninterpreted functions for operators that are introduced by Merz et al. in [9,10].

Remark 1. At present, Z3 is the default real arithmetic backend; however, other tools exist which likewise accept SMT-LIB input and could serve as alternatives. It must be noted that some of these tools (e.g., MetiTarski [13]) can only work with SMT-LIB inputs of a particular form and would not be able to handle problems in the untyped SMT encoding as described above.

3 Safety Verification of Cyber-Physical Systems

As an illustrative example of safety verification that involves real-valued variables, we will use a model of an oscillator. The motion of a simple harmonic oscillator, such as a mass m suspended from a spring (with spring constant k) can be described by a second-order differential equation $\ddot{x} + \omega^2 x = 0$, where $\omega = \sqrt{\frac{k}{m}}$ is the frequency of oscillation, the state variable x measures the displacement of the mass from the point of equilibrium and $\ddot{x}$ represents the second derivative of x with respect to time, i.e., the acceleration $\frac{d^2x}{dt^2}$. The dynamics of this system can be written down as a system of linear differential equations $\dot{x} = y,\ \dot{y} = -\omega^2 x$. For simplicity, let $m = 1$ and $k = 1$, so that the system becomes $\dot{x} = y,\ \dot{y} = -x$. The system can be geometrically represented as a *vector field* $\langle y, -x \rangle$ defined on the real plane (as shown in Fig. 2a). To reduce the amplitude of oscillations, a *damping term* $D(y)$ can be introduced into the system to yield a damped oscillator $\dot{x} = y,\ \dot{y} = -x - D(y)$ in which oscillations die down over time.

Let us consider a hybrid automaton (illustrated in Fig. 2b) with two modes evolving according the undamped (mode q_1) and damped oscillator dynamics (mode q_2). In this model, the system switches on damping when the displacement x falls below -2 (this could be done e.g., to prevent damage to the spring).Let us suppose that the initial displacement x_0 of the oscillator is only known to be within the bounds $-\frac{1}{2} \leq x_0 \leq \frac{1}{2}$ and the initial velocity y_0 is in the range $1 \leq y_0 \leq \frac{3}{2}$. From this set of initial conditions we wish to prove that damping need never be applied (i.e., the hybrid automaton in Fig. 2b never transitions into mode q_2). There are a number of ways in which one can prove the safety specification described above. A common approach (which does *not* involve computing solutions to the differential equation) is to exhibit an appropriate *inductive invariant*, i.e., a set of states $I \subseteq \mathbb{R}^2$ such that all trajectories starting inside the invariant remain within the invariant. A standard proof of safety using an inductive invariant involves showing three things: (1.) that the proposed invariant is indeed inductive (i.e., that the system cannot transition outside the invariant), (2.) that all possible initial states of the system lie within the invariant, and (3.) that the invariant contains no *unsafe* states that are deemed undesirable. In order to prove our property of interest, we can employ an inductive invariant given by formula $x^2+y^2 < 4 \wedge x^2+y^2 \geq 1$, which corresponds an annular region illustrated in Fig. 2a, where it is seen to include all the initial states (represented by the grey box) and none of the unsafe states (shown in red) from which the system may transition into mode q_2 where damping is applied.

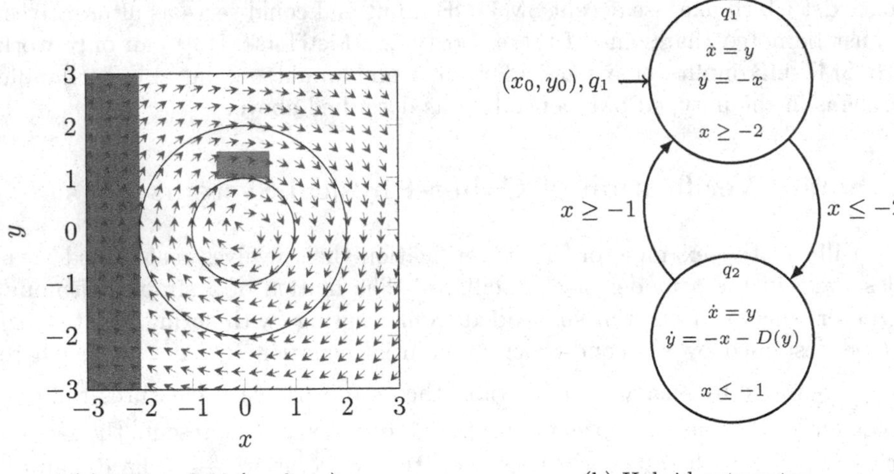

(a) Vector field (mode q_1)

(b) Hybrid automaton

Fig. 2. Hybrid system model of an oscillator

Several methods exist to check whether a proposed invariant is inductive (i.e., to solve (1.)); while these fall outside the scope of the present paper, these methods essentially reduce the problem to one of real arithmetic. In this example, the fact that x^2+y^2 is a conserved quantity can be established by checking that its time derivative $2x\dot{x}+2y\dot{y}$ is everywhere zero (i.e., $2xy-2yx=0$). For solving (2.) and (3.), the first-order theory of real arithmetic provides us with a formal language that is expressive enough to state properties such as inclusion or non-intersection of sets, provided that these are described using formulas that only involve *polynomials*. Establishing the inclusion of the initial states within the invariant and its non-intersection with the unsafe states in this example reduces to proving the following sentences:

$$\forall\, x, y \in \mathbb{R}.\ \underbrace{-0.5 \leq x \wedge x \leq 0.5 \wedge 1 \leq y \wedge y \leq 1.5}_{\text{Initial states}} \rightarrow \underbrace{x^2+y^2 < 4 \wedge x^2+y^2 \geq 1}_{\text{Invariant}},$$

$$\forall\, x, y \in \mathbb{R}.\ \neg \left(\underbrace{x \leq -2}_{\text{Unsafe}} \wedge \underbrace{x^2+y^2 < 4 \wedge x^2+y^2 \geq 1}_{\text{Invariant}} \right).$$

Figure 3 shows how these conjectures are represented in the TLA$^+$ syntax and solved using our implementation with Z3 as a real arithmetic backend.

```
EXTENDS TLAPS, Reals

(*
 * All possible initial states of the systems lie within the
 * proposed invariant Init => Inv. The conjecture is proven true.
 *)
THEOREM \A x,y \in Real: ((-0.5 <= x /\ x <= 0.5 /\ 1.0 <= y /\ y <= 1.5)
                          => ((x*x)+(y*y) < 4.0 /\ (x*x)+(y*y) >= 1.0))
                             BY Z3

(*
 * The invariant does not contain unsafe states.
 * ¬( Unsafe /\ Inv) The conjecture is proven true.
 *)
THEOREM \A x,y \in Real: ~((x <= - 2.0) /\ ((x*x) + (y*y) < 4.0  /\
                                          (x*x) + (y*y) >= 1.0)) BY Z3
```

Fig. 3. Hybrid system safety verification: real arithmetic conjectures (2.) and (3.)

Unlike hybrid automata, *discrete-time* dynamical systems can be modelled in TLA$^+$ in a straightforward way. Let us consider the following discrete-time system in which the state variables x and y take values in the real numbers:

$$x(t+1) = \frac{2x(t)}{3} + \frac{y(t)}{2},$$
$$y(t+1) = \frac{x(t)}{2} - \frac{y(t)}{3}.$$

Let us suppose that the system may be initialised from any state satisfying the formula $x^2 + y^2 \leq 1$ (i.e., $x(0)^2 + y(0)^2 \leq 1$) and that we wish to show that the absolute value of x can never exceed 1 as the system evolves. To prove this, let us take $x^2 + y^2 \leq 1$ as our candidate inductive invariant. The inclusion of all initial states within the invariant is trivial in this case, so it remains to show that (1.) no unsafe state satisfies $x^2 + y^2 \leq 1$, and (2.) $x^2 + y^2 \leq 1$ is an inductive invariant. To show (1.), one needs to prove that the invariant implies the safety of the system, i.e., that for all $x, y \in \mathbb{R}$ one has $x^2 + y^2 \leq 1 \rightarrow x \leq 1 \wedge x \geq -1$. To prove (2.) one needs to show that the set of states satisfying $x^2 + y^2 \leq 1$ is closed under the dynamics of the system. In TLA+ one may model the dynamics of such a system as follows:

```
x' = (2.0/3.0)*x + 0.5*y
y' = 0.5*x - (1.0/3.0)*y
```

where the primed symbols `x'` and `y'` stand for the value of the variables `x` and `y` in the next state. Showing that the invariant is inductive ultimately reduces to proving that the following implication holds for all $x, y, x', y' \in \mathbb{R}$:

$$\left(x^2 + y^2 \leq 1 \wedge x' = \frac{2}{3}x + \frac{1}{2}y \wedge y' = \frac{1}{2}x - \frac{1}{3}y\right) \rightarrow (x')^2 + (y')^2 \leq 1.$$

Proving safety specifications for discrete-time systems such as the one above in TLA+ can now be done conveniently with the help of the extended proof manager.

4 Conclusion

We have developed support in the TLA+ Proof Manager for handling first-order real arithmetic sentences. Real arithmetic problems arise naturally in the verification of hybrid and cyber-physical systems and our work represents a step towards facilitating their formal verification using TLA+. Currently, our implementation employs only Z3 as a real arithmetic backend; however, we note the potential for supporting additional backends in the future. In particular, tools such as MetiTarski [13] and dReal [4] can – in addition to serving as alternative real arithmetic backends – enable reasoning about *special functions* (such as $\sin, \cos, \ln, e$, etc., the presence of which makes real arithmetic *undecidable*). The TLA+ Proof Manager currently does not offer support for working with these kinds of functions and further extensions to the system could be pursued to enable this functionality.

References

1. Chaudhuri, K., et al.: GitHub: the TLA$^+$ proof manager. https://github.com/tlaplus/tlapm. Accessed December 2023
2. Denman, W., Muñoz, C.: Automated real proving in PVS via MetiTarski. In: Jones, C., Pihlajasaari, P., Sun, J. (eds.) FM 2014. LNCS, vol. 8442, pp. 194–199. Springer, Cham (2014). https://doi.org/10.1007/978-3-319-06410-9_14
3. Fulton, N., Mitsch, S., Quesel, J.-D., Völp, M., Platzer, A.: KeYmaera X: an axiomatic tactical theorem prover for hybrid systems. In: Felty, A.P., Middeldorp, A. (eds.) CADE 2015. LNCS (LNAI), vol. 9195, pp. 527–538. Springer, Cham (2015). https://doi.org/10.1007/978-3-319-21401-6_36
4. Gao, S., Kong, S., Clarke, E.M.: dReal: an SMT solver for nonlinear theories over the reals. In: Bonacina, M.P. (ed.) CADE 2013. LNCS (LNAI), vol. 7898, pp. 208–214. Springer, Heidelberg (2013). https://doi.org/10.1007/978-3-642-38574-2_14
5. Gunasekera, O.V.W.: GitHub: TLA$^+$ proof system with real arithmetic support. https://github.com/Ovini99/TLAPS_Real. Accessed December 2023
6. Lamport, L.: Hybrid systems in TLA$^+$. In: Grossman, R.L., Nerode, A., Ravn, A.P., Rischel, H. (eds.) HS 1991-1992. LNCS, vol. 736, pp. 77–102. Springer, Heidelberg (1993). https://doi.org/10.1007/3-540-57318-6_25
7. Lamport, L.: Specifying Systems: The TLA$^+$ Language and Tools for Hardware and Software Engineers. Addison-Wesley (2002). https://www.microsoft.com/en-us/research/uploads/prod/2018/05/book-02-08-08.pdf
8. Lamport, L.: Industrial use of TLA$^+$ (2019). https://lamport.azurewebsites.net/tla/industrial-use.html. Accessed March 2023
9. Merz, S., Vanzetto, H.: Harnessing SMT solvers for TLA$^+$ proofs. Electron. Commun. EASST **53** (2012). https://doi.org/10.14279/TUJ.ECEASST.53.766
10. Merz, S., Vanzetto, H.: Refinement types for TLA$^+$. In: Badger, J.M., Rozier, K.Y. (eds.) NFM 2014. LNCS, vol. 8430, pp. 143–157. Springer, Cham (2014). https://doi.org/10.1007/978-3-319-06200-6_11
11. Merz, S., Vanzetto, H.: Encoding TLA$^+$ into many-sorted first-order logic. In: Butler, M., Schewe, K.-D., Mashkoor, A., Biro, M. (eds.) ABZ 2016. LNCS, vol. 9675, pp. 54–69. Springer, Cham (2016). https://doi.org/10.1007/978-3-319-33600-8_3
12. Owre, S., Rushby, J.M., Shankar, N.: PVS: a prototype verification system. In: Kapur, D. (ed.) CADE 1992. LNCS, vol. 607, pp. 748–752. Springer, Heidelberg (1992). https://doi.org/10.1007/3-540-55602-8_217
13. Paulson, L.C.: MetiTarski: past and future. In: Beringer, L., Felty, A. (eds.) ITP 2012. LNCS, vol. 7406, pp. 1–10. Springer, Heidelberg (2012). https://doi.org/10.1007/978-3-642-32347-8_1
14. Wang, S., Zhan, N., Zou, L.: An improved HHL prover: an interactive theorem prover for hybrid systems. In: Butler, M., Conchon, S., Zaïdi, F. (eds.) ICFEM 2015. LNCS, vol. 9407, pp. 382–399. Springer, Cham (2015). https://doi.org/10.1007/978-3-319-25423-4_25

References

SMT-Based Assurance of Behavioral Specifications

Deductive Model Refinement

Douglas R. Smith[1(✉)] and Srinivas Nedunuri[2]

[1] Kestrel Institute, Palo Alto, CA 94304, USA
smith@kestrel.edu
[2] Sandia National Laboratories, Livermore, CA 94550, USA
snedunu@sandia.gov

Abstract. Deductive model refinement (hereafter simply "model refinement") is a uniform approach to generating correct-by-construction designs for algorithms and systems from formal specifications. Given an overapproximating model $\mathcal{M}$ of system dynamics and a set Φ of required properties, model refinement is an iterative process that eliminates behaviors of $\mathcal{M}$ that do not satisfy the required properties. The result of model refinement is a refined model $\mathcal{M}'$ that satisfies by construction the required properties Φ. The calculations needed to generate refinements of $\mathcal{M}$ typically involve quantifier elimination and extensive formula/term simplification modulo the underlying domain theories. This paper focuses on the enforcement of basic safety properties in the form of state, action, and path invariants. We have run a prototype implementation of model refinement based on the Z3 SMT solver over a variety of system and algorithm design problems.

Keywords: Refinement · model-based design · formal specification · reactive synthesis · function synthesis · program synthesis

1 Introduction

Formal specifications characterize the acceptable behaviors of a desired program. Among the various means for specifying requirements on a desired program are (1) *logical specifications* in which predicates expressed in a suitable logic decide the desired behaviors, and (2) *models* whose computable behaviors are a superset or overapproximation of the desired behaviors. We view logical specifications and models as having complementary strengths and believe that their combination can lead to simpler and more natural specifications of systems and algorithms.

This paper comes from a complementary line of formal development research that explores automatic transformations that map a specification or intermediate design to an equivalent form or to a correct-by-construction refinement. The field of *program synthesis* focuses on automatic generation of programs from formal specifications using such transformations. Obviously, any formal development process will benefit to the extent that refinement steps can be automatically generated. Human insight is still needed to choose appropriate transformations and to specify how to apply them.

N. Benz et al. (Eds.): NFM 2024, LNCS 14627, pp. 147–165, 2024.
https://doi.org/10.1007/978-3-031-60698-4_9

In this paper we propose a unifying synthesis framework, called *deductive model refinement* (or simply model refinement), that starts with a formal specification comprised of models and logical properties. From a given model and logical properties, we define a constraint system that characterizes refinements of the model that satisfy the logical properties. Solving the constraint system corresponds to eliminating undesired behaviors from the model. Model refinement serves to unify and extend previous work on function/algorithm synthesis with reactive system synthesis.

Given a model $\mathcal{M}$ that overapproximates desired behaviors and a set Φ of required properties, the goal of model refinement is to generate the least refinement $\mathcal{M}'$ of model $\mathcal{M}$ such that $\mathcal{M}'$ satisfies the specified properties Φ (where the refinement relation defines a lattice of models). If the set of legal initial states in $\mathcal{M}'$ differs from the initial states of $\mathcal{M}$, then the difference characterizes the set of initial states from which the system does not have any acceptable behaviors.

Overapproximating models can arise in a variety of ways. For control system problems, the model captures the dynamics of a physical asset (aka the "plant") to be controlled. In software system design, the model captures the APIs and possible operations of a component and perhaps a restricted grammar for expressing programs [1]. In general system design, a model can express a system design pattern [4,9,22]. In algorithm design, a model can reflect the imposition of a parametric solution pattern, such as an algorithm theory [29] or a sketch [34].

Model refinement techniques are common in science and engineering. Our approach is called *deductive model refinement* due to the use of deductive techniques to enforce logical requirement properties on a model. Examples of data-driven or inductive model refinement can be found in (1) statistical model estimation techniques that fit, say, a Bayesian Network model to given data, and (2) machine learning techniques for refining an artificial neural network model with training data. In these examples the model provides the abstract computational pattern and the data provides the requirements on the refined model.

This paper focuses on enforcement of basic safety properties. In [30], we introduce a wider fragment of temporal logic that can be reduced to the basic safety fragment. Most current work on the synthesis of reactive systems focuses on circuit design and starts with specifications in propositional Linear Temporal Logic (LTL) [3,13]. It is therefore limited to finite state models. Our approach to model refinement allows specifications that are first-order and uses a temporal logic of action (similar to TLA [15]) that is amenable to refinement, allowing possibly-infinite state spaces and allowing a broader range of applications to be tackled.

Model refinement is intended to support highly automated refinement-generating tools that produce correct-by-construction designs together with checkable proofs. One barrier to automation is the computational complexity of formula simplification in the application domain theories that support the specification. When the domain theories are decidable (e.g. by SMT solvers) and admit quantifier elimination, then model refinement can run fully automatically. We have used our Z3-based prototype to perform model refinement on a variety of examples, each solvable in a few seconds or minutes.

Our novel contributions include

1. a uniform framework for specifying algorithms and reactive systems by a combination of overapproximating behavioral models and logical specifications of required behavior,
2. a characterization of model refinement via a system of definite constraints that can be efficiently solved by fixpoint-iteration procedures,
3. a variety of examples to show the breadth of the technique,
4. a prototype implementation based on the Z3 SMT-solver [28].

After introducing basic concepts, the paper first focuses on reactive system synthesis as constraint-solving via iterated constraint propagation, with examples. Function specifications that arise during reactive system synthesis then provide a natural segue into a treatment of function/algorithm synthesis as generalized iterated constraint propagation over paths.

2 Preliminaries

2.1 Required Properties

We focus on safety properties formulated in a simple linear temporal logic of actions, similar to Lamport's TLA [15]. A *state* is a (type-consistent) map from variables to values. *State predicates* are boolean expressions formed over the variables of a state and the constants (including functions) relevant to an application domain. A state predicate p denotes a relation $[\![p]\!]$ over states, so $p(s)$ denotes the truth value $[\![p]\!](s)$ for state s. *Actions* are boolean expressions formed over variables, primed variables, and the constants (including functions) relevant to an application domain. An action a specifies a state transition and it denotes a predicate $[\![a]\!]$ over a pair of states, and $a(s,t)$ denotes the truth value $[\![a]\!](s,t)$ for states s and t. The expression $x' = x + 1 + y$ is a typical action where the unprimed variables refer to the first state and primed variables refer to the second state.

A *basic safety property* (or simply a safety property) has the form φ or $\Box\varphi$ where φ is a state predicate or an action. The truth of a safety property φ at position n of a trace σ (an infinite sequence of states), written $\sigma, n \models \varphi$, is defined as follows:

- $\sigma, n \models p$, for p a state predicate, if p holds at state $\sigma[n]$, i.e. $[\![p]\!](\sigma[n])$;
- $\sigma, n \models a$, for a an action, if a holds over the states $\sigma[n], \sigma[n+1]$, i.e. $[\![a]\!](\sigma[n], \sigma[n+1])$;
- $\sigma, n \models \Box\varphi$ if $\sigma, i \models \varphi$ for all $i \geq n$.

2.2 Behavioral Models

Formally, a model is a *labeled control flow graph* (LCFG) $\mathcal{M} = \langle \mathcal{V}, N, A, \mathcal{L} \rangle$ where

- $\mathcal{V}$: a countable set of variables; implicitly each variable has a type with a finite (typically first-order) specification of the predicates and functions that provides vocabulary for expressions and constrains their meaning via axioms. The aggregation of these variable specifications is called the *application domain theory* (or simply domain theory) of the problem at hand.
- N: a finite set of nodes. Associated with each node $m \in N$, we have a finite subset of observable variables $V(m) \subseteq \mathcal{V}$. N has a distinguished node m_0 that is the initial node. An LCFG is *arc-like* if it also has a designated final node m_f.
- A: a finite set of directed arcs, $A \subseteq N \times N$. Each node m has an identity self-transition $id_m = \langle m, m \rangle$, called *stutter*, that changes the values of no observable variables.
- $\mathcal{L}$: a set of labels. For each node $m \in N$, we have a label $L_m \in \mathcal{L}$ that is a state predicate over $V(m)$ representing a node invariant. For each arc $a = \langle m, n \rangle$, label $L_a \in \mathcal{L}$ is an action over $V(m)$, $V(n)$, and auxiliary variables e and u which are discussed below.

In reactive system design, it is commonly the case that the variables at all nodes are the same, so $V(m) = V(n)$ for all nodes $m, n \in N$ and all variables are global. In functional algorithm design it is typical that the variables at each node are disjoint, effectively treating all variables as local to a unique node. Most programming languages, of course, support models that have both global and local variables.

To simplify notation, we often write $L_m(st_m)$ to denote $st_m \models L_m(V(m))$ (and similarly for arc labels). A node m denotes the set of states $[\![m]\!] = \{st \mid L_m(st)\}$. The label L_{m_0} is the *initial condition* of the model and denotes the set of initial states.

Arc label L_a generally specifies a nondeterministic action, whose nondeterminism may be reduced under refinement. In reactive systems, which have a game-like character, some of the nondeterminism is due to the uncontrollable behavior of the environment or an adversarial agent. For refinement purposes, it is necessary to specify which parts of the nondeterminism are refinable and which are unrefinable. Accordingly, the label L_a of an action has the general form:

$$L_a(st_m, e, u, st_n) \equiv e \in E_a(st_m) \wedge U_a(st_m, u) \wedge st_n = f_a(st_m, u, e)$$

where

1. e is treated as an uncontrollable Environment or adversary input that ranges over the unrefinable set $E_a(st_m)$;
2. u is treated as a controllable value that satisfies the refinable constraint $U_a(st_m, u)$;
3. function f_a gives the deterministic response of the action.

The variability of the control value specifies the refinable part of $L_a(st_m, e, u, st_n)$. This kind of formulation of actions is common in modeling discrete and continuous control systems [35]. Let

$$[\![a]\!] = \{\langle st_m, st_n\rangle \mid \exists e, u.\ L_a(st_m, e, u, st_n)\}.$$

Note that e and u are independent of each other. Alternative formulations are easily made in which one depends on the other.

Semantics. A *trace* is a possibly infinite sequence of states. An LCFG $\mathcal{M} = \langle \mathcal{V}, N, A, \mathcal{L}\rangle$ generates a trace $tr = st_0, st_1, \ldots$ if

1. Initially, st_0 is a legal state of the initial node m_0, i.e. $st_0 \in [\![m_0]\!]$;
2. Inductively, if $i \geq 0$ and st_i is a legal state of node m, i.e. $st_i \in [\![m]\!]$, then there exists arc $a = \langle m, n\rangle$ where $\langle st_i, st_{i+1}\rangle \in [\![a]\!]$ and where st_{i+1} is a legal state of node n; i.e. $st_{i+1} \in [\![n]\!]$.

$[\![\mathcal{M}]\!]$ is the set of all traces that can be generated by $\mathcal{M}$.

A node m and a legal state st_m is *nonblocking* if there is an arc $a = \langle m, n\rangle$ and control choice u such that $U_a(st_m, u)$ and a transitions to a legal state of n regardless of the environment input. In game-theoretic terms, if all reachable nodes and states of the model are nonblocking, then the system has a winning strategy. A key part of model refinement is the elimination of blocking states in the model.

2.3 Specification and Refinement

Refinement of LCFG model $\mathcal{M}_1$ to model $\mathcal{M}_2$ is a preorder relation, written $\mathcal{M}_1 \sqsubseteq \mathcal{M}_2$, that holds when there exists a *simulation map* $\xi : \mathcal{M}_2 \rightarrow \mathcal{M}_1$ that maps the nodes and arcs of $\mathcal{M}_2$ to the nodes and arcs of $\mathcal{M}_1$; i.e. where $\xi : N^{\mathcal{M}_2} \rightarrow N^{\mathcal{M}_1}$ and $\xi : A^{\mathcal{M}_2} \rightarrow A^{\mathcal{M}_1}$ such that

1. Initial nodes are preserved: $\xi(m_0^{\mathcal{M}_2}) = m_0^{\mathcal{M}_1}$;
2. Observable variables: $V^{\mathcal{M}_2}(m) \supseteq V^{\mathcal{M}_1}(\xi(m))$ for each node $m \in N^{\mathcal{M}_2}$;
3. Node labels: $L_m^{\mathcal{M}_2} \implies L_{\xi(m)}^{\mathcal{M}_1}$ for each node $m \in N^{\mathcal{M}_2}$;
4. Arc labels: $L_a^{\mathcal{M}_2} \implies L_{\xi(a)}^{\mathcal{M}_1}$ for each arc $a \in A^{\mathcal{M}_2}$.

There are several kinds of transformations of models that generate refinements, including (1) strengthening the invariant at a node, and (2) strengthening the action at an arc. These are used in the model refinement procedure in the next section. A third transformation, *arc refinement*, replaces an arc by an arc-like LCFG. This transformation may be used when imposing a design pattern or program scheme as a constraint on how to achieve the action of the arc. An example of this is given in Sect. 5.1.

A *specification* $\mathcal{S} = \langle \mathcal{M}, \Phi\rangle$ is comprised of a model $\mathcal{M}$ and a set of properties Φ that we require to incorporate or enforce in $\mathcal{M}$. A specification denotes the set of traces generable by $\mathcal{M}$ that also satisfy all properties in Φ:

$$[\![\mathcal{S}]\!] = \{tr \mid tr \in [\![\mathcal{M}]\!] \wedge tr \models \Phi\} = [\![\mathcal{M}]\!] \cap [\![\Phi]\!].$$

Refinement of specification $\mathcal{S}$ to specification $\mathcal{T}$ is a preorder relation, written $\mathcal{S} \sqsubseteq \mathcal{T}$, that holds when there is a mapping ξ from traces of $\mathcal{T}$ to traces of $\mathcal{S}$ such that

$$\forall \sigma . \sigma \in [\![\mathcal{T}]\!] \implies \xi(\sigma) \in [\![\mathcal{S}]\!]$$

or more succinctly $\xi([\![\mathcal{T}]\!]) \subseteq [\![\mathcal{S}]\!]$.

Theorem 1. If (1) $\mathcal{S}_1 = \langle \mathcal{M}_1, \Phi_1 \rangle$ and $\mathcal{S}_2 = \langle \mathcal{M}_2, \Phi_2 \rangle$ are specifications, (2) $\xi : \mathcal{M}_2 \to \mathcal{M}_1$ is a simulation map, and (3) $\Phi_2 \implies \Phi_1$, then $\mathcal{S}_1 \sqsubseteq \mathcal{S}_2$.

The proof, given in [30], shows how ξ induces a map $\hat{\xi}$ of traces of $\mathcal{S}_2$ such that $\hat{\xi}([\![\mathcal{S}_2]\!]) \subseteq [\![\mathcal{S}_1]\!]$.

3 Model Refinement as Constraint Solving

Model refinement transforms a model $\mathcal{M}$ and required properties Φ into a model $\mathcal{M}'$ such that $\mathcal{M} \sqsubseteq \mathcal{M}' \wedge \mathcal{M}' \models \Phi$. We define now a constraint system whose solutions correspond to refinements of $\mathcal{M}$ that satisfy Φ. The intent is to find the greatest solution of the constraint system, which corresponds to the minimal refinement of $\mathcal{M}$ that satisfies Φ. In later sections we discuss several situations in which only a near-greatest solution can be found.

In formulating model refinement as a constraint satisfaction problem, we treat the node labels L_m and arc labels L_a as variables, whose assigned values are state and action predicates, respectively. We can view the constraint system as taking place in the Boolean lattice of formulas with implication as the partial order (i.e. a Tarski-Lindenbaum algebra). Each constraint provides an upper bound on feasible values of one variable. A feasible solution to the constraint system is an assignment of formulas to each variable that satisfies all the constraints of the system. We discuss below how to assure finite convergence of the constraint solving process as the lattice is typically of infinite height for nonpropositional logics.

For arc $a = \langle m, n \rangle$, arc label L_a, and node label L_n, let $wcp(L_a, L_n)$ be the *weakest controllable predecessor* predicate transformer which is defined by

$$wcp(L_a, L_n) \equiv \forall e.\, e \in E(st_m) \implies \exists st_n.\, st_n = f_a(st_m, e, u) \wedge L_n(st_n)$$

or, simply

$$wcp(L_a, L_n) \equiv \forall e.\, e \in E(st_m) \implies L_n(f_a(st_m, e, u)).$$

$wcp(L_a, L_n)$ is the weakest formula over $V(m) \bigcup \{u\}$ such that for any environment input e the transition a is assured to reach a state st_n satisfying the post-state predicate L_n. Its effect is to define the nonblocking states of node m

```
if φ is a state predicate
    then for all m ∈ N : L_m ← L_m ∧ φ
    else for all a ∈ A : L_a ← L_a ∧ φ
do
    for all a ∈ A : U_a ← U_a ∧ wcp(L_a, L_n)
    for all m ∈ N : L_m ← L_m ∧  ⋁_{a=⟨m,n⟩} ∃u. U_a
until L_m is unchanged for all nodes m ∈ N.
```

Fig. 1. Model Refinement Algorithm

– those states from which there is some control value that forces the transition to a legal state at n regardless of the environment input.

The constraint system is comprised of the following four sets of constraints for each required temporal property $\Box\varphi$:

1. **Node Localization:** $L_m \implies \varphi$ for each node $m \in N$ if φ is a state predicate expressed over the variables at m;
2. **Arc Localization:** $L_a \implies \varphi$ for each arc $a = \langle m, n\rangle \in A$ if φ is an action predicate expressed over the variables at m and n;
3. **Control Constraint:** $U_a \implies wcp(L_a, L_n)$ for each arc $a = \langle m, n\rangle$
4. **Node Invariant:** $L_m \implies \bigvee_{a=\langle m,n\rangle} \exists u.\, U_a$ for each node $m \in N$.

The Localization constraints (1) and (2) provide upper bounds on the node labels. The Control constraints (3) are the essentially synthetic aspect of model refinement as they serve to eliminate any state transitions in which the environment can force the system to a state not satisfying the safety properties. The Node Invariant constraints (4) serve to eliminate blocking states of a node with respect to all of its outgoing arcs. Given a specification $\mathcal{S} = \langle M, \Phi\rangle$, the model refinement transformation refines the specification by solving the constraint system. In other words, a solution to the constraints is a model that refines the input model and the solution process generates a refinement.

A straightforward algorithm for solving the constraint system over the labels on a model is presented in Fig. 1. The iteration converges to a fixpoint when the labels do not change in an iteration. Upon convergence to a refined model $\mathcal{M}'$, we have $[\![\mathcal{M}']\!] \subseteq [\![\mathcal{M}]\!] \cap [\![\Phi]\!]$, and in the case that the algorithm converges to a greatest fixpoint we have $[\![\mathcal{M}']\!] = [\![\mathcal{M}]\!] \cap [\![\Phi]\!]$. The algorithm in [21] provides a more efficient control strategy that exploits dependencies between the constraints.

The *derived initial condition* is the final refined invariant L_{m_0} which characterizes the set of nonblocking initial states from which the system can ensure that all behaviors satisfy the specified safety properties. In a model-checking scenario where the model doesn't check, the derived initial condition may provide a useful characterization of the model's failure.

The correctness of this algorithm is a consequence of Tarski's theorem. Each constraint has definite form $v \leq g(v)$ where g is monotone, so we can express solutions as fixpoints of $v = g(v)$. As we are looking for the most general (i.e. least refinement of the initial model), the algorithm aims to converge on the greatest fixpoint using a Kleene iteration. If the state space is finite, then the fixpoint iteration process will be finite too. In fact, the number of iterations is linear in the height of the lattice [21]. Techniques to improve the complexity of the algorithm and to guarantee convergence to a fixpoint are further discussed in [30].

Example: Packet Flow Control
In this example, based on [23], a buffer is used to control and smooth the flow of packets in a communication system. We model this problem as in discrete control theory with a plant (a buffer of length *buf*), environment input e, and control value u. The environment supplies a stream of packets that varies up to 4 packets per time unit. The plant is modeled by a single linear transition that updates the state of the plant. The goal is to assure that the system keeps no more than 20 packets in the buffer *buf* and keeps the outflow rate *out* at no more than 4 packets per time unit.

This is a classical discrete control problem with a single node and a single linear transition. It can be specified by the following TLA-like notation for an LCFG, which lists (1) the global state variables, (2) their initial invariants, (3) the one node, (4) the one arc and its initial action (dependent on environment input e and control value u), (5) the required safety properties, and (6) currently known theorems, which are empty here but are extended by the model refinement process.

Specification FC0
  Vars: $buf, out : Integer$
  Invariant: $0 \leq buf \wedge 0 \leq out$
  Node: m_0
  Arc: $a = \langle m_0, m_0 \rangle : -1 \leq u \leq 1 \ \wedge\ 0 \leq e \leq 4$
    $\wedge\ buf' = buf + e - out \ \wedge\ out' = out + u$
  Required Properties
    $buf = 0$
    $out = 0$
    $\Box\, 0 \leq buf \ \wedge\ buf \leq 20 \ \wedge\ 0 \leq out \ \wedge\ out \leq 4$
  Theorems
End Specification

The first two required properties determine the initial state values. For the last required property, the algorithm in Fig. 1 instantiates *wcp* to generate the following formula as an upper bound on the control condition

$$U(buf, out, u) \equiv -1 \leq u \leq 1 \ \wedge\ 0 \leq out + u \leq 4$$
$$\wedge\ \forall e.\, 0 \leq e \leq 4 \implies 0 \leq buf + e - out \leq 20.$$

This formula is in the language of integer linear arithmetic which admits quantifier elimination and our Z3-based prototype simplifies it to the equivalent of

$$1 \leq buf - out \leq 16 \ \wedge \ 0 \leq out + u \leq 4.$$

According to the algorithm in Fig. 1, the control condition $U(buf, out, u)$ strengthens to

$$-1 \leq u \leq 1 \ \wedge \ 1 \leq buf - out \leq 16 \ \wedge \ 0 \leq out + u \leq 4$$

and the state invariant strengthens to

$$0 \leq buf \ \wedge \ 0 \leq out \ \wedge \ 1 \leq out - buf \leq 16.$$

Next, our prototype simplifies the control condition with respect to the strengthened state invariant, and the control condition becomes

$$-1 \leq u \leq 1 \ \wedge \ 0 \leq out + u \leq 4.$$

Since the control condition for the sole transition has changed, the iteration continues. For this problem convergence happens after four iterations and generates the following refined model, in which the required properties are enforced by construction and so they become theorems of the model, as can be verified by a model checker.

Specification FC1
  Vars: $buf, out : Integer = 0$
  Invariant: $0 \leq out \leq 4 \wedge 0 \leq buf - out \leq 16$
    $\wedge - 3 \leq buf - 3 * out \leq 11 \wedge -6 \leq buf - 4 * out \leq 10$
  Node: m_0
  Arc: $a = \langle m_0, m_0 \rangle : \ -1 \leq u \leq 1 \wedge \ 0 \leq out + u \leq 4 \wedge \ 0 \leq e \leq 4$
    $\wedge \ -6 \leq buf - 4 * u - 5 * out \leq 6$
    $\wedge \ -1 \leq buf - 2 * u - 3 * out \leq 9$
    $\wedge \ buf' = buf + e - out \wedge \ out' = out + u$
  Theorems: $buf = 0 \wedge out = 0 \wedge \Box \ (0 \leq buf \leq 20 \wedge 0 \leq out \leq 4)$
End Specification

Again, note how the Required Properties of the initial model have been transformed into Theorems of the refined model, by construction. The strengthened state invariant on node m_0 is also the derived initial condition and specifies the set of initial states from which we have assurance that the system will keep within the required bounds regardless of environment inputs.

The refined transition now defines a somewhat complex polyhedron around the control values. If there are no more required properties to enforce, then the next step will be to synthesize a control function that selects a specific control value u in each given state. For game-like problems, this is also known as extracting a winning strategy for the system game modulo the derived initial conditions.

Our prototype model refinement system converges on the model above in a few seconds. The version of this problem in which the variables are Reals or Rationals, with an infinite state space, is also solved in a small number of iterations in a few seconds, with a different invariant polytope and derived initial condition defining the safe operating space.

Other Examples

The Cinderella-Stepmother game has been posed as a challenge problem for synthesis systems (cf. [2]). It is a turn-based game between Cinderella and her wicked stepmother. The game centers on a ring of five buckets that can each hold up to c units of water, where initially the buckets are empty. In each round of the game the stepmother adds one unit of water distributed over the buckets, and then Cinderella empties two adjacent buckets. If any of the buckets ever overflow, then the stepmother wins, otherwise Cinderella wins.

Specification Cinderella-Stepmother

Vars: $b_0, b_1, b_2, b_3, b_4, c : NonNegativeReal$

$e_0, e_1, e_2, e_3, e_4 : NonNegativeReal$

Invariant: $\bigwedge_{i=0,4} b_i = 0$

Nodes: m_C, m_S

Arc: $Add = \langle m_S, m_C \rangle : \sum_{i=0,4} b'_i = 1 + \sum_{i=0,4} b_i$

$\wedge \ \bigwedge_{i=0,4} b'_i = b_i + e_i$

Arc: $Empty = \langle m_C, m_S \rangle : b'_u = 0 \wedge b'_{(u+1)\%5} = 0$

Required Properties: $\Box \bigwedge_{i=0,4} b_i \leq c$

End Specification

Our specification for this game-like problem has two nodes, one for the turn or each player. The game is parametric on a real value $c > 0$ used to define the Stepmother's (antagonist's) task. In [2], a controller for the game is found using sketches as hints to the solver. It is conjectured that automatic solutions (i.e. without human-provided hints) are "unrealistic" for values of c in range [1.5,3] (the problem is relatively easy outside that range). Our model refinement prototype automatically generates winning strategies in that range using roughly a minute of CPU time.

Other problems for which we have synthesized code include the classic readers-writers problem, elevator control, model-repair [2], and a reactive controller for a secure enclave. The latter problem has time-bounded responsive requirements and in [30] we introduce transformations that reduce a collection of time-bounded temporal operators to basic safety properties. After that reduction then the model refinement algorithm can be applied.

4 Function Synthesis

Model refinement naturally gives rise to the specification of several functions. For example, in the final model of the Flow Control example, the action constrains the control choice u to satisfy

$$-1 \leq u \leq 1 \wedge 0 \leq out+u \leq 4 \wedge -6 \leq buf-4*u-5*out \leq 6 \wedge -1 \leq buf-2*u-3*out \leq 9. \quad (1)$$

To make that choice, we must synthesize a control function

$$FlowControl(\langle buf, out\rangle) = u \text{ such that } (1).$$

Generally, for each arc $a = \langle m, n\rangle$ in the final model, model refinement generates a specification for a control function for a that outputs a satisfying control value. The desired control function may be specified as

$$Control_a(st \mid L_m(st)) \;=\; u \text{ such that } U_a(st, u)$$

where $L_m(st)$ is the precondition and $U_a(st, u)$ is the postcondition. Algorithm or function synthesis is appropriate for this specification, since the behaviors are specified by a simple input-output relation which we treat as a safety property over traces of length 2 (input state followed by output state). A variety of techniques for function synthesis have been developed, many of which stem from the original work on deductive synthesis [6,12,17]. Later approaches to synthesis of functions exploit algorithm design patterns [29], sketches [34], and transformations from high-level function definitions [19].

Here, since the control variable u only takes on three values, a simple transformation to form a conditional function can be applied resulting in the following (see [30] for details).

$$\begin{aligned}
&controlFun(\langle buf, out\rangle \mid 0 \leq out \leq 4 \wedge 0 \leq buf - out \leq 16\\
&\qquad\qquad \wedge -3 \leq buf - 3*out \leq 11 \wedge -6 \leq buf - 4*out \leq 1)) =\\
&\quad \textbf{if } 4*out - buf > -5 \wedge 2*out - buf > -12\\
&\qquad\qquad \wedge out \geq 1 \wedge 5*out - buf > -3 \textbf{ then } -1\\
&\quad \textbf{else if } buf - 2*out > 0 \wedge out \leq 3 \textbf{ then } 0\\
&\quad \textbf{else } 1
\end{aligned}$$

5 Path Properties

In the previous section we discussed how function specification naturally arises during model refinement. In this section we present a general approach to function synthesis that generalizes the model refinement approach. Reactive synthesis tends to generate control systems with relatively flat structure whereas algorithm/function design generates smaller programs with deeper structure (via a hierarchy of subfunctions). Our intent is to have model refinement as the unifying framework for synthesizing both reactive systems and functions.

Some required properties are naturally expressed over the nodes of a path in the model, rather than being localized to a node (state invarient) or arc (action invariants). They express required properties that hold between values that are not near in time or space. We define *path properties* to be predicates over the variables of nodes along some path in the model. An action property is a special case of a path property since it is expressed over a path of length one. When necessary we prefix a variable with the node at which the value is referenced. If a variable is only accessible at one node or arc (i.e. it is local), the prefix can be omitted.

We define next some refinement rules that can be used to reduce path properties to action properties. The refinement rules work by propagating the path property through the structure of the path, resulting in the strengthening of the labels on particular arcs. The resulting refined path implies the path property by construction. At that point, the constraint system of Sect. 3 can be defined and solved.

Path properties may arise by the imposition of model substructure via arc refinement, where an arc is replaced by an arc-like LCFG (i.e. a submodel). This may happen when an action specifies a complex state change that requires, say, an iterative or recursive computation to complete. Suppose that we have a required property $\varphi_{m,p}(st_m, st_p)$ that relates the state at node m to the state at node p, where there exists a path from m to p in the model $\mathcal{M}$. Our strategy is to propagate φ through the structure of $\mathcal{M}$ until we have inferred properties that can be localized to the nodes and arcs of $\mathcal{M}$. For purposes of reasoning about path properties we proceed as if we have path labels in $\mathcal{M}$ for all pairs of nodes; e.g. $L_{m,p}$ is treated as the label expressing properties of the paths from node m to node p.

There are two propagation rules that reduce the scope of a path property, with the goal of reducing the property to action properties in the path: either propagate forward from node m toward p, or propagate backward from node p toward m. Rules for both are defined next. Each rule reduces the span of a path predicate by one, so we iterate their application until we generate a path predicate than spans a single arc, whereupon we can enforce it locally.

Forward Propagation: Let $\mathcal{S} = \langle \mathcal{M}, \Phi \rangle$ be a specification and let $\varphi_{m,p} \in \Phi$ be a path property from node m to node p. We can refine $\mathcal{S}$ to reduce the path property $\varphi_{m,p}$ as follows: (1) Delete $\varphi_{m,p}$ from Φ, and (2) for each arc $a = \langle m, n \rangle \in Arc$, add the path formula $wcPostSpec(L_a, \varphi_{m,p})$ to Φ where $wcPostSpec(L_a, \theta)$ is the *Weakest Controllable PostSpecification* of action L_a with respect to path formula θ over $V(m) \cup V(p)$ and is defined by

$$\forall st_m, u, e.\ L_m(st_m) \ \wedge\ U(st_m, u)\ \wedge\ e \in E(st_m) \implies \theta(f_a(st_m, u, e)).$$

wcPostSpec is the weakest path formula over $V(n) \cup V(p)$ such that for any transition instance of a from some state st_m to state st_n, there is some st_p such that $\theta(st_m, st_p)$. We repeat Forward Propagation until all path properties have been reduced to actions (and thus can be enforced by model refinement).

Backward Propagation: Let $\mathcal{S} = \langle \mathcal{M}, \Phi \rangle$ be a system specification and let $\varphi_{m,p} \in \Phi$ be a path formula from node m to node p. We can refine $\mathcal{S}$ to reduce the path property occurrences as follows: (1) Delete $\varphi_{m,p}$ from Φ, and (2) for each arc $a = \langle n, p \rangle \in Arc$ where there exists a path from m to n, add the path formula $wcPreSpec(L_a, \varphi_{m,p})$ to Φ where $wcPreSpec(L_a, \theta)$ is the *Weakest Controllable PreSpecification* of action L_a with respect to path formula θ over $V(m) \cup V(p)$ and is defined by

$$\forall u, e.\, L_n(st_n) \,\wedge\, U(st_n, u) \,\wedge\, e \in E(st_n) \implies \theta(st_m, f_a(st_n, u, e)).$$

wcPreSpec is the weakest path formula over $V(m) \cup V(n)$ such that for any transition instance of a from some state st_n to state st_p, there is some st_m such that $\theta(st_m, st_p)$. We repeat Backward Propagation until all path properties have been reduced to actions (and thus can be enforced by model refinement).

Both of these propagation rules work by propagating the path property φ through the transition a, whether forward or backwards. To get useful results, L_a must express a nontrivial constraint. These rules are often applied after one has chosen a candidate function/operation for transition a and then desires to infer the consequences. This process is analogous to SAT algorithms in which one chooses a variable and a value heuristically and then explores the consequences via boolean propagation and conflict-driven learning in the failure case. The choice of a simple operation that is natural in context, as an arc refinement, enables the propagation to go through. This is a choice and alternative choices lead to different designs, as illustrated in the next section.

5.1 Algorithm Design Example: Sorting

One feature of model refinement is that it subsumes a major part of the automated algorithm design work performed in earlier function synthesis systems such as KIDS [25]. In retrospect, the success of KIDS in algorithm design is partly due to its automated inference system which was designed to propagate output conditions through the structure of a chosen program scheme (i.e. an over-approximating model representing an algorithm class). To illustrate, consider the design of a sorting algorithm using a binary divide-and-conquer program scheme as a model. In a functional notation, the model can be expressed as

$$\begin{aligned} F(x{:}D) : (z{:}R) = \; & \textsf{if } primitive(x) \textsf{ then } direct(x) \\ & \textsf{else } compose \circ (F \times F) \circ decompose(x) \end{aligned}$$

and the required property is $bag(x) = bag(z) \wedge ordered(z)$, where x and z are lists of numbers, $bag(x)$ returns the bag or multiset of elements in list x, and $ordered(z)$ holds when list z is in sorted order. The property is simply an input/output predicate since the only observable behavior of an algorithm is its (uncontrollable) input and (controllable) output value. In a functional setting, there are no global variables and hence no global state. The input to each functional component is the environment input and the control value is the output of the action.

There are several common tactics for designing divide-and-conquer algorithms. One is to select a simple *decompose* operation on the input type, and then to calculate a *compose* operator that achieves the correct output. A dual tactic is to select a simple *compose* operation on the output type, and then calculate a *decompose* operator that achieves a decomposition of the input into parts that can be solved and composed to yield a correct solution.

We might represent the key recursive part of the scheme as a dataflow path:

$$\begin{array}{ccc} \langle x_0 \rangle & \xrightarrow{F(x_0,z_0)} & \langle z_0 \rangle \\ \downarrow {\scriptstyle decompose(x_0,x_1,x_2)} & & \uparrow {\scriptstyle compose(z_0,z_1,z_2)} \\ \langle x_1, x_2 \rangle & \xrightarrow{F(x_1,z_1)\times F(x_2,z_2)} & \langle z_1, z_2 \rangle \end{array}$$

where a node represents a state by the variables that exist in it (and their properties), and each arc specifies an action by a predicate over input and output variables. This particular model derives from a functional program, so the abstract "states" actually do not represent stored values, but the value flow at intermediate points in a computation. For simplicity and clarity, we use this graphical representation rather than perform the straightforward translation to the TLA-like notation used in previous examples.

In terms of the dataflow path, the goal constraint is a predicate over x_0 and z_0: $\varphi(x_0, z_0) \equiv bag(x_0) = bag(z_0) \wedge ordered(z_0)$. Suppose that we follow the second tactic and refine the model by choosing list concatenation as our *compose* operator: $compose \mapsto z_0 = z_1{+\!+}z_2$. The ultimate effect of this choice is to derive a variant of a quicksort algorithm. Note that in this case the environment input is the pair $\langle z_1, z_2 \rangle$ and the control value is the output z_0. The Backward Propagation Rule applies here since the goal property is not expressed over the input and output variables of *compose*, so we calculate:

$$\begin{array}{l} wcPreSpec(compose, \varphi(x_0, z_0)) \\ \equiv \quad \forall z_0.\, z_0 = z_1{+\!+}z_2 \implies bag(x_0) = bag(z_0) \wedge ordered(z_0) \\ \equiv \quad \{\text{ quantifier elimination on } z_0 \ \} \\ \quad\; bag(x_0) = bag(z_1{+\!+}z_2) \wedge ordered(z_1{+\!+}z_2) \\ \equiv \quad \{\text{ distributivity laws and simplification}\} \\ \quad\; bag(x_0) = bag(z_1) \cup bag(z_2) \wedge\ ordered(z_1) \wedge ordered(z_2) \wedge bag(z_1) \leq bag(z_2). \end{array}$$

where we have used domain-specific laws for distributing *bag* and *ordered* over list concatenation, and $b_1 \leq b_2$ holds when each element of bag b_1 is less than or equal to each element of bag b_2. As this remains a path predicate $\varphi(x_0, z_1, z_2)$ (i.e. not localizable to an arc), we continue by propagating this derived goal backward through the recursive calls:

$$\begin{array}{l} wcPreSpec(F \times F,\, \varphi(x_0, z_1, z_2)) \\ \equiv \quad \{\text{ unfold}\} \\ \quad \forall z_1, z_2.\, bag(x_1) = bag(z_1) \wedge ordered(z_1) \wedge bag(x_2) = bag(z_2) \wedge ordered(z_2) \\ \qquad\quad \implies bag(x_0) = bag(z_1) \cup bag(z_2) \\ \qquad\qquad\quad \wedge\, ordered(z_1) \wedge ordered(z_1) \wedge bag(z_1) \leq bag(z_2) \\ \equiv \quad \{\text{ simplification and quantifier elimination}\} \\ \quad bag(x_0) = bag(x_1) \cup bag(x_2) \wedge bag(x_1) \leq bag(x_2). \end{array}$$

This last predicate is expressed over the input/output variables of the *decompose* operator, so it can be localized and enforced by strengthening the *decompose* action to

$$bag(x_0) = bag(x_1) \cup bag(x_2) \wedge bag(x_1) \leq bag(x_2).$$

Note that this is a specification for (a version of) the well-known partition subalgorithm of Quicksort. It asserts that if we decompose the input list x_0 into two lists x_1 and x_2 whose collective elements are the same as the elements in x_0, and such that each element of x_1 is less-than-or-equal-to each element of x_2, then when we recursively sort x_1 and x_2, and then concatenate them, the result will be a sorted version of x_0. If we had included a well-founded order in the decompose operator, we would infer a derived initial condition of $length(x_0) > 1$ on *decompose*. This serves as a guard on the recursive path in the algorithm.

In summary, we have used propagation rules to infer a specification on the *decompose* action that, if realized by further refinement, is sufficient to establish the correctness of the whole algorithm.

6 Related Work

Our previous work on functional algorithm design used algorithm theories as over-approximating models for various classes of algorithms. Algorithm theories and design tactics [29] were implemented in KIDS [25] and Specware [14]. These synthesis systems used a form of model refinement to instantiate algorithm models for divide-and-conquer [24], global search, dynamic programming [26], and other classes. Synthesized applications include schedulers [31], SAT-solvers [33], and garbage collectors [32].

Sketching [34] is a currently popular program synthesis approach that can be seen as a special case of model refinement. The model is supplied in the form of a program template with holes for missing code. In the case of SyGuS [1], a grammar is given as an over-approximation to the missing code. The property to be enforced may be expressed using the language of an SMT-solver, so that guesses as to how to fill the hole can be verified. While the problem setup is similar to model refinement, the synthesis process is based on generate-and-test rather than predicate transformer-based calculation.

Model refinement is most obviously derived from the extensive literature on controller synthesis [8,20] and reactive system design [18]. Most current work on the synthesis of reactive systems focuses on circuit design and starts with specifications in propositional Linear Temporal Logic (LTL) or GR(1) [3,13]. Model refinement allows specifications that are first-order and uses a temporal logic of action that is amenable to refinement, allowing a broader range of applications to be tackled.

The algorithm derivation in Sect. 5 highlights a novel aspect of model refinement: the imposition of a design template rather than a plant or game model as it typical in reactive system design. Design templates in the systems world are often discussed as Design Patterns. The refinement mechanism is arc refinement (see Sect. 2.3) which refines a model arc by an arc-like LCFG, in effect, replacing the arc with a design pattern. The arc specification becomes a path property and the refinement rules in Sect. 5 are used to localize the property by strengthening arc labels along the path. It is typical of algorithm derivation that structure refinements are needed to implement arc/action specifications, resulting in the top-down synthesis of subalgorithms. Algorithms often have a deeper hierarchy of subcomputations than system control codes.

The model refinement constraints are a kind of Constrained Horn Clause (CHC) and specialized algorithms have been explored for these as a generalization of SMT solving [7,10,11]. The main application is finding inductive invariants for program verification. Our approach aims to find a maximal solution whereas CHC tools typically aim to find any solution, since any inductive invariant is sufficient to establish the specified verification condition.

Model checking [5] can be viewed as a special case of model refinement in which refinement of the model is not an option. Counter-example-driven model refinement is performed in CEGAR with the goal to prove a specific property on a model of a fixed underlying program. The goal of CEGAR is not to synthesize a correct program from properties but to verify properties of a given program.

7 Concluding Remarks

The starting point of this work is the observation that logical properties and computational models have complementary strengths for purposes of formally stating requirements on desired computer behavior. The key questions then are (1) how to combine these strengths into a coherent formalism for specifying requirements, and (2) how to calculate programs that are consistent with specifications stated in the formalism.

In this paper we have presented an instance of these general ideas, using (1) a first-order temporal logic of actions to specify logical properties and (2) labelled transition systems to express concrete and abstract computational models and their refinement order. For illustration purposes we have further focused on basic safety properties.

Physical plants (as in the Flow Control problem) and game-like problems (as in the Cinderella-Stepmother problem) provide concrete models upon which model refinement can propagate logical properties over actions. The imposition of abstract designs as abstract models (as in the Sorting example and more generally in the form of design patterns, algorithm schemas, sketches, etc.) naturally transforms property specifications into path predicates over abstract models. This paper has presented model refinement as a unified treatment of reactive and functional design using iterated constraint propagation of (1) path predicates over abstract models and (2) state/action predicates over concrete model steps/arcs.

While this paper provides a fairly general and mechanizable framework for user-guided, yet highly automated design, it also admits the possibility of high computational complexity or undecidability due to the expressiveness of the first-order formulas. By suitably restricting the domain of discourse to decidable theories, we can define a more automated design process. Our prototype implementation restricts constraints to the decidable theories in Z3, which is sufficient for a range of applications including the examples presented above. Extension to handle liveness properties ($\Diamond\varphi$) and reactivity properties ($\Box\Diamond\varphi$) can also be handled as definite constraint systems whose fixpoints can be found by Kleene iteration combined with widening. However, for practical purposes, reactive systems typically want guarantees of bounded-time responsiveness, which is a safety property (and therefore amenable to the techniques in this paper).

Model refinement is intended to be part of a library of refinement-generating transformations that are used to develop complex algorithms and systems. In our view, a practical synthesis environment generates a refinement chain from an initial specification down to compilable code. Each step of the refinement chain is generated by a transformation that is also capable of emitting proofs of the refinement relation between the pre- and post-specification [27,32]. Model refinement would tend to be used earlier in the refinement chain since it translates logical requirements into operational designs, by enforcing properties in the model. Other refinement-generating transformations are necessary to improve the performance of the evolving model including expression simplification, finite-differencing or incrementalization, and datatype refinements [16,25].

Treating a specification as a model plus required properties is a key aspect of model refinement. Models are essentially programs annotated with invariant properties. While temporal logics can be translated into automata (and vice-versa), for complex designs, the models can be much more compact than logic, especially when the nodes have rich properties and the control structure is complex. Initially, models serve to succinctly capture fixed behavioral structure in the problem domain, such as physical plant dynamics and information system APIs. During refinement, the model serves as the accumulation of the design decisions made so far. Another intended use of models is via the imposition of design patterns for algorithms and systems. Patterns from a library capture best-practice designs that might be difficult to find by search; e.g. when there is a delicate tradeoff between "ilities", such as between precision of output and runtime.

We are currently working on the design of a processor (model) that asynchronously receives and processes tasks for which we want to enforce capacity and timeliness properties. To enforce fairness and timeliness the design composes in an abstract scheduler (design pattern). We hope to report on this work in a future paper.

Acknowledgments. The authors would like to thank Alessandro Coglio, Grant Jurgenson, Christoph Kreitz, and the reviewers for their comments on this paper. This work has been sponsored in part by NSF under contract CCF-0737840, ONR under contract N00014-04-1-0727, and by the Laboratory Directed Research and Development program at Sandia National Laboratories, a multimission laboratory managed and operated by National Technology & Engineering Solutions of Sandia, LLC, a wholly owned subsidiary of Honeywell International Inc., for the U.S. Department of Energy's

National Nuclear Security Administration under contract DE-NA0003525. This paper describes objective technical results and analysis. Any subjective views or opinions that might be expressed in the paper do not necessarily represent the views of the U.S. Department of Energy or the United States Government.

Disclosure of Interests. The authors have no competing interests to declare that are relevant to the content of this article.

References

1. Alur, R., et al.: Syntax-guided synthesis. In: Proceedings of the IEEE International Conference on Formal Methods in Computer-Aided Design (FMCAD), pp. 1–17 (2013)
2. Beyene, T., Chaudhuri, S., Popeea, C., Rybalchenko, A.: A constraint-based approach to solving games on infinite. In: Proceedings of the 41st ACM SIGPLAN-SIGACT Symposium on Principles of Programming Languages, pp. 221–233 (2014)
3. Bloem, R., Jobstmann, B., Piterman, N., Pnueli, A., Saar, Y.: Synthesis of reactive(1) designs. J. Comput. Syst. Sci. **78**(3), 911–938 (2012)
4. Buschmann, F., Meunier, R., Rohnert, H., Sommerlad, P., Stal, M.: Pattern-Oriented Software Architecture, Volume 1: A System of Patterns. Wiley, Hoboken (1996)
5. Clarke, E.M., Grumberg, O., Peled, D.A.: Model Checking. MIT Press, Cambridge (2000)
6. Constable, R.L.: Constructive mathematics and automatic program writers. In: Information Processing 1971, pp. 229–233. IFIP, Ljubljana (1971)
7. Fedyukovich, G., Prabhu, S., Madhukar, K., Gupta, A.: Solving constrained horn clauses using syntax and data. In: 2018 Formal Methods in Computer Aided Design (FMCAD), pp. 1–9 (2018). https://doi.org/10.23919/FMCAD.2018.8603011
8. Filippidis, I., Dathathri, S., Livingston, S.C., Ozay, N., Murray, R.M.: Control design for hybrid systems with tulip: the temporal logic planning toolbox. In: 2016 IEEE Conference on Control Applications (CCA), pp. 1030–1041 (2016)
9. Gamma, E., Helm, R., Johnson, R., Vlissides, J.: Design Patterns: Elements of Reusable Object-Oriented Software. Addison-Wesley, Boston (1994)
10. Govind, V., Shoham, S., Gurfinkel, A.: Solving constrained horn clauses modulo algebraic data types and recursive functions. Proc. ACM Program. Lang. **6**(POPL), 1–29 (2022)
11. Grebenshchikov, S., Lopes, N.P., Popeea, C., Rybalchenko, A.: Synthesizing software verifiers from proof rules. In: Proceedings of the 33rd ACM SIGPLAN Conference on Programming Language Design and Implementation, pp. 405–416 (2012)
12. Green, C.: Application of theorem proving to problem solving. In: Proceedings of the First International Joint Conference on Artificial Intelligence, pp. 219–239 (1969)
13. Jacobs, S., Klein, F., Schirmer, S.: A high-level LTL synthesis format: TLSF v1.1. Electron. Proc. Theor. Comput. Sci. **229**, 112–132 (2016)
14. Kestrel Institute: Specware System and documentation (2003). http://www.specware.org/
15. Lamport, L.: The temporal logic of actions. ACM Trans. Program. Lang. Syst. **16**(3), 872–923 (1994)
16. Liu, Y.: Systematic Program Design: From Clarity to Efficiency. Cambridge University Press, Cambridge (2013)

17. Manna, Z., Waldinger, R.: A deductive approach to program synthesis. ACM Trans. Program. Lang. Syst. **2**(1), 90–121 (1980)
18. Pnueli, A., Rosner, R.: On the synthesis of a reactive module. In: Proceedings of the 16th ACM SIGPLAN-SIGACT Symposium on Principles of Programming Languages, pp. 179–190 (1989)
19. Püschel, M., et al.: SPIRAL: a generator for platform-adapted libraries of signal processing algorithms. Int. J. High Perform. Comput. Appl. **18**(1), 21–45 (2004)
20. Ramadge, P., Wonham, W.: The control of discrete event systems. Proc. IEEE **77**(1), 81–98 (1989)
21. Rehof, J., Mogensen, T.: Tractable constraints in finite semilattices. Sci. Comput. Program. **35**, 191–221 (1999)
22. Schmidt, D.C., Stal, M., Rohnert, H., Buschmann, F.: Pattern-Oriented Software Architecture, Volume 2: Patterns for Concurrent and Networked Objects. Wiley, Hoboken (2000)
23. Slanina, M., Sankaranarayanan, S., Sipma, H., Manna, Z.: Controller synthesis of discrete linear plants using polyhedra. Technical report REACT-TR-2007-01, Stanford University (2007)
24. Smith, D.R.: Top-down synthesis of divide-and-conquer algorithms. Artif. Intell. **27**(1), 43–96 (1985). (Reprinted in Rich, C., Waters, R. (eds.): Readings in Artificial Intelligence and Software Engineering. Morgan Kaufmann, Los Altos (1986))
25. Smith, D.R.: KIDS – a semi-automatic program development system. IEEE Trans. Softw. Eng. Spec. Issue Form. Methods Softw. Eng. **16**(9), 1024–1043 (1990). citeseer.ist.psu.edu/article/smith90kids.html
26. Smith, D.R.: Structure and design of problem reduction generators. In: Möller, B. (ed.) Constructing Programs from Specifications, pp. 91–124. North-Holland, Amsterdam (1991)
27. Smith, D.R.: Generating programs plus proofs by refinement. In: Meyer, B., Woodcock, J. (eds.) VSTTE 2005. LNCS, vol. 4171, pp. 182–188. Springer, Heidelberg (2008). https://doi.org/10.1007/978-3-540-69149-5_20
28. Smith, D.R.: Model refinement code (2021). https://github.com/KestrelInstitute/modelRefinement
29. Smith, Douglas R.., Lowry, Michael R..: Algorithm theories and design tactics. In: van de Snepscheut, J.. L.. A.. (ed.) MPC 1989. LNCS, vol. 375, pp. 379–398. Springer, Heidelberg (1989). https://doi.org/10.1007/3-540-51305-1_23. (reprinted in Science of Computer Programming **14**(2-3), 305–321 (1990)
30. Smith, D.R., Nedunuri, S.: Model refinement. Technical report 21.0, Kestrel Institute (2021). https://www.kestrel.edu/people/smith/pub/MR-TR.pdf
31. Smith, D.R., Parra, E.A., Westfold, S.J.: Synthesis of planning and scheduling software. In: Tate, A. (ed.) Advanced Planning Technology, pp. 226–234. AAAI Press, Menlo Park (1996)
32. Smith, D.R., Westbrook, E., Westfold, S.J.: Deriving concurrent garbage collectors: final report. Technical report, Kestrel Institute (2015). http://www.kestrel.edu/home/people/smith/pub/Crash-FR.pdf
33. Smith, D.R., Westfold, S.: Toward the synthesis of constraint solvers. Technical report, Kestrel Institute (2013). http://www.kestrel.edu/home/people/smith/pub/CW-report.pdf
34. Solar-Lezama, A.: The sketching approach to program synthesis. In: Hu, Z. (ed.) APLAS 2009. LNCS, vol. 5904, pp. 4–13. Springer, Heidelberg (2009). https://doi.org/10.1007/978-3-642-10672-9_3
35. Sontag, E.: Mathematical Control Theory. Springer, New York (1998). https://doi.org/10.1007/978-1-4612-0577-7

Symmetry-Based Abstraction Algorithm for Accelerating Symbolic Control Synthesis

Hussein Sibai[1(✉)], Sacha Huriot[1], Tyler Martin[1], and Murat Arcak[2]

[1] Washington University in St. Louis, St. Louis, USA
{sibai,h.sacha,martin.t}@wustl.edu
[2] University of California, Berkeley, Berkeley, USA
arcak@berkeley.edu

Abstract. We propose an efficient symbolic control synthesis algorithm for equivariant continuous-time dynamical systems to satisfy reach-avoid specifications. The algorithm exploits dynamical symmetries to construct lean abstractions to avoid redundant computations during synthesis. Our proposed algorithm adds another layer of abstraction over the common grid-based discrete abstraction before solving the synthesis problem. It combines each set of grid cells that are at a similar relative position from the targets and nearby obstacles, defined by the symmetries, into a single abstract state. It uses this layer of abstraction to guide the order by which actions are explored during synthesis over the grid-based abstraction. We demonstrate the potential of our algorithm by synthesizing a reach-avoid controller for a 3-dimensional ship model with translation and rotation symmetries in the special Euclidean group SE(2) (Code is available at: https://github.com/HusseinSibai/symmetric_control_synthesis/tree/public).

1 Introduction

Control synthesis is the problem of automatically generating a control signal that drives a dynamical system to satisfy a given specification. If solved, it offers a correct-by-construction approach to formally assuring that control systems behave as intended. Several promising approaches for synthesis have been proposed in the past for discrete and continuous-time dynamical systems and for reach-avoid and optimality specifications [10,16,19,21,22,29]. The main challenge for wider deployability is scalability, as these algorithms require expensive computational time and memory. They are known to suffer from what is colloquially known as the curse-of-dimensionality since their computational complexity grows at least exponentially with the state and input dimensions [29].

On the other hand, many control systems possess symmetries. A symmetry map of a dynamical system acts on its state space. When applied on the states visited by any of the system trajectories, a symmetry map results in another trajectory of the same system starting from a different initial state, potentially following different control and disturbance signals. A control synthesis algorithm explores the feasible control signals at each state and chooses a one that drives the system to satisfy the given specification. With symmetric dynamics, such an algorithm can infer the control that satisfies the

N. Benz et al. (Eds.): NFM 2024, LNCS 14627, pp. 166–185, 2024.
https://doi.org/10.1007/978-3-031-60698-4_10

specification at a given state without its usual comprehensive exploration if it knows the one that satisfies the specification at a symmetric state. For example, a vehicle with translation- and rotation-symmetric dynamics will likely need the same control to satisfy a reach-avoid specification when starting from states at a similar *relative* position from the reach and avoid sets. We exploit this simple, yet effective, intuition by constructing abstractions that combine such similar *concrete* states into the same *abstract* states. We use these abstractions to explore the control space more efficiently during control synthesis. We further use symmetries to compute fewer reachable sets from scratch using existing tools during the construction of the abstractions, which in turn can be efficiently transformed to obtain the rest of the reachable sets.

Abstractions have helped solving several formal verification and synthesis problems in various domains, e.g., [1,6,14,19,23,25]. Common abstractions for continuous-time dynamical systems are discrete transition models, e.g., [19,29]. Such discrete models are usually built by gridding the state, control, and time spaces. We call them *grid-based abstractions* (GA). Then, their non-deterministic discrete transitions are constructed by computing the bounded-time reachable sets, or corresponding over-approximations, of the continuous systems starting from the cells of the grid following constant control for a constant time interval, using reachability analysis tools, e.g., [7,18]. Such an abstraction results in discrete state and control sets with sizes exponential in their dimensions. To synthesize a reach-avoid controller for such an abstraction, the standard algorithm repetitively iterates, with an *arbitrary* order, over these sets. At each iteration, the algorithm extends the target or *reach* set with the discrete states that can reach it in one transition without intersecting with the *avoid* set [19,29]. Each iteration of the algorithm has an exponential time complexity in the state and input dimensions.

We further abstract the continuous-time system by combining the cells in the grid that are at *similar* relative positions to the reach and avoid sets. We call the new system the *symmetry-based abstraction* (SA). We use the SA to define an order over which different controls are explored during synthesis at every GA state. Such an order allows more efficient exploration of the action space during synthesis. The order will reflect the likelihood of control symbols satisfying the specification at a GA state given the experience at other GA states that are represented by the same SA state.

Moreover, we use symmetries to compute a set of reachable sets with cardinality equal to the number of cells in the grid over the control space times the number of cells in the non-symmetric dimensions of the state space. That is exponentially fewer than the ones used to compute the GA transitions in the traditional method (e.g., [19]). Also, each of the reachable sets we compute starts from an initial set of states that has uncertainty only in the non-symmetric dimensions of the state. These reachable sets are represented in the relative coordinates by construction and are sufficient to construct the SA. When a GA transition is needed during synthesis, it is sufficient to transform one of these pre-computed reachable sets using particular symmetry transformations (Corollary 1). Such transformations are potentially more efficient than computing the reachable set from scratch using existing reachability analysis tools [25,27,28].

The algorithm for constructing SA transforms each cell in the grid to a manifold where the symmetric coordinates are constant. Then, it finds the control symbol that results in the closest reachable set to the target that does not intersect the obstacles, when the cell is the initial set of states. All sets, i.e., the initial, reachable, target, and obstacles' ones, are represented in the relative coordinates based on the original concrete coordinates of the cell. The SA construction algorithm then maps the cells which share the same such control to the same SA state.

Before synthesis, we use the constructed SA to build a cache mapping every SA state to a set of pairs of non-negative integers, called *scores*, and control symbols. At first, every entry is initialized to a singleton set with the pair having the control symbol that was used to construct the corresponding SA state and its score being zero. During control synthesis for GA, this cache is used to define the order according to which control symbols are checked at every GA state. Particularly, if at a certain synthesis iteration a control symbol is found to be specification-satisfying for some GA state, the cache entry corresponding to its representative SA state is updated. Specifically, if that symbol exists in that cache entry, its score is incremented by one. Otherwise, a new pair is added to the entry with a score of one. The synthesis algorithm explores the symbols at a given GA state in a decreasing score order checking the controls that satisfied the specification for more GA states with the same representative SA state first.

Our algorithm preserves the guarantees of the traditional synthesis algorithm for GA. We present experimental results showing promising computational time savings when synthesizing a reach-avoid controller for a 3-dimensional ship model while exploiting its translation and rotation symmetries.

Related Work. Symmetries have been useful in numerous domains: from deriving conservation laws [20], analyzing contraction and stability [24], reinforcement and supervised learning algorithms [4,30], and interval integration of ODEs [5].

Symmetries have been used to efficiently design motion planners for vehicles to achieve reach-avoid specifications [8,17]. Particularly, they have been used to transform pre-computed reachable sets to obtain reachable sets starting from different initial sets. The plans these works synthesize start from a fixed initial set of states and assume given user-provided feedback controllers. Symmetries have also been used to reduce the dimensionality of dynamic programming problems when both the system dynamics and the cost function share the same symmetries [16]. In contrast, we do not assume a given feedback controller, and do not assume that the specification has the same symmetries as the dynamics. We aim to find the largest initial set in the state set from which the reach-avoid specification can be reached along with the associated controller.

Symmetries have also been useful to accelerate safety verification of continuous-time dynamical systems and hybrid automata [15,25,27,28]. More specifically, they have been used to reduce the dimensionality of reachable set computation problems, to efficiently cache reachable sets during verification, and to generate abstractions of hybrid automata. These works tackle the verification problem for closed dynamical systems, while we tackle the control synthesis problem for systems with inputs and disturbances.

2 Preliminaries

Notation. We denote by $\mathbb{N}$, $\mathbb{R}$ and $\mathbb{R}_{\geq 0}$ the sets of natural, real, and non-negative real numbers, respectively. $\forall n \in \mathbb{N}$, we define $[n] = \{0, \ldots, n-1\}$. For any $g : S \times \mathbb{R}_{\geq 0} \to S$, we denote by $g(s,\cdot) : \mathbb{R}_{\geq 0} \to S$ the function of $\mathbb{R}_{\geq 0}$ resulting from projecting g to having the first parameter fixed to $s \in S$. If S is a finite set, we denote its cardinality by $|S|$.

2.1 System and Problem Definitions

We consider control systems described with ordinary differential equations (ODEs):

$$\dot{x}(t) = f(x(t), u(t), w(t)), \tag{1}$$

where $x(t) \in \mathbb{R}^{n_x}$ is the *state* of the system at time $t \in \mathbb{R}_{\geq 0}$, $u : \mathbb{R}_{\geq 0} \to U \subset \mathbb{R}^{n_u}$ and $w : \mathbb{R}_{\geq 0} \to W \subseteq \mathbb{R}^{n_w}$ are two measurable functions representing control and disturbance inputs with U and W being compact sets, and $f : \mathbb{R}^{n_x} \times \mathbb{R}^{n_u} \times \mathbb{R}^{n_w} \to \mathbb{R}^{n_x}$ is a Lipschitz continuous function in x uniformly in u and w. Given any time bound $T \geq 0$, initial state $\mathbf{x}_0 \in \mathbb{R}^{n_x}$, input signal $u : [0,T] \to \mathbb{R}^{n_u}$, and a disturbance signal $w : [0,T] \to \mathbb{R}^{n_w}$, we assume that the corresponding *trajectory* of system (1) exists and is unique. We denote such a trajectory by: $\xi(\mathbf{x}_0, u, w; \cdot) : [0,T] \to \mathbb{R}^{n_x}$, and say that T is the duration of ξ. The trajectory ξ satisfies equation (1) almost everywhere and is equal to $\mathbf{x}_0$ at $t = 0$.

Given a time interval $[t_0, t_1] \subset \mathbb{R}_{\geq 0}$, a compact initial set $X_0 \subseteq X$, a fixed control function $u : \mathbb{R}_{\geq 0} \to \mathbb{R}^{n_u}$, and the interval disturbance set W, the *reachable set* of system (1) is defined as follows: $Reachset(X_0, u, W; [t_0, t_1]) := \{\xi(\mathbf{x}_0, u, w; t) \mid \mathbf{x}_0 \in X_0, t \in [t_0, t_1], w : \mathbb{R}_{\geq 0} \to W\}$, where every w in the equation above is a measurable signal. We abuse notation and denote the set of states that are reachable exactly at time t, i.e., $Reachset(X_0, u, W; [t,t])$, by $Reachset(X_0, u, W; t)$. It is generally undecidable to compute the exact reachable sets of nonlinear control systems [12]. Fortunately, significant progress resulted in numerous tools to over-approximate them (e.g., [7, 18]).

Given *reach* and *avoid* sets $X_r, X_a \subseteq \mathbb{R}^{n_x}$, a *reach-avoid* specification of system (1) requires its trajectories to eventually reach X_r, while avoiding being in X_a. The "reach set" X_r should not be confused with the "reachset", or equivalently, reachable set, that we defined earlier. Now, we formally define the problem as follows:

Problem 1. Given system (1) and *reach* and *avoid* sets of states $X_r, X_a \subseteq X$, find a set of initial states $X_0 \subseteq X$, preferably the largest one possible, and a controller $g : X \times \mathbb{R}_{\geq 0} \to U$ such that for any measurable disturbance function $w : \mathbb{R}_{\geq 0} \to W$, $\mathbf{x}_0 \in X_0$, $\exists t_r \in \mathbb{R}_{\geq 0}$, such that $\forall t \leq t_r$, $\xi(\mathbf{x}_0, g(\mathbf{x}_0, \cdot), w; t) \in X \backslash X_a$ and $\xi(\mathbf{x}_0, g(\mathbf{x}_0, \cdot), w; t_r) \in X_r$.

2.2 Transformation Groups and Equivariant Control Systems

A control system whose dynamics are unchanged under transformations of its state, control, and disturbance is called *equivariant*. Formally, fix a *transformation group* $\{h_\alpha = (\phi_\alpha, \chi_\alpha, \psi_\alpha)\}_{\alpha \in \mathscr{G}}$ on $\mathbb{R}^{n_x} \times \mathbb{R}^{n_u} \times \mathbb{R}^{n_w}$, where $\mathscr{G}$ is a Lie group with dimension r. Then, system (1) is called $\mathscr{G}$*-equivariant* if $\forall \alpha \in \mathscr{G}$, $\mathbf{x} \in \mathbb{R}^{n_x}$, $u \in \mathbb{R}^{n_u}$, and $w \in \mathbb{R}^{n_w}$, it satisfies $\frac{\partial \phi_\alpha}{\partial x}|_{x=\mathbf{x}} f(\mathbf{x}, u, w) = f(\phi_\alpha(\mathbf{x}), \chi_\alpha(u), \psi_\alpha(w))$ [16]. A trajectory or a reachset of a $\mathscr{G}$-equivariant system can be transformed using the corresponding transformation group to obtain more trajectories or reachsets, as shown in the following theorems.

Theorem 1 ([24]). *If system (1) is $\mathscr{G}$-equivariant, then $\forall \alpha \in \mathscr{G}$, $\mathbf{x}_0 \in \mathbb{R}^{n_x}$, $u : \mathbb{R}_{\geq 0} \to \mathbb{R}^{n_u}$, $w : \mathbb{R}_{\geq 0} \to \mathbb{R}^{n_w}$, and $t \in \mathbb{R}_{\geq 0}$, $\phi_\alpha(\xi(\mathbf{x}_0, u, w; t)) = \xi(\phi_\alpha(\mathbf{x}_0), \chi_\alpha \circ u, \psi_\alpha \circ w; t)$.*

Theorem 2 ([27,28]). *If system (1) is $\mathcal{G}$-equivariant, then $\forall\alpha \in \mathcal{G}$, $X_0 \subset \mathbb{R}^{n_x}$, $u : \mathbb{R}_{\geq 0} \rightarrow \mathbb{R}^{n_u}$, $w : \mathbb{R}_{\geq 0} \rightarrow \mathbb{R}^{n_w}$, and $[t_0,t_1] \subset \mathbb{R}_{\geq 0}$, $\phi_\alpha(Reachset(X_0,u,W;[t_0,t_1])) = Reachset(\ \phi_\alpha(X_0), \chi_\alpha \circ u, \psi_\alpha(W);[t_0,t_1])$. Moreover, if we let $ApprReachset(X_0,u,w;[t_0,t_1])$ be a set in $\mathbb{R}^{n_x}$ over-approximating the exact reachable set $Reachset(X_0,u,w;[t_0,t_1])$, Then, $Reachset(\phi_\alpha(X_0), \chi_\alpha \circ u, \psi_\alpha(W);[t_0,t_1]) \subseteq \phi_\alpha(ApprReachset(X_0,u,W;[t_0,t_1]))$.*

In the rest of the paper, we use *Reachset* for both the exact values and the over-approximations of reachable sets. We clarify when a distinction has to be made.

2.3 Cartan's Moving Frame and Computing Lower-Dimensional Reachsets

Assume that system (1) is $\mathcal{G}$-equivariant and that $\mathcal{G}$ is r-dimensional. Moreover, assume that $\forall\alpha \in \mathcal{G}$, ϕ_α can be split as $(\phi^a_\alpha, \phi^b_\alpha)$, defining the r and $n_x - r$ dimensions of the image of ϕ_α, respectively, such that ϕ^a_α is invertible. We call the first r dimensions the *symmetric coordinates* and the rest the *non-symmetric* ones. We select a c in the image of ϕ^a_α and define the cross-section $\mathcal{C} = \{\mathbf{x} \mid \phi^a_e(\mathbf{x}) = c\}$, a submanifold of $\mathbb{R}^{n_x}$. We assume that for each $\mathbf{x} \in \mathbb{R}^{n_x}$, there exists a unique $\alpha \in \mathcal{G}$ such that $\phi_\alpha(\mathbf{x}) \in \mathcal{C}$. We denote by $\gamma : X \rightarrow \mathcal{G}$ the function that maps each $\mathbf{x} \in X$ to its corresponding $\alpha \in \mathcal{G}$. We call γ a *moving frame*. This concept has been proposed by Cartan in 1937 [3] and has found numerous applications (e.g., [2,13,15,25–27]).

In the following corollary of Theorem 2, we show that when a moving frame is available, we can decompose the computation of a reachable set of system (1) starting from an initial set X_0 into the computation of another reachable set starting from the projection of X_0 to the cross-section $\mathcal{C}$ followed by a set of r-dimensional transformations. A version of the corollary for translation symmetry has been proposed in [28]. Also, a similar idea has been utilized for interval integration using general Lie symmetries in [5]. We present the proof of the corollary in Appendix A.

Corollary 1. *If system (1) is $\mathcal{G}$-equivariant where $\mathcal{G}$ is r-dimensional, γ is a corresponding moving frame, and $\forall\alpha \in \mathcal{G}$, ϕ^b_α is the map that projects x to its last $n_x - r$ coordinates and χ_α is the identity map, then $\forall X_0 \subset \mathbb{R}^{n_x}$, $u : \mathbb{R}_{\geq 0} \rightarrow \mathbb{R}^{n_u}$, and $[t_0,t_1] \subset \mathbb{R}_{\geq 0}$: $Reachset(X_0,u,W;[t_0,t_1]) \subseteq \cup_{\mathbf{x}_0 \in X_0} \phi_{\gamma(\mathbf{x}_0)}^{-1}(Reachset(\bar{X}_0,u,\bar{W};[t_0,t_1]))$, where $\bar{X}_0 = \cup_{\mathbf{x}_0 \in X_0} \phi_{\gamma(\mathbf{x}_0)}(\mathbf{x}_0)$ and $\bar{W} = \cup_{\mathbf{x}_0 \in X_0} \psi_{\gamma(\mathbf{x}_0)}(W)$.*

The set $\bar{X}_0$ in the corollary above belongs to the cross-section $\mathcal{C}$ determined by the moving frame γ. Thus, the projection of any $\bar{\mathbf{x}}_0 \in \bar{X}_0$ to its first r dimensions is equal to c. Computing the reachable set starting from $\bar{X}_0$, then transforming it using the maps ϕ_α is usually computationally cheaper than computing it starting from X_0 [28]. For instance, many reachability analysis tools, e.g., [7], refine, i.e., partition, the initial sets to decrease over-approximation errors. Consequently, having lower-dimensional initial sets can result in exponentially-fewer partitions when computing accurate reachable sets. The union over X_0 in the corollary can be over-approximated in a similar manner to computing reachable sets for discrete-time systems with uncertain parameters and initial states for a single time step. Finally, the assumption in the corollary that χ_α is an identity map is usually satisfied as the control input is mostly represented in the body coordinates in robotic systems, e.g., pushing the throttle or steering the wheel.

2.4 Discrete Abstractions of Continuous-Time Control Systems

In this section, we define discrete abstractions of continuous-time dynamical systems under reach-avoid specifications. When abstracting the transitions of continuous-time systems under reach-avoid specifications using discrete ones, it is important to distinguish the discrete states representing the continuous states that the continuous-time system *reaches* at the end of a time period from the ones it *visits* as it evolves over the time period. We only need the states that the system reaches to be inside the target set, but all of the states that it visits to be outside the avoid set. Without this distinction, the initial state will always be a potential *next* state in the discrete transition, and unless it is already in the target set, we would not be able to add the initial state to the extended target set. We define a transition map that makes such a distinction as follows.

Definition 1 (Non-deterministic discrete system). *A non-deterministic discrete system $\mathscr{A}$ is a tuple $(\mathscr{X}, \mathscr{U}, \delta)$, where $\mathscr{X}$ and $\mathscr{U}$ are two finite sets of symbols, and $\delta : \mathscr{X} \times \mathscr{U} \to 2^{2^{\mathscr{X}} \times \mathscr{X}}$ is a non-deterministic transition map.*

We denote δ when restricted to the first entries of the pairs in its image by $\delta.full$, representing the sets of states that $\mathscr{A}$ might *visit* in a transition, and when restricted to the second entries by $\delta.last$, representing the states that it might *reach* after the transition.

The semantics of a discrete system $\mathscr{A}$ are determined by its executions. An *execution* σ of $\mathscr{A}$ is a sequence of triples. The first entry of each triple is a finite set of symbols in $\mathscr{X}$, the second entry is a symbol contained in the first entry, and the last entry is a symbol in $\mathscr{U}$, or is equal to $\bot$, indicating the end of the execution. More formally, $\sigma := \langle(\{s_0\}, s_0, a_0), \ldots, (\{s_{l,j}\}_{j\in[z_l]}, s_l, \bot)\rangle$, where $s_0 \in \mathscr{X}$ is an initial state, and $\forall i \leq l$, z_i is the number of states that the system might visit in the ith step. Moreover, $(\{s_{i+1,j}\}_{j\in[z_{i+1}]}, s_{i+1}) \in \delta(s_i, a_i)$. Finally, we say that l is the *length* of σ.

Given reach and avoid sets of discrete states $\mathscr{X}_r$ and $\mathscr{X}_a$, respectively, we say that an execution σ of $\mathscr{A}$ satisfies the reach-avoid specification $(\mathscr{X}_r, \mathscr{X}_a)$ if $s_l \in \mathscr{X}_r$ and $s_{i,j} \notin \mathscr{X}_a$, for all $i \in [0, l]$ and $j \in [z_i]$.

To be able to relate the behaviors of system (1) and that of a discrete one, we use the concept of simulation relations [14]. We define *forward simulation relations* as follows.

Definition 2 (Forward simulation relation). *Fix (a) a discrete system $\mathscr{A} = (\mathscr{X}, \mathscr{U}, \delta)$; (b) an injective map $\beta : \mathscr{U} \to U$; (c) a time period $\tau > 0$; (d) a set of ordered pairs $\mathscr{R} \subseteq X \times \mathscr{X}$. We say that $\mathscr{R}$ is a* forward simulation relation *(FSR) from the tuple $(X, U, W, f, \beta, \tau)$ to $\mathscr{A}$, where f is the right-hand-side of system (1), if (1) $\forall \mathbf{x} \in X$: there exists $s \in \mathscr{X}$, where $(\mathbf{x}, s) \in \mathscr{R}$, and (2) $\forall \mathbf{x} \in X$ and $s \in \mathscr{X}$ such that $(\mathbf{x}, s) \in \mathscr{R}$, $a_0 \in \mathscr{U}$, $t_e \in [0, \tau]$, and a measurable $w : [0, t_e] \to W$: there exists an execution $\sigma = \langle(\{s_0\}, s_0, a_0), (\{s_{1,j}\}_{j\in[z_1]}, s_1, \bot)\rangle$ such that $\forall t \in [0, t_e]$, $\exists j \in [z_1]$ such that $(\xi(\mathbf{x}, u, w; t), s_{1,j}) \in \mathscr{R}$, where u is the input signal that is equal to $\beta(a_0)$ over $[0, t_e]$, and if $t_e = \tau$, then $(\xi(\mathbf{x}, u, w; \tau), s_1) \in \mathscr{R}$.*

Let $\mathscr{U}_c$ be the set of left-piecewise-constant functions which only switch at time periods of τ time units, mapping $\mathbb{R}_{\geq 0}$ to the set $\beta(\mathscr{U})$. Then, the existence of a FSR implies that for every trajectory ξ of system (1), with a control signal in $\mathscr{U}_c$, there exists a corresponding execution σ of the discrete system and σ is said to *represent* ξ. If an FSR exists, we say that $\mathscr{A}$ is an *abstraction* of $(X, U, W, f, \beta, \tau)$.

Next, given reach and avoid sets X_r and X_a for system (1), we *abstract* them to the sets $\mathscr{X}_r$ and $\mathscr{X}_a$ of discrete states in $\mathscr{X}$. Such sets are not unique, but should satisfy: (1) $\forall \mathbf{x} \in X$: if $\exists s \in \mathscr{X}_r$ such that $(\mathbf{x}, s) \in \mathscr{R}$, then $\mathbf{x} \in X_r$, and (2) $\forall \mathbf{x} \in X_a$: the set $\{s \in \mathscr{X} \mid (\mathbf{x}, s) \in \mathscr{R}\}$ is non-empty and is a subset of $\mathscr{X}_a$. If an execution of $\mathscr{A}$ satisfies the reach-avoid specification $(\mathscr{X}_r, \mathscr{X}_a)$, then all trajectories of system (1) represented by σ satisfy the specification (X_r, X_a). Further details are in Appendix B.

2.5 Discrete Control Synthesis

In this section, we present a control synthesis algorithm for discrete abstractions of system (1). First, we define a controller of a discrete system $\mathscr{A}$ to be a function $\mathscr{K}$ that maps $\mathscr{X}$ to the set $\mathscr{U} \cup \{\perp\}$. The *composition* of $\mathscr{A}$ and $\mathscr{K}$ results in a closed non-deterministic system, which we denote by the pair $(\mathscr{A}, \mathscr{K})$. It can only start from a state in the set $R := \{s \in \mathscr{X} | \mathscr{K}[s] \neq \perp\}$. The executions of $(\mathscr{A}, \mathscr{K})$ will have the same type as those of $\mathscr{A}$ with the actions taken following $\mathscr{K}$, i.e., $a_i = \mathscr{K}[s_i]$.

We say that $\mathscr{K}$ satisfies a specification of $\mathscr{A}$ if $\forall s \in R$, all executions starting from s of the system $(\mathscr{A}, \mathscr{K})$ satisfy the specification. A trivial one would map all $s \in \mathscr{X}$ to $\perp$, i.e., $R = \emptyset$. We seek non-trivial controllers with R covering large parts of $\mathscr{X}$.

If $\mathscr{A}$ is an abstraction of $(X, U, W, f, \beta, \tau)$ with a FSR $\mathscr{R}$, then a corresponding controller $\mathscr{K}$ *induces* a *zero-order-hold* controller g for system (1). The controller g periodically samples the state $\mathbf{x}$ of system (1) every τ time units and outputs $\beta(\mathscr{K}[s])$ for the next period, where $(\mathbf{x}, s) \in \mathscr{R}$ [29].

Given a discrete abstraction of system (1), one can use existing model checking tools to generate a corresponding controller $\mathscr{K}$, such as the one in Algorithm 1 (see [29]).

Algorithm 1. Discrete control synthesis for reach-avoid specifications

---

input: $\mathscr{A} = (\mathscr{X}, \mathscr{U}, \delta), \mathscr{X}_a, \mathscr{X}_r$
$\forall s \in \mathscr{X}, \mathscr{K}[s] \leftarrow \perp; R \leftarrow \mathscr{X}_r$
while R did not reach a fixed-point **do**
    $R \leftarrow \{s \in \mathscr{X} | \exists a \in \mathscr{U}, \delta.last(s,a) \subseteq R, \delta.full(s,a) \cap \mathscr{X}_a = \emptyset\}$
For each $s \in R$, assign $\mathscr{K}[s]$ to its corresponding $a \in \mathscr{U}$.
return: $\mathscr{K}$

Grid-Based Discrete Abstractions. A common approach to generate a discrete abstraction of system (1) is to grid the compact state and control sets X and U. The resulting sets of states and control values $\mathscr{X}_{grid}$ and $\mathscr{U}_{grid}$ have cardinalities equal to the number of cells in Q_x and Q_u, which we denote by $|Q_x|$ and $|Q_u|$. The sets of reach and avoid states $\mathscr{X}_{grid,r}$ and $\mathscr{X}_{grid,a}$ consist of the states corresponding to the cells in Q_x that are subsets of X_r and intersect X_a, respectively. The FSR $\mathscr{R}_{grid}$ maps any $\mathbf{x} \in X$ to the state in $\mathscr{X}_{grid}$ corresponding to the cell in Q_x that $\mathbf{x}$ belongs to. The function β_{grid} maps each state in $\mathscr{U}_{grid}$ to the center of a unique cell in Q_u. Throughout the paper, we fix $\mathscr{U}_{grid}$ and β_{grid} and use them for all abstractions and drop their *grid* annotation.

For any $(s_{grid}, a) \in \mathscr{X}_{grid} \times \mathscr{U}$, one can compute δ_{grid} for that pair by computing the reachable set of system (1) starting from the cell in Q_x corresponding to s_{grid} following $\beta(a)$ for τ time units, using one of the existing reachable set-computation tools, such as TIRA [18].

2.6 Symmetry-Based Discrete Transitions Computation

In Algorithm 2, we present a more efficient way to compute the entries of δ_{grid}. Algorithm 2 follows Corollary 1 and pre-computes the reachable sets starting from the cells of the grid $\bar{Q}_x$, which is Q_x projected onto the cross-section $\mathscr{C}$ defined by the moving frame γ. In other words, $\bar{Q}_x$ is a grid over the set $\cup_{\mathbf{x}\in X} \phi_{\gamma(\mathbf{x})}(\mathbf{x})$ that has the same resolution as Q_x. The reachable sets are computed assuming disturbance sets of the form $\bar{W}_j := \cup_{\mathbf{x}_0 \in X_j} \psi_{\gamma(\mathbf{x}_0)}(W)$, where $X_j = \cup_{i\in H_j} Q_{x,i}$ and H_j is the set of cells in Q_x that are projected to $\bar{Q}_{x,j}$ in $\bar{Q}_x$. It stores them in the data structure *ReachDict*. When a transition from an arbitrary $s_{grid} \in \mathscr{X}_{grid} \setminus \mathscr{X}_a \cup \mathscr{X}_r$ and $a \in \mathscr{U}$ is needed during synthesis, Corollary 1 can be used to transform the reachable set in *ReachDict* that starts from the projection of $Q_{x,i}$, the cell in Q_x corresponding to s_{grid}, to $\mathscr{C}$ from the relative coordinates back to the absolute ones. Computing reachable sets starting from lower-dimensional initial sets and transforming them is usually computationally cheaper than computing ones starting from higher-dimensional initial sets. In addition, using this approach enables the synthesis algorithm to compute exponentially-fewer reachable sets using reachability analysis engines, and transform the rest, potentially leading to significant speedups.

Algorithm 2. Symmetry-based discrete transitions computation

1: **for** $j \in [|\bar{Q}_x|]$ and $a \in \mathscr{U}$ **do** $ReachDict[j][a] \leftarrow Reachset(\bar{Q}_{x,j}, \beta(a), \bar{W}_j; [0,T])$

3 Symmetry-Based Abstraction

In this section, we describe a symmetry-based procedure that generates an abstraction $\mathscr{A}_{sym}$ for $\mathscr{A}_{grid}$, shown in Algorithm 4. It takes as input a set $\mathscr{X}_{rel}$ which has a one-to-one correspondence with $\mathscr{X}_{grid}$. We construct $\mathscr{X}_{rel}$ in Algorithm 3.

Algorithm 3. Generation of (state, avoid set, reach set) tuples in relative coordinates

1: **input:** $Q_x, X_r, X_a, \{\phi_\alpha\}_{\alpha\in\mathscr{G}}, \gamma$
2: $\mathscr{X}_{rel} \leftarrow \emptyset$
3: **for** $i \in [|Q_x|]$ **do**
4: $\quad \bar{Q}_{x,i} \leftarrow \cup_{\mathbf{x}\in Q_{x,i}} \phi_{\gamma(\mathbf{x})}(\mathbf{x})$; $\bar{X}_a \leftarrow \cup_{\mathbf{x}\in Q_{x,i}} \phi_{\gamma(\mathbf{x})}(X_a)$; $\bar{X}_r \leftarrow \cap_{\mathbf{x}\in Q_{x,i}} \phi_{\gamma(\mathbf{x})}(X_r)$
5: $\quad s_{rel} \leftarrow (\bar{Q}_{x,i}, \bar{X}_a, \bar{X}_r)$; $\mathscr{X}_{rel} \leftarrow \mathscr{X}_{rel} \cup \{s_{rel}\}$
6: **return:** $\mathscr{X}_{rel}$

From Absolute to Relative Coordinates. Similar to $\mathscr{A}_{grid}$, Algorithm 3 creates a discrete state for each cell in Q_x. For each $i \in [|Q_x|]$, it creates a state $s_{rel} \in \mathscr{X}_{rel}$, which is a triple. The first entry, $s_{rel}.\bar{Q}_x$, is the ith cell of Q_x, $Q_{x,i}$, projected onto $\mathscr{C}$ defined by γ. The set $s_{rel}.\bar{Q}_x$ is $Q_{x,i}$ represented in the frames defined by its own states. Recall from Sect. 2.3 that all states in $s_{rel}.\bar{Q}_x$ would have their first r dimensions equal to a constant c. The second entry of s_{rel}, $s_{rel}.\bar{X}_a$, represents the union of all the sets resulting from transforming X_a to the coordinate frames defined by the states in $Q_{x,i}$. Thus, for each $\mathbf{x} \in Q_{x,i}$, $s_{rel}.\bar{X}_a$ is an over-approximation of X_a transformed by $\phi_{\gamma(\mathbf{x})}$. The third element $s_{rel}.\bar{X}_r$ represents the intersection of all the sets resulting from transforming X_r to the frames defined by the states in $Q_{x,i}$. For each $\mathbf{x} \in Q_{x,i}$, $s_{rel}.\bar{X}_r$ is an under-approximation of X_r represented in the frame $\gamma(\mathbf{x})$, i.e., $\phi_{\gamma(\mathbf{x})}(X_r)$.

Algorithm 4. Symmetry-based abstraction construction

1: **input:** $\mathscr{X}_{rel}$, *ReachDict*, M
2: $\mathscr{X}_{sym} \leftarrow \{s_{sym,r}, s_{sym,a}\}$; $\forall s_{rel} \in \mathscr{X}_{rel}, \mathscr{R}_{gs}[s_{rel}] \leftarrow \perp$
3: **for** $s_{rel} \in \mathscr{X}_{rel}$ **do**
4:     **if** $s_{rel}.\bar{Q}_x \subseteq s_{rel}.\bar{X}_r$ **then** $\mathscr{R}_{gs}[s_{rel}] \leftarrow s_{sym,r}$, **continue**
5:     **else if** $s_{rel}.\bar{Q}_x \cap s_{rel}.\bar{X}_a \neq \emptyset$ **then** $\mathscr{R}_{gs}[s_{rel}] \leftarrow s_{sym,a}$, **continue**
6:     Let j be the index of s_{rel} in *ReachDict*
7:     $obstructed \leftarrow \emptyset$
8:     **while** $|obstructed| < M$ **do**
9:         $a^* \leftarrow \text{argmin}_{a \in \mathscr{U} \setminus obstructed}(ReachDict[j][a].last, s_{rel}.\bar{X}_r)$
10:         **if** $s_{rel}.\bar{X}_a \cap ReachDict[j][a].full \neq \emptyset$ **then** $obstructed \leftarrow obstructed \cup \{a^*\}$
11:         **else**
12:             **if** $(j, a^*) \notin \mathscr{X}_{sym}$ **then** $\mathscr{X}_{sym} \leftarrow \mathscr{X}_{sym} \cup \{(j, a^*)\}$;
13:             $\mathscr{R}_{gs}[s_{rel}] \leftarrow (j, a^*)$; **break**
14:     **if** $|obstructed| = M$ **then** $\mathscr{R}_{gs}[s_{rel}] \leftarrow s_{sym,a}$
15: **return:** $\mathscr{X}_{sym}$, $\mathscr{R}_{gs}$

Generating the Symmetry-Based Abstraction. Algorithm 4 is an abstraction procedure that takes as input the output $\mathscr{X}_{rel}$ of Algorithm 3, the dictionary *ReachDict* computed in Algorithm 2, and an integer $M \in [|\mathscr{U}|]$. It outputs a dictionary $\mathscr{R}_{gs}$ and a set $\mathscr{X}_{sym}$. $\mathscr{R}_{gs}$ maps every state in $\mathscr{X}_{rel}$ (equivalently, $\mathscr{X}_{grid}$) to some state in $\mathscr{X}_{sym}$. The subscript gs standing for *grid*-based to *symmetry*-based abstraction.

It proceeds as follows. It first initializes $\mathscr{X}_{sym}$ to be a set of two states: $s_{sym,r}$, the *reach* state, and $s_{sym,a}$, the *avoid* state. Then, it updates $\mathscr{R}_{gs}$ in line 4 to represent any $s_{rel} \in \mathscr{X}_{rel}$ whose $s_{rel}.\bar{X}_r$ contains $s_{rel}.\bar{Q}_x$ by $s_{sym,r}$ in $\mathscr{X}_{sym}$. Such states correspond to the cells in Q_x that are inside X_r. Similarly, it updates $\mathscr{R}_{gs}$ in line 5 to represent any s_{rel} whose $s_{rel}.\bar{X}_a$ intersects $s_{rel}.\bar{Q}_x$, by $s_{sym,a}$. These are the cells in Q_x which intersect X_a. It later maps more cells in Q_x to $s_{sym,a}$ in line 14. In our implementation of Algorithm 4, we store the *last* reachable sets in *ReachDict*$[j][:]$ in an R-tree [11][1] Now, if some s_{rel} is not mapped to $s_{sym,r}$ or $s_{sym,a}$, Algorithm 4 either maps it to another abstract state in $\mathscr{X}_{sym}$ or creates a new one in lines 6–14. Algorithm 4 first retrieves the index j of the cell $s_{rel}.\bar{Q}_x$ in the grid $\bar{Q}_x$ in line 6. Then, in lines 7–12, it finds the control

[1] We use https://github.com/libspatialindex/libspatialindex.

symbol that results in the closest reachable set in *ReachDict*$[j][:]$ to the relative target $s_{rel}.\bar{X}_r$ that does not intersect with relative obstacles $s_{rel}.\bar{X}_a$, according to some distance metric. Although this problem can be formulated as a quadratic program when using Euclidean distance, the number of constraints would be $O(|\mathscr{U}|)$, which is exponential in the input dimension, and thus computationally expensive. Instead, in our implementation of Algorithm 4, we approximate the minimizer. Our implementation first finds the closest point in the relative target, where the latter is a polytope, to the center of $s_{rel}.\bar{Q}_x$ by solving a simple quadratic program with the constraints being the half spaces of the polytope. Then, it retrieves a set of closest hyperrectangles of a predetermined size in the R-tree storing the last reachable sets in *ReachDict*$[j][:]$ and their associated control symbols. This computation is efficient as an R-tree is designed to optimize such a task [11]. We maintain a set of *visited* control symbols that have been investigated in previous iterations of the while-loop, and remove them from the retrieved set. At every iteration, we increase the size of the set we request from the R-tree, as some of the returned ones would have been visited in previous iterations. Algorithm 4 also maintains a set *obstructed* of control symbols that have been found to result in reachable sets that intersect $s_{rel}.\bar{X}_a$. After that, it iteratively checks if there exists an a^* among the retrieved control symbols results in a full reachable set that does not intersect $s_{rel}.\bar{X}_a$. If that is the case, a new abstract state, denoted by (j, a^*), is created if it is not already in $\mathscr{X}_{sym}$. After that s_{rel} is mapped to that state in $\mathscr{R}_{gs}$, i.e., it sets $\mathscr{R}_{gs}[s_{rel}]$ to (j, a^*). Otherwise, they are all added to *obstructed*. If $|obstructed|$ becomes equal to M, the while-loop terminates and s_{rel} is mapped to $s_{sym,a}$ in $\mathscr{R}_{gs}$.

4 Symmetry-Based Control Synthesis Algorithm

In this section, we present the main contribution of the paper: a control synthesis algorithm that exploits the symmetry-based abstraction as a guide to accelerate the search for specification-satisfying control symbols. The pseudocode is in Algorithm 5.

In addition to the outputs of Algorithms 2, 3, and 4, Algorithm 5 takes an upper bound N on the number of different subsets of $\mathscr{U}$ to be searched for a specification-satisfying control symbol for each state symbol in each synthesis iteration. It outputs a controller $\mathscr{K}_{rel}$ for $\mathscr{A}_{rel}$ (equivalently, $\mathscr{A}_{grid}$) satisfying the specification $(\mathscr{R}_{gs}^{-1}[s_{sym,r}], \mathscr{R}_{gs}^{-1}[s_{sym,a}])$.

Algorithm 5 proceeds as follows: it initializes the dictionary *cache* that maps each $s_{sym} \in \mathscr{X}_{sym}$ to a list of pairs of non-negative integers (scores) and control symbols in $\mathscr{U}$. That list is maintained to be sorted in decreasing order of the scores. For each such pair, the first element, i.e., the score, represents the number of times its second element, i.e., the control symbol, has been found to be specification-satisfying for a state in $\mathscr{R}_{gs}^{-1}[s_{sym}]$. The list is initialized to have a single pair $(0, s_{sym}[1])$, where $s_{sym}[1]$ is the second element, the control, in the pair defining s_{sym}. Also, as Algorithm 1, it initializes the set R to be $\mathscr{X}_{rel,r}$ and $\mathscr{K}_{rel}$ to a dictionary mapping every $s_{rel} \in \mathscr{X}_{rel}$ to $\bot$. In addition, Algorithm 5 initializes a set E to the set of states in $\mathscr{X}_{rel}$ that are not reach or avoid ones.

Algorithm 5 iteratively synthesizes $\mathscr{K}_{rel}$ in lines 4-17. Instead of searching $\mathscr{U}$ in an *arbitrary* order for a specification-satisfying control as Algorithm 1, Algorithm 5

Algorithm 5. Control synthesis using symmetry-based abstractions

1: **input:** $Q_x, Q_u, \mathscr{X}_{rel}, ReachDict, \mathscr{X}_{sym}, \mathscr{R}_{gs}, N$
2: $\forall s_{sym}, cache[s_{sym}] \leftarrow \{(0, s_{sym}[1])\}; \forall s_{rel} \in \mathscr{X}_{rel}, \mathscr{K}_{rel}[s_{rel}] \leftarrow \bot$
3: $R \leftarrow \mathscr{R}_{gs}^{-1}[s_{sym,r}]; E \leftarrow \mathscr{X}_{rel} \setminus (R \cup \mathscr{R}_{gs}^{-1}[s_{sym,a}]); progress \leftarrow 1$
4: **while** $progress$ **do**
5: $\quad progress \leftarrow 0$
6: $\quad$ **for** $s_{rel} \in E$ **do**
7: $\quad\quad A \leftarrow$ control symbols in $cache[\mathscr{R}_{gs}[s_{rel}]]$
8: $\quad\quad$ **for** $itr \in [N]$ **do**
9: $\quad\quad\quad$ **for** $a \in A$ **do**
10: $\quad\quad\quad\quad$ **if** $\delta_{rel}.last(s_{rel}, a) \subseteq R, \delta_{rel}.full(s_{rel}, a) \cap \mathscr{R}_{gs}^{-1}[s_{sym,a}] = \emptyset$ **then**
11: $\quad\quad\quad\quad\quad R \leftarrow R \cup \{s_{rel}\}; \mathscr{K}_{rel}[s_{rel}] \leftarrow a; progress \leftarrow 1;$
12: $\quad\quad\quad\quad\quad$ **if** $\exists\ count \geq 0, (count, a) \in cache[\mathscr{R}_{gs}[s_{rel}]]$ **then**
13: $\quad\quad\quad\quad\quad\quad cache[\mathscr{R}_{gs}[s_{rel}]].replace((count, a), (count+1, a))$
14: $\quad\quad\quad\quad\quad$ **else** $cache[\mathscr{R}_{gs}[s_{rel}]] \leftarrow cache[\mathscr{R}_{gs}[s_{rel}]].insert((1, a))$
15: $\quad\quad\quad\quad\quad$ **break**
16: $\quad\quad\quad$ **if** $s_{rel} \notin R$ **then** $A \leftarrow$ new (greedy or random) subset of $\mathscr{U}$
17: $\quad E \leftarrow$ neighborhood of newly added states to R
18: **return** $\mathscr{K}_{rel}$

searches $\mathscr{U}$ according to the order they appear in the cache. Particularly, it explores the symbols in $\mathscr{U}$ in batches. The batch at any iteration is stored in the set A. It is initialized at line 7 to be the list of control symbols appearing in the cache entry corresponding to the representative state $\mathscr{R}_{gs}[s_{rel}]$ of s_{rel} in $\mathscr{X}_{sym}$. That list is always sorted in the decreasing order of the scores. Thus, Algorithm 5 checks the control symbols with higher scores first in the for-loop in line 9. If none of the symbols in the cache are specification-satisfying, Algorithm 5 samples a new subset of control symbols in $\mathscr{U}$ to investigate in the next iteration of the for-loop at line 8. It either samples that batch greedily or uniformly at random. The greedy approach is the same one we followed during the abstraction process in Algorithm 4, i.e., the ones closest to the relative target.

If some $a \in A$ satisfies the specification for a state s_{rel}, then Algorithm 5 increments its score in $cache[\mathscr{R}_{gs}[s_{rel}]]$, if it exists, or adds a new pair $(1, a)$ to that entry of the cache, otherwise. In either case, when $cache[\mathscr{R}_{gs}[s_{rel}]]$ is modified, it is re-sorted to remain ordered in a decreasing order of scores.

In an ideal scenario, for any $s_{sym} \in \mathscr{X}_{sym}$, the greedy control $s_{sym}[1]$ found in the abstraction process would suffice for satisfying the specification for all $s_{rel} \in \mathscr{R}_{gs}^{-1}[s_{sym}]$. In that case, when Algorithm 5 terminates, $cache[s_{sym}]$ would be a singleton list containing the pair $(count, a)$, where $count = |\mathscr{R}_{gs}^{-1}[s_{sym}]|$ and $a = s_{sym}[1]$. However, that might not be the case in most scenarios. Different states in $\mathscr{R}_{gs}^{-1}[s_{sym}]$ might require different control to achieve the specification. The control symbol $s_{sym}[1]$ is a greedy choice to minimize the distance to the target. However, as well known from optimal control theory and dynamic programming, a greedy decision is not necessarily the optimal one. There are non-symmetric state coordinates and further away obstacles that affect the optimality of the control. Algorithm 5 adds states that are closer to the target to the extended target first, same as Algorithm 1. Thus, at a certain iteration of the while-loop in line 4 and iteration of the for-loop in line 6, the greedily-chosen control symbol might not satisfy the specification while the optimal one does, which requires the for-loop in line 8 to iterate until finding it.

Our intuition is that in most environments, states with the same symmetry-based abstract state will require a small set of control symbols to achieve the reach-avoid specification, resulting in cache entries with short lists after the termination of Algorithm 5. That allows considering large $\mathscr{U}$ without incurring the expense of exploring it fully in an arbitrary order for every state in $\mathscr{X}_{rel}$ at every synthesis iteration.

Additionally, after each synthesis iteration, a non-optimized algorithm such as Algorithm 1 would only remove the states that have been added to R in that iteration from E, i.e., update E to be $E \setminus R$. However, given all the reachable sets one would need to compute δ_{grid}, they can compute the maximum travelled distance in each dimension in one step starting from any state and following any control symbol. Notice that it would sufficient for Algorithm 5 to update E in line 17 to be the states in $\mathscr{X}_{rel}$ that correspond to cells in Q_x that are within these maximum per-dimension distances from the newly added states to R in the same synthesis iteration. That is because other states further away cannot be added to R in the next synthesis iteration as their reachable sets following any control cannot intersect the newly added states to R. This significantly reduces the number of states that Algorithm 5 has to explore. Now, assume that for any $\alpha \in \mathscr{G}$, ϕ_α is a rigid motion transformation, i.e., preserves the distance and angle measures. Then, the maximum travelled distance in each dimension in the reachable sets stored in *ReachDict* would be the same as that in all the reachable sets needed if one had to construct δ_{grid}, and thus there is no need to compute the latter. That is what we follow in our implementation of Algorithm 5.

Finally, consider the case when N and the subsets selected in line 16 are sufficiently large to cover all symbols in $\mathscr{U}$ in every iteration of the for-loop over E in line 6. Also, assume that computing the reachable sets for the transitions by transforming those in *ReachDict* using Corollary 1 results in the same over-approximation errors as computing them from scratch using existing tools. Then, Algorithm 5 would be the same as Algorithm 1 with the only two differences being the order by which the control symbols are explored and the restriction of the states to explore at a given iteration to those whose neighborhood has changed in the past iteration. Thus, it retains the same correctness guarantees as Algorithm 1.

5 Case Study

In this section, we describe our results from synthesizing a controller for a 1:30 scale model of a platform supply vessel using Algorithm 5. The dynamics of this model have been described in [9] and used as a case study in [19]. Its kinematics can be approximated using the ODE [9,19]: $\dot{\eta} = R(\theta)v + v_c$, where $\eta = [N;E;\theta] \in \mathbb{R}^3$ is the state of the ship representing its South-North and West-East position and its heading angle, respectively. The control input v is 3-dimensional. $R(\theta)$ is a rotation matrix that given θ, rotates v from the body coordinates to the global ones, where $\theta = 0$ points to the North. Finally, v_c represents the disturbance resulting from water-current velocities. We consider the same environment and reach-avoid specification of Meyer et al. [19], where the ship is required to dock while avoiding obstacles in a rectangular pier. We make a slight modification to represent boundaries as obstacles. Further details are in Appendix C.

Let $\mathcal{G}$ be $SE(2)$, the special Euclidean group, representing 2-dimensional rotations and 3-dimensional translations. Then, the kinematics of the ship are $\mathcal{G}$-equivariant, where the transformation group $\{h_\alpha = (\phi_\alpha, \chi_\alpha, \psi_\alpha)\}_{\alpha \in \mathcal{G}}$ is defined as follows: $\phi_\alpha(\eta) = R_\alpha^\intercal(\eta - \eta_\alpha)$, $\chi_\alpha(v) = Iv = v$, $\psi_\alpha(v_c) = R_\alpha^\intercal v_c$, where η_α and R_α are the 3-dimensional translation vector and rotation matrix corresponding to α. We define the moving frame γ to be the one that maps any $\mathbf{x} = [N; E; \theta]$ to the $\alpha \in \mathcal{G}$ with $R_\alpha = R(\theta)$ and $\eta_\alpha = \mathbf{x}$. Thus, $\mathcal{C}$ consists of a singleton state: the origin.

We implemented our algorithms in Python. We used TIRA [18] (implemented in Matlab) to compute the reachable sets in Algorithm 2. The reachable sets are represented as lists of time-annotated axis-aligned hyper-rectangles in $\mathbb{R}^3$. We used the Polytope library[2] to translate and rotate them. We ran Algorithm 4 in parallel to generate the symmetry-based abstractions. It is a naturally parallelizable algorithm since the concrete states determine their representative abstract states independent from each other. We ran the control synthesis part of Algorithm 5 sequentially, although it can be ran in parallel as well. We considered several choices of resolutions of the grid Q_x and fixed $|Q_u| = 9^3$ in all experiments. The results are shown in Table 1.

We ran Algorithm 5 using different parameters to identify the benefits of the different optimizations that we introduced. We call each choice a *strategy* and try 8 of them. Strat. 0 is the *baseline* and the traditional implementation of Algorithm 1 where states and controls are explored in an arbitrary order. Strat. 0.5 differs from Strat. 0 by exploring only 400 unique controls sampled uniformly at random i.i.d at every state in every synthesis iteration. The rest correspond to running Algorithm 5 with N and batch sizes chosen to explore all symbols (strategies 1, 3, 4, and 6) or 400 unique symbols (including those in the cache) (strategies 2 and 5) in $\mathcal{U}$ in the loop in line 8. We use the same number of allowed controls to explore in creating the abstractions in Algorithm 4. Strategies 1, 2, and 3 update E in line 17 to $E \setminus R$ while 4, 5, and 6 update it to the neighborhood of newly added states to R. Strategies 3 and 6 consider an arbitrary order of control symbols, instead of the greedy ones, for the abstraction and for control synthesis. In other words, for each $s_{rel} \in \mathcal{X}_{rel}$, Algorithm 4 following that strategy iterates over the control symbols according to their indices and the first symbol that does not result in collision is used for the abstraction. Similarly, Algorithm 5 following that strategy iterates over the controls in the cache first, and if none is specification-satisfying, it iterates over the rest in an arbitrary order. Moreover, we considered different grid resolutions for Q_x: 1 corresponds to $30 \times 30 \times 30$ (30 partitions per dimension); 2 corresponds to $50 \times 50 \times 50$; 3 corresponds to $60 \times 70 \times 50$; and 4 corresponds to $80 \times 100 \times 50$.

From Table 1, we can see that Strat. 5, the one that uses all optimizations we introduced (symmetry-abstraction for choosing and updating the cache, updating E to neighborhoods of newly added states to R, and considering only subset of $\mathcal{U}$ in the order of the scores) result in the least Tt with respect to all other strategies at almost no cost in #Ctr and |Path|. It results in a 1.7×, 1.5×, 1.5×, and 1.7× speedup over the benchmark runs for resolutions 1, 2, 3, and 4, respectively.

[2] https://pypi.org/project/polytope/.

Table 1. Experimental results. The table presents results from runs of Algorithm 5 with different parameters and resolutions of Q_x. It shows: # cells in Q_x that are not avoid or reach ones $|\mathcal{X}^*_{grid}| = |\mathcal{X}_{grid} \setminus \mathcal{X}_{grid,a} \cup \mathcal{X}_{grid,r}|$; # abstract states $|\mathcal{X}_{sym}|$; # states mapped to $s_{sym,a}$ in line 14 of Algorithm 4 (#CAO); total # states added to R during synthesis (#Ctr); min/average/median/max lengths of lists in *cache*; average of $|E|/(|\mathcal{X}^*_{grid}| - |R| + |\mathcal{X}_{grid,r}|)$ over synthesis iterations (Exp, for states-to-be-explored); average/max of the lengths of paths from states in R to the reach set (|Path|); the abstraction, synthesis, and total computation times in seconds (At, St, and Tt).

Str	Q_x	$\lvert\mathcal{X}^*_{grid}\rvert$	$\lvert\mathcal{X}_{sym}\rvert$	#CAO	#Ctr	*cache*	Exp	|Path|	At	St	Tt
0	1	6580	0	0	1750	–	1	4.6/11	–	2496	2496
1	1	6580	143	210	1750	1/1.5/1.0/13	1	4.6/11	108	3683	3791
2	1	6580	143	210	1750	1/1.5/1.0/12	1	4.6/11	105	2209	2315
3	1	6580	35	210	1750	1/2.9/2.0/17	1	4.6/11	94	2590	2685
4	1	6580	143	210	1750	1/1.5/1.0/13	0.40	4.6/11	106	3017	3123
5	1	6580	143	210	1750	1/1.5/1.0/16	0.40	4.7/11	105	1373	**1479**
6	1	6580	35	210	1750	1/2.9/2.0/17	0.40	4.6/11	97	2465	2562
0	2	34544	0	0	31056	–	1	10.2/28	–	11895	11895
1	2	34544	167	3488	31056	2/7.4/5.0/54	1	10.2/28	567	17096	17663
2	2	34544	167	3488	31056	1/7.3/4.5/47	1	10.4/30	515	9663	10179
3	2	34544	34	3488	31056	2/12.3/4/106	1	10.2/28	510	12072	12583
4	2	34544	167	3488	31056	2/6.7/5.0/37	0.32	10.2/29	581	13953	14534
5	2	34544	167	3488	31056	2/7.1/5.0/43	0.29	10.3/34	514	7335	**7850**
6	2	34544	34	3488	31056	2/11.6/4/97	0.32	10.2/29	517	11679	12197
0	3	58030	0	0	57180	–	1	11.0/32	–	20910	20938
5	3	58030	215	850	57180	1/7.1/4.0/50	.47	10.3/32	831	12999	**13832**
0	4	117340	0	0	105500	–	1	8.6/24	–	39204	39260
5	4	117340	149	11840	105500	1/12.5/8.0/67	0.28	8.4/25	1870	21117	**22989**

Also, we can see that resolutions 2, 3, and 4 were sufficient to find a specification-satisfying control for all states in $\mathcal{X}_{rel}$ corresponding to states in $\mathcal{X}^*_{grid}$ and the abstraction was able to find all states that cannot be controlled to satisfy the specification and map them to $s_{sym,a}$, before synthesis. Additionally, despite Strat. 6 (which explores control symbols in an arbitrary order for abstraction and synthesis) resulting in fewer abstract states than Strat. 5, the *cache* did not help it in decreasing St and resulted in a St similar to that of the benchmark. If we add the overhead of At, it required more computation time than the baseline. Its sub-optimality is also evident from the lengths of the lists in the cache being much longer than those of Strat. 5, which demonstrate that more states represented by the same abstract state required different controls to satisfy the specification. Moreover, Strat. 5 is significantly faster than Strat. 2, which shows the benefit of restricting E to the neighborhood of newly added states to R instead of exploring all remaining states in each synthesis iteration. Yet, we found that iterating over the newly added states to R after each synthesis iteration and taking the union of their neighborhoods, itself adds an overhead of computation time. Despite that overhead, it still resulted in more efficient computation time than without that optimization when combined with the symmetry-based abstraction and synthesis. Otherwise, the overhead seems to balance out its benefit (Strat. 6 versus Strat. 3). We also found that when exploring the control symbols during synthesis in a similar manner to how we construct the symmetry-based abstraction also adds an overhead for finding the closest reachable sets and for excluding those control symbols returned by the R-tree that are already explored. That overhead is worth it when exploring a subset of $\mathscr{U}$, i.e., small N and batch sizes (results of Strat. 2 and Strat. 5 versus Strat. 0.5). However, it is not when we are exploring all symbols in $\mathscr{U}$ (results of Strat. 1 and Strat. 4 versus the baseline).

6 Conclusions

We proposed an algorithm to accelerate symbolic control synthesis for continuous-time dynamical systems and reach-avoid specifications. Our algorithm exploits dynamical symmetries even in non-symmetric environments through an abstraction approach. Our algorithm uses the abstraction to explore control symbols more selectively during synthesis. Our approach is general; it allows exploitation of any symmetries in the form of Lie groups that the system possesses. We show experimental results demonstrating the effectiveness of our approach.

Acknowledgements. This work has been supported by the National Science Foundation under grant number CNS-2111688.

A Proof of Corollary 1

Corollary 1. *If system (1) is $\mathscr{G}$-equivariant where $\mathscr{G}$ is r-dimensional, γ is a corresponding moving frame, and $\forall \alpha \in \mathscr{G}$, ϕ^b_α is the map that projects x to its last $n_x - r$ coordinates and χ_α is the identity map, then $\forall X_0 \subset \mathbb{R}^{n_x}$, $u : \mathbb{R}_{\geq 0} \rightarrow \mathbb{R}^{n_u}$, and $[t_0, t_1] \subset \mathbb{R}_{\geq 0}$: $Reachset(X_0, u, W; [t_0, t_1]) \subseteq \cup_{\mathbf{x}_0 \in X_0} \phi_{\gamma(\mathbf{x}_0)}{}^{-1}(Reachset(\bar{X}_0, u, \bar{W}; [t_0, t_1]))$, where $\bar{X}_0 = \cup_{\mathbf{x}_0 \in X_0} \phi_{\gamma(\mathbf{x}_0)}(\mathbf{x}_0)$ and $\bar{W} = \cup_{\mathbf{x}_0 \in X_0} \psi_{\gamma(\mathbf{x}_0)}(W)$.*

Proof. The proof follows from applying Theorem 2 to the reachable sets starting from each initial state in X_0: $Reachset(X_0, u, W; [t_0, t_1]) =$

$$
\begin{aligned}
&\cup_{\mathbf{x}_0 \in X_0} Reachset(\mathbf{x}_0, u, W; [t_0, t_1]) \\
&\qquad \text{[by the definition of } Reachset\text{]} \\
&= \cup_{\mathbf{x}_0 \in X_0} \phi_{\gamma(\mathbf{x}_0)}{}^{-1}(Reachset(\phi_{\gamma(\mathbf{x}_0)}(\mathbf{x}_0), u, \psi_{\gamma(\mathbf{x}_0)}(W); [t_0, t_1])) \\
&\qquad \text{[by the definition of } Reachset \text{ and by Theorem 2]} \\
&= \cup_{\mathbf{x}_0 \in X_0} \phi_{\gamma(\mathbf{x}_0)}{}^{-1}(Reachset(\bar{\mathbf{x}}_0, u, \psi_{\gamma(\mathbf{x}_0)}(W); [t_0, t_1])) \\
&\qquad \text{[where } \bar{\mathbf{x}}_0 \in \mathscr{C}\text{]} \\
&\subseteq \cup_{\mathbf{x}_0 \in X_0} \phi_{\gamma(\mathbf{x}_0)}{}^{-1}(Reachset(\bar{X}_0, u, \bar{W}; [t_0, t_1])),
\end{aligned}
\tag{2}
$$

where the last step follows from the fact that $Reachset(\bar{\mathbf{x}}_0, u, \psi_{\gamma(\mathbf{x}_0)}(W)) \subseteq Reachset(\bar{X}_0, u, \bar{W}; [t_0, t_1])$ since $\bar{\mathbf{x}}_0 \in \bar{X}_0$ and $\psi_{\gamma(\mathbf{x}_0)}(W) \subseteq \bar{W}$.

B Specification Correspondence Between a Continuous-Time System and a Corresponding Discrete Abstraction

Theorem 3 below is an adaptation of Lemma 4.23 of [14] to our continuous-to-discrete abstraction setting. Theorem 3 shows that the existence of a FSR implies that for every trajectory ξ of system (1), there exists a corresponding execution σ of the discrete system. In that case, we say that $\mathscr{A}$ is an *abstraction* of $(X, U, W, f, \beta, \tau)$, with control signals constrained to be in $\mathscr{U}_c$, the set of left-piecewise-constant functions, which only switch at time periods of τ time units, mapping $\mathbb{R}_{\geq 0}$ to the set $\beta(\mathscr{U})$.

Theorem 3 (Executions correspondence). *For any $\mathbf{x} \in X, u \in \mathscr{U}_c$, measurable $w : \mathbb{R}_{\geq 0} \to W$, and time horizon $T \geq 0$: there exists an execution $\sigma = \langle(\{s_0\}, s_0, a_0), \ldots, (\{s_{l,j}\}_{j \in z_l}, s_l, \bot)\rangle$ of $\mathscr{A}$, where $k = \lceil \frac{T}{\tau} \rceil$, such that for all indices $i \in [l]$, $\beta(a_i) = u(i\tau)$, $(\xi(\mathbf{x}, u, w; i\tau), s_i) \in \mathscr{R}$, and for all indices $i \in [l]$, $\forall t \in [i\tau, \min\{(i+1)\tau, T\}]$, $\exists j \in [z_{i+1}]$ such that $(\xi(\mathbf{x}, u, w; t), s_{i+1,j}) \in \mathscr{R}$.*

We say that σ in Theorem 3 *represents* ξ. Also, we abuse notation and say that $\sigma \in \mathscr{R}(\xi)$ and $\xi \in \mathscr{R}^{-1}(\sigma)$. The proof of the theorem is similar to that of Lemma 4.23 of [14], and skip it here for conciseness.

In the following corollary of Theorem 3, we show that if a trajectory ξ of system (1) violates the reach-avoid specification (X_r, X_a), then any corresponding execution σ of $\mathscr{A}$, as defined in Theorem 3, violates the reach-avoid specification $(\mathscr{X}_r, \mathscr{X}_a)$ as well. Moreover, if an execution σ satisfies the reach-avoid specification $(\mathscr{X}_r, \mathscr{X}_a)$, then any trajectory ξ of system (1) that is related to σ in $\mathscr{R}$ satisfies the (X_r, X_a) specification.

Corollary 2 (Specification correspondence). *For any $\mathbf{x} \in X, u \in \mathscr{U}_c$, measurable $w : \mathbb{R}_{\geq 0} \to W$, and time horizon $T \geq 0$: if $\exists t \in [0, T]$ such that $\xi(\mathbf{x}, u, w; t) \in X_a$, let $i = \lfloor \frac{t}{\tau} \rfloor$, then $\exists j \in [z_i]$, such that $s_{i,j} \in \mathscr{X}_a$. Moreover, if $\nexists t \in [0, T]$ such that $\xi(\mathbf{x}, u, w; t) \in X_r$, then for all $\sigma \in \mathscr{R}(\xi)$, $\nexists i \in [\lceil \frac{T}{\tau} \rceil + 1]$ and $j \in [z_i]$ such that $s_{i,j} \in \mathscr{X}_r$. On the other hand, fix any execution σ of $\mathscr{A}$ of length $l \geq 1$. Then, if $\nexists i \in [l+1]$ and $j \in [z_i]$, such that $s_{i,j} \in \mathscr{X}_a$, then for all $\xi \in \mathscr{R}^{-1}(\sigma)$, $\nexists t \in [0, k\tau]$ such that $\xi(\mathbf{x}, u, w; t) \in X_a$. Moreover, if $s_l \in \mathscr{X}_r$, then for any $\xi \in \mathscr{R}^{-1}(\sigma)$ of duration $l\tau$, $\xi(\mathbf{x}, u, w; l\tau) \in X_r$.*

In addition to Theorem 3, the proof of Corollary 2 follows from the definition of $\mathscr{X}_r$ which under-approximates X_r and the definition of $\mathscr{X}_a$ which over-approximates X_a.

The following corollary of Corollary 2 shows that if the controller $\mathscr{K}$ of $\mathscr{A}$ satisfies a reach-avoid specification that abstracts the reach-avoid specification of system (1), then the controller it induces satisfies that specification of system (1).

Corollary 3. *If there exists a discrete abstraction $\mathscr{A}$ of $(X, U, W, f, \beta, \tau)$, an abstraction $(\mathscr{X}_r, \mathscr{X}_a)$ of (X_r, X_a), and a controller $\mathscr{K}$ that satisfies the discrete reach-avoid specification $(\mathscr{X}_r, \mathscr{X}_a)$ for $\mathscr{A}$ starting from a set $R \subseteq \mathscr{X}$, then the zero-order-hold controller induced by $\mathscr{K}$ satisfies the reach-avoid specification (X_r, X_a) for system (1) starting from the set $\mathscr{R}^{-1}(R) \subseteq X$.*

C Details of the Ship-Docking Case Study

The kinematics of a marine vessel can be approximated using the ODE [19]: $\dot{\eta} = R(\theta)\nu + \nu_c$, where $\eta = [N; E; \theta] \in \mathbb{R}^3$ is the state of the ship representing its South-North and West-East position and its heading angle, respectively. The control input ν is a 3-dimensional vector that determines the surge, sway, and yaw velocities of the ship. $R(\theta)$ is a rotation matrix that given the heading angle θ, rotates ν from body coordinates to the global coordinates where $\theta = 0$ points to the North. Finally, ν_c represents the disturbance resulting from water-current velocities. We consider the same environment and reach-avoid specification of Meyer et al. [19], where the ship is required to dock while avoiding obstacles in a rectangular pier. We make a slight modification to represent boundaries as obstacles. The original model of the ship is 6-dimensional. However, as shown in [19], three dimensions can be abstracted using another form of abstraction, called *continuous abstraction*.

We implemented our algorithms in Python. We used TIRA [18] (implemented in Matlab) to compute the reachable sets in Algorithm 2. The reachable sets are represented as lists of time-annotated axis-aligned hyper-rectangles in $\mathbb{R}^3$. Then, we transformed their hyper-rectangles to polytopes before translating and rotating them to obtain the reachable sets starting from the different cells in Q_x to get the relevant transitions in δ_{grid} during synthesis. We used the Polytope library[3] to perform such transformations. We over-approximate the union in Corollary 1 by transforming the reachable set in *ReachDict* using the frames corresponding to the vertices of the hyper-rectangle representing X_0, and then taking the bounding box of the resulting reachable sets.

We follow the experimental setup of [19]: we consider the rectangular state set $X = [0,10] \times [0,6.5] \times [-\pi,\pi]$ and input set $U = [-0.18, 0.18] \times [-0.05, 0.05] \times [-0.1, 0.1]$. We use a disturbance set $W = [\frac{-0.01}{\sqrt{2}}, \frac{0.01}{\sqrt{2}}]^3$ smaller than the one in [19], which was $[-0.01, 0.01]^3$, since after the rotations in Corollary 1, our W will become the set $\bar{W} = [-0.01, 0.01]^3$. For the reach-avoid specification, as [19], we consider the reach set $X_r = [7,10] \times [0,6.5] \times [\pi/3, 2\pi/3]$ and the avoid sets $X_a = X_{a,0} \cup X_{a,1}$, where $X_{a,0} = [2,2.5] \times [0,3] \times [-\pi,\pi]$ and $X_{a,1} = [5,5.5] \times [3.5,6.5] \times [-\pi,\pi]$. However, in contrast with [19], we add more avoid sets to represent the boundaries of X. The reason behind this change is to keep track of the environment boundaries in the symmetry-based abstraction. We do that as follows: first, we expand the boundaries of X by 3 units in each of the first two dimensions, resulting in $X = [-3, 13] \times [-3, 9.5] \times [-\pi, \pi]$. Then, we expand the two avoid sets and add four new obstacles at each side of X resulting in $X_a = \cup_{i \in [6]} X_{a,i}$, where $X_{a,0} = [2,2.5] \times [-3,3] \times [-\pi,\pi]$, $X_{a,1} = [5,5.5] \times [3.5,9.5] \times [-\pi,\pi]$, $X_{a,1} = [5,5.5] \times [3.5,9.5] \times [-\pi,\pi]$, $X_{a,2} = [-3,0] \times [-3,9.5] \times [-\pi,\pi]$, $X_{a,3} = [-3,13] \times [-3,0] \times [-\pi,\pi]$, $X_{a,4} = [-3,13] \times [-3,9.5] \times [-\pi,\pi]$, and $X_{a,5} = [10,13] \times [6.5,9.5] \times [-\pi,\pi]$. Since our environment is larger, having the same number of partitions per dimensions in Q_x as Meyer et al. [19] results in larger cells in our case. Hence, we consider a finer gridding ($80 \times 100 \times 50$ in the fourth resolution in our experiments) than the one in [19] ($50 \times 50 \times 50$), which roughly amounts to the same cell size. We choose τ to be 3 s. We modified TIRA [18] to generate the full reachable set instead of just the one at $T = \tau = 3$ seconds. Instead, it now results

[3] https://pypi.org/project/polytope/.

in a sequence of axis-aligned rectangles representing the reachable sets in the different sub-intervals of $[0, \tau]$. In our case study, we choose to partition $[0, \tau]$ to four intervals, resulting in reachable sets with four rectangles. Example reachable sets starting from the origin using the centers of the grid Q_u over U as constant control signals is shown in Fig. 1.

In strategies 1, 2, 4, and 5, we start with batches of size 3 and multiply that by 5 at the end of the for-loop in line 8 until the limit is reached (400 or all 9^3, depends on the strategy). We consider the greedy approach to update A except in the last one, at which we follow the random approach to sample 75 unique symbols to explore.

We ran all experiments on an 18 core Intel i9 7980xe with an AMD64 instruction set and stock speeds with ASUS multicore enhancement defaults, 80 GB of 2666 MHz ddr4 RAM with a 16 GB ZRAM partition, and Ubuntu 22.04 operating system.

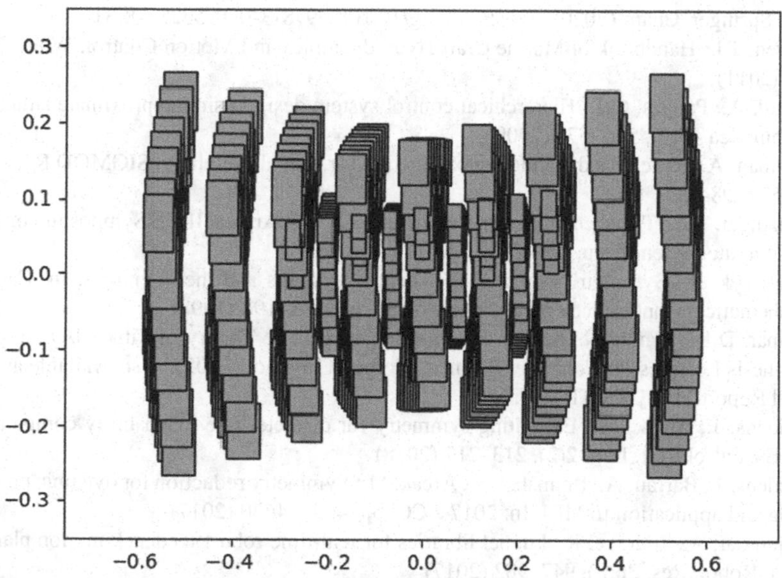

Fig. 1. *ReachDict*: set of reachable sets, projected into the position coordinates, for the ship example having the origin as the initial state following 9^3 different constant control signals (centers of the cells in Q_u that partitions U to 9 intervals in each of the three dimensions) for 3 s divided into 4 time steps.

References

1. Bogomolov, S., et al.: Assume-guarantee abstraction refinement meets hybrid systems. In: Yahav, E. (ed.) HVC 2014. LNCS, vol. 8855, pp. 116–131. Springer, Cham (2014). https://doi.org/10.1007/978-3-319-13338-6_10
2. Bonnabel, S., Martin, P., Rouchon, P.: Symmetry-preserving observers. IEEE Trans. Autom. Control **53**(11), 2514–2526 (2008)

3. Cartan, E.J., Leray, J.-L.: La théorie des groupes finis et continus et la géométrie différentielle traitées par la méthode du repère mobile : leçons professées à la sorbonne (1937)
4. Cohen, T.S., Welling, M.: Group equivariant convolutional networks. In: Proceedings of the 33rd International Conference on International Conference on Machine Learning, ICML 2016, vol. 48, pp. 2990–2999. JMLR.org (2016)
5. Damers, J., Jaulin, L., Rohou, S.: Lie symmetries applied to interval integration. Automatica **144**(C) (2022)
6. Doyen, L., Henzinger, T.A., Raskin, J.-F.: Automatic rectangular refinement of affine hybrid systems. In: Pettersson, P., Yi, W. (eds.) FORMATS 2005. LNCS, vol. 3829, pp. 144–161. Springer, Heidelberg (2005). https://doi.org/10.1007/11603009_13
7. Duggirala, P.S., Mitra, S., Viswanathan, M., Potok, M.: C2E2: a verification tool for stateflow models. In: Baier, C., Tinelli, C. (eds.) TACAS 2015. LNCS, vol. 9035, pp. 68–82. Springer, Heidelberg (2015). https://doi.org/10.1007/978-3-662-46681-0_5
8. Fan, C., Miller, K., Mitra, S.: Fast and guaranteed safe controller synthesis for nonlinear vehicle models. In: Lahiri, S.K., Wang, C. (eds.) CAV 2020. LNCS, vol. 12224, pp. 629–652. Springer, Cham (2020). https://doi.org/10.1007/978-3-030-53288-8_31
9. Fossen, T.I.: Handbook of Marine Craft Hydrodynamics and Motion Control. Wiley, Hoboken (2011)
10. Girard, A., Pappas, G.J.: Hierarchical control system design using approximate simulation. Automatica **45**(2), 566–571 (2009)
11. Guttman, A.: R-trees: a dynamic index structure for spatial searching. SIGMOD Rec. **14**(2), 47–57 (1984)
12. Henzinger, T.A.: The theory of hybrid automata. In: 11th Annual IEEE Symposium on Logic in Computer Science, pp. 278–292 (1996)
13. Jakubczyk, B.: Symmetries of nonlinear control systems and their symbols. In: Canadian Mathematical Conference Proceedings, vol. 25, pp. 183–198 (1998)
14. Kaynar, D.K., Lynch, N., Segala, R., Vaandrager, F.: The Theory of Timed I/O Automata. Synthesis Lectures on Computer Science. Morgan Claypool (2005). Also available as Technical Report MIT-LCS-TR-917, MIT
15. Maidens, J., Arcak, M.: Exploiting symmetry for discrete-time reachability computations. IEEE Control Syst. Lett. **2**(2), 213–217 (2018)
16. Maidens, J., Barrau, A., Bonnabel, S., Arcak, M.: Symmetry reduction for dynamic programming and application to MRI. In: 2017 ACC, pp. 4625–4630 (2017)
17. Majumdar, A., Tedrake, R.: Funnel libraries for real-time robust feedback motion planning. Int. J. Robot. Res. **36**(8), 947–982 (2017)
18. Meyer, P.-J., Devonport, A., Arcak, M.: TIRA: toolbox for interval reachability analysis. In: Proceedings of the 22nd ACM International Conference on Hybrid Systems: Computation and Control, HSCC 2019, pp. 224–229. ACM, New York (2019)
19. Meyer, P.-J., Yin, H., Brodtkorb, A.H., Arcak, M., Sørensen, A.J.: Continuous and discrete abstractions for planning, applied to ship docking. ArXiv, abs/1911.09773 (2020)
20. Noether, E.: Invarianten beliebiger differentialausdrücke. Nachrichten von der Gesellschaft der Wissenschaften zu Göttingen Mathematisch-Physikalische Klasse **1918**, 37–44 (1918)
21. Pola, G., Pepe, P., Benedetto, M.D.D.: Decentralized supervisory control of networks of nonlinear control systems. IEEE Trans. Autom. Control **63**(9), 2803–2817 (2018)
22. Reissig, G., Weber, A., Rungger, M.: Feedback refinement relations for the synthesis of symbolic controllers. IEEE Trans. Autom. Control **62**(4), 1781–1796 (2017)
23. Roohi, N., Prabhakar, P., Viswanathan, M.: HARE: a hybrid abstraction refinement engine for verifying non-linear hybrid automata. In: Legay, A., Margaria, T. (eds.) TACAS 2017. LNCS, vol. 10205, pp. 573–588. Springer, Heidelberg (2017). https://doi.org/10.1007/978-3-662-54577-5_33

24. Russo, G., Slotine, J.-J.E.: Symmetries, stability, and control in nonlinear systems and networks. Phys. Rev. E **84**(4), 041929 (2011)
25. Sibai, H., Li, Y., Mitra, S.: SceneChecker: boosting scenario verification using symmetry abstractions. In: Silva, A., Leino, K.R.M. (eds.) CAV 2021. LNCS, vol. 12759, pp. 580–594. Springer, Cham (2021). https://doi.org/10.1007/978-3-030-81685-8_28
26. Sibai, H., Mitra, S.: Symmetry-based abstractions for hybrid automata. IEEE Trans. Autom. Control 1–8 (2023)
27. Sibai, H., Mokhlesi, N., Fan, C., Mitra, S.: Multi-agent safety verification using symmetry transformations. In: TACAS 2020. LNCS, vol. 12078, pp. 173–190. Springer, Cham (2020). https://doi.org/10.1007/978-3-030-45190-5_10
28. Sibai, H., Mokhlesi, N., Mitra, S.: Using symmetry transformations in equivariant dynamical systems for their safety verification. In: Chen, Y.-F., Cheng, C.-H., Esparza, J. (eds.) ATVA 2019. LNCS, vol. 11781, pp. 98–114. Springer, Cham (2019). https://doi.org/10.1007/978-3-030-31784-3_6
29. Tabuada, P.: Verification and Control of Hybrid Systems: A Symbolic Approach, 1st edn. Springer, New York (2009). https://doi.org/10.1007/978-1-4419-0224-5
30. van der Pol, E., Worrall, D., van Hoof, H., Oliehoek, F., Welling, M.: MDP homomorphic networks: group symmetries in reinforcement learning. In: NeurIPS, vol. 33, pp. 4199–4210. Curran Associates, Inc. (2020)

SMT-Based Aircraft Conflict Detection and Resolution

Saswata Paul, Baoluo Meng(✉), and Christopher Alexander

GE Aerospace Research, Niskayuna, NY 12309, USA
{saswata.paul,baoluo.meng,christopher.alexander}@ge.com

Abstract. The integration of Unmanned Aircraft Systems (UAS) in the National Airspace System (NAS) for Urban Air Mobility (UAM) operations will create the need to develop robust, efficient, and verifiable tools and techniques for UAS Traffic Management (UTM). In this paper, we present a novel approach for strategic detection and resolution of airborne conflicts using Satisfiability Modulo Theories (SMT) solvers. Our approach takes a flight plan for an ownship, a set of immutable flight plans for traffic aircraft, and a set of constraints, and then returns a flight plan for the ownship that satisfies all constraints and is also conflict free with respect to the traffic aircraft. The constraints can relate to operational, business, or other aspects which must be considered while setting up the conflict resolution task as a constraint satisfaction problem. We present simulations of our approach using a prototype implementation based on dReal, an SMT solver that is specialized for solving non-linear real function problems, showing promising results.

Keywords: Urban Air Mobility · UAS Traffic Management · Autonomous Navigation · SMT-Based Deconfliction · Constraint Solving

1 Introduction

In the near future, Unmanned Aircraft Systems (UAS) will be integrated in the National Airspace System (NAS) for various applications such as package delivery and data collection. This will warrant the need for smarter autonomous air-traffic management (ATM) techniques better-suited to deal with high-density air traffic than traditional human-operated air-traffic control (ATC). Autonomous ATM systems can be deployed either in a centralized or a decentralized manner [16], but in both configurations such systems must be capable of ensuring *standard separation* [10] between the aircraft in order to prevent catastrophic incidents like *near mid-air collisions* (NMAC) [28]. Two types of approaches are commonly used for maintaining standard separation between aircraft—*tactical approaches* (*e.g.*, [23]), which are effective in resolving imminent conflicts between aircraft by using tactical maneuvers, and *strategic approaches* (*e.g.*, [32]), which can be used for detecting and resolving conflicts between aircraft by monitoring their flight plans either prior to or during their execution.

N. Benz et al. (Eds.): NFM 2024, LNCS 14627, pp. 186–203, 2024.
https://doi.org/10.1007/978-3-031-60698-4_11

The difference between tactical and strategic approaches is that the former allows for conflict detection with shorter *look-ahead* times while the latter involves analysis of potential hazards over longer look-ahead times [8]. Purely tactical maneuvers usually require almost instantaneous reactions from pilots and flight control computers. Such maneuvers may not always be feasible in the highly-dense urban airspaces of the future. A combination of strategic and tactical approaches can provide more flexibility and preparedness for aircraft operating in urban air mobility (UAM) scenarios.

In recent years, Satisfiability Modulo Theory (SMT) solvers have emerged as widely used and effective tools to reason about complex, real-world constraints. SMT checks if first-order logical formulas over one or more theories are satisfiable or not. A theory in this context could be finite sets and relations [21]. A decision procedure for a theory determines whether the constraints in the theory are satisfiable. SMT solvers consist of several theory solvers and can effectively decide the satisfiability of constraints over a combination of theories [18,21,34]. Due, in part, to the emergence of efficient decision procedures, SMT solvers have been used to design new applications for synthesis of system design [19], cybersecurity analysis [20,22,37], test case generation [17], and verification of machine learning systems [14], among others. dReal [13] is an SMT solver specializing in solving first-order logic formulas over real numbers. It can solve problems that involve a wide range of nonlinear operators including power, square root, and trigonometric functions[1]. dReal implements the framework of *δ-complete decision procedures* in which δ is a numerical error bound specified by the user. When dReal answers "unsat" on the input formulas, the formula is guaranteed to be unsatisfiable, whereas a "δ-sat" answer indicates that a δ-perturbed form of the input formula is satisfiable. The probability of a conflict being zero in real-life aerospace circumstances is not realistic due to uncertainties that exist in practical operating conditions of aerospace systems [36]. The notion of δ satisfiability, albeit conservative in our case, allows us to take into account such uncertainties as it guarantees that if dReal returns unsat, then there is no conflict. When it returns δ-sat, a potential conflict is identified, however, there is a chance that no conflict exists within an acceptable error margin δ. Since aerospace systems are safety-critical, for any conflict detection approach, it is acceptable to incorrectly detect conflicts within an acceptable error margin as long as it is guaranteed that all possible conflicts will be correctly detected.

Several approaches for strategic conflict management exist in the literature (*e.g.*, [3,33,35,40]). Paul *et al.* [31], presented a formally-verified strategic conflict detection and resolution algorithm that is capable of detecting conflicts between a given *flight plan* for an *ownship* and a set of traffic flight plans and generating resolutions to avoid such conflicts. A flight plan is simply a collection of *waypoints* in the 4 dimensional space where each waypoint is connected by a straight-line constant-velocity *flight segment*. Their conflict resolution approach involves assigning appropriate values of ground speed to the flight segments in

---

[1] Other SMT solvers, such as Z3 [7], which support non-linear arithmetic, do not fully support trigonometric functions, which is needed for this work.

the ownship's flight plan such that the ownship can maintain standard separation with the known traffic aircraft. They present a proof-of-concept software implementation for this task, and verify correctness properties for an independent formal specification of the implementation using an interactive theorem proving system. In this work, we build upon Paul *et al.*'s logic for conflict detection and resolution, but instead of specifying a concrete algorithm to solve the problem, we set up the task of conflict detection and resolution as a constraint satisfaction problem and use dReal to solve it. The use of an SMT solver for this purpose has two major advantages over Paul *et al.*'s approach. Firstly, the problem of conflict detection and resolution can be converted into a constraint-solving problem where it is sufficient to declaratively specify the desirable properties of a valid solution rather than concretely specifying the logical steps to generate the solution. The declarative paradigm allows the encoding of complex properties that can easily be verified for correctness and also makes it possible to encode a wide variety of desirable constraints in addition to conflict resolution. Secondly, a solution generated by an SMT solver can have a high degree of confidence associated with it since a satisfiable solution can be checked by straightforward means and *proof certificates* can be generated for an *unsatisfiable solution* that detail how to derive a contradiction from the inputs [15]. In addition, the proofs from an SMT solver can be independently checked by third-party theorem provers [11]. This high-degree of confidence provided by SMT solvers makes our approach more appropriate for *safety-critical* aerospace applications over Paul *et al.*'s approach, in which the unverified software may have differences with the formal specification used for verification.

The contributions of this paper are:

- it presents a novel approach for strategic conflict detection and resolution by setting up the task as a constraint satisfaction problem and using SMT solvers to find valid solutions,
- it presents an approach for encoding additional constraints in SMT-LIB to find valid solutions which are not just conflict-free but also satisfy some desirable aerodynamic, business, and operational constraints, and
- it presents simulations to showcase the effectiveness of the approach for realistic airborne collision detection and avoidance using an implementation based on the dReal SMT solver.

The rest of the paper is organized as follows: Sect. 2 details our approach; Sect. 3 provides simulations to show the effectiveness of our approach; Sect. 4 provides a discussion on applicable operations for our approach and potential areas of improvement; Sect. 5 discusses related work in the literature and Sect. 6 concludes the paper with a discussion on future work.

2 SMT-Based Conflict Detection and Resolution

Two aircraft are said to be in conflict at a point in time if their vertical and horizontal separations are less than two given thresholds H and D at that time [9]. These thresholds form a *"hockey-puck"* shaped volume around each aircraft called the *well-clear volume* [25] (Fig. 1). The intersections of well-clear volumes of two aircraft at any point in time is constituted as an NMAC.

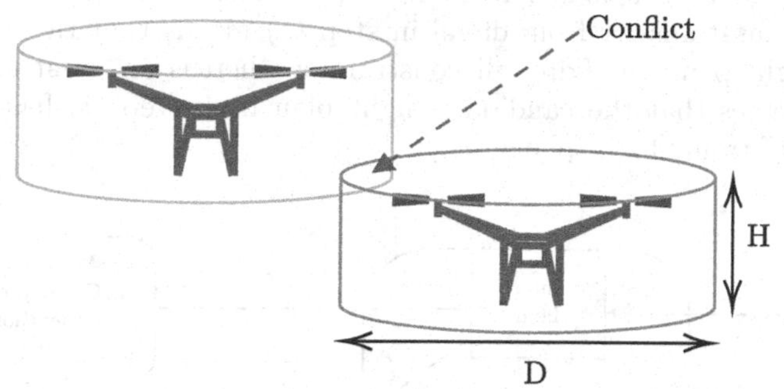

Fig. 1. Conflicts are caused by the intersection of well-clear volumes.

The problem for conflict detection and resolution can, therefore, be stated as— *"given a flight plan for an ownship F_o, a horizontal threshold D, a vertical threshold H, and a set of flight plans for traffic aircraft Φ, generate a conflict-free flight plan $\bar{F_o}$ if there is any conflict between F_o and any element of Φ"*[2]. [3]The problem can be made more challenging by imposing a set of aerodynamic, operational, or business constraints (see Sect. 2.1) on the solution flight plans[4].

Our approach for conflict detection and resolution consists of two consecutive steps which are designed as separate constraint satisfaction problems:

1. *Generating valid candidate flight plans* - A candidate flight plan is a flight plan that takes into account all the aerodynamic, business, or operational constraints that are imposed on $\bar{F_o}$. It may or may not have conflicts with the given set of traffic flight plans Φ. We generate all possible candidate flight plans by encoding the constraints in SMT-LIB and repeatedly pushing the negation of each identified candidate to the context of dReal until a satisfiable solution is returned by dReal.[5]. A satisfying solution from dReal is converted to a candidate flight plan.
2. *Analyzing the generated candidates for conflict* - As the potential candidates are generated, we check each one of them for possible conflicts with the elements of Φ. We encode the constraints for conflict detection in SMT-LIB and

[2] We use the definition of [31] where $\bar{F_o}$ has the same spatial configuration as F_o.

[3] This problem statement aligns well with the *discovery and synchronization service* (DSS) based concept of operation for UAM where a *provider of services for UAM* (PSU) has to prove awareness of other PSUs with active operations in an area for its proposed operation to be accepted by the DSS of that area [6].

[4] These constraints can also take into account factors like the aerodynamic capabilities of the ownship (*e.g.*, fixed wing vs rotorcraft, flight-surface damage, etc.).

[5] In this paper, the solution space is finite and bounded by a set of discrete ground speeds allowed for the ownship (see Sect. 2.1).

use dReal to check if a particular candidate for $\bar{F}_o$ is conflict-free or not. A candidate is returned as an output if and only if it is identified to be conflict-free from all elements of Φ.

Every candidate that is generated in step (1) is sent to step (2) for conflict analysis. An unsat answer from dReal in step (1) means that there is no valid candidate flight plan satisfying all constraints; whereas an unsat answer from step (2) indicates that the candidate flight plan from step (1) has no conflict with the set of traffic flight plans.

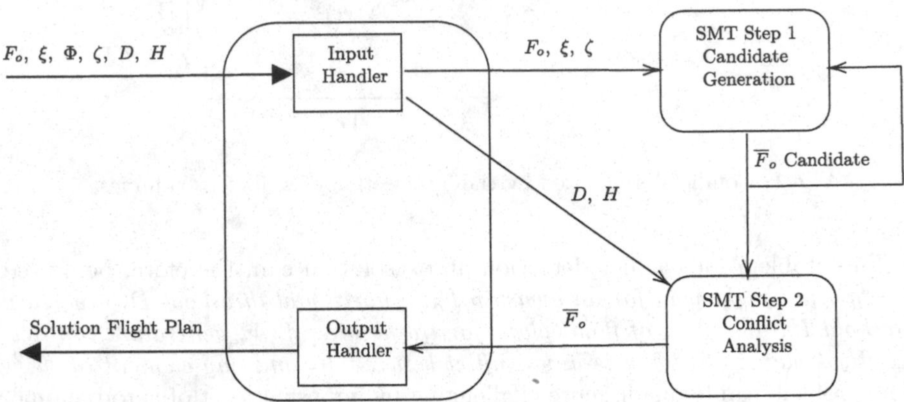

Fig. 2. Schematics of the SMT-based conflict detection and resolution approach.

2.1 Generating Valid Candidate Flight Plans

As defined earlier, for a conflict to occur at a point in time, the well-clear volumes of two aircraft need to intersect at that time. Therefore, $\bar{F}_o$ can be guaranteed to be conflict-free if it does not have concurrent horizontal and vertical threshold violations with any element of Φ. Many different strategies can be used for ensuring this invariant, *e.g.*, either the waypoints can be spatially shifted or the velocities in the flight segments of $\bar{F}_o$ can be chosen to prevent concurrent horizontal and vertical violations. A valid strategy can be specified as a constraint satisfaction problem by identifying the appropriate constraints and the resulting solution space will be constraint-dependent. For simplicity, we adopt Paul *et al.*'s approach of varying the velocities in the flight segments to avoid conflicts [31]—there is a set of ground speeds ξ that the ownship can fly with, but it cannot deviate spatially from its original flight plan F_o. An appropriate ground speed from ξ is assigned to each segment of F_o and then the vertical speed is adjusted to ensure that the 3D profile of $\bar{F}_o$ remains similar to that of F_o. Therefore, only the temporal profile changes for the solution flight plan. The solution space for valid candidates, therefore, is all possible permutations of ground speed assignments to the different segments of F_o.

The approach that is taken for generating valid candidates is as follows: a set ζ of useful realistic constraints are identified and encoded in SMT-LIB for dReal to solve. A δ-sat answer from dReal indicates that there exists a valid candidate flight plan that satisfies all constraints. The negation of the solution is then pushed to the context of dReal to generate a different satisfying solution. This process continues until dReal can no longer find any valid candidates (Table 1).

Table 1. The notations used for describing the conflict detection logic.

Notation	Description	SMT Declaration
$s_{x,t,X}$	Position of an aircraft in the x axis	(declare-const s_x_t_X Real)
$s_{y,t,X}$	Position of an aircraft in the y axis	(declare-const s_y_t_X Real)
$s_{z,t,X}$	Position of an aircraft in the z axis	(declare-const s_z_t_X Real)
$v_{xy,t,X}$	Velocity of an aircraft in the xy plane	(declare-const v_xy_t_X Real)
$v_{z,t,X}$	Velocity of an aircraft in the z axis	(declare-const v_z_t_X Real)
$\lambda_{t,X}$	True heading of an aircraft in the xy plane	(declare-const l_t_X Real)
$v_{x,t,X}$	Velocity of an aircraft in the x axis	(declare-const v_x_t_X Real)
$v_{y,t,X}$	Velocity of an aircraft in the y axis	(declare-const s_y_t_X Real)
$s_{x,t}$	Relative position in the x axis	(declare-const s_x_t Real)
$s_{y,t}$	Relative position in the y axis	(declare-const s_y_t Real)
$v_{x,t}$	Relative velocity in the x axis	(declare-const v_x_t Real)
$v_{y,t}$	Relative velocity in the y axis	(declare-const v_y_t Real)
$s_{z,t}$	Relative position in the z axis	(declare-const s_z_t Real)
$v_{z,t}$	Relative velocity in the z axis	(declare-const v_z_t Real)

Aerodynamic, Operational, and Business Constraints: We list here a set of generic constraints for generating valid candidates in step 1[6]:

1. *Constraint on the velocity difference between consecutive segments:*
From an aerodynamic perspective, aircraft cannot accelerate or decelerate instantaneously. Therefore, a valid flight plan should ensure that the difference in velocity between consecutive segments is within some practical threshold that depends on the aircraft model in question. Given the set of segments S in a flight plan, this constraint can therefore be defined as:

$$\varphi_{\text{vel}} \equiv \forall s_1, s_2 \in S : |v_{xy,s_2} - v_{xy,s_1}| \leq \Gamma_{\text{vel\_change}}$$

where v_{xy,s_1} and v_{xy,s_2} are the velocities in s_1 and s_2, and $\Gamma_{\text{vel\_change}}$ is the threshold of velocity change.
An example SMT encoding for this constraint is illustrated below, where *v_xy_1* and *v_xy_2* are velocity variables for the two consecutive segments 1 and 2 , respectively, and 40 is the allowed threshold of the velocity change for the two segments.

```
(assert ( <= (abs (- v_xy_1, v_xy_2)) 40))
```

[6] Depending on the use case, the constraints can be adjusted accordingly.

2. *Constraint on the arc length required for turns:*

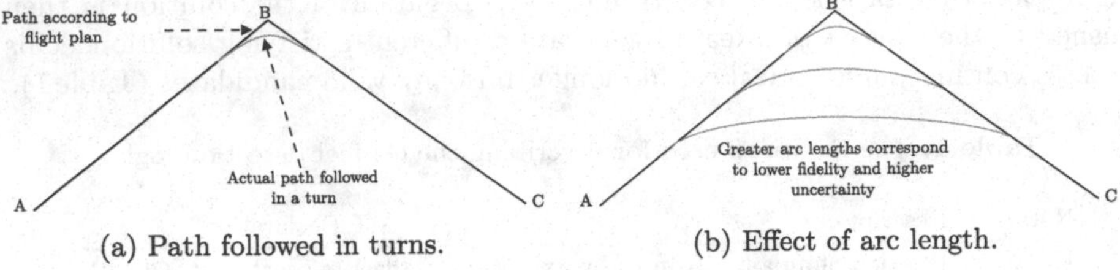

(a) Path followed in turns. (b) Effect of arc length.

Fig. 3. Uncertainty involved in turns at waypoints.

At each waypoint in a flight plan, an aircraft changes its heading and makes a turn towards the next waypoint. Due to aerodynamic restrictions, aircraft may not instantaneously change direction and need to follow arc-shaped paths while making such turns (Fig. 3). The larger the length of the arc, the more the aircraft deviates from the planned straight line segments in the flight plan (Fig. 3). To minimize this uncertainty, it is desirable to ensure that the required *arc lengths* $\bar{a}$ for the turns remain as small as possible. The required arc length $\bar{a}$ depends on the *radius of turn* r_Φ, the change in heading $\Delta\lambda$, and the ground speed v (Eq. 1). In the absence of wind[7], the radius of the turn depends on the ground speed v_{xy} and the *bank angle* ϕ of a turn (Eq. 2) [27].

$$\bar{a} = \frac{(\Delta\lambda) r_\phi}{v_{xy}} \tag{1}$$

$$r_\Phi = \frac{v_{xy}^2}{G \tan\phi} \tag{2}$$

The relationship between $\bar{a}$ and v_{xy} can now be stated as:

$$\bar{a} = \frac{(\Delta\lambda) v_{xy}}{G \tan\phi}$$

For simplicity, we can assume two things—to reduce the arc length, the aircraft will use the smallest possible bank angle ϕ_s for the turns and the aircraft will maintain a velocity $\bar{v}_{xy}$ equal to the average of the velocities in the two segments corresponding to a turn. Therefore a constraint on the arc length can now be specified in terms of the velocities of any two consecutive segments s_1 and s_2.

$$\varphi_{\text{arclen}} \equiv \forall s_1, s_2 \in S : |\frac{(\lambda_{s2} - \lambda_{s1})\bar{v}_{xy}}{G \tan\phi_s}| \leq \Gamma_{\text{arclen}}$$

where λ_{s1} and λ_{s2} are the headings in s_1 and s_2 respectively.

[7] For simplicity, in this paper we assume the absence of wind. However, more complicated constraints may be designed by factoring in wind.

3. *Constraint on the total fuel cost:*
The total fuel cost $\psi_{f,F}$ for a flight plan F can be computed by Eq. 3 where $\mathcal{T}_F$ represents the total flight time and ρ_f represents the fuel consumption rate of the aircraft model [26,39].
$$\psi_{f,F} = \mathcal{T}_F \rho_f \tag{3}$$
A constraint on the total fuel consumption for a solution flight plan $\bar{F}_o$ can be defined as follows:
$$\varphi_{\texttt{fuel}} \equiv \psi_{f,\bar{F}_o} \leq \Gamma_{\texttt{fuel}}$$

4. *Constraint on operational costs:*
Airline companies often associate some operational costs (Eq. 4) to a flight plan F by using an *operational cost index* ρ_o that accounts for the costs of aircraft maintenance, crew salary, etc. [24].
$$\psi_{o,F} = \mathcal{T}_F \rho_o \tag{4}$$
A constraint that takes into consideration these costs can be specified as:
$$\varphi_{\texttt{op}} \equiv \psi_{o,\bar{F}_o} \leq \Gamma_{\texttt{op}}$$

5. *Constraint on the total flight time:*
A constraint on the total time of flight for a solution $\bar{F}_o$ can be imposed for operational, business, or performance reasons.
$$\varphi_{\texttt{TOF}} \equiv \mathcal{T}_{\bar{F}_o} \leq \Gamma_{\texttt{TOF}}$$

6. *Constraint on the total delay:*
A constraint on the total delay caused by a solution flight plan $\bar{F}_o$ with respect to the original flight plan F_o can be imposed to ensure that an optimal solution is generated.
$$\varphi_{\texttt{delay}} \equiv \mathcal{T}_{\bar{F}_o} - \mathcal{T}_{F_o} \leq \Gamma_{\texttt{delay}}$$

2.2 Analyzing the Generated Candidates for Conflict

Once a valid candidate has been generated, it needs to be checked for conflicts with the available set of traffic flight plans Φ. This can be done by using a purely geometric framework that has a relative coordinate system which considers intervals when both aircraft maintain constant-velocity flights [12].

In a given interval of time $[t_0, t_1]$, it is possible to detect if two aircraft A and B have a violation of the horizontal and/or vertical thresholds D and H. For this, it is required to know the states of each aircraft at time t_0 as follows [12]:
$$\langle s_{x,t_0,A}, s_{y,t_0,A}, s_{z,t_0,A}, v_{xy,t_0,A}, v_{z,t_0,A}, \lambda_{t_0,A} \rangle$$
$$\langle s_{x,t_0,B}, s_{y,t_0,B}, s_{z,t_0,B}, v_{xy,t_0,B}, v_{z,t_0,B}, \lambda_{t_0,B} \rangle$$

where $s_{x,t,X}$, $s_{y,t,X}$, $s_{z,t,X}$, $v_{xy,t,X}$, $v_{z,t,X}$, and $\lambda_{t,X}$ represent the coordinates in the 3D space, the horizontal and vertical velocities, and the horizontal heading respectively for an aircraft X at time t. For the well-clear volumes of A and B to intersect at any time, both the horizontal threshold and the vertical threshold need to be violated at that time. Therefore, in order for a conflict to be present in an interval $[t_0, t_1]$, it is necessary that there exists some time $t_C : t_0 \leq t_C \leq t_1$ when both horizontal and vertical thresholds are violated. Below, we describe the mathematical logic to detect these violations independently.

Horizontal Threshold Violation

To detect violation of the horizontal threshold, we first find the x and y components of the horizontal velocities of both A and B as follows:

$$\begin{aligned} v_{x,t_0,A} &= v_{xy,t_0,A}\cos(\lambda_{t_0,A}) \\ v_{y,t_0,A} &= v_{xy,t_0,A}\sin(\lambda_{t_0,A}) \\ v_{x,t_0,B} &= v_{xy,t_0,B}\cos(\lambda_{t_0,B}) \\ v_{y,t_0,B} &= v_{xy,t_0,B}\sin(\lambda_{t_0,B}) \end{aligned}$$

Their relative positions and velocities in the xy plane are then calculated as:

$$\begin{aligned} s_{x,t_0} &= s_{x,t_0,A} - s_{x,t_0,B} \\ s_{y,t_0} &= s_{y,t_0,A} - s_{y,t_0,B} \\ v_{x,t_0} &= v_{x,t_0,A} - v_{x,t_0,B} \\ v_{y,t_0} &= v_{y,t_0,A} - v_{y,t_0,B} \end{aligned}$$

Now, given the relative horizontal positions and the relative horizontal velocities, it is possible to find the times at which the horizontal threshold D is violated by finding the roots of Eq. 5 where $a = v_{x,t_0}^2 + v_{y,t_0}^2$, $b = 2(s_{x,t_0}v_{x,t_0} + s_{y,t_0}v_{y,t_0})$, and $c = s_{x,t_0}^2 + s_{y,t_0}^2 - D^2$. If any root t' is found such that $t_0 \leq t_0 + t' \leq t_1$, then the horizontal threshold is violated at time $t_0 + t'$.

$$at^2 + bt + c = 0 \tag{5}$$

Vertical Threshold Violation

To detect vertical threshold violation, the relative vertical position and velocity for the aircraft are computed as follows:

$$\begin{aligned} s_{z,t_0} &= s_{z,t_0,A} - s_{z,t_0,B} \\ v_{z,t_0} &= v_{z,t_0,A} - v_{z,t_0,B} \end{aligned}$$

Now, at any time t, the vertical separation is given by $s_{z,t_0} + v_{z,t_0}(t - t_0)$. Therefore, for a vertical threshold violation to exist at a time t, Eq. 6 needs to be satisfied.

$$|s_{z,t_0} + v_{z,t_0}(t - t_0)| \leq H \tag{6}$$

The Conflict Constraint. The conflict-detection logic described earlier works if and only if both aircraft maintain constant-velocity flight paths in the interval $[t_0, t_1]$. Therefore, given two flight plans F_a and F_b for a traffic aircraft, the temporal dimension must be discretized into a set of consecutive intervals I_{F_a,F_b} where it is known that both aircraft maintain constant-velocities [31]. Each of these intervals can then be checked for conflicts independently in order to determine if there is a conflict between the two flight plans. The $\texttt{conflict}(\bar{F_a}, F_b)$ predicate returns *true* if and only if at some interval $[t_0, t_1] \in I_{F_a,F_b}$ there is some time t_C such that $t_C - t_0$ satisfies Eq. 5 and t_C satisfies Eq. 6.

Given a set of traffic flight plans Φ, any correct solution $\bar{F_o}$ should satisfy the constraint that it will be conflict-free from any member of the set Φ. Therefore, the conflict constraint can be specified as:

$$\varphi_{\texttt{conflict}} \equiv \forall F_i \in \Phi : \neg\texttt{conflict}(\bar{F_o}, F_i)$$

Detecting Conflicts with Stationary Objects. The conflict detection approach using flight plans can be easily generalized to detect conflicts with stationary objects. This can be done by modeling an object as a well-clear volume with a flight plan consisting of a single waypoint, and at all times, the volume remains stationary at that same waypoint. *E.g.*, if an obstacle is present at the 3D position $\langle s_{x,o}, s_{y,o}, s_{z,o}\rangle$, then its state at any time t can be represented by $\langle s_{x,o}, s_{y,o}, s_{z,o}, 0.0, 0.0, 0.0\rangle$. This will allow the conflict detection logic described above to work for detecting conflicts with such an object. The horizontal and vertical thresholds for stationary objects can be chosen as appropriate.

3 Simulations

3.1 Simulated Example

In this section, we present a hypothetical example in which our approach has been used to detect and resolve a potential conflict between three flight plans F_A, F_B and F_C for three aircraft A, B, and C respectively.

F_A consists of the series of waypoints $F_{A_1} = \langle -50,100,4,30,0,0\rangle$, $F_{A_2} = \langle -49,60,4,30,0,79.38987707834347\rangle$, and $F_{A_3} = \langle 0,0,4,30,0,233.09249935504437\rangle$ $F_{A_4} = \langle 120,0,4,30,0,471.1877374502825\rangle$; F_B consists of the series of waypoints $F_{B_1} = \langle 120,0,4,30,0,0\rangle$, $F_{B_2} = \langle 0,0,4,30,0,238.0952380952381\rangle$, and $F_{B_3} = \langle -50,-55,4,30,0,385.5760788424455\rangle$; and F_C consists of the series of waypoints $F_{C_1} = \langle 0,50,4,30,0,0\rangle$, $F_{C_2} = \langle 100,60,4,30,0,294.9616814944148\rangle$, and $F_{C_3} = \langle 120,70,4,30,0,339.3281096194106\rangle$. where a waypoint is represented by a tuple ⟨*x axis position in feet, y axis position in feet, z axis position in feet, groundspeed in knots (kts), vertical velocity in feet per second (fps), time of record*⟩. We use a 3D Euclidean coordinate system where each unit on the x, y, and z axis is 100 ft apart, so our Java-based tool takes ground speed in knots as an input and converts it to fps/100 using the ratio 0.0168. Well-clear volumes are configured with 60 ft horizontal and 10 ft vertical separation. For this simulation all aircraft are initially traveling at 30 kts. This simple example has an overlap of well-clear volumes between F_A and F_B at roughly 233 s. We consider A as the ownship with the allowed groundspeed values for A being 10, 15, 20 and 25 kts and try to create a flight plan for A that avoids conflicts with B and C (Fig. 4).

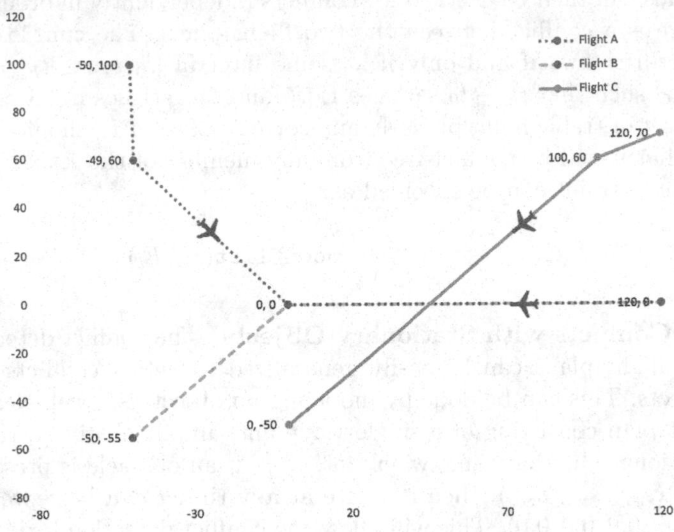

Fig. 4. 2D top-view of the flight plans.

We designed a Java-based tool that takes user inputs and converts the data into SMT-LIB using some pre-defined parameterized patterns. The software has components that act as the input handler and output handler (as shown in Fig. 2) and communicates with dReal running on a docker container. It breaks down the problem into parts wherever applicable and all computations are encoded in SMT-LIB and sent to dReal to generate possible results. Figure 5 and Fig. 6 show a sample SMT-LIB code and the corresponding dReal output from one of the many intermediate steps in the computation of our example.

Running our tool on the data, without any additional business constraints, generated an alternate flight plan $\bar{F_A}$ for A containing the series of waypoints $\bar{F_{A_1}} = \langle -50{,}100{,}4{,}10{,}0{,}0.0 \rangle$, $\bar{F_{A_2}} = \langle -49{,}60{,}4{,}10{,}0{,}238.16963123503044 \rangle$, $\bar{F_{A_3}} = \langle 0{,}0{,}4{,}10{,}0{,}699.2774980651332 \rangle$, and $\bar{F_{A_4}} = \langle 120{,}0{,}4{,}10{,}0{,}1413.5632123508476 \rangle$.

While the generated flight plan verifiably avoids a conflict between flights, the alteration caused a delay in the flight. In practice, the SMT proposal rules could be expanded to include business constraints, including flight time restrictions. We then added a constraint on the total flight time for A to 600 s and reran the tool. This time, the resulting flight plan $\bar{F_A}'$ increased the velocity of A to the maximum allowable velocity of 25 kts in all segments, with the waypoint configurations for $\bar{F_A}'$ being: $\bar{F_{A_1}} = \langle -50{,}100{,}4{,}25{,}0{,}0.0 \rangle$, $\bar{F'_{A_2}} =$

```
(assert (= s0_len (sqrt (+ (* (- w1_x w0_x) (- w1_x w0_x))
    (* (- w1_y w0_y) (- w1_y w0_y))))))
(assert (= t1 (+ t0 (/ s0_len s0_v))))
(assert (= allowed_v0 (* 0.0168 10.0)))
(assert (or (or (or (or  (= s0_v allowed_v0))
    (= s0_v allowed_v1)) (= s0_v allowed_v2)) (= s0_v allowed_v3)))
```

Fig. 5. Snippet from SMTLIB code used for finding the appropriate groundspeed in a segment as generated by our tool.

```
delta-sat with delta = 0.001
s0_v : [0.1679999999999998, 0.1680000000000004]
s1_v : [0.1679999999999998, 0.1680000000000004]
s2_v : [0.1679999999999998, 0.1680000000000004]
w0_x : [-50, -50]
w0_y : [100, 100]
w1_x : [-49, -49]
w1_y : [60, 60]
w2_x : [0, 0]
w2_y : [0, 0]
w3_x : [120, 120]
w3_y : [0, 0]
s0_len : [40.012498047485103, 40.012498047485117]
s1_len : [77.466121627457241, 77.466121627457269]
s2_len : [119.99999999999999, 120.00000000000001]
t0 : [0, 0]
t1 : [238.16963123503029, 238.16963123503049]
t2 : [699.2774980651327, 699.27749806513339]
t3 : [1413.5632123508467, 1413.5632123508478]
allowed_v0 : [0.1679999999999998, 0.1680000000000004]
allowed_v1 : [0.2519999999999995, 0.2520000000000006]
allowed_v2 : [0.3359999999999997, 0.3360000000000008]
allowed_v3 : [0.4199999999999993, 0.4200000000000001]
```

Fig. 6. dReal output for the SMTLIB encoding in Fig. 5

$\langle -49{,}60{,}4{,}25{,}0{,}95.26785249401217\rangle$, $\bar{F'_{A_3}} = \langle 0{,}0{,}4{,}25{,}0{,}279.7109992260533\rangle$, and $\bar{F'_{A_4}} = \langle 120{,}0{,}4{,}10{,}0{,}565.425284940339\rangle$.

The computation of the above example involved the generation of 2 candidate flight plans. The total number of assertions involved was 95, with 18 of them being variable assignments. Both the candidates were evaluated, but the first candidate to complete evaluation was chosen as the result (Fig. 7).

```
(assert (= TOF (- t3 t0)))
(declare-fun T_TOF () Real)
(assert (= T_TOF 600.0))
(assert (<= TOF T_TOF))
```

Fig. 7. SMTLIB code snippet for adding a constraint on total flight time of A.

3.2 Performance Benchmarking

Currently, we have designed a prototype JAVA tool that has a limited interface for users. The tool takes flight plan inputs via the interface or as configuration files and calls dReal using a docker container in the background. Users can input new data in real-time and generate follow-up flight plans using the tool. However, the performance can be somewhat limited by the bottleneck of the dReal docker container. This simulation was conducted using the docker image of the latest dReal release on the linux/arm64/v8 platform. Execution time of the dReal process was captured using Docker's command line interface container inspection functionality to omit infrastructure startup time. It is expected that the execution time of the SMT process will decrease when run on a supported platform or with a standalone install. 100 runs of the dReal process to create a flight plan in compliance with the 600 s flight time business constraint averaged 190 ms with a standard deviation of roughly 4 ms. Execution time of 100 dReal flight segment conflict detection processes averaged 770 ms with a standard deviation of 156 ms. Additional performance benchmarking and analysis, and enhancements to optimize the tool, is planned as future work.

4 Discussion

The conflict detection and resolution approach presented in this paper can be used for autonomous air-traffic management for UAM scenarios where UAS must coordinate with each other in the absence of a centralized controller. Such autonomous ATM approaches have been presented in [6] and [29]. [6] presented an UTM Concept of Operations (UTM ConOps) where UAS operators must consult a *lookup table* with the flight plans of other UAS and compute and propose a conflict-free flight plan that must then be approved. Similarly, [29] proposed a decentralized admission control (DAC) approach, where autonomous aircraft have to decide on a set of *safe* (conflict-free) flight plans and coordinate with the help of distributed algorithms before entering an airspace. Our approach can be used to compute the conflict-free flight plans in both these scenarios.

There are currently some limitations to our approach. Firstly, the strategy to compute new conflict-free flight plans only changes the flight plan of the ownship and does not adjust the plans of traffic plans. This limits the possibilities of optimizing the usage of the four-dimensional airspace and also restricts the possible solution space. The solution space is also constrained by the number of discrete ground speed values that are allowed for the ownship. Further, we do not consider the effect of wind on trajectories, which can have a significant impact [30]. Improvements can be made to the approach by using optimization techniques like counterexample guided abstraction refinement (CEGAR) [4], which allows lazy generation of candidates and refinement of constraints when conflicts are identified; and determining more efficient termination and evaluation criterion that can identify similarities between potential candidates and use this knowledge to increase efficiency. Theoretically, the approach presented in this paper can be used for any number of flight plans of any length. However, practically, the efficiency is limited by the software implementation and its interactions with the backend SMT solver. The optimization techniques used within the SMT solver can also create performance bottlenecks. We aim to investigate and address these limitations in future work.

5 Related Work

Several approaches to strategic conflict management for aircraft exist in the literature. Alejo *et al.* [1] presented a one-at-a-time strategy for conflict detection and resolution using Particle Swarm Optimization. There exists work in the literature on strategic conflict management. Zhang *et al.* [40] proposed an approach for coordination of autonomous drones passing through an intersection by minimizing fuel consumption and avoiding conflicts. Yang *et al.* [38] presented an optimization-based approach in which probabilistic reach sets are determined to generate solutions. Pritchett *et al.* [33] proposed an approach based on game theory that allows aircraft to coordinate and decide on a set of compatible flight plans. Sacharny *et al.* [35] presented a lane-based approach for scheduling aircraft trajectories that can be used by UAS Service Suppliers. Ayhan *et al.* [2] proposed an approach for conflict resolution by using historical trajectory data to change one or more trajectories involved in a conflict. Balachandran *et al.* [3] proposed an approach for automatic merging and spacing of UAS in urban environments by introducing new waypoints to delay arrival times. Colbert *et al.* [5] presented Polysafe, which is a strategic algorithm for conflict detection between polynomial trajectories.

Our approach improves upon the existing work by converting the task to a constraint satisfaction problem that can be solved by state-of-the-art SMT solvers. This allows us to declaratively encode arbitrary aerodynamic or operational constraints and makes the approach appropriate for safety-critical UAM applications as the solutions generated by SMT solvers can be easily verified and machine-checkable proofs can be generated from SMT solvers.

6 Conclusion

We presented an SMT-based approach for generating conflict-free flight plans for an aircraft in the presence of known traffic aircraft. Our approach supports imposing operational or business constraints on the solution flight plans, making it a more versatile conflict-resolution technique than tactical solutions. Moreover, the use of SMT solvers also allows for the verification of the solutions by independent third-party proof verification tools or by directly generating proof certificates from the SMT solvers.

Our solution space is currently limited to the possible permutations of allowed ground speed for the ownship. A potential direction of future work, therefore, would be to extend our SMT-based approach to support other strategies that can allow for more robust and efficient solution spaces. Another direction of future work would be to include the capability to directly generate a proof certificate for every solution flight plan that is generated by the toolchain to increase people's confidence in the results. It will also be valuable to investigate a CEGAR approach for the lazy generation of candidate flight plans in order to increase the efficiency and accuracy of the conflict resolution process.

Acknowledgement. The authors would like to thank GE Aerospace Research for supporting the work and the reviewers of NFM 2024 for their detailed and constructive comments that helped improve the final manuscript.

References

1. Alejo, D., Cobano, J.A., Heredia, G., Ollero, A.: Collision-free 4D trajectory planning in unmanned aerial vehicles for assembly and structure construction. J. Intell. Robot. Syst. **73**(1), 783–795 (2014)
2. Ayhan, S., Costas, P., Samet, H.: Prescriptive analytics system for long-range aircraft conflict detection and resolution. In: Proceedings of the 26th ACM SIGSPATIAL International Conference on Advances in Geographic Information Systems, pp. 239–248 (2018)
3. Balachandran, S., Manderino, C., Muñoz, C., Consiglio, M.: A decentralized framework to support UAS merging and spacing operations in urban canyons. In: 2020 International Conference on Unmanned Aircraft Systems (ICUAS), pp. 204–210. IEEE (2020)
4. Clarke, E., Grumberg, O., Jha, S., Lu, Y., Veith, H.: Counterexample-guided abstraction refinement. In: Emerson, E.A., Sistla, A.P. (eds.) CAV 2000. LNCS, vol. 1855, pp. 154–169. Springer, Heidelberg (2000). https://doi.org/10.1007/10722167_15
5. Colbert, B.K., Slagel, J.T., Crespo, L.G., Balachandran, S., Munoz, C.: Polysafe: a formally verified algorithm for conflict detection on a polynomial airspace. IFAC-PapersOnLine **53**(2), 15615–15620 (2020)
6. Craven, N., et al.: Report: X3 Simulation with National Campaign-Developmental Test (NC-DT) Airspace Partners. Technical report, National Aeronatics and Space Administration (2021). https://aviationsystems.arc.nasa.gov/publications/2021/NASA-TM-20210011098.pdf. Accessed 25 June 2021
7. de Moura, L., Bjørner, N.: Z3: an efficient SMT solver. In: Ramakrishnan, C.R., Rehof, J. (eds.) TACAS 2008. LNCS, vol. 4963, pp. 337–340. Springer, Heidelberg (2008). https://doi.org/10.1007/978-3-540-78800-3_24
8. Dowek, G., Munoz, C., Carreño, V.: Provably safe coordinated strategy for distributed conflict resolution. In: AIAA Guidance, Navigation, and Control Conference and Exhibit, p. 6047 (2005)
9. Dowek, G., Munoz, C., Geser, A.: Tactical conflict detection and resolution in a 3-d airspace. Technical report INSTITUTE FOR COMPUTER APPLICATIONS IN SCIENCE AND ENGINEERING HAMPTON VA (2001)

10. Durand, N., Alliot, J.M., Noailles, J.: Automatic aircraft conflict resolution using genetic algorithms. In: Proceedings of the 1996 ACM Symposium on Applied Computing, pp. 289–298 (1996)
11. Ekici, B., et al.: SMTCoq: a plug-in for integrating SMT solvers into Coq. In: Majumdar, R., Kunčak, V. (eds.) CAV 2017. LNCS, vol. 10427, pp. 126–133. Springer, Cham (2017). https://doi.org/10.1007/978-3-319-63390-9_7
12. Galdino, A.L., Muñoz, C., Ayala-Rincón, M.: Formal verification of an optimal air traffic conflict resolution and recovery algorithm. In: Leivant, D., de Queiroz, R. (eds.) WoLLIC 2007. LNCS, vol. 4576, pp. 177–188. Springer, Heidelberg (2007). https://doi.org/10.1007/978-3-540-73445-1_13
13. Gao, S., Kong, S., Clarke, E.M.: dReal: an SMT solver for nonlinear theories over the reals. In: Bonacina, M.P. (ed.) CADE 2013. LNCS (LNAI), vol. 7898, pp. 208–214. Springer, Heidelberg (2013). https://doi.org/10.1007/978-3-642-38574-2_14
14. Irfan, A., et al.: Towards verification of neural networks for small unmanned aircraft collision avoidance. In: 2020 AIAA/IEEE 39th Digital Avionics Systems Conference (DASC), pp. 1–10. IEEE (2020)
15. Katz, G., Barrett, C., Tinelli, C., Reynolds, A., Hadarean, L.: Lazy proofs for DPLL (T)-based SMT solvers. In: 2016 Formal Methods in Computer-Aided Design (FMCAD), pp. 93–100. IEEE (2016)
16. Krozel, J., Peters, M., Bilimoria, K.D., Lee, C., Mitchell, J.S.: System performance characteristics of centralized and decentralized air traffic separation strategies. Air Traffic Control Q. **9**(4), 311–332 (2001)
17. Li, M., et al.: Requirements-based automated test generation for safety critical software. In: 2019 IEEE/AIAA 38th Digital Avionics Systems Conference (DASC), pp. 1–10. IEEE (2019)
18. Liang, T., Reynolds, A., Tinelli, C., Barrett, C., Deters, M.: A DPLL(T) theory solver for a theory of strings and regular expressions. In: Biere, A., Bloem, R. (eds.) CAV 2014. LNCS, vol. 8559, pp. 646–662. Springer, Cham (2014). https://doi.org/10.1007/978-3-319-08867-9_43
19. Meng, B., et al.: Towards a correct-by-construction design of integrated modular avionics. In: Conference on Formal Methods in Computer-Aided Design – FMCAD, p. 221 (2023)
20. Meng, B., et al.: Verdict: a language and framework for engineering cyber resilient and safe system. Systems **9**(1), 18 (2021)
21. Meng, B., Reynolds, A., Tinelli, C., Barrett, C.: Relational constraint solving in SMT. In: de Moura, L. (ed.) CADE 2017. LNCS (LNAI), vol. 10395, pp. 148–165. Springer, Cham (2017). https://doi.org/10.1007/978-3-319-63046-5_10
22. Meng, B., Viswanathan, A., Smith, W., Moitra, A., Siu, K., Durling, M.: Synthesis of optimal defenses for system architecture design model in MaXSMT. In: Deshmukh, J.V., Havelund, K., Perez, I. (eds.) NFM 2022. LNCS, vol. 13260, pp. 752–770. Springer, Cham (2022). https://doi.org/10.1007/978-3-031-06773-0_40
23. Munoz, C., Narkawicz, A., Chamberlain, J.: A TCAS-ii resolution advisory detection algorithm. In: AIAA Guidance, Navigation, and Control (GNC) Conference, p. 4622 (2013)
24. Murrieta-Mendoza, A., Botez, R.M., Patrón, R.S.F.: Flight altitude optimization using genetic algorithms considering climb and descent costs in cruise with flight plan information. Technical report SAE Technical Paper (2015)
25. Narkawicz, A., Muñoz, C., Dutle, A.: Sensor uncertainty mitigation and dynamic well clear volumes in DAIDALUS. In: 2018 IEEE/AIAA 37th Digital Avionics Systems Conference (DASC), pp. 1–8. IEEE (2018)

26. National Aeronatics and Space Administration: Range and Fuel Consumption Activity. https://www.grc.nasa.gov/www/k-12/BGP/Devon/range_fuel_act.htm. Accessed 18 June 2021
27. Paul, S.: Emergency Trajectory Generation for Fixed-Wing Aircraft. Master's thesis, Rensselaer Polytechnic Institute (2018)
28. Paul, S., Agha, G.A., Patterson, S., Varela, C.A.: Verification of eventual consensus in synod using a failure-aware actor model. In: Dutle, A., Moscato, M.M., Titolo, L., Muñoz, C.A., Perez, I. (eds.) NFM 2021. LNCS, vol. 12673, pp. 249–267. Springer, Cham (2021). https://doi.org/10.1007/978-3-030-76384-8_16
29. Paul, S., et al.: Formal verification of safety-critical aerospace systems. IEEE Aerosp. Electron. Syst. Mag. **38**(5), 72–88 (2023). https://doi.org/10.1109/MAES.2023.3238378
30. Paul, S., Hole, F., Zytek, A., Varela, C.A.: Wind-aware trajectory planning for fixed-wing aircraft in loss of thrust emergencies. In: 2018 IEEE/AIAA 37th Digital Avionics Systems Conference (DASC), pp. 1–10 (2018).https://doi.org/10.1109/DASC.2018.8569842
31. Paul, S., Patterson, S., Varela, C.A.: Conflict-aware flight planning for avoiding near mid-air collisions. In: The 38th AIAA/IEEE Digital Avionics Systems Conference (DASC 2019). San Diego, CA (2019).https://doi.org/10.1109/DASC43569.2019.9081658
32. Peters, A., Balachandran, S., Duffy, B., Smalling, K., Consiglio, M., Muñoz, C.: Flight test results of a distributed merging algorithm for autonomous UAS operations. In: 2020 AIAA/IEEE 39th Digital Avionics Systems Conference (DASC), pp. 1–7. IEEE (2020)
33. Pritchett, A.R., Genton, A.: Negotiated decentralized aircraft conflict resolution. IEEE Trans. Intell. Transp. Syst. **19**(1), 81–91 (2017)
34. Reynolds, A., Iosif, R., Serban, C., King, T.: A decision procedure for separation logic in SMT. In: Artho, C., Legay, A., Peled, D. (eds.) ATVA 2016. LNCS, vol. 9938, pp. 244–261. Springer, Cham (2016). https://doi.org/10.1007/978-3-319-46520-3_16
35. Sacharny, D., Henderson, T.C.: A lane-based approach for large-scale strategic conflict management for UAS service suppliers. In: 2019 International Conference on Unmanned Aircraft Systems (ICUAS), pp. 937–945. IEEE (2019)
36. Shone, R., Glazebrook, K., Zografos, K.G.: Applications of stochastic modeling in air traffic management: methods, challenges and opportunities for solving air traffic problems under uncertainty. Eur. J. Oper. Res. (2020)
37. Siu, K., et al.: Architectural and behavioral analysis for cyber security. In: 2019 IEEE/AIAA 38th Digital Avionics Systems Conference (DASC), pp. 1–10. IEEE (2019)
38. Yang, Y., Zhang, J., Cai, K.Q., Prandini, M.: Multi-aircraft conflict detection and resolution based on probabilistic reach sets. IEEE Trans. Control Syst. Technol. **25**(1), 309–316 (2016)

39. Young-Brown, F.: FUEL BURN RATES FOR PRIVATE AIRCRAFT (2015). https://www.sherpareport.com/aircraft/fuel-burn-private-aircraft.html. Accessed 18 June 2021
40. Zhang, Y.J., Malikopoulos, A.A., Cassandras, C.G.: Optimal control and coordination of connected and automated vehicles at urban traffic intersections. In: 2016 American Control Conference (ACC), pp. 6227–6232. IEEE (2016)

Formal Methods for Learning-Enabled Systems

Towards Formal Verification of Neural Networks in Cyber-Physical Systems

Federico Rossi(✉), Cinzia Bernardeschi, Marco Cococcioni, and Maurizio Palmieri

Department of Information Engineering, University of Pisa, Pisa, Italy
federico.rossi@ing.unipi.it,
{cinzia.bernardeschi,marco.cococcioni,maurizio.palmieri}@unipi.it

Abstract. Machine Learning approaches have been successfully used for the creation of high-performance control components of cyber-physical systems, where the control dynamics result from the combination of many subsystems. However, these approaches may lack the trustworthiness required to guarantee their reliable application in a safety-critical context. In this paper, we propose an approach to automatically translate entire feed-forward fully-connected neural networks into first-order logic formal models that can be used to analyse the prediction of the network. The approach exploits the Prototype Verification System theorem prover to model neural networks based on non-linear activation functions and prove the safety bounds of the output under safety-critical conditions. Finally, we show the application of the proposed approach to a model-predictive controller for autonomous driving.

Keywords: Formal methods · PVS · Neural Networks · Cyber-Physical Systems · Trustworthiness

1 Introduction

Neural network integration is becoming more and more common in the current cyber-physical systems (CPS) landscape, changing the capabilities of these systems in a variety of fields, such as industrial automation [1], smart grids, autonomous vehicles [2], and healthcare. Deep learning models in particular, which use neural networks, do remarkably well in difficult tasks like decision-making, picture identification, and natural language processing. However, there are issues with reliability and safety when using them in safety-critical CPS.

Manuscript submitted for publication.

Work funded by: the PNRR - M4C2 - Investimento 1.3, Partenariato Esteso PE00000013 - "FAIR - Future Artificial Intelligence Research" - Spoke 1 "Human-centered AI" under the NextGeneration EU programme; the European High Performance Computing Joint Undertaking (JU) under Framework Partnership Agreement No 800928 and Specific Grant Agreement No 101036168 (EPI SGA2); the Italian Ministry of University and Research (MUR) in the framework of the FoReLab and CrossLab projects (Departments of Excellence).

N. Benz et al. (Eds.): NFM 2024, LNCS 14627, pp. 207–222, 2024.
https://doi.org/10.1007/978-3-031-60698-4_12

The need to guarantee neural network trustworthiness in CPS has led to an increasing interest in formal verification techniques [3]. Formal verification provides a level of confidence vital for applications where errors can have serious repercussions by offering a methodical and mathematical technique to evaluating the accuracy and adherence to specifications of complex systems.

Figure 1 summarises the approach proposed in this paper, which takes as input the trained model, a fully connected feed-forward neural network resulting from well-known training algorithms, and automatically produces its formal representation that allows the verification of user-defined properties with a theorem prover such as PVS [4]. The formal verification of the trained model is a semi-automatic process that combines automatic procedures of the theorem prover with user knowledge.

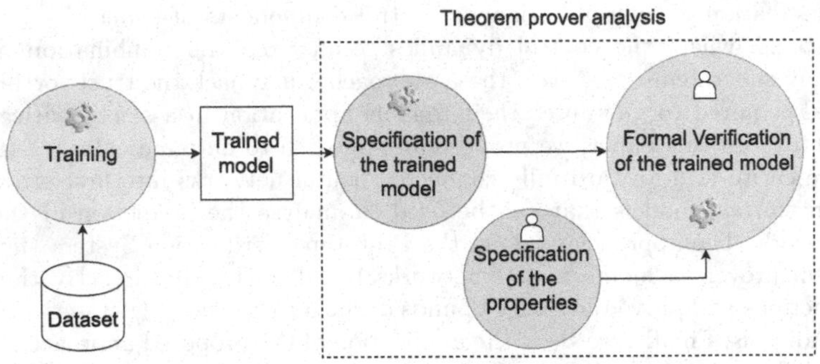

Fig. 1. Execution flow of the proposed approach.

2 Related Works

Other works have targeted the formal verification of neural networks exploiting several different theories, all leveraging the rectified linear unit (ReLU) activation function in feed-forward neural networks. In [5] authors propose an efficient method to verify relu-based deep (fully-connected) neural networks using Satisfiability Modulo Theory (SMT). In [6] authors proposed a similar SMT approach to verification of multi layer perceptron, using a piece-wise linear activation function to abstract sigmoid-based feed-forward neural networks. In [7] authors proposed an SMT approach to verify properties of piece-wise linear feed-forward neural networks, again using ReLU-like activation functions. Similarly, in [8] authors proposed an evolution of [5], aimed at expanding verification capabilities to convolutional and pooling layer, again, based on ReLU activation functions. Other approaches like [9] exploit boolean satisfiability theory to verify properties of neural network using SAT solvers. In [10] authors used the Coq prover[1] to provide means to verify feed-forward neural networks.

[1] https://coq.inria.fr/.

Other works targeted different class of activation functions and neural networks, including convolutional layers or non-linear activation functions. In particular, [11,12] authors used hybrid automata to formalize sigmoid-based neural networks. In [13–15] the authors empirically evaluate the reachability set of a neural network using a Monte-Carlo like simulation method. In [16] authors propose a geometrical polyhedron-based verification method on several deep learning models to evaluate the reachability set of a neural network, which can be applied only when the ReLU activation function is used. In [17–19] authors show an approach to formal verification of neural networks and"learning enabled" components when considered in a closed control loop system.

In this work, we aim to generalise the approach of formal verification of feed-forward neural networks including the capability of using non-linear, exponential-based, activation functions such as the hyperbolic tangent and the sigmoid using the Prototype Verification System[2] (PVS), that employs sequent calculus axioms and inference rules with the NASA-lib PVS library.

3 Background

This Section provides details on the PVS and neural networks that will be extensively used in the remaining of this work.

3.1 PVS Language

PVS is a mechanized environment for formal specification and verification. A PVS *specification* is a combination of one or more *theories*, where a theory is a set of formulas, variable declarations, and function declarations. The PVS language provides a large set of base types for variables, including naturals, integers, reals, booleans, and their operations, each defined in the fundamental library *prelude*, implicitly imported in every PVS theory. Complex and advanced data types, such as the matrices used in this work, have been provided by the Nasalib extensions [20]. Function declarations are in the form `foo(arg: T1): T2`, where *foo* is the name, *arg* is the argument of type *T1*, and *T2* is the type returned by the function. The formulas are the sentences (named *THEOREM* or *LEMMA*) that users should prove to guarantee that a certain property of the system described in the specification holds starting from some valid *AXIOMS*. The proof system of PVS is based on the sequent calculus [21].

3.2 Neural Network

Considering a generic neural network, we can express the input-output relation as follows:

$$nn : R^{m\times n} \rightarrow R^{p\times q}, \tag{1}$$

[2] https://pvs.csl.sri.com.

where (m, n) and (p, q) are, respectively, the input and output shape of the neural network. For instance, if we consider a regression problem, when the network is trained to approximate a function of n arguments and one output, the shapes will be $(1, n)$ and $(1, 1)$. Going into details, we can now consider the less general feed-forward network model. This network can be summarised with Eq. (1) as well; however, we can furtherly express the single fully-connected layers l_i functions follows:

$$l_i : R^{m_i \times n_i} \rightarrow R^{p_i \times q_i}, \tag{2}$$

where (m_i, n_i) and (p_i, q_i) are, respectively, the input and output shape of the layer l_i. Again, in the example of a regression problem, the shapes will be $(1, n_i)$ and $(1, q_i)$. Typically a neural network layer has a set of weights W and biases B. Biases can be considered as an additional degree of freedom of the neural network parameters. Let W_i, B_i be the weights and the biases of the fully-connected layer l_i, the function that furtherly expresses Eq. (2) is the following:

$$l_i(X) = \sigma_i\left(X \times W_i + B_i\right), \tag{3}$$

where σ_i is a generic activation function, $\times$ is the matrix-matrix multiplication operation and $+$ is the matrix sum operation. In the case of a regression problem, $X \in R^{1,m_i}$, $W_i \in R^{m_i,n_i}$ and $B_i \in R^{1,n_i}$. Consequently, the layer result $l_i(X) \in R^{1,m_i} \rightarrow R^{1,n_i}$.

A n-layer feed-forward neural network is composed of a series of fully-connected layers $l_1, l_2, ..., l_n$. Each of these layers applies the transformation expressed in (3) to the output of the previous layer or, in the case of the input layer l_1, to the input data I. We can then express the relation (1) exploiting this concept:

$$nn(I) = l_n(\, l_{n-1}(\, ...\, l_2(\, l_1(I)))). \tag{4}$$

For example, a 3-layer neural network can be expressed as follows:

$$nn(I) = l_3(\, l_2\, (\, l_1(I))) = \sigma(\, \sigma(\, \sigma(W_1 \times I + B_1) \times W_2 + B_2) \times W_3 + B_3). \tag{5}$$

3.3 PyTorch

In this work we use the PyTorch python framework [22] to create, train, and manipulate neural networks. A fully-connected neural network can be created using PyTorch as shown in Listing 1.1, where an example of a neural network (called *Sequential* by PyTorch) with a hyperbolic tangent activation function is declared. The network has 3 fully-connected layers (called *Linear* by PyTorch) and each of them has 100 × 100 parameters.

```
Sequential(
    Linear(100, 100),
    Tanh(),
    Linear(100, 100),
    Tanh(),
    Linear(100, 100),
    Tanh()
)
```

Listing 1.1. PyTorch example of a fully-connected neural network.

4 Translation of Neural Networks to Formal Models

Once we have the representation shown in (4) we can then formalise the application of each layer as a PVS function, exploiting the `matrices` PVS theory to represent both two-dimensional matrices and 1-dimensional vectors. In particular, given a layer $l_i : R^{1\times m_i} \rightarrow R^{1\times n_i}$ as shown in Eq. (3), we can formalise its weights and biases as in Listing 1.2. In PVS dimensional matrices are represented by the `MatrixMN` type and can be initialised with nested lists (e.g. a 2×2 matrix can be initalised as `(: (: 1,1 :), (: 2,2 :) :)`, where `(: :)` is the Lisp notation for a list).

```
wi: MatrixMN(m,n) = (:(: w11, w12, ... , w1n :), ... , :)
bi: MatrixMN(1,n) = (: b1, b2, ..., bn :)
```

Listing 1.2. PVS formalisation for a fully connected layer.

Layer activation functions can be straightforwardly implemented using their mathematical definition as in Listing 1.3. We can generalise ReLU-like functions [23], as general piece-wise linear functions, also known as *leaky relu*. A leaky relu behaves as the identity function for positive values of the argument (i.e. $y = x, x \geq 0$) and as a straight line with a positive slope for negative values of the argument (i.e. $y = nslope \times x, x \leq 0$). The ReLU function is a particular case of the leaky relu where $nslope = 0$, as shown in Listing 1.3.

```
leaky_relu(x: real, nslope: real):
    real = IF x >= 0 THEN x
           ELSE nslope*x ENDIF
relu(x: real) : real = leaky_relu(x,0)
```

Listing 1.3. PVS formalisation for piece-wise linear activation functions.

S-shaped functions such as the sigmoid and hyperbolic tangent functions can be represented as well exploiting the definition of the exponential function in PVS (`exp`) as in Listing 1.4. The hyperbolic tangent can be defined using the sigmoid function as a building block.

```
sigmoid(x: real): real =
    1/(1 + exp(-x))
tanh(x: real): real =
    2*sigmoid(2*x) - 1
```

Listing 1.4. PVS formalisation of s-shaped, sigmoid-based activation functions.

The application of these scalar functions to an entire matrix is formalised as in Listing 1.5, where `act_fun` is one of the scalar functions seen before.

```
act(M: Matrix): MatrixMN(rows(M),columns(M)) =
    form_matrix(LAMBDA (i,j:nat):
        act_fun(entry(M)(i,j)), rows(M), columns(M));
```

Listing 1.5. PVS formalisation for generic activation function on a matrix.

Finally, wrapping everything up, we formalise the entire network forward pass as in Listing 1.6 and Eq. (4).

```
net(input: Matrix): Matrix =
    act(act(input*w1+b1)*w2+b2)*w3+b3 ...
```

Listing 1.6. PVS formalisation for generic activation function on a matrix.

4.1 Network Constraints and Properties

Since we are interested in proving properties on the network, we can express some constraints on the input layer arguments and a theorem for the output of the entire network. We can constrain the neural network inputs in a certain range so that the i-th input x_i is constrained as $x_i \in [lb_i, ub_i]$. In the theorem we identify the i-th output of the neural network as `entry( net(... )(0,i)` and we can put a constraint on each of them, joining the constraints with a disjunctive or a conjunctive clause.

```
x1: TYPE = { r: real | r>=lb1 AND r<=ub1 }
x2: TYPE = { r: real | r>=lb2 AND r<=ub2 }
...
xn: TYPE = { r: real | r>lbn AND r<=ubn }
network_bounds: THEOREM
  FORALL (x0in: x1,x1in: x2, ...):
        entry( net( (:(:x0in,x1in, ... :):) ) )(0,0) <= ... AND
        entry( net( (:(:x0in,x1in, ... :):) ) )(0,1) <= ...
```

Listing 1.7. PVS constraints for the input variables and theorem on the output.

4.2 Linking PVS and PyTorch Together

The previous approach can produce a functioning and provable theory for a feed-forward neural network; however, it is not tractable to manually write a theory when number and size of layers scale up. Therefore we developed a Python-based tool that can automatically generate an entire PVS theory starting from a pre-trained PyTorch neural network model. The algorithmic complexity of generating a PVS theory from a network model is $\mathcal{O}(n_p)$, where n_p is the number of parameters in the model (e.g. generating the theory for the network in Listing 1.1 takes $2s$ on a 3 GHz desktop processor). For example, starting from a very simple neural network, suppose we have a single-layer neural network as shown in Fig. 2. The correspondent PyTorch model summary is shown in Listing 1.8.

```
Sequential(
    Linear(in_features=2, out_features=2, bias=True),
    ReLU(),
    Linear(in_features=2, out_features=1, bias=True)
)
```

Listing 1.8. PyTorch code for a simple network model with two hidden neurons.

If we run said model through our tool we produce the theory shown in Listing 1.9. We added some constraints on the input variables and a theorem for the network output.

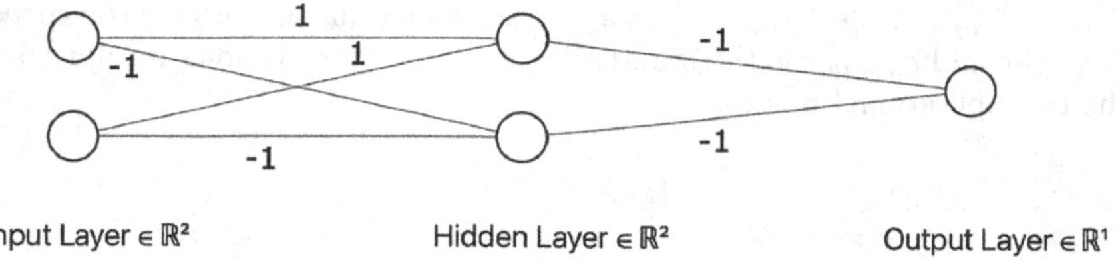

Fig. 2. Simple neural network with two hidden neurons and ReLU activation function

```
mlp: THEORY
BEGIN
    IMPORTING matrices@matrices
    linear0: MatrixMN(2,2) = (:(:1,-1:),(:1,-1:):)
    linear2: MatrixMN(2,1) = (:(:-1:),(:-1:):)

    relu(x: real): real = IF x > 0 THEN x ELSE 0 ENDIF
    act(M: Matrix): MatrixMN(rows(M),columns(M)) =
    net(input: Matrix): Matrix = act(input*linear0)*linear2
    % Manually added
    x1: TYPE = { r: real | r>=-2 AND r<=2}
    x2: TYPE = { r: real | r>=-2 AND r<=2}
    network_bounds: THEOREM
    FORALL (x: x1, y: x2):
        entry(net( (:(:x,y:):) ))(0,0) >= -5
END mlp
```

Listing 1.9. Full PVS theory for the simple network shown before.

In Listing 1.9 there is the complete theory generated with the manual addition of constraints on the two inputs. Doing so, we were able to prove the `network_bounds` theorem mostly automatically, starting from the original PyTorch model. In the next section, we will cover a more complex use case, with a bigger fully connected network, to highlight the potential capabilities of our approach.

5 Use Case: Adaptive Cruise Control with MPC

In this section, we consider an autonomous driving application, where a neural network is trained using simulated data and then we verify some of its properties using the approach shown in the previous section. In particular, we consider the simple scenario[3] shown in Fig. 3, where the autonomous driving system sets the acceleration of the *ego car*, sensing the speed and position of the *lead car*. This problem is solved, for example, by employing a model-predictive controller (MPC) to regulate the speed of the *ego* car in two operational modes: i) following the set velocity v_{set} and ii) maintaining a safe distance from the lead car equal

[3] https://it.mathworks.com/help/mpc/ug/adaptive-cruise-control-using-model-predictive-controller.html.

to $d_{safe} = t_{gap} * v_{ego} + d_{default}$, where t_{gap} is a time constant, v_{ego} is the speed of the *ego* car and $d_{default}$ is the standstill spacing. Figure 3 shows an illustration of the two operational modes.

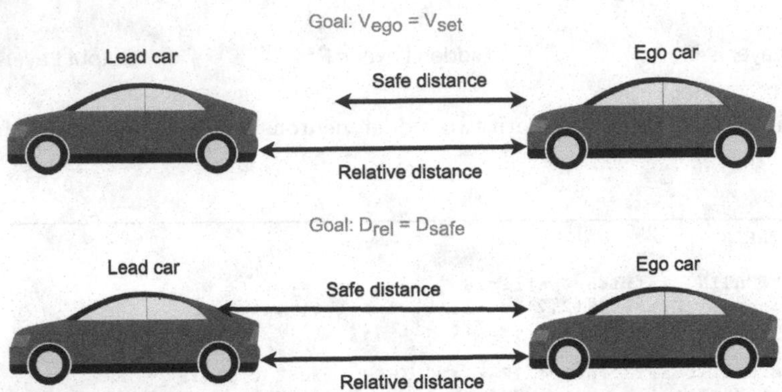

Fig. 3. Scheme for the MPC controlled cruise control application.

The MPC controller accepts three inputs, nominally, the longitudinal velocity of the ego car, relative distance, and relative velocity of the lead car. Then it has only one output, i.e. the controlled quantity, that is the acceleration control given to the ego car. As a consequence, it is possible to replace the MPC controller with a surrogate model based on a neural network with the following structure:

$$n(v_{ego}, d_{rel}, v_{rel}) = a_{ego}. \tag{6}$$

Therefore we can simulate the use case scenario using the approach proposed in [1] to generate a set of tuples $v_{ego}, d_{rel}, v_{rel}, a_{ego}$ to be used as input and output data for the training process. Due to the nature of the application we set up a regression problem based on a feed-forward non-linear neural network as shown in Fig. 4, with 9 hidden neurons.

5.1 Modelling and Proving Properties for the Neural Network

We used the tool shown in Sect. 4 to model both the network based on the hyperbolic tangent activation function and the network based on the LeakyReLU one as a PVS theory. Listing 1.10 shows the PVS theory of the network with *tanh*, where the manually added bounds are the minimum and maximum values shown during the training phase. We selected some properties of the trained model to be proved using the theory described in Sect. 3.

Safety Property: Deceleration. For instance, we want to ensure that, when the relative distance between ego and lead car is less than a safety value d_s, the controller always outputs a deceleration command (i.e. the output is less than or equal to zero). To prove this we express the following theorem:

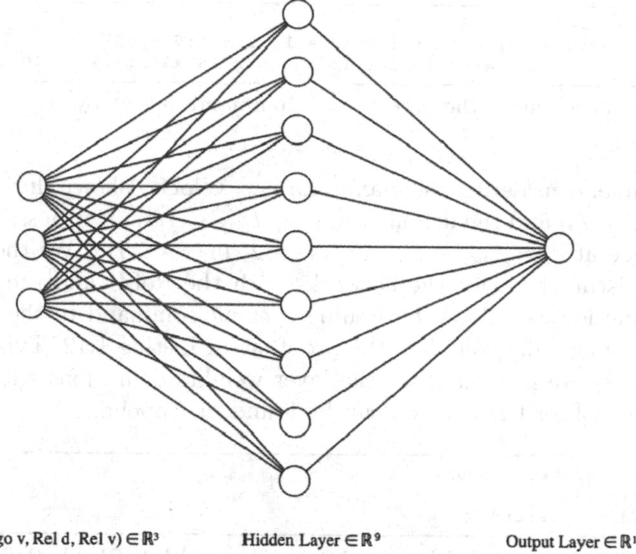

Fig. 4. Neural network for solving the MPC regression problem.

```
cruisenn: THEORY
    BEGIN
    IMPORTING matrices@matrices
    linear0: MatrixMN(3,9) = (:
                                    (:2.599972,...,-0.726693:),
                                    (:-1.584255,...,0.327811:),
                                    (:3.008755,...,-0.316700:)
                                :)
    linear_bias0: MatrixMN(1,9) = (:(:3.842371,...,-0.274796:):)
    linear2: MatrixMN(9,1) = (:
                                    (:-0.615591:),
                                    (:-0.016017:),
                                    ...,
                                    (:0.001300:)
                                :)
    linear_bias2: MatrixMN(1,1) = (:(:-1.154893:):)

    sigmoid(x: real): real = 1/(1 + exp(-x))
    tanh(x: real): real = 2*sigmoid(2*x) - 1
    act(M: Matrix): MatrixMN(rows(M),columns(M))  =
        form_matrix(LAMBDA (i,j:nat): tanh(entry(M)(i,j)), rows(M),
     columns(M));
    net(input: Matrix): Matrix = act(input*linear0+linear_bias0)*linear2+
     linear_bias2

  %%% Manually added part
    %ego velocity
    x0inreal: TYPE = { r: real | r>= 20 AND r<= 25 }
    %rel position
    x1inreal: TYPE = { r: real | r>= 0 AND r<= 50 }
    %rel velocity
    x2inreal: TYPE = { r: real | r>= -2 AND r<=2 }
 END cruisenn
```

Listing 1.10. Full PVS theory for the MPC neural network.

```
should_decelerate: THEOREM
  FORALL (x0in: x0inreal,x1in: x1inreal,x2in: x2inreal):
  x1in < d_s IMPLIES entry( net( (:(:x0in,x1in,x2in:):) ) )(0,0) <= 0
```

Listing 1.11. Theorem on the deceleration command output by the neural network controller.

For example, considering the maximum v_{ego} velocity shown during the training ($v_{ego} = 25\,\text{m/s}$) and the default time gap $t_{gap} = 1.4\,\text{s}$, it is possible to set the safety distance at $d_s = t_{gap} \times v_{ego} = 1.4\,\text{s} \times 25\,\text{m/s} = 35\,\text{m}$. We then prove the theorem in Listing 1.11, for the networks with the ReLU and the LeakyReLU activation function as follows, by issuing a *grind* command to the prover, that is able to automatically complete the proof, as in Listing 1.12. Type-check constraints (TCCs) are generated for the layer weights definitions with `MatrixMN`: a scheme of proof for these TCCs can be found in Appendix A.

```
should_decelerate : PROOF
(then (grind))
QED should_decelerate
```

Listing 1.12. Proof of the deceleration property with the LeakyRelu network.

Network Output Bounds. We can also prove general properties on the upper and lower bound of the network output, in particular when we may have constraints on the controller output to the actuator. For instance, suppose we want to prove that the trained model output always falls in the range $[a, b]$.

```
network_bounds: THEOREM
    FORALL (x0in: real,x1in: real,x2in: real):
     entry( net( (:(:x0in,x1in,x2in:):) ) )(0,0) > a AND
     entry( net( (:(:x0in,x1in,x2in:):) ) )(0,0) < b
```

Listing 1.13. Theorem on the deceleration command output by the neural network controller.

For the neural networks with ReLU and LeakyReLU activation functions the proof is identical to the one shown in Listing 1.12.

Instead, to prove this for the neural network with sigmoid-based activation functions we need to leverage the properties of the sigmoid function and express the output of the network as in Eq. (7), where x_1, x_2, x_3 are the neural network inputs and all the other terms are fixed coefficients that depend on the neural network weights.

$$nn(I) = c + \sum_{i=0}^{N} a_i \times \sigma(k_i + p_i \times x_1 + q_i \times x_2 + r_i \times x_3) \tag{7}$$

Within the prover, we can provide lemmas to set an upper bound and a lower bound to the sigmoid components, depending on the coefficient a_i, and then, as a consequence, we can provide an upper and lower bound to the network output. For instance, if the neural network output is $a_1 \times \sigma(x_1) - b_1 \times \sigma(x_2)$ we can put a broad upper bound $a_1 \times \sigma(x_1) - b_1 \times \sigma(x_2) < a$ and a broad lower bound $a_1 \times \sigma(x_1) - b_1 \times \sigma(x_2) > -b_1$. This means, for instance, that we can prove the boundaries shown in Listing 1.13 when $a = -10, b = 9$. We can thus define two lemmas for the sigmoid bounds as in Listing 1.14 (proof can be found in Appendix B).

```
sigmoid_lb: LEMMA
    FORALL(x: real): sigmoid(x) >= 0
sigmoid_ub: LEMMA
    FORALL(x: real): sigmoid(x) <= 1
```

Listing 1.14. Sigmoid bounds lemmas.

Hereafter we report the proof for the theorem in Listing 1.13 that exploits the two lemmas defined before as shown in Listing 1.15.

```
network_ub : PROOF
(then (skeep)(grind)
(rewrite* sigmoid_lb)
(rewrite* sigmoid_ub)
(assert))
QED network_ub
```

Listing 1.15. Theorem on the deceleration command output by the neural network controller.

6 Conclusions

In this work, we illustrated an approach to automatically formalise a neural network model as a PVS theory that linearly scales with the network parameter count and introduced a series of lemmas and strategies to prove simple properties on fully-connected feed-forward networks. In particular, we demonstrated that using this approach with PVS we could prove some safety properties on non-linear or piecewise activation function networks other than ReLU (e.g. sigmoid, tanh and LeakyRelu). Finally, we proved some properties on the obtained neural network controller, to guarantee an expected behaviour of the neural network. Some limitations remain in place and will be addressed in future extensions of the work: i) full-precision real arithmetic does not scale well with number of neurons and/or layers, hence the tool suffers from bigger networks ii) the tool itself is limited to generation of fully-connected layers iii) state-of-the-art works using different provers/verification techniques must be taken into account for a fair comparison. Future work will also include new neural network layers such as convolution and pooling layers. Furthermore we plan to use the information given by the prover to act back on the neural network weights and training process.

A Proving the Type-Checking Constraints (TCCs)

When type-checking the theory presented in Listing 1.9 we generate a TCC for each linear layer that must be proved before proceeding with the rest of the theory:

```
linear0_TCC1: OBLIGATION
  length[list[real]]((: (: 1, -1 :), (: 1, -1 :) :)) = 2
    AND
  FORALL (i: below(length[list[real]]((: (: 1, -1 :), (: 1, -1 :) :)))):
       length[real](nth[list[real]]((: (: 1, -1 :), (: 1, -1 :) :), i))
    = 2
```

Listing 1.16. TCC for the first fully connected layer.

```
linear2_TCC1: OBLIGATION
  length[list[real]]((: (: -1 :), (: -1 :) :)) = 2
    AND
  FORALL (i: below(length[list[real]]((: (: -1 :), (: -1 :) :)))):
       length[real](nth[list[real]]((: (: -1 :), (: -1 :) :), i)) = 1
```

Listing 1.17. TCC for the second fully connected layer.

In Listing 1.18 we report a simple proof scheme to prove such TCC.

```
linear2_TCC1 : PROOF
(spread (split)
  ((then (grind))
   (then (skeep)(typepred i)(expand nth)(lift-if)
    (spread (split)
     ((then (flatten)(grind))
      (then (flatten)(expand nth)(lift-if)
       (spread (split)
        ((then (flatten)(grind))
         (then (flatten)(expand nth)(lift-if)
          (spread (split)
           ((then (flatten)(grind))
            (then (flatten)(grind)))))))))))))
QED linear2_TCC1
```

Listing 1.18. Proof for the TCC reported in Listing 1.17.

A similar proof can be carried out with other, similar TCCs for fully connected layers.

B Dealing with Transcendental Activation Functions

As shown in Sect. 3, we managed to model several activation functions. In particular we showed two classes of activation functions: i) piece-wise linear activation functions such as ReLU and Leaky ReLU, ii) S-shaped sigmoid-based activation functions such as the hyperbolic tangent. While modelling the first class is straightforward with base PVS real arithmetic, the second class must be addressed differently.

The S-shaped functions are typically based on the e^x transcendental function. PVS Nasalib offers two way to express the exponential function: i) infinite (or truncated) summation series ii) Inverse function of the natural logarithm ln. In the first case we have the following formulation:

$$e^x_n = \sum_{i=0}^{n} \frac{x^i}{i!}, \tag{8}$$

where n is the n-th term where the series is truncated. We can obtain the mathematical expression for e^x as follows:

$$\lim_{n \to \infty} e^x_n = e^x. \tag{9}$$

In PVS, this is represented by the function **exp_estimate(x,n)**. In the second case, $ln(x)$ is defined as follows:

$$ln(x) = \int_1^x \frac{1}{x}, \tag{10}$$

and e^x is defined as follows in PVS:

$$e^x = \{p_y | x = ln(p_y)\} \tag{11}$$

The formulation in Eq. (11) allows, alongside with a series of lemmas, to express computations between exponential functions without actually computing the real value associated with them. Obviously, this can lead to an unfinished proof if there are no ways to further simplify a given expression using the aforementioned lemmas. In this case we can combine this expression the definition in Eq. (8). We provide a lemma that put a correspondence between the two expressions in PVS:

```
exp_deff: AXIOM
    FORALL (x:real): exp(x) = exp_estimate(x,10)
```

Listing 1.19. Axiom for the correspondence (approximated) between the exact exponent function and its estimation in PVS.

Let us take now the neural network shown in Fig. 4 and try to prove this simple property:

```
value_tester: LEMMA
    entry( net( (:(:2,2,2:):) ) )(0,0) >= -5
```

Listing 1.20. Simple property on a tanh-based neural network.

We can then use **grind** to reach a proof state where the prover needs the lemma we specified in Listing 1.19. Then, we use **lemma exp_deff**, **inst?** and **grind** to apply estimation and simplification in the sequents. This can be iteratively done for all the occurrences of **exp** in the sequents. A proof scheme can be found hereafter.

```
value_tester : PROOF
(then (grind) (rewrite* exp_deff)(grind))
QED value_tester
```

Listing 1.21. Proof scheme for the proof of theory shown in 1.20.

We can exploit this lemma to prove further properties of the exponential function and, as a consequence of the exponential-based activation functions such as the sigmoid and the hyperbolic tangent; indeed, the sigmoid function can be defined as $\sigma(x) = \frac{\exp x}{(1+\exp x)}$. Listing 1.22 shows two lemmas that define basic properties of exponential functions.

```
exp_gt_0: LEMMA
    FORALL (x:real): exp(x) > 0
```

Listing 1.22. Exponential function property lemma.

Listing 1.23 shows the proof scheme for the two aforementioned lemmas; the proof is completed by rewriting the exp with its series definition.

```
exp_gt_0 : PROOF
(then (skeep) (rewrite exp_deff)
(lift-if) (split)
(("1" (flatten) (grind)) ("2" (flatten) (grind) (field))))
QED exp_gt_0
```

Listing 1.23. Proof scheme for the proof of lemmas shown in 1.22.

These two lemmas can be then used to prove other properties on the sigmoid function and, in particular, its bounds, as shown in Listing 1.24.

```
sigmoid_lb: LEMMA FORALL (x:real): sigmoid(x) > 0
sigmoid_ub: LEMMA FORALL (x:real): sigmoid(x) < 1
```

Listing 1.24. Exponential function property lemmas.

These three lemmas can be proven by issuing a **field** command to the prover after an initial **skeep** as shown in Listing 1.25.

```
sigmoid_lb : PROOF
(then (skeep) (field) )
QED sigmoid_lb
sigmoid_ub : PROOF
(then (skeep) (field) )
QED sigmoid_ub
```

Listing 1.25. Proof scheme for the proof of lemmas shown in 1.24.

References

1. Bernardeschi, C., Cococcioni, M., Palmieri, M., Rossi, F.: Training neural networks in cyber-physical systems using design space exploration and co-simulation. In: 2023 International Conference on Electrical, Communication, and Computer Engineering (ICECCE 2023), pp. 1–7 (2023)
2. Cococcioni, M., Rossi, F., Ruffaldi, E., Saponara, S., de Dinechin, B.D.: Novel arithmetics in deep neural networks signal processing for autonomous driving: challenges and opportunities. IEEE Signal Process. Maga. **38**(1), 97–110 (2021)
3. Urban, C., Miné, A.: A review of formal methods applied to machine learning. CoRR arxiv:2104.02466 (2021)
4. Owre, S., Rajan, S., Rushby, J., Shankar, N., Srivas, M.: PVS: combining specification, proof checking, and model checking. In: Alur, R., Henzinger, T.A. (eds.) CAV 1996. LNCS, vol. 1102, pp. 411–414. Springer, Heidelberg (1996). https://doi.org/10.1007/BFb0031813

5. Katz, G., Barrett, C., Dill, D.L., Julian, K., Kochenderfer, M.J.: Reluplex: an efficient smt solver for verifying deep neural networks. In: Majumdar, R., Kunčak, V. (eds.) CAV 2017. LNCS, vol. 10426, pp. 97–117. Springer, Cham (2017). https://doi.org/10.1007/978-3-319-63387-9_5
6. Pulina, L., Tacchella, A.: An abstraction-refinement approach to verification of artificial neural networks. In: Touili, T., Cook, B., Jackson, P. (eds.) CAV 2010. LNCS, pp. 243–257. Springer, Heidelberg (2010). https://doi.org/10.1007/978-3-642-14295-6_24
7. Ehlers, R.: Formal verification of piece-wise linear feed-forward neural networks. In: D'Souza, D., Kumar, K.N. (eds.) ATVA 2017. LNCS, vol. 10482, pp. 269–286. Springer, Cham (2017). https://doi.org/10.1007/978-3-319-68167-2_19
8. Katz, G., et al.: The marabou framework for verification and analysis of deep neural networks. In: Dillig, I., Tasiran, S. (eds.) CAV 2019. LNCS, vol. 11561, pp. 443–452. Springer, Cham (2019). https://doi.org/10.1007/978-3-030-25540-4_26
9. Narodytska, N., Kasiviswanathan, S., Ryzhyk, L., Sagiv, M., Walsh, T.: Verifying properties of binarized deep neural networks. In: Proceedings of the AAAI Conference on Artificial Intelligence, vol. 32, no. 11 (2018)
10. Aleksandrov, A., Völlinger, K.: Formalizing piecewise affine activation functions of neural networks in coq. In: Rozier, K.Y., Chaudhuri, S. (eds.) NFM 2023. LNCS, vol. 13903, pp. 62–78. Springer, Cham (2023). https://doi.org/10.1007/978-3-031-33170-1_4
11. Ivanov, R., Weimer, J., Alur, R., Pappas, G.J., Lee, I.: Verisig: verifying safety properties of hybrid systems with neural network controllers. In: Proceedings of the 22nd ACM International Conference on Hybrid Systems: Computation and Control, HSCC 2019, pp. 169-178. Association for Computing Machinery, New York (2019)
12. Ivanov, R., Carpenter, T., Weimer, J., Alur, R., Pappas, G., Lee, I.: Verisig 2.0: verification of neural network controllers using taylor model preconditioning. In: Silva, A., Rustan, K., Leino, M. (eds.) CAV 2021. LNCS, vol. 12759, pp. 249–262. Springer, Cham (2021). https://doi.org/10.1007/978-3-030-81685-8_11
13. Huang, C., Fan, J., Li, W., Chen, X., Zhu, Q.: Reachnn: reachability analysis of neural-network controlled systems. ACM Trans. Embed. Comput. Syst. **18**(5s), 1–22 (2019)
14. Fan, J., Huang, C., Chen, X., Li, W., Zhu, Q.: Reachnn*: a tool for reachability analysis of neural-network controlled systems. In: Van Hung, D., Sokolsky, O. (eds.) ATVA 2020. LNCS, vol. 12302, pp. 537–542. Springer, Cham (2020). https://doi.org/10.1007/978-3-030-59152-6_30
15. Xiang, W., Tran, H.-D., Johnson, T.T.: Output reachable set estimation and verification for multilayer neural networks. IEEE Trans. Neural Netw. Learn. Syst. **29**(11), 5777–5783 (2018)
16. Lopez, D.M., Choi, S.W., Tran, H.D., Johnson, T.T.: NNV 2.0: the neural network verification tool. In: Enea, C., Lal, A. (eds.) CAV 2023. LNCS, vol. 13965, pp. 397–412. Springer, Cham (2023). https://doi.org/10.1007/978-3-031-37703-7_19
17. Bak, S., Tran, H.D.: Neural network compression of acas xu early prototype is unsafe: closed-loop verification through quantized state backreachability. In: Deshmukh, J.V., Havelund, K., Perez, I. (eds.) NFM 2022. LNCS, vol. 13260. Springer, Cham (2022). https://doi.org/10.1007/978-3-031-06773-0_15
18. Lopez, D.M., Althoff, M., Forets, M., Johnson, T.T., Ladner, T., Schilling, C.: Arch-comp23 category report: artificial intelligence and neural network control systems (ainncs) for continuous and hybrid systems plants. In: EPiC Series in Computing, vol. 96, pp. 89–125. EasyChair (2023)

19. Lopez, D.M., Johnson, T.T., Bak, S., Tran, H.D., Hobbs, K.L.: Evaluation of neural network verification methods for air-to-air collision avoidance. J. Air Transport. **31**(1), 1–17 (2023)
20. Dutertre, B.: Elements of mathematical analysis in PVS. In: Goos, G., Hartmanis, J., van Leeuwen, J., von Wright, J., Grundy, J., Harrison, J. (eds.) TPHOLs 1996. LNCS, vol. 1125, pp. 141–156. Springer, Heidelberg (1996). https://doi.org/10.1007/bfb0105402
21. Raymond Merrill Smullyan: First-Order Logic. Dover publications, Mineola (1995)
22. Paszke, A., et al.: Pytorch: an imperative style, high-performance deep learning library. In Advances in Neural Information Processing Systems, vol. 32, pp. 8024–8035. Curran Associates, Inc. (2019)
23. Agarap, A.F.: Deep learning using rectified linear units (relu). arXiv preprint arXiv:1803.08375 (2018)

Approximate Conformance Verification of Deep Neural Networks

P. Habeeb[1(✉)] and Pavithra Prabhakar[2]

[1] Indian Institute of Science, Bangalore, India
habeebp@iisc.ac.in
[2] Kansas State University, Manhattan, KS 66506, USA
pprabhakar@ksu.edu

Abstract. We consider the problem of approximate conformance checking on deep neural networks. More precisely, given two neural networks and a conformance bound ϵ, we need to check if the neural network outputs are within ϵ given the same inputs from the input set. Our approach reduces the approximate conformance checking problem to a reachability analysis problem using transformations of neural networks. We provide experimental comparison of ϵ-conformance checking based on our approach using various reachability analysis tools as well as other alternate ϵ-conformance checking algorithms. We illustrate the benefits of our approach as well as identify reachability analysis tools that are conducive for conformance checking.

Keywords: Neural networks · Verification · Conformance checking

1 Introduction

Neural networks are being widely used in a variety of applications specifically in safety critical domains such as self-driving cars [2] and air traffic collision avoidance systems [1]. On one hand, providing strong guarantees of correctness is important, while on the other hand, these systems are continually evolving to accomplish increased performance, to incorporate newly available data or to optimize certain parameters such as the network size. From the safety perspective, it is important to enforce that the newly trained system still conforms with the original system in terms of behaviors. In this paper, we explore the problem of conformance between two networks.

Conformance checking of two neural network amounts to checking that their input-output behaviors are the same. However, this is often too strict a constraint, since the systems differ slightly due to retraining. Hence, we are interested in approximate conformance checking wherein a parameter ϵ characterizes the approximation bound. Specifically, given two neural networks, N_1 and N_2, with the same set of input and output nodes, an input region $\mathcal{I}$ and a conformance bound ϵ, the conformance problem consists of checking if $\forall x \in \mathcal{I}, \|N_1(x) - N_2(x)\| < \epsilon$. In other words, the neural network conformance problem checks that the output value difference between two neural networks for any input in the given region is always less than the given ϵ.

N. Benz et al. (Eds.): NFM 2024, LNCS 14627, pp. 223–238, 2024.
https://doi.org/10.1007/978-3-031-60698-4_13

The ϵ-conformance problem has been explored using a symbolic interval analysis technique, ReluDiff [8], and a geometric path enumeration-based technique, StarDiff [10]. However, ReluDiff only works with structurally equivalent neural networks and is designed to check the conformance between network pairs with very small differences in edge weight values. StarDiff [10] is an extension of the geometric paths enumeration algorithm [1]; while it is able to determine violation of ϵ-conformance on network pairs quickly, it often takes longer to conclude conformance. In general, the conformance problem is coNP-complete. Further, an SMT-based approach [4] has been explored, however, it is slower with respect to the other approaches.

Our broad approach to conformance checking is to reduce the problem to reachability analysis of neural networks and and exploit the recent progress in techniques and tools for neural network verification. More precisely, we transform the given networks N_1 and N_2 into a single network N, that simulates the joint behavior of N_1 and N_2. The output of N on input u is the pair of outputs from N_1 and N_2 on u. Hence, by performing the reachability analysis of N on a set of inputs I, we obtain the set of pairs of outputs of N_1 and N_2 on inputs from I, that is, O. To check ϵ-conformance, we need to check whether $\|v_1 - v_2\| < \epsilon$ for every pair $(v_1, v_2) \in O$ in the output. Therefore, the systems N_1 and N_2 are ϵ-conformance if and only if the constraint, there exists $(v_1, v_2) \in O$, with $\|v_1 - v_2\| \geq \epsilon$, is not satisfiable.

We have implemented the transformation of the neural networks in Python, and experimented with several reachability analysis tools. We also compare our approach with ReluDiff and StarDiff. We evaluated on 27 pairs of networks taken from the ACAS Xu benchmark [5]. Our experiments show that our approach based on reachability analysis using *nnenum* [1] tool performs better than all other approaches both in terms of the conformance checking time and the number of network pairs for which conformance or non-conformance was successfully determined.

2 Conformance Checking of Neural Networks

In this section, we describe the definition of the neural network, its semantics, and the conformance-checking problem. A neural network consists of multiple neurons organized as layers, including an input layer, an output layer and one or more hidden layers. Neurons in adjacent layers are connected with weighted edges; each neuron in the network, except for those in the input layer, has an activation function and a bias value. The following subsection presents preliminaries regarding neural networks and the operations performed on them before formally defining the neural network components.

2.1 Preliminaries

Let $\mathbb{R}$ denote the set of real numbers, and $\mathbb{N}$ denote the set of natural numbers. Given a set A, $|A|$ represents the number of elements of A. Given a non-negative integer k, let $[k]$ denote the set $\{0, \ldots, k\}$, and $(k]$ denote the set $\{1, \cdots, k\}$. ReLU activation function is defined as $ReLU(x) = max(0, x)\ \forall x \in \mathbb{R}$. For any set S, a valuation over S is a function $f : S \longrightarrow \mathbb{R}$. We define $Val(S)$ to be the set of all valuations over S. Given $l, u \in \mathbb{N}$ such that $l < u$, then $[l, u]$ denote the set $\{l, l+1, \ldots, u-1, u\}$. Given two sets S_1 and S_2, the operation $\uplus$ represents the disjoint union of S_1 and S_2. For a vector v, $\|v\|$ is the maximum absolute value of elements in v. Given two functions $f : A \rightarrow B$ and $g : B \rightarrow C$, the composition of f and g, $g \circ f : A \rightarrow C$, is given by, for all $a \in A$, $g \circ f(a) = g(f(a))$. Let $n \in \mathbb{N}$. For $x \in \mathbb{R}^n$, let x_i denote the projection of x onto i^{th} component, that is, $x = (x_1, x_2, ..., x_n)$. For $x \in \mathbb{R}^n$ and $y \in \mathbb{R}^m$, $x \diamond y = (x_1, \cdots, x_n, y_1, \cdots, y_m) \in \mathbb{R}^{n+m}$.

Definition 1. *(Neural Network). A neural network is a tuple* $N = (k, Act, \{S_i\}_{i\in[k]}, \{W_i\}_{i\in(k]}, \{B_i\}_{i\in(k]}, \{\sigma_i\}_{i\in(k]})$, *where*

- $k \in \mathbb{N}$ *represents the number of layers (except the input layer);*
- Act *is a set of activation functions, and every* $f \in Act$ *has* $\mathbb{R}$ *as its domain and range;*
- $\forall i \in [k], S_i$ *is a set of neurons of layer* i, *and* $\forall i \neq j, S_i \cap S_j = \emptyset$;
- $\forall i \in (k], W_i : S_{i-1} \times S_i \rightarrow \mathbb{R}$ *is the weight function that captures the weights on the edges between the neurons at layer* $i-1$ *and* i;
- $\forall i \in (k], B_i : S_i \rightarrow \mathbb{R}$ *is the bias function that associates a bias value with neurons of layer* i;
- $\forall i \in (k], \sigma_i : S_i \rightarrow Act$ *is an activation association function that associates an activation function with each neuron of layer* i.

The layers S_0 and S_k are called the input and the output layers respectively; rest of the layers are called the hidden layers. We fix the following notations for the rest of the paper. Any neural network denoted by N is the network $N = (k, Act, \{S_i\}_{i\in[k]}, \{W_i\}_{i\in(k]}, \{B_i\}_{i\in(k]}, \{\sigma_i\}_{i\in(k]})$ and for any $j \in \mathbb{N}$, $N_j = (k_j, Act, \{S_i^j\}_{i\in[k_j]}, \{W_i^j\}_{i\in(k_j]}, \{B_i^j\}_{i\in(k_j]}, \{\sigma_i^j\}_{i\in(k_j]})$. For notational convenience, we simplify the notation assuming the values that i iterates over are clear from the context. For example, for any $j \in \mathbb{N}$, we will write a neural network N_j with k_j layers as $N_j = (k_j, Act, S_i^j, W_i^j, B_i^j, \sigma_i^j)$.

As an example, consider the neural network N_1 in Fig. 1; it consists of an input layer with two neurons, two hidden layers with three neurons each, and an output layer with two neurons. The weights on the edges are shown, the biases are zero, and the activation functions are all ReLU.

Next, we define the executions of a neural network as a sequence of valuations, each of which corresponds to values assigned to the neurons in a layer. Given a valuation v for a layer $i-1$, $[\![N]\!]_i(v)$ denotes the valuation obtained for the layer i according to the semantics of N, which is defined below.

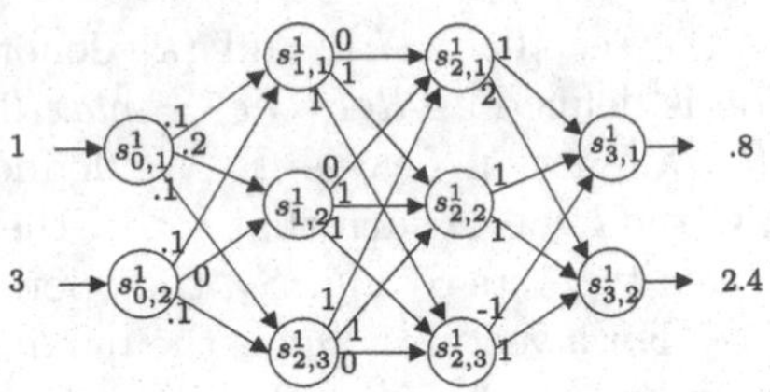

Fig. 1. Neural Network N_1.

Definition 2. *(Semantics of a Neural Network). Given a neural network N, the semantics of the layer i, $i \neq 0$, is the function $[\![N]\!]_i$: $Val(S_{i-1}) \to Val(S_i)$, where for any $v \in Val(S_{i-1})$, $[\![N]\!]_i(v) = v'$, is given by*

$$\forall s' \in S_i, v'(s') = \sigma_i(s')((\sum_{s \in S_{i-1}} W_i(s, s')v(s)) + B_i(s'))$$

We define the semantics of neural network N by the function $[\![N]\!]$: $Val(S_0) \to Val(S_k)$ as a composition of functions corresponding to individual layers as $[\![N]\!] = [\![N]\!]_k \circ [\![N]\!]_{k-1} \circ \ldots \circ [\![N]\!]_1$.

For input values of 1 for $s^1_{0,1}$ and 3 for $s^1_{0,2}$, the neural network N_1 produces output values of 0.8 and 2.4 for neurons $s^1_{3,1}$ and $s^1_{3,2}$, respectively.

Let us fix some more notations for the rest of the paper. For a neural network N, let $S_i = \{s_{i,1}, s_{i,2}, \cdots, s_{i,r_i}\}$ for each $0 \leq i \leq k$. Since any valuation $v \in Val(S_i)$ is a map $v : S_i \to \mathbb{R}$, and we have defined the ordering of the nodes in every layer, from now on we consider $v \in Val(S_i)$ as an element of $\mathbb{R}^{|S_i|}$. Hence the semantic of a neural network can be considered as the following function $[\![N]\!] : \mathbb{R}^{|S_0|} \to \mathbb{R}^{|S_k|}$.

The approximate conformance checking problem is: given two neural networks with the same number of input and output neurons, a set of valuations for the input layer, and an $\epsilon \in \mathbb{R}_{\geq 0}$, check whether the difference between output neuron values of corresponding nodes in both networks is in the range $(-\epsilon, \epsilon)$.

Problem 1. (**ϵ-conformance**). Given two neural networks, N_1 and N_2, a set of input valuations $\mathcal{I} \subseteq Val(S^1_0)$, and a conformance bound $\epsilon \in \mathbb{R}_{\geq 0}$, the ϵ-conformance problem involves verifying whether, $\forall v \in \mathcal{I}$, the condition $\|[\![N_1]\!](v) - [\![N_2]\!](v)\| < \epsilon$ holds.

Strict-conformance or *exact-conformance* is a special case of ϵ-conformance where the value of $\epsilon = 0$; that is, two networks are strictly equivalent if their outputs are the same for the given input valuations.

Since our goal is to compare two neural networks, all the neural networks considered in the paper are assumed to have the same number of nodes in their input and output layers. In particular, for neural networks N, N_1, N_2, $|S_0| = |S^1_0| = |S^2_0| = n$ and $|S_k| = |S^1_{k_1}| = |S^2_{k_2}| = m$.

3 Conformance Checking Algorithm

In this section, we present reachability-based methods for solving the ϵ-conformance problem. This method consists of two steps: first, we create a merged network of the networks being analyzed, and then we perform a reachability analysis on the combined network. First, we explain the process of constructing the merged network and provide proof of the correctness of the construction. Then in the following subsection, we explain our reachability-based analysis.

3.1 Append Hidden Layer

In this section, we describe a helper function which we use to construct the merged network in the next subsection. Given a neural network N and a positive integer r, the append hidden layer function, *append*(N, r), adds r hidden layers, each having the same number of neurons as the last hidden layer before the output layer, effectively repeating the last hidden layer r times. The weights on the newly added edges are zero, except for the edges between corresponding nodes in adjacent layers, which have a weight of 1. The bias value on each newly added neuron is set to zero, and the activation function on each new node is ReLU. Even though we are using the ReLU activation function for newly added neurons, the values of neurons in the recently added layers are equal to those of their corresponding neurons in the last hidden layer of the original network because these neurons get values after the application of the activation function. Now, we formally define the append hidden layer function.

Definition 3. *(Append Hidden Layer): Given a neural network* $N_1 = (k_1, Act, S_i^1, W_i^1, B_i^1, \sigma_i^1)$ *and an append count* $r \in \mathbb{N}$, *the append hidden layer function append*(N_1, r) *returns a neural network* $N_2 = (k_2, Act, S_i^2, W_i^2, B_i^2, \sigma_i^2)$, *where*

- $k_2 = k_1 + r$,
- *for each* $i \in [k_1 - 1]$, $S_i^2 = S_i^1$, *for each* $i \in [k_1, k_2 - 1]$, $S_i^2 = S_{k_1-1}^1$, *and* $S_{k_2}^2 = S_{k_1}^1$;
- *for each* $i \in (k_1 - 1]$, *the functions* W_i^2 *and* W_i^1 *are the same, for each* $i \in [k_1, k_2 - 1]$, $W_i^2(s_{i-1,l}^2, s_{i,m}^2) = 1$ *if* $l = m$, *and* 0 *otherwise, and* $W_{k_2}^2(s_{k_2-1,i}^2, s_{k_2,j}^2) = W_{k_1}^1(s_{k_1-1,i}^1, s_{k_1,j}^1)$;
- *for each* $i \in (k_1 - 1]$, *the functions* B_i^2 *and* B_i^1 *are the same, for each* $i \in [k_1, k_2 - 1]$, B_i^2 *is a zero function,* $B_{k_2}^2(s_{k_2,j}^2) = B_{k_1}^1(s_{k_1,j}^1)$, *and*
- *all activation functions are ReLU.*

As an example of the append operation, Fig. 2 shows the neural network resulting from *append*$(N_1, 1)$, where N_1 refers to the neural network shown in Fig. 1, and the newly added neurons are highlighted. The correctness of the *append*(N_1, r) construction, where $r \in \mathbb{N}$, is established by the following lemma. It asserts that, for a given input valuation, the output values computed by both N_1 and *append*(N_1, r) are the same, thereby establishing the soundness of the append operation.

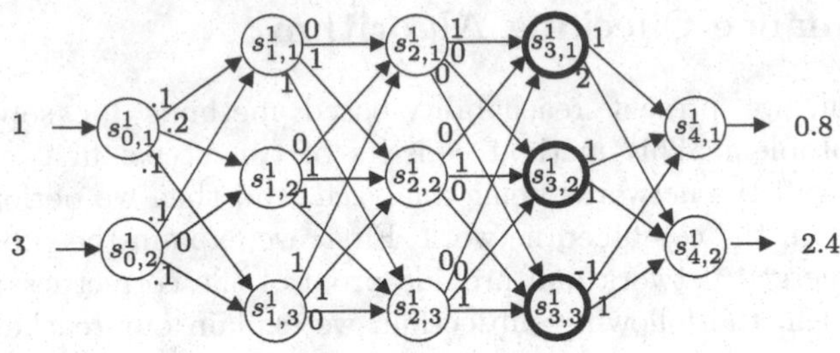

Fig. 2. Append hidden layer example: *append*$(N_1, 1)$.

Lemma 1. *Given a neural network* $N_1 = (k_1, Act, S_i^1, W_i^1, B_i^1, \sigma_i^1)$, *and an append count* $r \in \mathbb{N}$, *let* $append(N_1, r) = N_2 = (k_2, Act, S_i^2, W_i^2, B_i^2, \sigma_i^2)$, *then* $[\![N_2]\!] = [\![N_1]\!]$.

Proof. Note that nodes and edges from the input layer to layer $k_1 - 1$ are the same in both N_1 and N_2, so from the definition of $[\![N]\!]_i$, we get $[\![N_2]\!]_i = [\![N_1]\!]_i$, $\forall 1 \leq i \leq k_1 - 1$. Similarly, it is easy to see that $\forall v \in Val(S_{k_1-1}^1), [\![N_2]\!]_i(v) = v, \forall k_1 \leq i \leq k_2 - 1$, because $\forall k_1 \leq i \leq k_2 - 1$, $B_i^2(s_{i,j}) = 0$, $W_i^2(s, s') = 0$ for all $s_{i-1,j}$ and $s'_{i,k}$ such that $k \neq j$, and $W_i^2(s, s') = 1$ for all $s_{i-1,j}$ and $s'_{i,k}$ such that $k = j$. Finally, for the output layer, for any $v \in \mathbb{R}^{|S_{k-1}^1|}$, $[\![N_2]\!]_{k_2}(v) = [\![N_1]\!]_{k_1}(v)$, because the weights on the edges to the neurons in the output layer and biases associated with the neurons in the output layer are the same for both N_1 and N_2. Hence, from the definition of $[\![N]\!]$ we can see that $[\![N_2]\!](v) = [\![N_1]\!](v), \forall v \in \mathbb{R}^n$.

3.2 Merge Networks

The merge operation combines two neural networks with the same or different topology, where the input and output layers have the same number of nodes, into a single network. The values computed by both networks can be derivable from the merged network. To achieve this, the merge function first ensures that both networks have the same number of layers. This is accomplished by using the *append* hidden layer function, as defined in the previous subsection. The *append* hidden layer function adds the necessary number of layers to the network with the smallest layer count. Then, it creates a new neural network, such that neurons in each layer is the union of neurons in the corresponding layers of input networks. Edges and weights in the new network are the unions of edges and weights from both networks, and additional edges with zero weights are added to ensure that the new network is fully connected. We formally defined the merge operation in the Definition 4.

Definition 4. *(Merge Two Networks): Given two neural networks,* $N_1 = (k_1, Act, S_i^1, W_i^1, B_i^1, \sigma_i^1)$, $N_2 = (k_2, Act, S_i^2, W_i^2, B_i^2, \sigma_i^2)$, *with* $|S_1^1| = |S_1^2|$, $|S_{k_1}^1| = |S_{k_2}^2|$, *and* $k_1 = k_2$, *the merge operation* $merge(N_1, N_2)$ *returns a new network* $N_3 = (k_3, Act, S_i^3, W_i^3, B_i^3, \sigma_i^3)$ *where,*

- $k_3 = k_1 (= k_2)$.
- $S_0^3 = S_0^1$, *for each* $i \in [1, k_3], S_i^3 = S_i^1 \uplus S_i^2$.
- *We define the weight functions as follows. For all the edges that are present in one of the neural networks, the weights on those edges remain the same, the rest of the edges are given the weight* 0.
 Further, for each $i \in [|S_0^2|], j \in [|S_1^2|], W_1^3(s_{0,i}^1, s_{1,j}^2) = W_1^2(s_{0,i}^2, s_{1,j}^2)$;
- *For all the nodes, the bias values remain the same.*
- *For all the nodes, the activation function remain the same.*

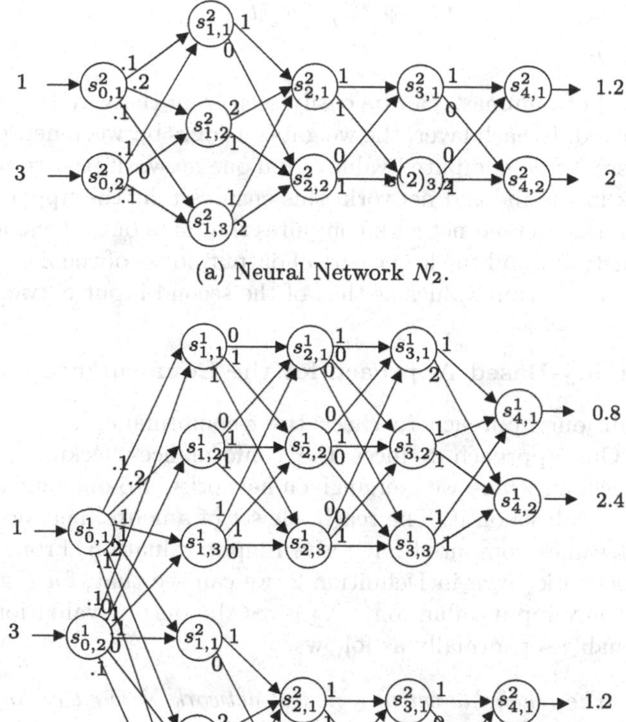

(a) Neural Network N_2.

(b) Merged Network $merge(append(N_1, 1), N_2)$.

Fig. 3. Merge Example.

Figure 3b depicts the result of merging networks $append(N_1, 1)$ in Fig. 2 and N_2 in Fig. 3a. We omitted edges from neurons of N_1 to neurons of N_2 because their weights are set to zero and do not impact the output computation.

Given two neural networks and their merged network, the output values computed by the input networks for a given input valuation can be determined from the values of the corresponding neurons in the merged network's output layer. The values computed by the upper output neurons (neurons in the output layer of the merged network and output nodes of the first input network) match the output values of the first input network. Similarly, the values computed by the lower output neurons (neurons in the output layer of the merged network and output nodes of the second input network) match the output values of the second input network.

Lemma 2. *Given two neural networks* N_1 *and* N_2 *with* $k_1 = k_2$*, let* $N_3 = merge(N_1, N_2)$*. Then* $\forall v \in \mathbb{R}^n (= \mathbb{R}^{|S_0^1|})$*,* $[\![N_3]\!](v) = v_1 \diamond v_2$ *where* $v_1 = [\![N_1]\!](v)$ *and* $v_2 = [\![N_2]\!](v)$*.*

Proof. The proof of Lemma 2 can be easily seen from the way the merged network is constructed. In each layer, the weights on edges between neurons of input networks are zero, so no computed values from one network pass to nodes of the second network in the merged network; this ensures that the upper part of the output nodes in the merged network computes the same output value as that of the first input network and the lower part of output nodes of the merged network computes the same output values as that of the second input network.

3.3 Reachability-Based Approach for the Conformance Checking

Now, we explain our approach to check the ϵ-conformance between two neural networks. Our approach reduces the conformance-checking problems to reachability-checking, where we merge given networks into one network and run the reachability analysis on it. The reachable set of a neural network is nothing but the output values computed for a given input valuation. From the semantics of neural network given in Definition 2, we can see that, for a given neural network N, for any input valuation, $[\![N]\!]$ gives the output valuation of N. We define the reachable set formally as follows.

Definition 5. *The reachable set of a neural network* N *w.r.t an input set* $\mathcal{I} \subseteq \mathbb{R}^n$ *is*

$$\mathcal{R}_N(\mathcal{I}) = \{[\![N]\!](v) | v \in \mathcal{I}\}.$$

To check the ϵ-conformance between two given neural networks, we first compute the reachable set of the merged network and then find out the maximum difference between the corresponding neurons using the reachable set computed. If the maximum difference is always less than the given ϵ, then the given networks are ϵ-conformant to each other.

Theorem 1. *Let* N_1 *and* N_2 *be two neural networks with* $k_1 = k_2$*. Let* $N_3 = merge(N_1, N_2)$*. Given a set of input valuations* $\mathcal{I} \subseteq Val(S_0^1)$*, and a conformance bound* $\epsilon > 0$*,* N_1 *and* N_2 *satisfy* ϵ*-conformance property if and only if* $\forall v \in \mathcal{I}$ $|([\![N_3]\!](v))_i - ([\![N_3]\!](v))_{m+i}| < \epsilon, \forall 1 \leq i \leq m$*.*

Proof. Note that N_1 and N_2 satisfy the ϵ-conformance property if and only if $|(\llbracket N_1 \rrbracket(v))_i - (\llbracket N_2 \rrbracket(v))_i| < \epsilon, 1 \leq i \leq m$. Let $v_0 \in \mathcal{I}$. By Lemma 2, $\llbracket N_3 \rrbracket(v_0) = v_1 \diamond v_2$, where $v_1 = \llbracket N_1 \rrbracket(v)$ and $v_2 = \llbracket N_2 \rrbracket(v)$. Hence, N_1 and N_2 satisfy the ϵ-conformance property if and only if $|(\llbracket N_3 \rrbracket(v_0))_i - (\llbracket N_3 \rrbracket(v_0))_{m+i}| < \epsilon, \forall 1 \leq i \leq m$.

We use the range of N_3 (defined in Definition 5) to compute the expression given in the theorem.

4 Implementation and Experiments

We implemented the conformance-checking algorithm in Python and utilized existing neural network reachability analysis tools to compute the reach set. Algorithm 1 gives a high-level overview of our ϵ-conformance checking algorithm. Inputs to the algorithm are two neural networks, N_1 with k_1 layers and N_2 with k_2 layers, conformance bound ϵ, input region $\mathcal{I}$, and the timeout c. First, in Lines (1–2), we make sure that both networks have the same number of layers using our *append*() function defined in Definition 3. The tools we compare in our experiments require both networks to have the same number of layers. Next, the algorithm merges N_1 and N_2 to a single network N_3 using our merge function *merge*(N_1, N_2) defined in Definition 4. The *computeReachSet*() function runs the reachability check tool for c time unit and returns the outputs. The output values are either the reach set returned or the timeout. If the reach set is returned, we check whether the maximum difference between corresponding output nodes is less than or equal to the given ϵ. If the maximum value is less than the given ϵ, then the networks satisfy the ϵ-conformance property; otherwise, networks do not satisfy the ϵ-conformance property.

Algorithm 1. ϵ-Conformance Checking Algorithm.

Input: NN1 N_1: k_1 layers, NN2 N_2: k_2 layers, conformance bound ϵ, input region $\mathcal{I}$, timeout c.
Output: Conformant, Unconformant, TimeOut

1: $N_1' = append(N_1, |k_1 - max(k_1, k_2)|)$
2: $N_2' = append(N_2, |k_2 - max(k_1, k_2)|)$
3: $N_3 = merge(N_1', N_2')$
4: $reachSet = computeReachSet(N_3, \mathcal{I}, c)$
5: **if** *reachSet* is not timeout **then**
6:     **if** the maximum output difference in *reachSet* $< \epsilon$ **then**
7:         return *Conformant*.
8:     **else**
9:         return *Unconformant*.
10:     **end if**
11: **else**
12:     return *timeout*.
13: **end if**

Next, we explain our experimental setup. All experiments were conducted on an Ubuntu machine with an Intel(R) Core(TM) i5-10210U 1.60 GHz CPU and 8GB RAM. We consider 27 pairs of neural networks from Airborne Collision System X Unmanned (ACAS Xu) [5] benchmark suite, and 9 input sets which correspond to the properties $P1$ (= $P2$), $P3$, $P4$, $P5$, $P6$, $P7$, $P8$, $P9$, and $P10$ from the nnenum benchmarks [1]. These networks are trained to replace the lookup table operation system for midair collisions of unmanned aircraft. The suite contains a total of 45 neural networks, and each of them has five inputs: the distance from the ownship to the intruder, the angle to the intruder relative to the ownship heading direction, the heading angle of the intruder relative to the ownship heading direction, the speed of ownship, and the speed of intruder. The output layer consists of five output nodes, with one for each possible advisory: clear-of-conflict, weak left, weak right, strong left, and strong right. The action with the minimum score is the action advised. These networks also contain five hidden layers, each of which has 50 neurons. We randomly selected 27 pairs of networks from the 2025 ACAS Xu network benchmark for the ϵ-conformance experiments with the initial set provided by nine ACAS Xu properties (P1 - P10) taken from [1]. We consider two values for the approximation bound ϵ.

We compare our approach with two other approaches, namely, ReluDiff [8] and StarDiff [10], which are alternate methods for checking ϵ-conformance. ReluDiff [8] considers differential verification of two closely related networks using interval analysis and consists of approximate forward interval analysis pass followed by a backward pass that iteratively refines the approximation until the desired property is verified. StarDiff [10] extends a geometric path enumeration algorithm to the setting of multiple neural networks. While StarDiff checks that output values at each of the nodes in the first neural network is within ϵ of the corresponding nodes of the other neural network, ReluDiff focuses on one output node, that is, checks if the values at a specific output node in the two networks are within ϵ. For our method, we consider two reachability analysis tools, namely, $\alpha-\beta-CROWN$ [11], and nnenum [1]. $\alpha-\beta-CROWN$ [11] is a neural network verifier based on an efficient linear bound propagation framework and branch and bound techniques. nnenum [1] is a neural network verification tool that computes reachable sets by propagating star-set overapproximations. The results are tabulated in Table 1, 2, 3 and Table 4. We consider two experiments with nnenum, one where we consider only one specific output node, and the other where we consider all output nodes; there are reported in columns named nnenum and nnenumAll in the tables.

Table 1 and Table 2 report the number of pairs for which conformance or non-conformance was successfully determined, and the time taken for the same, respectively. Each row corresponds to 27 pairs of networks with respect to the input set provided by Pis, with $\epsilon = 0.05$ and a time out of 180 s. Table 3 and Table 4 report the experiments with $\epsilon = 0.5$.

Our algorithm using the *nnenum* [1] and the $\alpha-\beta-CROWN$ [11] tools determined conformance/non-conformance for more number of network pairs and took less time for determining the same as compared to the existing confor-

Table 1. Number of networks out of 27 for which conformance/non-conformance was determined. $\epsilon = 0.05$. Timeout = 180 s.

	Exsting Tools		Our Approach		
Property	ReluDiff	StarDiff	$\alpha-\beta-CROWN$	nnenum	nnenumAll
P1, P2	7	15	9	19	22
P3	6	25	26	27	27
P4	11	27	27	27	26
P5	6	23	27	24	27
P7	0	23	12	14	23
P8	0	23	9	14	25
P9	15	21	23	27	26
P10	22	1	26	25	26
Total	67	158	159	177	202

Table 2. Total time taken to check 27 networks. $\epsilon = 0.05$. Timeout = 180 s.

	Exsting Tools		Our Approach		
Property	ReluDiff	StarDiff	$\alpha-\beta-CROWN$	nnenum	nnenumAll
P1, P2	3638.3	2873.3	3394.4	1774.9	1514.7
P3	3574.6	785.1	566	227	101.2
P4	3031.3	170	84.2	87.9	252.4
P5	3445.8	1316	226.7	660.2	104.5
P7	4860	1350.1	2845.3	2423.9	978.5
P8	4860	1192.3	3299.6	2531.4	498.7
P9	2296	1106.4	938.8	496.9	723.7
P10	2089.6	4816.3	673.6	1060.2	1254.9
Total	27795.6	13609.5	12028.6	9262.4	5428.6

mance checking tools *ReluDiff* and *StarDiff*, with the approach using *nnenum* tool performing the best. Our experiments using SMT-based tool [4] timed out for all the networks, hence, we do not report it in the tables. The size of the ϵ also affects the number of networks for which conformance/non-conformance was determined successfully; more network pairs can be verified for conformance when the ϵ is smaller.

5 Application of Conformance Checking to Closed-Loop Systems

We consider the effect of swapping ϵ-conformant neural networks employed as controllers in a closed-loop system. Specifically, we want to check whether the

Table 3. Number of networks out of 27 for which conformance/non-conformance was determined. $\epsilon = 0.5$. Timeout = 180 s.

	Exsting Tools		Our Approach		
Property	ReluDiff	StarDiff	$\alpha-\beta-CROWN$	nnenum	nnenumAll
P1, P2	3	0	14	16	7
P3	23	18	27	27	27
P4	26	25	27	27	26
P5	26	5	27	26	24
P7	0	0	0	0	0
P8	0	0	0	0	0
P9	24	0	26	26	23
P10	27	1	25	26	24
Total	119	49	146	148	131

Table 4. Total time taken to check 27 networks. Epsilon = 0.5. Timeout = 180 s.

	Exsting Tools		Our Approach		
Property	ReluDiff	StarDiff	$\alpha-\beta-CROWN$	nnenum	nnenumAll
P1,P2	4571	4860	2691.1	3361.3	4271.4
P3	1075.1	2063	228.4	227	102.4
P4	371	1393.4	44.9	50.8	235.8
P5	1284	4504	169.4	344.7	730.3
P7	4860	4860	4860	4860	4860
P8	4860	4860	4860	4860	4860
P9	2994.4	4860	473.1	1185.9	1629.7
P10	536.1	4818.1	636.5	629.4	878.3
Total	20551.6	32218.5	13963.4	15519.1	17567.9

behaviours of two systems are approximately equivalent when the controller is replaced by an ϵ-conformant neural network. We consider simple closed-loop systems consisting of a plant modeled as linear dynamical systems with system matrices $A \in \mathbb{R}^{n\times n}$ and $B \in \mathbb{R}^{n\times d}$, and the controller modeled as a neural network as shown in Fig. 4. The neural network controller takes the plant's state at time k, $x(k)$, as input and computes the plant's control input $u(k)$, and the plant updates its state based on the received control input to $x(k+1)$. The system starts with a given initial state $x(0) = x_0$.

5.1 Case Study: Automatic Rocket Landing System

As a case study to gain insight into the deviation of system states, we consider a simple rocket landing system. In this system, the rocket's internal control

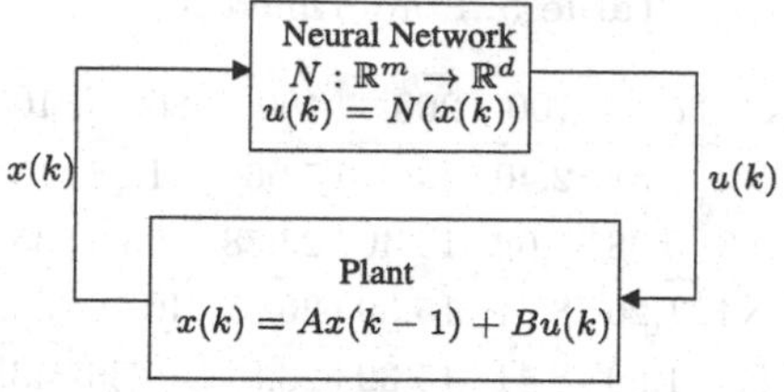

Fig. 4. Closed Loop System with NN Control.

system hands over the maneuver task to the automatic landing system at a particular height from the ground. The automated landing system aims to reduce the rocket's velocity by applying thrust and achieve a smooth landing on the ground.

The system's state is a two-dimensional real-valued vector $[p, v]$, representing the rocket's position (distance from the ground) and velocity. The neural network controller takes the system's current state and outputs the amount of thrust that should be applied to the system. The following equations describe the dynamics of the plant:

$$x(k) = Ax(k-1) + Bu(k)$$

where $x(k) = [p, v]$ represents the position and velocity at time k, and $u(k)$ is the output of the neural network at step k. The system matrices are given below,

$$A = \begin{bmatrix} 1 & -\tau \\ 0 & 1 \end{bmatrix}, \textit{and } B = \begin{bmatrix} 0 \\ -100\tau \end{bmatrix},$$

where $\tau = 0.001$ is the sampling period.

We trained the reinforcement-learning-based neural network controller using the Deep Deterministic Policy Gradient (DDPG) method [7]. To generate training scenarios, we implemented the rocket landing system as an environment in the OpenAI Gym toolkit [3]. The initial position and velocity of the rocket are randomly chosen from the intervals [50, 60] and [45, 55], respectively. The termination condition is either velocity ≤ 0 or position ≤ 0. The reward function $\rho(p, v)$ is given below,

$$\rho(p, v) = -(p + v) + I_1(p, v) + I_2(p, v) + r(\textit{safeLanding}) + r(\textit{collision}),$$

where $I_1(p, v)$ returns a reward of 20 if $p \in [3, 6] \wedge v \in [2, 5]$, it returns a reward of 0 if $p \notin [3, 6] \wedge v \notin [2, 5]$. Otherwise, it returns a reward of –100. Similarly, $I_2(p, v)$ returns a reward of 20 if $p \in [1, 3) \wedge v \in [1, 2)$, returning a reward of 0 if $p \notin [1, 3) \wedge v \notin [1, 2)$. Otherwise, it returns a reward of –100. $r(\textit{safeLanding})$ returns a reward of 10000 if $p = 0 \wedge v = 0$, and $r(\textit{collision})$ return a reward of –500 if $(p < 0 \wedge v > 0) \vee (p > 0 \wedge v <= 0)$.

A total of five networks have been trained for 100 epochs; details of each network are as follows: N1 (2, 500, 400, 300, 1), N2 (2, 500, 400, 1), N3 (2, 500, 400, 300, 200, 1), N4 (2, 500, 400, 300, 200, 100, 1), and N5 (2, 500, 400,

Table 5. State Difference

Nets	ϵ	100	200	400	800	1000
N1, N2	0.38	2.40	4.38	7.96	11.58	15.02
N1, N3	0.98	7.62	13.40	23.58	35.03	35.70
N1, N4	1.26	8.41	15.39	26.87	40.76	47.73
N1, N5	1.59	8.41	15.39	26.87	40.36	43.61
N2, N3	0.72	5.22	9.01	15.62	23.45	20.68
N2, N4	1.00	6.00	11.01	18.90	29.17	32.70
N2, N5	1.31	6.00	11.01	18.90	28.78	28.58
N3, N4	0.30	0.78	1.99	3.28	5.72	12.02
N3, N5	0.68	0.78	1.99	3.28	5.32	7.90

300, 200, 100, 100, 1), where the numbers in parenthesis represent the number of nodes in each layer. We evaluated our method on ten pairs of systems using these networks. We ran each individual system with an initial position of 55 and an initial velocity of 50 and recorded the maximum difference in states at a given step of the execution. Table 5 shows the maximum difference in system states at different execution steps 100, 200, 400, 800 and 1000. The first column lists the names of neural networks used in the two systems, the second column is the ϵ value for which the network pair is conformant for input valuation for the position is in [0, 60] and for the velocity is in [45, 55], and the remaining columns give the maximum state difference after the specified execution step.

The experimental results show that although the neural network states are close for a small value of ϵ, the state deviation increases with the number of steps. The reason is that after each step, the inputs to the neural networks deviate, thereby, their outputs are no more guaranteed to be within ϵ. Specifically, ϵ-conformance as defined in the paper does not apply to the setting of closed-loop systems, since the two neural network receive varying inputs in subsequent iterations.

6 Related Works

In this section, we briefly explain some of the existing tools to check the ϵ-conformance between two neural networks. SMT-based approach [4] for the conformance-checking between two neural networks encodes the input neural networks as two SMT formulas, ϕ_1 and ϕ_2, the conformance constraint as another formula Φ, and then checks the satisfiability of $\phi_1 \wedge \phi_2 \wedge \neg\Phi$. If the solver returns UNSAT, then the input NNs satisfy the conformance property; otherwise, they do not satisfy the conformance property. As seen in our experiments (not reported here) SMT-based approach underperforms with respect to the existing approaches.

ReluDiff introduced interval analysis-based techniques to check conformance between two networks that are structurally equivalent. The main focus of the ReluDiff tool is to check equivalence between neural networks with slight changes in the edge weights, such as truncating a 32-bit value to a 16-bit value. This tool used a forward interval analysis pass using the symbolic interval analysis followed by a backward pass that iteratively refines the approximation until the desired property is verified. The authors improved this work using a more fine-grained approximation in [9]. The ReluDiff tool works better if the neural networks differ by small weight changes, such as changing edge weights from 32 to 16 bits.

The StarDiff project [1] extended the single neural network geometric path enumeration algorithm to a setting with multiple neural networks. This paper also proved that the conformance problem for neural networks is coNP-complete. The mixed-integer linear program (MILP)-based technique [6] encodes networks and conformance properties as an optimization problem and utilizes Gurobi to solve it.

7 Conclusion

In this work, we presented an approach to check the approximate conformance between two neural networks using the reachability analysis on a transformed network. Our approach, using the existing reachability analysis tools for neural networks, outperforms all the existing approaches developed specifically for the conformance checking between neural networks. We apply our approach to conformance checking of neural networks used as controllers in closed-loop control systems. Though the neural networks are approximately conformant, we do not obtain bounds on the conformance between the two closed-loop systems. This may require generalizing the notion of approximate conformance. We plan to explore that in the future.

Acknowledgements. This work was partially supported by NSF Grant No. 2008957 and an Amazon Research Award. We would like to thank Lipsy Gupta for discussions and feedback on the paper.

References

1. Bak, S., Tran, H.D., Hobbs, K., Johnson, T.T.: Improved geometric path enumeration for verifying relu neural networks. In: Lahiri, S., Wang, C. (eds.) CAV 2020. LNCS, vol. 12224, pp. 66–96. Springer, Heidelberg (2020). https://doi.org/10.1007/978-3-030-53288-8_4
2. Bojarski, M., et al.: End to end learning for self-driving cars. CoRR **abs/1604.07316** (2016). http://arxiv.org/abs/1604.07316
3. Brockman, G., et al.: Openai gym (2016)
4. Eleftheriadis, C., Kekatos, N., Katsaros, P., Tripakis, S.: On neural network equivalence checking using SMT solvers. In: Bogomolov, S., Parker, D. (eds.) FORMATS 2022, vol. 13465, pp. 237–257. Springer, Heidelberg (2022). https://doi.org/10.1007/978-3-031-15839-1_14

5. Julian, K.D., Kochenderfer, M.J., Owen, M.P.: Deep neural network compression for aircraft collision avoidance systems. J. Guid. Control. Dyn. **42**(3), 598–608 (2019)
6. Kleine Büning, M., Kern, P., Sinz, C.: Verifying equivalence properties of neural networks with relu activation functions. In: Simonis, H. (ed.) CP 2020. LNCS, vol. 12333, pp. 868–884. Springer, Heidelberg (2020). https://doi.org/10.1007/978-3-030-58475-7_50
7. Lillicrap, T.P., et al.: Continuous control with deep reinforcement learning. arXiv preprint arXiv:1509.02971 (2015)
8. Paulsen, B., Wang, J., Wang, C.: Reludiff: differential verification of deep neural networks. In: Rothermel, G., Bae, D. (eds.) ICSE 2020: 42nd International Conference on Software Engineering, Seoul, South Korea, 27 June–19 July 2020, pp. 714–726. ACM (2020). https://doi.org/10.1145/3377811.3380337
9. Paulsen, B., Wang, J., Wang, J., Wang, C.: Neurodiff: scalable differential verification of neural networks using fine-grained approximation. In: 2020 35th IEEE/ACM International Conference on Automated Software Engineering (ASE), pp. 784–796. IEEE (2020)
10. Teuber, S., Büning, M.K., Kern, P., Sinz, C.: Geometric path enumeration for equivalence verification of neural networks. In: 2021 IEEE 33rd International Conference on Tools with Artificial Intelligence (ICTAI), pp. 200–208. IEEE (2021)
11. Wang, S., et al.: Beta-CROWN: efficient bound propagation with per-neuron split constraints for complete and incomplete neural network verification. In: Advances in Neural Information Processing Systems, vol. 34 (2021)

Compositional Inductive Invariant Based Verification of Neural Network Controlled Systems

Yuhao Zhou(✉) and Stavros Tripakis

Northeastern University, Boston, MA, USA
{zhou.yuhao,stavros}@northeastern.edu

Abstract. The integration of neural networks into safety-critical systems has shown great potential in recent years. However, the challenge of effectively verifying the safety of Neural Network Controlled Systems (NNCS) persists. This paper introduces a novel approach to NNCS safety verification, leveraging the inductive invariant method. Verifying the inductiveness of a candidate inductive invariant in the context of NNCS is hard because of the scale and nonlinearity of neural networks. Our compositional method makes this verification process manageable by decomposing the inductiveness proof obligation into smaller, more tractable subproblems. Alongside the high-level method, we present an algorithm capable of automatically verifying the inductiveness of given candidates by automatically inferring the necessary decomposition predicates. The algorithm significantly outperforms the baseline method and shows remarkable reductions in execution time in our case studies, shortening the verification time from hours (or timeout) to seconds.

Keywords: Formal Verification · Inductive Invariant · Neural Networks · Neural Network Controlled Systems

1 Introduction

Neural Network Controlled Systems (NNCSs) are closed-loop systems that consist of an *environment* controlled by a *neural network* (NN). Advancements in machine learning have made NNCSs more widespread in safety-critical applications, such as autonomous cars, industrial control, and healthcare [47]. While many methods exist for the formal verification of standard closed-loop systems [8], the scale and nonlinearity of NNs makes the direct application of these methods to NNCSs a challenging task.

In this paper, we study formal verification of safety properties of NNCSs, using the *inductive invariant method* [28]. In a nutshell, the method consists in coming up with a state predicate *IndInv* which is *inductive*, an *invariant*, and implies safety (see Sect. 2, Conditions (4), (5) and (6)). The most important property, and often the most difficult to check, is inductiveness. In the case of

N. Benz et al. (Eds.): NFM 2024, LNCS 14627, pp. 239–255, 2024.
https://doi.org/10.1007/978-3-031-60698-4_14

NNCSs, checking inductiveness amounts to checking the validity of the following formula, where $Next_{NNC}$ and $Next_{ENV}$ are the transition relation predicates of the NN controller and of the environment, respectively, and ϕ' is the state predicate ϕ applied to the next-state (primed) variables:

$$(IndInv \wedge Next_{NNC} \wedge Next_{ENV}) \implies IndInv' \tag{1}$$

The problem that motivates our work is that checking formula (1) is infeasible in practice using state-of-the-art tools. On the one hand, generic tools such as SMT solvers [9] cannot handle formula 1 directly, typically due to the size and complexity of the NN and corresponding $Next_{NNC}$ predicate. On the other hand, specialized NN verification tools [45,46] also cannot handle formula (1) directly, typically due to limitations in being able to deal with closed-loop systems and the environment transition relation $Next_{ENV}$ (which, for example, might be non-deterministic).

This paper proposes a *compositional* method to deal with this problem. The key idea is the following: instead of checking formula (1) *monolithically*, we propose to break it up into two separate conditions:

$$(IndInv \wedge Next_{NNC}) \implies Bridge \tag{2}$$
$$(Bridge \wedge Next_{ENV}) \implies IndInv' \tag{3}$$

where *Bridge* is a new state predicate that needs to be invented (we propose a technique to do this automatically). Not only are each of the formulas (2) and (3) smaller than the monolithic formula (1) they can also be handled by the corresponding specialized tool: formula (2) by a NN verifier, and formula (3) by an SMT solver.

In Sect. 3 we elaborate our approach. We propose a technique to construct *Bridge* predicates automatically, and show how this technique can also be used to establish the validity of Condition (2) by construction. We also present a heuristic that can falsify inductiveness compositionally in some cases when formula (1) is not valid. We incorporate these techniques into an algorithm that checks inductiveness of candidate *IndInv* predicates for NNCSs.

Our experimental results (Sect. 4) indicate that our algorithm consistently terminates, effectively verifying or falsifying the inductiveness of the given candidate in both deterministic and non-deterministic environment setups, for NNs of sizes up to 2×1024 neurons, in a matter of seconds. This is in contrast to the monolithic method, which times out after one hour for all our experiments with NNs larger than 2×56 neurons.

2 Preliminaries and Problem Statement

Symbolic Transition Systems: The systems considered in this paper can be modeled as *symbolic transition systems* (STSs), like the ones shown in Fig. 1. An STS is defined by: (1) a set of *state variables*, each of appropriate type; (2) a predicate *Init* over the state variables, specifying the set of possible *initial*

State variable : $s \in \mathbb{Z}$
Init : $s = 0$
Next : $(s = 3 \implies s' = 0) \wedge$
$(s \neq 3 \implies s' = s + 1)$
Safe : $0 \leq s \leq 3$

(a) Mod-4 counter

State variable : $s \in \mathbb{Z}$
Init : $s = 0$
NN function : $f_{NN} : \mathbb{Z} \to \mathbb{R}$
$Next_{NNC}$: $a = f_{NN}(s)$
$Next_{ENV}$: $(a \geq 0 \implies s' = 0) \wedge$
$(a < 0 \implies s' = s + 1)$
Next : $Next_{NNC} \wedge Next_{ENV}$
Safe : $0 \leq s \leq 3$

(b) Mod-4 counter with NN controller

Fig. 1. Two STSs. The one in Fig. 1b is a NNCS: function f_{NN} (defined elsewhere) models a neural network controller.

states; and (3) a predicate *Next* over current and next (primed) state variables, specifying the *transition relation* of the system. For example, the STS shown in Fig. 1a models a counter modulo-4. This system has one state variable s of type integer ($\mathbb{Z}$). Its *Init* predicate specifies that s is initially 0. *Next* specifies that at each transition, s is incremented by one until we reach $s = 3$, upon which s is reset to 0 (primed variable s' denotes the value of state variable s at the next state). The *Safe* predicate defines the set of *safe* states (used later).

A *state* is an assignment of values to all state variables. We use the notation $x \models P$ to denote that state x satisfies state predicate P, i.e., that P evaluates to true once we replace all state variables in P by their values as given by x. A *transition* is a pair of states (x, x') that satisfies the predicate *Next*, denoted $(x, x') \models Next$. We also use notation $x \to x'$ instead of $(x, x') \models Next$, when *Next* is clear from context. A *trace* is an infinite sequence of states $x_0, x_1, \cdots$ such that $x_0 \models Init$ and $x_i \to x_{i+1}$ for all $i \geq 0$. A state x is *reachable* if there exists a trace $x_0, x_1, \cdots$, such that $x = x_i$ for some i. We use *Reach*(M) to denote the set of all reachable states of an STS M.

Invariants: In this paper we are interested in the verification of safety properties, and in particular *invariants*, which are state predicates that hold at all reachable states. Formally, for an STS M, an invariant is a state predicate *Inv* such that $Reach(M) \subseteq \{s \mid s \models Inv\}$. Predicates $s \geq 0$ and $0 \leq s \leq 3$ are both invariants of the STS of Fig. 1a.

Inductive Invariants: A standard technique for checking whether a given state predicate *Safe* is an invariant of a given STS is to come up with an *inductive invariant* stronger than *Safe*, that is, with a state predicate *IndInv* which satisfies the following conditions [28]:

$$Init \implies IndInv \quad (4)$$

$$(IndInv \wedge Next) \implies IndInv' \quad (5)$$

$$IndInv \implies Safe \quad (6)$$

where *IndInv'* denotes the predicate *IndInv* where state variables are replaced by their primed, next-state versions. Condition (4) states that *IndInv* holds at all initial states. Condition (5) states that *IndInv* is *inductive*, that is, if *IndInv* holds at a state s, then it also holds at any successor of s. We call Condition (5) the *inductiveness condition*. Condition (6) states that *IndInv* is stronger than *Safe*. Conditions (4) and (5) imply that all reachable states satisfy *IndInv*, which together with Condition (6) implies that they also satisfy *Safe*.

Neural Networks: At its core, a *neural network* (NN) is a function, receiving inputs and producing outputs. Mathematically, the output $z^{(i)}$ of each layer in a feed-forward NN with L layers can be expressed as:

$$z^{(i)} = \sigma_i(W^{(i)} z^{(i-1)} + b^{(i)}), \quad i = 1, 2, \cdots, L,$$

where $W^{(i)}$ and $b^{(i)}$ represent the weight matrix and bias vector for the i-th layer, respectively, and σ_i is the activation function for that layer. Our paper considers feed-forward NNs with ReLU activation functions, where $\text{ReLU}(x) = \max(0, x)$.

Neural Network Controlled Systems: In this paper, we are interested in safety verification for *neural network controlled systems* (NNCSs). A NNCS is a STS consisting of a *neural network controller* and an *environment*, in closed-loop configuration. Formally, a NNCS is a STS whose transition relation predicate *Next* is of the form $Next_{NNC} \wedge Next_{ENV}$, where $Next_{NNC}$ is a predicate capturing the NN controller, and $Next_{ENV}$ is a predicate capturing the transition relation of the environment. We assume that $Next_{NNC}$ is always of the form $\boldsymbol{a} = f_{NN}(\boldsymbol{s})$, where f_{NN} is the function modeling the NN controller, $\boldsymbol{s}$ is the vector of state variables of the environment (which are the inputs to the NN controller), and $\boldsymbol{a}$ is the vector of outputs of the NN controller (which are the inputs to the environment). Then, $Next_{ENV}$ is a predicate on $\boldsymbol{s}$, $\boldsymbol{s}'$, and $\boldsymbol{a}$. Note that the only state variables in the NNCS are $\boldsymbol{s}$. Variables $\boldsymbol{a}$ are not state variables, but just temporary variables that can be eliminated and replaced by $f_{NN}(\boldsymbol{s})$, according to the equation $\boldsymbol{a} = f_{NN}(\boldsymbol{s})$. We assume that for any assignment of $\boldsymbol{s}$ and $\boldsymbol{a}$, there always exists an assignment of $\boldsymbol{s}'$ such that $Next_{ENV}$ is satisfied; that is, the system is deadlock-free.

An example NNCS is shown in Fig. 1b. In this simple example, the output a of the NN controller controls the environment to either reset the state variable s to 0 (if $a \geq 0$) or increment it by 1 (if $a < 0$).

Safety Verification Problem for NNCS: The problem we study in this paper is the safety verification problem for NNCS, namely: *given a NNCS M and a safety predicate Safe, check whether Safe is an invariant of M.*

3 Our Approach

To solve the safety verification problem for NNCSs, we will use the inductive invariant method described in Sect. 2. In particular, our approach assumes that a *candidate* inductive invariant is given, and our focus is to *check* whether this candidate is indeed a valid inductive invariant stronger than *Safe*, i.e., whether it satisfies Conditions (4), (5), and (6). Specifically, we focus on checking *inductiveness*, i.e., Condition (5), because this is the most challenging condition to check.

In the case of NNCS, Condition (5) instantiates to:

$$(\mathit{IndInv} \wedge \mathit{Next}_{NNC} \wedge \mathit{Next}_{ENV}) \implies \mathit{IndInv}'. \tag{7}$$

A naive approach is to attempt to check Condition (7) directly: we call this the *monolithic method*. Unfortunately, as we will show in Sect. 4, the monolithic method does not scale. This is typically because of the size of the Next_{NNC} part of the formula, which encodes the NN controller, and tends to be very large. To address this challenge, we introduce a *compositional method* for checking inductiveness, described next.

3.1 Our Approach: Compositional Method

Our compositional method is centered around two key ideas: (i) automatically construct a *bridge predicate*, denoted *Bridge*; and (ii) replace the monolithic inductiveness Condition (7) by two separate conditions:

$$(\mathit{IndInv} \wedge \mathit{Next}_{NNC}) \implies \mathit{Bridge} \tag{8}$$

$$(\mathit{Bridge} \wedge \mathit{Next}_{ENV}) \implies \mathit{IndInv}' \tag{9}$$

By transitivity of logical implication, it is easy to show the following:

Theorem 1 (Soundness). *If Conditions (8) and (9) hold then Condition (7) holds.*

The completeness of our method follows from the fact that in the worst case we can set *Bridge* to be equal to $\mathit{IndInv} \wedge \mathit{Next}_{NNC}$.

Theorem 2 (Completeness). *If Condition (7) holds then we can find Bridge such that Conditions (8) and (9) hold.*

As it turns out (c.f. Section 4) checking Conditions (8) and (9) separately scales much better than checking Condition (7) monolithically. However, this relies on finding a "good" bridge precidate. Setting *Bridge* to $\mathit{IndInv} \wedge \mathit{Next}_{NNC}$ is not helpful, because then Condition (9) becomes identical to the monolithic Condition (7). Thus, a necessary step is finding a bridge predicate that satisfies Conditions (8) and (9), while remaining manageable. In Sect. 3.2, we present an automatic technique for doing so. But first, we examine bridge predicates in more depth.

Naive Bridge Predicates are Incomplete: A natural starting point for constructing the bridge predicate is to define it only over the output variables $\boldsymbol{a}$ of the NN controller. We call this a *naive bridge predicate.* Unfortunately, naive bridge predicates might be insufficient, as we show next. Consider the system shown in Fig. 1b. Suppose we set $Next_{NNC}$ to:

$$((0 \leq s \leq 2) \land a = -1) \lor (s = 3 \land a = 1) \lor ((s < 0 \lor s > 3) \land (a = -1 \lor a = 1))$$

It can be checked that the set of reachable states of this system is $0 \leq s \leq 3$. Therefore, $0 \leq s \leq 3$ is also an inductive invariant of this system. A naive bridge predicate that satisfies Condition (8) could be $a = 1 \lor a = -1$. This is, in fact, the strongest naive bridge predicate that satisfies Condition (8), as it captures all the possible values of a. Therefore, if this naive bridge predicate does not satisfy Condition (9), then no naive bridge predicate that satisfies both Conditions (8) and (9) exists. Indeed, Condition (9) is violated by this naive bridge, as it becomes

$$((a = 1 \lor a = -1) \land (a \geq 0 \implies s' = 0) \land (a < 0 \implies s' = s + 1)) \\ \implies (0 \leq s' \leq 3)$$

which is false when $s = 3$, $a = -1$ and $s' = 4$. So, no naive bridge predicate can satisfy both Condition (8) and (9). This suggests that naive bridge predicates are insufficient. The solution is to allow bridge predicates to refer both to the inputs and outputs of the NN controller:

Generalized Bridge Predicates are Complete: A *generalized bridge predicate* is a predicate defined over both the output variables $\boldsymbol{a}$ as well as the input variables $\boldsymbol{s}$ of the NN controller (the inputs $\boldsymbol{s}$ are the same as the state variables of the environment). Continuing our example above, a generalized bridge predicate could be: $((0 \leq s \leq 2) \land a = -1) \lor (s = 3 \land a = 1)$. Then, Conditions (8) and (9) become:

$$\begin{aligned} &((0 \leq s \leq 3) \quad \land \\ &((0 \leq s \leq 2) \land a = -1) \lor (s = 3 \land a = 1) \lor ((s < 0 \lor s > 3) \land (a = -1 \lor a = 1))) \\ &\implies (((0 \leq s \leq 2) \land a = -1) \lor (s = 3 \land a = 1)) \end{aligned} \tag{10}$$

$$\begin{aligned} &(((0 \leq s \leq 2) \land a = -1) \lor (s = 3 \land a = 1)) \land (a \geq 0 \implies s' = 0) \\ &\land \ (a < 0 \implies s' = s + 1)) \\ &\implies (0 \leq s' \leq 3). \end{aligned} \tag{11}$$

and it can be checked that both are valid, which shows that this generalized bridge predicate is sufficient.

In general, and according to Theorem 2, a generalized bridge predicate is sufficient, since we can set *Bridge* to $IndInv \land Next_{NNC}$, and the latter predicate is over $\boldsymbol{s}$ and $\boldsymbol{a}$. But it is important to note that a bridge that works need not be the "worst-case scenario" predicate $IndInv \land Next_{NNC}$. Indeed, the bridge of our example is not, and neither are the bridges constructed by our tool for the case studies in Sect. 4.

3.2 Automatic Inference of Generalized Bridge Predicates

The key idea of our automatic bridge inference technique is to synthesize a generalized bridge predicate such that Condition (8) holds *by construction* (i.e., it does not need to be checked). To explain how this works, let us first define, given a predicate A over both $\boldsymbol{s}$ and $\boldsymbol{a}$, and predicate B over only $\boldsymbol{s}$, the *set of postconditions*, denoted AllPosts(A, B), to be the set of all predicates C over $\boldsymbol{a}$ such that $(A \wedge B) \implies C$ is valid.

Then, our algorithm will construct a bridge predicate the has the form:

$$Bridge = (p_1 \wedge \psi_1) \vee (p_2 \wedge \psi_2) \vee \cdots \vee (p_n \wedge \psi_n) \tag{12}$$

where each p_i is a predicate over $\boldsymbol{s}$, and each ψ_i is a predicate over $\boldsymbol{a}$, such that the following conditions hold:

$$(p_1 \vee p_2 \vee \cdots \vee p_n) \iff IndInv \tag{13}$$

$$\forall i = 1, ..., n,\ \psi_i \in \text{AllPosts}(Next_{NNC}, p_i) \tag{14}$$

Condition (13) ensures that the set of all p_i's is a *decomposition* of the candidate inductive invariant *IndInv*, i.e., that their union, viewed as sets, "covers" *IndInv*. This decomposition need not be a partition of *IndInv*, i.e., the p_i's need not be disjoint. Condition (14) ensures that each ψ_i is a postcondition of the corresponding p_i w.r.t. the NN controller (note that ψ_i is not necessarily the strongest postcondition).

Now, from (12) and (13), Condition (8) becomes:

$$((p_1 \vee p_2 \vee \cdots \vee p_n) \wedge Next_{NNC}) \implies ((p_1 \wedge \psi_1) \vee (p_2 \wedge \psi_2) \vee \cdots \vee (p_n \wedge \psi_n))$$

which is equivalent to

$$\left(\bigvee_{i=1}^{n} (p_i \wedge Next_{NNC})\right) \implies \left(\bigvee_{j=1}^{n} (p_j \wedge \psi_j)\right) \tag{15}$$

which is equivalent to

$$\bigwedge_{i=1}^{n} \left((p_i \wedge Next_{NNC}) \implies (\bigvee_{j=1}^{n} (p_j \wedge \psi_j)) \right) \tag{16}$$

But observe that $(p_i \wedge Next_{NNC}) \implies p_i$ trivially holds, for each $i = 1, ..., n$. And note that $(p_i \wedge Next_{NNC}) \implies \psi_i$ also holds, since by construction, $\psi_i \in$ AllPosts$(Next_{NNC}, p_i)$. Therefore, $(p_i \wedge Next_{NNC}) \implies (p_i \wedge \psi_i)$ holds for each i, which implies that (16) holds by construction. Therefore, we have:

Theorem 3 (Condition (8) holds by construction). *For any bridge predicate that is in form of Condition (12), if this predicate satisfies Conditions (13) and (14), then Condition (8) holds by construction.*

Next, consider Condition (9). From (12), Condition (9) becomes:

$$\Big(((p_1 \wedge \psi_1) \vee (p_2 \wedge \psi_2) \vee \cdots \vee (p_n \wedge \psi_n)) \wedge \mathit{Next}_{ENV}\Big) \implies \mathit{IndInv}' \quad (17)$$

which is equivalent to:

$$\left(\bigvee_{i=1}^{n} (p_i \wedge \psi_i \wedge \mathit{Next}_{ENV})\right) \implies \mathit{IndInv}' \quad (18)$$

which is equivalent to:

$$\bigwedge_{i=1}^{n} ((p_i \wedge \psi_i \wedge \mathit{Next}_{ENV}) \implies \mathit{IndInv}') \quad (19)$$

which means that checking Condition (9) can be replaced by checking n smaller conditions, namely, $(p_i \wedge \psi_i \wedge \mathit{Next}_{ENV}) \implies \mathit{IndInv}'$, for $i = 1, ..., n$.

The algorithm that we present below (Algorithm 1) starts with $n = 1$ and $p_1 = \mathit{IndInv}$. It then computes some $\psi_1 \in \text{AllPosts}(\mathit{Next}_{NNC}, p_1)$ and checks whether $(p_1 \wedge \psi_1 \wedge \mathit{Next}_{ENV}) \implies \mathit{IndInv}'$ is valid. If it is, then $p_1 \wedge \psi_1$ is a valid bridge and inductiveness holds. Otherwise, p_1 is *split* into several p_i's, and the process repeats.

3.3 Heuristic for Falsifying Inductiveness

An additional feature of our algorithm is that it is often capable to *falsify* inductiveness and thereby prove that it does not hold. This allows us to avoid searching hopelessly for a bridge predicate when none exists, because the candidate invariant is not inductive.

Directly falsifying Condition (7) faces the same scalability issues as trying to prove this condition monolithically. On the other hand, falsifying Conditions (8) or (9) is not sufficient to disprove inductiveness. The failure to prove these conditions might simply mean that our chosen bridge predicate does not work.

Therefore, we propose a practical heuristic which inherits the decomposition ideas described above. This heuristic involves constructing: (i) a satisfiable *falsifying state predicate* over $\boldsymbol{s}$, denoted *FState*; and (ii) a predicate over the output of the NN controller $\boldsymbol{a}$, denoted *FPred*, such that the following conditions hold:

$$\mathit{FState} \implies \mathit{IndInv} \quad (20)$$

$$(\mathit{FState} \wedge \mathit{Next}_{NNC}) \implies \mathit{FPred} \quad (21)$$

$$(\mathit{FState} \wedge \mathit{FPred} \wedge \mathit{Next}_{ENV}) \implies \neg \mathit{IndInv}' \quad (22)$$

Intuitively, *FState* identifies a set of states which satisfy *IndInv* but violate *IndInv′* after a transition. *FPred* captures the outputs of the NN controller when its inputs satisfy *FState*. The conjunction of (21) and (22) implies:

$$(\mathit{FState} \wedge \mathit{Next}_{NNC} \wedge \mathit{Next}_{ENV}) \implies \neg \mathit{IndInv}' \quad (23)$$

In turn, (23) and (20) together imply that Condition (7) does not hold. This leads us to the following theorem:

Theorem 4 (Falsifying Inductiveness). *If FState is satisfiable, and if Conditions (20), (21), and (22) hold, then Condition (7) does not hold.*

Our falsification approach aligns well with the composite structure of a NNCS, and is compositional, because it allows to check separately the NN transition relation $Next_{NNC}$ in (21) and the environment transition relation $Next_{ENV}$ in (22).

3.4 Algorithm

The aforementioned ideas are combined in Algorithm 1, which implements our compositional inductiveness verification approach for NNCSs. Line 7 ensures that ψ is a postcondition of p w.r.t. the NN controller. In practice we use a *NN verifier* to compute the postcondition (see Sect. 4). Lines 15 and 16 ensure Condition (13), together with the fact that the initial p is *IndInv* (Line 3). Line 9 ensures that the bridge predicate is in form of Condition (12). Therefore, by Theorem 3, Algorithm 1 ensures Condition (8) by construction.

Line 8 corresponds to checking (19) compositionally, i.e., separately for each i. In practice, we use an *SMT solver* for this check (see Sect. 4).

For falsification, to use Theorem 4, we set $FState = p$ and $FPred = \psi$. The splitting process at Line 15 guarantees that p is satisfiable. Condition (20) then becomes $p \implies IndInv$, which holds by construction because of Condition (13). Condition (21) becomes $p \wedge Next_{NNC} \implies \psi$, which holds because $\psi \in \text{AllPosts}(Next_{NNC}, p)$. Condition (22) becomes $(p \wedge \psi \wedge Next_{ENV}) \implies \neg IndInv'$, which is checked in Line 11.

If the algorithm can neither prove $(p \wedge \psi \wedge Next_{ENV}) \implies IndInv'$, nor falsify inductiveness, then it splits p into a disjunction of satisfiable state predicates, ensuring Condition (12). Our implementation utilizes various splitting strategies. The specific splitting strategies employed in our case studies are elaborated in Sect. 4. After splitting, all resulting state predicates are added into the queue Q. Consequently, the queue becomes empty if and only if the validity of every conjunct in Condition (19) is proved. Therefore, an empty queue indicates that inductiveness holds.

Termination: The algorithm terminates either upon successfully proving or upon falsifying inductiveness. However, termination is not guaranteed in all cases. In infinite state spaces, the algorithm may keep splitting predicates ad infinitum. In practice, as observed in our case studies, the algorithm consistently terminated (see Sect. 4).

Algorithm 1: Compositional Inductiveness Checking for NNCS

Input: Transition relations $Next_{NNC}$, $Next_{ENV}$; Candidate Inductive Invariant $IndInv$

Output: Verification result: (True with bridge predicate $Bridge$) or (False with falsifying state predicate)

Function `CheckInductiveness`($Next_{NNC}$, $Next_{ENV}$, $IndInv$):
- $Bridge := False$;
- $Q := \{IndInv\}$;
- **while** $Q \neq \emptyset$ **do**
  - Let $p \in Q$;
  - $Q := Q \setminus \{p\}$;
  - Let $\psi \in \text{AllPosts}(Next_{NNC}, p)$;
  - **if** $(p \wedge \psi \wedge Next_{ENV}) \implies IndInv'$ *holds* **then**
    - $Bridge := Bridge \vee (p \wedge \psi)$;
  - **end**
  - **else if** $(p \wedge \psi \wedge Next_{ENV}) \implies \neg IndInv'$ *holds* **then**
    - **return** *(False, p)* ;
  - **end**
  - **else**
    - Split p into $p_1, p_2, \cdots, p_k$ such that $p \iff (p_1 \vee p_2 \vee \cdots \vee p_k)$;
    - $Q := Q \cup \{p_1, p_2, \cdots, p_k\}$;
  - **end**
- **end**
- **return** *(True, Bridge)* ;

4 Evaluation

In the experiments reported below, we evaluate our compositional method by comparing it against the monolithic method which uses Z3 to check Condition 7 directly. We remark that we also attempted to use specialized NN verifiers such as [45] to check inductiveness monolithically, but this proved infeasible. Specifically, we tried two ways of encoding checking inductiveness as an NN verification problem: (i) Encoding $Next_{ENV}$ and Condition (7) into the NN's input and output constraints. This approach was impractical for our case studies since $Next_{ENV}$ involves arithmetic applied simultaneously to both the input and output of the NN controller, e.g., ($x' = x + 0.1a$). Such constraints are beyond the capability of existing NN verifiers such as [5,25,26,45]. (ii) Encoding both the NN controller and the environment into a single NN. Our trials revealed that current NN verifiers support only a limited range of operators for defining a NN, restricting this approach as well. Notably, the operators we required, such as adding the NN's input to its output, are not typically supported. Although these limitations might diminish as NN verifiers evolve, an additional complication arises from the fact that $Next_{ENV}$ might be non-deterministic (as in our second set of case studies). Encoding non-deterministic transition relations into a NN remains a significant challenge because NNs are typically deterministic functions.

In our evaluation, we do not attempt to systematically compare our tool against NNCS reachability analysis tools, e.g. [16,23,35,41], primarily because these tools perform verification over a bounded time horizon through reachability analysis, while our method is based on inductive invariants and enables the verification of safety properties over an infinite time horizon. However, following the recommendation of an anonymous Reviewer, we did execute some of the aforementioned tools on the 2D maze case studies described in Sect. 4.2 that follows. In summary, in many of our experiments, tools such as JuliaReach [6] and NNV [41] have been able to successfully verify safety within a bounded time horizon. For example, it took NNV a few seconds to perform a 50-step reachability analysis on the deterministic 2D maze with the largest NN controller that we used (2×1024 neurons). However, both JuliaReach and NNV also failed to verify safety in some instances, due to the overapproximation of the reach set. Our experiments with JuliaReach and NNV will be reported in the extended version of this paper [48].

4.1 Implementation and Experimental Setup

We implemented Algorithm 1 in a prototype tool – the source code and models needed to reproduce our experiments are available at https://github.com/YUH-Z/comp-indinv-verification-nncs. We use the SMT solver Z3 [9] for the validity checks of Lines 8 and 11 of Algorithm 1. To compute the postcondition ψ (Line 7 of Algorithm 1), we use AutoLIRPA [46], which is the core engine of the NN verifier α-β-CROWN [45]. AutoLIRPA computes a postcondition $\psi \in \text{AllPosts}(\mathit{Next}_{NNC}, p)$, i.e., guarantees that $(p \wedge \mathit{Next}_{NNC}) \implies \psi$, but it does not generally guarantee that ψ is the strongest possible postcondition.

In our case studies reported below, each candidate inductive invariant is a union of hyperrectangles, which aligns with the constraint types supported by mainstream NN verifiers such as [5,25,26,45].

Our splitting strategy (Line 15 of Algorithm 1) follows a binary scheme, dividing hyperrectangles at their midpoints along each dimension. For example, the interval $[1, 2]$ would be split into $[1, 3/2]$ and $[3/2, 2]$. This straightforward strategy turns out to be effective in our case studies.

Our experiments were conducted on a machine equipped with a 3.3 GHz 8-core AMD CPU, 16 GB memory, and an Nvidia 3060 GPU. Z3 ran on the CPU and AutoLIRPA on the GPU with CUDA enabled, both using default configurations.

4.2 Case Studies and Experimental Results

We ran our experiments on two sets of examples, a *deterministic 2D maze*, and a *non-deterministic 2D maze*, as described below.

Deterministic 2D Maze: In this example, the environment has two state variables x and y of type real ($\mathbb{R}$), representing an object's 2D position. The

Table 1. Experimental results: *Det* and *NDet* indicate the results for the deterministic and non-deterministic 2D maze case studies, respectively. All execution times are in seconds. T.O. represents an one-hour timeout. The *Verified?* column shows whether the compositional method successfully terminated, either by proving (T) or by disproving (F) inductiveness. *#Splits* reports the total number of splits performed. *#SMT* and *#NNV queries* report the total number of calls made to Z3 and AutoLIRPA, respectively.

NN size	Verified?		Monolithic execution time		Compositional execution time		#Splits		#SMT queries		#NNV queries	
	Det	NDet	Det	NDet	Det	NDet	Det	NDet	Det	NDet	Det	NDet
2 × 32	T	T	51.59	39.73	0.73	0.83	12	14	61	71	49	57
2 × 40	T	T	113.69	296.61	0.70	0.66	13	13	66	66	53	53
2 × 48	T	T	410.14	3002.20	0.52	0.42	10	8	51	41	41	33
2 × 56	T	T	1203.76	T.O	0.42	0.46	8	9	41	46	33	37
2 × 64	T	T	T.O.	T.O	0.76	0.61	15	12	76	61	61	49
2 × 128	F	T	T.O.	T.O	2.21	1.43	64	28	225	141	160	113
2 × 256	T	T	T.O.	T.O	1.68	1.18	27	23	136	116	109	93
2 × 512	T	T	T.O.	T.O	3.04	2.30	60	45	301	226	241	181
2 × 1024	T	T	T.O.	T.O.	1.94	5.23	38	102	191	511	153	409

NN controller $f_{NN} : \mathbb{R}^2 \rightarrow \mathbb{R}^2$ outputs $(a, b) = f_{NN}(x, y)$, guiding the object's horizontal and vertical movement. The initial state is set within $0.3 \leq x \leq 0.4$ and $0.6 \leq y \leq 0.7$. The transition relation $Next_{ENV}$ of the environment is deterministic and defined by $x' = x + 0.1a$ and $y' = y + 0.1b$. The controller's goal is to navigate the object to ($0.8 \leq x \leq 0.9$ and $0.8 \leq y \leq 0.9$), while keeping it within a safe region of ($0.22 \leq x \leq 0.98$ and $0.54 \leq y \leq 0.98$), which is the safety property we want to prove.

As NN controllers, we used two-layer feed-forward NNs with ReLU activations, trained via PyTorch [31] and Stable-Baselines3 [33]. We trained NN controllers of various sizes, ranging from 2 × 32 to 2 × 1024 neurons. To standardize the comparison among the systems containing different NN controllers, for each system, we check the same candidate inductive invariant, defined as $0.25 \leq x \leq 0.95$ and $0.55 \leq y \leq 0.95$. For this candidate and for the *Init* and *Safe* predicates defined above, it is easy to see that Conditions (4) and (6) hold. So our experiments only check the inductiveness Condition (7).

The results are reported in Table 1: for this case study, the relevant columns are those marked as *Det*. The compositional method successfully terminated in all cases, and proved inductiveness for all NN configurations, except for 2 × 128, for which inductiveness does not hold, and in which case the compositional method managed to falsify it. In terms of performance, the monolithic method requires around one minute even for the smallest NN configurations, and times out after one hour for the larger configurations; while the compositional method terminates in all cases in a couple of seconds. A key metric of the compositional method is the number of splits, which is determined by the number of times Line 15 of Algorithm 1 is executed. This metric is crucial as it impacts the number of queries made to the SMT solver and to the NN verifier, typically the most time-consuming steps in the algorithm. Additionally, the number of splits indicates the size of the bridge predicate, where fewer splits suggest smaller bridge predicates.

Non-deterministic 2D Maze: This case study is similar to the deterministic 2D maze, with the difference that the environment's transition relation is non-deterministic, specifically, defined as $x' = x + 0.1c \cdot a$ and $y' = y + 0.1c \cdot b$, where c is a constant of type real, non-deterministically ranging between 0.5 and 1.0. This non-determinism simulates the noise within the system.

The NN controllers in this set of experiments, while maintaining the same architecture and size as in the deterministic case studies, were retrained from scratch to adapt to the new transition relation. The candidate inductive invariant is the same as in the deterministic case study, ensuring consistency in our comparative analysis.

The results are shown in Table 1, columns marked by *NDet*. As demonstrated by the results, our compositional method successfully verified inductiveness in all configurations, in a matter of seconds.

5 Related Work

A large body of research exists on NN verification, including methods that verify NN input-output relations, using SMT solvers [22,25,26] or MILP solvers [40], as well as methods that employ abstract-interpretation techniques [17,38], symbolic interval propagation [44], dual optimization [13], linear relaxation [46], and bound propagation [45]. [29] formally verifies equivalence and adversarial robustness of binarized NNs by SAT solvers. [14] propose an SMT based approach for checking equivalence and approximate equivalence of NNs.

These and other techniques and the corresponding tools focus on NN verification at the *component level*, that is, they verify a NN in isolation. In contrast, we focus on *system-level* verification, that is, verification of a closed-loop system consisting of a NN controller and an environment.

System-level verification approaches have also been proposed in the literature. A number of methods capture NNCSs as *hybrid systems*: in [24] the NN is transformed into a hybrid system and the existing tool Flow* [7] is used to verify the resulting hybrid system. In [21] the NN is approximated using Bernstein polynomials, while [23] employs Taylor models, and uses various techniques to reduce error. In [15] NNCSs are modeled as transition systems, and existing NN verifiers like Marabou [26] are used for bounded model checking. These methods are adept at proving safety properties within a bounded time horizon. The ARCH-COMP series of competitions includes categories for verifying continuous and hybrid systems with neural network components [27]. The tools [2,6,12,16,20,24,41] that participated in these competitions are designed to verify properties within a bounded time horizon by reachability analysis. In contrast, our approach is designed to verify safety properties over an infinite time horizon using inductive invariants instead of reachability. Also, our approach works for a discrete-time rather than continuous-time model. In [4], the authors perform time-unbounded safety verification of NNCS within a conventional reinforcement learning setting that features a finite set of possible actions by computing polyhedral overapproximations of the reach set using MILP techniques. In contrast, our method does not assume a finite action space and uses inductive invariants.

Our approach can handle non-deterministic environments. While the non-deterministic case is less studied than deterministic NNCSs, some of the tools mentioned above, e.g., [2,41], can also handle non-determinism, albeit with a fundamentally different technique than ours (reachability instead of inductive invariants). The verification of non-deterministic NNCSs has also been studied in [1], which leverages MILP solvers for the verification task.

In addition to verification, various methods for testing NNCSs have been explored. Simulation-based approaches for NNCS analysis, including falsification, fuzz testing, and counterexample analysis, were introduced by [11,42]. [19] proposed a method to explore the state space of hybrid systems containing neural networks.

Our work is also related to research on automatic inductive invariant discovery, which is a hard, generally undecidable, problem [30]. Recently, several studies have proposed techniques for automatic inductive invariant discovery for distributed protocols [18,36], while [34] applies deep learning techniques to infer loop invariants for programs. [3] proposes a heuristic for inferring simple inductive invariants in NNCSs, within the context of communication networking systems. Such systems possess unique traits not commonly found in general NNCSs. These specific traits enable using a NN verifier to check a weaker condition instead of directly verifying the inductiveness condition. In contrast, our method does not depend on specific properties of specialized NNCSs.

Our work is also related to *barrier certificates*, an alternative technique for verifying continuous-time systems [32,39]. In [43] the authors synthesize barrier certificates by solving an optimization problem subject to bilinear matrix inequalities. In [10] the authors propose a method that uses barrier certificates to synthesize neural network controllers which are safe by design. [37] presents an approach to verifying NNCSs by constructing barrier certificates.

6 Conclusions

We present a compositional, inductive-invariant based method for NNCS verification. Our method allows to to verify safety properties over an infinite time horizon. The key idea is to decompose the monolithic inductiveness check (which is typically not supported by state-of-the-art NN verifiers, and does not scale with state-of-the-art SMT solvers) into several manageable subproblems, which can be each individually handled by the corresponding tool. Our case studies show encouraging results where the verification time is reduced from hours (or timeout) to seconds.

Future work includes augmenting our method's capabilities to suit a broader range of NNCS applications. We also plan to explore the automatic generation of candidate inductive invariants (in addition to bridges) for NNCSs.

Acknowledgments. We would like to thank the anonymous Reviewers of the submitted version of this paper for their helpful feedback. This work has been supported in part by NSF CCF award #2319500.

References

1. Akintunde, M.E., Botoeva, E., Kouvaros, P., Lomuscio, A.: Formal verification of neural agents in non-deterministic environments. Auton. Agents Multi-Agent Syst. **36**, 6 (2022)
2. Althoff, M.: An introduction to CORA 2015. In: Proceedings of the Workshop on Applied Verification for Continuous and Hybrid Systems (2015)
3. Amir, G., Schapira, M., Katz, G.: Towards scalable verification of deep reinforcement learning. In: Formal Methods in Computer Aided Design (FMCAD) (2021)
4. Bacci, E., Giacobbe, M., Parker, D.: Verifying reinforcement learning up to infinity. In: Proceedings of the International Joint Conference on Artificial Intelligence. International Joint Conferences on Artificial Intelligence Organization (2021)
5. Bak, S.: nnenum: verification of ReLU neural networks with optimized abstraction refinement. In: NASA Formal Methods Symposium (2021)
6. Bogomolov, S., Forets, M., Frehse, G., Potomkin, K., Schilling, C.: JuliaReach: a toolbox for set-based reachability. In: Proceedings of the 22nd ACM International Conference on Hybrid Systems: Computation and Control (2019)
7. Chen, X., Ábrahám, E., Sankaranarayanan, S.: Flow*: an analyzer for non-linear hybrid systems. In: Sharygina, N., Veith, H. (eds.) CAV 2013. LNCS, vol. 8044, pp. 258–263. Springer, Heidelberg (2013). https://doi.org/10.1007/978-3-642-39799-8_18
8. Clarke, E.M., Henzinger, T.A., Veith, H., Bloem, R. (eds.): Handbook of Model Checking. Springer, Heidelberg (2018). https://doi.org/10.1007/978-3-319-10575-8
9. De Moura, L., Bjørner, N.: Z3: an efficient SMT solver. In: International conference on Tools and Algorithms for the Construction and Analysis of Systems (2008)
10. Deshmukh, J.V., Kapinski, J.P., Yamaguchi, T., Prokhorov, D.: Learning deep neural network controllers for dynamical systems with safety guarantees. In: 2019 IEEE/ACM International Conference on Computer-Aided Design (ICCAD). IEEE (2019)
11. Dreossi, T., et al.: VerifAI: a toolkit for the formal design and analysis of artificial intelligence-based systems. In: Dillig, I., Tasiran, S. (eds.) CAV 2019. LNCS, vol. 11561, pp. 432–442. Springer, Heidelberg (2019). https://doi.org/10.1007/978-3-030-25540-4_25
12. Dutta, S., Chen, X., Jha, S., Sankaranarayanan, S., Tiwari, A.: Sherlock-a tool for verification of neural network feedback systems: demo abstract. In: Proceedings of the 22nd ACM International Conference on Hybrid Systems: Computation and Control (2019)
13. Dvijotham, K., Stanforth, R., Gowal, S., Mann, T.A., Kohli, P.: A dual approach to scalable verification of deep networks. In: UAI (2018)
14. Eleftheriadis, C., Kekatos, N., Katsaros, P., Tripakis, S.: On neural network equivalence checking using SMT solvers. In: 20th International Conference on Formal Modeling and Analysis of Timed Systems (FORMATS 2022) (2022)
15. Eliyahu, T., Kazak, Y., Katz, G., Schapira, M.: Verifying learning-augmented systems. In: Proceedings of the 2021 ACM SIGCOMM 2021 Conference (2021)

16. Fan, J., Huang, C., Chen, X., Li, W., Zhu, Q.: ReachNN*: a tool for reachability analysis of neural-network controlled systems. In: Automated Technology for Verification and Analysis (2020)
17. Gehr, T., Mirman, M., Drachsler-Cohen, D., Tsankov, P., Chaudhuri, S., Vechev, M.: Ai2: safety and robustness certification of neural networks with abstract interpretation. In: 2018 IEEE Symposium on Security and Privacy (SP) (2018)
18. Goel, A., Sakallah, K.: On symmetry and quantification: a new approach to verify distributed protocols. In: NASA Formal Methods Symposium (2021)
19. Goyal, M., Duggirala, P.S.: Neuralexplorer: state space exploration of closed loop control systems using neural networks. In: Hung, D.V., Sokolsky, O. (eds.) ATVA 2020. LNCS, vol. 12302, pp. 75–91. Springer, Heidelberg (2020). https://doi.org/10.1007/978-3-030-59152-6_4
20. Huang, C., Fan, J., Chen, X., Li, W., Zhu, Q.: POLAR: a polynomial arithmetic framework for verifying neural-network controlled systems. In: Bouajjani, A., Holik, L., Wu, Z. (eds.) ATVA 2022, pp. 414–430. Springer, Heidelberg (2022). https://doi.org/10.1007/978-3-031-19992-9_27
21. Huang, C., Fan, J., Li, W., Chen, X., Zhu, Q.: ReachNN: reachability analysis of neural-network controlled systems. ACM Trans. Embed. Comput. Syst. (TECS) (2019)
22. Huang, X., Kwiatkowska, M., Wang, S., Wu, M.: Safety Verification of Deep Neural Networks. In: Majumdar, R., Kuncak, V. (eds.) CAV 2017. LNCS, vol. 10426, pp. 3–29. Springer, Heidelberg (2017). https://doi.org/10.1007/978-3-319-63387-9_1
23. Ivanov, R., Carpenter, T., Weimer, J., Alur, R., Pappas, G., Lee, I.: Verisig 2.0: verification of neural network controllers using taylor model preconditioning. In: Silva, A., Leino, K.R.M. (eds.) CAV 2021. LNCS, vol. 12759, pp. 249–262. Springer, Heidelberg (2021). https://doi.org/10.1007/978-3-030-81685-8_11
24. Ivanov, R., Weimer, J., Alur, R., Pappas, G.J., Lee, I.: Verisig: verifying safety properties of hybrid systems with neural network controllers. In: Proceedings of the 22nd ACM International Conference on Hybrid Systems: Computation and Control (2019)
25. Katz, G., Barrett, C., Dill, D.L., Julian, K., Kochenderfer, M.J.: Reluplex: an efficient smt solver for verifying deep neural networks. In: Majumdar, R., Kuncak, V. (eds.) CAV 2017. LNCS, vol. 10426, pp. 97–117. Springer, Heidelberg (2017). https://doi.org/10.1007/978-3-319-63387-9_5
26. Katz, G., et al.: The marabou framework for verification and analysis of deep neural networks. In: Dillig, I., Tasiran, S. (eds.) CAV 2019. LNCS, vol. 11561, pp. 443–452. Springer, Heidelberg (2019). https://doi.org/10.1007/978-3-030-25540-4_26
27. Lopez, D.M., Althoff, M., Forets, M., Johnson, T.T., Ladner, T., Schilling, C.: ARCH-COMP23 category report: artificial intelligence and neural network control systems (AINNCS) for continuous and hybrid systems plants. In: Proceedings of 10th International Workshop on Applied Verification of Continuous and Hybrid Systems (ARCH23). EPiC Series in Computing (2023)
28. Manna, Z., Pnueli, A.: Temporal Verification of Reactive Systems: Safety. Springer, New York (1995). https://doi.org/10.1007/978-1-4612-4222-2
29. Narodytska, N., Kasiviswanathan, S., Ryzhyk, L., Sagiv, M., Walsh, T.: Verifying properties of binarized deep neural networks. In: Proceedings of the AAAI Conference on Artificial Intelligence (2018)
30. Padon, O., Immerman, N., Shoham, S., Karbyshev, A., Sagiv, M.: Decidability of inferring inductive invariants. ACM SIGPLAN Not. **51**, 217–231 (2016)
31. Paszke, A., et al.: Pytorch: an imperative style, high-performance deep learning library. In: Advances in Neural Information Processing Systems (2019)

32. Prajna, S., Jadbabaie, A.: Safety verification of hybrid systems using barrier certificates. In: Alur, R., Pappas, G.J. (eds.) HSCC 2004. LNCS, vol. 2993, pp. 477–492. Springer, Heidelberg (2004). https://doi.org/10.1007/978-3-540-24743-2_32
33. Raffin, A., Hill, A., Gleave, A., Kanervisto, A., Ernestus, M., Dormann, N.: Stable-baselines3: reliable reinforcement learning implementations. J. Mach. Learn. Res. **22**, 1–8 (2021)
34. Ryan, G., Wong, J., Yao, J., Gu, R., Jana, S.: CLN2INV: learning loop invariants with continuous logic networks. arXiv preprint arXiv:1909.11542 (2019)
35. Schilling, C., Forets, M., Guadalupe, S.: Verification of neural-network control systems by integrating Taylor models and zonotopes. In: AAAI (2022)
36. Schultz, W., Dardik, I., Tripakis, S.: Plain and simple inductive invariant inference for distributed protocols in TLA+. In: Formal Methods in Computer-Aided Design (FMCAD) (2022)
37. Sha, M., et al.: Synthesizing barrier certificates of neural network controlled continuous systems via approximations. In: ACM/IEEE Design Automation Conference. IEEE (2021)
38. Singh, G., Gehr, T., Mirman, M., Püschel, M., Vechev, M.: Fast and effective robustness certification. Adv. Neural Inf. Process. Syst. **31**, 1–12 (2018)
39. Sogokon, A., Ghorbal, K., Tan, Y.K., Platzer, A.: Vector barrier certificates and comparison systems. In: Havelund, K., Peleska, J., Roscoe, B., de Vink, E. (eds.) FM 2018. LNCS, vol. 10951, pp. 418–437. Springer, Heidelberg (2018). https://doi.org/10.1007/978-3-319-95582-7_25
40. Tjeng, V., Xiao, K.Y., Tedrake, R.: Evaluating robustness of neural networks with mixed integer programming. In: ICLR (2019)
41. Tran, H.D., et al.: NNV: the neural network verification tool for deep neural networks and learning-enabled cyber-physical systems. In: Lahiri, S., Wang, C. (eds.) CAV 2020. LNCS, vol. 12224, pp. 3–17. Springer, Heidelberg (2020). https://doi.org/10.1007/978-3-030-53288-8_1
42. Viswanadha, K., Kim, E., Indaheng, F., Fremont, D.J., Seshia, S.A.: Parallel and multi-objective falsification with scenic and verifai. In: Runtime Verification: 21st International Conference (2021)
43. Wang, Q., Chen, M., Xue, B., Zhan, N., Katoen, J.P.: Synthesizing invariant barrier certificates via difference-of-convex programming. In: Silva, A., Leino, K.R.M. (eds.) CAV 2021. LNCS, vol. 12759, pp. 443–466. Springer, Heidelberg (2021). https://doi.org/10.1007/978-3-030-81685-8_21
44. Wang, S., Pei, K., Whitehouse, J., Yang, J., Jana, S.: Formal security analysis of neural networks using symbolic intervals. In: 27th USENIX Security Symposium (USENIX Security 2018). USENIX Association (2018)
45. Wang, S., et al.: Beta-crown: efficient bound propagation with per-neuron split constraints for neural network robustness verification. Adv. Neural Inf. Process. Syst. **34**, 29909–29921 (2021)
46. Xu, K., et al.: Automatic perturbation analysis for scalable certified robustness and beyond. Adv. Neural Inf. Process. Syst. **33**, 1129–1141 (2020)
47. Zhang, J., Li, J.: Testing and verification of neural-network-based safety-critical control software: a systematic literature review. Inf. Softw. Technol. **123**, 106296 (2020)
48. Zhou, Y., Tripakis, S.: Compositional inductive invariant based verification of neural network controlled systems. arXiv eprint arxiv:2312.10842 (2023)

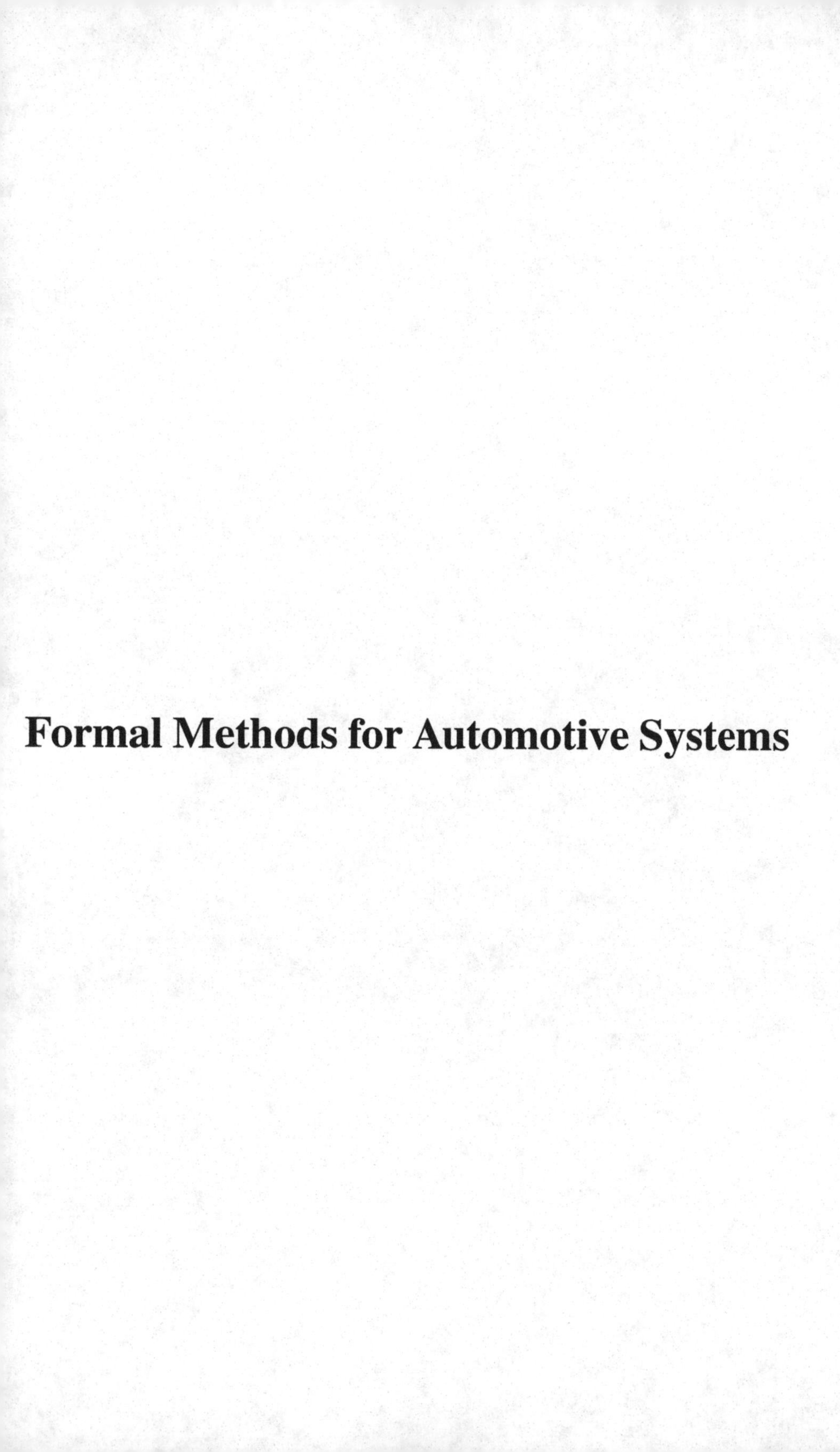

Formal Methods for Automotive Systems

Tree-Based Scenario Classification

A Formal Framework for Measuring Domain Coverage When Testing Autonomous Systems

Till Schallau[1(✉)], Stefan Naujokat[1], Fiona Kullmann[1], and Falk Howar[1,2]

[1] TU Dortmund University, Dortmund, Germany
till.schallau@tu-dortmund.de

[2] Fraunhofer ISST, Dortmund, Germany

Abstract. Scenario-based testing is envisioned as a key approach for the safety assurance of automated driving systems. In scenario-based testing, relevant (driving) scenarios are the basis of tests. Many recent works focus on specification, variation, generation, and execution of individual scenarios. In this work, we address the open challenges of classifying sets of recorded test drives into such scenarios and measuring scenario coverage in these test drives. Technically, we specify features in logic formulas over complex data streams and construct tree-based classifiers for scenarios from these feature specifications. For such specifications, we introduce CMFTBL, a new logic that extends existing linear-time temporal logics with aspects that are essential for concise specifications that work on field-recorded data. We demonstrate the expressiveness and effectiveness of our approach by defining a family of related scenario classifiers for different aspects of urban driving.

1 Introduction

One of the open challenges in developing automated driving systems is assuring their safety [20]. For several years, research has focused on structured approaches to assure the safety of autonomous driving systems [9,21]. The recently published ISO 21448 [14] norm (Safety of the Intended Functionality) transfers the conceptual framework of system safety approaches (e.g., ISO 26262 [13]) to the assurance of a vehicle's safety under all environmental conditions and possible faults that are triggered by the environment [25]. The idea is to identify relevant driving situations and potential triggers and then use these as a basis for testing the safety of a vehicle or its driving software. Many recent works focus on defining notions of safety [33], formalizing what constitutes scenarios [31,35], and on testing safety in specified scenarios [23].

Recent standardization efforts target the specification of so-called operational design domains (ODDs) [34] that define the anticipated environmental conditions for autonomous driving systems at a high level (e.g., weather conditions, road types and parameters, etc.). To combine works and results on testing individual scenarios into compelling arguments about the safety of an autonomous driving

N. Benz et al. (Eds.): NFM 2024, LNCS 14627, pp. 259–278, 2024.
https://doi.org/10.1007/978-3-031-60698-4_15

system in its operational design domain, we need tools for describing sets of relevant scenarios in some ODD and methods for analyzing coverage of these scenarios in driving tests as, e.g., stated in the ASAM OpenODD concept [2].

In this paper, we present an approach to the specification of scenario sets through the definition and recognition of scenario features. These features can then be used to classify observed scenarios in recorded test drives. Moreover, we can compute the set of possible combinations of features from our specification. This enables us to provide coverage metrics and to identify counterfactual scenarios, i.e., scenarios that were not observed but could be observed. Technically, we specify features in logic formulas over complex data streams and construct tree-based classifiers from these feature specifications that describe sets of scenarios, emerging from the combinatorial combination of features. We extend an existing modal logic to express features that can be found in ODD standards, in the 6-layer model of driving scenarios [31], and in the classification of driving maneuvers (e.g., intersection, sunny, oncoming traffic, left-turn maneuver, etc.).

For the demonstration of the expressiveness and effectiveness of our approach, we conduct a case study: we specify a small set of features and use test drives in a randomized simulation to analyze the observed scenario classes and the coverage that can be achieved in this setup. We also demonstrate how to decompose and analyze coverage for individual features or layers of the 6-layer model.

Summarizing, the contribution of this paper is threefold:

1. We introduce the Counting Metric First Order Temporal Binding Logic (CMFTBL), a formal logic for describing properties over recorded sequences of scenes. The logic extends upon existing temporal logics in multiple aspects that are essential for concise specifications that work on field-recorded data: firstly, the logic allows us to express imprecise specifications (in the spirit of "most of the time"); secondly, it is defined over complex structured domains for capturing scenes, and thirdly, it allows binding term evaluations to variables for access in nested parts of formulas (cf. Sect. 3).
2. We present a method for specifying and classifying sets of scenarios that is conceptually inspired by recent works and standardization efforts around operational design domains (ODDs) and technically inspired by feature models [30], where features of scenarios are specified using the CMFTBL logic (cf. Sect. 4.1).
3. The specification of features for sets of scenarios enables several quantitative and qualitative analyses on recorded driving data, e.g., scenario coverage, missing scenarios, missing combination of features, and distribution of combinations of features. In contrast to other works, these metrics focus on sets of scenarios and not on the parameters of one scenario (cf. Sect. 4.2).

Related Work. The presented approach is related to various existing works on the safety of automated driving systems, as well as works that utilize logic for specifying properties of safety-critical systems.

Amersbach and Winner [1] present an approach for estimating the required number of concrete scenarios for achieving scenario coverage based on real-world driving and accident data. Their analysis shows that more scenarios are required than would be feasible to test. Therefore, they propose to group concrete parameter combinations in so-called functional (i.e., abstract) scenario specifications (e.g., lane-change, following). Similar to this, Jafer et al. [15] introduce the Aviation Scenario Definition Language (ASDL), which allows for graphically specifying abstract and concrete flight scenarios. The conformance of the defined scenarios to predefined rules is verified using state charts and a model checker [4]. Our work provides classifiers for such abstract features of a scenario.

Li et al. [17] generate abstract scenarios with the goal of maximizing the coverage of k-way combinatorial testing for various scenario categories (e.g., weather, road type, ego-action). While their scenario categories are related to our scenario features, they do not provide classifiers for categories but aim to generate concrete instances of abstract scenarios.

Variants of temporal logics are commonly used for specifying properties of autonomous systems and their operational environments: Esterle et al. [7] formalize traffic rules for highway situations using Linear Temporal Logic (LTL). Rizaldi et al. [24] also formalize German overtaking rules using the same logic. Others formalize similar traffic rules, such as interstate traffic [19] or intersections [18], using the Metric Temporal Logic (MTL), as LTL is not capable of modeling duration. In a different direction of works, Schumann et al. [32] use MTL and LTL in their R2U2 framework for runtime System Health Management. Johannsen et al. [16] demonstrate how they extend this approach to transform previously intractable "first order" specifications (i.e., self-reference, unboundedness, and explicit counting) into Mission-time Linear Temporal Logic (MLTL) formulas without the need for extensions. This is done by parameterizing specifications based on restrictions of the evaluation domain. Dokhanchi et al. [5] introduce a *freeze frame quantifier* in their Timed Quality Temporal Logic (TQTL) to refer to objects in some time frame. We use a similar operator for modeling relations of objects over time (e.g., lane changes). Finally, the FRET framework [10] internally also works with LTL formulas. It can be used to define and analyze formal requirements in the restricted natural language FRETISH [11]. Similar to our goal of providing concise specification mechanisms, this work aims at making formal specification languages accessible to domain experts.

Outline. The paper is structured as follows. Section 2 outlines an example that motivates our approach. The formal logic for defining scenario properties is introduced in Sect. 3. Sect. 4 then introduces the formalism for scenario classifier trees and the calculation of coverage metrics and analyses on such trees. The results of our case study are presented in Sect. 5. The paper concludes in Sect. 6.

Extended Version, Implementation, and Reproduction Package. We provide an extended version of this paper [28], the open-source framework implementation[1], and a reproduction package on Zenodo [29]. For more technical introductions to the framework, please refer to [26] and [27].

[1] https://github.com/tudo-aqua/stars.

2 Motivational Example

We illustrate our approach to analyzing test drives in an urban environment. For this, we utilize a database of recorded test drives as the foundation. Recordings consist of sequences of *scenes* that are split into meaningful *segments*, e.g., based on regions of a map. A single scene is the snapshot of the state and the observed environment of the ego vehicle, comprising map data, position, and velocity of the ego vehicle, stationary objects, and moving objects around the ego vehicle. We record segments (i.e., sequences of scenes) at fixed intervals.

Our task is to decide whether this database of test drives covers sufficiently many relevant *scenarios* (i.e., archetypes of driving situations), or at least classify the test drives to identify the encountered scenarios. A scenario, in this case, would be a basic driving task, like making an unprotected left turn on a three-way intersection, and it could have variants, e.g., presence of oncoming traffic or pedestrians.

Figure 1 shows an example of a scene with three road users on a T-junction. The ego vehicle is planning to turn left. It currently stops at the stop line of the stop sign on the ego vehicle's lane. The other car follows its lane, going straight over the junction, and crossing the trajectory of the ego vehicle. The ego vehicle's destination lane contains a crosswalk with a pedestrian currently crossing the road. Thus, the pedestrian is crossing the trajectory of the ego vehicle.

Fig. 1. Simulation in CARLA [6]: the ego vehicle (red, dotted) stops at a stop sign. The trajectory of its planned left turn is crossed by an oncoming vehicle (green, dashed) and by a pedestrian (blue, solid). (Color figure online)

When analyzing the segment, we can observe specific maneuvers, environmental properties, and features from the viewpoint of the ego vehicle: road type is *T-junction*; ego is *turning left*; there is *oncoming traffic*; a *stop sign* is present; the ego vehicle does *stop at the stop line*, since it *must yield* to another vehicle; a *pedestrian is crossing* the destination lane; the weather is *sunny* during *daytime*.

These features can be formally described by formulas in a temporal logic over sequences of scenes. Then, we can use a set of features to classify segments: the combination of identified features (i.e., corresponding formulas that hold) defines the scenario class. The segment is one concrete *instance* of this scenario class. Assuming that features are not entailed by other features, we obtain 2^n scenario classes from n features. For the more realistic case that some dependencies exist between features (e.g., no overtaking without multiple lanes), we can use trees to model taxonomies of features and still compute possible scenario classes and check if they exist in our data. Variations of features in the example could be: the ego vehicle *drives straight* instead of turning left, there is *no oncoming traffic*, or *no pedestrian is crossing the road.* Based on these three variations (neglecting the other properties for the sake of simplicity), a total of $2^3 = 8$ possible scenario classes are observable. We can use this information to compute missing scenario classes or to measure scenario class coverage on a set of test drives. In our example, one scenario class was observed. Given the eight possible scenario classes, we obtain a scenario class coverage of 12.5%. Section 4 formalizes these concepts.

3 A Temporal Logic for Properties of Scenarios

We base scenario classifiers on the environment representation that is usually produced by the perception sub-system of an automated vehicle: a map of the road network and typed objects with positions, velocities, and observed states. We express properties of recorded sequences of scenes (i.e., momentary snapshots of the environment of the ego vehicle) in a formal logic. We use logic structures to describe scenes over a given signature of domain-specific functions and relations (e.g., positions, lanes, vehicles, velocities, etc.). We extend Metric First-Order Temporal Logic (MFOTL) [3] with a *minimum prevalence operator* that allows to express that a property holds for a certain fraction of all future states (within a finite trace), a corresponding past time version, and a *binding operator* that binds the value of a term at the current time to a variable. While the prevalence operators extend the expressiveness of MFOTL, binding is a shorthand for existentially quantified formulas of a certain form. We also introduce evaluation over complex data structures (in the form of further notational shorthands and conventions) to more easily capture the properties of scenes. We name our extension Counting Metric First-Order Temporal Binding Logic (CMFTBL).

A signature σ is a tuple $\langle \mathcal{C}, \mathcal{F}, \mathcal{R}, \text{ar}\rangle$, where $\mathcal{C}$ is a set of named constants, $\mathcal{F}$ is a set of function symbols, $\mathcal{R}$ is a set of relation symbols, and ar : $(\mathcal{F} \cup \mathcal{R}) \mapsto \mathbb{N}_0$ defines an arity for each function symbol $f \in \mathcal{F}$ and relation symbol $r \in \mathcal{R}$. A σ-structure $\mathfrak{D}$ is a pair $\langle \mathcal{D}, I\rangle$ of a domain $\mathcal{D}$ and interpretations of constants, functions, and relations with $I(c) \in \mathcal{D}$ for $c \in \mathcal{C}$, ar(f)-ary function $I(f) : \mathcal{D}^{\text{ar}(f)} \rightarrow \mathcal{D}$ for $f \in \mathcal{F}$, and $I(r) \subseteq \mathcal{D}^{\text{ar}(r)}$ for $r \in \mathcal{R}$. We write an interval of the set of non-empty intervals $\mathcal{I}$ over $\mathbb{N}$ as $[b, b') := \{a \in \mathbb{N} | b \leq a < b'\}$, where $b \in \mathbb{N}, b' \in \mathbb{N} \cup \{\infty\}$ and $b < b'$.

Formulas in CMFTBL over the signature σ, intervals $\mathcal{I}$, and the countably infinite set of variables $\mathcal{V}$ (assuming $\mathcal{V} \cap (\mathcal{C} \cup \mathcal{F} \cup \mathcal{R}) = \emptyset$) are inductively defined as follows:

(i) A *term* t is either a constant c, a variable v, or for $f \in \mathcal{F}$ and terms $t_1, \cdots, t_{\text{ar}(f)}$ the application $f(t_1, \cdots, t_{\text{ar}(f)})$.

(ii) For $r \in \mathcal{R}$ and terms $t_1, \cdots, t_{\text{ar}(r)}$, the predicate $r(t_1, \cdots, t_{\text{ar}(r)})$ is a *formula*.

(iii) For $x \in \mathcal{V}$ and $d \in \mathcal{D}$, if t is a term, φ and ψ are formulas, then $(\neg\varphi), (\varphi \vee \psi)$, $(\exists x : \varphi)$, and $(\downarrow^t_x \varphi)$ are formulas, where $\downarrow^t_x$ evaluates t in the current state and binds the result to variable x.

(iv) For $I \in \mathcal{I}$ and $p \in \mathbb{R}$, if φ and ψ are formulas, then next ($\bigcirc_I \varphi$), previously ($\bullet_I \varphi$), until ($\varphi\ U_I\ \psi$), since ($\varphi\ S_I\ \psi$), min. prevalence ($\nabla_I^p \psi$), and past min. prevalence ($\blacktriangledown_I^p \psi$) are formulas.

The pair $\langle \mathfrak{D}, \boldsymbol{\tau} \rangle$ is a *finite temporal structure* over the signature σ, where $\mathfrak{D} = (\mathfrak{D}_0, \mathfrak{D}_1, \cdots, \mathfrak{D}_n)$ is a finite sequence of structures (i.e., scenes) over σ and $\boldsymbol{\tau} = (\tau_0, \tau_1, \cdots, \tau_n)$ is a finite sequence of non-negative rational numbers $\tau_i \in \mathbb{Q}^+$ with length n. The elements in the sequence $\boldsymbol{\tau}$ are (increasing) *timestamps.* Furthermore, the interpretations of relations $r^{\mathfrak{D}_0}, r^{\mathfrak{D}_1}, \cdots, r^{\mathfrak{D}_n}$ in a temporal structure $\langle \mathfrak{D}, \boldsymbol{\tau} \rangle$ corresponding to a predicate symbol $r \in \mathcal{R}$ may change over time. The same is true for functions. Constants $c \in \mathcal{C}$ and the domain $\mathcal{D}$, on the other hand, do not change over time. More formally, we assume for all $0 \leq i < n$ that $\tau_i < \tau_{i+1}$ and for $\mathfrak{D}_i = \langle \mathcal{D}_i, I_i \rangle$ and $\mathfrak{D}_{i+1} = \langle \mathcal{D}_{i+1}, I_{i+1} \rangle$ that $\mathcal{D}_i = \mathcal{D}_{i+1}$. Moreover, $c^{\mathfrak{D}_i} = c^{\mathfrak{D}_{i+1}}$ for each constant symbol $c \in \mathcal{C}$.

A *valuation* is a mapping $v : \mathcal{V} \to \mathcal{D}$ from variables to domain elements. We write $v[x \mapsto d]$ for the valuation v that maps x to d. All other variables are not affected in the valuation v. We abuse notation by applying a valuation v also to constant symbols $c \in \mathcal{C}$, with $v(c) = c^{\mathfrak{D}}$. We evaluate a term t for valuation v and structure $\mathfrak{D}$, denoted by $\beta[t, v, \mathfrak{D}]$ as follows. For constants and variables x, let $\beta[x, v, \mathfrak{D}] = v(x)$. For the function application $a = f(t_1, \cdots, t_{\mathrm{ar}(f)})$, let

$$\beta[a, v, \mathfrak{D}] = f^{\mathfrak{D}}(\beta[t_1, v, \mathfrak{D}], \cdots, \beta[t_{\mathrm{ar}(f)}, v, \mathfrak{D}]).$$

We define the semantics of CMFTBL in terms of the relation $(\mathfrak{D}, \boldsymbol{\tau}, v, i) \models \varphi$ inductively, as shown in Table 1, where $|\boldsymbol{\tau}|$ denotes the number of timestamps in the temporal structure $\langle \mathfrak{D}, \boldsymbol{\tau} \rangle$ and is mostly used as an upper bound for intervals of temporal operators. The temporal structure $\langle \mathfrak{D}, \boldsymbol{\tau} \rangle$ satisfies formula φ iff $(\mathfrak{D}, \boldsymbol{\tau}, \emptyset, 0) \models \varphi$.

For $I \in \mathbb{I}$ and the common Boolean constant $\top$ (for true), we define the usual syntactic shorthands of operators as follows:

$$\begin{aligned}
(\varphi \wedge \psi) &:= \Big(\neg((\neg\varphi) \vee (\neg\psi))\Big) && \text{logical and} \\
(\varphi \Rightarrow \psi) &:= ((\neg\varphi) \vee \psi) && \text{implication} \\
(\forall x : \varphi) &:= (\neg(\exists x : \neg\varphi)) && \text{all quantifier} \\
(\Diamond_I \varphi) &:= (\top\ U_I\ \varphi) && \text{eventually} \\
(\Box_I \varphi) &:= \Big(\neg(\Diamond_I(\neg\varphi))\Big) && \text{always} \\
(\blacklozenge_I \varphi) &:= (\top\ S_I\ \varphi) && \text{once} \\
(\blacksquare_I \varphi) &:= \Big(\neg(\blacklozenge_I(\neg\varphi))\Big) && \text{historically}
\end{aligned}$$

Analogously, we define maximum prevalence operators based on minimum prevalence:

$$\begin{aligned}
(\triangle_I^p \varphi) &:= (\nabla_I^{1-p} \neg\varphi) && \text{max. prevalence} \\
(\blacktriangle_I^p \varphi) &:= (\blacktriangledown_I^{1-p} \neg\varphi) && \text{past max. prevalence}
\end{aligned}$$

Table 1. Definition of the semantics of the Counting Metric First-Order Temporal Logic (CMFTBL), given inductively by the relation $(\mathfrak{D}, \boldsymbol{\tau}, v, i) \models \psi$. The newly introduced operators are *minimum prevalence* $(\nabla_I^p \psi)$, *past minimum prevalence* $(\blacktriangledown_I^p \psi)$, and *binding* $(\downarrow_x^t \psi)$.

$(\mathfrak{D}, \boldsymbol{\tau}, v, i) \models r(t_1, ..., t_{a(r)})$	iff $(\beta(t_1, v, \mathfrak{D}_i), \cdots, \beta(t_{\mathrm{ar}(r)}, v, \mathfrak{D}_i)) \in r^{\mathfrak{D}_i}$
$(\mathfrak{D}, \boldsymbol{\tau}, v, i) \models (\neg \psi)$	iff $(\mathfrak{D}, \boldsymbol{\tau}, v, i) \not\models \psi$
$(\mathfrak{D}, \boldsymbol{\tau}, v, i) \models (\psi \vee \psi')$	iff $(\mathfrak{D}, \boldsymbol{\tau}, v, i) \models \psi$ or $(\mathfrak{D}, \boldsymbol{\tau}, v, i) \models \psi'$
$(\mathfrak{D}, \boldsymbol{\tau}, v, i) \models (\exists x : \psi)$	iff $(\mathfrak{D}, \boldsymbol{\tau}, v[x \mapsto d], i) \models \psi$, for some $d \in \mathcal{D}$
$(\mathfrak{D}, \boldsymbol{\tau}, v, i) \models (\bigcirc_I \psi)$	iff $\tau_{i+1} - \tau_i \in I$ and $(\mathfrak{D}, \boldsymbol{\tau}, v, i+1) \models \psi$
$(\mathfrak{D}, \boldsymbol{\tau}, v, i) \models (\bullet_I \psi)$	iff $i > 0$, $\tau_i - \tau_{i-1} \in I$, and $(\mathfrak{D}, \boldsymbol{\tau}, v, i-1) \models \psi$
$(\mathfrak{D}, \boldsymbol{\tau}, v, i) \models (\psi\ U_I\ \psi')$	iff for some $j \geq i, \tau_j - \tau_i \in I, (\mathfrak{D}, \boldsymbol{\tau}, v, j) \models \psi'$, and $(\mathfrak{D}, \boldsymbol{\tau}, v, k) \models \psi$, for all $k \in \mathbb{N}$ with $i \leq k < j$
$(\mathfrak{D}, \boldsymbol{\tau}, v, i) \models (\psi\ S_I\ \psi')$	iff for some $j \leq i, \tau_i - \tau_j \in I, (\mathfrak{D}, \boldsymbol{\tau}, v, j) \models \psi'$, and $(\mathfrak{D}, \boldsymbol{\tau}, v, k) \models \psi$, for all $k \in \mathbb{N}$ with $j < k \leq i$
$(\mathfrak{D}, \boldsymbol{\tau}, v, i) \models (\nabla_I^p \psi)$	iff $(\mathfrak{D}, \boldsymbol{\tau}, v, j) \models \psi$, for at least fraction p of indices $i \leq j \leq \lvert\boldsymbol{\tau}\rvert$ with $\tau_j - \tau_i \in I$
$(\mathfrak{D}, \boldsymbol{\tau}, v, i) \models (\blacktriangledown_I^p \psi)$	iff $(\mathfrak{D}, \boldsymbol{\tau}, v, j) \models \psi$, for at least fraction p of indices $0 \leq j \leq i$ with $\tau_i - \tau_j \in I$
$(\mathfrak{D}, \boldsymbol{\tau}, v, i) \models (\downarrow_x^t \psi)$	iff $(\mathfrak{D}, \boldsymbol{\tau}, v[x \mapsto \beta(t, v, \mathfrak{D}_i)], i) \models \psi$

We obtain non-metric variants of the temporal operators for interval $[0, \infty)$. In addition to these commonly used patterns, we introduce several notational conventions to ease presentation.

Let $isVehicle \in \mathcal{R}$ be a unary relation. We define the set of all vehicles $\mathcal{V} \subseteq \mathcal{D}$ as $\{d \in \mathcal{D} \mid isVehicle(d)\}$. Analogously, we define the set of pedestrians as $\mathcal{P}$, and the set of actors $\mathcal{A} := \mathcal{P} \cup \mathcal{V}$ with $\mathcal{P} \cap \mathcal{V} = \emptyset$. We also use a notation reminiscent of object-relational element associations. For instance, for some vehicle $v \in \mathcal{V}$ and the relations $\{isEgo, isLane, onLane\} \subseteq \mathcal{R}$, we use shorthand notations like, e.g., $v.isEgo$ for $isEgo(v)$ and $v.lane$ for the unique $l \in \mathcal{D}$ where $isLane(l) \wedge onLane(v, l)$.

Formulas used for specifying features in a tree-based classifier usually consist of one unary relation that needs to hold for the ego vehicle. For such an $r \in \mathcal{R}$ and $\varphi := \exists v \in \mathcal{V} : \Box(v.isEgo) \wedge r(v)$, we write $ego.r$ instead of the entire formula φ. As an example, consider *ego.obeyedSpeedLimit* to model that the ego vehicle obeys the speed limit at all times. Using our notational conventions, the relation is defined as follows:

$$obeyedSpeedLimit(v) := \Box(v.speed \leq v.lane.speedLimitAt(v.pos))$$

The associations *v.speed* and *v.pos* are functions as introduced before and *speedLimitAt* is a function from a position number and a lane to a speed limit number. For numbers, we assume the relations $\{eq, neq, lt, gt, leq, geq\} \in \mathcal{R}$ to represent the common mathematical comparators $\{=, \neq, <, >, \leq, \geq\}$, which we also allow as notation shortcuts.

With these notational conventions, we can concisely specify traffic rules and environmental features using CMFTBL formulas and evaluate those on sequences of scenes. We express each predicate of our case study (cf. Sect. 5) in this way. For comparison, consider the formula for "the ego vehicle obeys the speed limit at all times" without these syntactic conventions:

$$\begin{aligned}\varphi_{osl} := \exists v \in \mathcal{D} : \Box(isVehicle(v) \wedge isEgo(v)) \wedge \\ \Box\Big(\exists l \in \mathcal{D} : \exists p \in \mathcal{D} : isLane(l) \wedge onLane(v, l) \wedge \\ leq\big(speed(v), speedLimitAt(p, l)\big)\Big)\end{aligned}$$

We conclude this section with two example formulas from our case study that utilize the operators introduced by CMFTBL. Consider a relation *isInJunction* that decides whether a vehicle $v \in \mathcal{V}$ primarily drives through a junction during the analyzed segment. For this, we require the road the vehicle drives on to be categorized as a junction "for the most part" (e.g., 80%) of the segment. To express this, we need the newly introduced minimum prevalence operator.

$$isInJunction(v) := \nabla^{0.8}(v.lane.road.isJunction) \tag{1}$$

We utilize the binding operator to detect a lane change for a given vehicle $v \in \mathcal{V}$. We bind the lane of vehicle v at the current timestamp to a new variable l. In nested formulas, which might evaluate other (here, later) timestamps, we can compare the vehicle's lane value to l to detect a lane change.

$$changedLane(v) := \downarrow_{l}^{v.lane} (\Diamond(l \neq v.lane)) \tag{2}$$

4 Classifiers for Scenarios and Metrics on Sets of Scenarios

We want to use CMFTBL formulas to express features of scenarios and classify recorded driving data into scenario classes. Formally, we assume recorded driving data to be given as temporal structures $\langle \mathfrak{D}, \boldsymbol{\tau} \rangle$ over some fix basic signature $\langle \mathcal{C}, \mathcal{F}, \mathcal{R}, \text{ar} \rangle$. This basic signature encodes the set of properties that is provided as information in the data (i.e., objects with positions) and classifications on a road network with information about lanes, signs, and signals. For the scope of this paper, we additionally assume that the recorded data is already segmented into sequences. We use $\mathfrak{S}$ to denote a set of segments of form $\langle \mathfrak{D}, \boldsymbol{\tau} \rangle$. In practice, segmentation could either be done based on a map or based on classification.

4.1 Classifiers for Scenarios

We organize features hierarchically in trees to account for dependencies between features (a lane change, e.g., can only occur on a multi-lane road). This enables us to capture the taxonomies of features found in the 6-layer model or in draft standards for specifying operational design domains.

Definition 1 (Tree-Based Scenario Classifier). *A tree-based scenario classifier (TSC)* $\mathbb{T}$ *is a tuple* $\langle \mathcal{Q}, q_r, \Gamma, \lambda_l, \lambda_u \rangle$ *with set of nodes* $\mathcal{Q}$ *(i.e., the modeled features), root node* $q_r \in \mathcal{Q}$*, set of edges* Γ *of type* (q, q', φ) *where* $q, q' \in \mathcal{Q}$ *are source and destination, CMFTBL formula* φ *is the edge condition, lower bounds for sub-features of nodes* $\lambda_l : \mathcal{Q} \to \mathbb{N}_0$*, and upper bounds for sub-features of nodes* $\lambda_u : \mathcal{Q} \to \mathbb{N}_0$*.*

We write $q \xrightarrow{\varphi} q'$ for (q, q', φ). We require $\mathbb{T}$ to be a tree rooted at q_r. For $q \in \mathcal{Q}$, let $c(q) = \{q' \mid q \xrightarrow{\varphi} q' \in \Gamma\}$ denote the children of q. Bounds must be $0 \leq \lambda_l(q) \leq \lambda_u(q) \leq |c(q)|$.

Inspired by feature models, we name certain types of nodes $q \in \mathcal{Q}$ depending on their lower and upper bounds (abbreviated notation with parentheses):

(A)ll	$\lambda_l(q) = \lambda_u(q) = \lvert c(q)\rvert$	**(O)ptional**	$\lambda_l(q) = 0 \wedge \lambda_u(q) = \lvert c(q)\rvert$
E(X)clusive	$\lambda_l(q) = \lambda_u(q) = 1$	**(a..b)-Bounded**	$\lambda_l(q) = a \wedge \lambda_u(q) = b$
Leaf ()	$\lambda_l(q) = \lambda_u(q) = 0$		

We introduce these bounds on sub-features to compute the number of combinatorial combinations, i.e., the number of observable scenario classes (cf. Sect. 4.2). A more precise approach to computing possible scenarios would be to compute satisfiable combinations of features. Such an approach, however, does not seem feasible or meaningful. Even if the satisfiability of some fragment of CMFTBL can be established, there is no mechanism to constrain acceptable models to realistic segments. A much more useful analysis in the context of our approach (which it does indeed provide), is to determine which segments (if any) are classified with feature combinations that are invalid according to the explicit definitions in the TSC. This information can then be used to refine the tree or find errors in the data.

Figure 2 shows one of the TSCs developed for our case study (cf. Sect. 5) as a simple example. All nodes (except for the root node) model features of urban driving scenarios. In this example, we focus on different features corresponding to road types. The nodes are labeled with a short description of the feature, followed by the node type (that defines the upper and lower bounds for the number of children in classes modeled by this TSC) in parentheses. Each edge from source to destination is labeled with a formula to recognize the destination node's feature. For better readability of the figure, we omit all formulas except for the always true $\top$ as well as two references to the formulas (1) and (2) presented in Sect. 3.

We can now describe individual scenario classes for a scenario classifier.

Definition 2 (Scenario Class). *For a given tree-based scenario classifier* $\mathbb{T} = \langle \mathcal{Q}^o q^o_r, \Gamma^o, \lambda^o_l, \lambda^o_u \rangle$*, a scenario class is a tree* $T = \langle \mathcal{Q}, q_r, \Gamma \rangle$ *with set of nodes* $\mathcal{Q} \subseteq \mathcal{Q}^o$*, root node* $q_r = q^o_r$*, and set of edges* Γ *of type* (q, q') *such that* $(q, q', \varphi) \in \Gamma^o$*. We require the number of children* $c(q)$ *for every node* $q \in \mathcal{Q}$ *to be within the lower and upper bounds of* q *in* $\mathbb{T}$*.*

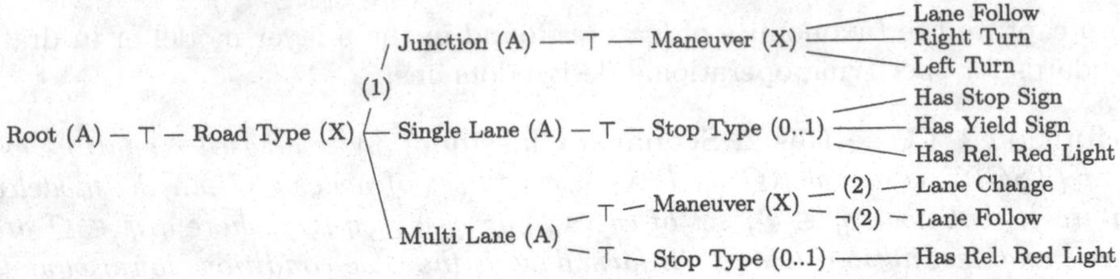

Fig. 2. Simple example classifier from our case study. Edge labels (1) and (2) refer to the formulas shown in Sect. 3.

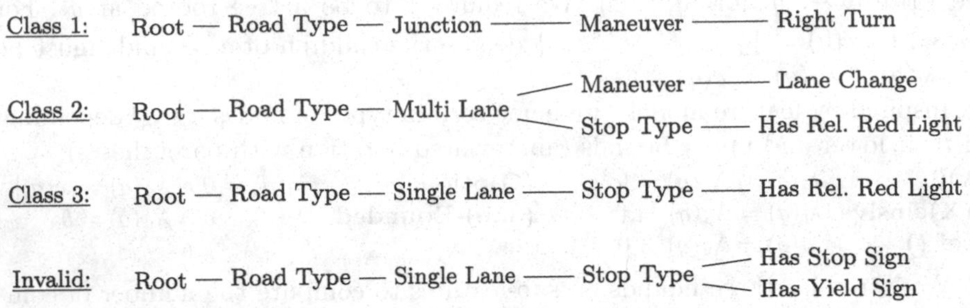

Fig. 3. Scenario classes (3 of the total 11) modeled by the TSC shown in Fig. 2. The invalid class violates the bounds of the single lane *Stop Type (0..1)* node.

Let $\mathcal{T}_{\mathbb{T}}$ denote the (finite) set of all scenario classes for tree-based classifier $\mathbb{T}$, and let $\mathcal{W}$ denote the (infinite) set of observable segments of driving data $\langle \mathfrak{D}, \boldsymbol{\tau} \rangle$. We denote the classification function that maps observed driving data $\langle \mathfrak{D}, \boldsymbol{\tau} \rangle$ to a scenario class T based on the tree-based scenario classifier $\mathbb{T}$ by $C_{\mathbb{T}} : \mathcal{W} \rightarrow \mathcal{T}_{\mathbb{T}}$. For recorded data segment $\mathcal{S} = \langle \mathfrak{D}, \boldsymbol{\tau} \rangle$, we compute $C_{\mathbb{T}}(\mathcal{S}) = \langle \mathcal{Q}, q_r, \Gamma \rangle$ by computing the set $\mathcal{Q}$ of nodes, which uniquely determines the set of transitions. We initialize $\mathcal{Q}$ as $\{q_r^o\}$ and then add every node q' for which $q \in \mathcal{Q}$ and $(q, q', \varphi) \in \Gamma^o$ with $\mathcal{S} \models \varphi$ until a fixed point is reached. We assume that bounds permit a valid class to be computed for every realistic segment $\mathcal{S}$ and lift $C_{\mathbb{T}}$ to sets of segments by letting $C_{\mathbb{T}}(\mathfrak{S})$ denote the set of observed scenario classes for $\mathfrak{S}$.

In total, the TSC presented in Fig. 2 models 11 different scenario classes, i.e., subsets of feature nodes that comply with the bounds given by the node types. As the main node *Road Type* is an (X)-node (with bounds $\lambda_l = \lambda_u = 1$), the possible scenario classes are the 3 junction maneuvers plus the 4 single lane stop type variants (stop sign, yield sign, relevant red light, or none of these) plus 4 possible combinations of multi-lane features (lane change with relevant red light, lane change without relevant red light, etc.). Figure 3 shows three example classes as well as one invalid class where stop sign and yield sign are both recognized at the same time, which violates the bounds of the single lane *Stop Type (0..1)* node. Finding such invalid classes in the analyzed data either indicates errors in the TSC modeling (i.e., in the formulas or bounds) or faulty data (e.g., errors in map data).

4.2 Coverage Metrics for Sets of Scenarios

Given a set of recorded segments $\mathfrak{S}$ and a classifier $\mathbb{T}$, we want to analyze and quantify *if and to what degree* the recorded data covers possible scenarios. We start by showing how to compute the number of scenario classes for a tree-based scenario classifier $\mathbb{T} = \langle \mathcal{Q}, q_r, \Gamma, \lambda_l, \lambda_u \rangle$. Let $\Gamma_q = \{(q, q', \varphi) \in \Gamma\}$ be the set of edges originating in q, and $[\Gamma_q]^{\lambda_l(q)..\lambda_u(q)} =_{def} \bigcup_{i=\lambda_l(q)}^{\lambda_u(q)} [\Gamma_q]^i$ be the set of all subsets of these edges with size within the lower and upper bounds of q. We define the size $|\mathbb{T}| = |q_r|$ recursively as:

$$|q| =_{def} \sum_{G \in [\Gamma_q]^{\lambda_l(q)..\lambda_u(q)}} \left(\prod_{(q,q',\varphi) \in G} |q'| \right)$$

The primary metric we are considering is **scenario class coverage** (SCC), expressing the ratio between the number of observed scenario classes and the number of classes modeled by classifier $\mathbb{T} = \langle \mathcal{Q}, q_r, \Gamma, \lambda_l, \lambda_u \rangle$. For a set of recorded segments $\mathfrak{S}$, we define SCC as:

$$\text{SCC}(\mathfrak{S}, \mathbb{T}) =_{def} \frac{|\mathcal{C}_{\mathbb{T}}(\mathfrak{S})|}{|\mathbb{T}|}$$

It can be expected that gaining high coverage on TSCs with (potentially multiple combinations of) rare events requires an increasingly high amount of test scenarios. To measure the individual rarity of the modeled environmental conditions, from which explanations for coverage gaps might be derived, we introduce a metric for **absolute feature occurrence** (afo):

$$\text{afo}(\mathfrak{S}, q) =_{def} \left|\{\langle \mathcal{Q}, q_r, \Gamma \rangle \in \mathcal{C}_{\mathbb{T}}(\mathfrak{S}) \mid q \in \mathcal{Q}\}\right|$$

In addition to coverage, which only considers if a scenario class has been observed, we define **scenario instance count** (sic) to count how often a certain class has been encountered in a set of scenarios:

$$\text{sic}(\mathfrak{S}, t) =_{def} \left|\{\mathcal{S} \in \mathfrak{S} \mid \mathcal{C}_{\mathbb{T}}(\mathcal{S}) = t\}\right|$$

Similar to calculating the size of a TSC, we can enumerate all possible scenario classes and use them to identify **class instance missings**, i.e., classes as which no $\overline{\mathcal{S}} \in \mathfrak{S}$ is classified. However, gaining meaningful insights from large sets of missing classes is difficult. Therefore, we also analyze **feature pair misses**, i.e., pairs of TSC nodes that do not exist together in any observed class.

5 Evaluation

We designed our evaluation as a single case mechanism experiment [37] that validates the presented approach. We aim at 1) demonstrating that we can express relevant properties of ODDs in CMFTBL, 2) evaluating to which degree we

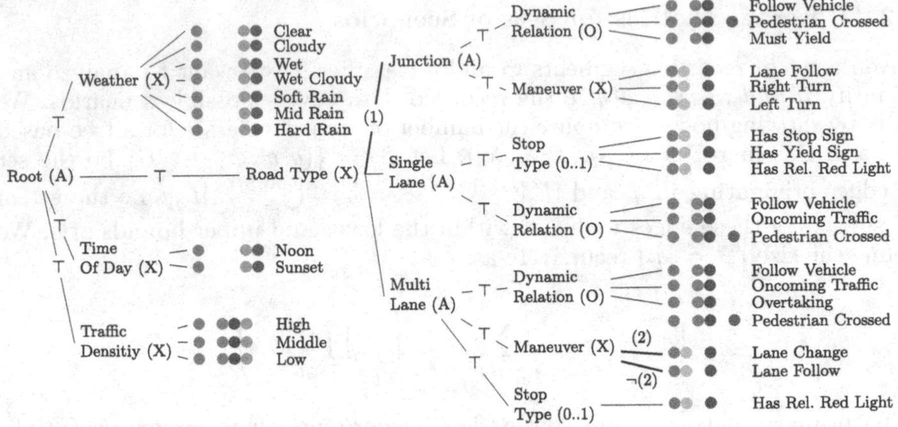

Fig. 4. Tree-Based Scenario Classifiers modeled for our experiments. Features (as well as their paths to the root node) are included in a TSC, if they are marked with a corresponding colored circle. Bold edges with labels (1) and (2) refer to the formulas shown in Sect. 3. Formulas for other features are omitted. Based on the *full TSC* classifier, which contains all evaluated features, we define multiple subsets based on the 6-layer model of scenario classification. In total, we define six classifiers: ● *full TSC*, ● *layer 1+2*, ● *layer 4*, ● *layer 1+2+4*, ● *layer (4)+5*, and ● *pedestrian.*

can achieve scenario class coverage, and 3) evaluating whether coverage analysis generates valuable insights about missing classes. To this end, we identify and model features for an urban driving environment, define a family of related tree-based scenario classifiers based on those features, and use these classifiers for analyzing simulated urban traffic. We chose features to model the types of properties (or labels) that are envisioned for specifications of operational design domains (ODDs) as described in BSI 1883 [34] or OpenODD [2]. The remainder of this section discusses the features and classifiers developed for our case study, details the experimental setup, presents results from the simulated experiments, and provides initial answers to the above questions.

Classifiers for the 6-Layer Model. To construct tree-based scenario classifiers (TSCs) for our case study, we evaluated the 6-layer model of scenario classification by Scholtes et al. [31] and extracted observable features. In Fig. 4, we visualize all TSCs developed for this case study at once, using colored circles to indicate the features included in each TSC. The hierarchic organization of the complete set of features extracted from the 6-layer model resulted in the *full TSC*, while the others focus on individual layers or combinations of layers. Please note: the *layer 1+2* TSC marked with ● is the one we already presented as an example in Sect. 4.1 (cf. Fig. 2).

We define features as CMFTBL predicates and formulas. In total, we define 51 predicates (including sub-predicates) to completely express the detection of the modeled features for our experiments. We use the min. prevalence operator

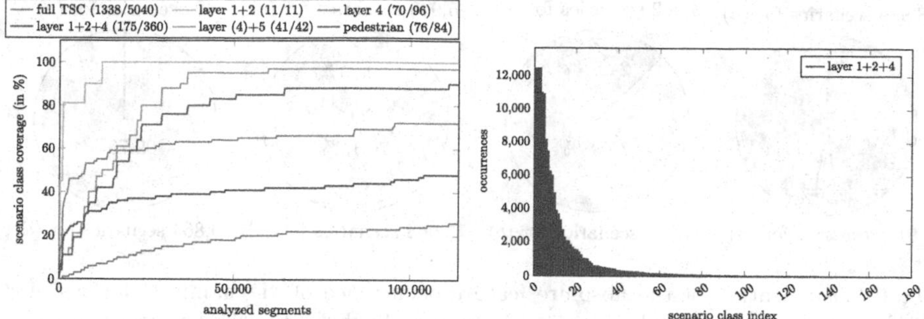

(a) Scenario class coverage over the course of the 113,767 analyzed segments

(b) Distribution of the observed scenario classes for the *layer 1+2+4* classifier set

Fig. 5. Coverage of scenario classes and distribution of segments over classes

in 16 predicates to model that some feature holds for most of the time during a segment. For more examples of predicates, please refer to our implementation[2] and the preprint version of this paper [28].

Experimental Setup. For recording and classifying scenario runs, we built a toolchain based on the CARLA simulator [6] and our analysis framework [26].

Based on the classifications of recorded runs, we calculate coverage and the other metrics introduced in Sect. 4.2. Moreover, we analyze saturation by counting class coverage over time.

For our experiments, we record 100 simulation runs of 5 min each. In every run, a random map, daytime, and weather is chosen and up to 200 vehicles and 30 pedestrians are spawned randomly on the map. All vehicles are driven by CARLA's autopilot. We analyze each simulation run multiple times: once with each vehicle being considered to be *the ego vehicle*. Overall, this results in 113, 767 segments representing 1, 104 h of driving data. The analysis of this data with all classifiers and predicates discussed above takes 118 min on a single core of a 2021 Apple M1 Pro SoC.

Experimental Results. We visualize our results for scenario class coverage over the course of analyzed segments in Fig. 5a. Each colored curve represents the coverage result of one classifier from Fig. 4 and shows its class coverage percentage in relation to its respective observed scene sequences. The legend also shows the final count of observed scenario classes for each classifier after analyzing all 113, 767 segments and the number of possible classes. The *layer 1+2* classifier covers 100% of scenario classes after 12, 233 analyzed segments. Furthermore, *layer (4)+5* almost fully covers its possible scenario classes after

[2] https://github.com/tudo-aqua/stars-carla-experiments/blob/main/src/main/kotlin/tools/aqua/stars/carla/experiments/predicates.kt.

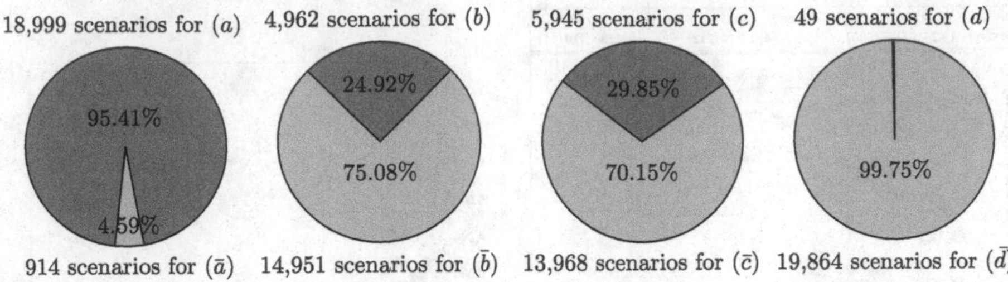

Fig. 6. Visualization of the absolute feature occurrence of "Dynamic Relations" for "Multi-Lane" roads. We define $a=$ "Oncoming Traffic", $b=$ "Pedestrian Crossed", $c=$ "Following Leading Vehicle" and $d=$ "Overtaking".

around 59,409 segments but misses one scenario class and therefore only reaches 97% coverage. The *pedestrian* classifier covers over 90% of relevant scenario classes. The classifiers *layer 4* and *layer 1+2+4* cover 72% and 48% of relevant scenario classes, respectively. Finally, the reference classifier *full TSC* reaches a coverage of 26%.

Figure 5b visualizes the scenario instance count metric of the 175 observed scenario classes for the *layer 1+2+4* classifier. The plot shows a long-tail distribution in which 85,120 segments of the total 113,767 segments are classified into only 15 scenario classes. The remaining 28,647 segments are classified into the remaining 160 classes. The three most common scenario classes are each observed about 11,000 times. The other classifiers show similar long-tail distributions.

Our analysis provides detailed insights into specific scenario classes regarding the underlying features and their combinations. To demonstrate the results, Figs. 6 and 7 visualize analyses on the *Dynamic Relation* features of the *Multi-Lane* node of the TSC (cf. Fig. 4). For better readability in the figures, we label the observable features as $a=$ "*Oncoming Traffic*", $b=$ "*Pedestrian Crossed*", $c=$ "*Following Leading Vehicle*" and $d=$ "*Overtaking*". We also write (x) or $(\bar{x})$ if feature x was observed or not observed, respectively. For example, the combination $(a{\cdot}b{\cdot}c{\cdot}\bar{d})$ describes the scenario classes in which *Oncoming Traffic*, *Pedestrian Crossed* and *Following Leading Vehicle* are observed, while *Overtaking* is not observed.

Absolute Feature Occurrence. Figure 6 visualizes the individual absolute occurrences of each observable feature for the *Dynamic Relations* on *Multi-Lane* roads. The percentages are based on the 19,913 analyzed segments classified as containing the *Multi-Lane* feature. Here, *Oncoming Traffic* (a) appears in 95.41% of the total occurrences. *Pedestrian Crossed* (b) and *Following Leading Vehicle* (c) are similarly present with a coverage of 24.92% and 29.85%, whereas *Overtaking* (d) is only encountered in 0.25% of the analyzed segments.

Feature Combinations. As the classifiers (cf. Fig. 4) define the *Dynamic Relation* node as *Optional*, all combinations of the four children form valid scenario classes. Figure 7 shows the distribution for these combinations. It can be seen

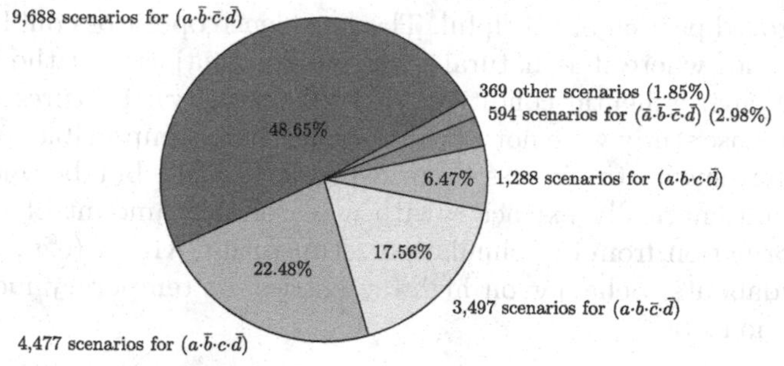

Fig. 7. Distribution of all feature combinations of "Dynamic Relations" for "Multi-Lane" roads. We define $a=$ "Oncoming Traffic", $b=$ "Pedestrian Crossed", $c=$ "Following Leading Vehicle" and $d=$ "Overtaking".

that 98.14% of observed scenarios are covered by the following five feature combinations: $(a{\cdot}\bar{b}{\cdot}\bar{c}{\cdot}\bar{d})$, $(a{\cdot}\bar{b}{\cdot}c{\cdot}\bar{d})$, $(a{\cdot}b{\cdot}\bar{c}{\cdot}\bar{d})$, $(a{\cdot}b{\cdot}c{\cdot}\bar{d})$, and $(\bar{a}{\cdot}\bar{b}{\cdot}\bar{c}{\cdot}\bar{d})$. The 369 *other scenarios* are composed of the following combinations: 152 scenarios for $(\bar{a}{\cdot}\bar{b}{\cdot}c{\cdot}\bar{d})$, 143 scenarios for $(\bar{a}{\cdot}b{\cdot}\bar{c}{\cdot}\bar{d})$, 37 scenarios for $(a{\cdot}\bar{b}{\cdot}\bar{c}{\cdot}d)$, 25 scenarios for $(\bar{a}{\cdot}b{\cdot}c{\cdot}\bar{d})$, 9 scenarios for $(a{\cdot}b{\cdot}\bar{c}{\cdot}d)$, and 3 scenarios for $(a{\cdot}\bar{b}{\cdot}c{\cdot}d)$. The five feature combinations that never occurred – $(a{\cdot}b{\cdot}c{\cdot}d)$, $(\bar{a}{\cdot}b{\cdot}c{\cdot}d)$, $(\bar{a}{\cdot}b{\cdot}\bar{c}{\cdot}d)$, $(\bar{a}{\cdot}\bar{b}{\cdot}c{\cdot}d)$, and $(\bar{a}{\cdot}\bar{b}{\cdot}\bar{c}{\cdot}d)$ – each include feature (d), which directly stems from the overall low occurrence of only 0.25% for feature (d).

Missing Feature Combinations. As discussed, our method yields precise information on which scenario classes never occurred. However, a detailed analysis is not feasible, as the full TSC analysis resulted in 3,702 unseen classes. With the analysis of feature pair misses, we instead focus on predicate combinations that never occurred. This results in the information that the following five predicate combinations were never observed together: (Overtaking & Lane Change), (Overtaking & Has Red Light), (Has Stop Sign & High Traffic), (Has Yield Sign & High Traffic), and (Has Yield Sign & Middle Traffic).

5.1 Discussion

We discuss the experimental results in the context of the three contributions outlined in Sect. 1.

Specification of Scenario Classes: With our hierarchic structuring of properties into scenario classifier trees, we were able to express and organize many relevant features for common driving situations considered in the proposals for operational design domains [34] and approaches like the 6-layer model [31], as well as classify recorded driving data according to the different scenario classes defined by such trees. While our TSC approach (as well as the framework implementation) is generally independent of the logic used to evaluate driving data,

CMFTBL proved particularly helpful. The prevalence operator could be used to detect properties where it is natural to formulate "majority of the time" constraints (like environmental conditions or traffic density). Features we did not include in our case study were not left out because it was impossible (or even particularly inconvenient) to express them using CMFTBL, but because we were not able to automatically extract – with a reasonable amount of effort – the required information from our simulation setup with CARLA (e.g., yield priorities in roundabouts, behavior on highway entries, or temporary modifications like construction work).

Analysis Time: We analyzed a total of 1,104 h of data from simulated test drives, which took a little over 118 min. With a total of 113,767 segments, we have on average 34.93 s of driving data per segment and 62.23 ms of computation time per segment evaluation. While a more comprehensive scenario classifier would contain more features, due to the tree-based structure of our classifier, whole sub-trees get cut off from evaluation if a condition does not hold (e.g., none of the *single-lane* features of Fig. 4 are evaluated when the segment is recognized as a *junction*). The obtained results thus indicate that our approach is generally feasible with regard to computation time. Even in-vehicle analysis of properties while driving (i.e., after completing a segment) seems possible.

Analyses/Metrics: Our experiments show that we can achieve scenario coverage with hierarchical classifiers. Even though the features evaluated with the classifiers are limited in scope, they already model more than 5.000 situations in urban driving. In our experiments, we achieve high coverage and saturation of observed scenario classes. This is in contrast to Hartjen et al. [12], who analyze saturation effects in observed maneuvers of multiple vehicles including and around the ego vehicle. In their analysis, the amount of observed unique sequences shows no significant saturation over time, indicating that individual maneuvers induce a space that is too big to be feasible for analyzing scenario coverage.

Our detailed analyses proved particularly useful for the interpretation of the coverage levels our classifiers converge to: all five feature combinations that are not encountered at all throughout our data combine a *layer 1+2* feature with a *layer 4* feature. Due to the combinatorial nature of our classifier concept, about half of all combinations in the *layer 1+2+4* classifier remain undetected. We can utilize this information and investigate why certain feature pairs are missed. For instance, in the three maps we included in our experiments, only a single junction on a small side road has a yield sign. We are less likely to detect middle or high traffic density on this road. These insights can be used to plan test drives or as a basis for analyzing the relevance of specified scenarios in some real environment.

5.2 Threats to Validity

To test our approach, we generated data with CARLA, as this allowed us to produce a large set of test drives using automated scripts.

Internal Validity. We have not tested our approach on a set of ground truth data to check our predicates against pre-labeled data. However, we manually inspected rendered videos of the generated data set to match the actual driving situations we addressed with our formulas.

External Validity. As stated in Sect. 2, we focused on analyzing urban driving scenarios. With our map selection, we could define all relevant predicates for our experiments. However, other typical urban driving situations comprise, e.g., interstate-like roads with on-ramps or roundabouts. In another set of experiments, we successfully adapted the formalizations of interstate traffic done by [19] and analyzed their coverage in simulated driving data. For roundabouts, the main challenge is that the underlying OpenDRIVE data (used by the maps in CARLA) does not explicitly specify a roundabout's lane layout.

Concept Validity. When analyzing more complex situations, the specification might get too large for our approach to be practically usable. Especially as data from the real world can contain errors and deviations, various complex predicates and classification trees might become necessary. Our experiments use the perfect world perception provided by CARLA, which removes the uncertainties of real sensor data. Analyzing real-world data requires the intelligent handling of such uncertainties. Predicates then need to consider that the environmental perception, such as object tracking, has uncertainty. Current research is already addressing problems in regards to environmental perception [36], such as sensor fusion [8], or object reference generation [22]. We are confident that with further results and insights, we can use our *min. prevalence* operator to deal with uncertainties or sensor errors in the analyzed data.

6 Conclusion

We have presented a temporal logic for expressing features of driving scenarios over complex data streams and combining such features into tree-based scenario classifiers that structure the operational design domain of an autonomous driving system into relevant scenario classes. On recorded driving data, tree-based scenario classifiers enable an analysis of scenario class coverage, metrics, and qualitative analyses that uncover and explain misses. We have evaluated our technique in simulated urban driving experiments. The results show that we are capable of achieving full coverage for some scenario classifiers and can reason about the observed features of the analyzed set of recorded test drives.

References

1. Amersbach, C., Winner, H.: Defining required and feasible test coverage for scenario-based validation of highly automated vehicles. In: ITSC 2019, pp. 425–430. IEEE, New York (2019). https://doi.org/10.1109/itsc.2019.8917534
2. Association for Standardization of Automation and Measuring Systems: ASAM OpenODD: Concept Paper v1.0 (2021). https://www.asam.net/index.php?eID=dumpFile&t=f&f=4544&token=1260ce1c4f0afdbe18261f7137c689b1d9c27576

3. Basin, D., Klaedtke, F., Müller, S., Zălinescu, E.: Monitoring metric first-order temporal properties. J. ACM **62**(2), 1–45 (2015). https://doi.org/10.1145/2699444
4. Chhaya, B., Jafer, S., Durak, U.: Formal verification of simulation scenarios in aviation scenario definition language (ASDL). Aerospace **5**(1), 10 (2018). https://doi.org/10.3390/aerospace5010010
5. Dokhanchi, A., Amor, H.B., Deshmukh, J.V., Fainekos, G.: Evaluating perception systems for autonomous vehicles using quality temporal logic. In: Colombo, C., Leucker, M. (eds.) RV 2018. LNCS, vol. 11237, pp. 409–416. Springer, Heidelberg (2018). https://doi.org/10.1007/978-3-030-03769-7_23
6. Dosovitskiy, A., Ros, G., Codevilla, F., Lopez, A., Koltun, V.: CARLA: an open urban driving simulator. In: PMLR 2017, vol. 78, pp. 1–16. PMLR (2017), https://proceedings.mlr.press/v78/dosovitskiy17a.html
7. Esterle, K., Gressenbuch, L., Knoll, A.C.: Formalizing traffic rules for machine interpretability. In: CAVS 2020, pp. 1–7. IEEE (2020). https://doi.org/10.1109/CAVS51000.2020.9334599
8. Fadadu, S., et al.: Multi-view fusion of sensor data for improved perception and prediction in autonomous driving. In: WACV 2022. IEEE, New York (2022). https://doi.org/10.1109/wacv51458.2022.00335
9. Felbinger, H., et al.: Comparing two systematic approaches for testing automated driving functions. In: ICCVE 2019. IEEE, New York (2019). https://doi.org/10.1109/iccve45908.2019.8965209
10. Giannakopoulou, D., Pressburger, T., Mavridou, A., Rhein, J., Schumann, J., Shi, N.: Formal requirements elicitation with FRET. In: REFSQ 2020 (2020). https://ceur-ws.org/Vol-2584/PT-paper4.pdf
11. Giannakopoulou, D., Pressburger, T., Mavridou, A., Schumann, J.: Generation of formal requirements from structured natural language. In: Madhavji, N., Pasquale, L., Ferrari, A., Gnesi, S. (eds.) REFSQ 2020. LNCS, vol. 12045, pp. 19–35. Springer, Heidelberg (2020). https://doi.org/10.1007/978-3-030-44429-7_2
12. Hartjen, L., Philipp, R., Schuldt, F., Friedrich, B.: Saturation effects in recorded maneuver data for the test of automated driving. 13. Uni-DAS e.V. Workshop Fahrerassistenz und automatisiertes Fahren pp. 74–83 (2020). https://www.uni-das.de/images/pdf/fas-workshop/2020/FAS_2020_HARTJEN.pdf
13. ISO Central Secretary: Road vehicles - functional safety - part 1: Vocabulary. Standard ISO 26262-1:2018, International Organization for Standardization, Geneva, CH (2018). https://www.iso.org/standard/68383.html
14. ISO Central Secretary: Road vehicles - safety of the intended functionality. Standard ISO 21448:2022, International Organization for Standardization, Geneva, CH (2022). https://www.iso.org/standard/77490.html
15. Jafer, S., Chhaya, B., Durak, U.: Graphical specification of flight scenarios with aviation scenario definition language (ASDL). In: AIAA Modeling and Simulation Technologies Conference. American Institute of Aeronautics and Astronautics (2017). https://doi.org/10.2514/6.2017-1311
16. Johannsen, C., Kempa, B., Jones, P.H., Rozier, K.Y., Wongpiromsarn, T.: Impossible made possible: encoding intractable specifications via implied domain constraints. In: Cimatti, A., Titolo, L. (eds.) FMICS 2023, vol. 14290, pp. 151–169. Springer, Heidelberg (2023). https://doi.org/10.1007/978-3-031-43681-9_9
17. Li, C., Cheng, C.H., Sun, T., Chen, Y., Yan, R.: ComOpT: combination and optimization for testing autonomous driving systems. In: ICRA 2022. IEEE, New York (2022). https://doi.org/10.1109/icra46639.2022.9811794

18. Maierhofer, S., Moosbrugger, P., Althoff, M.: Formalization of intersection traffic rules in temporal logic. In: IV 2022. IEEE, New York (2022). https://doi.org/10.1109/iv51971.2022.9827153, IV 2022
19. Maierhofer, S., Rettinger, A.K., Mayer, E.C., Althoff, M.: Formalization of interstate traffic rules in temporal logic. In: IV 2020., pp. 752–759. IEEE, New York (2020). https://doi.org/10.1109/IV47402.2020.9304549, IV 2020
20. Mariani, R.: An overview of autonomous vehicles safety. In: 2018 IEEE International Reliability Physics Symposium (IRPS). IEEE, New York (2018). https://doi.org/10.1109/irps.2018.8353618
21. Mauritz, M., Howar, F., Rausch, A.: Assuring the safety of advanced driver assistance systems through a combination of simulation and runtime monitoring. In: Margaria, T., Steffen, B. (eds.) ISoLA 2016. LNCS, vol. 9953, pp. 672–687. Springer, Heidelberg (2016). https://doi.org/10.1007/978-3-319-47169-3_52
22. Philipp, R., Zhu, Z., Fuchs, J., Hartjen, L., Schuldt, F., Howar, F.: Automated 3d object reference generation for the evaluation of autonomous vehicle perception. In: ICSRS 2021. IEEE, New York (2021). https://doi.org/10.1109/icsrs53853.2021.9660660
23. Riedmaier, S., Ponn, T., Ludwig, D., Schick, B., Diermeyer, F.: Survey on scenario-based safety assessment of automated vehicles. IEEE Access **8**, 87456–87477 (2020).https://doi.org/10.1109/ACCESS.2020.2993730
24. Rizaldi, A., et al.: Formalising and monitoring traffic rules for autonomous vehicles in isabelle/HOL. In: Polikarpova, N., Schneider, S. (eds.) iFM 2017. LNCS, vol. 10510, pp. 50–66. Springer, Heidelberg (2017). https://doi.org/10.1007/978-3-319-66845-1_4
25. Saberi, A.K., Hegge, J., Fruehling, T., Groote, J.F.: Beyond SOTIF: black swans and formal methods. In: SysCon 2020, pp. 1–5. IEEE, New York (2020). https://doi.org/10.1109/SysCon47679.2020.9275888
26. Schallau, T., Mäckel, D., Naujokat, S., Howar, F.: STARS: a tool for measuring scenario coverage when testing autonomous robotic systems. In: Sangchoolie, B., Adler, R., Hawkins, R., Schleiss, P., Arteconi, A., Mancini, A. (eds.) EDCC 2024. LNCS, vol. 2078, pp. 62–70. Springer, Heidelberg (2024). https://doi.org/10.1007/978-3-031-56776-6_6
27. Schallau, T., Naujokat, S.: Validating behavioral requirements, conditions, and rules of autonomous systems with scenario-based testing. Electron. Commun. EASST **82** (2023). https://doi.org/10.14279/tuj.eceasst.82.1222
28. Schallau, T., Naujokat, S., Kullmann, F., Howar, F.: Tree-based scenario classification: a formal framework for coverage analysis on test drives of autonomous vehicle. https://doi.org/10.48550/arXiv.2307.05106
29. Schallau, T., Naujokat, S., Kullmann, F., Howar, F.: Tree-based scenario classification: a formal framework for coverage analysis on test drives of autonomous vehicles - replication artifact (2023). https://doi.org/10.5281/zenodo.8131947
30. Schobbens, P.Y., Heymans, P., Trigaux, J.C.: Feature diagrams: a survey and a formal semantics. In: RE 2006. IEEE, New York (2006). https://doi.org/10.1109/re.2006.23
31. Scholtes, M., et al.: 6-layer model for a structured description and categorization of urban traffic and environment. IEEE Access **9**, 59131–59147 (2021). https://doi.org/10.1109/access.2021.3072739
32. Schumann, J., Moosbrugger, P., Rozier, K.Y.: R2U2: monitoring and diagnosis of security threats for unmanned aerial systems. In: Bartocci, E., Majumdar, R. (eds.) RV 2015. LNCS, vol. 9333, pp. 233–249. Springer, Heidelberg (2015). https://doi.org/10.1007/978-3-319-23820-3_15

33. Schütt, B., Steimle, M., Kramer, B., Behnecke, D., Sax, E.: A taxonomy for quality in simulation-based development and testing of automated driving systems. IEEE Access **10**, 18631–18644 (2022). https://doi.org/10.1109/ACCESS.2022.3149542
34. The British Standards Institution: Operational Design Domain (ODD) taxonomy for an automated driving system (ADS) - Specification. Specification PAS 1883:2020 (2020). https://www.bsigroup.com/globalassets/localfiles/en-gb/cav/pas1883.pdf
35. Ulbrich, S., Menzel, T., Reschka, A., Schuldt, F., Maurer, M.: Defining and substantiating the terms scene, situation, and scenario for automated driving. In: ITSC 2015. IEEE, New York (2015). https://doi.org/10.1109/itsc.2015.164
36. Velasco-Hernandez, G., Yeong, D.J., Barry, J., Walsh, J.: Autonomous driving architectures, perception and data fusion: a review. In: ICCP 2020. IEEE, New York (2020). https://doi.org/10.1109/iccp51029.2020.9266268
37. Wieringa, R.J.: Single-case mechanism experiments. In: Design Science Methodology for Information Systems and Software Engineering, pp. 247–267. Springer, Heidelberg (2014). https://doi.org/10.1007/978-3-662-43839-8_18

Validation of Reinforcement Learning Agents and Safety Shields with ProB

Fabian Vu(✉), Jannik Dunkelau(✉), and Michael Leuschel

Mathematisch-Naturwissenschaftliche Fakultät Institut für Informatik, Heinrich-Heine-Universität Düsseldorf, Düsseldorf, Germany
{fabian.vu,jannik.dunkelau,leuschel}@uni-duesseldorf.de

Abstract. Reinforcement learning (RL) is an important machine learning technique to train agents that make decisions autonomously. For safety-critical applications, however, the decision-making of an RL agent may not be intelligible to humans and thus difficult to validate, verify and certify.

This work presents a technique to link a concrete RL agent with a high-level formal B model of the safety shield and the environment. This allows us to run the RL agent in the formal method tool ProB, and particularly use the formal model to surround the agent with a safety shield at runtime. This paper also presents a methodology to validate the behavior of RL agents and respective safety shields with formal methods techniques, including trace replay, simulation, and statistical validation. The validation process is supported by domain-specific visualizations to ease human validation. Finally, we demonstrate the approach for a highway simulation.

Keywords: AI · Reinforcement Learning · B Method · Validation · Shielding

1 Introduction and Motivation

Artificial intelligence (AI) and machine learning (ML) [42] are increasingly used to develop software applications. One popular ML technique is reinforcement learning (RL) [31] which also finds use in safety-critical domains such as the automotive domain [27], the railway domain [21], and the aviation domain [24]. Hereby, an *agent* learns to make autonomous decisions within an *environment* to maximize an accumulated *reward*. In a trial-and-error approach, the agent receives a reward as feedback for actions taken based on their observed outcome and uses this feedback to optimize its *decision policy*.

The work of Fabian Vu is part of the KI-LOK project funded by the "Bundesministerium für Wirtschaft und Energie"; grant # 19/21007E, and the IVOIRE project funded by "Deutsche Forschungsgemeinschaft" (DFG) and the Austrian Science Fund (FWF) grant # I 4744-N.

N. Benz et al. (Eds.): NFM 2024, LNCS 14627, pp. 279–297, 2024.
https://doi.org/10.1007/978-3-031-60698-4_16

In the context of safety-critical applications, it is important to *verify* and *validate* an RL agent's learned behavior. As RL agents typically are black boxes, their decision-making may be unintelligible and hard to reason about. Validation and verification of RL agents is thus an ongoing research topic [6,14,34]. *Safety shields* [4] is a runtime monitoring and verification technique to ensure the safety of RL agents. A safety shield intervenes when a dangerous situation might occur, i.e., its task is to avoid or prevent dangerous situations. Safety shields are related to Sha's concept of "using simplicity to control complexity" [29] where a simpler system monitors and intervenes in a complex system when rules are violated.

This work presents a technique to link a concrete RL agent with a high-level formal model of the B method [2] for the RL agent and its environment with a safety shield. This allows us to run the RL agent in the ProB [16,17] animator and model checker, and use the formal model as a safety shield at runtime. While ProB also supports verification of the formal model via model checking, we focus on the validation of RL agents with other formal methods techniques such as trace replay, simulation, and statistical validation. With trace replay, it is possible to re-play a single execution run to reason about the RL agent's decisions. Trace replay also checks whether an execution run is feasible; thus, one can validate whether a safety shield has out-ruled a dangerous situation. Using SimB [38], one can run the RL agent in ProB in real-time, or as Monte Carlo simulation. Based on multiple simulated runs, one can apply statistical validation such as computing the likelihood of violating certain properties, and estimating probabilities, averages, and sums. Finally, we demonstrate the applicability and efficacy of this methodology in a highway environment [15]. In this context, we evaluate how safety shields in this work improve the safety and the achieved reward for the RL agent. We also use the insights gained from this technique, to improve the safety shield and the reward function.

2 Background

The B Method. The B method [2] is a formal method for specifying and verifying software systems. The B language is based on set theory and first-order logic, and makes use of *general substitution* for state modifications as well as *refinement calculus* to model *state machines* at various levels of abstraction.

Within a B model, the modeler has to specify an `INVARIANT` clause which contains a predicate to provide typing for variables and define (safety) properties which must be fulfilled in each state of the model. The `INITIALISATION` contains substitutions (also

Listing 1. B Model for Coin Toss

```
MACHINE CoinToss
SETS Side = {Heads, Tails, None}
VARIABLES lastToss
INVARIANT lastToss ∈ Side
INITIALISATION lastToss := None
OPERATIONS
  toss = lastToss :∈ {Heads, Tails}
END
```

called statements) to describe the model's initial states, assigning values to each machine variable. Within the `OPERATIONS` clause, a modeler can specify operations with respective *guards* and substitutions. When the guard is true, the operation's substitution can be executed by modifying the model's current state. Listing 1 shows a simple B model for a coin toss with an operation `toss` that chooses between `Heads` and `Tails` non-deterministically.

In this paper, we use established tools from the B landscape, namely ProB and SimB. ProB [16,17] is an animator, constraint solver, and model checker for formalisms such as B, Event-B, TLA$^+$ or CSP. It provides capabilities such as animation, trace replay [5], simulation [38], and different model checking techniques [13,23] to *verify* and *validate* formal models. SimB [37,38] is a simulator with support for timing, probabilities, and live user interaction. SimB also provides statistical validation techniques such as hypothesis testing and value estimation for probabilities, averages, and sums.

Reinforcement Learning. Reinforcement Learning [31] is a machine learning paradigm in which an agent learns to maximize a cumulative reward function via a feedback loop with its *environment* in a trial-and-error manner. The agent interacts with its environment through a set of available actions which can alter the environment's state. The respective actions are chosen via a gradually learned *policy* which dictates the agent's decision-making process. The benefits of actions are quantified by a *reward* function evaluated in the successor states. By estimating the *value* (i.e. predicted long-term reward) of actions, instead of only the immediate reward of the next state, a policy can make short-term trade-offs which lead to higher long-term rewards.

In this work, we use the Deep Q-Network (DQN) algorithm [20] which mixes deep learning with Q learning [40]. Given a state-action pair (s, a), the idea behind Q learning revolves around learning an action-value function $Q(s, a)$ that estimates the long-term value of executing action a in state s [31]. In the DQN algorithm, the learning of the Q function is done by a deep neural network [20].

Safety Shields. Safety shields [4] is a formal technique to ensure the safety of an agent at runtime. More precisely, the agent is surrounded by a *safety shield* which intervenes to prevent/avoid dangerous actions. Safety shields align with Sha's concept of "using simplicity to control complexity" [29] where a simpler system monitors and enforces properties/rules in a complex system. Two techniques are pre-shielding and post-shielding [12]. In the pre-shielding approach, actions are shielded before execution and then provided to an RL agent to choose the next action from. In post-shielding, actions are corrected to safe ones when the agent's decisions are considered unsafe. In shield synthesis [12] the safety shield is synthesized via training from the underlying environment and RL agent.

The Highway Environment. The highway environment [15] is an available environment for training RL agents to navigate a particular vehicle on a highway. We refer to that vehicle as the *ego vehicle*. The observed environment contains positional information (x/y-coordinate) and velocities (in x/y direction) of all

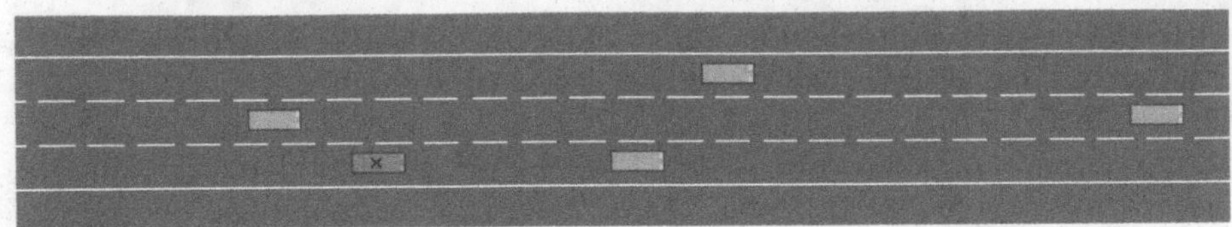

Fig. 1. Screenshot from the highway environment. The green box (manually marked with an X, on the bottom line to the left) represents the ego vehicle controlled by the RL agent, while the blue boxes are surrounding vehicles. (Color figure online)

vehicles. There is information about whether the ego vehicle has crashed, and the reward resulting from the current state. Hereby, the reward function favors driving fast and on the right-most lane. The environment is simulated in a frequency of one frame per second, following the default configuration. Hence, each second the RL agent observes the current state and reacts accordingly. As the goal is to learn a policy which lets the ego vehicle drive fast and collision-free, the agent has to learn when to accelerate or decelerate, and when to switch lanes to keep momentum. The agent's action space consists of 5 actions: `IDLE`, `LANE_LEFT`, `LANE_RIGHT`, `FASTER`, and `SLOWER`. Figure 1 displays a visualization of an exemplary environment state.

3 Formal Models for Reinforcement Learning Agents

This section presents a technique to use formal models for the validation of RL agents. Based on a trained RL agent, a modeler creates a formal model which captures the RL agent's actions/decisions, and the environment's state. In this work, we do not formally model the internal decision-making process of the RL agent. This means that the decisions are still made by the RL agent, while its decision and the resulting environment's state are synchronized with the formal model. Adding the agent's actions as machine operations in the formal model, we can also define rules in the formal model to use it as a safety shield (discussed in detail in Sect. 3.2).

Figure 2 illustrates the interaction between the formal model and the RL agent with Shielding. During the RL agent's runtime, there is a sensor capturing the RL agent's environment. The environment is updated in the formal model and the RL agent accordingly. At runtime, the formal model is used to compute the set of actions that are considered to be safe, which is then passed to the RL agent. From these safe actions, the RL agent then chooses the one with the highest estimated long-term reward. This action is then executed in the environment.

Using a formal model at runtime gives us the ability to apply formal method tools and techniques to the RL agent. This enables us to evaluate and uncover weaknesses in the reward function and (possible) safety shields. Furthermore, this work is not limited to RL, but caters to other AI and real-time systems.

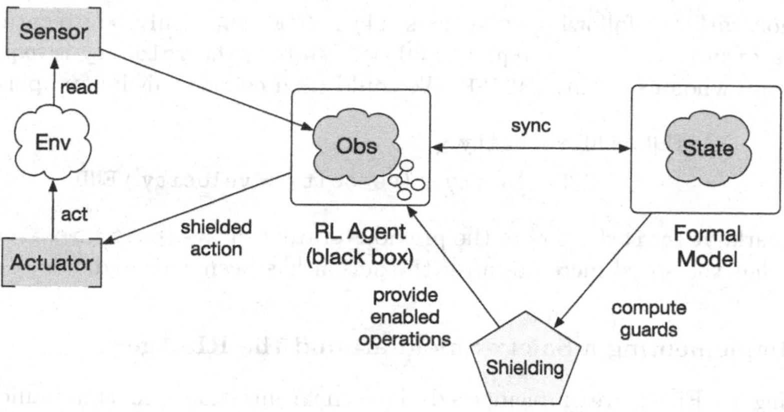

Fig. 2. Interaction between Formal Model, RL Agent with Shielding, and the Environment; shielding process works similarly to pre-shielding [12].

3.1 Creation of the Formal Model

The formal B model contains (1) the current state of the environment, and (2) the agent's actions. The environment's current state is represented using *sets*, *constants*, and *variables* in the formal model.

Let us assume that the RL agent can execute the actions $a_1, \ldots, a_m$. For each action a_j with $j \in \{1, \ldots, m\}$, we introduce a respective operation o_j which consists of a guard g_{o_j} and a state-altering substitution s_{o_j}:

$$o_j = \texttt{PRE}\ g_{o_j}\ \texttt{THEN}\ s_{o_j}\ \texttt{END}$$

Each operation's guard g_{o_j} defines whether the operation is considered safe for execution; we use this to encode a safety shield. The guards must hence be encoded in such a way that at least one operation is always enabled. Otherwise, the agent runs at risk of being unable to act at all in certain cases, as it will only be able to execute actions with their corresponding guards enabled. This property can be checked by techniques that are made available in this work.[1] Within the substitution s_{o_j}, the variables are assigned to a possible value wrt. their expected domain. The `INITIALISATION` substitution is encoded similarly. With this encoding, it is also possible to validate the implementation of the RL agent. Let us assume that v_i is a variable whose value changes after executing an action o_j. Within s_{o_j}, one could then encode:

- an assignment by value *val* ($v_i := val$),
- a non-deterministic assignment via a domain set S ($v_i :\in S$), or
- a non-deterministic assignment via a domain predicate P ($v_i :| (P)$).

Let us assume that we create a formal B model for the highway environment in Sect. 2 using a variable `velocity`. Assume we would like to encode a `FASTER`

[1] Cf. relative deadlock freedom [1, Chapter 14] for a proof-based approach.

operation with the following conditions: (1) `FASTER` shall only be executable if the `velocity` is less than or equal to 30 m/s, and (2) the `velocity` is expected to increase when executing `FASTER`. We could then encode this by an operation:

$$\texttt{FASTER} = \texttt{PRE velocity} \leq 30$$
$$\texttt{THEN velocity} :| (\texttt{velocity} > \texttt{velocity}') \texttt{ END}$$

Remark: $\texttt{velocity}'$ refers to the previous state; thus, $\texttt{velocity} > \texttt{velocity}'$ means that the speed increases after the action has been executed.

3.2 Implementing a Safety Shield around the RL Agent

Referring to Fig. 2, we implemented the synchronization and communication (including shielding) between the formal model and the RL agent in ProB and SimB. The simulation is done by the RL agent and synchronized with the simulation in ProB and SimB. As mentioned before, the formal B model encodes safety shields in the operations' guards to apply pre-shielding [12]. The decision process with shielding is illustrated in Fig. 3. For each executed action, the following steps are performed:

1. The current state of the environment and the last executed action is captured by the RL agent, and provided to ProB.
2. ProB synchronizes the internal state of the animated formal model to match the current observation provided by the environment. Based on the encoding of the operations (discussed in Sect. 3.1), ProB also checks that the target state matches the desired effect of the provided action.
3. Based on the current state, ProB computes enabled operations by evaluating their guards. Actions where the guard is violated in the current state are deemed unsafe.
4. ProB provides a list of enabled operations to the RL agent.[2]
5. Based on the current observation, the RL agent predicts the enabled operation/action with the highest reward.
6. The chosen action is subsequently executed by an actuator.
7. The environment changes according to the action and the respective reward is computed.

Referring to the highway environment in Sect. 2, an example of the shielding process in Fig. 3 could be as follows: First, the RL agent observes the environment containing other vehicles and provides the information to ProB. Second, ProB computes `SLOWER` and `LANE_LEFT` as operations that are considered to be safe and provides the shielded actions to the RL agent. Finally, the RL agent executes the enabled action with the highest reward which can be `SLOWER`, for example. The environment updates accordingly, and the reward is returned to the RL agent. Without a safety shield, the RL agent could predict `FASTER` with the highest reward and execute the action although it could be evaluated as unsafe.

[2] Note that at least one operation must always be enabled as discussed before.

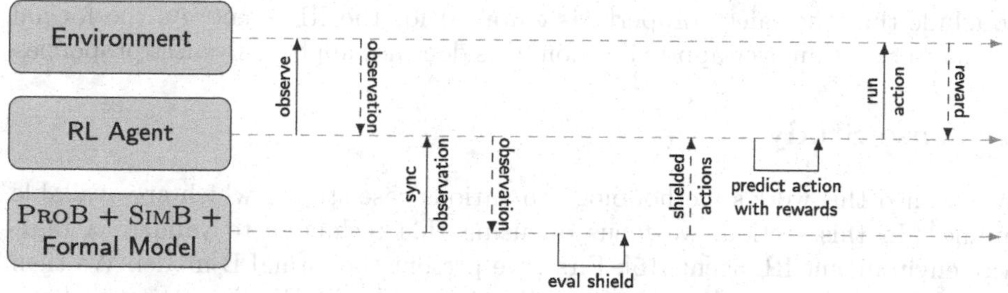

Fig. 3. Shielding the RL Agent with a Formal Model. The general control loop captures the current environmental state over which a set of enabled actions are computed by ProB, matching the safety shield's specification. The RL agent chooses the enabled action which has the highest reward for execution.

Section 4 shows that manually encoded safety shields can improve the RL performance over unshielded agents. However, we do not promote manually encoded shields but rather demonstrate the possibility of using a formal specification as a shield. In cases where this is not suitable, we recommend the synthesis of safety shields based on safety guarantees instead [12].

3.3 Validatability and Verifiability

This work facilitates simulating and reasoning about the RL agents' execution runs, despite their black-box nature. Based on a single execution run, one can evaluate the behavior with trace replay. If the agent behaves correctly in a critical situation, we can understand which decisions were particularly important. We can also assess errors leading to a safety-critical situation. With trace replay, one can evaluate which dangerous scenarios are avoided by safety shields. If the execution of an operation in a trace is blocked by a safety shield, the safety shield was effective in avoiding this particular dangerous scenario.

Given multiple execution runs, one can apply statistical validation techniques, e.g., estimation of certain values (probabilities, averages, and sums) and the likelihood of certain properties. This allows us to validate the choice of the reward function as well as the behavior and impact of safety shields.

By encoding expected domains for the variables' values after executing an operation, this work allows us to validate the implementation of the RL agent. We can also validate that the RL agent and its environment match the encoded domains. Consequently, the formal model together with the encoded safety shield can be seen as an over-approximation of the RL agent and its environment. In the future, we intend to use those validated domains as assumptions to (1) prove the formal model under these assumptions, and (2) also restrict the state space to make model checking easier to apply. With these techniques, one could then check safety properties (including invariants) on the formal model. When the formal model, and thus also the safety shield fulfill the safety property, one can conclude that the safety property is enforced for the RL agent. As the formal model works as an over-approximation, this does not apply to liveness properties.

4 Case Study

We applied this work's methodology to various case studies which are available online[3]. In this section, we focus on using this technique to validate a highway environment RL agent [15]. First, we present the formal B model. We then describe how we train the agent, and how we apply SIMB's simulation and statistical validation. We then apply trace replay, and domain-specific visualization to reason about the agent's decisions.

4.1 Formal B Model for Highway Environment

In the formal B model, we define variables storing the set of present vehicles (`PresentVehicles`), and total functions mapping each vehicle to its respective x and y-coordinates (`VehiclesX`, `VehiclesY`), and its velocities (`VehiclesVx`, `VehiclesVy`) and accelerations (`VehiclesAx`, `VehiclesAy`) in x and y-directions. The accelerations are computed from the current and previous observations wrt. the elapsed time between these two observations (one second). To make the formal model easier to understand, we define a set of `Vehicles` which includes the `EgoVehicle`. We further introduce a `Crash` and a `Reward` variable for validation purposes. Note that the encoding of the formal model in this section differs from the more abstract illustration described in Sect. 3.1.

Table 1. Encoding of Shield for Highway Agent

Action	Disabling Condition (Guard)
`LANE_LEFT`	Action is not executable if there is a vehicle on a lane further left which (1) is between 10 m and 30 m in front and drives slower (2) is between 10 m behind and 10 m in front (3) is between 10 m and 20 m behind and drives faster
`LANE_RIGHT`	Action is not executable if there is a vehicle on a lane further right which (1) is between 10 m and 30 m in front and drives slower (2) is between 10 m behind and 10 m in front (3) is between 10 m and 20 m behind and drives faster
`FASTER`	Action is not executable if distance to front vehicle is less than 40 m
`IDLE`	Action is not executable if distance to front vehicle is less than 30 m
`SLOWER`	Action is not executable if distance to front vehicle is less than 10 m and (1) `LANE_LEFT` is enabled or (2) `LANE_RIGHT` is enabled

[3] https://github.com/hhu-stups/reinforcement-learning-b-models.

Listing 2. `FASTER` Operation in B Model for Highway Environment; each vehicle's position corresponds to its center, each vehicle's length is 5 m, each vehicle's width is 2 m; therefore we encode $[0.0, 45.0]$ in x-direction and $[-3.5, 3.5]$ in y-direction to formulate that the distance to the vehicle in front is less than 40 m.

```
1  FASTER =
2  PRE
3    EgoVehicle ∈ dom(VehiclesVx) ∧
4    ¬(∃v. (v ∈ PresentVehicles \ {EgoVehicle} ∧
5    VehiclesX(v) > 0.0 ∧ VehiclesX(v) < 45.0  ∧
6    VehiclesY(v) < 3.5 ∧ VehiclesY(v) > -3.5))
7  THEN
8    Crash :∈ BOOL ||
9    PresentVehicles :| (PresentVehicles ∈ ℙ(Vehicles) ∧
10     EgoVehicle : PresentVehicles) ||
11   VehiclesX :∈ Vehicles → ℝ ||
12   VehiclesY :∈ Vehicles → ℝ ||
13   VehiclesVx :| (VehiclesVx ∈ Vehicles → ℝ ∧
14     (Crash = FALSE ⟹
15     VehiclesVx(EgoVehicle) ≥
16     VehiclesVx'(EgoVehicle) - 0.05)) ||
17   VehiclesVy :∈ Vehicles → ℝ ||
18   VehiclesAx :| (VehiclesAx ∈ Vehicles → ℝ ∧
19     (Crash = FALSE ⟹ VehiclesAx(EgoVehicle) ≥ -0.05)) ||
20   VehiclesAy :∈ Vehicles → ℝ ||
21   Reward :∈ ℝ
22 END
```

Corresponding to the agent's action space, we encoded 5 actions into the formal B model: `IDLE`, `LANE_LEFT`, `LANE_RIGHT`, `FASTER`, and `SLOWER`. Table 1 shows the description of the guards for all operations that we use as safety shield in our experiments. The `SLOWER` action is guaranteed to be enabled if no other guard would hold. Listing 2 shows the `FASTER` operation in our formal model with a safety shield. The guard (see lines 3–6) for shielding the `FASTER` action states that `FASTER` is not enabled if the distance to the vehicle in front is less than 40 m. As each vehicle's position corresponds to its center, and its length is 5 m, we encode 45 m in the formula. In lines 13–16, we encode that the expected speed remains the same or increases with a tolerance of –0.05 m/s. Likewise, the acceleration should be positive with the same tolerance (see lines 18–19).

4.2 Training the Agents

We compare two trained DQN agents for the environment, both are trained over the `highway fast-v0` environment with three lanes. The first agent uses default configurations for the environment and the reward function. We will refer to this agent as Base agent. The reward function rewards the agent based on the resulting environment state caused by its last action. The environment's default rewards are –1 for a collision, 0.1 when the agent is on the right-most lane, and 0.0–0.5 for a speed between 20–30 m/s (linearly scaled over the speed interval).

As it turned out, the agent's driving behavior proved to be rather risky, preferring speed over collision avoidance in certain cases and thus ending up with a high collision rate of almost 60 % (see Table 3). In response, we changed the penalty for collisions from –1 to –2. We also adjusted the reward for driving on the right-most lane from 0.1 to 0.2 to further the desired behavior of prioritizing the right-most lane. The agent trained with this altered reward function will be referred to as HIGHER PENALTY.

For the DQN, we used a neural network with two hidden layers of 256 neurons each and a learning rate of 0.0005. The discount factor was set to 0.9 which affects the value of future rewards [31]: A reward received in k steps will only be 0.9^{k-1} times as valuable as if received immediately. The exploration rate decayed linearly from 1.0 to 0.05 within the first 6000 of a total of 20,000 training steps, indicating the ratio of actions which are taken randomly rather than following the thus far learned policy. This randomness is meant to overcome local maxima in the learned policy by regularly bypassing greedy behavior. The agents were each trained within 15 min.

4.3 Statistical Validation

Now, we apply SIMB's statistical validation techniques to validate safety properties for the highway agent. For this, we evaluate 1000 execution runs per agent, once with and without a safety shield. We choose an episode length of 60 s for each run with a frequency of one observation per second. An episode might end earlier than 60 s if an accident occurs.

To estimate the RL agents' quality, we first gathered statistics over the resulting traces to get a feeling for how well the agents act in the first place. We measured averages of episode length, speed, distance traveled per episode, time on the right lane per episode, and reward. The results are shown in Table 2. One can see that HIGHER PENALTY increases the average episode length to over 53 s, an increase of 14 s (+36.5 %) to BASE. This indicates that the higher penalty was indeed a sensible choice. Further, we already see the benefits of shielding.

Table 2. Estimation of Average Values, Application of SIMB Validation Techniques, and the Result of Validation; Values represent average metric values with standard deviation.

Metric	BASE		HIGHER PENALTY	
	no shield	with shield	no shield	with shield
Episode Length	38.85 ± 22.41	56.71 ± 11.47	53.02 ± 15.32	59.16 ± 5.54
Velocity [m/s]	23.37 ± 2.17	21.49 ± 0.94	21.14 ± 0.79	20.95 ± 0.63
Distance [m]	876.35 ± 477.62	1213.30 ± 244.48	1117.18 ± 321.71	1238.04 ± 122.12
On Right Lane [s]	31.69 ± 22.29	42.26 ± 20.51	47.07 ± 17.85	48.73 ± 17.52
Total Reward	30.41 ± 17.39	42.88 ± 8.86	39.90 ± 11.77	44.20 ± 4.42

Table 3. Safety Properties, Application of SIMB Validation Techniques, and the Result of Validation. Percentages represent ratio of measured traces fulfilling the safety property.

Safety Property		BASE		HIGHER PENALTY	
		no shield	with shield	no shield	with shield
SAF1:	The agent must avoid collisions with other vehicles	45.4 %	91.8 %	78.5 %	97.4 %
SAF2:	The agent must drive faster than 20 m/s	93.4 %	91.4 %	76.9 %	83.0 %
SAF3:	The agent must drive slower than 30 m/s	95.2 %	98.8 %	100.0 %	100.0 %
SAF4:	The agent should decelerate at a maximum of 5 m/s^2	100.0 %	100.0 %	100.0 %	100.0 %
SAF5:	The agent should accelerate at a maximum of 5 m/s^2	100.0 %	100.0 %	100.0 %	100.0 %
SAF6:	To each other vehicle, the agent should keep a lateral safety distance of at least 2 m and a longitudinal safety distance of at least 10 m	6.4 %	49.2 %	41.6 %	70.5 %

Table 3 lists the safety properties we validated with SIMB and the corresponding results for both agents with and without safety shields. The safety properties **SAF1**–**SAF6** cover the following aspects:

- **SAF1** is the main property and states that the agent must avoid collisions with other vehicles.
- **SAF2** and **SAF3** check that the agent drives with an appropriate speed.
- **SAF4** and **SAF5** check that the agent does not change speed by acceleration or braking abruptly.
- **SAF6** check that the agent should maintain appropriate distances from other cars to have enough room for reactions when accelerating, braking, and switching lanes.

Note that the validation objectives are not necessarily favored by the reward function, i.e., the agent is unaware of these specifications. For instance, **SAF6** is not rewarded during training. We intentionally validate untrained properties to show how the approach might capture such instances.

When evaluating **SAF1**, we found that the RL agent causes significantly fewer accidents if it is penalized more severely for accidents during training. We are also able to reduce the accident rate by encoding a safety shield. Especially for BASE, the accident rate with a safety shield could be reduced to be safer than HIGHER PENALTY without a safety shield. Despite the safety shield, collisions still occur in HIGHER PENALTY. From the corresponding simulated traces, our technique discovered that almost all scenarios with collisions consist of the ego vehicle approaching another vehicle in front while performing `SLOWER` and driving at the set minimum speed of 20 m/s: the front vehicle drives even slower leading to the collision. Our technique also discovered that setting a lower minimum speed, e.g. 19 m/s, is also not an appropriate solution. In this case, the ego vehicle sometimes drives slower than all other vehicles which leads to all other vehicles driving away at the front of the highway. This means the ego vehicle drives alone at the back of the highway without any collisions. There is also another rare scenario leading to a collision (in the experiments it was 1 of the 1000 simulated traces): the ego vehicle collides with another vehicle on the other side of the highway, i.e. the ego vehicle and another vehicle drive in the opposite outer lanes and both switch to the center lane simultaneously.

Driving too slow does not seem to be a factor in crashes (see **SAF2**). Sometimes, the actual speed might be slightly below the desired minimum speed, especially for HIGHER PENALTY. While this seems to work against the environment's specification, we did not correct this with the safety shield, as there might be situations where it is sensible to brake and drive slower. Furthermore, BASE agent sometimes drives slightly too fast, i.e., exceeding the speed limit of 30 m/s (see **SAF3**). As shown in the values for **SAF6**, it seems that maintaining safe distances is significantly more important to avoid accidents rather than exceeding the speed limit. In all four variations, the RL agent never accelerates or decelerates heavily, i.e., **SAF4** and **SAF5** are never violated. This is to be expected as the encoded acceleration range for the agent is [–5,5] by default. Thus, with the validation of **SAF4** and **SAF5**, we also validated the implementation of the RL agent. Relating the validation results to Table 2 again, we see that with safety shields:

- The average speed is slower, but the distance traveled and the average episode length are greater. An interesting result here is that BASE with a safety shield achieves a lower crash rate than HIGHER PENALTY without a safety shield even with a higher average speed.
- The safety distances are maintained more often which seems to be the main reason for fewer crashes. Especially, BASE with a safety shield maintains safety distances better than HIGHER PENALTY without a safety shield.
- The cumulative reward is higher with a smaller standard deviation.
- The agent drives on the right lane more often.

Thus, our results highlight the safety capabilities of the employed shield and how pre-shielding can alleviate shortcomings during training. This helped us to calibrate the reward function better. Note that this work does not demonstrate that the manual encoding of the safety shield is perfect; in the future, we will consider shield synthesis [12]. However, we show that one can use a formal specification as a safety shield and that it achieves better RL performance than without.

4.4 Validation by Trace Replay

Now, we discuss validating the agent's behavior with trace replay, highlighting the role of safety shields. For easier understanding, we employ a domain-specific visualization [41] for the highway environment. We focus on two different, observed scenarios[4].

Figure 4 shows a scenario where the ego vehicle approaches another vehicle and slows down. Here, the agent was able to detect the vehicle in front and brake in time. The safety distance to the vehicle in front is hence kept and an accident could be avoided. Further, the RL agent seems to be aware of another vehicle in the center lane as it decides to slow down rather than switch lane. The scenario shown in Fig. 4 was simulated without safety shields. When re-playing this trace with safety shields being activated, the trace is still feasible. So, in this scenario, the RL agent behaves correctly without intervention by safety shields.

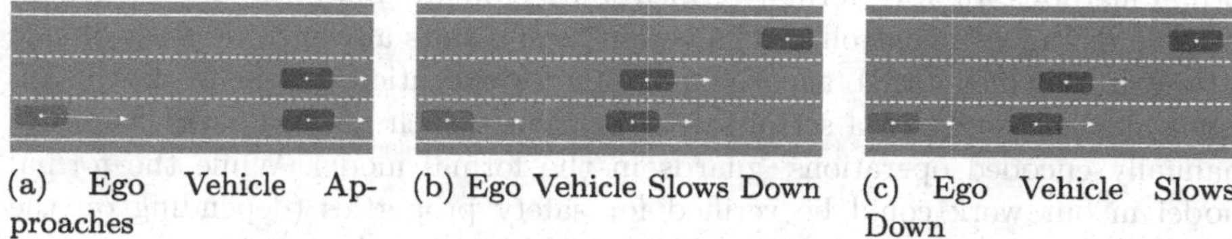

(a) Ego Vehicle Approaches (b) Ego Vehicle Slows Down (c) Ego Vehicle Slows Down

Fig. 4. Example for Approaching Scenario; white arrows show the direction of the velocity vector.

A second scenario is shown in Fig. 5. Here, the agent switches to the center lane while keeping a high velocity. After switching, the ego vehicle has to slow down as it is approaching another vehicle in front. As the agent does not brake in time, it collides with the vehicle in front. This scenario was also simulated without safety shields. When trying to re-play the trace with safety shields, the trace is not feasible anymore, especially when the RL agent tries to execute `LANE_LEFT`. Thus, a collision could have been avoided in this scenario by using safety shields.

Of course, the question of why the agent behaves in the observed manner cannot be answered completely. While the RL agent seems to behave in certain ways that correspond to similar human intuition, there still is no way to properly find reason in the agent's behaviors. This is due to the black box nature of neural networks underlying our DQN approach. While explainable AI methods from research [35] might offer insights, there are no guarantees they may accurately capture black box agents [26] and different explainers might even yield conflicting explanations. These problems with explainable AI emphasize the need for proper validation tools for RL agents, as outlined in this work.

---

[4] A scenario is a sequence of events which alters the system's state. Scenarios as static exports [36] available at: https://hhu-stups.github.io/highway-env-b-model/.

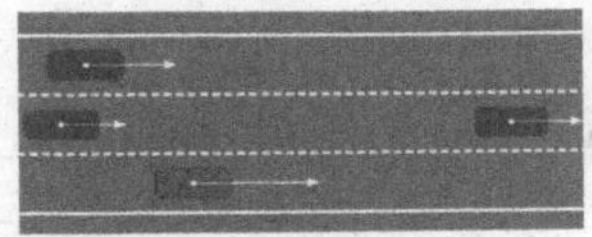

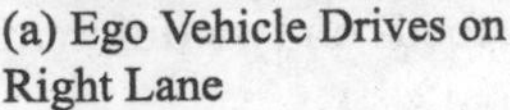

(a) Ego Vehicle Drives on Right Lane

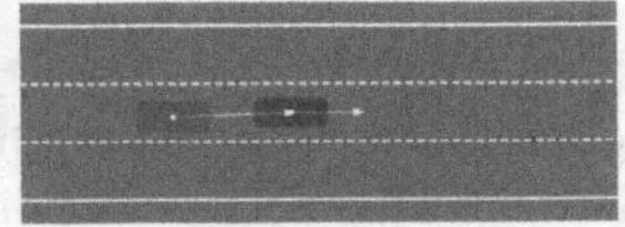

(b) Ego Vehicle Switches to Center Lane

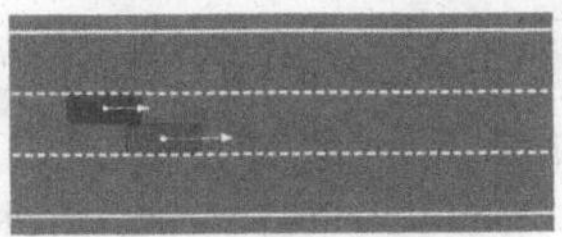

(c) Ego Vehicle Crashes

Fig. 5. Example for Crash Scenario; white arrows show the direction of the velocity vector.

5 Related Work

This section compares this work with other works in the field of formal methods for AI, with a stronger focus on RL.

Justified Speculative Control (JSC) [6] is a technique to achieve safe RL with formal methods. In JSC, formal verification results are obtained and integrated into the RL agent's controller. The verification results also provide a set of safe actions from which an RL agent can choose for execution. In our work, the RL agent also chooses from a set of safe operations which are computed from the manually encoded operations' guards in the formal model. While the formal model in our work could be verified for safety properties (depending on the model's state space), the creation of the shield is driven by requirements rather than verification results. Still, we can detect and avoid dangerous situations.

Sha [29] presented an approach to "use simplicity to control complexity" in which a simpler system monitors a complex system at runtime, and intervenes when certain rules are violated. Sha's concept is independent of reinforcement learning; the given example is about a complex Boeing flight system that was checked for laws by a simple, reliable controller. Based on Sha's concept, Phan et al. [22] presented a *neural simplex architecture* (NSA) for reinforcement learning. The NSA consists of a pre-certified *decision module* which switches between the complex unverified *neural controller* and a verified *baseline controller* if the former tries to execute a potentially dangerous action. Referring to Sha, the RL agent can be viewed as the complex system, and the formal model with the safety shield as the simple controlling system in our work. Furthermore, the safety shield influences every decision for the RL agent as ProB uses the formal model to compute actions that are deemed to be safe.

Shield synthesis [12] is a runtime verification technique which also aims to achieve safe RL. After modeling the environment as a Markov Chain, a shield is synthesized which may take over the agent's decision-making for a (possibly limited) number of steps. The shield acts once the probability of reaching an unsafe state shortly exceeds a given threshold. In our technique, we encoded shields by hand rather than synthesizing them. While the burden of precisely formulating the shielding conditions is now placed on the modeler, we can assume the RL agent's internal decision-making process as black box. However, we do not guarantee that the shield will be returning control to the agent eventually. In shield synthesis, there is also the concept of enforcing temporal properties, especially LTL properties [4]. Assuming that the formal model's state space is finite, one could also use ProB's LTL model checker [23] in our approach, to verify LTL properties on the RL agent (with shielding). When the formal model fulfills a safety property, then we know that this safety property is also enforced for the RL agent. However, this is not the case for liveness properties.

Deep RL is implemented using neural networks for which there are also verification approaches [8,9,28], including techniques such as abstract interpretation [7], SMT solving [10], and proving [25]. Our work mainly focuses on validation and does not yet tackle the challenge of verifying the RL agent extensively. In the future, we should investigate how to achieve and guarantee better safety of RL agents in our approach.

Search-based testing [33] is a technique which uses a depth-first search to find safety-critical states. The RL agent is then brought into a situation close to the safety-critical state to test how well it avoids this state. The technique also applies *fuzz testing* to achieve better coverage of the RL agent's behavior. *Differential safety testing* [32] is another technique to test RL agents for safety, which makes use of automata learning [18,19], probabilistic model checking [3], and statistical methods. With Monte Carlo simulation, our work simulates multiple different scenarios. Based on the resulting execution runs, our work can estimate certain values and compute the likelihood of fulfilling certain safety properties. The results are then used to evaluate and improve the safety shield and the reward function. However, we have not yet navigated the RL agent into critical situations for testing purposes.

Wang et al. [39] presented a safety-falsification method which works as an adversary for the RL agent. The technique uses metric temporal logic formulas to enforce the RL agent to violate safety properties. As these properties are difficult to integrate into the reward function, safety-falsification helps the RL agent to train adversarial behavior. As we do not use a safety shield during training, our RL agents also experience the consequences of bad behaviour in the form of reward penalties.

Shalev-Shwartz et al. [30] presented a formal model for safe behavior of self-driving cars, called responsibility-sensitive safety (RSS). This model was later extended and translated to Event-B [11]. The rules of RSS in general and the Event-B model, in particular, could be integrated as safety shields into our approach in the future.

6 Conclusion and Future Work

This work presented a technique to validate RL agents with formal methods tools and techniques. We create a formal model at a high-level abstraction and link it with the RL agent. This allows to use the formal specification as a safety shield for the RL agent. Furthermore, the formal model encodes the RL agent's expected external behavior, i.e., the RL agent's actions and its environment. It is then possible to apply validation techniques like trace replay, simulation, or statistical validation.

In this work, we successfully demonstrated our technique using the formal B method with the tools ProB and SimB on a highway environment. With trace replay, and real-time simulation, we can replay the agent's situation and reason about its decisions. Here, we also demonstrated that dangerous scenarios are avoided by safety shields in the formal model. Applying statistical validation techniques, we can estimate the likelihood of fulfilling various safety requirements, e.g., the likelihood of crashes or not maintaining safety distances. We also estimate certain values, e.g., the average reward, the average speed, the average distance of one episode, the average time on the right lane of one episode, or the average episode length of the RL agent on the highway. With the gained knowledge, we improved safety shields which again increased safety. Safety shields were effective in reducing the likelihood of crashes at the cost of reducing the average velocity, overall increasing the safety of the model. With the manually encoded safety shields in the formal model, we also achieve higher rewards for the agent. We were even able to validate the reward function, highlighting where we needed to adjust the respective weights. Furthermore, we were able to validate the implementation of the RL agent. All models, including highway environment, are available online at:

https://github.com/hhu-stups/reinforcement-learning-b-models

While our approach enables various validation techniques, verification has yet not been tackled actively. We aim to validate and better understand the RL agent's behavior to collect assumptions about the agent and its environment. Based on this, we plan to verify the model with techniques like model checking or proving. Assuming that safety properties are fulfilled for the formal model, we can also conclude these properties for the RL agent, as the formal model is encoded as an over-approximation of the RL agent. As future work, one could further investigate how our approach can be extended by shielding over LTL properties.

Acknowledgements. We would like to thank Davin Holten for his initial experiments showing the feasibility of ProB's techniques — especially of SimB — for the highway RL agent.

References

1. Abrial, J.R.: Modeling in Event-B: System and Software Engineering. Cambridge University Press, Cambridge (2010). https://doi.org/10.1017/CBO9781139195881
2. Abrial, J.R., Hoare, A.: The B-Book: Assigning Programs to Meanings. Cambridge University Press, Cambridge (2005). https://doi.org/10.1017/CBO9780511624162
3. Aichernig, B.K., Tappler, M.: Probabilistic black-box reachability checking (extended version). Form. Methods Syst. Des. **54**(3), 416–448 (2019). https://doi.org/10.1007/s10703-019-00333-0
4. Alshiekh, M., Bloem, R., Ehlers, R., Könighofer, B., Niekum, S., Topcu, U.: Safe reinforcement learning via shielding. In: Proceedings AAAI, pp. 2669–2678. AAAI Press (2018). https://doi.org/10.1609/aaai.v32i1.11797

5. Bendisposto, J., et al.: PROB2-UI: a java-based user interface for ProB. In: Lluch Lafuente, A., Mavridou, A. (eds.) FMICS 2021. LNCS, vol. 12863, pp. 193–201. Springer, Cham (2021). https://doi.org/10.1007/978-3-030-85248-1_12
6. Fulton, N., Platzer, A.: Safe reinforcement learning via formal methods: toward safe control through proof and learning. In: Proceedings AAAI, pp. 6485–6492. AAAI Press (2018). https://doi.org/10.1609/aaai.v32i1.12107
7. Gehr, T., Mirman, M., Drachsler-Cohen, D., Tsankov, P., Chaudhuri, S., Vechev, M.: Ai2: safety and robustness certification of neural networks with abstract interpretation. In: 2018 IEEE Symposium on Security and Privacy (SP), pp. 3–18. IEEE (2018). https://doi.org/10.1109/SP.2018.00058
8. Huang, X., Kwiatkowska, M., Wang, S., Wu, M.: Safety verification of deep neural networks. In: Majumdar, R., Kunčak, V. (eds.) CAV 2017. LNCS, vol. 10426, pp. 3–29. Springer, Cham (2017). https://doi.org/10.1007/978-3-319-63387-9_1
9. Huang, X., Ruan, W., Tang, Q., Zhao, X.: Bridging formal methods and machine learning with global optimisation. In: Riesco, A., Zhang, M. (eds.) Formal Methods and Software Engineering. ICFEM 2022. LNCS, vol. 13478, pp. 1–19. Springer, Cham (2022). https://doi.org/10.1007/978-3-031-17244-1_1
10. Katz, G., Barrett, C., Dill, D.L., Julian, K., Kochenderfer, M.J.: Reluplex: an efficient SMT solver for verifying deep neural networks. In: Majumdar, R., Kunčak, V. (eds.) CAV 2017. LNCS, vol. 10426, pp. 97–117. Springer, Cham (2017). https://doi.org/10.1007/978-3-319-63387-9_5
11. Kobayashi, T., Bondu, M., Ishikawa, F.: Formal modelling of safety architecture for responsibility-aware autonomous vehicle via event-b refinement. In: Proceedings FM'2023, pp. 533–549 (2023). https://doi.org/10.1007/978-3-031-27481-7_30
12. Könighofer, B., Lorber, F., Jansen, N., Bloem, R.: Shield synthesis for reinforcement learning. In: Margaria, T., Steffen, B. (eds.) ISoLA 2020. LNCS, vol. 12476, pp. 290–306. Springer, Cham (2020). https://doi.org/10.1007/978-3-030-61362-4_16
13. Krings, S.: Towards Infinite-State Symbolic Model Checking for B and Event-B. Ph.D. thesis, Heinrich Heine Universität Düsseldorf, August 2017
14. Landers, M., Doryab, A.: Deep reinforcement learning verification: a survey. ACM Comput. Surv. **55**(14s) (2023). https://doi.org/10.1145/3596444
15. Leurent, E.: An Environment for Autonomous Driving Decision-Making (2018). https://github.com/eleurent/highway-env
16. Leuschel, M., Butler, M.: ProB: a model checker for B. In: Araki, K., Gnesi, S., Mandrioli, D. (eds.) FME 2003. LNCS, vol. 2805, pp. 855–874. Springer, Heidelberg (2003). https://doi.org/10.1007/978-3-540-45236-2_46
17. Leuschel, M., Butler, M.: ProB: an automated analysis toolset for the B method. STTT **10**(2), 185–203 (2008). https://doi.org/10.1007/s10009-007-0063-9
18. Mao, H., Chen, Y., Jaeger, M., Nielsen, T.D., Larsen, K.G., Nielsen, B.: Learning Markov decision processes for model checking. In: Proceedings QFM, pp. 49–63. EPTCS 103, Open Publishing Association (2012). http://dx.doi.org/10.4204/EPTCS.103.6
19. Mao, H., Chen, Y., Jaeger, M., Nielsen, T.D., Larsen, K.G., Nielsen, B.: Learning deterministic probabilistic automata from a model checking perspective. Mach. Learn. **105**(2), 255–299 (2016). https://doi.org/10.1007/s10994-016-5565-9
20. Mnih, V., et al.: Human-level control through deep reinforcement learning. Nature **518**(7540), 529–533 (2015). https://doi.org/10.1038/nature14236
21. Peer, E., Menkovski, V., Zhang, Y., Lee, W.J.: Shunting trains with deep reinforcement learning. In: Proceedings SMC, pp. 3063–3068. IEEE (2018). https://doi.org/10.1109/SMC.2018.00520

22. Phan, D.T., Grosu, R., Jansen, N., Paoletti, N., Smolka, S.A., Stoller, S.D.: Neural simplex architecture. In: Lee, R., Jha, S., Mavridou, A., Giannakopoulou, D. (eds.) NFM 2020. LNCS, vol. 12229, pp. 97–114. Springer, Cham (2020). https://doi.org/10.1007/978-3-030-55754-6_6
23. Plagge, D., Leuschel, M.: Seven at one stroke: LTL model checking for high-level specifications in B, Z, CSP, and more. STTT **12**(1), 9–21 (2010). https://doi.org/10.1007/s10009-009-0132-3
24. Razzaghi, P., et al.: A Survey on Reinforcement Learning in Aviation Applications (2022). https://doi.org/10.48550/arXiv.2211.02147
25. Ruan, W., Huang, X., Kwiatkowska, M.: Reachability analysis of deep neural networks with provable guarantees. In: Proceedings IJCAI, pp. 2651–2659 (2018). https://doi.org/10.24963/ijcai.2018/368
26. Rudin, C.: Stop explaining black box machine learning models for high stakes decisions and use interpretable models instead. Nat. Mach. Intell. **1**(5), 206–215 (2019). https://doi.org/10.1038/s42256-019-0048-x
27. Sallab, A., Abdou, M., Perot, E., Yogamani, S.: Deep reinforcement learning framework for autonomous driving. Electron. Imaging **29**(19), 70–76 (2017). https://doi.org/10.2352/ISSN.2470-1173.2017.19.AVM-023
28. Seshia, S.A., Sadigh, D., Sastry, S.S.: Toward verified artificial intelligence. Commun. ACM **65**(7), 46–55 (2022). https://doi.org/10.1145/3503914
29. Sha, L.: Using simplicity to control complexity. IEEE Softw. **18**(4), 20–28 (2001). https://doi.org/10.1109/MS.2001.936213
30. Shalev-Shwartz, S., Shammah, S., Shashua, A.: On a formal model of safe and scalable self-driving cars. CoRR **abs/1708.06374** (2017). http://arxiv.org/abs/1708.06374
31. Sutton, R.S., Barto, A.G.: Reinforcement Learning: An Introduction. MIT Press, Cambridge (2018)
32. Tappler, M., Aichernig, B.K.: Differential safety testing of deep RL agents enabled by automata learning. In: Steffen, B. (eds.) Bridging the Gap Between AI and Reality. AISoLA 2023. LNCS, vol. 14380, pp. 138–159 Springer, Cham (2024). https://doi.org/10.1007/978-3-031-46002-9_8
33. Tappler, M., Cano Cordoba, F., Aichernig, B., Könighofer, B.: Search-based testing of reinforcement learning. In: Proceedings IJCAI, pp. 503–510 (2022). https://doi.org/10.24963/ijcai.2022/72
34. Tran, H.D., Cai, F., Diego, M.L., Musau, P., Johnson, T.T., Koutsoukos, X.: Safety verification of cyber-physical systems with reinforcement learning control. ACM Trans. Embed. Comput. Syst. **18**(5s), 1–22 (2019). https://doi.org/10.1145/3358230
35. Vouros, G.A.: Explainable deep reinforcement learning: state of the art and challenges. ACM Comput. Surv. **55**(5), 1–39 (2022). https://doi.org/10.1145/3527448
36. Vu, F., Happe, C., Leuschel, M.: Generating interactive documents for domain-specific validation of formal models. STTT (2024). https://doi.org/10.1007/s10009-024-00739-0
37. Vu, F., Leuschel, M.: Validation of formal models by interactive simulation. In: Glässer, U., Creissac Campos, J., Méry, D., Palanque, P. (eds.) ABZ 2023. LNCS, vol. 14010, pp. 59–69. Springer, Cham (2023). https://doi.org/10.1007/978-3-031-33163-3_5
38. Vu, F., Leuschel, M., Mashkoor, A.: Validation of formal models by timed probabilistic simulation. In: Raschke, A., Méry, D. (eds.) ABZ 2021. LNCS, vol. 12709, pp. 81–96. Springer, Cham (2021). https://doi.org/10.1007/978-3-030-77543-8_6

39. Wang, X., Nair, S., Althoff, M.: Falsification-based robust adversarial reinforcement learning. In: Proceedings ICMLA, pp. 205–212. IEEE (2020). https://doi.org/10.1109/ICMLA51294.2020.00042
40. Watkins, C.J., Dayan, P.: Q-learning. Mach. Learn. **8**, 279–292 (1992). https://doi.org/10.1007/BF00992698
41. Werth, M., Leuschel, M.: VisB: a lightweight tool to visualize formal models with SVG graphics. In: Raschke, A., Méry, D., Houdek, F. (eds.) ABZ 2020. LNCS, vol. 12071, pp. 260–265. Springer, Cham (2020). https://doi.org/10.1007/978-3-030-48077-6_21
42. Zhou, Z.-H.: Machine Learning. Springer, Singapore (2021). https://doi.org/10.1007/978-981-15-1967-3

Contract-Driven Runtime Adaptation

Eunsuk Kang[1(✉)], Akila Ganlath[2], Shatadal Mishra[2], Florin Baiduc[3], and Nejib Ammar[2]

[1] Carnegie Mellon University, Pittsburgh, USA
eskang@cmu.edu
[2] Toyota Motor North America R&D, InfoTech Labs, Ann Arbor, USA
{akila.ganlath,shatadal.mishra,nejib.ammar}@toyota.com
[3] Woven Planet Holdings, Tokyo, Japan
florin.baiduc@woven-planet.global

Abstract. For safe and reliable operation, modern cyber-physical systems (CPS) rely on various assumptions about the environment, such as the reliability of the underlying communication network and the behavior of other, uncontrollable agents. In practice, however, the environment may *deviate* over time, possibly violating one or more of these assumptions. Ideally, in these scenarios, it would be desirable for the system to provide some level of guarantee about its critical requirements. In this paper, we propose a *contract-based* approach to dynamically adapting the behavior of a system component in response to an environmental assumption violation. In particular, we extend the well-known notion of *assume-guarantee contracts* with an additional concept called the *weakening operator*, which describes how the component temporarily weakens its original guarantee to compensate for a violated assumption. Building on this type of contract, which we call an *adaptive contract*, we propose a runtime system for automatically detecting assumption violations and adapting the component behavior. We present a prototype implementation of our adaptation framework on the CARLA simulator and demonstrate its feasibility on an automotive case study.

1 Introduction

To ensure critical requirements, systems rely on various assumptions about their deployment environment. For instance, a driving-assistance system in an autonomous vehicle leverages information about its surroundings (e.g., the distance to and the velocity of the leading vehicle) to maintain a safe distance and minimize the risk of collision. Timely and accurate access to this information, in turn, depends on the performance of the underlying communication network and the reliability of the in-vehicle sensors.

In practice, modern cyber-physical systems (CPS) are deployed in a highly dynamic, uncertain environment where one or more of these assumptions may occasionally fail to hold. An inclement weather, for example, may prevent a sensor from delivering accurate information about the surroundings; a congestion in a traffic area may increase the latency of the network and cause a delay

N. Benz et al. (Eds.): NFM 2024, LNCS 14627, pp. 298–313, 2024.
https://doi.org/10.1007/978-3-031-60698-4_17

in message delivery. Ideally, a robust system would recognize a violation of an assumption and respond appropriately by triggering a fail-safe or fail-operational mechanism (e.g., slow down the vehicle or switch to a manual driver control mode in case of a critical sensor failure).

Contract-based design [1] is a systematic, rigorous methodology for the development of CPS. In this approach, a component is assigned a *contract* that describes its properties or behaviors that are expected by other components (e.g., the client of a service). In this paper, we investigate a type of contract called *assume-guarantee (AG) contract*, where a component is assigned (1) an *assumption*, A, that it makes about its environment (e.g., expected condition over its inputs) and (2) a *guarantee*, G, that it promises to the environment. The concept of AG contracts have been leveraged for a number of different use cases, including verification [23], synthesis [9,13], testing [3], and runtime monitoring [24]. Informally, a well-accepted interpretation of an AG contract [1] is that the component promises to provide the specified guarantee *if* the assumption holds (i.e., $A \Rightarrow G$). One limitation of this interpretation is that an AG contract does not say anything about how the component behaves in case of the assumption violation: Under the standard logical interpretation, $\neg A$ implies anything, meaning that the component may choose to behave in an arbitrary manner and still fulfill its assigned contract.

In this paper, we propose the concept of *adaptive contracts*, which can be used to specify how a component responds to abnormal conditions or changes in the environment, in addition to specifying the expected guarantee under the normative environment. Our intuition is that even if the assumption is violated, the component may still be able to provide some level of guarantee, depending on the degree of the violation. To capture this, our approach extends a standard AG contract with an additional element called the *weakening operator*, which describes the level of *weakened* guarantee that the component promises in case of an assumption violation. Given a component with a contract $C = (A, G)$, suppose that the environment fails to satisfy the original assumption A but satisfies a weaker assumption A' (e.g., the latency of the vehicular communication network increases from 50 to 100 ms). Then, the weakening operator ω maps A' to a corresponding *weakened* guarantee G' that specifies the level of guarantee that the component promises to satisfy under A' (e.g., the vehicle maintains a safe distance at a decreased average velocity, thus temporarily sacrificing its performance in response to the increased network latency).

Building on this notion of an adaptive contract, we propose a runtime mechanism for detecting assumption violations and automatically adapting the behavior of a component in response. In particular, given contract $C = (A, G)$, where A and G are expressed using *Signal Temporal Logic (STL)* [17], we demonstrate how the weakening operator can be specified declaratively as a constraint over the *robustness of satisfaction* [7] of the assumption and guarantee. Furthermore, we show how the task of finding G' for given A' can be formulated as a *mixed-integer linear programming (MILP)* problem.

To demonstrate the feasibility of the proposed approach, we have developed a prototype of the contract-based runtime adaptation mechanism on top of the

CARLA simulator [8]. In particular, we show how our approach can be used to specify a contract for an *adaptive cruise control (ACC)* feature (which relies on assumptions about the reliability of the vehicular network) and enable the component to adjust its guarantee dynamically when these assumptions are violated. Our preliminary experiments show that our adaptation method can be used to achieve an acceptable level of safety during assumption violations.

The paper makes the following contributions:

- The concept of an *adaptive contract*, which extends assume-guarantee contracts with the notion of a *weakening operator* that describes how the component should adjust its guarantee in response to an assumption violation (Sect. 4),
- A runtime adaptation mechanism that leverages MILP to automatically adjust component guarantees (Sect. 5), and
- A prototype implementation of the proposed adaptation mechanism on top of the CARLA simulator and its demonstration on a case study involving ACC (Sect. 6).

2 Motivating Example

As a running example, consider an ACC feature inside a vehicle. When activated, this feature is designed to perform two tasks: (1) continually adjust the acceleration of the ego vehicle to maintain a steady *gap distance* to the leading vehicle and (2) reduce the chance of collision by ensuring that the *time-to-collision (TTC)* is always above some safe threshold (e.g., 3 s). Task (2) is fulfilling a safety requirement, while task (1) is intended to achieve an optimal traffic flow. ACC relies on an internal communication network to receive information about the status of the leading vehicle, such as its relative acceleration, relative velocity, and the relative distance ahead with respect to the ego vehicle.

The system designer assigns an AG contract $C = (A, G)$ to describe the specification of the ACC feature, where A states that the network ensures timely delivery of the information about the leading vehicle (with an upper bound on the message delivery time) and G says that ACC will perform the above two tasks, as long as the assumption A holds. Formally, the contract can also be specified by using a specification language such as STL [17]; e.g., $C = (\varphi_A, \varphi_G)$, where $\varphi_A \equiv \Box(\texttt{delay} \leq 100\,\text{ms})$ and $\varphi_G \equiv \Box(\Diamond(\texttt{gapDist} \leq 20\,\text{m})) \wedge \Box(\texttt{ttc} \geq 3s)$. This contract specification could then be used as part of a runtime monitor to ensure that the environment satisfies its assumption, or that the ACC component fulfills its guarantee as expected.

One limitation of an AG contract, however, is that it does not say anything about what the component should do when its assumption is violated; this is left up to the designer to decide, by devising additional mechanisms to handle those situations. Our approach addresses this by augmenting the AG contract with an additional concept, called the weakening operator, that describes how the component should adapt its behavior in response to an assumption violation. For the ACC feature, this operator specifies how the system should adjust its guarantee on the TTC and optimal gap distance when the network experiences a delay. In particular, one possible adaptation strategy is to temporarily increase the gap distance to compensate for the network delay, thus weakening part of its original guarantee (i.e., $\square(\lozenge(\texttt{gapDist} \leq 20\,\mathrm{m} + k))$ for some non-negative value k) but still ensuring safety ($\square(\texttt{ttc} \geq 3s)$).

There are important benefits to including this adaptive behavior as part of a component specification. First, this information can be used as part of a runtime adaptive framework that monitors for assumption violation and systematically adjusts the behavior of the component in response. Second, other components in the system may rely on the guarantee provided by C; when its assumption is violated, it may be useful for C to provide some partial guarantee to those components (instead of completely discarding G). Lastly, an adaptive contract encourages the designer to explicitly consider situations in which assumptions are violated and how to respond to them, which may help improve the overall resiliency of the system.

3 Preliminaries

Contract-based Design. *Contract-based design* is a promising methodology for developing CPS [1] by enabling a compositional, "divide and conquer" paradigm where a system is designed as a hierarchy of components, and verification is done on individual components before being composed to provide end-to-end system guarantees.

In the contract framework [1], a *component* M is a basic unit of a system, characterized by a set of *variables* V and a set of *behaviors* (denoted $beh(M)$) expressed over V. Variables are further classified into *input* and *output* variables: Output variables represent those that the component can directly control (e.g., the acceleration of a vehicle), while input variables are observed from the environment but not directly controllable (e.g., the speed of a surrounding vehicle observed through a sensor). Components can be connected to each other through one or more variables and form a larger, composite system.

An *assume-guarantee contract* C is given by pair (A, G), where A and G are *sets* of behaviors for the assumption and guarantee, respectively. Assumptions and guarantees can be expressed in different formalisms, such as temporal logics (e.g., LTL [20], STL [17]) or state machines. Component M *implements* contract C (denoted $M \models C$) if M satisfies its guarantee whenever the assumption holds, i.e., $A \cap beh(M) \subseteq G$. Contract C is *compatible* if there exists a valid environment for M, i.e., if and only if $A \neq \emptyset$, where $\emptyset$ is the empty set. In addition, C is said to be *consistent* if there exists a feasible implementation M for it.

Signal Temporal Logic (STL). In CPS, the behavior of a component can be captured by real-valued *signals*. Formally, a signal s is a function $\mathbf{s} : T \to D$ defined over a finite or infinite set of time, $T \subseteq \mathbb{R}_{\geq 0}$, to a tuple of k real numbers, $D \subseteq \mathbb{R}^k$. Intuitively, the value of signal $\mathbf{s}(t) = (v_1, \dots, v_k)$ represents the state variables of the system at time t, e.g, v_1 might represent the time-to-collision (TTC) between the ego vehicle and its leading vehicle. For convenience, $\mathbf{s}_i(t)$ denotes the i-th component of the signal at time t (for $1 \leq i \leq k$).

STL [17] is an extension of linear-temporal logic (LTL) [20] that can be used to specify time-varying requirements of a system over real-valued signals. The atomic expression in STL is called a *signal predicate.* A signal predicate μ is a formula of form $f_\mu(\mathbf{s}(t)) \geq 0$, where f_μ is a function from D to $\mathbb{R}$, i.e., the predicate μ is true if and only if $f_\mu(\mathbf{s}(t))$ is at least zero. The overall syntax of an STL formula φ is defined as:

$$\varphi := \mu \mid \neg\varphi \mid \varphi \wedge \varphi \mid \varphi\, \mathcal{U}_{[a,b]} \varphi$$

where $a, b \in \mathbb{R}$, $a < b$, and $\neg$, $\wedge$, and $\mathcal{U}$ are the negation, conjunction, and until operators, respectively. Informally, $\varphi_1 \mathcal{U}_{[a,b]} \varphi_2$ states that φ_1 must hold *until* φ_2 becomes true within time interval $[a, b]$. The operator $\mathcal{U}_{[a,b]}$ can be used to define other temporal operators: $\Diamond_{[a,b]}\varphi := True\ \mathcal{U}_{[a,b]}\varphi$ and $\Box_{[a,b]}\varphi := \neg\Diamond_{[a,b]}\neg\varphi$.

Robustness. Typically, the semantics of temporal logic such as LTL are defined over a *binary* notion of formula satisfaction. STL also supports a *quantitative* notion of satisfaction called *robustness*, which indicates how "close" the system is from satisfying or violating a property. Formally, the robustness of signal $\mathbf{s}$ with respect to formula φ at time t, denoted $\rho(\varphi, \mathbf{s}, t)$, is defined as:

$$\begin{aligned}
\rho(\mu, \mathbf{s}, t) &\equiv f_\mu(\mathbf{s}(t)) \qquad \rho(\neg\varphi, \mathbf{s}, t) \equiv -\rho(\varphi, \mathbf{s}, t) \\
\rho(\varphi_1 \wedge \varphi_2, \mathbf{s}, t) &\equiv \min\{\rho(\varphi_1, \mathbf{s}, t), \rho(\varphi_2, \mathbf{s}, t)\} \\
\rho(\varphi_1 \mathcal{U}_{[a,b]} \varphi_2, \mathbf{s}, t) &\equiv \sup_{t' \in [t+a, t+b]} \min\{\rho(\varphi_2, \mathbf{s}, t'), \inf_{t'' \in [t,t']} \rho(\varphi_1, \mathbf{s}, t'')\} \\
\rho(\Diamond_{[a,b]}\varphi, \mathbf{s}, t) &\equiv \sup_{t_1 \in [t+a, t+b]} \rho(\varphi, \mathbf{s}, t_1) \\
\rho(\Box_{[a,b]}\varphi, \mathbf{s}, t) &\equiv \inf_{t_1 \in [t+a, t+b]} \rho(\varphi, \mathbf{s}, t_1)
\end{aligned}$$

where $\inf_{x \in X} f(x)$ is the greatest lower bound of function $f : X \to \mathbb{R}$ (and sup the least upper bound). The robustness of predicate μ captures the amount by which signal $\mathbf{s}$ at time t is above or below the value of $f_\mu(\mathbf{s}(t))$. For example, consider predicate $\mu \equiv \mathtt{ttc}(t) - 3 \geq 0$, which captures the property that "the TTC between the ego and leading vehicles is at least 3.0 s." If, at time t, the TTC signal is $\mathtt{ttc}(\mathrm{t}) = 1\,\mathrm{s}$, then robustness value $\rho(\mu, a, t) = -2$ indicates that the system is 2.0 s below the desired safe threshold. In the case of robustness of $\Box_{[a,b]}(\mathtt{ttc}(t) - 3 \geq 0)$, it represents the value within interval $[a, b]$ at which the TTC is furthest away from 3.0 s.

4 Adaptive Contracts

While AG contracts are a powerful design and analysis tool, once the component design and corresponding contracts are set, they are sensitive to un-modeled or non-provisioned changes. In particular, an AG contract does not say anything about how the component will behave when perturbations in the environment lead to a violation of the original assumption. These perturbations can be the result of diverse events: hardware failures, frayed wires, unexpected network congestion, or malicious attacks. In isolation, this can have catastrophic impacts depending on the nature of the component, and in a hierarchical structure, the effects may cascade or propagate to other components and the system as a whole.

An *adaptive contract* extends an assume-guarantee with an additional concept called the *weakening operator* (denoted ω), which describes how the component (implementing the contract) responds to a violation of the assumption by the environment. Formally:

Definition 1 (Adaptive Contract). *An adaptive contract C is tuple (A, G, ω), where A and G are sets of behaviors representing its assumption and guarantee, respectively; ω is a function of type $\mathbb{M}_A \rightarrow \mathbb{M}_G$, where $\mathbb{M}_A$ and $\mathbb{M}_G$ are distance metrics for assumptions and guarantees, respectively.*

For a given assumption, A, and the actual behavior manifested by the environment, A' (where A' is weaker than A), let $d_A \in \mathbb{M}_A$ be the distance between A' and A, representing the degree by which the environment violates A. Then, $w(d_A) = d_G \in \mathbb{M}_G$ represents the *maximum degree of weakening* in its guarantee; i.e., the degree by which the original guarantee G may be compromised to a weaker guarantee, G'.

Intuitively, $C = (A, G, \omega)$ is a contract stipulating that any component M implementing C must be designed with a mechanism for providing some level of guarantee even when its assumption is violated. In particular, when A is violated by degree d_A, component M should continue to provide a level of guarantee G' that is no weaker than G by degree $\omega(d_A) = d_G$.

We note a couple of special cases. For some $d_A \in \mathbb{M}_G$ where $d_A \neq 0$, if $\omega(d_A) = 0$ (i.e., no weakening of the guarantee is allowed), any component M implementing C must achieve the original guarantee G even under the assumption violation. If $w(d_A) = \infty$ for some d_A (i.e., the guarantee can be weakened by any arbitrary amount), it means that M needs not provide any guarantee at all when the environment deviates from its assumed behavior by degree d_A. This latter case represents the semantics of a standard AG contract, which leaves unspecified the behavior of the component under an assumption violation.

Realization in STL. The concept of weakening operator ω is general and can be realized through different representations of distance metrics $\mathbb{M}_A$ and $\mathbb{M}_G$. Given our choice of STL as the formalism for specifying A and G, we define ω as a function of type $\mathbb{R} \rightarrow \mathbb{R}$, whose domain and range correspond to the robustness of the satisfaction of the assumption and guarantee, respectively. We define the meaning of the weakening operator for STL-based adaptive contracts as follows:

Definition 2 (Robustness-based Weakening Operator). *Given adaptive contract $C = (\varphi_A, \varphi_G, \omega)$ for STL formulas φ_A and φ_G, and weakening operator $\omega : \mathbb{R} \rightarrow \mathbb{R}$, $\omega(d_A) = d_G$ for d_A, $d_G \in \mathbb{R}$ if and only if the following holds:*

For every signal $\boldsymbol{s}$ and time t, if $\rho(\varphi_A, \boldsymbol{s}, t) \leq 0$ and $-\rho(\varphi_A, \boldsymbol{s}, t) \leq d_A$, then $-\rho(\varphi_G, \boldsymbol{s}, t) \leq d_G$.

In other words, as long as the environment violates its assumption (φ_A) no more than by d_A, any component implementing C must ensure that its guarantee (φ_G) is violated by no more than d_G.

For example, consider contract $C = (\varphi_A, \varphi_G, \omega)$ for the ACC component, where $\varphi_A \equiv \Box(\mathtt{delay} \leq 100\,\text{ms})$ and $\varphi_G \equiv \Box(\mathtt{ttc} \geq 3s) \wedge \Box(\Diamond(\mathtt{gapDist} \leq 20\,\text{m}))$. Suppose that the condition of the network deteriorates and the assumption about the maximum message delay no longer holds; in particular, let us assume that the new observed delay is $(100 + x)ms$ for some $x > 0$. Thus, for signal $\mathbf{s}$ that represents the observed system execution and current time t, $\rho(\varphi_A, \mathbf{s}, t) = -x$.

To ensure safety (i.e., $\mathtt{ttc} \geq 3s$) despite the fact that its information about the leading vehicle may be outdated (by x ms), the ego vehicle must behave more conservatively. To do so, the ACC feature compromises the other part of its guarantee, by maintaining a larger gap distance of $(20 + y)$ meters (for some $y > 0$). With this new behavior, ACC is violating its original guarantee by y; i.e., $\rho(\varphi_G, \mathbf{s}, t) = -y$.

Then, this adaptive behavior of ACC can be represented by $\omega(x) = y$, which informally says that "if the network delay is increased by no more than x ms, then the ACC component will ensure safety with an increase in the gap distance that is no greater than y m".

Specifying the Weakening Operator. As mentioned earlier, the weakening operator ω is a function that maps the degree of an assumption violation (d_A) to the maximum allowed degree of relaxation in the guarantee (d_G). In our approach, ω is specified *symbolically* as a logical constraint R_ω that describes the relationship between variables $d_A, d_G \in \mathbb{R}$ where $w(d_A) = d_G$. Formally:

For every $d_A, d_G \in \mathbb{R}$, $w(d_A) = d_G$ if and only if $R_\omega(d_G, d_A)$ holds true.

Our approach does not prescribe a particular language or type of constraint for specifying R_ω; this will depend on the capability of the underlying reasoning engine to be used as part of the runtime adaptation mechanism. For the particular mechanism that we propose in Sect. 5, we assume that the expressions in R_ω can be encoded as MILP constraints.

Back to our running ACC example, recall that the two parameter values, x and y, correspond to the degrees by which the original assumption and guarantee associated with the contract are violated, respectively. One way to define the relationship between x and y is as follows:

$$R_\omega(x, y) \iff R_1(x, y) \wedge R_2(x, y) \tag{1}$$

$$R_1(x, y) \iff \mathtt{timeToCollision(x)} \geq 3 \tag{2}$$

$$R_2(x, y) \iff 20 + y \leq \mathtt{estLeadingDist(x)} \tag{3}$$

Here, on line (2), `timeToCollision(x)` is an auxiliary function that estimates the time-to-collision between the leading and ego vehicles, taking into account the additional network delay of x ms. On (3), `estLeadingDist(x)` is a function that computes a conservative estimate of the distance between the leading and ego vehicle, assuming that the leading vehicle continually decelerates

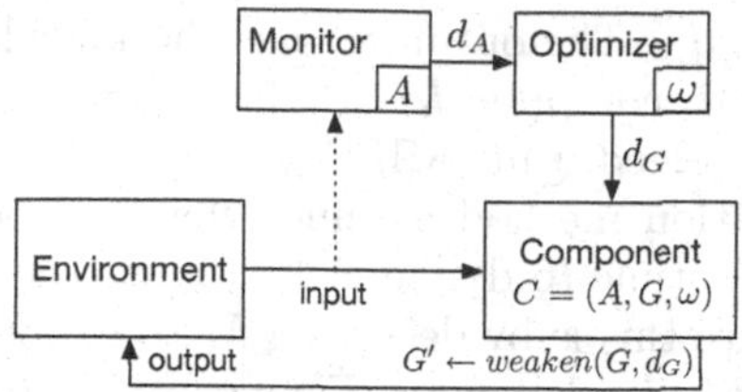

Fig. 1. Conceptual overview of the runtime adaptation framework.

for the time duration x. Due to limited space, we provide the definition of `estLeadingDist(x)` only:

`estLeadingDist(x)`

$$= (\text{leading vehicle displacement}) - (\text{ego vehicle displacement})$$
$$= (dist_l + v_l * x + 0.5 * \texttt{ACC}_{\texttt{dec}} * x^2) - (v_e * x + 0.5 * a_e * x^2)$$

where $dist_l$ is the current distance to the leading vehicle, v_l and v_e are the velocities of the leading and ego vehicles, respectively, a_e is the current acceleration of the ego vehicle, and $\texttt{ACC}_{\texttt{dec}}$ is a constant that represents the lowest acceleration value for the leading vehicle. In addition, $dist_l$, v_l, v_e are designated as input variables (i.e., observed from the environment) while a_e is an output variable (i.e., directly controllable by the ACC component). Given that the ego vehicle has possibly outdated information about the acceleration of the leading vehicle (due to the network delay), the gap distance is estimated by assuming the most conservative value for it (i.e., full deceleration, $\texttt{ACC}_{\texttt{dec}}$).

Constraint R_ω captures how the ACC component weakens its guarantee on the gap distance to compensate for the increased network delay (x) by adjusting the acceleration of the ego vehicle. In particular, larger the delay x is, lower the acceleration a_e will be, to keep the time-to-collision above 3 s. This, in turn, results in the vehicle keeping a larger gap distance—thus, a larger value for y.

5 Runtime Adaptation Framework

In this section, we describe an approach for using adaptive contracts as part of a runtime system that detects a violation of an environmental assumption and automatically adjust the behavior of the component in response.

Runtime Architecture. Figure 1 shows the architecture of our proposed runtime adaptation system, consisting of two major parts: (1) a *monitor* and (2) an *optimizer*. Attached to component M with contract $C = (\varphi_A, \varphi_G, \omega)$, the monitor continuously observes the inputs into M and attempts to detect a violation of the assumption by the environment. In particular, the monitor evaluates the robustness of the satisfaction of φ_A over some sequence of input observations $\mathbf{s}_{in}$; if the violation has occurred, it also extracts the robustness value as the degree of assumption violation, d_A. The optimizer has the knowledge of the weakening operator ω and uses it to compute $d_G = \omega(d_G)$; we describe in the following section how this task is solved using MILP.

Our runtime adaptation method assumes that the behavior of component M can be modified at runtime to dynamically adjust the guarantee that it provides. One way to achieve this is by designing M to expose parameters that can be reconfigured to modify its behavior. For example, an ACC controller may be configured with parameters that represent the expected performance of the vehicle, such as the cruise speed and gap distance [14]; the degree of weakening produced by the optimizer, d_G, could be used to determine the new parameter values. Another way to support dynamic behavior modification is to temporarily override M's behavior with a new sequence of actions to fulfill G'; in the following section, we show how these alternative actions can be synthesized (along with d_G) using MILP.

Finally, when the monitor detects that the environment has resumed satisfying its assumption, the optimizer instructs the component to revert its behavior back to the original one to satisfy G.

MILP-based Adaptation. As stated earlier, when the monitor detects that the environment has violated its assumption by degree d_A, the next step in the adaptation process is to determine how the component should adjust its guarantee; i.e., determine $d_G = \omega(d_A)$. There are different methods to achieving this task, depending on the representation of the operator ω. In this paper, given $\omega(d_A, d_G)$ that is expressed as a symbolic constraint $R_\omega(d_A, d_G)$, we propose a method that formulates this task as a MILP problem.

Our adaptation process produces two outputs: (1) d_G and (2) a sequence of control actions $u_1, ..., u_H \in U$ that the component should execute in order to provide the weakened guarantee. For example, in the ACC example, these actions would correspond to a sequence of acceleration commands that ACC should generate in order to maintain a new gap distance. To produce these outputs, the optimizer carries out a task that is similar to *model predictive control (MPC)* [5], exploring possible sequences of actions over given *prediction horizon* H and evaluating them with respect to the desired property $\varphi_{G'}$. In particular, we adapt the STL-based MPC approach developed by Raman et al. [21], where they also use MILP to generate a sequence of control actions; for details on how to encode STL expressions as MILP, we refer the reader to [21].

Given current system state s_0, prediction horizon $H \in \mathbb{Z}$, predictive model $\mathcal{M}$, and the degree of assumption violation, d_A, the adaptation task is formulated as the following MILP problem:

$$\text{Find } u_1, ..., u_H \in U, d_G \in \mathbb{R} \tag{4}$$

$$\text{that minimizes } d_G \tag{5}$$

$$\text{subject to } R(d_A, d_G) \wedge \tag{6}$$

$$\mathbf{s}' = \mathit{predict}(\mathcal{M}, s_0, [u_1, ..., u_H]) \wedge \tag{7}$$

$$-\rho(\varphi_G, \mathbf{s}', 0) \leq d_G \tag{8}$$

Expressions on (6)–(8) are constraints that must be satisfied by the solution to the variables $u_1, ..., u_H$ and d_G. On (6), $R(d_A, d_G)$ is the constraint that relates the degree of assumption violation with that of guarantee weakening (as described in Sect. 4). Function *predict* on (7) takes model $\mathcal{M}$ and produces a predictive signal, $\mathbf{s}'$, that describes how the system might evolve over the horizon H given a possible sequence of actions $u_1, ..., u_H$. Then, the constraint on (8) states that over this predicted execution, the system must provide a level of guarantee that is no weaker than by d_G.

A predictive model ($\mathcal{M}$) takes the current state of the system s_0 and control action $u \in U$, and produces the next state. Inside *predict*, this model is executed repeatedly over $u_1, ..., u_H$ to produce the predictive signal $\mathbf{s}'$. This model can be specified as a transition system, a dynamical model, or a lookup table [25] that maps each (state, action) pair to the corresponding next state.

Finally, (5) stipulates that the degree of weakening d_G should be minimized. This optimization objective is to ensure that the original guarantee is weakened no more than needed to satisfy the constraints; minimizing this is desirable since in general, weaker guarantees mean a lower or degraded level of functionality.

Example. Recall contract $C = (\varphi_A, \varphi_G, \omega)$ for the ACC component, where $\varphi_A \equiv \Box(\texttt{delay} \leq 100\,\text{ms})$ and $\varphi_G \equiv \Box(\texttt{ttc} \geq 3s) \wedge \Box(\Diamond(\texttt{gapDist} \leq 20\,\text{m}))$. The predictive model $\mathcal{M}$ is specified as a dynamical model that describes how the velocity of the ego vehicle and the distance to the leading vehicle evolve based on a given command for setting the ego acceleration (i.e., the control action u). When the monitor detects that the network delay exceeds the original threshold (e.g., 500 ms), it computes the degree of violation d_A as (500–100) = 400 ms. The optimizer then takes this value and generates the corresponding MILP problem for computing d_G, where $R(d_A, d_G)$ encodes the constraints (1)–(3) from Sect. 4. Finally, the underlying MILP solver computes $d_G = 2$, suggesting that the behavior of the ACC component should be adjusted to maintain a larger gap of 22 m instead of the original 20 m to achieve the safe TTC threshold of 3 s.

6 Case Study

We have developed a prototype implementation of the proposed runtime adaptation framework and applied it to a case study involving a realistic implementation of ACC. We take the component M_{acc} to be the composition of (1) the ACC functions `estLeadingDist`, `timeToCollision` and (2) a proportional-integral-derivative (PID) controller to track the safe relative distance set-point $\texttt{gapDist}_{\texttt{des}}$. The component takes input signals from a ranging sensor (e.g., RADAR), which provides the current relative distance and velocity, and produces an acceleration command generated by the PID controller.

The design goal for M_{acc} is to fulfill the *safety* and *performance* requirements, similar to those described in Sect. 2. In particular, the adaptive contract assigned to M_{acc} is as follows: $C = (\varphi_A, \varphi_G, \omega)$, where $\varphi_A \equiv \Box(\texttt{delay} \leq T)$ and $\varphi_G \equiv \Box(\texttt{gapDist} \geq 5m) \wedge \Box(\Diamond(\texttt{gapDist} \leq 20\,\text{m}))$. Note that for simplicity, instead of

Fig. 2. Test scenario for evaluation of the ACC case study

`ttc` from the running example, we use `gapDist` to specify the safety requirement. We assume that the PID controller has been tuned to enforce these requirements based on expected ranges of `delay`. In our experiments, we allow this network latency to vary outside the design-stage ranges, resulting in a violation of φ_A and motivating the need for contract adaptation.

Recall that the contract guarantee G can be broken into two parts: $\varphi_G \equiv \varphi_{G_{safety}} \wedge \varphi_{G_{perf}}$. Hence, weakening either one of the two requirements would amount to weakening the overall component guarantee. As satisfying the safety requirement are paramount to automotive engineers, we weaken $\varphi_{G_{perf}}$ in favor of $\varphi_{G_{safety}}$ by allowing the ACC component to temporarily increase its tracking distance in response to an increased network delay: $\texttt{gapDist}_{\texttt{des}} \leftarrow \texttt{gapDist}_{\texttt{des}} + \texttt{d}_{\texttt{G}}$; that is, the *runtime adaptation* for the ACC component is realized by adjusting the setpoint of the PID controller.

Implementation in CARLA. The component M_{acc} is implemented as a node in ROS2 [16] and deployed in CARLA [8], a high-fidelity simulator for autonomous vehicles, which serves as the environment for M_{acc}. The component obtains information about the vehicle and environment through simulated sensors and generates throttle commands. The parameters (e.g., `gapDist`) for the ACC component are configurable during runtime. The sensor network delay is implemented by buffering messages before they are delivered to M_{acc}.

In accordance with Fig. 1, the Monitor is realized as a ROS2 node wrapping the Runtime Assurance Monitoring Tool (RTAMT) [19], a software library for automatic generation and deployment of monitors for STL specifications. In addition, the Optimizer is implemented as a ROS2 node wrapping MiniZinc, an open-source constrained optimization toolchain that provides a high-level modeling language for encoding and solving MILP constraints [18].

Experiments. We developed a car following scenario in CARLA as the test environment for our experiments. In this scenario, the leading vehicle starts from rest and tracks a predefined path of length 244 m with a constant speed set-point of 35 m/s. This is enforced by the default PID controllers provided by CARLA for both the lateral and longitudinal dynamics. The ego vehicle starts from rest at a fixed distance behind the leading vehicle, as can be seen in Fig. 2. The lateral control is managed by the default PID controller while the longitudinal control

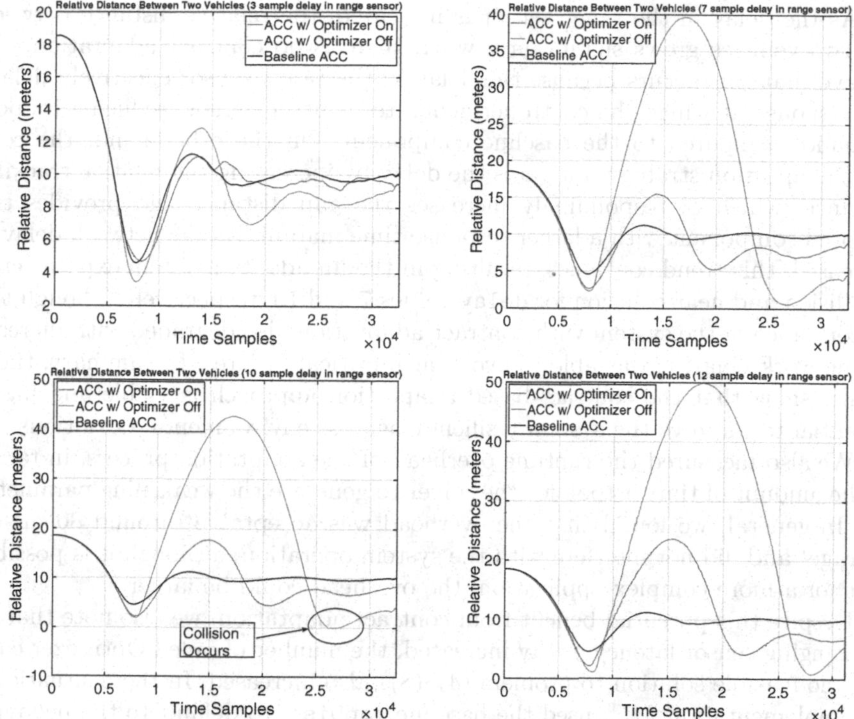

Fig. 3. Relative distance between two vehicles. The controller with and without contract adaptation is shown in red and blue, respectively; the black plot represents the baseline controller behavior without time delay (i.e., adaptation is never triggered). From top left, in a clockwise fashion, the delay samples are 3, 7, 10 and 12. (Color figure online)

is provided by M_{acc} component, which is activated at the start of the scenario. The scenario terminates when the leading vehicle reaches a preset destination at the end of the path.

Experiments were performed by simulating the above scenario under varying amounts of network delay in the range sensor samples; for each `delay`, the scenario was simulated twice, with and without the adaptation enabled (i.e., without the adaption, the ACC component would try to maintain its original set-point, ignoring the delay). Delay was added to the range sensor by buffering the signal by 3, 7, 10 and 12 samples, respectively, for each experiment.

Results. Figure 3 shows the performance of the proposed approach, where the relative distance between the leading and ego vehicles is plotted for the different scenarios. The system performance without contract adaptation is shown in red lines in the plots whereas the performance of the contract adaptation framework is shown in blue. As a reference, the baseline relative distance is shown in black, for where there is no network delay and no contract adaptation (baseline ACC).

As the delay in the range sensor is increased, the relative distance between the two vehicles grows significantly when there is no contract adaptation. We believe that this occurs because the delay in the range sensor effectively delays the response at which the controller generates control signals, reducing its performance compared to the baseline component. On the other hand, the contract adaptation strategy mitigates the delay by increasing the relative tracking distance, which correspondingly increases the gap distance and provides the adapted component with a larger response time margin. As the network delay is increased, this trend continues, resulting in the un-adapted system experiencing a collision and near-collision for `delay` values 7 and 10, respectively. Though the performance of the system with contract adaptation also degraded with increasing network delay, it was able to avoid such critical failures. In summary, these results show that the contract-based adaptation approach is viable and has a potential to improve the system resiliency against environmental deviations.

We also measured the runtime overhead of the adaptation process, in terms of the amount of time it took for the solver to generate the weakening parameter d_G. In general, we found that the overhead was acceptable (around 80 ms on average) and did not interfere with the system operation, although it is possible that for a more complex application, the overhead could be larger.

Despite this potential benefit from contract adaptation, we also note that as the ranging sensor latency `delay` increased, the number of failed Optimizer calls (e.g. no feasible solution to problem (4)–(8)) also increased. In these situations, the implementation M_{acc} used the baseline `gapDist`, to default to the behavior of the system without adaptation. In addition, there was significant variance in the solver computation time when such a solution existed. As part of future work, we plan to further investigate this phenomenon, including the impact of different solvers, solver configurations, and alternative MILP formulations.

7 Related Work

The problem of responding to faulty or unexpected environmental behaviors is not new. One closely related concept is that of *graceful degradation* [10], which refers to mechanisms for maintaining system functionality at a reduced level in presence of an unexpected component or environmental failure. Although this is a well-studied topic, there is relatively little prior work on formal specification of graceful degradation (with the work by Merlihy and Wing [12] being a notable exception but for distributed systems). An adaptive contract can be regarded as a component specification that explicitly indicates the level of degraded functionality that the component can provide under abnormal environmental conditions.

The concept of the weakening operator was in part inspired by the concept of *stability* in control theory [15], which stipulates that bounded disturbances in a system input should result in bounded disturbances in the output. Within formal methods, researchers have proposed definitions of *robustness* (not to be confused with the robustness of satisfaction in STL) that capture a similar concept [2,11, 26]. For example, Bloem et al. propose a notion of robustness that relates the number of incorrect environment inputs and system outputs [2]; Tabuada et al. propose a different notion of robustness that assigns costs to certain inputs and outputs (e.g., a high cost may be assigned to an input that deviates significantly from the expected behavior) and states that an input with a small cost should only result in an output with a proportionally small cost [26]. As far as we know, these works mainly focus on design-stage verification or synthesis rather than leveraging these notions of robustness for monitoring and behavior adaptation.

Self-adaptive systems refer to systems that are capable of dynamically adjusting their behaviors in response to changes in the environment [27]. Among the prior works in this area, closest to our work are those that leverage temporal logics to specify the system requirements to be achieved during adaptation [4,6,22,28]. Requirement relaxation (or weakening) has also been investigated in the context of self-adaptation; most notably, RELAX [28] is a framework based on fuzzy logic that supports specifications of requirements that explicitly capture uncertainty about possible system behavior. RELAX can be used to support self-adaptation mechanisms where the system dynamically adjusts its behavior to accommodate for uncertainty or changes in the environment. One interesting future direction that we plan to explore is to leverage RELAX as another type of requirements specification language (instead of STL) to support contract-based adaptation. The work by Chu et al. [6] proposes a method for weakening component guarantees that is also based on STL, although their goal is to dynamically resolve *feature interactions* (i.e., unexpected conflicts among components), rather than weakening a guarantee in response to an environmental deviation.

8 Limitations and Future Work

We have proposed the notion of an *adaptive contract*, which explicitly captures how a component behaves in response to the violation of an assumption by the environment. In addition, we have presented an approach for dynamically adapting the behavior of the component by leveraging an adaptive contract specified in STL and an encoding of the adaptation task in MILP, demonstrating its feasibility through a car-following case study in the automotive domain.

Although these results show a promise, further research is needed to overcome a number of challenges to make this type of adaptation approach effective under realistic settings. First, the process of solving MILP problems can be computationally expensive and introduce a variable amount of runtime overhead. We plan to explore alternative methods that leverage domain-specific heuristics or offline learning to enable more efficient adaptation. Second, our approach currently assumes that the system is able to satisfy the weakened (as well as the original) guarantees. In practice, however, it is possible for these guarantees to be violated due to a fault within the system; thus, augmenting the type of runtime architecture that we have presented with monitoring of guarantees (in addition to assumptions) is an interesting extension that would provide an additional layer of assurance.

Furthermore, we have only studied the application of an adaptive contract to a single component (e.g., ACC); an interesting follow-up work could investigate how the *composition* of multiple adaptive contracts can enable reasoning about the end-to-end robustness of a system against environmental disturbances. Finally, under certain "good" environmental conditions (e.g., higher than expected network performance), it may be possible to apply a similar type of adaptation to *strengthen* the guarantee (instead of weakening it), to provide an optimal level of system functionality by enabling dynamically flexible component specifications. We plan to investigate a hybrid adaptation framework that is capable of both weakening and strengthening component guarantees.

References

1. Benveniste, A., et al.: Contracts for system design. Found. Trends Electron. Des. Autom. **12**(2–3), 124–400 (2018)
2. Bloem, R., Chatterjee, K., Greimel, K., Henzinger, T.A., Jobstmann, B.: Specification-centered robustness. In: International Symposium on Industrial Embedded Systems (SIES) (2011)
3. Blundell, C., Giannakopoulou, D., Pasareanu, C.S.: Assume-guarantee testing. ACM SIGSOFT Softw. Eng. Notes **31**(2) (2006)
4. Calinescu, R., Grunske, L., Kwiatkowska, M.Z., Mirandola, R., Tamburrelli, G.: Dynamic QoS management and optimization in service-based systems. IEEE Trans. Softw. Eng. **37**(3), 387–409 (2011)
5. Camacho, E., Alba, C.: Model Predictive Control. Advanced Textbooks in Control and Signal Processing. Springer, London (2013). https://doi.org/10.1007/978-3-319-24853-0
6. Chu, S., et al.: Runtime resolution of feature interactions through adaptive requirement weakening. In: IEEE/ACM Symposium on Software Engineering for Adaptive and Self-Managing Systems (SEAMS), pp. 115–125. IEEE (2023)
7. Donzé, A., Maler, O.: Robust satisfaction of temporal logic over real-valued signals. In: FORMATS (2010)
8. Dosovitskiy, A., Ros, G., Codevilla, F., Lopez, A., Koltun, V.: CARLA: an open urban driving simulator. In: Annual Conference on Robot Learning (2017)
9. Ghasemi, K., Sadraddini, S., Belta, C.: Compositional synthesis via a convex parameterization of assume-guarantee contracts. In: HSCC (2020)
10. González, O., Shrikumar, H., Stankovic, J.A., Ramamritham, K.: Adaptive fault tolerance and graceful degradation under dynamic hard real-time scheduling. In: RTSS (1997)
11. Henzinger, T.A., Otop, J., Samanta, R.: Lipschitz robustness of finite-state transducers. In: FSTTCS (2014)
12. Herlihy, M., Wing, J.M.: Specifying graceful degradation. IEEE Trans. Parallel Distrib. Syst. **2**(1), 93–104 (1991)
13. Iannopollo, A., Tripakis, S., Sangiovanni-Vincentelli, A.L.: Specification decomposition for synthesis from libraries of LTL assume/guarantee contracts. In: DATE, pp. 1574–1579 (2018)
14. Kesting, A., Treiber, M., Schönhof, M., Helbing, D.: Adaptive cruise control design for active congestion avoidance. Transp. Res. Part C: Emerg. Technol. **16**(6), 668–683 (2008)

15. Kirk, D.: Optimal Control Theory: An Introduction. Dover Books on Electrical Engineering Series. Dover Publications, New York (2004)
16. Macenski, S., Foote, T., Gerkey, B., Lalancette, C., Woodall, W.: Robot operating system 2: design, architecture, and uses in the wild. Sci. Robot. **7**(66) (2022)
17. Maler, O., Nickovic, D.: Monitoring temporal properties of continuous signals. In: FORMATS, pp. 152–166 (2004)
18. Nethercote, N., Stuckey, P.J., Becket, R., Brand, S., Duck, G.J., Tack, G.: Minizinc: towards a standard CP modelling language. In: International Conference on Principles and Practice of Constraint Programming (CP), pp. 529–543 (2007)
19. Nickovic, D., Yamaguchi, T.: RTAMT: Online robustness monitors from STL (2020). https://arxiv.org/abs/2005.11827
20. Pnueli, A.: The temporal logic of programs. In: Annual Symposium on Foundations of Computer Science (FOCS), pp. 46–57 (1977)
21. Raman, V., Donzé, A., Maasoumy, M., Murray, R.M., Sangiovanni-Vincentelli, A.L., Seshia, S.A.: Model predictive control with signal temporal logic specifications. In: IEEE Conference on Decision and Control (CDC) (2014)
22. Rodrigues, A., Caldas, R.D., Rodrigues, G.N., Vogel, T., Pelliccione, P.: A learning approach to enhance assurances for real-time self-adaptive systems. In: SEAMS (2018)
23. Saoud, A., Girard, A., Fribourg, L.: On the composition of discrete and continuous-time assume-guarantee contracts for invariance. In: European Control Conference, ECC, pp. 435–440 (2018)
24. Sokolsky, O., Zhang, T., Lee, I., McDougall, M.: Monitoring assumptions in assume-guarantee contracts. In: PrePost@IFM (2016)
25. Sundström, C., Frisk, E., Nielsen, L.: Diagnostic method combining the lookup tables and fault models applied on a hybrid electric vehicle. IEEE Trans. Control Syst. Technol. **24**(3), 1109–1117 (2016)
26. Tabuada, P., Balkan, A., Caliskan, S.Y., Shoukry, Y., Majumdar, R.: Input-output robustness for discrete systems. In: EMSOFT, pp. 217–226 (2012)
27. Weyns, D.: An Introduction to Self-adaptive Systems: A Contemporary Software Engineering Perspective. Wiley-IEEE Computer Society, Hoboken (2020)
28. Whittle, J., Sawyer, P., Bencomo, N., Cheng, B.H.C., Bruel, J.: RELAX: a language to address uncertainty in self-adaptive systems requirement. Requir. Eng. **15**(2), 177–196 (2010)

Topllet: An Optimized Engine for Answering Metric Temporal Conjunctive Queries

Lukas Westhofen[1(✉)], Christian Neurohr[1], Jean Christoph Jung[2], and Daniel Neider[2,3]

[1] German Aerospace Center (DLR) e.V., Institute of Systems Engineering for Future Mobility, Oldenburg, Germany
{lukas.westhofen,christian.neurohr}@dlr.de

[2] TU Dortmund University, Dortmund, Germany
{jean.jung,daniel.neider}@tu-dortmund.de

[3] Center for Trustworthy Data Science and Security, University Alliance Ruhr, Dortmund, Germany

Abstract. We present TOPLLET, a software tool for answering Metric Temporal Conjunctive Queries over temporal knowledge bases with ontologies formulated in expressive Description Logics. Its main use case is the formal specification of requirements and their evaluation against test data when confronted with a highly complex operational domain of the system under test, e.g., urban automated driving. It is implemented as a module in the well-established reasoner OPENLLET, which offers good performance in the core reasoning tasks (such as consistency checks) but lacks support for temporal properties. Although the underlying problem of answering queries in the examined logics is ExpTime-hard, this work shows how we practically tackle this theoretical complexity. Despite being the first implementation of the task, TOPLLET already exhibits satisfactory performance due to our optimizations.

Keywords: Temporal Conjunctive Queries · Description Logics · Temporal Logics

1 Introduction

Automated systems are expected to take over increasingly more complex and safety-critical tasks from humans. Accordingly, their operational domains (ODs) grow from a limited set of conditions to highly involved contexts, possibly involving untrained humans interacting with the system. An example is automated driving systems (ADSs), where the OD progresses steadily towards complex

This work was partially funded by the German Federal Ministries of Education and Research ('AutoDevSafeOps') and Economic Affairs and Climate Action ('VVM - Verification & Validation Methods for Automated Vehicles Level 4 and 5').

N. Benz et al. (Eds.): NFM 2024, LNCS 14627, pp. 314–321, 2024.
https://doi.org/10.1007/978-3-031-60698-4_18

urban environments. Demonstrating safety within these ODs can be considered a road block for release. While conclusively proving safety is likely impossible, type approval (demonstrating adherence to regulatory requirements to certified authorities) demands at least partial evidence thereof. A standard approach to demonstrate readiness of a system prior to its release is system-level testing, where requirements are formally specified, the system is run in a test environment, and the requirements are evaluated. This approach requires powerful means of formally specifying and evaluating requirements.

Our tool, TOPLLET, available at https://github.com/lu-w/topllet, provides a solution to exactly this problem: It implements a tailored version of *Linear Temporal Logic over Finite Traces* (LTL_f) over *Temporal Knowledge Bases* (TKBs). The latter allow storing data as unary and binary relations as well as background knowledge about the OD in form of ontologies formulated in *Description Logics* (DLs). Our temporal logic, termed *Metric Temporal Conjunctive Queries* (MTCQs), enables querying this model using LTL_f operators with an interval-constrained until, thus being similar to Mission-Time LTL (MLTL) [11]. We give an informal introduction to TKBs and MTCQs in Sect. 2.

In 2013, theoretical work has proven the underlying problem of temporal querying (over infinite traces) of TKBs with ontologies formulated in expressive DLs to be ExpTime-hard, depending on the DL fragment [1]. In light of practically applicable implementations for reasoning over highly expressive DLs (which is N2ExpTime-complete [10]) we suspect that temporal querying can also be tamed for relevant settings. As of now, the community has however focused on implementing temporal querying over so-called lightweight DLs: Software tools like MeTeoR [15], Ontop-temporal [5], and OptiqueVQS [14] operate on ontologies with restricted expressiveness (OWL2 RL resp. QL) and do not suffice to capture complex ODs. With TOPLLET (presented in Sect. 3) we advance querying TKBs with ontologies formulated in *expressive* DLs towards practice. Section 4 shows promising results of TOPLLET on our benchmarks.

2 Background

We now explain TKBs and MTCQs intuitively by example as to provide intuition about the task that TOPLLET solves. For formal details, we refer to Baader et al. [1] and Westhofen et al. [16]. A typical use case for TOPLLET is requirements for urban automated driving, and our introductory example is concerned with granting right of way to bicyclists or mopeds on crossings. We have three components: a) an ontology, b) temporal data, c) a temporal query.

Ontology. First, we gather relevant background knowledge in our ontology:

1. Crossings are equivalent to everything that connects at least three lanes.
2. Every two wheeled vehicle is a bicycle or moped.
3. Everything that is left of something is also to the side thereof.

In TOPLLET, we can use any DL fragment up to the expressive logic $\mathcal{SRIQ}^{(\mathcal{D})}$ [7] for formalizing ontologies. Specifically, TOPLLET supports the Web Ontology Language 2 (OWL2) [17], which captures a superclass of $\mathcal{SRIQ}^{(\mathcal{D})}$. In the OWL2 functional-style syntax, our example ontology is formalized as:

1. `EquivalentClasses(:Crossing ObjectMinCardinality(3 :connects :Road))`
2. `SubClassOf(:TwoWheeledVehicle ObjectUnionOf(:Bicycle :Moped))`
3. `SubPropertyOf(:toTheLeftOf :toTheSideOf)`

Data. For the data, let us assume a test run yielded a finite time trace. The perception identified five so-called individuals (concrete objects): the system `:s`, a two-wheeled vehicle `:t`, and a space `:c` connecting the distinct roads `:r0`, `:r1`, `:r2`, with `:r0` and `:r1` being orthogonal. Over three time points we further observed:

t_0: `:s` is to the left of and parallel to `:t`, `:s` and `:t` intersect `:r0`;
t_1: `:s` intersects `:r0`, `:t` intersects `:c`;
t_2: `:s` intersects `:r1`.

In TOPLLET, temporal data are finite sequences of non-temporal data. Each element in the sequence represents a discrete time point by assigning classes to and binary relations between individuals.

Query. The final component is the query, representing the requirement: "Anyone who intends to turn on a crossing shall let bicycles or mopeds enter the intersection first if they drive parallel to them." In TOPLLET, we use MTCQs:

```
G # fixes the global types of the answers
(
  (:System(?x) & :Road(?q) & :Road(?p) & :orthogonal(?q, ?p))
  &
  ((:Moped(?y)) | (:Bicycle(?y)))
)
  &
(
  F
  (
    (:intersects(?x,?p) & :toTheSideOf(?x,?y) & :parallel(?x,?y))
      &
    F_[0,20] (:intersects(?x,?q))
  ) # if, somewhen, x turns from p to q with y being parallel to it before
    ->
  ( # then, x has to be on p until y is on the crossing (grant right of
    way)
    (:intersects(?x,?p))
      U
    (:intersects(?y,c) & :Crossing(c) & :connects(c,?p) & :connects(c,?q))
  )
)
```

It uses the temporal operators `G` (globally), `F` (eventually), `F_[a,b]` (interval-constrained eventually), and `U` (until) as well as Boolean operators `&` (conjunction), `|` (disjunction), and `->` (implication). The query asks for individuals `x`, `y` in the data s.t. `x` is a system that, if it is in a crossing situation with a two-wheeler `y` being parallel and to the side of `x`, grant right of way to `y` before turning.

TOPLLET identifies individuals to answer MTCQs over a given TKB. More specifically, it returns exactly those assignments from the answer variables (prefixed by ?) to individuals in the data that guarantee, i.e., under any interpretation, the query to hold in the TKB. For our example, these contain any system and moped or bicycle for which the system granted right of way, if needed. An answer is also valid if no granting is necessary. For the given data, the only answer is $\mathtt{x} \mapsto \mathtt{:s}, \mathtt{y} \mapsto \mathtt{:t}, \mathtt{p} \mapsto \mathtt{:r0}, \mathtt{q} \mapsto \mathtt{:r1}$. Any assignment not guaranteeing the constraints of the MTCQ is not returned.

3 TOPLLET

We implemented TOPLLET on top of OPENLLET, an established non-temporal DL reasoner written in Java. OPENLLET supports reasoning over OWL2 knowledge bases, such as consistency checking and tree-shaped conjunctive query answering [13]. TOPLLET depends on several Java libraries, e.g., OWLAPI [6] and automatalib [9], as well as two software tools, MLTL2LTLF and LYDIA [2]. It has been tested on mainstream Linux distributions and requires at least Java 17 with moderate hardware. To provide evidence for the correctness of our implementation, we distribute a test suite with the tool.

The task of TOPLLET is to answer an MTCQ over a given TKB containing an (expressive) ontology and data. Its main interface is via the command line[1]:

```
topllet [-c CATALOG] <QUERY> <TKB>
```

where `CATALOG` is an optional OASIS XML catalog, `QUERY` is a file containing an MTCQ, and `TKB` is a file with a list of file paths to (non-temporal) OWL2-files.

For MTCQs, we rely on an extension of the standard LTL_f grammar [3,16][2]. A valid query was already given in Sect. 2. For theoretical reasons, the MTCQ has to be *tree-shaped*, i.e., if we view each CQ in the MTCQ as a graph with the relations being edges and quantified variables being nodes, it is tree-shaped [8]. Note that tMTCQs are only a mild restriction compared to full MTCQs as the tree-shape affects only role sequences consisting solely of quantified variables.

The OWL2 format is concerned with non-temporal knowledge bases, and we are not aware of any temporal extension. Hence, we propose a simple mechanism: A TKB is a list of OWL2 files, one for the data at each time point.

TOPLLET is implemented as the module `openllet-mtcq` in OPENLLET, which is shown together with existing modules and external dependencies in Fig. 1. We changed various modules of OPENLLET. For example, the query model was completely rewritten with generics to enable different query types with low code redundancy. Figure 1 also shows MLTL2LTLF, a tool we developed for translating MLTL to LTL_f [11], available at https://github.com/lu-w/mltl2ltlf.

Our architecture enables the following, abstract workflow:

(a) input via CLI,

[1] TOPLLET also offers a Java API, with a usage example given in the repository.
[2] A detailed syntax explanation can be found at https://github.com/lu-w/topllet.

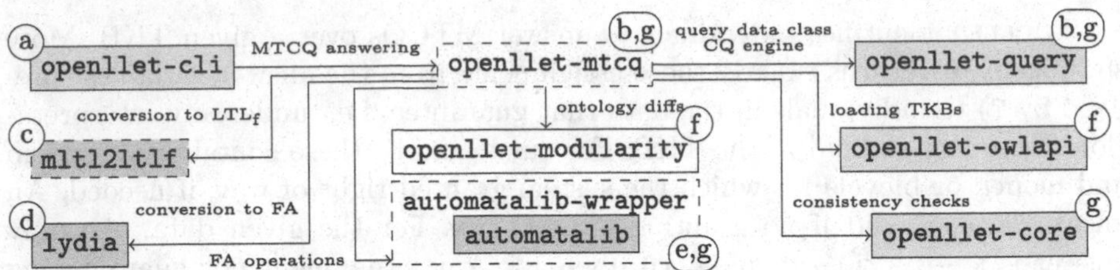

Fig. 1. Modules of TOPLLET, with external dependencies (gray), new developments (dashed), and adapted modules of OPENLLET (blue). The core module, `openllet-mtcq`, is displayed in yellow. The workflow (a) to (g) is mapped. (Color figure online)

(b) parse the MTCQ and build the propositional abstraction of its negation,
(c) convert the output of b) to an LTL$_f$ formula using MLTL2LTLF,
(d) convert the LTL$_f$ formula to a finite automaton (FA) using LYDIA [2],
(e) parse the FA using AUTOMATALIB [9],
(f) parse the data and ontology, and
(g) find an accepting run in the FA by reading the current data and computing the satisfiable answers to each edge of each currently active state.

By checking satisfiability of the negated formula, we find *counterexamples* to reject a potential answer ('candidate'). Hence, we accept a candidate iff. no accepting run was found.

A large part of the implementation's complexity and novelty lies in the final step g). For this, we need to compute satisfiable answers to so-called Boolean conjunctions of CQs (BCQs). Alas, it is theoretically unsound to use the built-in CQ engine of OPENLLET for this. To the date of writing, we are not aware of any implementation for answering BCQs over expressive DLs. Thus, we implemented a procedure due to Baader et al. [1] and Horrocks and Tessaris [8]. Here, the BCQ gets transformed into data assertions (for the positive query atoms) and a union of CQs (UCQ). Again, we are not aware of any answering engine for UCQs over expressive DLs. We hence added our own implementation to TOPLLET. This engine transforms UCQs into a conjunctive normal form (CNF), which is then answered one-by-one through transformation to data assertions. It relies on the so-called rolling-up procedure [8], which is already implemented in OPENLLET.

Due to the high theoretical complexity, we implemented several optimizations: Firstly, we prevent expensive BCQ checks by executing the optimized CQ engine of OPENLLET and transfer its results to (un)satisfiability of the BCQ, if theoretically possible. This approach is highly optimized [12] and, in practice, avoids the BCQ check for over 98% of the candidates. If we absolutely must check a BCQ, we intensively cache results as to avoid duplicate checking. Secondly, we merge different paths through the FA that lead to the same state with different sets of (un)satisfiable answer candidates. Finally, we changed the `QueryResult` of OPENLLET to a semi-symbolic version, which is only resolved on iteration.

4 Performance

As TOPLLET is the first tool for querying TKBs with ontologies formulated in expressive DLs, there is neither competition for comparison nor existing benchmarks. Figure 2 therefore shows absolute performance of TOPLLET on our custom benchmark set, which is available at https://github.com/lu-w/topllet-benchmarks. These benchmarks are similar to the example of Sect. 2 but have a scaling parameter N denoting the number of two-wheelers. Our results were obtained on a laptop computer with an AMD Ryzen 7 PRO 3700U CPU and 12 GB available RAM. Since the performance of TOPLLET is linear in the number of time points, we report the time spent per time point. Our experience shows typical data to have 10 to 30 s sampled with 5 to 20 Hz. For practical applications, we can thus estimate the number of time points to be less than 10^3. Even for large data sets ($N = 30$ has a search space of 1 256 640 candidates), query answering is feasible in several seconds per time point in the data, with an exponential dependency between the data size and run time. On larger data, BCQ checks (which can not rely on the same optimizations as CQ answering) are causing the majority of this run time. Note that it is spent on only a fraction of the search space: for $N = 30$, approx. 0.004% was, on average over all time points, analyzed by BCQ checks. In summary, TOPLLET is already mature enough for answering MTCQs over non-trivial data sizes.

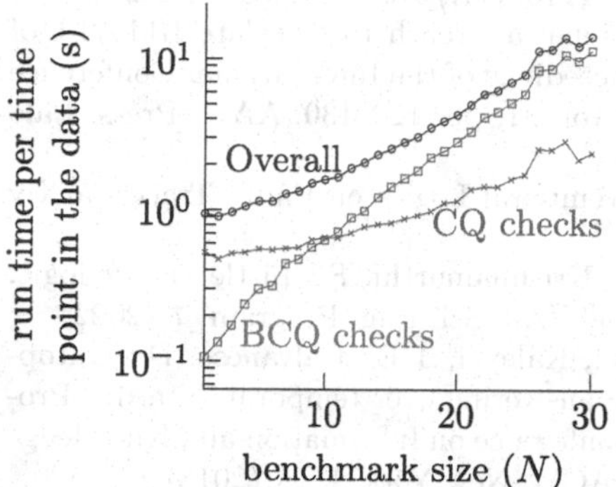

Fig. 2. Log-scaled wall clock run time, including input loading, together with the share of BCQ and CQ checks on run time.

5 Conclusion and Future Work

We presented TOPLLET, a software tool for answering tree-shaped MTCQs over TKBs with ontologies in expressive DLs. It is based on OPENLLET and uses its consistency check, query rolling-up, and CQ answering features. As TOPLLET is the first of its kind, we are still at the beginning of practically approaching the ExpTime-hard problem. With TOPLLET, we strive towards this goal.

We conducted early experiments with TOPLLET on real-world traffic data from intersections and a few example requirements by the authors. The data were generated by a measurement vehicle and a video feed from a drone. While performance was reasonable, for applying TOPLLET on larger requirement suites, we find that future work must further decrease run time, e.g., by parallelization or incremental reasoning over time. Our experience also shows LTL_f to be a sufficient temporal basis for MTCQs. However, misconceptions in semantics may lead to specification of faulty LTL formulae [4], which is currently also investigated for LTL_f. Orthogonally, for the ontology language, users may also require temporal axioms. Improving the usability of our inputs is hence in order.

References

1. Baader, F., Borgwardt, S., Lippmann, M.: Temporalizing ontology-based data access. In: Bonacina, M.P. (ed.) CADE 2013. LNCS (LNAI), vol. 7898, pp. 330–344. Springer, Heidelberg (2013). https://doi.org/10.1007/978-3-642-38574-2_23
2. De Giacomo, G., Favorito, M.: Compositional approach to translate LTLf/LDLf into deterministic finite automata. In: Proceedings of the International Conference on Automated Planning and Scheduling, vol. 31, pp. 122–130. AAAI Press, Palo Alto, USA (2021)
3. Favorito, M.: A Standard Grammar for Temporal Logics on Finite Traces. arXiv preprint arXiv:2012.13638 (2020)
4. Greenman, B., Saarinen, S., Nelson, T., Krishnamurthi, S.: Little tricky logic: misconceptions in the understanding of LTL. Art Sci. Eng. Program. **7** (2022)
5. Güzel Kalayci, E., Xiao, G., Ryzhikov, V., Kalayci, T.E., Calvanese, D.: Ontop-temporal: a tool for ontology-based query answering over temporal data. In: Proceedings of the 27th ACM International Conference on Information and Knowledge Management, pp. 1927–1930. CIKM '18, ACM, New York, USA (2018)
6. Horridge, M., Bechhofer, S.: The OWL API: a java API for OWL ontologies. Semant. Web **2**(1), 11–21 (2011)
7. Horrocks, I., Kutz, O., Sattler, U.: The irresistible SRIQ. In: Grau, B.C., Horrocks, I., Parsia, B., Patel-Schneider, P.F. (eds.) Proceedings of the OWLED*05 Workshop on OWL: Experiences and Directions, Galway, Ireland, 11–12 November 2005. CEUR Workshop Proceedings, vol. 188. CEUR-WS.org (2005)
8. Horrocks, I., Tessaris, S.: A conjunctive query language for description logic aboxes. In: Proceedings of the Seventeenth National Conference on Artificial Intelligence and Twelfth Conference on Innovative Applications of Artificial Intelligence, pp. 399–404. AAAI Press, Palo Alto, USA (2000)
9. Isberner, M., Howar, F., Steffen, B.: The open-source LearnLib. In: Kroening, D., Păsăreanu, C.S. (eds.) CAV 2015. LNCS, vol. 9206, pp. 487–495. Springer, Cham (2015). https://doi.org/10.1007/978-3-319-21690-4_32
10. Kazakov, Y.: RIQ and SROIQ are harder than SHOIQ. In: Proceedings of the Eleventh International Conference on Principles of Knowledge Representation and Reasoning, pp. 274–284. KR'08, AAAI Press (2008)
11. Li, J., Vardi, M.Y., Rozier, K.Y.: Satisfiability checking for mission-time LTL. In: Dillig, I., Tasiran, S. (eds.) CAV 2019. LNCS, vol. 11562, pp. 3–22. Springer, Cham (2019). https://doi.org/10.1007/978-3-030-25543-5_1
12. Sirin, E., Parsia, B.: Optimizations for answering conjunctive ABox queries: first results. In: Proceedings of the 2006 International Workshop on Description Logics (DL'06), pp. 215–222 (2006)
13. Sirin, E., Parsia, B., Grau, B.C., Kalyanpur, A., Katz, Y.: Pellet: a practical OWL-DL reasoner. J. Web Semant. **5**(2), 51–53 (2007)
14. Soylu, A., et al.: Querying industrial stream-temporal data: An ontology-based visual approach. J. Ambient Intell. Smart Environ. **9**(1), 77–95 (2017)
15. Wang, D., Hu, P., Wałega, P.A., Grau, B.C.: MeTeoR: practical reasoning in datalog with metric temporal operators. In: Proceedings of the AAAI Conference on Artificial Intelligence, vol. 36, pp. 5906–5913. AAAI Press, Palo Alto, USA (2022)

16. Westhofen, L., Neurohr, C., Jung, J.C., Neider, D.: Answering temporal conjunctive queries over description logic ontologies for situation recognition in complex operational domains. In: Finkbeiner, B., Kovacs, L. (eds.) Tools and Algorithms for the Construction and Analysis of Systems. TACAS 2024. LNCS, vol. 14570, pp. 167–187. Springer, Cham (2024). https://doi.org/10.1007/978-3-031-57246-3_10
17. World Wide Web Consortium: OWL 2 Web Ontology Language, Structural Specification and Functional-Style Syntax (Second Edition), December 2012

A Formal Verification Framework for Runtime Assurance

J. Tanner Slagel(✉), Lauren M. White, Aaron Dutle, César A. Muñoz, and Nicolas Crespo

NASA Langley Research Center, Hampton, VA 23666, USA
j.tanner.slagel@nasa.gov

Abstract. The simplex architecture is an instance of Runtime Assurance (RTA) where a trusted component takes control of a safety-critical system when an untrusted component violates a safety property. This paper presents a formalization of the simplex RTA framework in the language of hybrid programs. A feature of this formal verification framework is that, for a given system, a specific instantiation can be created and its safety properties are guaranteed by construction. Instantiations may be kept at varying levels of generality that allow for black box components, such as ML/AI-based controllers, to be modeled. The framework is written in the Prototype Verification System (PVS) using Plaidypvs, an embedding of differential dynamic logic in PVS. As a proof of concept, the framework is illustrated on an automatic vehicle braking system.

Keywords: Runtime Assurance · Hybrid Programs · Plaidypvs · PVS

1 Introduction

Runtime Assurance (RTA) is a design-time architecture for safety-critical systems where an internal monitor takes action upon detecting a violation of a property [2]. The simplex architecture is an instance of RTA where control of the overall system is handed to a trusted controller when an untrusted one violates a safety property [9]. Simplex RTA is emerging as a method for allowing AI/ML and other unverified software to be integrated into safety-critical applications.

This paper presents a formalization of a simplex RTA framework in the Prototype Verification System (PVS) [7] using an embedding of differential dynamic logic (dL) called Plaidypvs [10]. A novel feature of this framework is that it can be instantiated at different levels of abstraction. This feature allows for the formal verification of a system with an untrusted black box component, such as an AI/ML controller.

1.1 Runtime Assurance

Runtime *verification* is the use of a *monitor* to check safety properties of a system at runtime [4,6]. If a property is violated, the monitor may send a signal

N. Benz et al. (Eds.): NFM 2024, LNCS 14627, pp. 322–328, 2024.
https://doi.org/10.1007/978-3-031-60698-4_19

to perform some action or to alert a user. Runtime *Assurance* is the design-time integration of runtime verification into a system to provide some guarantee on the overall system.

Arguably, the most common application of Runtime Assurance is in the *simplex* architecture [9]. In this architecture, a system has an *advanced* controller (AC) and a *reversionary* controller (RC). The system is allowed to operate with the AC until a runtime monitor detects that some property has been violated and then the RC takes over. Assuming that the monitor can detect improper functioning with enough time for the RC to correct the impending problem, and that the RC is trusted, this use of RTA allows for the integration of untrusted—but possibly more performant—controllers in a safe way. This is of particular interest with the rise of AI/ML technology and the desire to integrate it in safety-critical systems like aircraft. To this end, ASTM and NASA have each published guidelines on the use of RTA in such systems [1,2]. Due to the ubiquity of the simplex RTA framework, the term RTA will be used to represent a simplex architecture in the remainder of the paper.

This paper does not address the many difficulties in deploying RTA to an industrial-level system [3]. Instead, the focus is on the formal verification of the simplex RTA *framework* in the language of hybrid programs. Employing the Plaidypvs formalization in PVS allows for the verification of the general framework and then, by specializing some components of the hybrid program, to verify instances of the framework while keeping the untrusted component essentially a black box.

1.2 Plaidypvs

Plaidypvs (**P**roperly **A**ssured **I**mplementation of **D**ifferential Dynamic Logic for Hybrid **P**rogram **V**erification and **S**pecification) [10][1] is a formal embedding of Differential Dynamic Logic [8] that allows for the formal specification of, and reasoning about, hybrid programs within the PVS interactive theorem prover. Hybrid programs are used to model hybrid systems, i.e., systems with both continuous and discrete behavior, which often arise in safety- and mission-critical applications [5].

In Plaidypvs, reasoning can be done on the executions of a hybrid program using universal and existential quantifiers denoted by *allruns* $[\cdot]$ and *someruns* $\langle\cdot\rangle$ respectively. For a given hybrid program α and a Boolean expression P on environments, $[\alpha]P$ (respectively, $\langle\alpha\rangle P$) asserts that every (respectively, some) run of the hybrid program α ends at a value that satisfies P.

Hybrid programs are syntactically defined as a datatype $\mathcal{H}$ in Plaidypvs according to the grammar

$$\alpha ::= \mathbf{x} := \ell \mid \mathbf{x}' = \ell \,\&\, P \mid ?P \mid x := * \mid \alpha_1; \alpha_2 \mid \alpha_1 \cup \alpha_2 \mid \alpha_1^*$$

[1] Plaidypvs is available as part of the NASA PVS library at https://github.com/nasa/pvslib/tree/master/dL.

where $\mathbf{x} := \ell$ is a discrete assignment, $\mathbf{x}' = \ell$ is a differential system symbolizing a continuous evolution, and P is a Boolean expression. The expression $?P$ represents a check of the Boolean expression P, $x := *$ is an arbitrary assignment of the variable x, the expression $\alpha_1; \alpha_2$ represents sequential execution of two subprograms, $\alpha_1 \cup \alpha_2$ symbolizes a nondeterministic choice between two subprograms, and finally α_1^* represents a fixed but unknown number of repetitions of a hybrid program.

Plaidypvs uses a predicate called the dL-sequent denoted $\Gamma \vdash \Delta$, where Γ and Δ are lists of Boolean expressions. This predicate is defined by the Boolean formula

$$\bigwedge_i \Gamma_i(e) \to \bigvee_j \Delta_j(e),$$

where $\Gamma_i(e)$ and $\Delta_j(e)$ represent the i-th and j-th Boolean expressions of Γ and Δ, respectively, evaluated in the environment e.

2 RTA Framework in Plaidypvs

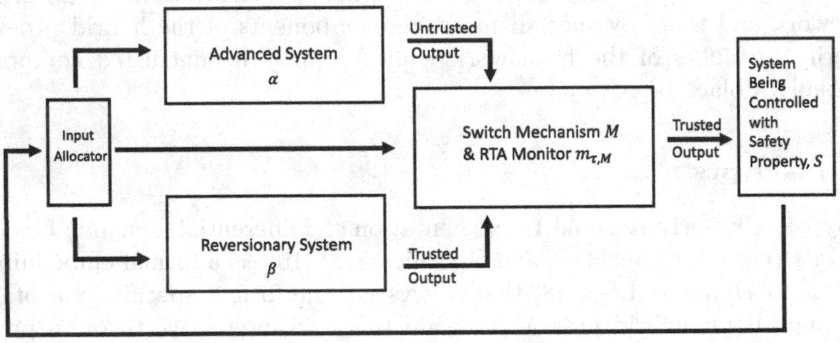

Fig. 1. The simplex RTA framework. In this work the advanced and reversionary systems are denoted by hybrid programs α and β respectively.

This section presents a general framework for RTA in Plaidypvs where the entire system, including trusted and untrusted components, are modeled as hybrid programs. In this architecture, it is assumed the monitor does not instantaneously detect when the switch condition is violated, but rather samples at least every $\tau \in \mathbb{R}_{\geq 0}$ amount of time. This assumption models real-world systems where the monitor is checked with discrete samples.

To model this sampling, the notion of a monitored hybrid program is introduced. This monitored hybrid program can be defined as a function $m_{\tau,M}$, where τ is the maximum allowed amount of time between samples and M is the switch condition. This function takes a hybrid program α and produces a hybrid program that has the same dynamics as α but is restricted to the runs where M

has been true within τ units of time of the final state. For a hybrid program α the associated monitored hybrid program is defined as:

$$m_{\tau,M}(\alpha) = \begin{cases} (?M; t := 0; (\mathbf{x}' = \ell, t' = 1 \,\&\, P \wedge t \leq \tau))^* & \text{if } \alpha = (\mathbf{x}' = \ell \,\&\, P), \\ m_{\tau,M}(\alpha_1); m_{\tau,M}(\alpha_2) & \text{if } \alpha = \alpha_1; \alpha_2, \\ m_{\tau,M}(\alpha_1) \cup m_{\tau,M}(\alpha_2) & \text{if } \alpha = \alpha_1 \cup \alpha_2, \\ (m_{\tau,M}(\alpha_1))^* & \text{if } \alpha = \alpha_1^* \\ \alpha & \text{otherwise.} \end{cases}$$

Here, it is required that the variable t does not appear in the hybrid program α.

Figure 1 shows the general RTA framework, which has been specified and verified in Plaidypvs.[2] Let the advanced and reversionary components be modeled by hybrid programs α and β, respectively, and let S be a Boolean expression describing the safety property that must be always satisfied by the RTA system. The function $m_{\tau,M}$ enforces that the hybrid program does not evolve for more than $\tau \in \mathbb{R}_{\geq 0}$ units of time without the switch condition property M being checked. In this system, the RTA framework can be written as the hybrid program:

$$((?M; m_{\tau,M}(\alpha)) \cup (?\neg M; \beta))^* . \tag{1}$$

This RTA structure enforces the switch to β when it is detected that the switch condition property M is not satisfied. Note that β is allowed to run for as long as it wants regardless of the value of M. The switch back to the advanced system α is not specified in this paper but can be defined within Plaidypvs. For instance, one enforcement of a switchback is to replace β with a monitored reversionary system $m_{\tau,\neg N}(\beta)$ checking for a switchback condition N. With the assumption that N is an invariant of β, N implies M, and the existence of a run of $m_{\tau,\neg N}(\beta)$ where N is true, it can be shown a switchback to the advanced system occurs.

Given an RTA system, a primary goal is to know that the safety property S is always satisfied, written in Plaidypvs as:

$$[((?M; m_{\tau,M}(\alpha)) \cup (?\neg M; \beta))^*]\, S.$$

To prove this invariant property, a general rule was specified and proven in Plaidypvs that relates the safety of the overall system to safety of its individual components:

$$\frac{\Gamma \vdash S \wedge (M \vee G) \quad S \vdash [m_{\tau,M}(\alpha)](S \wedge (G \vee M)) \quad G \vdash [\beta^*]S}{\Gamma \vdash [((?M; m_{\tau,M}(\alpha)) \cup (?\neg M; \beta))^*]S}\ (\mathbf{RTA}),$$

where $G \in \mathcal{B}$ is a user-instantiated condition that represents a property that carries over when switching between the advanced system to the reversionary

[2] The formal development presented in this paper, including examples, is available at https://github.com/nasa/pvslib/tree/master/dL/dL_RTA.

system. This switch property G is used to capture conditions that will allow the reversionary controller to satisfy S after detecting the monitor is violated.

The rule **RTA** takes the RTA system in Formula (1) and generates three subgoals. The first subgoal $\Gamma \vdash S \wedge (M \vee G)$ corresponds to the initial state of the system. The safety property S must be true to start, and either the monitoring condition M or the switch property G must hold. The second subgoal $S \vdash [m_{\tau,M}(\alpha)](S \wedge (G \vee M))$ is the proof condition that if the system is in a safe initial point, every monitored run of the advanced system will satisfy S (recall that a *monitored* run of α is terminated within τ of the M failing to hold), and have the property that if the monitoring condition M is not true, then the switch condition G holds—since $G \vee M \iff (\neg M \rightarrow G)$. The third subgoal $G \vdash [\beta^*]S$ requires proving that when starting from the switch condition being true, the reversionary system may run any finite number of times and the safety property S is satisfied.

3 A Simple Example

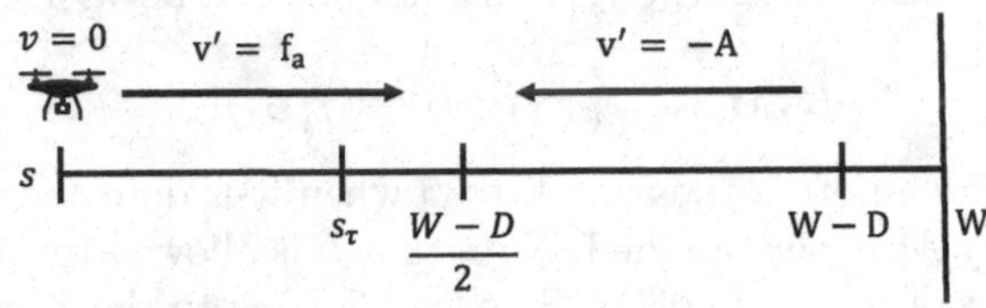

Fig. 2. A simple hysteresis controller set-up, which is an instantiation of the general RTA framework.

Consider the one-dimensional braking example in Fig. 2, where a vehicle whose position and velocity are given by the variables s and v, respectively, is governed by an RTA system. The advanced controller is given by

$$\alpha := (s' := v, v' := f_a), \tag{2}$$

where $f_a \in \mathcal{R}$ is any positive acceleration function bounded by $A \in \mathbb{R}_{>0}$. Note that f_a is not specifically defined, but is a black box component with only the requirement that it is bounded by A. The reversionary braking system is given by

$$\beta := (s' := v, v' := -A). \tag{3}$$

The switching condition M is a check on the position and velocity. Given a sampling rate τ, the full RTA system is a variant of the hysteresis controller, having the form of Formula (1).

Let the vehicle start with $s = 0$ and $v = 0$, and as a safety property, require that the vehicle does not go within a given distance $D \in \mathbb{R}_{>0}$ to a wall $W \in \mathbb{R}$ (assuming that $W - D > 0$). The RTA property is then

$$s = 0, v = 0 \rightarrow \left[(?M; m_{\tau,M}(\alpha) \cup ?\neg M; \beta)^*\right](s \leq W - D). \tag{4}$$

Using the values

$$\tau = \sqrt{\frac{W - D}{A}} \tag{5}$$

$$M = s \leq s_\tau \wedge v \leq \sqrt{A(W - D)} \tag{6}$$

$$s_\tau = \frac{(\sqrt{A(W - D)} - \tau)^2}{2}, \tag{7}$$

allows Formula (4) to be proven in Plaidypvs. In fact, the proof process itself was crucial in discovering the requirement on the maximum time between samples, τ, to guarantee the safety property for the system. Furthermore, it illuminates an important aspect of runtime verification, that the amount of drift in the system between samples must be accounted for to ensure correctness. This is shown in the term s_τ corresponding the position component of the switch condition M. This term is specified so that even in the worst case, where the sampling rate is such that the position is sampled right before M is violated and the next sample occurs τ time after the previous, the switch condition allows the reversionary controller to take over with enough time so that a distance D away from the wall is maintained.

Proving the property is done by applying the **RTA** rule with

$$G = s \leq \frac{W - D}{2} \wedge v \leq \sqrt{A(W - D)},$$

which yields the three subgoals

$$s = 0, v = 0 \vdash s \leq W - D \wedge (M \vee G) \tag{8}$$

$$s \leq W - D \vdash [m_{\tau,M}\,(\alpha)] s \leq W - D \wedge (M \vee G) \tag{9}$$

$$G \vdash [(\beta)^*]\,(s \leq W - D) \tag{10}$$

each of which are then proven within Plaidypvs.

4 Conclusion

This paper presents a general framework for RTA, which has been formalized in Plaidypvs. The formalization allows the designer of a safety-critical system to prove safety properties of the entire RTA system based on properties of its individual components. A simple braking example illustrates the use of this emerging idea. Particularly, this framework extracts and reveals requirements of the underlying system being modeled. Future work will apply this RTA framework to more complex examples in the aerospace domain, to extract safety requirements, including the delicate interplay between sample rates of sensors and monitoring specifications. Using the temporal extension of Plaidypvs that includes the trace semantics of hybrid programs [11], examples will be developed where temporal properties are shown for the system. Additionally, the trace semantics of hybrid program will allow a rigorous connection to be made between a hybrid program and its analogous monitored hybrid program. Plaidypvs allows more complicated RTA structures to be modeled at a generic level. This could include multiple components such as secondary reversionary controller or even a system made of several simplex RTA structures, which creates the need for modeling concurrency in Plaidypvs.

References

1. ASTM International: Standard practice for methods to safely bound behavior of aircraft systems containing complex functions using run-time assurance, ASTM F3269-21 (2021). https://doi.org/10.1520/F3269-21
2. Brat, G., Pai, G.: Runtime assurance of aeronautical products: preliminary recommendations. Technical Memorandum (2023). https://ntrs.nasa.gov/citations/20220015734
3. Goodloe, A.: Challenges in high-assurance runtime verification. In: Margaria, T., Steffen, B. (eds.) ISoLA 2016. LNCS, vol. 9952, pp. 446–460. Springer, Cham (2016). https://doi.org/10.1007/978-3-319-47166-2_31
4. Havelund, K.: Using runtime analysis to guide model checking of java programs. In: Havelund, K., Penix, J., Visser, W. (eds.) SPIN 2000. LNCS, vol. 1885, pp. 245–264. Springer, Heidelberg (2000). https://doi.org/10.1007/10722468_15
5. Jeannin, J., et al.: A formally verified hybrid system for safe advisories in the next-generation airborne collision avoidance system. Int. J. Softw. Tools Technol. Transf. **19**(6) (2017). https://doi.org/10.1007/978-3-662-46681-0_2
6. Kim, M., Viswanathan, M., Ben-Abdallah, H., Kannan, S., Lee, I., Sokolsky, O.: Formally specified monitoring of temporal properties. In: Euromicro Conference on Real-Time Systems. Euromicro RTS. IEEE (1999). https://doi.org/10.1109/EMRTS.1999.777457
7. Owre, S., Rushby, J.M., Shankar, N.: PVS: a prototype verification system. In: Kapur, D. (ed.) CADE 1992. LNCS, vol. 607, pp. 748–752. Springer, Heidelberg (1992). https://doi.org/10.1007/3-540-55602-8_217
8. Platzer, A.: Differential dynamic logic for hybrid systems. J. Autom. Reason. **41**(2) (2008). https://doi.org/10.1007/s10817-008-9103-8
9. Seto, D., Krogh, B., Sha, L., Chutinan, A.: The simplex architecture for safe online control system upgrades. In: Proceedings of the 1998 American Control Conference. ACC, vol. 6, pp. 3504–3508 (1998). https://doi.org/10.1109/ACC.1998.703255
10. Slagel, J.T., Moscato, M.M., White, L., Muñoz, C., Balachandran, S., Dutle, A.: Embedding differential dynamic logic in PVS. In: International Conference on Logical and Semantic Frameworks, with Applications. LSFA (2023). https://ntrs.nasa.gov/citations/20220019093
11. White, L., Titolo, L., Slagel, J.T., Muñoz, C.: A temporal differential dynamic logic formal embedding. In: ACM SIGPLAN International Conference on Certified Programs and Proofs. CPP (2024). https://doi.org/10.1145/3636501.3636943

Formal Methods for Robotics

SMT-Based Dynamic Multi-Robot Task Allocation

Victoria Marie Tuck[1(✉)], Pei-Wei Chen[1(✉)], Georgios Fainekos[2], Bardh Hoxha[2], Hideki Okamoto[2], S. Shankar Sastry[1], and Sanjit A. Seshia[1]

[1] UC Berkeley, Berkeley, CA 94704, USA
{victoria_tuck,pwchen,shankar_sastry,sseshia}@berkeley.edu
[2] Toyota Motor North America, Research & Development, Ann Arbor, MI 48105, USA
{georgios.fainekos,bardh.hoxha,hideki.okamoto}@toyota.com

Abstract. Multi-Robot Task Allocation (MRTA) is a problem that arises in many application domains including package delivery, warehouse robotics, and healthcare. In this work, we consider the problem of MRTA for a dynamic stream of tasks with task deadlines and capacitated agents (capacity for more than one simultaneous task). Previous work commonly focuses on the static case, uses specialized algorithms for restrictive task specifications, or lacks guarantees. We propose an approach to Dynamic MRTA for capacitated robots that is based on Satisfiability Modulo Theories (SMT) solving and addresses these concerns. We show our approach is both sound and complete, and that the SMT encoding is general, enabling extension to a broader class of task specifications. We show how to leverage the incremental solving capabilities of SMT solvers, keeping learned information when allocating new tasks arriving online, and to solve non-incrementally, which we provide runtime comparisons of. Additionally, we provide an algorithm to start with a smaller but potentially incomplete encoding that can iteratively be adjusted to the complete encoding. We evaluate our method on a parameterized set of benchmarks encoding multi-robot delivery created from a graph abstraction of a hospital-like environment. The effectiveness of our approach is demonstrated using a range of encodings, including quantifier-free theories of uninterpreted functions and linear or bitvector arithmetic across multiple solvers.

Keywords: Multi-Robot Task Allocation · Satisfiability Modulo Theories · Capacitated Robots · Incremental Solving · Cyber-Physical Systems · Robotics

1 Introduction

Multi-robot systems have the potential to increase productivity by providing point-to-point pickup and delivery services, referring to the assignment to a team

P.-W. Chen—Denotes significant contribution.

N. Benz et al. (Eds.): NFM 2024, LNCS 14627, pp. 331–351, 2024.
https://doi.org/10.1007/978-3-031-60698-4_20

of robots of pickup and drop-off locations for transporting items under some optimization criteria and constraints. Such services have already revolutionised warehouse management [24] by eliminating long travel times between locations for workers. New mobile robot systems are being developed for point-to-point pickup and delivery in environments where human-robot interaction is more likely – such as in healthcare facilities [5,11,20]. Even though multi-robot systems in warehouses and healthcare settings share many similarities, the latter require a higher level of assurance. Formal methods provides this level of assurance by finding an assignment to robots if and only if one exists.

In this paper, we study the application of Satisfiability Modulo Theories (SMT) [2] to the Multi-Robot Task Assignment (MRTA) [3,15] problem for point-to-point pickup and delivery. We assume that the robots can execute only a limited number of concurrent tasks and assume that tasks are generated online, have a strict deadline, and each require only one robot. Although, as often used in warehouse settings, a gridworld abstraction may be applicable in a healthcare environment, the dynamic nature of the environment is better addressed through coarser abstractions (regions) within which local motion planning can be employed [21,23]. We therefore represent the environment by a weighted graph with nodes representing regions in the environment and weights the worst case cost (time) to move from region to region without any dynamic obstacles. Dynamic obstacles operating at shorter time scales, e.g., humans walking, could be avoided using local motion planning with safety guarantees [13,17]. Note that this work focuses on solving the high-level planning part and leaves local motion planning and collision avoidance to downstream planners.

Satisfiability Modulo Theories (SMT) [2] is a generalization of the Boolean satisfiability problem that answers the question whether a formula in first-order logic with background theories is satisfiable. Problems can be encoded as SMT formulas and passed to SMT solvers to determine satisfiability. Such solvers are widely used in industrial-scale applications (e.g., [18]). Given the progress in SMT solving, our aim is to study the feasibility and scalability of solving the aforementioned instance of the MRTA problem with an SMT formulation. There are several reasons for investigating an SMT approach to MRTA: 1) at its core, MRTA is a combinatorial problem with arithmetic constraints, 2) an SMT formulation can be easily adapted to handle different variants of the MRTA problem [3,15], e.g., with complex task dependencies [9], and 3) even satisfying solutions without guaranteed optimality are relevant for this application since hierarchical planning methods [21,23] can refine a non-optimal high level plan to an optimal (with respect to distance traveled) local motion plan.

Our contributions are:

- a general, SMT-based framework leveraging quantifier-free theories of uninterpreted functions and bitvector or linear arithmetic for dynamic, capacitated MRTA via incremental solving;
- an approach to manage complexity by dynamically changing the number of free variables to fit the needs of the problem;
- theoretical results of completeness and soundness;

- and an experimental analysis of the runtime of our approach across different solvers (cvc5, Z3, and Bitwuzla) for a series of static (one set of tasks) and dynamic (tasks arriving online) benchmarks and showing that solver and setting used affects whether or not incremental solving is beneficial.

2 Related Work

Multi-Robot Task Allocation (MRTA) refers to the class of problems that encompasses many variants of the point-to-point pickup and delivery scheduling and path planning for multi-robot systems. For example, pickup and delivery tasks may have deadlines, robots may have to form a team to complete the task, or each robot may have different capacity constraints. For a detailed taxonomy for task allocation problems with temporal constraints, please refer to [15].

Most heuristic-based MRTA algorithms search for a plan for each robot such that all tasks are completed while minimizing some objective. [12] employs a hybrid genetic algorithm where local search procedures are used as mutation operators to solve for tasks with an unlimited fleet of capacity-constrained robots. [19] uses a nearest-neighbor based approach to cluster nearby nodes and constructs routes for each of the clusters by mapping it to a traveling salesman problem (TSP) while minimizing overall package delivery time. [4] adopts a marginal-cost heuristic and a meta-heuristic improvement strategy based on large neighborhood search to simultaneously perform task assignment and path planning while minimizing the sum of differences between the actual complete time and the earliest complete time over all tasks. The above heuristic-based approaches are often scalable on problems with up to 2000 tasks, but are not able to provide completeness guarantees, i.e., with hard deadlines. Moreover, heuristics are often tightly tied to a specific problem setting which makes it non-trivial to extend to other settings. For a recent review on state-of-the-art optimization-based approaches to the MRTA problem, we direct readers to Chakraa et al. [3].

In contrast, many approaches that provide strong guarantees do not scale well. [16] formulates the MRTA problem as a Mixed-Integer Linear Programming (MILP) problem to simultaneously optimize task allocation and planning in a setting where capacity-constrained robots are assigned to complete tasks with deadlines in a grid world. However, the proposed method suffers in computational performance when problem size grows large – the approach is able to handle 20 tasks with 5 agents but the execution time is unavailable in the paper. [10] promises globally optimal solution in a hospital setting by exhaustively searching through possible combinations of locations of interest and choosing capacity-constrained robots with minimum travel distances to complete tasks. The approach is able to solve 197 periodic tasks over a duration of 8 h, but the runtime information for each solve is unknown. [7] is an linear-time temporal logic-based approach that provides strong guarantees and appears to scale well. However, its reliance on temporal logic may impact its ability to scale when length of the plans is large in time, whereas we represent time abstractly. Additionally, their approach does not allow for assigning robots new tasks before they have finished previous tasks, which our structure supports.

In this work, we are interested in the specification satisfaction problem, which is similar to the problem of minimizing cost where the cost goes to infinity if any of the constraints are not satisfiable. In contrast to the heuristic-based approach, our proposed approach is able to give completeness guarantees if solutions do not exist, while still achieving superior performance compared to those that give strong guarantees.

Symbol	Description
$\mathcal{M}_j$	The jth set of tasks in a task stream $\mathbb{S}$
t_j	Arrival time for the jth set of tasks
$\mathcal{M}$	Cumulative set of tasks until current time
μ_m	Task id for a task
t_m	Arrival time for task m
T_m	Deadline for task m
$\mathcal{S}_n$	Action sequence of an agent n
$\mathcal{S}_n^k$	Prefix of length k of agent n's action sequence
s_n^k	The kth element of agent n's action sequence
Π	A plan for a set of agents $\mathcal{N}$ and set of tasks $\mathcal{M}$
(i_d^n, t_d^n, l_d^n)	Action tuple for agent n at action point d
$Loc(i_d^n)$	Converts an action id to a location id
Γ	List of assumption vars limiting number of available action points
ρ	Time taken to pick up/drop off items
D_{min}, D_{max}	Min/max number of action points needed by task set $\mathcal{M}$
$start_m, end_m$	Start/end time for task m
n_m	Agent that completes task m
K_n	Each agent's capacity for tasks at once
$\mathcal{E}_j$	Encoding at the jth iteration of the algorithm
M, W, P, D	Move, wait, pick, drop actions
$s \in S$	Location in a set of system locations
$\sigma \in \Sigma$	Location id in set of location ids corresponding to the location set
$\mathcal{D}_k(\mathcal{S}_n)$	Duration of a prefix of length k of agent n's action sequence
$C_k(\mathcal{S}_n)$	Load of an agent n at the kth element in their action sequence

3 Problem Formulation

We use $\mathbb{Z}_{++}$ to denote the set of strictly positive integers.

3.1 Workspace Model

We assume we are given a finite set of designated system locations $s \in S$ each with a unique id $\sigma \in \Sigma \subset \mathbb{Z}_+$ where $s \in \mathbb{R}^2$. For example, each system location

s is a spot in a building where a robot can start, pick up an object, or drop off an object. We are given a complete, weighted, undirected graph $G = (V, E)$ where $V = \Sigma$ and $E = \{(\sigma_i, \sigma_j, w_{i,j}) | \sigma_i \in \Sigma, \sigma_j \in \Sigma, w_{i,j} \in \mathbb{Z}_+\}$ where $w_{i,j}$ is 0 *if and only if* $\sigma_i = \sigma_j$. The weight of the edge between vertices σ_i and σ_j is $w_{i,j}$. This weight $w_{i,j}$ denotes the travel time between the two points, which satisfies the triangle inequality with respect to all other sites s_k, i.e., $w_{i,k} + w_{k,j} \geq w_{i,j}\ \forall \sigma_k \in \Sigma$.

3.2 System Model

A task m is a tuple $(\mu_m, \sigma_{m,i}, \sigma_{m,f}, t_m, T_m)$ where $\mu_m \in \mathbb{Z}_+$ is the task's unique id, $\sigma_{m,i}, \sigma_{m,f} \in \Sigma$ are the starting and ending location ids, respectively, and $t_m, T_m \in \mathbb{Z}_+$ are the arrival time and deadline, respectively. i and f stand for initial and final, respectively. Each task is to move a corresponding object, which takes up one unit of capacity.

Sets of tasks arrive as a sequence of incoming tasks $\mathbb{S}$ called the task stream. Each entry of the task stream is a tuple $(\mathcal{M}_j, t_j)$. The first entry $\mathcal{M}_j$ of the tuple is an ordered set of tasks, and the second entry is the arrival time of the set. The arrival time t_m for any task in the set is the same as the set's arrival time ($t_j = t_m\ \forall m \in \mathcal{M}_j$). We use the same time in both contexts to more easily reference the arrival time depending on if we are reference a task in the set or the entire set. Assume $t_0 = 0$. We assume the stream is finite with a known total number of tasks M_{max}. We require that this sequence is monotonically increasing with respect to the second element of $(\mathcal{M}_j, t_j)$. Let $\overline{\mathcal{M}}_j = \bigcup_{j'=0}^{j} \mathcal{M}_{j'}$ be the total set of tasks that have arrived. We constrain the task id of the first task to be zero and all following tasks to have ids that increment by one. More formally, $\forall m \in \mathcal{M}_j$, $\mu_m \in \{|\overline{\mathcal{M}}_{j-1}|, \ldots, |\overline{\mathcal{M}}_j| - 1\}$ with $\overline{\mathcal{M}}_{-1} = \emptyset$. We use $M = |\overline{\mathcal{M}}_j|$ for the current total number of tasks where M will change with the context. We will sometimes notate a set of tasks as $\mathcal{M}$. We require that the unique task ids start at 0 and increase by 1 for every new task that arrives.

There exists a finite, zero-indexed, ordered set $\mathcal{N}$ of N agents. Each agent n has a unique id $\nu_n \in \{0, \ldots, N-1\}$ and a starting position $n_s \in S$ that may not be unique. Each agent has a capacity K_n for tasks at one time.

We define a set of actions $\mathcal{A}$ that a robot can take as $\mathcal{A} = (M, \sigma) \cup (\{P, D\}, \mu_m) \cup (W, t)$. The action (M, σ) designates that the robot is moving to location s with id σ, $(\{P, D\}, \mu_m)$ designates that the robot is picking up (P) or dropping off (D) the task m with id μ_m, and (W, t) has the agent wait in the same position for a time $t \in \mathbb{Z}_{++}$. We use the short-hand that $P_\mu = (P, \mu)$ and similar for drop. Each of $\{\mathbf{M}, \mathbf{W}, \mathbf{P}, \mathbf{D}\}$ represent all actions of that type, e.g. $\mathbf{M} = \{(M, \sigma) | \sigma \in \Sigma\}$. We assume the pick and drop actions each take a pre-specified time of $\rho \in \mathbb{Z}_{++}$.

The following definitions are used to define types of plans and the goals of our algorithm. Figure 1 shows the input, example output plans, and an example workspace. We use $\mathcal{S}_n^k$ to denote the prefix of length k of agent n's action sequence. $\mathbb{1}_\alpha$ is an indicator function that is 1 when α is true and 0 otherwise.

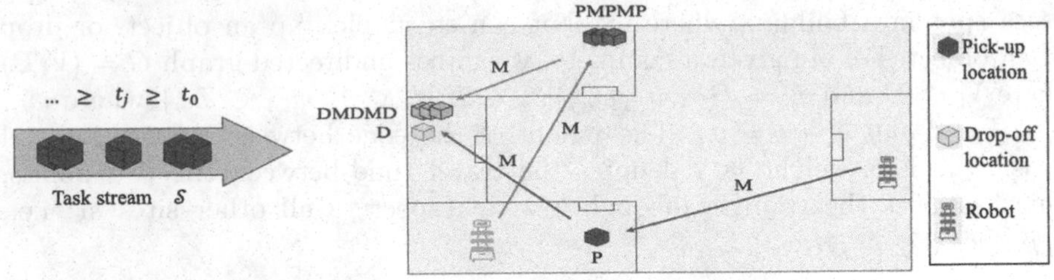

Fig. 1. A task stream of sets of tasks arrives with monotonically increasing arrival times. Five system sites are shown. Example tasks and robot paths are shown on the right with P, D, and M used to represent the actions succinctly. The result action sequence for the right robot is (M,P,M,D) and (M,P,M,P,M,P,M,D,M,D,M,D). The moves between picks or drops at the same location are used to keep a consistent structure in the plan but take no time.

Definition 1. ***Action sequence.*** *An action sequence $\mathcal{S}_n$ is a finite sequence beginning with element $k = 1$ where each element $s_n^k \in \mathcal{S}_n$ is an action ($s_n^k \in \mathcal{A}$).*

Definition 2. ***Plan.*** *A plan Π for the set of agents $\mathcal{N}$ and set of tasks $\mathcal{M}$ is an action sequence $\mathcal{S}_n$ with length k_n for each agent n.*

Definition 3. ***Duration of an action sequence.*** *We compute the duration of a prefix $\mathcal{S}_n^k$ of $\mathcal{S}_n$ as*

$$\mathcal{D}_k(\mathcal{S}_n) = \Sigma_{l=1}^k w_{\sigma_{l-1},\sigma_l} \mathbb{1}_{s_n^l \in \mathbf{M}} + \rho(\mathbb{1}_{s_n^l \in \mathbf{P}} + \mathbb{1}_{s_n^l \in \mathbf{D}}) + t_l \mathbb{1}_{s_n^l \in \mathbf{W}}$$

where $\sigma_0 = n_s$ and σ_l and t_l are the location ids and times, respectively, of action l. $\sigma_l = \sigma_{m,i}$ for a pick action and $\sigma_{m,f}$ for a drop action. σ_l for a wait is the most recent location.

Definition 4. ***Load of an action sequence.*** *We compute the load of a prefix $\mathcal{S}_n^k$ of $\mathcal{S}_n$ as $C_k(\mathcal{S}_n) = \Sigma_{j=1}^k(\mathbb{1}_{s_n^j \in \mathbf{P}} - \mathbb{1}_{s_n^j \in \mathbf{D}})$.*

Definition 5. ***Consistent action sequence.*** *A plan Π is made of consistent action sequences $\Phi_1(\Pi)$ if for each agent's sequence it starts with a move or wait; no capacity constraints are violated; any pick ($P_m = (P, \mu_m)$) and drop ($D_m = (D, \mu_m)$) actions for a task m are immediately preceded by the move to that point (A move that will require no time is still added if the agent "moves" to its current location.); pick precedes drop; drop follows pick; no two moves occur in a row; and any object in a sequence is only picked and dropped once (ϕ_1). An empty sequence is consistent.*

$$
\begin{aligned}
\phi_1(\mathcal{S}_n) =& \Big(\mathcal{S}_n = \emptyset\Big) \bigvee \qquad (1)\\
&\Big(\Big(s_n^1 \in \mathbf{M} \cup \mathbf{W}\Big) \wedge \Big(\forall \kappa \in \{1, ..., k_n\}.\ (0 \leq C_\kappa(\mathcal{S}_n)) \wedge (C_\kappa(\mathcal{S}_n) \leq K_n)\Big)\\
&\wedge \Big(s_n^{k_n} \notin \mathbf{M}\Big) \wedge \Big(\forall \kappa \in \{1, ..., k_n - 1\}.\ s_n^\kappa \in \mathbf{M} \Rightarrow s_n^{\kappa+1} \notin \mathbf{M}\Big)\\
&\bigwedge \Big(\forall m \in \mathcal{M},\ \forall \kappa \in \{2, ..., k_n\}.\ \Big((s_n^\kappa = P_m) \Rightarrow ((s_n^{\kappa-1} = M_{\sigma_{m,i}})\\
&\wedge (\bigvee\nolimits_{\kappa' > \kappa} s_n^{\kappa'} = D_m) \wedge (\forall \kappa' \neq \kappa \in \{1, ..., k_n\}.\ s_n^{\kappa'} \neq P_m))\Big)\\
&\wedge \Big((s_n^\kappa = D_m) \Rightarrow ((s_n^{\kappa-1} = M_{\sigma_{m,f}}) \wedge (\bigvee\nolimits_{\kappa' < \kappa} s_n^{\kappa'} = P_m)\\
&\wedge (\forall \kappa' \neq \kappa \in \{1, ..., k_n\}.\ s_n^{\kappa'} \neq D_m))\Big)\Big)\Big)
\end{aligned}
$$

$$
\Phi_1(\Pi) = \forall \mathcal{S}_n \in \Pi,\ \phi_1(\mathcal{S}_n) \qquad (2)
$$

Definition 6. ***Completed task.*** *Tasks with id μ_m in taskset $\mathcal{M}$ are completed $\Phi_{2,\mathcal{M}}$ by a plan Π if for each task there exists a single agent n with a consistent action sequence $\mathcal{S}_n \in \Pi$ that picks and drops the action. Additionally, the drop action must be before the deadline, and the time before moving to the pick action must be greater than or equal to the start time t_m ($\phi_{2,m}$). We define the predicates $\phi_{pickup}(m, \mathcal{S}_n)$ and $\phi_{dropoff}(m, \mathcal{S}_n)$ as*

$$
\phi_{pickup}(m, \mathcal{S}_n) = \exists \kappa_p \in \{1, ..., k_n\}.\ s_n^{\kappa_p} = P_m \qquad (3)
$$

$$
\phi_{dropoff}(m, \mathcal{S}_n) = \exists \kappa_d \in \{1, ..., k_n\}.\ s_n^{\kappa_d} = D_m \qquad (4)
$$

$$
\begin{aligned}
\phi_{2,m}(\Pi) =& \exists \mathcal{S}_n \in \Pi \qquad (5)\\
&st.\ \phi_1(\mathcal{S}_n) \wedge \phi_{pickup}(m, \mathcal{S}_n) \wedge \phi_{dropoff}(m, \mathcal{S}_n)\\
&\wedge (\forall n' \neq n \in \mathcal{N}.\ \neg\phi_{pickup}(m, \mathcal{S}_{n'}) \wedge \neg\phi_{dropoff}(m, \mathcal{S}_{n'}))\\
&\wedge (\mathcal{D}_{\kappa_d}(\mathcal{S}_n) \leq T_m) \wedge (\mathcal{D}_{\kappa_p - 2}(\mathcal{S}_n) \geq t_m)
\end{aligned}
$$

$$
\Phi_{2,\mathcal{M}}(\Pi) = \forall m \in \mathcal{M}.\ \phi_{2,m}(\Pi) \qquad (6)
$$

Definition 7. *We define $\Pi \models \Phi$ to hold when $\Phi(\Pi)$ is true.*

Definition 8. ***Valid Plan.*** *We define a valid plan Π for the set of agents $\mathcal{N}$ and set of tasks $\mathcal{M}$ as one where each agent's $\mathcal{S}_n$ is consistent and all tasks $m \in \mathcal{M}$ are completed. An empty plan is considered valid when $\mathcal{M} = \emptyset$. This can be written as $\Pi \models \Phi_1 \wedge \Phi_{2,\mathcal{M}}$.*

Definition 9. ***Updated plan.*** *A valid plan $\hat{\Pi}$ with agent sequence lengths $\hat{k_n}$ is updated at a time t from a previous valid plan Π with agent sequence lengths k_n if the following conditions hold. In each agent's action sequence there is an equivalent prefix $\hat{\mathcal{S}}_n^\kappa$ to that in Π where the prefix is all of $\mathcal{S}_n$ in Π followed by a wait action or $(s_n^\kappa \in \mathbf{P} \cup \mathbf{D}) \wedge \mathcal{D}_k(\mathcal{S}_n) \geq t$. This means that past actions and the* *current action are unchanged. A plan can only be updated at a system location s. A valid initial plan $\hat{\Pi}$ is always considered updated from an empty previous plan Π: $\forall n \in \mathcal{N}, \mathcal{S}_n = ()$. This empty plan will sometimes be notated as Π_{-1}. We also require that each agent's action sequence is efficient and does not contain extra waits.*

$$\begin{aligned}\Phi_{3,t,\Pi}(\hat{\Pi}) = \forall n \in \mathcal{N}, &\Bigg((\mathcal{S}_n^{k_n} = \mathcal{S}_n^{\hat{k}_n}) \\ &\wedge \Big((\mathcal{S}_n = \hat{\mathcal{S}}_n) \vee (\hat{s}_n^{k_n+1} = (W, t - \mathcal{D}_{k_n}(\mathcal{S}_n))) \Big) \Bigg) \\ &\bigvee \Bigg(\Big(\exists \kappa \in \{1, ..., k_n\}.\ (\mathcal{S}_n^{\kappa} = \hat{\mathcal{S}_n^{\kappa}}) \wedge (\mathcal{D}_{\kappa}(\mathcal{S}_n) \geq t) \wedge (s_n^{\kappa} \in \mathbf{P} \cup \mathbf{D}) \Big) \\ &\wedge \Big(\forall \kappa\ \in \{1, ..., k_n\}.\ \mathcal{D}_{\kappa}(\hat{\mathcal{S}}_n) \geq t, s_n^{\kappa} \notin \mathbf{W} \Big) \Bigg)\end{aligned} \tag{7}$$

Definition 10. ***Soundness.*** *Let $\Phi^j = \Phi_1 \wedge \Phi_{2,\overline{\mathcal{M}}_j} \wedge \Phi_{3,t_j,\Pi_{j-1}}$. An algorithm is sound for a given finite task stream of length J if $\forall j = 0, ..., J$, $(result_j = sat) \Rightarrow (\Pi_j \models \Phi^j)$.*

Definition 11. ***Completeness.*** *An algorithm is complete for a given finite task stream of length J, if $\forall j = 0, ..., J$, $(\Pi_j \models \Phi^j) \Rightarrow (result_j = sat)$.*

3.3 Problem Statement

Given a set of agents $\mathcal{N}$, task stream $\mathbb{S}$ including a known number of total tasks, and travel time graph G, after each element j in the task stream arrives at t_j, find a valid plan Π_j updated from a previous plan Π_{j-1} if one exists.

4 Summary of Approach

4.1 Preliminaries

We assume a basic understanding of propositional and first-order logic. *Satisfiability Modulo Theories* (SMT), a generalization of the Boolean satisfiability problem, is the satisfiability problem for formulas with respect to a first-order theory, or combinations of first-order theories. SMT solvers, such as Z3 [6] and cvc5 [1], are used to solve SMT formulas, where a model is returned if the SMT formula is satisfiable or otherwise reports unsatisfiability. Below we briefly introduce three theories of interest in the paper.

The theory of Equality Logic and Uninterpreted Functions (**EUF**) introduces the binary equality (=) predicate and uninterpreted functions, which maintains the property of functional congruence stating that function outputs should be the same when function inputs are the same. The theory of BitVectors (**BV**) incorporates fixed-precision numbers and operators, e.g. the bitwise AND operator. Note that the modulus operator with a constant 2 can be replaced by a bitwise

AND operation using a constant 1. The theory of Linear Integer Arithmetic (**LIA**) introduces arithmetic functions and predicates and constrains variables to only take integer values. Note that $v = x \mod k$, where x is a variable and k and v are constants, can be translated into $x = k \cdot n + v$ with a fresh integer variable n. In this paper, we only consider quantifier-free (QF) SMT formulas, and abbreviate Quantifier-Free Bit Vector Theory (Linear Integer Arithmetic) with Uninterpreted Functions as QF_UFBV (QF_UFLIA).

4.2 Encoding Literals

We introduce the notion of an **action id** i to describe what action an agent is taking. The first N action ids represent going to the corresponding agent number's starting position. For each following pair of values j, the values correspond to picking up and dropping off the jth object, respectively.

Each agent n in $\mathcal{N}$ is allowed D action tuples where a tuple for an action point $d = (i_d^n, t_d^n, l_d^n)$. i_d^n is the id of the action being taken, t_d^n is the time by which the action corresponding to the action id i_d^n has been completed, and l_d^n is the agent's load at the time t_d^n after completing the action with id i_d^n.

For each task $m \in \mathcal{M}$, we define the task start $start_m$ and end end_m times with agent n completing the task n_m. This creates a tuple $(start_m, end_m, n_m)$.

4.3 Incremental Solving

For tasks arriving online, we must re-solve our SMT problem given the new tasks. We implement this using push and pop functionalities provided by SMT solvers to retain information about previous solves. We push constraints onto the stack and pop them before adding new tasks as explained in AddTasks(). Past action points are constrained to be constant in SavePastState().

We use assumptions-based incremental solving to adjust the number of action points used. This allows us to force the solver to start with the minimum number necessary and search for the sufficient number needed for a sat result if one exists. We assume we are either given a list $\mathcal{K}$ of action point counts or will construct a reasonable list by starting with the $D_{min}(\mathcal{M}) = 2\lceil \frac{|\mathcal{M}|}{N} \rceil$ and incrementing by two to $D_{max} = 2M_{max} + 1$ inclusive. The last value of the user provided list must be D_{max}. More about D_{max} is explained in Sect. 5. From this, we define an assumption list Γ of booleans the same length as $\mathcal{K}$. An element $\Gamma[k]$ is used as an input to the solver to designate how many action points to use. $D = D_{max}$ in the encoding to allow for using the max number of action points if necessary to find a satisfying assignment.

4.4 SMT Encoding

Figure 2 includes the types of constraints that are used in our encoding. We include all for the initial solve and then some are iteratively removed and added for additional solves as explained in Algorithm 1. Assume t_{max} is set large enough to be greater than the maximum deadline of any task to appear plus maximum travel time between any two points. For our completeness argument, we will assume that $D = D_{max} = 2M_{max} + 1$.

For readability, we define the following symbols:

$$\mathrm{p}_d^n = ITE((i_d^n \,\&\, 1 = mod(N,2)) \wedge (i_d^n > N), 1, 0) \tag{8}$$

$$\mathrm{d}_d^n = ITE((i_d^n \,\&\, 1 = abs(mod(N,2) - 1)) \wedge (i_d^n > N), 1, 0) \tag{9}$$

$$\mathrm{dl}_d^{n,m} = (\bigvee\nolimits_{d'=d+1}^{D-1} i_{d'}^n = 2\mu_m + N + 1) \vee False \tag{10}$$

$$\mathrm{as}^{n,m} = \bigvee\nolimits_{d=1}^{D-1} i_d^n = 2\mu_m + N \tag{11}$$

$$valid_{i,d}^n = (N \leq i_d^n) \wedge (i_d^n < 2M + N) \tag{12}$$

E.1 initializes the action tuples; E.2, E.3, and E.6 relate action tuple pairs; E.4 restricts the uninterpreted functions, E.5 and E.7 bound action point values, E.8 restricts the task uninterpreted functions, E.9–E.11 relate action and task tuples; and E.12 restricts task tuples. Note that $mod(N, 2)$ and $abs(mod(N, 2) - 1)$ are pre-computed and are within {0, 1}.

4.5 Overall Algorithm

Algorithm 1 defines the overall algorithm. Figure 3 shows a flowchart of Algorithm 1. We define the following functions for use in the algorithm:

- Push($\mathcal{E}$), Pop($\mathcal{E}$): Refers to pushes and pops for incremental solving.
- Solve($\mathcal{E}, \alpha$): Solves the encoding $\mathcal{E}$ assuming $\alpha \in \Gamma$ returning the Result $\in$ sat, unsat, unknown and satisfying assignment $\mathcal{O}$ if available.
- GetPlan($\mathcal{O}$): Taking each agent's action points in order, for each action point d after the 1st where $i_d^n \neq \nu_n$, let $\mu_m = \lfloor \frac{i_d^n - N}{2} \rfloor$. If $t_d^n - t_{d-1}^n > w_{Loc(i_d^n), Loc(i_{d-1}^n)} + \rho$, add $(W, t_d^n - w_{Loc(i_d^n), Loc(i_{d-1}^n)} - \rho)$. Add $(M, \sigma_{m,i})$, (P, μ_m) if $mod(i_d^n - N, 2) = 0$ and $(M, \sigma_{m,f}), (D, \mu_m)$ if $mod(i_d^n - N, 2) = 1$.
- SavePastState($t_j, \mathcal{E}, \mathcal{O}$): For each agent, loop from $d = 0$ to $d = D - 1$, calling Add($(i_d^n, t_d^n, l_d^n) = \mathcal{O}_{j-1}((i_d^n, t_d^n, l_d^n)), \mathcal{E}, \emptyset, \emptyset$) until $(\mathcal{O}_{j-1}(t_d^n) \geq t_j) \mid (d + 1 < D \& i_{d+1}^n = n)$ at which point $d + 1$ is saved into δ_{ν_n}. Return the updated encoding and $\delta_{n \in \mathcal{N}}$.

In Algorithm 1, lines 1 and 2 add constraints that do not use task or arrival time information. Lines in between 3 and 22 contain code run after waiting for each task set to arrive. For each task set other than the 0th, line 5 saves the state of action points that have occurred in the past or that an agent is currently completing. In lines 6–8, we add constraints relating to the incoming set of tasks, pushing as necessary so that constraints can be popped later. The constraints that are pushed and popped are those that are based on new information (t_j and $\mathcal{M}_j$). In lines 9 to 17, we iteratively increase the number of action points used until the problem returns sat or the sufficient number of action points is reached in which case if the problem still returns unsat it will continue to return unsat

$$\mathcal{E}^{base}(\mathcal{N}, G, \Gamma, D, K_n, t_{max}) =$$

$$(\bigwedge_{n\in\mathcal{N}}(i_0^n, t_0^n, l_0^n) = (\nu_n, 0, 0) \bigwedge_{k=0}^{|\mathcal{K}|-2} \Gamma[k] \Rightarrow (i_{\mathcal{K}[k]}^n = \nu_n) \tag{E.1}$$

$$\bigwedge_{n\in\mathcal{N}} \bigwedge_{d=1}^{D-2} (i_d^n = \nu_n) \Rightarrow (i_{d+1}^n = \nu_n) \tag{E.2}$$

$$\bigwedge_{n\in\mathcal{N}} \bigwedge_{d=1}^{D-1} (l_d^n = l_{d-1}^n + \mathrm{p}_d^n - \mathrm{d}_d^n) \wedge (\neg(i_d^n = \nu_n) \Rightarrow (\neg(i_{d-1}^n = i_d^n))) \tag{E.3}$$

$$\bigwedge_{\sigma_1\in V} \bigwedge_{\sigma_2\in V} Dist(\sigma_1, \sigma_2) = w_{\sigma_1,\sigma_2} \bigwedge_{n\in\mathcal{N}} Loc(\nu_n) = n_s \tag{E.4}$$

$$\bigwedge_{n\in\mathcal{N}} \bigwedge_{d=1}^{D-1} (l_d^n \geq 0) \wedge (l_d^n \leq K_n) \wedge (i_d^n \geq 0) \wedge (i_d^n = \nu_n) \Rightarrow (t_d^n = t_{max})) \tag{E.5}$$

$$\mathcal{E}^{update}(\mathcal{N}, \delta, t_j, D, M) =$$

$$(\bigwedge_{n\in\mathcal{N}} \bigwedge_{d=\delta_n}^{D-1} (i_d^n \geq N) \Rightarrow$$
$$(t_d^n = ITE(t_{d-1}^n \leq t_j, t_j, t_{d-1}^n) + Dist(Loc(i_{d-1}^n), Loc(i_d^n)) + \rho) \tag{E.6}$$

$$\bigwedge_{n\in\mathcal{N}} \bigwedge_{d=1}^{D-1} \neg(i_d^n = \nu_n) \Rightarrow (valid_{i,d}^n)) \tag{E.7}$$

$$\mathcal{E}^{tasks}(\mathcal{N}, \mathcal{M}, D) =$$

$$(\bigwedge_{m\in\mathcal{M}}(Loc(2\mu_m + N) = \sigma_{m,i}) \wedge (Loc(2\mu_m + N + 1) = \sigma_{m,f}) \tag{E.8}$$

$$\bigwedge_{n\in\mathcal{N}} \bigwedge_{d=1}^{D-1} \bigwedge_{m\in\mathcal{M}} (i_d^n = 2\mu_m + N) \Rightarrow ((start_m = t_d^n) \wedge \mathrm{dl}_d^{n,m}) \tag{E.9}$$

$$\bigwedge_{n\in\mathcal{N}} \bigwedge_{d=1}^{D-1} \bigwedge_{m\in\mathcal{M}} (i_d^n = 2\mu_m + 1 + N) \Rightarrow (end_m = t_d^n) \wedge (n_m = \nu_n) \tag{E.10}$$

$$\bigwedge_{n\in\mathcal{N}} \bigwedge_{m\in\mathcal{M}} (n_m = \nu_n) \Rightarrow \mathrm{as}^{n,m} \tag{E.11}$$

$$\bigwedge_{m\in\mathcal{M}} (n_m \geq 0) \wedge (n_m < N) \wedge (start_m \geq t_m + \rho) \wedge (end_m \leq T_m)) \tag{E.12}$$

Fig. 2. Constraints used in the encoding developed in Algorithm 1

as is discussed in Sect. 5. Lines 10 to 12 increase the number of action points until the necessary number for the total number of tasks is reached. Lines 13 through 17 check the encoding with the given assumption, returning a plan if sat and incrementing the index into the action point count list if not sat. Line 21 pops the most recent model.

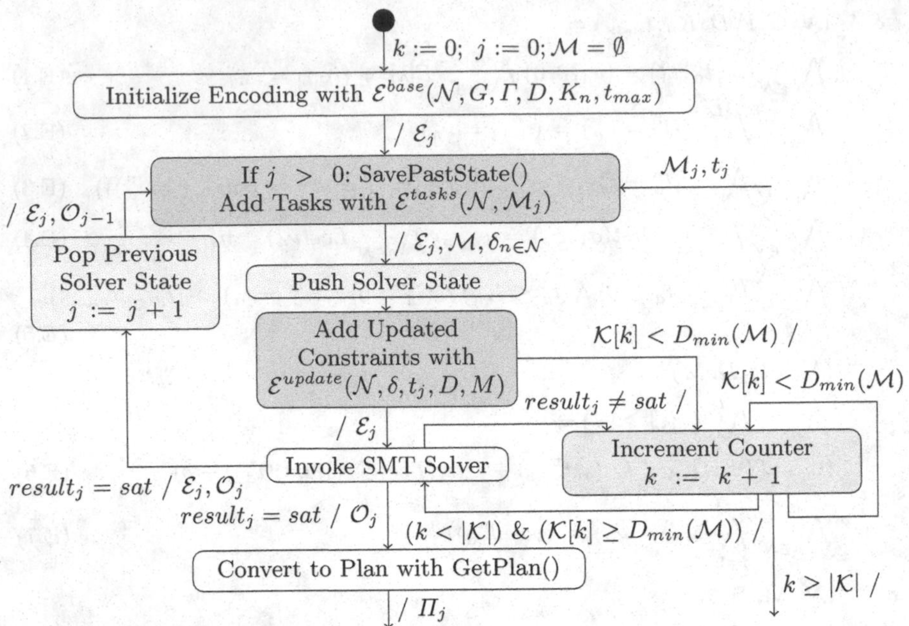

Fig. 3. Flow chart of Algorithm 1 starting at the black circle. A / B denotes a conditional A and a changed variable B. On the right is the assumption block to manage problem size. The third row from the top (in yellow) shows pushes and pops of the solver state. (Color figure online)

Algorithm 1. Overall Algorithm

```
M, E_0, k, j ← ∅, E_0, 0, 0
E_j ← E^base(N, G, Γ, D_max, K_n, t_max)
WaitForTaskSet (M_j, t_j)
if j > 0
    E_j, δ ← SavePastState(t_j, E_j, O)
E_j, M ← E_j ∪ E^tasks(N, M_j), M ∪ M_j              // Add constraints for new tasks
Push(E_j)
E_j ← E_j ∪ E^update(N, δ, t_j, D_max, |M|)          // Update constraints due to new tasks
while k < |K|
    if K[k] < D_min(M)                               // Increment k if num of action points
        k ← k + 1                                    // is smaller than minimum needed
        continue
    result_j, O_j = Solve(E_j, Γ[k])                 // Invoke SMT solver
    if result_j = sat
        Π_j = GetPlan(O_j)
        break
    k ← k + 1                                        // Unsat case – more action points may be needed
if result_j ≠ sat
    return unsat
j ← j + 1
E_j ← Pop(E_{j−1})
GoTo 3
```

5 Theoretical Results

In this section, we prove soundness and completeness for Algorithm 1 as described in Definition 10 and 11. We assume the solver used is sound and complete for the theories of bitvectors, uninterpreted functions, and linear integer arithmetic. Due to space constraint, additional proofs have been moved to the appendix in the extended version.[1]

5.1 Soundness

We first state two lemmas about our algorithm providing consistent action sequences and completing tasks given an initial task set of $\mathcal{M}_0$. To help in proving soundness, we also define strictly monotonically increasing action point times as $\phi = \forall n \in \mathcal{N}\ \forall d = 1, \ldots, D-1$ st. $i^n_d \neq n, t^n_{d-1} < t^n_d$.

Lemma 1. ***Consistency of action sequences.*** *If* $result_0$ *is sat,* $\phi \wedge \Pi_0 \models \Phi_1$.

Proof. (Sketch) We show only move/pick or move/drop pairs will be added to each action sequence if it is not empty. Therefore, the first action will be a move, there will be no consecutive moves, and corresponding moves will proceed picks/drops. Then, each second action can be mapped to the id for an action point, which constrains picks to be before drops and vice versa. We next show action point times are unique per agent by arguing that the alternative would require assigning two different times to the same task start or end time. This allows us to show picks and drops only occur once. Finally, we map loads of the action sequence to loads in the encoding to show capacity is adhered to.

Lemma 2. ***Completion of tasks.*** *If* $result_0$ *is sat,* $\Pi_0 \models \Phi_{2,\mathcal{M}}$ *for* $\mathcal{M} = \mathcal{M}_0$.

Proof. (Sketch) We first show that if $result_0$ is sat, by construction each task should be started by an agent and be completed by the same agent. Moreover, no two agents can start or complete the same task because that would imply that two distinct values are assigned to n_m in E.10. Finally, by construction the action point times satisfy the start time and deadline constraints, and by mapping time values to durations of subsequences we can prove that all timing constraints are satisfied.

We next state three lemmas that combined state that a sat result for iteration $j+1$ means our algorithm will fulfill Φ^j provided a previous result of sat also led to the plan fulfilling Φ^j.

Lemma 3. ***Plans are updated.*** *Assume* $(result_j = sat) \Rightarrow (\phi \wedge \Pi_j \models \Phi^j)$. *If* $result_{j+1}$ *is sat,* $\Pi_{j+1} \models \Phi_{3,t_{j+1},\Pi_j}$.

[1] Link to extended version: https://arxiv.org/abs/2403.11737.

Proof. (Sketch) We are updating from a valid plan if $(result_j = sat)$. Consider two cases per agent: 1) The duration of the previous action sequence is less than t_{j+1}. SavePastState($\cdot$) will save action points that only have times in the past, so either the new action sequence will be the same or will include a wait. This is because the time between the last action point of the previous assignment and the first changed action point will be greater than just a travel time plus a pick/drop. 2) Duration is greater than or equal to t_{j+1}. The time of the last action point copied from the previous assignment will be $\geq t_{j+1}$, so there will be an equivalent prefix, and no new waits will be added.

Lemma 4. ***Updated consistency.*** *Assume* $(result_j = sat) \Rightarrow (\phi \wedge \Pi_j \models \Phi^j)$. *If* $result_{j+1}$ *is sat,* $\Pi_{j+1} \models \Phi_1$.

Proof. (Sketch) Much of the proof can be repeated from that of Lemma 1. The key differences are the potential for added wait actions. Therefore, simple pairs of a move and pick/drop will now occasionally be a wait, move, and pick/drop. The waits will shift the mapping between actions and action id number but the statements from before still hold i.e., that a task is picked before dropped and vice versa. Action point times are still strictly monotonically increasing. We show this by remembering that the saved action point times are strictly monotonically increasing. We know that the new ones will be strictly monotonically increasing and greater than t_{j+1}, so the whole sequence will be, and we can claim pick and drop actions only occur once as before.

Lemma 5. ***Updated completion.*** *Assume* $(result_j = sat) \Rightarrow (\phi \wedge \Pi_j \models \Phi^j)$. *If* $result_{j+1}$ *is sat,* $\Pi_{j+1} \models \Phi_{2,j+1}$ *where* $\overline{\mathcal{M}}_{j+1} = (\bigcup_{j'=0}^{j+1} \mathcal{M}_{j'})$.

Proof. (Sketch) Much of the proof can be repeated from that of Lemma 2. For tasks that are completed before the arrival time t_j of new tasks, the duration constraints are satisfied. For all action points that take place after t_j, since the encoding still constrains that each task m starts after $start_m$ and ends before end_m and we are able to map action point times to durations, the timing constraints will be fulfilled.

In Theorem 1 and the following proof, we use the above lemmas to build an inductive argument that our algorithm is sound.

Theorem 1. ***Soundness of Algorithm.*** *Algorithm 1 is sound.*

Proof. Assuming $result_0 = sat$, the initial plan $\Pi_0 \models \Phi_{3,t,\emptyset}$ by definition. By Lemmas 1 and 2, $\phi \wedge \Pi_0 \models \Phi_1 \wedge \Phi_{2,\overline{\mathcal{M}}_j}$ where $\overline{\mathcal{M}}_j = \mathcal{M}_0$. We have therefore shown a base case that $(result_0 = sat) \Rightarrow (\phi \wedge \Pi_0 \models \Phi^0)$.

We will next make an inductive argument to show that at each iteration we are building a valid, updated plan with strictly monotonically increasing action point times. We need to show for $j \geq 1$ that $((result_{j-1} = sat) \Rightarrow (\Pi_{j-1} \models \Phi^{j-1})) \Rightarrow (result_j = sat \Rightarrow \Pi_j \models \Phi^j)$. We have two cases: 1) $result_{j-1} = sat$ and 2) $result_{j-1} \neq sat$. By construction, the algorithm will end and return unsat if $result_{j-1} \neq sat$ for $j > 0$, so if $result_{j-1} \neq sat$ then $result_j \neq sat$ for $j > 0$ then each implication is true proving the statement for this case. For $j > 0$, if we assume $(result_{j-1} = sat \Rightarrow \Pi_{j-1} \models \Phi^{j-1}) \wedge (result_{j-1} = \text{sat})$, then by Lemmas 3, 4, and 5, $result_j = sat$ implies $\phi \wedge \Pi_j \models \Phi^j$ and $result_j \neq sat$ trivially satisfies the formula. This implies the desired statement of soundness: $(result_j = sat) \Rightarrow (\Pi_j \models \Phi^j)$.

5.2 Completeness

In the following three lemmas, we state first that D_{max} is the maximum number of action points needed for an encoding provided the max number of tasks that will arrive is known. Then, we show that given we start with this maximum number of action points our algorithm is complete. Finally, we state that we will reach this number of action points in our algorithm if necessary. This allows us to then prove completeness.

Lemma 6. ***Maximum number of action points.*** *If an assignment $\mathcal{O}$ does not exist for an encoding $\mathcal{E}$ when $D = D_{max} = 2M + 1$ of action points then no assignment $\mathcal{O}$ exists for $D > D_{max}$.*

Proof. As shown in Lemma 1, pick and drop ids will only occur once per task in an agent's assignment in a satisfying $\mathcal{O}$. By construction, action point ids must be either $i^n_d = n$ or $i^n_d \geq N \wedge i^n_d < 2M + N$. Therefore, for an agent n, the maximum number of action points that can be assigned to a value other than n is $2M$. Adding in the constrained 0th action point, the total is $2M + 1 = D_{max}$ where $i^n_d = n$ for $d = d' \geq D_{max}$. Therefore, adding an extra action point does not add new free variables, so an unsat result cannot turn sat by adding more action points.

Lemma 7. ***Conditional Completeness.*** *Assume $\Gamma[|\mathcal{K}| - 1]$. If $D = D_{max}$, Algorithm 1 is complete.*

Proof. (Sketch) We want to show that for each iteration j in Algorithm 1, if given a plan Π_j for which $\Pi_j \models \Phi^j$, we can find a satisfying assignment $\mathcal{O}_j$. We know from Lemma 6 that the maximum number of action points for our assignment is $D = D_{max}$ per agent. Now we need to create the assignment from the given plan.

Take the action sequence for each agent n. Set the initial action point tuple $(i^n_0, t^n_0, l^n_0) = (\nu_n, 0, 0)$. Find the 1-indexed subsequence of indices of pick and drop actions. For each element k in the subsequence, let $i^n_k = 2\mu_m + N$ or $i^n_k = 2\mu_m + N + 1$ where μ_m is the id of the task that is picked or dropped, respectively. Set $t^n_k = \mathcal{D}_k(\mathcal{S}_n)$ and $l^n_d = \mathcal{C}_k(\mathcal{S}_n)$. For the task m, if $s^k_n \in \mathbf{P}$, set $start_m = \mathcal{D}_k(\mathcal{S}_n)$. If $s^k_n \in \mathbf{D}$, set $end_m = \mathcal{D}_k(\mathcal{S}_n)$. Set $n_m = \nu_n$. Set all remaining action points to $(\nu_n, t_{max}, 0)$. In the full proof in the Appendix, we show that this assignment is satisfying by going through constraints in the encoding.

Lemma 8. ***Increment to D_{max}.*** *Following Algorithm 1, k will eventually be such that the number of free action points $D = D_{max}$.*

Proof. An action point d is free if it is not constrained to have $i_d^n = \nu_n$. By inspection we see that the while loop in Lines 11 and 17 increases the index into the action point list which changes the assumes until the last one which then places no restriction on the encoding. By construction, the encoding can use all D_{max} action points when no assumptions are present.

Theorem 2. ***Completeness of Solve.*** *Algorithm 1 is complete.*

Proof. By Lemma 8, we will reach $D = D_{max}$. By Lemma 7, we know that given a sufficiently large $D = D_{max}$, the algorithm is complete.

6 Experimental Analysis

In this section, we evaluate the performance of our approach for initial solves and incremental solves for tasks arriving online. Specifically, we aim to answer the following research questions:

RQ1: How does the initial solve scale with respect to the number of tasks, number of agents, and number of action points? How does it scale with respect to different theory encodings?
RQ2: How does incremental solving scale, and is it more effective than non-incremental solving at handling tasks arriving online? How does task set batch size affect the performance?

For the initial solve, we generated benchmarks using the Z3Py API for initial solve in both QF_UFLIA and QF_UFBV. For conciseness, we abbreviate these as LIA and BV, respectively. For incremental solving, we implement the encoding in BV using both Z3Py and the Bitwuzla [14] Python API. For BV benchmarks, variables are encoded using small-domain encoding.[2]

Our workspace model represents an indoor setting with hallways and twenty rooms. It aims to reflect the complexities and challenges robots face in navigating complicated indoor settings. System locations were chosen from critical regions and travel time between pairs of locations were calculated with the approach in [21]. Agents' start locations and tasks start and end locations are uniformly randomly sampled from the system locations. Our evaluation consists of two sets of benchmarks, discussed separately in Sect. 6.1 and 6.2. We use Z3, Bitwuzla, and cvc5 as state-of-the-art SMT solvers. In the following, we abbreviate *S-T* as a solver setting where solver S runs on some benchmarks in theory T. All experiments were run on an AWS EC2 c5.4xlarge instance with 16 Intel Xeon Platinum cores running at 3.0 GHz with 16 GB RAM. All solvers were given a 3600 s timeout on each query.

[2] Link to implementation and benchmarks: https://github.com/victoria-tuck/SMrTa.

6.1 RQ1: Performance of Initial Solve and Comparison on Theories

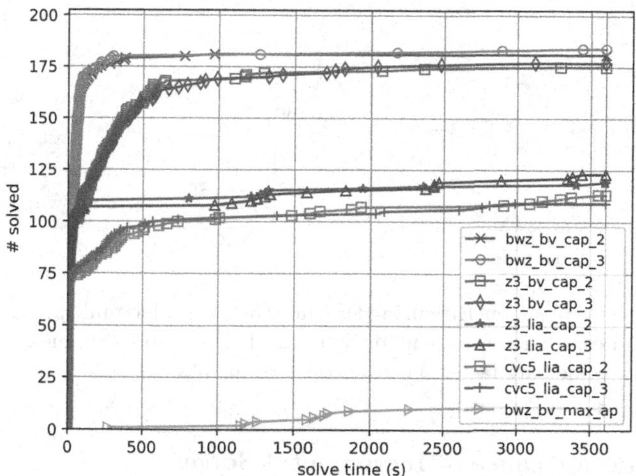

Fig. 4. Cactus plot for solver runtimes. Red line represents the 3600 s timeout. (Color figure online)

We create a set of 200 benchmarks with number of tasks ranging from 10 to 30 and number of agents from 5 to 20 both with an interval of 5 and ten instances for each combination. Task deadlines are sampled from a uniform distribution. Minimum number of action points were used. We ran both Z3-BV and Z3-LIA, Bitwuzla-BV, and cvc5-LIA on the initial solve benchmarks with max capacity c equal to 2 or 3.

Figure 4 shows the cactus plot for each solver. Solvers running on BV benchmarks consistently outperformed those running on LIA. Bitwuzla-BV performed the best, solving 184 and 181 instances, followed by Z3-BV solving 177 and 175 with $c = 3$ and 2 respectively. Solvers in general seem to perform better with larger max capacity, and we speculatively believe the constraint of $c = 3$ to be easier to solve. We also conducted an experiment using the maximum number of action points (`bwz_bv_max_ap` in Fig. 4) to show that action point number significantly affects performance.

Figure 5 shows the relation between problem size and solver performance for Bitwuzla-BV and Z3-BV with $c = 3$. In both plots, runtime grows as number of tasks grows, and when the number of tasks is fixed, a larger number of agents, which implies a smaller minimum number of action points, tend to lead to faster runtimes. Bitwuzla-BV generally outperforms Z3-BV on benchmarks with $M > 25$, while Z3-BV outperforms Bitwuzla-BV on those with $M < 15$.

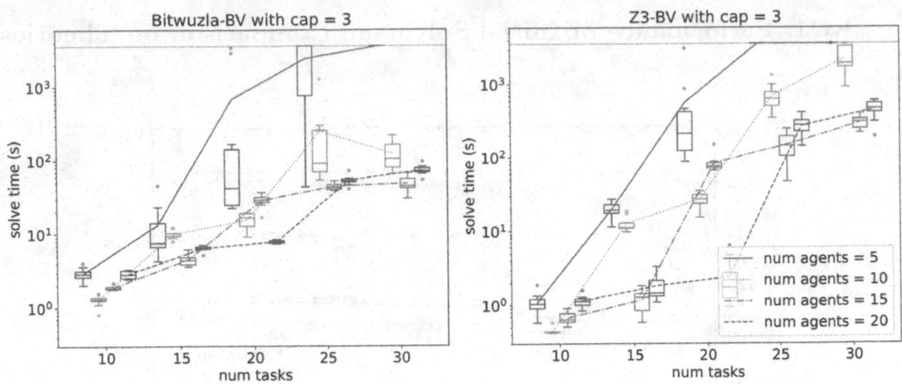

Fig. 5. Runtime analysis on Bitwuzla-BV and Z3-BV under multiple settings. Boxes represent quantiles, circles represent outliers, and lines represent means of runtimes. Observe that runtimes are faster when number of agents is larger.

6.2 RQ2: Performance of Incremental Solve

We create a set of 20 benchmarks with 20 agents that simulate a real world scenario where tasks arrive continuously. With a total of 200 tasks, we assume that each task arrives every 8 time units, and expires in $t \sim U(300, 500)$ time units after its arrival. We use batch (task set) sizes $b \in \{1, 10\}$. For each batch size b, the algorithm collects tasks and invokes the solver every b tasks. Due to the superior performances in the initial solve, only Bitwuzla-BV and Z3-BV with $c = 2$ were considered. Tasks are added incrementally via push/pop functionality, and action points are added using assumption variables according to the approach shown in Algorithm 1. For non-incremental solving, we copy all assertions of the incremental solver without the pushes/pops to a newly instantiated solver and assert the assumption variables.

We timed the execution of both solvers using incremental solving and non-incremental solving. The number of total free action points across agents was also recorded as an indicator of query difficulty. Figure 6 shows the results of running Bitwuzla-BV and Z3-BV with batch size equal to 1 and 10 with 200 tasks and 20 agents. We observed that performances on incremental and non-incremental solving depend greatly on the solver and batch size – Z3-BV significantly outperforms Bitwuzla-BV on incremental solving especially when batch sizes are small, as shown in the blue line in Fig. 6b, while Bitwuzla-BV performs better on non-incremental solves with larger batch sizes, as shown in the orange line in Fig. 6c. Empirically, Z3-BV took around 260 s on average to solve for 200 tasks. Based on the observations, we suggest using Z3-BV/Bitwuzla-BV with incremental/non-incremental solving when batch sizes are small/large.

Notice that there are peaks in runtime across all settings. These peaks occur when the minimum number of action points required increases. With 20 agents and batch size equal to 1 (10), a peak occurs every 20 (2) batches as an additional action point is needed every 20 tasks. We speculate this to be due to an increase of the search space when extra action points are introduced (shown via red lines in Fig. 6). Note that runtime does not correlate to the number of action points that have to be assigned to complete all available tasks, which is an indicator of the number of un/re-assigned tasks (shown in green in Fig. 6).

In comparison to heuristic-based approaches [19], those approaches will be faster but lack the guarantees of our approach. Additionally, when comparing others with guarantees [4,16], these lack runtime information.

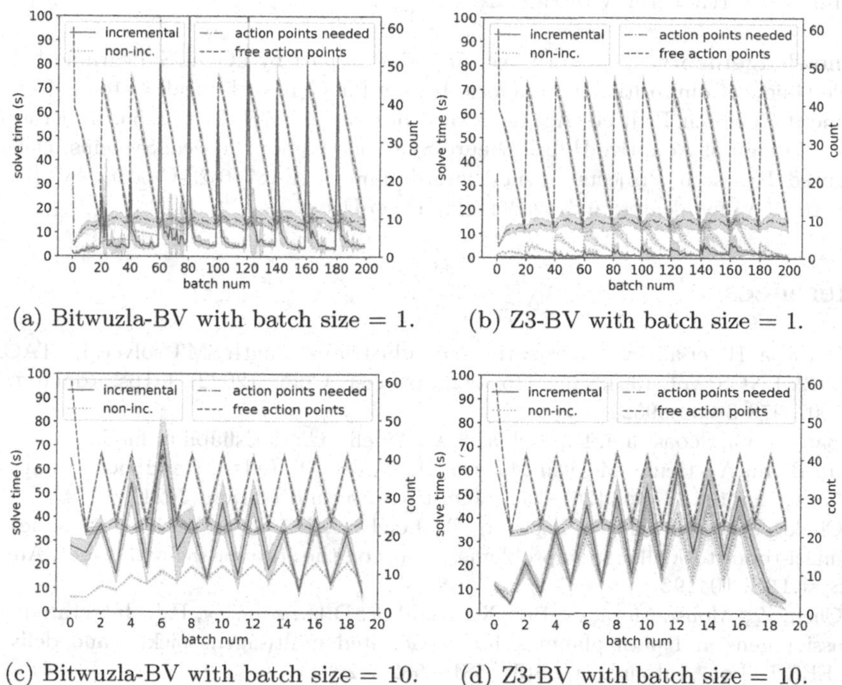

(a) Bitwuzla-BV with batch size = 1. (b) Z3-BV with batch size = 1.

(c) Bitwuzla-BV with batch size = 10. (d) Z3-BV with batch size = 10.

Fig. 6. Performance comparison for incremental v.s. non-incremental solves with $cap = 2$.

7 Conclusion and Future Work

In this work, we present a SMT-based approach to the problem of Dynamic Multi-Robot Task Allocation with capacitated agents. Our algorithm handles online tasks and iteratively adjusts the size of the problem in order to manage computational complexity. We show its efficacy on problems of up to 20 agents and 200 tasks, showing the potential for our approach to be used in longer settings. Future work includes extending to stochastic settings to better accommodate dynamic environments where a probabilistic guarantee of adherence is desired potentially using probabilistic logics [8], and to connect our approach to lower-level motion planning algorithms (e.g., similar to the work on satisfiability modulo convex programming [22]). Further extensions include allowing agents to pass objects to one another, and, specifically for hospital settings, representing complicated features like elevators. We also believe that this problem setting can act as an SMT benchmark because, for example, without managing action points as in our approach, large numbers of action points do create problems that are very difficult to solve as shown in Fig. 4. In conclusion, we show SMT-based approaches can be useful in handling the computational complexity of this combinatorial domain in an extendable way and that our framework provides a baseline for further study of this area.

Acknowledgements. This work was supported in part by LOGiCS: Learning-Driven Oracle-Guided Compositional Symbiotic Design for Cyber-Physical Systems, Defense Advanced Research Projects Agency award number FA8750-20-C-0156; by Provably Correct Design of Adaptive Hybrid Neuro-Symbolic Cyber Physical Systems, Defense Advanced Research Projects Agency award number FA8750-23-C-0080; by Toyota under the iCyPhy Center; and by Berkeley Deep Drive.

References

1. Barbosa, H., et al.: cvc5: a versatile and industrial-strength SMT solver. In: TACAS 2022. LNCS, vol. 13243, pp. 415–442. Springer, Cham (2022). https://doi.org/10.1007/978-3-030-99524-9_24
2. Barrett, C., Sebastiani, R., Seshia, S.A., Tinelli, C.: Satisfiability modulo theories. In: Biere, A., Heule, M., van Maaren, H., Walsh, T. (eds.), Handbook of Satisfiability, chapter 33, pp. 1267–1329. IOS Press, second edition (2021)
3. Chakraa, H., Guerin, F., Leclercq, E., Lefebvre, D.: Optimization techniques for multi-robot task allocation problems: review on the state-of-the-art. Robot. Auton. Syst.**168**, 104492
4. Chen, Z., Alonso-Mora, J., Bai, X., Harabor, D.D., Stuckey, P.J.: Integrated task assignment and path planning for capacitated multi-agent pickup and delivery. IEEE Robot. Autom. Lett. **6**(3), 5816–5823 (2021)
5. Das, G.P., Mcginnity, T.M., Coleman, S.A., Behera, L.: A distributed task allocation algorithm for a multi-robot system in healthcare facilities. J. Intell. Robot. Syst. **80**, 33–58 (2015)
6. de Moura, L., Bjørner, N.: Z3: an efficient SMT solver. In: Ramakrishnan, C.R., Rehof, J. (eds.) TACAS 2008. LNCS, vol. 4963, pp. 337–340. Springer, Heidelberg (2008). https://doi.org/10.1007/978-3-540-78800-3_24
7. Gavran, I., Majumdar, R., Saha, I.: Antlab: a multi-robot task server. ACM Trans. Embed. Comput. Syst. (TECS) **16**(5s), 1–19 (2017)
8. Hansson, H., Jonsson, B.: A logic for reasoning about time and reliability. Form. Aspects Comput. **6**, 02 (1995)
9. Hekmatnejad, M., Pedrielli, G., Fainekos, G.: Optimal task scheduling with nonlinear costs using SMT solvers. In: IEEE International Conference on Automation Science and Engineering (CASE) (2019)
10. Jeon, S., Lee, J.: Vehicle routing problem with pickup and delivery of multiple robots for hospital logistics. In: 2016 16th International Conference on Control, Automation and Systems (ICCAS), pp. 1572–1575. IEEE (2016)

11. Jeon, S., Lee, J., Kim, J.: Multi-robot task allocation for real-time hospital logistics. In: IEEE International Conference on Systems, Man, and Cybernetics (SMC), pp. 2465–2470 (2017)
12. Lopes, R.B., Ferreira, C., Santos, B.S.: A simple and effective evolutionary algorithm for the capacitated location-routing problem. Comput. Oper. Res. **70**, 155–162 (2016)
13. Majd, K., Yaghoubi, S., Yamaguchi, T., Hoxha, B., Prokhorov, D., Fainekos, G.: Safe navigation in human occupied environments using sampling and control barrier functions. In: IEEE/RSJ International Conference on Intelligent Robots and Systems (IROS) (2021)
14. Niemetz, A., Preiner, M.: Bitwuzla. In: Computer Aided Verification–35th International Conference, CAV, pp. 3–17. Springer, Cham (2023). https://doi.org/10.1007/978-3-031-37703-7_1
15. Nunes, E., Manner, M., Mitiche, H., Gini, M.: A taxonomy for task allocation problems with temporal and ordering constraints. Robot. Auton. Syst. **90**, 55–70 (2017). Special Issue on New Research Frontiers for Intelligent Autonomous Systems
16. Okubo, T., Takahashi, M.: Simultaneous optimization of task allocation and path planning using mixed-integer programming for time and capacity constrained multi-agent pickup and delivery. In: 2022 22nd International Conference on Control, Automation and Systems (ICCAS), pp. 1088–1093. IEEE (2022)
17. Parwana, H., et al.: Feasible space monitoring for multiple control barrier functions with application to large scale indoor navigation (2023). https://arxiv.org/abs/2312.07803
18. Rungta, N.: A billion SMT queries a day (Invited Paper). In: Shoham, S., Vizel, Y. (eds.) Computer Aided Verification. CAV 2022. LNCS, vol. 13371, pp. 3–18. Springer, Cham (2022). https://doi.org/10.1007/978-3-031-13185-1_1
19. Sarkar, C., Paul, H.S., Pal, A.: A scalable multi-robot task allocation algorithm. In: 2018 IEEE International Conference on Robotics and Automation (ICRA), pp. 5022–5027. IEEE (2018)
20. Schüle, M., Kraus, J.M., Babel, F., Reißner, N.: Patients' trust in hospital transport robots: evaluation of the role of user dispositions, anxiety, and robot characteristics. In: 17th ACM/IEEE International Conference on Human-Robot Interaction (HRI), pp. 246–255 (2022)
21. Shah, N., Srivastava, S.: Using deep learning to bootstrap abstractions for hierarchical robot planning. In: 21st International Conference on Autonomous Agents and Multiagent Systems (AAMAS) (2022)
22. Shoukry, Y., Nuzzo, P., Sangiovanni-Vincentelli, A.L., Seshia, S.A., Pappas, G.J., Tabuada, P.: SMC: satisfiability modulo convex programming. Proc. IEEE **106**(9) (2018)
23. Uwacu, D., Yammanuru, A., Morales, M., Amato, N.M.: Hierarchical planning with annotated skeleton guidance. IEEE Robot. Autom. Lett. (RAL) **7**, 11055–11061 (2022)
24. Wurman, P.R., D'Andrea, R., Mountz, M.: Coordinating hundreds of cooperative, autonomous vehicles in warehouses. AI Mag. **29**(1), 9 (2008)

Control Barrier Function Toolbox: An Extensible Framework for Provable Safety

Andrew Schoer[1(✉)], Helena Teixeira-Dasilva[1,3], Christian So[2], Makai Mann[1], and Roberto Tron[2]

[1] MIT Lincoln Laboratory, Lexington, MA, USA
{andrew.schoer,makai.mann}@ll.mit.edu
[2] Boston University, Boston, MA, USA
{cbso,tron}@bu.edu
[3] Washington University in St. Louis, St. Louis, MO, USA
h.teixeira-dasilva@wustl.edu

Abstract. The need for safety is ubiquitous, however, guaranteeing safety can be difficult for systems with non-trivial dynamics. Control barrier functions (CBFs) are an active area of research for safety-critical control systems. Generally, the application of CBFs has been limited to those with the controls expertise required to write the safety constraints from scratch. An analogous technique for stabilization, Control Lyapunov functions (CLFs), can be paired with CBFs to find safe and stabilizing controls. Our CBF Toolbox, written in Python, enables easy construction of CBF and CLF constraints to provide safety guarantees in simulation and hardware demonstrations. Additionally, the CBF Toolbox serves as a useful tool to teach the theory, and explore the impact of CBFs and CLFs on control systems. We discuss the basic theory and organization of the toolbox, a simple software example, and a robotics demonstration to land a quadrotor on a moving platform with the CBF Toolbox.

Keywords: control barrier function · control Lyapunov function · safety

1 Introduction

In recent years, control barrier functions (CBFs) have become a popular technique used to provide mathematical guarantees that ensure the safety of autonomous systems. CBF techniques can be quite powerful and versatile, however, due to their relative novelty, there is no standard software implementation. As a result, this technology is often limited to use by controls experts. This

Roberto Tron was partly supported by NSF award CPS-1932162.
 The NASA University Leadership Initiative (grant #80NSSC20M0163) provided funds to assist the authors with their research, but this article solely reflects the opinions and conclusions of its authors and not any NASA entity.

N. Benz et al. (Eds.): NFM 2024, LNCS 14627, pp. 352–358, 2024.
https://doi.org/10.1007/978-3-031-60698-4_21

paper presents the Control Barrier Function Toolbox, a Python package that allows both the novice and the expert alike to design systems with safety guarantees provided by CBF constraints. The toolbox can pair CBF techniques with similarly formulated control Lyapunov functions (CLFs) to provide liveness guarantees which ensures an action moves an agent toward its goal. The relationships between objects in the CBF Toolbox are represented as a graph. This graph is used to automatically encode CBF and CLF constraints into a quadratic program (QP) to find safe and stabilizing controls for the autonomous agent(s) at every time step of the simulation or hardware implementation.

The Control Barrier Function Toolbox is an effective instructional tool for students who are new to control systems. It can be used out-of-the-box by those with only a cursory knowledge of controls, but its design allows for deeper exploration if desired. As a Python package, it can easily interface with ROS for robotics demonstrations, or be paired with other packages from the rich library of Python packages. Through the use of automatic differentiation, the software simplifies the synthesis of CBF and CLF constraints. In addition to students, this toolbox is also useful to researchers and engineers looking to enforce safety constraints for autonomous systems, or to provide a baseline of simple CBF techniques. Whether it is for educational purposes, engineering safety, or controls research, the CBF Toolbox aims to make control barrier functions and related techniques accessible.

2 Background

Dynamics. The dynamics of an object define how it moves through its state space, $\mathcal{X} \subset \mathbb{R}^n$. All dynamics that are built into the CBF Toolbox must be written in control affine form,

$$\dot{x} = f(x) + g(x)u, \tag{1}$$

where $x \in \mathcal{X} \subset \mathbb{R}^n$ is the state and $u \in \mathcal{U} \subset \mathbb{R}^m$ is the control input.

Control Barrier Functions. Control barrier functions (CBFs) provide a mathematical framework to enforce the forward invariance of a safe set. In other words, a CBF provides theoretical safety guarantees for a system by ensuring that it remains within a set of safe states. The safe set is defined by a continuously differentiable barrier function, $h(x)$, that is zero on the boundary, positive in the safe set, and negative in the unsafe set. A CBF constraint has the form

$$\mathcal{L}_f h(x) + \mathcal{L}_g h(x)u \geq -\alpha(h(x)), \tag{2}$$

where the left side of the inequality are the Lie derivatives of the barrier function $h(x)$ along f and g, and $\alpha(\cdot)$ is a class $\mathcal{K}$ function. Any control $u \in \mathcal{U}$ for the system (1) that satisfies inequality (2) is guaranteed to be safe. See [1] for a more in-depth discussion.

Control Lyapunov Functions. Control Lyapunov functions (CLFs) provide a mathematical framework to compute controls that asymptotically stabilize a system to an equilibrium point. A continuously differentiable Lyapunov function, $V(x)$, can be used to prove stability of an equilibrium point. A CLF constraint has the form

$$\mathcal{L}_f V(x) + \mathcal{L}_g V(x) u \leq -\gamma(V(x)), \tag{3}$$

where the left side are the Lie derivatives of the Lyapunov function $V(x)$ along f and g, and $\gamma(\cdot)$ is a class $\mathcal{K}$ function. Any control $u \in \mathcal{U}$ for the system (1) that satisfies inequality (3) is guaranteed to be asymptotically stabilizing. See [3,8] for a more in-depth discussion.

Control Synthesis. A standard approach to generating a control input u that satisfies (2) and (3) is to formulate an optimization problem. Any solution that satisfies a CBF constraint is guaranteed to remain safe with respect to the associated obstacle, and one that satisfies a CLF constraint is guaranteed to move an agent toward the associated goal. These two objectives can be in conflict if it is unsafe to move an agent toward its goal. For safety-critical scenarios, the CLF constraint is relaxed to ensure that safety is not compromised. This can be formulated as a quadratic program (QP),

$$\begin{aligned} u(x) = \underset{(u,\delta)\in\mathbb{R}^{m+1}}{\operatorname{argmin}} \quad & \frac{1}{2} u^T H u + \rho\delta^2 \\ \text{s.t.} \quad & \mathcal{L}_f h(x) + \mathcal{L}_g h(x) u \geq -\alpha(h(x)) \\ & \mathcal{L}_f V(x) + \mathcal{L}_g V(x) u \leq -\gamma(V(x)) + \delta, \end{aligned} \tag{4}$$

where the output is the safe control $u(x)$, δ is a CLF slack variable, H is a weighting matrix on the control space, ρ is a coefficient to relax liveness, and all other variables are as discussed above [2]. The objective function finds the minimum energy trajectory.

3 Organization

The CBF Toolbox is a Python package that simplifies encoding control barrier functions. The classes that form the core functionality of the CBF Toolbox are shown in Fig. 1. A user defines a scenario by connecting instances of subclasses of `Vertex` (we provide `Agent`, `Obstacle`, and `Goal`) with subclassess of `Edge` (we provide `CBF` and `CLF`). When a scenario is built into a `Simulation` object, a graph connecting `Vertex` objects with the `Edge` objects is automatically instantiated at each time step to generate the QP in (4) which is used to find satisfying control inputs to each `Agent`.

As can be seen in Fig. 1, four parameters are needed to define an arbitrary `Dynamics` model: the drift field, $f(x)$, the control fields, $g(x)$, the dimension of the state vector n, and the dimension of the control vector m. We provide `Single_integrator` and `Unicycle` dynamics. All `Vertex` objects have a `Shape` which encodes its associated barrier or Lyapunov function for use by connected `Edge` objects. The provided subclasses of `Shape` are `Point`, `Ellipsoid`, `Sphere` and `HalfPlane` which can be combined to handle many types of obstacles and goals. The classes `Vertex` and `Edge`, `Dynamics` and `Shape` are all designed to be extensible.

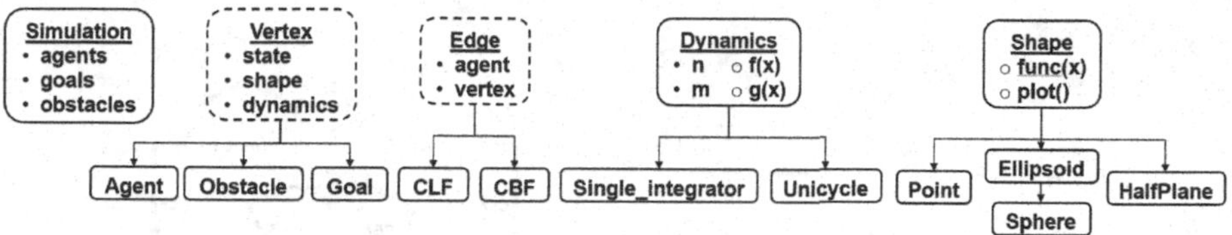

Fig. 1. A diagram that shows the hierarchies of the classes in the current release of the CBF Toolbox. Dashed lines denote abstract classes. The • are attributes of a class, and the ○ are definable functions.

The CBF and CLF constraints require derivatives which are automatically calculated using JAX [4]. Gurobi is the optimization package currently used to solve QPs [5], although future work could use a solver-agnostic framework. To support the hardware demonstration in Sect. 5, we leverage a number of other software tools including ROS [9] and Pixhawk [6], but code to integrate these tools is not currently provided with CBF Toolbox, but could be in the future.

4 Software Example

We illustrate how to create a simple software simulation using the CBF Toolbox with the code sample shown in Listing 1. This example shows two autonomous agents that will swap positions while avoiding an obstacle and each other.

```
1  # Define two agents with goals to swap positions
2  agt0=Agent(state=[0.,0.], radius=.5, dynamics=SingleInt2d())
3  agt1=Agent(state=[5.,4.], radius=.5, dynamics=SingleInt2d())
4  goal0=Goal([5.,4.])
5  goal1=Goal([0.,0.])
6  # Create an ellipsoidal obstacle between the agents
7  ellipse=Ellipsoid([1.,0.5], rotation=45)
8  obst=Obstacle([2.,2.], ellipse, SingleInt2d())
9  # Add everything to a simulation object and simulate
10 s=Simulation()
11 s.add_agent(agent=agt0, control=goal0)
12 s.add_agent(agent=agt1, control=goal1)
13 s.add_obstacle(obst=obst)
14 s.simulate(num_steps=100, dt=0.1)
```

Listing 1. Code for scenario with a two agents and a single obstacle

We define two `Agent` objects with single integrator dynamics on lines 2–3, and their corresponding `Goal` objects on line 4–5. We define a ellipsoidal `Obstacle` on lines 7–8. We define the `Simulation` object, and subsequently add all `Agent`, `Goal`, and `Obstacle` objects before running the simulation for 100 time steps on lines 10–14. Figure 2(a) shows the trajectories of the agent and obstacle part way through the simulation, and Fig. 2(b) shows the graph of relationships between objects. Figure 3 shows the CBF and CLF values throughout the simulation.

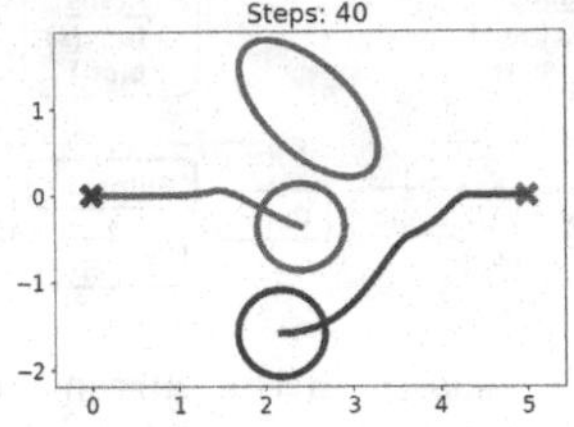

(a) Agent1 takes a wide route to avoid the `Obstacle` and Agent0

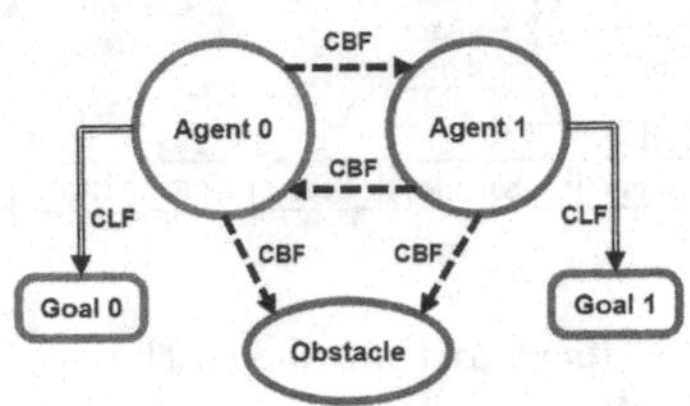

(b) `Vertex` objects relate to each other through `Edge` objects

Fig. 2. Two visualizations from the example in Listing 1

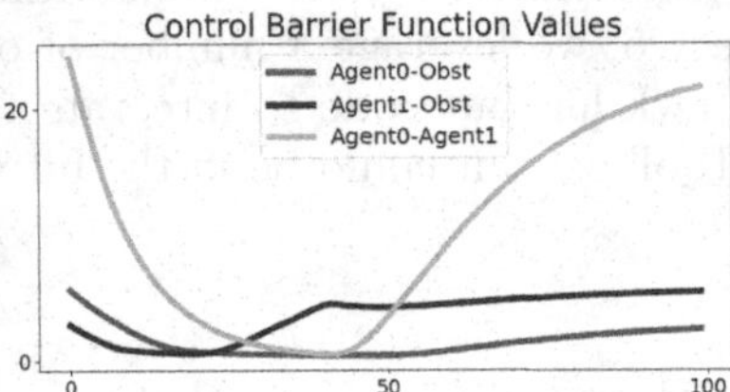

(a) CBF constraints enforce that the distance between two objects is never negative

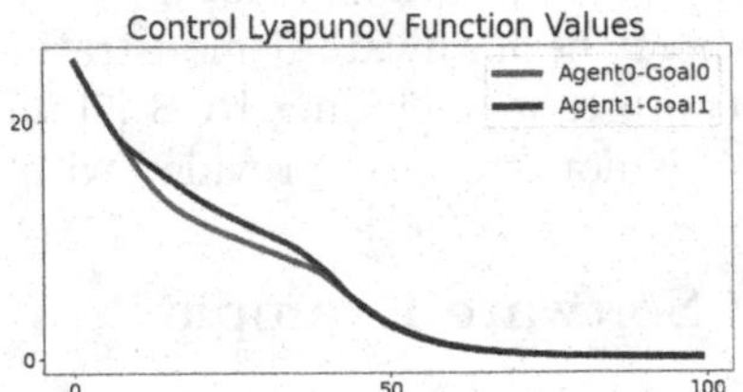

(b) CLF constraints enforces that the Agent-Goal distance moves toward zero

Fig. 3. These plots show the CBF and CLF values from the example in Listing 1

5 Hardware Experiment

We used the CBF Toolbox to safely land a quadrotor on a platform on the back of a Boston Dynamics Spot robot moving along a trajectory unknown to the quadrotor. Our hardware setup included an OptiTrack motion capture system to provide state estimates of the objects in our operational space. A ROS node running the CBF Toolbox code used the positions from OptiTrack to find safe and stabilizing velocity commands to send to the quadrotor. CBF constraints were used to avoid obstacles, and a CLF constraint was used to guide the quadrotor to the platform. Although a quadrotor has a complex dynamics model, we used a reduced-order, three dimensional single integrator model that allowed us to enforce safety constraints on the quadrotor's position by giving it velocity

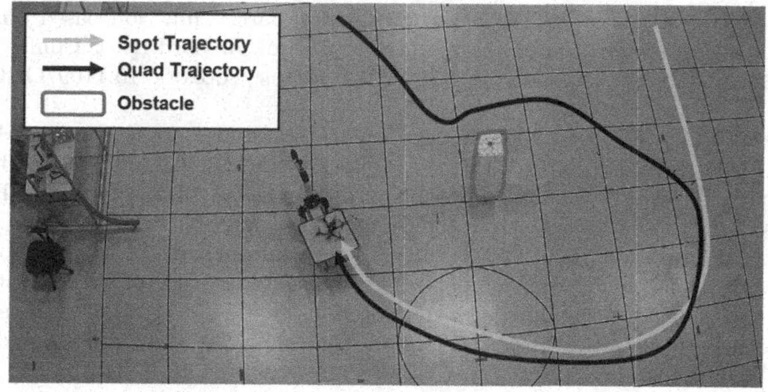

Fig. 4. The quadrotor must avoid the obstacle while moving to its goal

commands [7]. This model is sufficient as long as the autopilot controller tracking velocity commands to the quadrotor is not overwhelmed by large instantaneous changes in velocities. We demonstrated several successful landings on the moving platform while avoiding obstacles in the space. Figure 4 shows a snapshot from an overhead camera of one of these landing experiments with the trajectories of the quadrotor and robot overlaid.

The CBF Toolbox is useful in hardware demonstrations, but its limits should be understood. Every experimental setup should be carefully tested to ensure that the level of safety that the CBF Toolbox can provide is sufficient. Although the controls that are calculated are theoretically safe, assumptions begin to breakdown outside of the simulation environment. Errors can be introduced from various sources including uncertainty in your state estimation, low battery levels in your robots, and network latency to name a few. Additionally, as the scenario becomes more complex, the time needed to solve the quadratic program can become a limiting factor.

6 Conclusion

The CBF Toolbox is a Python package that makes makes using control barrier functions simple. Using object oriented design, and automatic differentiation software, this package builds CBF and CLF constraints from the user defined scenario, and solves a quadratic program to find safe and stabilizing controls for autonomous systems. The primary goal of the CBF Toolbox is to lower the barrier of entry to CBF and related techniques to make them more accessible to a broad audience of students, researchers, and engineers.

References

1. Ames, A.D., Coogan, S., Egerstedt, M., Notomista, G., Sreenath, K., Tabuada, P.: Control barrier functions: theory and applications. In: 2019 18th European control conference (ECC), pp. 3420–3431. IEEE (2019)

2. Ames, A.D., Grizzle, J.W., Tabuada, P.: Control barrier function based quadratic programs with application to adaptive cruise control. In: 53rd IEEE Conference on Decision and Control, pp. 6271–6278 (2014). https://doi.org/10.1109/CDC.2014.7040372
3. Artstein, Z.: Stabilization with relaxed controls. Nonlinear Anal. Theory, Methods Appl. **7**(11), 1163–1173 (1983). https://doi.org/10.1016/0362-546X(83)90049-4
4. Bradbury, J., et. al.: JAX: composable transformations of Python+NumPy programs (2018). http://github.com/google/jax
5. Gurobi Optimization, LLC: (2023). https://www.gurobi.com
6. Meier, L., Tanskanen, P., Fraundorfer, F., Pollefeys, M.: Pixhawk: A system for autonomous flight using onboard computer vision. In: 2011 IEEE International Conference on Robotics and Automation, pp. 2992–2997 (2011).https://doi.org/10.1109/ICRA.2011.5980229
7. Molnár, T., Ames, A.: Safety-critical control with bounded inputs via reduced order models, pp. 1414–1421 (2023). https://doi.org/10.23919/ACC55779.2023.10155871
8. Sontag, E.D.: A 'universal' construction of artstein's theorem on nonlinear stabilization. Syst. Control Lett. **13**(2), 117–123 (1989). https://doi.org/10.1016/0167-6911(89)90028-5
9. Stanford Artificial Intelligence Laboratory et al.: Robotic operating system. https://www.ros.org

Robotics: A New Mission for FRET Requirements

Gricel Vázquez[1(✉)], Anastasia Mavridou[2], Marie Farrell[3], Tom Pressburger[4], and Radu Calinescu[1]

[1] Department of Computer Science, University of York, York, UK
gricel.vazquez@york.ac.uk
[2] KBR Inc., NASA Ames Research Center, Moffett Field, USA
[3] Department of Computer Science, The University of Manchester, Manchester, UK
[4] NASA Ames Research Center, Moffett Field, USA

Abstract. Mobile robots are used to support planetary exploration and safety-critical environments such as nuclear plants. Central to the development of mobile robots is the specification of complex required behaviors known as missions. In this paper, we use NASA's Formal Requirements Elicitation Tool (FRET) to specify functional robotic mission requirements. To examine the applicability of FRET in the mobile robotics domain, we studied robotic mission patterns specified in Linear Temporal Logic (LTL). These patterns were originally derived from a large repository that included patterns from the literature and consultation with industrial experts. We extend this repository with those found during our extensive literature review. Although FRET has been successfully used in the past in case studies within the aerospace domain, mobile robot requirements present new challenges in their specification. To this end, our work provides a methodological basis for using FRET in the specification of robotic mission requirements.

1 Introduction

Mobile robots can help to separate humans from hazards and inaccessible environments, such as nuclear plants [14] and planetary exploration [12]. For example, NASA's Curiosity and Perseverance rovers are mobile robots that explore Mars, enabling us to gather data and execute missions that are currently out of reach for human astronauts. Central to the development of such systems is the elicitation and specification of mission functional requirements that guide

N. Benz et al. (Eds.): NFM 2024, LNCS 14627, pp. 359–376, 2024.
https://doi.org/10.1007/978-3-031-60698-4_22

the design and analysis process. Robotic mission requirements typically describe the high-level tasks that the robotic system must accomplish and how it should react in specific situations. These requirements are typically written in ambiguous natural language making their understanding and specification error-prone.

Formal languages, rooted in rigorous semantics, provide the means to precisely describe and reason about intended behavior; however, they are less intuitive than natural language. Even for experts, translating mission requirements into a formal language, like temporal logic, can be challenging [19,32]. To bridge the gap between intuitive natural language descriptions and unambiguous formal languages, specification patterns have been proposed by the research community. Recent work in [35] presents a collection of 22 temporal logic specification patterns for robotic missions, resulting from a systematic literature review and consultation with industrial partners and domain experts.

NASA's Formal Requirements Elicitation Tool (FRET) provides support for users to write their system's requirements using a restricted natural language. These requirements are automatically provided with temporal logic semantics that is more amenable to analysis and verification than the natural language requirements would be [9,19]. The ability to automatically generate temporal logic formalization from (structured) natural language requirements is useful, particularly in domains where those specifying the requirements may not be experts in logical formalization.

Our objective in this paper is to examine whether FRET, which has been used on aerospace use cases (e.g., [19,32,37]), can be adopted more generally in the robotics domain. Although FRET has been used effectively in specific robotic use cases [9,21], we examine the generalizability of FRET for mission specifications of mobile robots.

We begin by exploring the specification patterns identified in [35]. We examined the literature to find a more up-to-date set of patterns, which resulted in extending the original set with 6 new specification patterns and their associated temporal logic formalizations. We specify these patterns using FRET [23].

Specifically, this paper contributes:

1. A set of six newly identified robotic mission specification patterns that were derived from a systematic literature review (Sect. 2)
2. The specification using FRET of the patterns identified in [35], as well as our newly identified patterns (Sect. 3).
3. A study of the expressibility and applicability of FRET for robotic missions in Sect. 4.

2 Systematic Review: Identification of Robotic Patterns

We present our work on adding new robotic mission patterns to the set of patterns from [35], which, to the best of our knowledge, is the most extensive repository targeting robotic missions for mobile robots and their translation into Linear Temporal Logic (LTL) specifications. Each pattern is characterized by (i) a name; (ii) a description of the mission requirement; (iii) a template of the

Table 1. The venue sources used to obtain the primary studies for our literature review. We include the total number of publications per venue, which were identified using the queries defined in Sect. 2.

i	Venues	Acronyms	Type	Num publ.
i.1	International Journal of Robotics Research	IJRR	Journal	29
i.2	Transactions on Software Eng.	TSE	Journal	1
i.3	Robotics and Automation Letters	RA-L	Journal	369
i.4	Transactions on Robotics	T-RO (Trob)	Journal	63
i.5	Transactions on Automation Science and Eng.	T-ASE	Journal	0
i.6	Software Eng. for Adaptive and Self-Managing Sys.	SEAMS	Conf. & Symposium	0
i.7	Symposium on Applied Computing	SAC	Conf. & Symposium	2
i.8	Foundations of Software Engineering	ESEC/FSE	Conf. & Symposium	0
i.9	Intelligent Robots and Systems	IROS	Conference	133
i.10	Int. Conference on Robotics and Automation	ICRA	Conference	137
i.11	Int. Conference on Automation Science and Eng.	CASE	Conference	32
i.12	International Conference on Advanced Robotics	ICAR	Conference	15
i.13	International Conference on Software Engineering	ICSE	Conference	9
i.14	Int. Conf. on Model Driven Eng. Languages and Sys.	MODELS	Conference	3
i.15	Simulation, Modeling and Progr. for Aut. Robots	SIMPAR	Conference	2
i.16	Software Engineering and Formal Methods	SEFM	Conference	2
ii	Library/Search engine			
ii.1	IEEE Computer Society digital library			22
ii.2	Google Scholar search			16
			TOTAL	835

mission specification in temporal logic; (iv) variations of the pattern describing possible minor changes; (v) examples of how it is used and occurrences in the literature; and (vi) its relationship to other patterns. We refer to the original set from [35] as the *Initial Patterns*, and our enlarged set simply as *Patterns*.

LTL Background. We briefly review future time LTL operators [6,10] used throughout the paper. The **X** operator refers to the next time point, i.e., $\mathbf{X}\phi$ is true iff ϕ holds at the next time point. The **F** operator refers to at least one future time point, i.e., $\mathbf{F}\phi$ is true iff ϕ holds at some future time point including the present time. **G** is true iff ϕ is always true in the future. $\phi\mathbf{U}\psi$ is true iff ψ holds at some point t in the future and for all time points t' such that $t' < t$, ϕ is true. $\phi\mathbf{W}\psi$ has similar semantics but does not require that ψ holds at some point in the future, i.e., ψ remains false. The release operator $\phi\mathbf{V}\psi$ is defined as $!((!\phi)\mathbf{U}(!\psi))$.[1] This means that either ψ never holds and ϕ holds forever or that ψ occurs at time t and ϕ holds at all time points t' such that $t' \leq t$.

2.1 Methodology: Systematic Review

We conducted a systematic review following the guidelines in [8] and [28]. We scanned 835 primary studies gathered from a list of well-known venues and

[1] We use $(\wedge, \vee, \neg)$ and $(\&, |, !)$ indistinguishably for the usual logical operators.

digital resources. Our search spanned the last five years (2018–2022). Before 2018, we relied on the extensive review from which the original mission patterns were conceived [35]. Our literature review focuses on the identification of robotic mission specifications and seeks to answer the following **exploratory questions**:

- (RQ1) What types of logics are used in the specification of these mission requirements?
- (RQ2) For studies that use LTL, what types of missions do they describe and how are these specified?
- (RQ3) Are there any newly-identified patterns that are not already captured by the *Initial Patterns* repository?

Search Strategy. To identify the most relevant publications, we obtained an initial set of studies from (a) well-known high-impact venues in the areas of robotics and automation and (b) Google Scholar and IEEE Computer Society digital library. The first source provided high-impact papers ensuring the quality of the results, while search engines provided a wider search of the literature.

The list of venues is shown in Table 1. Papers were gathered from the DBLP database, filtering by year and venue, using the query: "*robot|MRS$ task|schedule|allocation|mission|adapt*"[2], where spaces mean logic *and*'s, | logic *or*'s and $ looks for exactly the word before this sign. For Google Scholar and IEEE Library, only the top 25 results sorted by relevance were considered. For both engines, we used the query "*(robots OR robot OR MRS) AND (task OR tasks OR schedule OR scheduling OR allocation OR mission OR missions OR adapt OR adaptation).*"

Inclusion Criteria. We identified 835 *primary studies* after removing: 1) duplicates; 2) papers focusing on robotic hardware development rather than missions; and 3) two papers related to the *Initial Patterns*. We focus our literature review on formally specified missions, in comparison with the *Initial Patterns* repository [35], which considers missions described either in natural language or formally. We wanted to assess how often formalisms are used in robotic missions and gather information about the different logics used in the robotic missions domain. Such information is valuable for developing and identifying requirement specification patterns and extending formalization tools, such as FRET. As expected, the majority of papers do not use formalisms for mission specification.

Data Items. For the studies that use LTL in the formalizations, we collected the following data:

- **Title**. Title and reference to the paper.
- **Summary**. English language Description of the LTL mission requirements.
- **Mission**. Set of LTL formulae that describe the mission requirements.
- **Pattern**. If the pattern already exists in *Initial Patterns*, then we provide its name. Otherwise, we introduce the name of the newly-identified pattern.

For each study, we manually extracted the mission specifications defined in temporal logic. We next present our findings concerning the three exploratory questions.

[2] MRS stands for Multi-Robot Systems.

2.2 Answering the Research Questions

At the beginning of this section, we outlined three research questions that we discuss, in light of our findings from the literature search, below.

(RQ1) What types of logics are used in the specification of these mission requirements?

We identified 16 papers that formally specify mission requirements; five use LTL and the rest use different logics. We encourage the reader to explore the background sections of these papers for a deeper understanding of these logics. Signal temporal logic (STL) is frequently used for the specification of robotic missions [27,41,42]. In [41], STL is used to declare tasks for the collaborative manipulation of robotic arms. A fragment of LTL, called capability temporal logic (CaTL), is used in [30] to generate specifications with absolute or relative timing of task completion, repetition frequencies, and different types of task interdependence, like sequencing or synchronization. In [25] a new specification language for mission specifications called Event-based Signal Temporal Logic, which is an extension of STL, is proposed. In [26], the authors implement a framework for the satisfiability of robotic missions described in an extended version of the Event-based STL logic by adding the ability to specify discrete uncontrolled event reactions. Metric temporal logic (MTL) was used in [38] for the specification of robotic manipulators. While FRET currently supports MTL, we are extending the pattern repository on *mobile* robot missions. Hence, the study of *motion planning* on robotic manipulators is deferred for future work.

For self-adapting mobile service robots, in [11], probabilistic computational tree logic (PCTL) encodes mission optimization metrics such as time or energy consumption. A repository of mission patterns defined in RPCTL, i.e., PCTL extended with rewards, is provided in [36] as a continuation of the *Initial Patterns* augmented with quantitative reasoning by adding the probabilistic and reward operators. RPCTL is also used in [44]. A variant of LTL, called sc-LTL, is used in [47] for the specification of missions to guide the multi-task planning problem using a Q-learning based approach. Finally, five studies formalize robotic mission specifications in LTL [5,18,33,40,46], which we detail next.

(RQ2) For studies that use LTL, what type of missions do they describe and how are these specified?

Table 2 presents the five studies with LTL formulae. The first column presents the LTL formulae; the second the corresponding pattern, if it exists; the third column provides an English description. The last column contains the reference to the corresponding research paper. In [18], the authors present a heuristic technique for updating robotic plans as new tasks are allocated. The robot tasks consist of moving boxes, pulling levers, travelling between locations and scanning rooms. In [5], the specification of multi-robot systems with collaborative tasks is studied. Continuing, [33] proposes a decentralized planner for part knowledge called MAP-mAKER, evaluated on two case studies: one with robots in a residential facility and the other as a services provider. Next, [40] studies the allocation and planning of tasks with multiple robots in four variants of an office environment; while [46] describes MRS missions in which robots have limited local information. Its case study consists of picking and dropping a box at different locations and performing activities such as scanning and taking pictures.

(RQ3) Are there identified patterns that are not already captured by the*Initial Patterns* repository?

From the gathered set of 42 formulae (first column, Table 2), 23 were already defined by a pattern in the *Initial Patterns* repository and one could not be identified as a pattern (identified in the second column as NA). For the remaining 17 formulae, we proposed a new set of six patterns: (1) *Visit with reaction*, (2) *Weak sequenced visit*, (3) *Continuous visit with reaction*, (4) *Weak patrolling*, (5) *Deliver with visit*, (6) *Maintain safe state* (depicted in column two within square brackets [ ]). The mission specification that is not defined as a pattern follows the form: $\mathbf{F}(l_1 \wedge a \wedge \mathbf{X}((a_1 \mathbf{U} a_2) \wedge \mathbf{F}\ a))$, where $\{a, a_1, a_2\}$ is a set of actions and l_1 is a reachable location. This is a very specific behaviour where action a is performed at location l_1, followed by two actions a_1,a_2 in a given order, performing action a again in the future; hence, this is not considered a pattern.

Formalization of New Patterns. Let $R = \{r_1, r_1, ..., r_n\}$ be a set of robots and $A = \{a_1, a_2, ..., a_m\}$ a set of actions that robots can perform, where a_i holds when any robot $r_j \in R$ executes action a_i. Let $L = \{l_1, l_2, ..., l_{n_1}\}$ be a set of locations and l_k holds when a robot reaches this location. We use the notation $l_\#$ to indicate any location in L, $a_\#$ any action in A, $(l_\#)^\omega$ an infinite trace of locations, and $(a_\#)^*$ a finite trace of actions. We define a logical disjunction of the set of locations to be visited as $d_x = \bigvee_{j=1}^{n_2} s_j$ where $s_j \in S$ belongs to a subset of locations $S \subseteq L$ and n_2 is the number of elements in S. For example, if locations l_1 or l_2 or l_4 are to be visited, then $d_1 = l_1|l_2|l_4$, which holds when any of these locations are visited. We denote $\{d_x\} = S$ the set of locations in d_x. For the previous example $\{d_1\} = \{l_1, l_2, l_4\}$. We define $g_{i,k} = l_i \wedge a_k$ as the visit of location l_i where a_k action is performed. Let $l_{\#-\{1,2,3\}}$ be any location except for locations l_1, l_2 or l_3; we define the new patterns as:

Visit with reaction: Visit a set of locations in an unspecified order. When at that location, an action must be carried out. In this case, we use the conjunction to assemble a formula with multiple locations and actions.

$$\bigwedge_{i=1}^{n} \mathbf{F}(l_i \wedge a_i), \texttt{ where } a_i \in A$$

Example: Action a_1 must be done at location l_1 and action a_2 at location l_2, at least once. An example of a trace that satisfies the mission requirement is $l_\# \rightarrow \{l_2, a_2\} \rightarrow l_\# \rightarrow \{l_1, a_1\} \rightarrow (l_\#)^\omega$. The trace $l_\# \rightarrow a_2 \rightarrow l_2 \rightarrow \{l_1, a_1\} \rightarrow (l_\#)^\omega$ violates the requirement as action a_2 is never carried out when visiting l_2.

Weak sequenced visit: Visit n locations in a specific order, where the ith location $i \leq n$ exists in $\{d_i\}$. It does not prohibit the interleaving of locations.

Table 2. Collection of LTL mission specifications extracted from the systematic review. New patterns are depicted in bold square brackets **[ ]**.

Temporal Logic Formula	Pattern name (from *Patterns*)	Definition	Ref.
(!dropoff U (room2 ∧ pickup)) (!dropoff U (room3 ∧ dropoff)) F(room3 ∧ pulllever) GF(room1 ∧ scan ∧ usecamera)	Wait **[Visit with reaction]** Patrolling	Pick up box from room2, drop it off in room3; pull the lever in room3. Repeatedly scan and take a picture in room1.	[18]
(!(room1scan) U (room4scan)) F(room1 ∧ scan)	Wait **[Visit with reaction]**	Scan in room4, then scan in room 1.	
GF(room2 ∧ scan) GF(room5 ∧ scan)	Patrolling Patrolling	Repeatedly travel between room2 and room5 and scan in those rooms.	
F(room1 ∧ usecamera) F(room4 ∧ pickup)	**[Visit with reaction]** **[Visit with reaction]**	Take a picture in room1 and pick up a box in room4, in any order.	
G(F(loadcarrier))	Patrolling	Periodically robot r1 loads debris on r2.	[33]
G(F(detectload ∧ F(unload)))	Sequenced patrolling	Robot r2 load debris and later unload.	
G(F(takesnapshot ∧ F(sendinfo)))	Sequenced patrolling	Robot r3 repeatedly takes and sends pictures.	
F(s1 ∧ (F(s2 | s3)))	**[Weak ordered visit]**	Reach a destination where service s1 is provided, then perform either s2 or s3.	
G(F(s4 | s5))	**[Weak patrolling]**	Visit s4 or s5 infinitely often.	
F(desk ∧ default ∧ X((carrybin U dispose) ∧ F(default))) F(desk ∧ emptybin ∧ X(desk ∧ default)) G(carrybin ⇒ !public)	NA **[Cont. visit with reaction]** Instant reaction	Robot by the desk while not loaded. Carry the bin until garbage is disposed and put it away again to reach the default state. Place empty paper bin next to the desk. Avoid public areas while carrying a bin.	[40]
F(printer) F(kitchen) G(battery_20)	Visit Visit **[Maintain safe state]**	Refill supplies at the printer room and the kitchen. Ensure sufficient battery.	
F(p ∧ carry U (d10 ∧ X!carry)) F(p ∧ carry U (d7 ∧ X!carry)) F(p ∧ carry U (d5 ∧ X!carry)) G(carry ⇒ !public) F(printer)	**[Deliver after visit]** **[Deliver after visit]** **[Deliver after visit]** Instant reaction Visit	Distribute copies (p) to desks d10, d7, d5, and avoid public areas while carrying the document. Printer has sufficient paper.	
F(m1 ∧ photo) F(m4 ∧ photo) F(m6 ∧ photo) G(!meeting ⇒ !camera) F(d5 ∧ carry U (d3 ∧ X!carry)) G(carry ⇒ !public) F(d11 ∧ guide U (m6 ∧ X!guide))	**[Visit with reaction]** **[Visit with reaction]** **[Visit with reaction]** Instant reaction **[Deliver after visit]** Instant reaction **[Deliver after visit]**	Take a photo in rooms m1, m4, and m6. Deliver document from d5 to d3. Guide a person at d11 to room m6. Turned off camera while not in meeting rooms. Document is not delivered through any public areas.	
(GF(t1)) (GF(t4)) G(w ∧ !o) (GF(t2)) (GF(t3))	Patrolling Patrolling **[Maintain safe state]** Patrolling Patrolling	Robots persistently survey locations t1, t2, t3 and t4. Always remain in the working space w and avoid obstacles in o.	[46]
F(r1t1) ∧ F(r2t2) ∧ F(r3t3) ∧ F(r4t4) (!r1t1 U r4t4) F(t4 ∧ F(t3))	Visit Wait Ordered visit	Each robot has a local task to perform. Robot r1 do task t1 only after r4 do t4. Do task t3 after t4.	[5]

$$\underbrace{\mathbf{F}(d_1 \wedge (\mathbf{F}(d_2 \wedge (\mathbf{F}(d_3 \wedge ...(\mathbf{F}(d_n)))))))}_{\text{F } d_i \text{ nested n times}}$$

Example: An instance of this property where $d_1 = l_1$ and $d_2 = l_2|l_3$ is written as $\mathbf{F}(l_1 \wedge \mathbf{F}(l_2|l_3))$. The traces $l_1 \rightarrow l_\# \rightarrow l_2 \rightarrow (l_\#)^\omega$ and $l_1 \rightarrow l_\# \rightarrow l_3 \rightarrow (l_\#)^\omega$ satisfy the instance of this property as l_2 or l_3 holds after l_1. The trace $l_2 \rightarrow (l_1)^\omega$ does not satisfy the requirement as l_2 never holds after l_1.

Continuous visit with reaction: Visit a location for n consecutive steps. During the visit, perform an action at each time step.

$$\underbrace{\mathbf{F}(g_{1,1} \wedge (\mathbf{X}(g_{1,2} \wedge (\mathbf{X}(g_{1,3} \wedge ...(\mathbf{X}(g_{1,n})))))))}_{\text{X } g_{1,i} \text{ nested n times}}$$

Example: Location l_1 must be visited and perform action a_1 when arriving, and a_2 at the next time step. In this case, $g_{1,1} = l_1 \wedge a_1$ and $g_{1,2} = l_1 \wedge a_2$, hence the specification is written as $\mathbf{F}(l_1 \wedge a_1 \wedge (\mathbf{X}(l_1 \wedge a_2)))$. The trace $\{l_1, a_2\} \rightarrow \{l_2, a_2\} \rightarrow \{l_1, a_1\} \rightarrow \{l_1, a_2\} \rightarrow (l_\#)^\omega$ satisfies the requirement. The trace $\{l_1, a_1\} \rightarrow \{l_2, a_2\} \rightarrow (l_\#)^\omega$ violates it as the robot exits l_1 before doing a_2.

Weak patrolling: Visit infinitely often one or more locations within $\{d_i\}$.

$$\bigwedge_{i=1}^{n}(\mathbf{G}(\mathbf{F}(d_i)))$$

Example: At least one of locations l_1, l_2 or l_3 must be visited infinitely often. In this case, $d_1 = l_1|l_2|l_3$ and the specification is written as $\mathbf{G}(\mathbf{F}((l_1 \mid l_2 \mid l_3))$. The traces $l_1 \rightarrow (l_\# \rightarrow l_2)^\omega$ and $l_3 \rightarrow l_\# \rightarrow (l_1)^\omega$ satisfy the requirement, as at least one location is visited infinitely often. The trace $l_2 \rightarrow l_4 \rightarrow (l_{\#-\{1,2,3\}})^\omega$ does not satisfy the requirement.

Deliver after visit: Eventually start action one and, if not at the specified location, start action two. If not at the specified location, continue performing action two until the specified location is visited and stop performing action two afterwards.

$$\mathbf{F}(a_1 \wedge a_2\mathbf{U}(l_i \wedge \mathbf{X}!a_2)), \ \texttt{where} \ \ a_{1,2} \in A$$

Example: When a_1 happens, then carry an object (a_2) until location l_1 is reached. The trace $(\{a_1, a_2\} \rightarrow \{!a_1, a_2\})^* \rightarrow (a_2)^* \rightarrow l_1 \rightarrow !a_2 \rightarrow (l_\#)^\omega$ satisfies this property at some point as action a_2 holds until it arrives at location l_1 and, at the next time step, a_2 is false. Notice that when l_i is reached, the action a_2 can be true or false. The trace $\{a_1, a_2\} \rightarrow \{l_1, !a_2\} \rightarrow (a_2)^\omega$ does not satisfy the requirement because $!a_2$ does not hold after l_1.

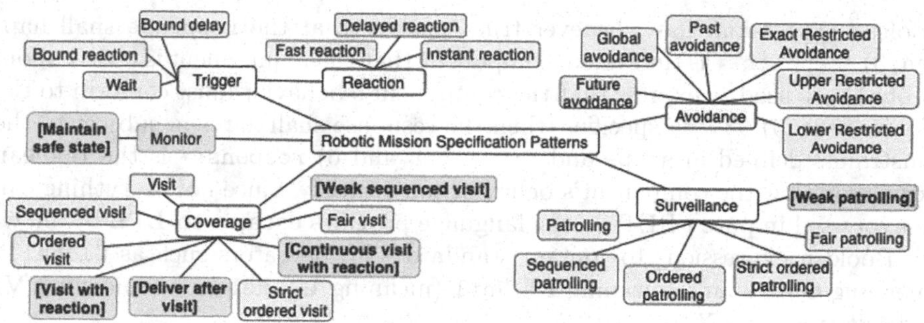

Fig. 1. *Patterns* for robotic missions for mobile robots organized in five categories: coverage, surveillance, avoidance, trigger and monitor. New patterns are depicted in yellow within square brackets [ ]. The rest are from the original catalogue [35].

Maintain safe state: Check that an action holds at every time point, for instance, for monitoring purposes; this formalization is also called an *invariant.*

$$\bigwedge_{i=i}^{n} \mathbf{G}(a_i)$$

Example: Measure the battery energy at all times to maintain it at least at 20%, where a_1 holds if the battery energy is $\geq$20%. A trace that satisfies the specification is $a_1 \rightarrow (l_{\#}, a_1)^{\omega}$, while the trace $l_1 \rightarrow (a_1)^{\omega}$ violates it because a_1 does not hold at the first time point.

We define *actions* as activities that the robots must execute within their operational domain, such as avoiding obstacles. Additionally, for the pattern *maintain safe state*, these actions include non-functional activities such as ensuring that the battery charge maintains a specific charge level.

Figure 1 shows the *Patterns* grouped into five categories: Coverage, Surveillance, Avoidance, Monitor, and Trigger. Note that Reaction is a subcategory of Trigger. As this robotic mission pattern catalogue is intended to grow as new patterns are identified, in this paper, we propose the *Monitor* category to capture the continuous monitoring of some mission-related parameter or behaviour, for instance, continual monitoring of battery energy level and maintaining the temperature within a specified range. The rest of the categories are taken from [35].

3 Expressing Robotic Missions in FRET

In this Section, we study the specification of *Patterns* in FRET.

FRETish Background: A FRETish requirement comprises up to six elements (of which the elements marked with a * are mandatory): 1) `scope` specifies the time intervals where the requirement is enforced; 2) `condition` is a

Boolean expression that whenever true specifies that the **response** shall happen; 3) component* is the system component that the requirement is levied upon; 4) **shall*** is used to express that the component's behavior must conform to the requirement; 5) timing specifies when the response shall happen, subject to the constraints defined in **scope** and condition and 6) **response*** is the Boolean expression that the component's behavior must satisfy. Since not everything can be expressed in pure FRETish, the language provides **escape-to-LTL** by allowing Boolean expressions to contain standard LTL operators such as **Globally** (meaning **G**), **Future** (meaning **F**), **Untl** (meaning **U**), **Releases** (meaning **V**) and **Nxt** (meaning **X**).

Table 3 shows how we specified the robotic mission *Patterns* in FRETish. The shaded rows indicate new patterns identified by this work that are not included in the *Initial Patterns* and are also not supported by the toolset that accompanies them, PsALM [34]. The second column contains the name of the pattern and the corresponding LTL formulation. Since both PsALM and FRET tools work on instantiated versions of the patterns, we present the formulations instantiated for a specific number of locations. For example, Table 3 lists the instantiated version of the `Visit` pattern for two locations `l0`, `l1`. The third column contains the pattern written as FRETish requirement(s). The plus (+) sign is used when multiple requirements are needed to express a single pattern. In certain cases, e.g., `Ordered Visit`, a pattern can be written as the composition of an existing pattern, e.g., `Sequenced Visit`, with additional FRETish requirements.

Table 3: Robotic Mission Patterns in FRETish.

#	Instantiated Pattern	Requirement(s) in FRETish
1	**Visit** F l0 ∧ F l1	robot **shall** eventually **satisfy l0** + robot **shall** eventually **satisfy l1**
2	**Sequenced Visit** F (l0 ∧ (F l1))	robot **shall** eventually **satisfy l0 & Future(l1)**
3	**Ordered Visit** F (l0 ∧ (F l1)) ∧ (! l1) U (l0)	**Sequenced Visit pattern** + robot **shall** until l0 **satisfy !l1**
4	**Strict Ordered Visit** F (l0 ∧ (F l1)) ∧ (! l1) U (l0) ∧ (! l0) U (l0 ∧ X (! l0 U (l1)))	**Ordered Visit pattern** + robot **shall** immediately **satisfy Untl((!l0), l0 & Nxt(Untl(!l0,!l1)))**
5	**Fair Visit** F l0 ∧ F l1 G (l0 ⇒ X ((! l0) W l1)) ∧ G (l1 ⇒ X ((! l1) W l0))	**Visit pattern** + whenever l0 robot **shall** at the next timepoint **satisfy Releases(l1,!l0 | l1)** + whenever l1 robot **shall** at the next timepoint **satisfy Releases(l0,!l1 | l0)**
6	**[Visit With Reaction]** F(l0 ∧ action)	robot **shall** eventually **satisfy l0 & action**
7	**[Weak Sequenced Visit]** F(l0 ∧ F(l1 ∨ l2))	robot **shall** eventually **satisfy l0 & (Future(l1 | l2))**
8	**[Continuous Visit With Reaction]** F((l0 ∧ a1) ∧ (X (l0 ∧ a2)))	robot **shall** eventually **satisfy (l0 & a1) & (Nxt(l0 & a2))**
9	**[Deliver After Visit]** F(a1 ∧ a2 U (l0 ∧ X !a2))	robot **shall** eventually **satisfy a1 & Untl(a2, l0 & Nxt(!a2))**

<table>
<tr><td>10 Patrolling
(G F l0) ∧ (G F l1)</td><td><code>whenever true robot shall eventually satisfy l0</code>
+ <code>whenever true robot shall eventually satisfy l1</code></td></tr>
<tr><td>11 Sequenced Patrolling
G (F (l0 ∧ (F l1)))</td><td><code>robot shall always satisfy Future(l0 & Future(l1))</code></td></tr>
<tr><td>12 Ordered Patrolling
G (F (l0 ∧ (F l1))) ∧
!l1 U l0 ∧
G(l1 ⇒ X((!l1) U l0))</td><td>Sequenced Patrolling pattern
+ <code>robot shall until l0 satisfy !l1</code>
+ <code>robot shall eventually satisfy l1</code>
+ <code>whenever l1 robot shall at the next timepoint satisfy Untl(!l1,l0)</code></td></tr>
<tr><td>13 Strict Ordered Patrolling
G (F(l0 ∧ (F l1))) ∧
!l1 U l0 ∧
G(l1 ⇒ X((!l1) U l0)) ∧
G(l0 ⇒ X (!l0 U l1))</td><td>Ordered Patrolling pattern
+ <code>whenever l0 robot shall at the next timepoint satisfy (Untl(!l0,l1))</code></td></tr>
<tr><td>14 [Weak Patrolling]
G (F (l0 ∨ l1))</td><td><code>whenever true robot shall eventually satisfy l0 | l1</code></td></tr>
<tr><td>15 Fair Patrolling
(G F l0) ∧ (G F l1) ∧
G (l0 ⇒ X ((! l0) W l1)) ∧
G (l1 ⇒ X ((! l1) W l0))</td><td>Patrolling pattern
+ <code>whenever l0 robot shall at the next timepoint satisfy Releases(l1,!l0 | l1)</code>
+ <code>whenever l1 robot shall at the next timepoint satisfy Releases(l0, !l1 | l0)</code></td></tr>
<tr><td>16 Past Avoidance
(!l0) U p</td><td><code>robot shall until p satisfy !l0</code>
+ <code>robot shall eventually satisfy p</code></td></tr>
<tr><td>17 Global Avoidance
G(!(l0))</td><td><code>robot shall never satisfy l0</code></td></tr>
<tr><td>18 Future Avoidance
G((c) ⇒ (G(!l0)))</td><td><code>whenever c robot shall never satisfy l0</code></td></tr>
<tr><td>19 Upper Restricted Avoidance
!F(l0 ∧ X(F(l0 ∧X(F(l0)))))
at most n times where n=2</td><td><code>robot shall immediately satisfy ! Future(l0 & Nxt(Future(l0 & Nxt(Future(l0))))</code></td></tr>
<tr><td>20 Lower Restricted Avoidance
F(l0 ∧ X(F(l0 ∧X(F(l0)))))
at least n times where n=3</td><td><code>robot shall eventually satisfy (l0 & Nxt(Future(l0 & Nxt(Future(l0)))))</code></td></tr>
<tr><td>21 Exact Restricted Avoidance
(!l0) U (l0 ∧ (X(!l0 U (l0 ∧ (X(!l0 U l0 ∧ X(G !l0)))))))
exactly n=3 times</td><td><code>robot shall immediately Untl (!l0, l0 & (Nxt(Untl (!l0, l0 & (Nxt(Untl(!l0, l0 & Nxt(Globally !l0)))))))</code></td></tr>
<tr><td>22 Instant Reaction
G(p1 ⇒ p2)</td><td><code>whenever p1 robot shall immediately satisfy p2</code></td></tr>
<tr><td>23 Delayed Reaction
G(p1 ⇒F(p2))</td><td><code>whenever p1 robot shall eventually satisfy p2</code></td></tr>
<tr><td>24 Prompt Reaction
G(p1 ⇒ X(p2))</td><td><code>whenever p1 robot shall at the next timepoint satisfy p2</code></td></tr>
<tr><td>25 Bound Reaction
G(p1 ⟺ p2)</td><td><code>robot shall always satisfy p1 <-> p2</code></td></tr>
<tr><td>26 Bound Delay
G(p1 ⟺ X(p2))</td><td><code>robot shall always satisfy p1 <-> Nxt(p2)</code></td></tr>
<tr><td>27 Wait
l0 U p</td><td><code>robot shall until p satisfy l0</code>
+ <code>robot shall eventually satisfy p</code></td></tr>
<tr><td>28 [Maintain Safe Space]
G action</td><td><code>robot shall always satisfy action</code></td></tr>
</table>

4 Discussion

Prior uses of FRET have typically been in the aerospace domain. However, FRET has also been studied in robotic applications, including inspection [9] and grasping [21]. Nevertheless, neither of these prior works systematically evaluated the expressibility of requirements for robotic systems as we do in this paper.

4.1 Expressibility of FRETish for Robotic Mission Requirements

The robotic mission requirements that we studied in this paper can be different from aerospace requirements written previously in FRET [15,19,32,37]. Their difference lies mainly in the unique nature and intrinsic complexity of robotic missions that require complex LTL specifications, e.g., nested temporal operators and reachability properties based on multiple locations.

We were able to specify all 28 patterns using FRET, however, in 13 cases (Table 3 rows 2, 4, 7–9, 11–13, 15, 19–21, 26), we had to use FRET's escape-to-LTL feature for patterns with nested temporal operators in `Sequenced Visit` and `Untl` and `Nxt` In future work, we will study how to extend FRET to capture these patterns in pure FRETish. One way would be to compositionally build complex patterns that require nesting of operators from simpler ones. Prior work makes a first step toward this by refactoring FRETish requirements that share repeated segments [20].

Table 3 shows that in certain cases, multiple FRETish requirements are needed to specify a single pattern. This decomposition of a pattern is beneficial for analysis purposes - performance-wise and also analysis feedback can be more targeted to specific sub-requirements - but also simplifies and makes the FRETish requirements easier to understand. To this end, FRET also helps users think of semantic subtleties and make intentional decisions when writing requirements. Consider the `Ordered Visit` pattern that uses the *strong until* $\mathbf{U}$ operator. The FRETish language provides the until keyword as a timing field option, however its semantics is that of weak until $\mathbf{W}$[3]. To be able to express strong until, e.g., $p\ \mathbf{U}\ q$ we need two requirements in FRETish, i.e., one that expresses $p\ \mathbf{W}\ q$ and a second that expresses $\mathbf{F}\ q$. As a result, when writing a requirement with the until keyword, the user must decide whether this is the intended semantics of the requirement or whether the intended semantics should be strong until instead. In the latter case, the user needs to intentionally add an extra requirement (see row 16, Table 3).

Finally, there might be multiple semantically equivalent ways of specifying the same pattern in FRETish, however, due to space limitations, we only present a single option per pattern in Table 3.

4.2 Comparing *Patterns* with FRETish Robotic Requirements in the Wild

Prior work contains FRETish requirements that were specified for a rover inspection mission [9]. We observe that some of these (system-level) requirements correspond to the `Maintain safe space` pattern that we have identified. For

[3] According to FRET developers, this was a design choice after studying that when the until keyword was used in a requirement, in most cases it meant *weak until*.

example, `Rover shall always satisfy speed <= 10`. Further, [9] also has component-level requirements that fit this pattern. Our focus in this paper is on requirements at the system and mission levels.

Other related work uses FRET in the specification of requirements for a robotic grasping system [21]. Here, we found instances of the `Maintain safe space` pattern as well as instances of the `Global avoidance` pattern. For example, `SV shall always satisfy !collide(SV, TGT)`. We note that here the global avoidance pattern is phrased differently than we have shown in Table 3, which uses the `never` timing in FRET. However, these two structures, one using logical negation and the other using never timing, are semantically equivalent. Although this robotic system is somewhat different from the mobile robots that we focus our work on, it is interesting that these safety-related patterns appear.

Finally, in recent work on the NASA Ames Research Center project Troupe, which aims at developing a fleet of rovers capable of autonomously mapping their environment [43], we found instances of the `Maintain safe space` and `Delayed reaction` patterns. The latter, however, uses a bounded version of the `eventually` timing operator, i.e., `within 1 s`.

More work is needed to examine the applicability of the *Patterns* more widely, both for robotics and whether similar patterns are useful in other critical systems. That said, their appearance in the aforementioned works demonstrates their relevance. Providing a set of generic patterns thus gives developers and engineers a starting point for eliciting requirements for robotic missions using FRET.

4.3 On PsALM and FRET

PsALM [34] was specifically developed to support predefined robotic patterns, i.e., those in the *Initial Patterns* catalogue. FRET is a requirements elicitation tool that supports the use of predefined templates but also authoring and understanding of requirements written from scratch in structured natural language. For example, to enable compositional analysis, a user would need to write component-level requirements complementary to the mission-level ones as demonstrated in [9]. If a developer intends to only use predefined *Patterns* to synthesize temporal formulae, then they can use either tool. The selection of a tool also depends on the intended purpose beyond this formalization stage. PsALM can generate inputs for multiple planners, simulators and model checkers. In contrast, FRET supports the generation of input for model checkers and runtime monitoring tools. Moreover, when using pure FRETish, FRET can generate both pure future-time and pure past-time LTL formulae (the PsALM mission catalogue is currently restricted to future-time LTL). By leveraging the pure past-time LTL translation, we can further perform realizability checking or other types of analysis with tools that can only digest pure past-time LTL.

4.4 Threats to Validity

We limited our search terms to those specified in Sect. 2.1 but it is possible that slightly different terms might have yielded different results. These mission patterns are defined for mobile robots transitioning between locations to perform tasks. Hence, in comparison to [35], we decided to explicitly include the search terms for the *scheduling* and *allocation* of tasks. It is also true that limiting ourselves to the 25 entries deemed most relevant by the search engine might have resulted in some interesting papers being omitted. However, we note that a larger literature review of formal specification and verification of autonomous robotic systems also travelled five pages deep in their chosen search engine (also Google scholar) [31]. Their review was older and more general than ours, spanning papers published from 2007–2018. Future work might analyse the papers found during their review (which revealed temporal logics as a popular specification formalism for robotics) in light of the patterns that we identified.

In [33], the authors refer to previous studies on specification patterns [16,24, 29] but we couldn't find a reference to the specific guideline they follow. Hence, we followed the guidelines for Systematic Reviews in Software Engineering from [8,28]. Had we opted for a collection of search engines, rather than just Google Scholar, this may have impacted the patterns that we derived. Our results are thus limited to those that are identified using Google's algorithms. Notably, the venues that our papers were drawn from were robotics, rather than formal methods venues. Including more venues where temporal logic papers appear, such as Formal Methods Europe or SAFECOMP for example, might have provided a richer set of temporal logic formulas.

Limiting our search to papers published at mostly academic venues might have resulted in gaps in the patterns that we identified. Our future work will seek to validate these patterns alongside industrial partners to ensure that our patterns are applicable and that additional patterns, including those that were potentially overlooked by our literature review, are identified and added to our catalog. For instance, we will seek to extensively validate these patterns and extract new patterns through missions and robotic projects at NASA, such as Troupe [7]. Two other sources we will consider for the extraction of additional robotic patterns in future work are well-known robotics competitions and large-scale studies. Robotic competitions such as RoboCup [3] and the DARPA Robotics Challenge [2] provide insights into state-of-the-art robotic missions, and large-scale case studies such as those conducted by Amazon Robotics offer real-world applications to investigate. For instance, the deployment of multiple mobile robots in an Amazon warehouse setting [1] presents opportunities to formalize complex robot interactions and mission strategies through FRETish, and ultimately, logic languages. This further validation and expansion of our catalog of patterns will help to ensure the maximum impact of this work whilst encouraging a wider uptake of FRET in robotics development.

5 Related Work

The specification of patterns in temporal logic is not a new concept. Developing sets of commonly occurring patterns is useful to guide developers in specifying their systems [16,24,39]. Existing tools should ideally express commonly occurring patterns to encourage their uptake and ensure that they are applicable in relevant domains. Robotic systems are frequently built of multiple (often pre-existing) components, each with its own requirements [13]. Identifying and expressing frequently used patterns thus enables uniformity and reuse.

Recently, several efforts have focused on creating repositories of robotic missions gathered from industry and literature that can be easily reused and implemented. For example, ROBOMAX [4] is a dynamic repository of robotic systems with self-adaptation capabilities that researchers can expand with new missions. ROBOMAX contains missions described in natural language.

Other works use temporal logic formalizations for the description of robotic missions and in particular for the planning of mobile robots [17,22]. Many of these were considered in the creation of mission patterns. However, these patterns do not support reasoning about quantities such as the cost to complete a mission or the probability of mission success without failure. As the need for qualitative requirements grows [44,45], a second set of robotic patterns, presented in [36], expands the mission patterns of [35] with quantitative semantics adding probabilities and rewards to capture uncertainty in robotic mission specifications. We did not use this second repository as FRET does not currently support probabilistic requirements.

6 Conclusion

This paper contributes (1) newly identified robotic mission patterns that were derived from a systematic literature review. The paper studies (2) the specification in FRETish of 28 distinct patterns, both newly identified in this paper and previously described in [35]. Finally, (3) we discuss and examine the implication that these patterns have for the design and applicability of FRET, by examining its expressibility and comparing these patterns with pre-existing sets of FRETish requirements. The catalog presented in Table 3 provides a methodological basis for roboticists wishing to use FRET to specify functional mission requirements for robots that are engaged in common tasks such as patrolling. Previously, FRET has been predominantly used for aerospace systems case studies. This paper illustrates that FRET can be more widely applicable, focusing on the mobile robotics domain.

In future work, we will explore additional sources of robotic missions. This will entail examining large-scale robotic applications, gaining insights into robotic missions through interviews with industrial developers, and investigating existing missions from projects at NASA and robotic competitions. We also plan to study the applicability of these patterns to other autonomous systems, such as within the context of Unmanned Aircraft Systems (UAS).

Acknowledgements. G. Vázquez performed part of this work during her internship with KBR Inc. at NASA Ames Research Center. M. Farrell's work is supported by a Royal Academy of Engineering Research Fellowship. A. Mavridou is supported by NASA Contract No. 80ARC020D001. T. Pressburger is supported by NASA's System-Wide Safety project in the Airspace Operations and Safety Program.

References

1. Amazon AWS and Amazon Robotics, case study. https://aws.amazon.com/solutions/case-studies/amazon-robotics-case-study/. Accessed 08 Mar 2024
2. DARPA Robotics Challenge website. https://www.darpa.mil/about-us/timeline/darpa-robotics-challenge. Accessed 08 Mar 2024
3. Robocup federation official website. https://www.robocup.org. Accessed 08 Mar 2024
4. Askarpour, M., et al.: Robomax: robotic mission adaptation exemplars. In: Software Engineering for Adaptive and Self-Managing Systems, pp. 245–251. IEEE (2021)
5. Bai, R., Zheng, R., Liu, M., Zhang, S.: Multi-robot task planning under individual and collaborative temporal logic specifications. In: Intelligent Robots and Systems, pp. 6382–6389. IEEE (2021)
6. Baier, C., Katoen, J.: Principles of Model Checking. MIT press, Cambridge (2008)
7. Benz, N., Sljivo, I., Vlastos, P.G., Woodard, A., Carter, C., Hejase, M.: The troupe system: an autonomous multi-agent rover swarm. In: AIAA SCITECH 2024 Forum, p. 2894 (2024)
8. Biolchini, J., Mian, P., Candida, A.N., Travassos, G.H.: Systematic review in software engineering. Technical report 05, System engineering and computer science department COPPE/UFRJ (2005)
9. Bourbouh, H., et al.: Integrating formal verification and assurance: an inspection rover case study. In: Dutle, A., Moscato, M.M., Titolo, L., Muñoz, C.A., Perez, I. (eds.) NFM 2021. LNCS, vol. 12673, pp. 53–71. Springer, Cham (2021). https://doi.org/10.1007/978-3-030-76384-8_4
10. Bozzano, M., Cavada, R., Cimatti, A., Dorigatti, M., Griggio, A., Mariotti, A., Micheli, A., Mover, S., Roveri, M., Tonetta, S.: nuxmv 2.0.0 user manual. Fondazione Bruno Kessler, Technical report, Trento, Italy (2019)
11. Cámara, J., Schmerl, B., Garlan, D.: Software architecture and task plan co-adaptation for mobile service robots. In: Software Engineering for Adaptive and Self-Managing Systems, pp. 125–136 (2020)
12. Cardoso, R.C., et al.: A review of verification and validation for space autonomous system. Current Robot. Rep. **2**(3), 273–283 (2021)
13. Côté, C., Létourneau, D., Michaud, F., Brosseau, Y.: Software design patterns for robotics: Solving integration problems with marie. In: Workshop of Robotic Software Environment (2005)
14. Devlin-Hill, B., Calinescu, R., Cámara, J., Caliskanelli, I.: Towards scalable multi-robot systems by partitioning the task domain. In: Pacheco-Gutierrez, S., Cryer, A., Caliskanelli, I., Tugal, H., Skilton, R. (eds.) TAROS 2022. LNCS, vol. 13546, pp. 282–292. Springer, Cham (2022). https://doi.org/10.1007/978-3-031-15908-4_22
15. Dutle, A., et al.: From requirements to autonomous flight: an overview of the monitoring icarous project. In: Formal Methods for Autonomous Systems (2020)
16. Dwyer, M.B., Avrunin, G.S., Corbett, J.C.: Patterns in property specifications for finite-state verification. In: International Conference on Software engineering, pp. 411–420 (1999)
17. Fainekos, G.E., Kress-Gazit, H., Pappas, G.J.: Temporal logic motion planning for mobile robots. In: Robotics and Automation, pp. 2020–2025. IEEE (2005)
18. Fang, A., Kress-Gazit, H.: Automated task updates of temporal logic specifications for heterogeneous robots. In: Robotics and Automation, pp. 4363–4369. IEEE (2022)

19. Farrell, M., Luckcuck, M., Sheridan, O., Monahan, R.: FRETting about requirements: formalised requirements for an aircraft engine controller. In: Gervasi, V., Vogelsang, A. (eds.) REFSQ 2022. LNCS, vol. 13216, pp. 96–111. Springer, Cham (2022). https://doi.org/10.1007/978-3-030-98464-9_9
20. Farrell, M., Luckcuck, M., Sheridan, O., Monahan, R.: Towards refactoring FRETish requirements. In: Deshmukh, J.V., Havelund, K., Perez, I. (eds.) NASA Formal Methods Symposium. LNCS, vol. 13260, pp. 272–279. Springer, Cham (2022). https://doi.org/10.1007/978-3-031-06773-0_14
21. Farrell, M., Mavrakis, N., Ferrando, A., Dixon, C., Gao, Y.: Formal modelling and runtime verification of autonomous grasping for active debris removal. Front. Robot. AI **8**, 639282 (2022)
22. Gavran, I., Majumdar, R., Saha, I.: Antlab: a multi-robot task server. ACM Trans. Embed. Comput. Syst. **16**(5s), 1–19 (2017)
23. Giannakopoulou, D., Mavridou, A., Rhein, J., Pressburger, T., Schumann, J., Shi, N.: Formal requirements elicitation with FRET. In: Requirements Engineering: Foundation for Software Quality (2020)
24. Grunske, L.: Specification patterns for probabilistic quality properties. In: Software Engineering, pp. 31–40 (2008)
25. Gundana, D., Kress-Gazit, H.: Event-based signal temporal logic synthesis for single and multi-robot tasks. IEEE Robot. Autom. Lett. **6**(2), 3687–3694 (2021)
26. Gundana, D., Kress-Gazit, H.: Event-based signal temporal logic tasks: execution and feedback in complex environments. IEEE Robot. Autom. Lett. **7**(4), 10001–10008 (2022)
27. Innes, C., Ramamoorthy, S.: Automated testing with temporal logic specifications for robotic controllers using adaptive experiment design. In: Robotics and Automation, pp. 6814–6821. IEEE (2022)
28. Keele, S.: Guidelines for performing systematic literature reviews in software engineering. Technical report EBSE (2007)
29. Konrad, S., Cheng, B.H.: Real-time specification patterns. In: Software Engineering, pp. 372–381 (2005)
30. Leahy, K., et al.: Scalable and robust algorithms for task-based coordination from high-level specifications (scratches). IEEE Trans. Robot. **38**(4), 2516–2535 (2021)
31. Luckcuck, M., Farrell, M., Dennis, L.A., Dixon, C., Fisher, M.: Formal specification and verification of autonomous robotic systems: a survey. ACM Comput. Surv. **52**(5), 1–41 (2019)
32. Mavridou, A., et al.: The ten lockheed martin cyber-physical challenges: formalized, analyzed, and explained. In: Requirements Engineering, pp. 300–310. IEEE (2020)
33. Menghi, C., Garcia, S., Pelliccione, P., Tumova, J.: Multi-robot LTL planning under uncertainty. In: Havelund, K., Peleska, J., Roscoe, B., de Vink, E. (eds.) FM 2018. LNCS, vol. 10951, pp. 399–417. Springer, Cham (2018). https://doi.org/10.1007/978-3-319-95582-7_24
34. Menghi, C., Tsigkanos, C., Berger, T., Pelliccione, P.: PsALM: specification of dependable robotic missions. In: Software Engineering, pp. 99–102. IEEE (2019)
35. Menghi, C., Tsigkanos, C., Pelliccione, P., Ghezzi, C., Berger, T.: Specification patterns for robotic missions. IEEE Trans. Softw. Eng. **47**(10) (2019)
36. Menghi, C., et al.: Mission specification patterns for mobile robots: providing support for quantitative properties. IEEE Trans. Softw. Eng. (2022)
37. Pressburger, T., Katis, A., Dutle, A., Mavridou, A.: Authoring, analyzing, and monitoring requirements for a lift-plus-cruise aircraft. In: Ferrari, A., Penzenstadler, B. (eds.) REFSQ 2023. LNCS, vol. 13975, pp. 295–308. Springer, Cham (2023). https://doi.org/10.1007/978-3-031-29786-1_21

38. Saha, S., Julius, A.A.: Task and motion planning for manipulator arms with metric temporal logic specifications. IEEE Robot. Autom. Lett. **3**(1), 379–386 (2017)
39. Salamah, S., Gates, A., Kreinovich, V.: Validated templates for specification of complex LTL formulas. Syst. Softw. **85**(8), 1915–1929 (2012)
40. Schillinger, P., Bürger, M., Dimarogonas, D.V.: Simultaneous task allocation and planning for temporal logic goals in heterogeneous multi-robot systems. Robot. Res. **37**(7), 818–838 (2018)
41. Sewlia, M., Verginis, C.K., Dimarogonas, D.V.: Cooperative object manipulation under signal temporal logic tasks and uncertain dynamics. IEEE Robot. Autom. Lett. **7**(4), 11561–11568 (2022)
42. Silano, G., Baca, T., Penicka, R., Liuzza, D., Saska, M.: Power line inspection tasks with multi-aerial robot systems via signal temporal logic specifications. IEEE Robot. Autom. Lett. **6**(2), 4169–4176 (2021)
43. Sljivo, I., Perez, I., Mavridou, A., Schumann, J., Vlastos, P.G., Carter, C.: Dynamic assurance of autonomous systems through ground control software. In: AIAA/Scitech (2024)
44. Vázquez, G., Calinescu, R., Cámara, J.: Scheduling multi-robot missions with joint tasks and heterogeneous robot teams. In: Fox, C., Gao, J., Ghalamzan Esfahani, A., Saaj, M., Hanheide, M., Parsons, S. (eds.) TAROS 2021. LNCS (LNAI), vol. 13054, pp. 354–359. Springer, Cham (2021). https://doi.org/10.1007/978-3-030-89177-0_36
45. Vázquez, G., Calinescu, R., Cámara, J.: Scheduling of missions with constrained tasks for heterogeneous robot systems. In: Formal Methods for Autonomous Systems (2022)
46. Yu, P., Dimarogonas, D.V.: Distributed motion coordination for multirobot systems under LTL specifications. IEEE Trans. Robot. **38**(2), 1047–1062 (2021)
47. Zhang, H., Kan, Z.: Temporal logic guided meta q-learning of multiple tasks. IEEE Robot. Autom. Lett. **7**(3), 8194–8201 (2022)

Safe Planning Through Incremental Decomposition of Signal Temporal Logic Specifications

Parv Kapoor[1(✉)], Eunsuk Kang[1], and Rômulo Meira-Góes[2]

[1] Carnegie Mellon University, Pittsburgh, PA, USA
parvk@cs.cmu.edu, eunsukk@andrew.cmu.edu

[2] Pennsylvania State University, State College, PA, USA
romulo@psu.edu

Abstract. *Trajectory planning* is a critical process that enables autonomous systems to safely navigate complex environments. *Signal temporal logic (STL)* specifications are an effective way to encode complex, temporally extended objectives for trajectory planning in cyber-physical systems (CPS). However, the complexity of planning with STL using existing techniques scales exponentially with the number of nested operators and the time horizon of a given specification. Additionally, poor performance is exacerbated at runtime due to limited computational budgets and compounding modeling errors. Decomposing a complex specification into smaller subtasks and incrementally planning for them can remedy these issues. In this work, we present a method for decomposing STL specifications to improve planning efficiency and performance. The key insight in our work is to encode all specifications as a set of basic constraints called *reachability* and *invariance constraints*, and schedule these constraints sequentially at runtime. Our experiment shows that the proposed technique outperforms the state-of-the-art trajectory planning techniques for both linear and non-linear dynamical systems.

Keywords: Signal Temporal Logic · Planning · Cyber Physical Systems

1 Introduction

Most autonomous robots interacting with the physical world need to achieve complex objectives while dealing with uncertainty and stochasticity in their environment. This problem is exacerbated by short response times expected while ensuring runtime efficiency. Hence, formulating these complex objectives accurately is a crucial step in realizing the desired behaviors for robotic operations.

Temporal logics such as *linear temporal logic (LTL)* [19] and *signal temporal logic (STL)* [16] provide a precise way to encode objectives that are expressed in a natural language. STL has received special attention in the community due to its rich quantitative semantics that can quantitatively measure satisfaction of a

N. Benz et al. (Eds.): NFM 2024, LNCS 14627, pp. 377–396, 2024.
https://doi.org/10.1007/978-3-031-60698-4_23

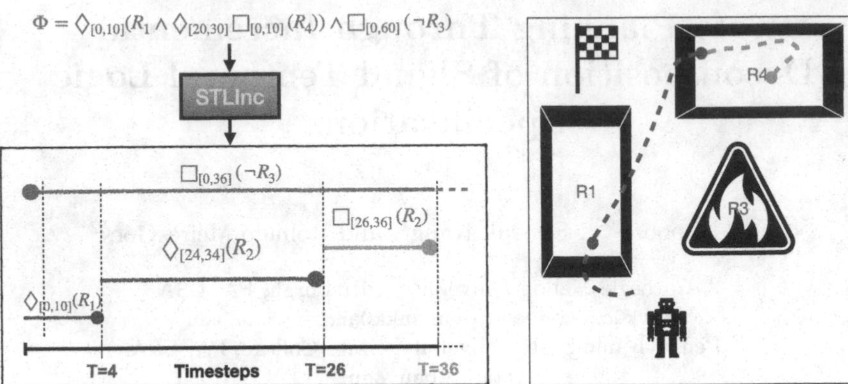

Fig. 1. Left: An STL specification ϕ with multiple nested temporal operators and a possible decomposition into subtasks. **Right**: A sample trajectory that satisfies ϕ in a planar environment.

given property that encodes an objective. Additionally, it can be used to describe complex properties over real valued signals such as state trajectories arising from continuous dynamical systems. For robotic planning, STL can be used to describe complex behaviors with concrete time deadlines such as those found in trajectory planning and task planning. Planners can use these specifications to generate specification-conforming behavior.

A significant amount of common robotic objectives can be interpreted as a sequence of subtasks. It has been shown that incremental subtask planning can be done more efficiently compared to planning for a composite task [5,7,18]. However, when STL is used to represent these composite tasks, incremental planning becomes challenging. This issue is because STL semantics can encode the sequential nature of tasks but does not expose this structure to the planner. In such cases, the planners are forced to work with complex long-horizon specifications. When the horizon of the specification is longer than the planning horizon, planners can often generate suboptimal or violating plans. This problem is exacerbated when planning occurs at runtime with computational constraints and compounding modeling errors [2].

In this work, we propose a theory to decompose long-horizon, arbitrarily nested specifications into sub-specifications that can be satisfied incrementally. We define recursive rules for decomposition and propose a novel scheduling algorithm for incremental task planning. The key insight here is to "divide and conquer" STL requirements while ensuring, by construction, that the resulting plan satisfies the original composite specification. We illustrate the effectiveness of our proposed approach over an experiment involving robot exploration problems with linear and non-linear dynamics. Our preliminary experiment shows that our approach is able to more efficiently generate plans for complex, composite specifications in comparison to the existing state-of-the-art STL-based planning methods. In addition, our decomposition technique is agnostic to the underlying system dynamics and the choice of planner, and can potentially be adapted by different planners.

The key contributions of this paper are:

- A method for decomposing an STL specification into a set of smaller STL specifications that represent subtasks (Sect. 4.2);
- A planning algorithm that incrementally schedules and executes these subtasks (Sects. 4.3 and 4.4);
- An evaluation of the proposed approach over a benchmark of motion planning tasks (Sect. 5).

2 Motivation

We illustrate the problem of planning from complex specifications using an example from the motion planning domain. We use a planning problem similar to the one defined in [14].

As illustrated in Fig. 1, the goal of the agent (robot) is to visit regions R_1 and R_4 sequentially while avoiding an unsafe region, R_3. Additionally, upon reaching R_4, the agent needs to stay in it for 10 time steps. We combine three common motion planning patterns such as sequenced visit, stabilization, and global avoidance to create a specification with timed deadlines as follows:

$$\begin{aligned}\Phi &= \phi_1 \wedge \phi_2\\ \phi_1 &= \Diamond_{[0,10]}(R_1 \wedge \Diamond_{[20,30]}\Box_{[0,10]}(R_4))\\ \phi_2 &= \Box_{[0,60]}(\neg R_3)\end{aligned}$$

The state-of-the-art (SOTA) technique for planning from Φ, originally proposed in [20], involves encoding the STL specification and the system dynamics as Mixed Integer Program (MIP) constraints and solving the constrained optimization problem in a receding horizon fashion. A new binary decision variable is introduced for each atomic proposition per time step in the STL specification. A known drawback of this technique is its exponential worst-case complexity with respect to the number of binary variables [12]. Various encoding modifications have been suggested to enhance the efficiency of the technique by reducing the number of variables and constraints [12,21].

However, even with reduced variable encoding, current methods excel primarily with short-horizon specifications. When encoding nested temporal operators, a large number of additional variables and constraints are needed to capture the relationship between different temporal operators, in contrast to non-nested operators, where temporal constraints associated with each operator are considered independently. For example, let us take the subformula $\Diamond_{[20,30]}\Box_{[0,10]}(R_4)$ from ϕ_1. For encoding this subformula into an MIP, we would need 11 (outer eventually) + 121 (inner always) = 132 binary variables.[1] In general, as the nesting depth increases, the number of variables can increase exponentially.

[1] For the outer $\Diamond$ clause, 11 binary variables are introduced to encode that the inner $\Box$ clause is satisfied within interval [20,30]; for each time point in [0,10] interval, another set of 11 variables are introduced, thus resulting in 11*11 = 121 variables.

In this work, we propose a technique to improve the scalability of STL planning algorithms through decomposition of STL specifications. Our idea is inspired by human planning, where long-term goals are achieved by breaking tasks into incremental sub-goals [8]. Concretely, by decomposing the specification, we effectively remove the complexity of nested operators and also reduce the length of the lookahead horizon.

A possible decomposition of the specification Φ into four subtasks is as follows:

$$\begin{aligned} sch_1 &= \Diamond_{[0,10]}(R1) \wedge \Box_{[0,10]}(\neg R_3) \\ sch_2 &= \Diamond_{[t_{R1}+20,t_{R1}+30]}(R_4) \wedge \Box_{[t_{R1}+20,t_{R1}+30]}(\neg R_3) \\ sch_3 &= \Box_{[t_{R4}+0,t_{R4}+10]}(\neg R_3 \wedge R_4) \\ sch_4 &= \Box_{[t_{R42},60]}(\neg R_3) \end{aligned}$$

Here, the symbolic time variables $(t_{R1}, t_{R4}, t_{R42})$ indicate when those subtasks get satisfied. More specifically, t_{R4} indicates when the agent reaches Region 1 and t_{R42} indicates when the agent has been inside Region 4 for 10 timesteps after reaching it. These variables then shift the time intervals of the other constraints that depend on them (e.g., time t_{R1} from sch_1 is used to concretize the time intervals for sch_2, whose time of satisfaction, in turn, influences sch_3). These subtasks have shorter time horizons and no nested temporal operators, resulting in MIP constraints that are less complex than those that would result from composite specifications. As shown later in Sect. 5, this decomposition-based approach has potential to significantly improve the efficiency of planning.

3 Preliminaries

STL is a logical formalism used to define properties of continuous time real valued signals [16]. A signal $\mathbf{s}$ is a function $\mathbf{s} : \mathbb{T} \rightarrow \mathbb{R}^n$ that maps a time domain $T \subseteq \mathbb{R}_{\geq 0}$ to a real valued vector. Then, an STL formula is defined as:

$$\phi := \mu \mid \neg\phi \mid \phi \wedge \psi \mid \phi \vee \psi \mid \phi \ \mathcal{U}_{[a,b]} \ \psi$$

where μ is a predicate on the signal $\mathbf{s}$ at time t in the form of $\mu \equiv \mu(\mathbf{s}(t)) > 0$ and $[a, b]$ is the time interval (or simply I). The *until* operator $\mathcal{U}$ defines that ϕ must be true until ψ becomes true within a time interval $[a, b]$. Two other operators can be derived from *until*: *eventually* ($F_{[a,b]} \ \phi := \top \ \mathcal{U}_{[a,b]} \ \phi$) and *always* ($G_{[a,b]} \ \phi := \neg F_{[a,b]} \ \neg\phi$).

Definition 1. *Given a signal s_t representing a signal starting at time t, the Boolean semantics of satisfaction of $s_t \models \phi$ are defined inductively as follows:*

$$\begin{aligned} s_t \models \mu &\iff \mu(s(t)) > 0 \\ s_t \models \neg\varphi &\iff \neg(s_t \models \varphi) \\ s_t \models \varphi_1 \wedge \varphi_2 &\iff (s_t \models \varphi_1) \wedge (s_t \models \varphi_2) \\ s_t \models F_{[a,b]}(\varphi) &\iff \exists t' \in [t+a, t+b] \ s.t. \ s_{t'} \models \varphi \\ s_t \models G_{[a,b]}(\varphi) &\iff \forall t' \in [t+a, t+b] \ s.t. \ s_{t'} \models \varphi \end{aligned}$$

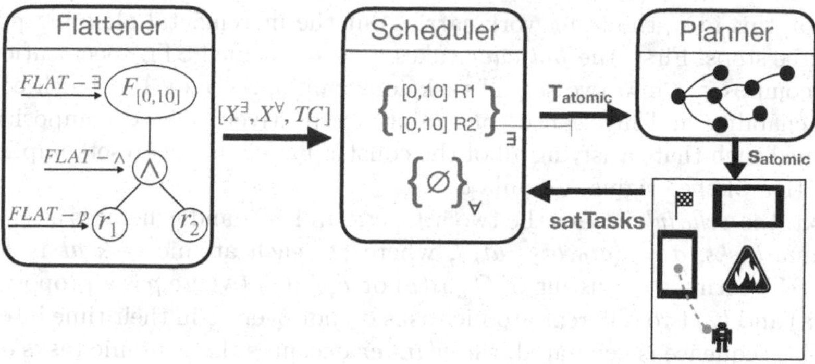

Fig. 2. Overview of the STLINC approach

Apart from the Boolean semantics, quantitative semantics are defined for a signal to compute a real-valued metric indicating *robustness*, i.e., the strength of satisfaction or violation.

Definition 2. *Given a signal s_t representing a signal starting at time t, the quantitative semantics of satisfaction of $s_t \models \phi$ are defined inductively as follows:*

$$\begin{aligned}
\rho(s_t, \mu_c) &= \mu(x_t) - c \\
\rho(s_t, \neg\varphi) &= -\rho(s_t, \varphi) \\
\rho(s_t, \varphi_1 \wedge \varphi_2) &= \min(\rho(s_t, \varphi_1), \rho(s_t, \varphi_2)) \\
\rho(s_t, F_{[a,b]}(\varphi)) &= \max_{t' \in [t+a, t+b]} \rho(s'_t, \varphi) \\
\rho(s_t, G_{[a,b]}(\varphi)) &= \min_{t' \in [t+a, t+b]} \rho(s'_t, \varphi)
\end{aligned}$$

For example, suppose that we are given (1) $\phi \equiv \mathrm{G}_{[0,3]}(\texttt{distToR3}(t) \geq 3.0)$, which states that the agent should maintain at least 3.0 m away from region R_3 for the next 4 time steps and (2) signal s_t that contains sequence $\langle 3.0, 2.5, 3.0, 3.5 \rangle$ for `distToR3`. Evaluting the robustness of satisfaction of ϕ over s_t would result in a value of -0.5, implying that the agent violates the property by a degree of 0.5 (i.e., it fails to stay away from R_3 by 0.5 m).

4 Approach

4.1 Basic Concepts and Definitions

The overview of our planning framework (STLINC) is shown in Fig. 2. The key idea behind this approach is that a bounded STL formula in our fragment can be decomposed into a finite set of the following two types of *task constraints*, each of which is associated with time interval $I = [a, b]$ and state proposition p.

Reachability: The system ensures that p holds over at least one time step t within I.

Invariance: The system ensures that p holds over every step t within I.

Based on this idea, the framework carries out the incremental planning process over three steps. First, the *flattener* takes a user-specified STL specification (ϕ) and decomposes it into two sets of task constraints, $\mathcal{X}^{\exists}$ and $\mathcal{X}^{\forall}$, which contain the reachability and invariance constraints, respectively. The decomposition is performed such that satisfying all of the constraints in these two sets implies the satisfaction of the original formula ϕ.

Next, the *scheduler* takes the two sets, $\mathcal{X}^{\exists}$ and $\mathcal{X}^{\forall}$, and generates a sequence of *atomic tasks*, $\sigma = \langle at_0, at_1 ... at_k \rangle$, where (1) each atomic task *at* is a non-nested STL formula consisting of $G_{[a,b]}(p)$ or $F_{[a,b]}(p)$ (where p is a propositional formula) and (2) two different atomic tasks do not overlap in their time intervals. After this sequence is generated, the *planner* executes these atomic tasks one by one in the designated order. Once all tasks are executed, the system will have fulfilled $\mathcal{X}^{\exists}$ and $\mathcal{X}^{\forall}$, thus satisfying the original goal of ϕ. The rest of this section describes each of the three steps in detail.

STL Fragment. Our approach is designed to handle specifications written in the following fragment of STL:

$$\phi ::= F_{[a,b]}(\phi) \mid G_{[a,b]}(\phi) \mid \phi_1 \wedge \phi_2 \mid p$$
$$p ::= p_1 \wedge p_2 \mid p_1 \vee p_2 \mid \neg p \mid \mu$$

where p is a propositional formula that does not contain any temporal operator, and μ is an atomic proposition. We target this STL fragment as (1) it signficantly simplifies the decomposition process and (2) it is still expressive enough to capture many common behavioral patterns in the robotics planning domain [17]. Note that the fragment allows a nesting of temporal operators of an arbitrary depth, which is important for specifying sequential tasks. For example, the objective of *visiting* locations in a particular order can be defined as:

$$\phi \equiv F_{[1,5]}(l_1 \wedge F_{[1,10]}(l_2 \wedge F_{[1,7]}(l_3)))$$

where l_1, l_2, l_3 represent the locations to be visited.

Task Constraints. As mentioned at the beginning of the section, an STL formula imposes two types of constraints over system behavior: *reachability* and *invariance* constraints, which are formally defined as follows:

Definition 3 (Reachability set). *A reachability set, $\mathcal{X}^{\exists} \in \mathbb{P}(\mathbb{T} \times \mathbb{T} \times \mathbb{U})$ is a set of tuples of form (l, h, p), each stating that there exists some time t in interval $[l, h]$, inclusively, such that proposition p holds over the system state at time t.*

Definition 4 (Invariance set). *An invariance set, $\mathcal{X}^{\forall} \in \mathbb{P}(\mathbb{T} \times \mathbb{T} \times \mathbb{U})$, is a set of tuples of form (l, h, p), each stating that for every time t in interval $[l, h]$, inclusively, proposition p holds over the system state at time t.*

$$\frac{\phi = p}{\mathcal{X}^{\exists} = \{(0,0,p)\} \quad \mathcal{X}^{\forall} = \emptyset \quad TC = \emptyset} \text{FLAT-}p \qquad \frac{\begin{array}{c}\phi = \phi_1 \wedge \phi_2 \\ (\mathcal{X}_1^{\exists}, \mathcal{X}_1^{\forall}, TC_1) = \text{FLAT}(\phi_1) \\ (\mathcal{X}_2^{\exists}, \mathcal{X}_2^{\forall}, TC_2) = \text{FLAT}(\phi_2)\end{array}}{\begin{array}{c}\mathcal{X}^{\exists} = \mathcal{X}_1^{\exists} \cup \mathcal{X}_2^{\exists} \\ \mathcal{X}^{\forall} = \mathcal{X}_1^{\forall} \cup \mathcal{X}_2^{\forall} \\ TC = TC_1 \cup TC_2\end{array}} \text{FLAT-}\wedge$$

$$\frac{\phi = F_{[a,b]}\phi_1 \qquad (\mathcal{X}_1^{\exists}, \mathcal{X}_1^{\forall}, TC_1) = \text{FLAT}(\phi_1)}{\begin{array}{l}\mathcal{X}^{\exists} = \{(t+l, t+h, p) \mid \exists (l,h,p) \in \mathcal{X}_1^{\exists}\} \\ \mathcal{X}^{\forall} = \{(t+l, t+h, p) \mid \exists (l,h,p) \in \mathcal{X}_1^{\forall}\} \\ TC = TC_1 \cup \{(a,b,t)\}\end{array}} \text{FLAT-}\exists$$

$$\frac{\phi = G_{[a,b]}\phi_1, \quad (\mathcal{X}_1^{\exists}, \mathcal{X}_1^{\forall}, TC_1) = \text{FLAT}(\phi_1)}{\begin{array}{l}\mathcal{X}^{\exists} = \{(k+l, k+l, p) \mid \exists (l,h,p) \in \mathcal{X}_1^{\exists} \wedge k \in [a,b]\} \\ \mathcal{X}^{\forall} = \{(a+l, b+h, p) \mid \exists (l,h,p) \in \mathcal{X}_1^{\forall}\} \\ TC = TC_1\end{array}} \text{FLAT-}\forall$$

Fig. 3. Flattening rules

We introduce an additional set of constraints that specify intervals over symbolic time variables that are introduced during the flattening of F formulas:

Definition 5 (Time variable intervals). *A time variable interval set, $TC \in \mathbb{P}(\mathbb{T} \times \mathbb{T} \times \mathbb{T})$, is a set of tuples of the form (l, h, v), each stating that symbolic time variable v takes a value in the interval $[l, h]$, inclusively.*

4.2 Flattening

Given an input STL specification, ϕ, the goal of *flattening* is to construct two sets of constraints—reachability and invariance sets—whose satisfaction also implies the satisfaction of ϕ. Flattening is applied recursively based on the structure of ϕ, as shown through the rules in Fig. 3. Along with $\mathcal{X}^{\forall}$ and $\mathcal{X}^{\exists}$, each recursive step produces an additional auxiliary output TC, which is later used by the scheduler to resolve symbolic time variables.

Flat-*p*. In the basic case where $\phi = p$, flattening generates one reachability constraint that requires p to be satisfied at the current time (i.e., $l = h = 0$). Hence, the reachability set for ϕ is $(0, 0, p)$.

Flat-$\wedge$. Given cojunctive formula $\phi = \phi_1 \wedge \phi_2$, the invariance set for ϕ is the union of $\mathcal{X}_1^{\forall}$ and $\mathcal{X}_2^{\forall}$; i.e., every invariance constraint in ϕ_1 and ϕ_2 must be satisfied. Similarly, the reachability set for ϕ is the union of $\mathcal{X}_1^{\exists}$ and $\mathcal{X}_2^{\exists}$; i.e., every reachability constraint in ϕ_1 and ϕ_2 must be satisfied.

Flat-$\exists$. Given $\phi = F_{[a,b]}(\phi_1)$, for each constraint $(l_1, h_1, p_1) \in \mathcal{X}_1^{\exists}$, flattening involves shifting interval $[l_1, h_1]$ by a symbolic time variable $t \in [a, b]$. This bound on t is encoded by adding a tuple (a, b, t) to TC. Intuitively, this can be understood from the following transformation similar to the one in [13]:

$$F_{[a,b]}(F_{[c,d]}(\phi_1)) = F_{[a+c,b+d]}(\phi_1)$$

Here, instead of adding a and b directly to the upper and lower bound, respectively of time interval $[c, d]$, we add a symbolic variable that can take a value between a and b. For example, given specification $\phi = F_{[2,5]}(p)$, $\mathcal{X}^\exists$ would contain constraint $(t + 0, t + 0, p)$ and TC would contain $(2, 5, t)$.

As another example, consider specification $\phi = F_{[2,5]}(p_2 \wedge F_{[1,3]}(p_1))$. When the FLAT-∃ rule is applied, the resulting $\mathcal{X}^\exists$ contains $(t_2 + t_1 + 0, t_2 + t_1 + 0, p1)$ and $(t_2, t_2, p2)$, and TC contains $\{(1, 3, t_1), (2, 5, t_2)\}$. Here, t_1 is introduced when FLAT-∃ rule is applied to the innermost F operator ($F_{[1,3]}$); t_2 is then introduced when FLAT-∃ is applied for outermost F operator ($F_{[2,5]}$).

The flattening of an F formula applied to an invariance set is handled similarly. Consider a specification of the form

$$\phi \equiv F_{[a,b]}(\phi_1) = F_{[a,b]}(G_{[c,d]}(p))$$

with $\mathcal{X}_1^\forall = \{(c, d, p)\}$. Here, according to the Boolean STL semantics, there exists a $t \in [a, b]$ such that $\forall t' \in [t + c, t + d]$, p must be satisfied. Hence, in the resulting invariance set for ϕ, the time interval for the existing invariance constraint is shifted by t. This bound on t is encoded by adding a tuple (a, b, t) to TC. For example, given specfcation $\phi = F_{[2,5]}(G_{[3,10]}(p))$, $\mathcal{X}^\forall$ would contain constraint $(t + 3, t + 10, p)$ and TC would contain $(2, 5, t)$.

Flat-∀. The flattening of an ∀ formula over $\mathcal{X}_1^\exists$ is handled in the following way. Consider a specification of the form:

$$\phi \equiv G_{[a,b]}(\phi_1) = G_{[a,b]}(F_{[c,d]}(p))$$

with $\mathcal{X}_1^\exists = \{tc\} = \{(t_1, t_1, p)\}$ and $TC = \{(c, d, t_1)\}$. Since ϕ states that constraint tc must hold at every time step between $[a, b]$, the idea is to create multiple reachability constraints of form $(t_1 + k, t_1 + k, p)$, one for each time value k in interval $[a, b]$. For example, let $\phi = G_{[1,100]}(F_{[1,5]}(p))$. After flattening, $\mathcal{X}^\exists$ for ϕ would contain 100 reachability constraints, each in form of $(t_1 + k, t_1 + k, p)$ for $1 \leq k \leq 100$.

The flattening of an ∀ over $\mathcal{X}_1^\forall$ is handled in the following way. Consider a specification of the form

$$\phi \equiv G_{[a,b]}(\phi_1) = G_{[a,b]}(G_{[c,d]}(p))$$

with $\mathcal{X}_1^\forall = \{tc\} = \{(c, d, p)\}$. Since ϕ states that constraint tc must hold at every time step between $[a, b]$, by shifting the interval of each constraint by $[a, b]$, the resulting formula $\mathcal{X}^\forall$ is constructed as $\{(a + c, b + d, p)\}$. Intuitively, this can be understood from the following transformation similar to the one in [13]:

$$G_{[a,b]}(G_{[c,d]}(\phi_1)) = G_{[a+c,b+d]}(\phi_1)$$

We now introduce a theorem that establishes the soundness of our flattening operation with respect to a given STL specification.

Lemma 1. *Let ϕ be an input STL specification, and let ($\mathcal{X}^{\exists}$, $\mathcal{X}^{\forall}$, TC) be the output of $flatten(\phi)$. Then, for every signal s_t:*

$$\forall v \in \mathcal{V}(vars(TC)) \bullet \forall x \in \mathcal{X}^{\exists} \cup \mathcal{X}^{\forall} \bullet s_t \models Inst(x, v) \implies s_t \models \phi$$

where vars is a function that returns the set of all symbolic variables in TC, $\mathcal{V}(\mathcal{X})$ is the set of all possible assignments of values to variables in $\mathcal{X}$ (restricted to values in their respective time intervals), and $Inst(x, v)$ instantiates symbolic variables in constraint x with the values from v.

In other words, if every possible reachability or invariance constraint is satisfied over a particular signal, then the original specification ϕ must also hold over the same signal.

4.3 Symbolic Time Resolution

The $\mathcal{X}^{\exists}$ and $\mathcal{X}^{\forall}$ constraints generated from flattening may contain multiple symbolic variables. To enable scheduling, STLINC first attempts to resolve as many of these variables as possible by applying substitution rules to the constraints.

Algorithm 1 shows the sketch of the *symbolic time resolution (STR)* process. As inputs, it takes the output of the flattening procedure—the $\mathcal{X}^{\exists}$ and $\mathcal{X}^{\forall}$ constraints, and the time intervals over symbolic time variables. As outputs, it produces (1) a new pair of $\mathcal{X}^{\exists}$ and $\mathcal{X}^{\forall}$, with some of the time variables replaced by concrete time values, and (2) time variable intervals (TC') that specifies, for each concrete constraint produced in (1), an interval during which the constraint must be satisfied. This latter set of time intervals are used to enforce conjunctive constraints (i.e., $\phi_1 \wedge \phi_2$) to be satisfied simultaneously.

The algorithm iterates through the time variables in the bottom-up order (i.e., starting with the variables that appear in the lower part of an AST for a given STL expression). For each constraint that contains variable t (line 4), STR applies two types of substitutions, depending on whether the constraint is a reachability or an invariance constraint.

Invariance Constraints. An invariance constraint, $x = (l, h, p)$, with time variable $t \in [a, b]$ represents an STL expression $F_{[a,b]}(G_{[l,h]}\ p)$ (where t appears in l and h, and p is an atomic proposition). Intuitively, this expression can be regarded a kind of "reach and stay" task, where the system must first reach a state where p holds within time interval $[a+l, b+l]$, and then continue to satisfy p for the following $(h-l)$ time steps. The rule APPLYFG takes constraint x and interval tc, and produces a new pair of reachability and invariance constraints, as follows:

$$\text{APPLYFG}(x = (l, h, p), tc = (a, b, t)) = ((a + l, b + l, p), (t_{sat}, t_{sat} + h - l, p))$$

where t_{sat} is a new symbolic variable that represents the time at which p is satisfied between $(a + l, b + l)$.

Algorithm 1. Symbolic Time Resolution (STR)

1: **Input**: Flattened constraints $\mathcal{X}^{\exists}, \mathcal{X}^{\forall}$, time variable intervals TC
2: **Output**: Modified constraints $\mathcal{X}^{\exists}, \mathcal{X}^{\forall}$, new time variable intervals TC'
3: $TC' = \emptyset$
4: **for** $tc = (a, b, t)$ in TC **do**
5: $\quad \mathcal{X}_t^{\forall} := \text{FILTER}(\mathcal{X}^{\forall}, t)$, $\mathcal{X}_t^{\exists} := \text{FILTER}(\mathcal{X}^{\exists}, t)$
6: $\quad$ **for** $x = (l, h, p)$ in $\mathcal{X}_t^{\forall}$ **do**
7: $\quad\quad (y^{\exists}, y^{\forall}) := \text{APPLYFG}(x, tc)$
8: $\quad\quad \mathcal{X}^{\exists} := \mathcal{X}^{\exists} \cup \{y^{\exists}\}$
9: $\quad\quad \mathcal{X}^{\forall} := (\mathcal{X}^{\forall} - \{x\}) \cup \{y^{\forall}\}$
10: $\quad\quad TC' := TC' \cup \{(t + l, t + l, \text{T-SAT}(y^{\exists})), (t + l + 1, t + h, \text{T-SAT}(y^{\forall}))\}$
11: $\quad$ **end for**
12: $\quad$ **for** $x = (l, h, p)$ in $\mathcal{X}_t^{\exists}$ **do**
13: $\quad\quad y^{\exists} := \text{APPLYFF}(x, tc)$
14: $\quad\quad \mathcal{X}^{\exists} := (\mathcal{X}^{\exists} - \{x\}) \cup \{y^{\exists}\}$
15: $\quad\quad TC' := TC' \cup \{(t + l, t + h, \text{T-SAT}(y^{\exists}))\}$
16: $\quad$ **end for**
17: **end for**
18: **return** $(\mathcal{X}^{\exists}, \mathcal{X}^{\forall}, TC')$

In addition, STR adds two time variable intervals (line 10) to ensure that: (1) the new reachability constraint, $y^{\exists}$, is satisfied exactly at $(t + l)$ and (2) the invariance constraint, $y^{\forall}$, is satisfied subsequently for the following $(l - h)$ steps. Here, $\text{T-SAT}(y)$ returns a symbolic time variable representing the time of satisfaction of constraint y.

Consider the example in Fig. 4. One of the invariance constraints that flattening generates is $(t + 1, t + 5, r_1)$, which depends on time variable $t \in [1, 20]$. The application of APPLYFG results in constraints stating that (1) the system must satisfy p within [2,21], and (2) from the point of the satisfaction of this constraint (t_2), it must hold p true for the following $(5 - 1) = 4$ steps. Note that the other invariance constraint, $(1, 35, \neg r_3)$, remains untouched, as it does not depend on any time variable.

Reachability Constraints. A reachability constraint, $x = (l, h, p)$, with time variable $t \in [a, b]$ represents an STL expression $F_{[a,b]}(F_{[l,h]}\ p)$. When a pair of F operators are nested in this manner, they can be simplified by using the following substitution rule:

$$\text{APPLYFF}(x = (l, h, p), tc = (a, b, t)) \equiv (l + a, h + b, p)$$

The resulting reachability constraint, $y^{\exists}$, replaces the existing constraint in $\mathcal{X}^{\exists}$ (line 14). In addition, a new time variable interval is added to ensure that $y^{\exists}$ is satisfied between $(t + l)$ and $(t + h)$.

For the example in Fig. 4, flattening produces one reachability constraint, $(t + t', t + t', r_2)$. During the first iteration of the outermost loop (line 4), STR selects $tc = (5, 15, t')$ and applies APPLYFF to the constraint, producing a new

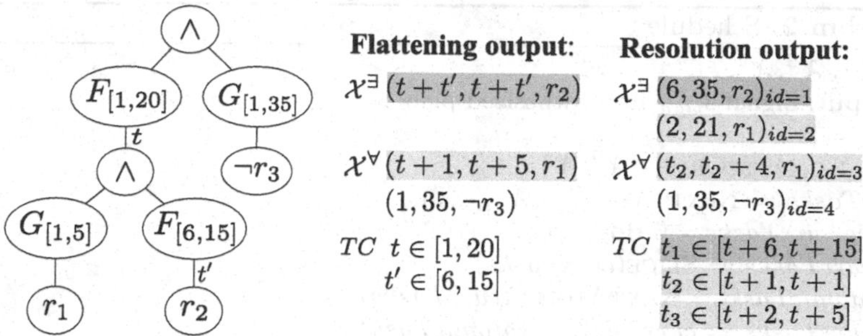

Fig. 4. An AST for an example STL specification, $F_{[1,20]}(G_{[1,5]}(r_1) \wedge F_{[6,15]}(r_2)) \wedge G_{[1,35]}(\neg r_3)$, with outputs from the flattening and symbolic time resolution steps. Each constraint resulting from the resolution step is assigned an identifier (*id*); a symbolic time variable that represents the time of satisfying the constraint is annotated with *id* as the subscript (i.e., t_2 represents the satisfaction of reachability constraint $(2, 21, r_1)$).

reachability constraint $(t + 5, t + 15, r_2)$. In next iteration, STR selects $tc = (1, 20, t)$ and applies ApplyFF to $(t + 5, t + 15, r_2)$, producing an additional reachability constraint $(6, 35, r_2)$.

Note that at the end of resolution for the example (Fig. 4), variable t appears in multiple intervals in TC'. In the following section, we describe how StlInc schedules tasks to generate concrete values for the time variables incrementally one-by-one, ultimately synthesizing a plan that satisfies the original STL formula.

Lemma 2. *Let* $(\mathcal{X}^{\exists}, \mathcal{X}^{\forall}, TC)$ *be the output of* $flatten(\phi)$ *and* $(\mathcal{X}_2^{\exists}, \mathcal{X}_2^{\forall}, TC')$ *be the output of* $STR(\mathcal{X}^{\exists}, \mathcal{X}^{\forall}, TC)$. *Then, for every signal* s_t*:*

$$\forall v \in \mathcal{V}(vars(TC')) \bullet (\forall x_2 \in \mathcal{X}_2^{\exists} \cup \mathcal{X}_2^{\forall} \bullet s_t \models Inst(x_2, v)) \implies (\forall x \in \mathcal{X}^{\exists} \cup \mathcal{X}^{\forall} \bullet s_t \models Inst(x, v))$$

In other words, if every reachability and invariance constraint generated from STR is satisfied under some instantiation (v) of symbolic time variables in TC', then the original set of flattened constraints must also be satisfied under the same condition.

4.4 Scheduling

Given the output from the resolution step (the two constraint sets, $\mathcal{X}^{\exists}, \mathcal{X}^{\forall}$ and the time interval variables, TC'), the goal of the scheduler is synthesize a plan that satisfies the original STL specification ϕ. To achieve this, the scheduler iteratively interacts with a *planner* that is capable of synthesizing a plan to satisfy an *atomic task* formula of form $F_{[a,b]}(\phi_1) \wedge G_{[a,b]}(\phi_2)$, where ϕ_1 and ϕ_2 are quantifier-free STL expressions. The scheduling process is incremental: The scheduler generates a sequence of atomic tasks formulas and invokes the planner

Algorithm 2. Schedule

1: **Input**: $\mathcal{X}^{\exists}, \mathcal{X}^{\forall}, TC'$
2: **Output**: Signal $\mathbf{s}_{plan}$ for synthesized plan
3: $\mathbf{s}_{plan} = \langle\rangle$
4: $\prec := \textsc{ComputeOrder}(\mathcal{X}^{\exists}, \mathcal{X}^{\forall}, TC')$
5: $currTasks := \textsc{NextTasks}(\mathcal{X}^{\exists}, \mathcal{X}^{\forall}, \prec, \emptyset)$
6: **while** $currTasks \neq \emptyset$ **do**
7: $\quad currTasks := \textsc{Slice}(currTasks)$
8: $\quad atomicTask := \textsc{NextAtomic}(currTasks)$
9: $\quad currTasks := currTasks - \{atomicTask\}$
10: $\quad \mathbf{s}_{atomic} := \textsc{Plan}\ (atomicTask)$
11: $\quad$ **if** $\mathbf{s}_{atomic} = \langle\rangle$ **then break end if**
12: $\quad \mathbf{s}_{plan} := \mathbf{s}^\frown \mathbf{s}_{atomic}$
13: $\quad$ satTasks := $\textsc{ExtractTime}(\mathbf{s}_{atomic})$
14: $\quad currTasks := currTasks \cup \textsc{NextTasks}(\mathcal{X}^{\exists}, \mathcal{X}^{\forall}, \prec, satTasks)$
15: **end while**
16: **return** $\mathbf{s}_{plan}$

to solve them one-by-one, using information (i.e., the time of satisfaction of a reachability or invariance constraint) generated by the planner to resolve any dependencies on symbolic time variables that were introduced during the flattening and resolution steps. The scheduling algorithm (Algorithm 2) comprises of three major parts: ordering, slicing of constraints, and planning of atomic tasks.

Ordering. In the first step (line 4), the scheduler computes a partial order ($\prec$) among the given reachability and invariance constraints, to determine which of these constraints must be satisfied before others. In particular, given a pair of constraints, x_1 and x_2, $x_1 \prec x_2$ if and only if the time of satisfaction of x_1 necessarily precede that of x_2, based on the time intervals that are assigned to those constraints in $\mathcal{X}^{\exists}$ or $\mathcal{X}^{\forall}$.

If one or more of x_1 and x_2 depends on another symbolic variable, t, for satisfaction, then the information in TC' is used to determine the presence of a precedence relationship. Consider t_1 and t_3 from Fig. 4; after resolution, the satisfaction of these two constraints depend on the symbolic variable t (as specified in TC'). Although the value of t is unknown, it can be determined that for any possible value of t, t_3 will necessarily be satisfied before t_1 (i.e., $t_3 \prec t_1$). Overall, for this example, ComputeOrder determines that $t_2 \prec t_3 \prec t_1$. Note that t_4 does not appear in this ordering as it needs to be satisfied in parallel with these other constraints.

Slicing. The scheduler then determines the first set of constraints (or tasks) to be carried out based on the order $\prec$ (line 5). In general, the time intervals over these constraint may overlap with each other in an arbitrary way. Recall, however, that each atomic task to be solved by the planner must be in form $F_{[a,b]}(\phi_1) \wedge G_{[a,b]}(\phi_2)$. Thus, the scheduler must first convert the constraints in *currTasks* into a set of atomic tasks constraint; this step involves *slicing* one or more constraints in *currTasks* (line 7).

Due to limited space, we provide the full details of the slicing algorithm in the appendix. We briefly illustrate it here using an example, shown in Fig. 5. For our running example, the first set of constraints to be fulfilled is $\{t_2 = (2, 21, r_1), t_4 = (1, 35, \neg r_3)\}$. To generate atomic tasks out of these, the SLICE operation slices t_4 into three constraints, t_{4a}, t_{4b}, t_{4c}; this, in turn, results in the following three atomic tasks:

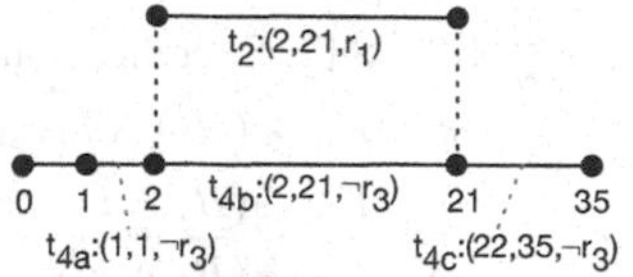

Fig. 5. A slicing example.

$$G_{[1,1]}(\neg r_3) \qquad F_{[2,21]}(r_2) \wedge G_{[2,21]}(\neg r_3) \qquad G_{[22,35]}(\neg r_3)$$

However, the slicing step may introduce dependencies among the atomic tasks, especially for the constraints in $\mathcal{X}^{\exists}$. For example, suppose that task $F_{[2,21]}(r_2)$ is further split into two slices, $F_{[2,12]}(r_2)$ and $F_{[12,21]}(r_2)$. Since r_2 needs to be satisfied only once in interval $[2, 21]$, we would need to ensure that we are not over-constraining the space of possible behaviors by requiring r_2 to be satisfied twice, as the slices would imply. To achieve this, we keep track of dependencies among constraints, which are used by the scheduler to remove unnecessary atomic tasks (e.g., remove $F_{[12,21]}(r_2)$ once r_2 is satisfied between $[2, 12]$). This dependency management is handled inside NEXTTASKS (Algorithm 2, Line 14).

Planning Atomic Tasks. Once atomic tasks have been generated through slicing, the scheduler selects the next atomic task and invokes the planner (lines 8–10). If the planner is able to synthesize a plan that satisfies the atomic task, it returns a signal that represents the satisfying trajectory, which is then appended to the cumulative signal $\mathbf{s}_{plan}$ (line 12); if not, the scheduler terminates by returning the signal that contains a partially satisfactory plan (line 11).

From the synthesized signal, the scheduler extracts the constraints from $\mathcal{X}^{\exists}$ and $\mathcal{X}^{\forall}$ that were satisfied, along with the concrete time values for their satisfaction (line 13). This information (*satTasks*) is then used to determine the next increment of constraints to be solved.

Finally, when all of the constraints in $\mathcal{X}^{\exists}$ and $\mathcal{X}^{\forall}$ have been satisfied, the scheduler terminates by returning $\mathbf{s}_{plan}$ as the final plan.

Lemma 3. *Let s_{plan} be the output of Schedule($\mathcal{X}^{\exists}$, $\mathcal{X}^{\forall}$, TC') and v be an assignment of values to symbolic time variables in TC', which are determined during the scheduling step. Then, the following statement holds:*

$$\forall x \in \mathcal{X}^{\exists} \cup \mathcal{X}^{\forall} \bullet s_{plan} \models Inst(x, v)$$

In other words, the synthesized plan, s_{plan}, satisfies all of the reachability and invariance constraints that were generated from the preceding flattening and STR steps.

Table 1. Benchmark STL specifications created from motion planning patterns. Here, R: Reach, A: Avoid, SV: Sequenced Visit, SB: Stabilization.

	STL Specification	Pattern
ϕ_1	$F_{[0,15]}(R_1) \wedge F_{[5,25]}(R_2) \wedge F_{[20,30]}(R_3) \wedge G_{[0,40]}(\neg O_1)$	R+A
ϕ_2	$F_{[0,15]}(R_1 \wedge F_{[0,15]}(R_2)) \wedge G_{[0,40]}(\neg O_1)$	SV+A
ϕ_3	$F_{[0,15]}(R_1 \wedge F_{[0,15]}(R_2 \wedge F_{[0,20]}(R_3 \wedge F_{[0,15]}(R_1))))$	SV
ϕ_4	$F_{[0,15]}G_{[0,10]}(R_1) \wedge F_{[0,35]}(R_2) \wedge G_{[0,40]}(\neg O_1)$	R+A+SB
ϕ_5	$F_{[0,15]}(R_1 \wedge F_{[0,20]}G_{[0,10]}(R_2))$	SV+SB

Building on Lemmas 1, 2, and 3, we finally introduce a theorem to state that our proposed approach generates a plan that satisfies the given specification ϕ:

Theorem 1. *Given specification ϕ and s_{plan} as the output of the scheduling algorithm, $s_{plan} \models \phi$.*

5 Evaluation

This section begins with a detailed description of our experimental setup, including specifications and implementation details, alongside the research questions we aim to address. Following this, we present our findings and conclude with a discussion of our approach over the benchmarks.

5.1 Experimental Setup

Specifications. We investigated multiple motion planning STL specifications from [6,17]. Based on the most common planning patterns, such as Reach (R), Avoid (A), Stabilisation (SB), Sequenced Visits (SV) etc., we created representative STL benchmark specifications as outlined in Table 1. These specifications are defined over STL subformulas of the form R_i or O_i where R_i / O_i is satisfied if the agent is inside Region i or Obstacle i. These subformulas are defined in a similar fashion using conjunction of linear and nonlinear predicates as done in [12]. Please refer to [12] for more information on how these are defined for rectangular/circular regions.

Implementation Details. We investigate planning from benchmark specifications in two robot exploration environments (similar to Fig. 1), namely LinEnv and NonLinEnv created using STLPY [12]. STLPY has the functionality to encode any arbitrary STL formula, dynamics and actuation limits into constraints and use existing state-of-the-art solvers (Gurobi [10], SNOPT [9], etc.,) to generate satisfying plans. Our two environments are both planar but differ in underlying dynamics governing the robot. LinEnv has linear dynamics (Double Integrator) whereas NonLinEnv has nonlinear dynamics (Unicycle). We benchmark our technique against existing MICP methods (for linear dynamics) and other gradient-based techniques like SNOPT (for non-linear dynamics). We use Python to implement our tool[2] while using stlpy and Drake [23] to encode the STL constraints. Additionally, we use Gurobi or SNOPT to solve the final constrained optimization problem. All experiments were run on a workstation with an Intel Xeon W-1350 processor and 32 GB RAM.

Benchmarks and Research Questions. We compare against the state-of-the-art techniques proposed in [4] (which we call *standard MICP*) and [12] (*reduced MICP*). Since the standard MICP encoding is only defined for environments with linear dynamics, we compare our technique against reduced MICP encoding for NonLinEnv. Reduced MICP claims better performance over standard MICP for long horizon and complex specifications due to their efficient encoding of disjunction and conjunction with fewer binary variables. However, standard MICP is faster for short-horizon specifications due to solver-specific presolve routines that leverage the additional binary variables for simplification.

Since our focus is on both short- and long-horizon specification with deep levels of temporal operator nesting, we benchmark against both techniques. The two main metrics we are concerned with are the time taken for solving and the final robustness values. To make the comparison fair, the total time taken by our technique includes the time taken by the flattener, scheduler, and solvers.

The two main research questions we investigate in this paper are:

1. **RQ1**: Does our decomposition technique result in shorter solve times?
2. **RQ2**: Does our decomposition technique result in higher robustness scores?

5.2 Results

Table 2 summarizes the results for StlInc performance compared to the baselines. In the tables, N represents the horizon of the specification and D represents the maximum depth of temporal nesting; TO represents a timeout, which means the solver did not terminate despite running it for 30 min. In those cases, the solver's output plan robustness is represented as -inf (which means no solution was found in the given time).

For LinEnv for all the specifications, our robustness values are comparable to the two techniques but our solve times are either lower or comparable to the baselines. Additionally, for specification ϕ_3, which has the deepest temporal nesting, our method significantly outperforms both baseline methods that experience timeouts.

For NonLinEnv for ϕ_1 and ϕ_4, the baseline encoding performs better in terms of solving time but StlInc only does slightly worse. However, for specification ϕ_2, ϕ_3 and ϕ_5, StlInc significantly outperforms the baselines.

[2] https://github.com/parvkpr/MCTSTL.

Table 2. StlInc Performance Benchmarking for LinEnv and NonLinEnv against standard MICP [4] and reduced MICP [12].

Spec	N	D	Solve time (s)					Robustness				
			LinEnv			NonLinEnv		LinEnv			NonLinEnv	
			[4]	[12]	StlInc	[12]	StlInc	[4]	[12]	StlInc	[12]	StlInc
ϕ_1	40	0	**0.845**	2.698	0.891	**0.890**	1.464	0.500	0.500	**0.500**	**0.430**	0.572
ϕ_2	30	1	2.459	TO	**0.402**	12.674	**0.892**	0.491	-inf	**0.491**	-inf	**0.594**
ϕ_3	60	3	TO	TO	**0.874**	15.829	**1.554**	-inf	-inf	**0.228**	-inf	**0.065**
ϕ_4	40	2	**0.318**	0.330	0.629	**1.049**	1.131	**0.494**	0.500	0.500	0.470	**0.364**
ϕ_5	40	2	2.829	28.490	**0.694**	83.193	**1.776**	0.500	0.500	**0.500**	-inf	**0.596**

Summary. Our technique excels significantly for nesting depths > 1 in both LinEnv and NonLinEnv. However, for nesting depths < 1, the baseline techniques outperform us due to marginal overhead from flattening, scheduling, and solver invocations. The encoding for these specifications involves fewer binary variables, and the preprocessing overhead of using StlInc outweighs the performance benefits. Nevertheless, the experiment suggests that our technique is more efficient for multi-step tasks with deep temporal nesting, outperforming baselines by an order of magnitude.

6 Related Work

Trajectory synthesis from STL specifications is an active area of research for which multiple approaches have been proposed in the past few years [1,2,15,20,21]. One of the first papers in this direction involved translating STL specifications into constraints within a Mixed Integer Linear Program (MILP) [20]. This approach is sound and complete but faces scalability challenges for long-horizon specifications. To remedy this drawback, the original encoding has been modified by focusing on abstraction-based techniques [22] and reducing binary variables via logarithmic encoding [12]. Most of these techniques focus on reducing the MILP's complexity to observe performance benefits. Recently, the focus has shifted to developing techniques that leverage robustness feedback as a heuristic for trajectory synthesis instead of using MILP. These techniques involve using reinforcement learning [1,11], search-based techniques [3] and control barrier functions [15] to generate STL satisfying trajectories. While these methods offer greater scalability, they are not complete and frequently struggle to accommodate complex specifications because of the intrinsically non-convex optimization problem posed by robustness semantics.

In this work, we focus on MILP-based techniques due to their completeness guarantees and improve their scalability by modifying input STL specifications themselves. However, since we perform structural manipulation of the specifications themselves, our decomposition technique is planner-agnostic and can also use learning- or search-based planners. Decomposition of STL specifications has been studied before in [13,24]. However, our work differs from existing work in multiple ways. In [24], the authors restrict themselves to an STL fragment that does not allow nesting of temporal operators, while a key contribution of our work is handling deep nested specifications. In [13], the authors perform structural manipulation using a tree structure. However, their focus is on multi-agent setups and they handle nested operators conservatively, especially for the eventually operator. This conservative notion generates specification satisfying behavior but it can be overly restrictive. Our interpretation is more flexible and in line with the Boolean semantics defined for the same operators.

7 Limitations and Future Work

In this work, we propose a structural manipulation-based technique for the temporal decomposition of STL specifications, enabling the incremental fulfillment of these specifications. We show our method generates correct-by -construction trajectories that satisfy deeply nested specifications with long time horizons for which existing baseline STL planning techniques struggle.

While the proposed approach is promising, our current decomposition technique does not handle disjunction. Additionally, the technique is sound but not complete, and designed to prioritize satisfaction over optimality. This limitation stems from incremental planning of objectives, which can be locally optimal compared to global planning, which considers the entire problem space. In future work, we aim to enrich our scheduling algorithm with backtracking capability, which can generate multiple satisfying plans, to overcome this limitation. Furthermore, for probabilistic systems, we plan to employ conformal prediction techniques to overcome compounding modeling error issues. Another avenue for future work is to adapt our theory to accommodate learning and heuristic-based approaches, such as reinforcement learning. Finally, our decomposition theory can potentially be employed for other STL applications, such as falsification, testing and runtime assurance and we plan to investigate that in the future.

Acknowledgements. We'd like to thank our reviewers for their insightful feedback. This work was supported in part by the National Science Foundation Award CCF-2144860.

A Appendix

A.1 Slicing Algorithm and Illustration

Our slicing algorithm is illustrated in Algorithm 3 and its application is demonstrated using the running example. In this example, the first set of constraints to be fulfilled is $\{t_2 = (2, 21, r_1), t_4 = (1, 35, \neg r_3)\}$. In the first step (line 3), we identify the lowest and the highest time bounds out of all the constraints in *currTasks* (which, for the example, would be 1 and 35). Then, in lines 5 to 11, for the horizon, we identify which constraints are active at each given time step. After this step, in lines 14 to 29, we first create "slices", which involves generating multiple time intervals out of time steps where similar constraints are active. Then, we create constraints of type $\mathcal{X}^s$ and $\mathcal{X}^\forall$ out of them by combining propositions of constraints of the same type. For the running example, these time slices would be [1,1], [2,21] and [22,35]. Finally, the constraints are converted into the following three atomic tasks:

$$G_{[1,1]}(\neg r_3) \qquad F_{[2,21]}(r_2) \wedge G_{[2,21]}(\neg r_3) \qquad G_{[22,35]}(\neg r_3)$$

Algorithm 3. SLICE

Input: Set of currTasks $\mathcal{X}^c$
Output: Set of atomic tasks constraints $\mathcal{X}^{c'}$
$t_{min}, t_{max} :=$ HORIZON($currTasks$)
$active := \langle\rangle$
for t in $[t_{min}, t_{max}]$ **do**
  $active_t := \langle\rangle$
  for $x = (l, h, p)$ in $\mathcal{X}^c$ **do**
    if t in $[l, h]$ **then** $active_t := active_t^\frown \langle x \rangle$ **end if**
  end for
  $active := active^\frown active_t$
end for
$t_{low} := t_{min}$
$\mathcal{X}^{c'} = \{\}$
for t in $[t_{min} + 1, t_{max}]$ **do**
  if $active[t-1]! = active[t]$ **then**
    $\mathcal{X}^{temp} := active[t-1]$
    $\mathcal{X}_\exists^{temp} := \{(t_{low}, t-1, \top)\}$
    $\mathcal{X}_\forall^{temp} := \{(t_{low}, t-1, \top)\}$
    for $x = (l, h, p)$ in $\mathcal{X}^{temp}$ **do**
      if x in $\mathcal{X}^\exists$ **then**
        $\mathcal{X}_\exists^{temp}.p := \mathcal{X}_\exists^{temp}.p \wedge p$
      else
        $\mathcal{X}_\forall^{temp}.p := \mathcal{X}_\forall^{temp}.p \wedge p$
      end if
    end for
    $\mathcal{X}^{c'} := \mathcal{X}^{c'} \cup \mathcal{X}_\exists^{temp} \cup \mathcal{X}_\forall^{temp}$
    $t_{low} := t$
  end if
end for
return $\mathcal{X}^{c'}$

References

1. Aksaray, D., Jones, A., Kong, Z., Schwager, M., Belta, C.: Q-learning for robust satisfaction of signal temporal logic specifications (2016)
2. Aloor, J.J., Patrikar, J., Kapoor, P., Oh, J., Scherer, S.: Follow the rules: online signal temporal logic tree search for guided imitation learning in stochastic domains. In: 2023 IEEE International Conference on Robotics and Automation (ICRA), pp. 1320–1326 (2023). https://doi.org/10.1109/ICRA48891.2023.10160953

3. Aloor, J.J., Patrikar, J., Kapoor, P., Oh, J., Scherer, S.: Follow the rules: online signal temporal logic tree search for guided imitation learning in stochastic domains. In: 2023 IEEE International Conference on Robotics and Automation (ICRA), pp. 1320–1326. IEEE (2023)
4. Belta, C., Sadraddini, S.: Formal methods for control synthesis: an optimization perspective. Ann. Rev. Control, Robot. Auton. Syst. **2**(1), 115–140 (2019)
5. Botea, A., Ciré, A.A.: Incremental heuristic search for planning with temporally extended goals and uncontrollable events. In: Proceedings of the 21st International Joint Conference on Artificial Intelligence, pp. 1647–1652. IJCAI'09, Morgan Kaufmann Publishers Inc., San Francisco, CA, USA (2009)
6. Chen, Y., Gandhi, R., Zhang, Y., Fan, C.: NL2TL: transforming natural languages to temporal logics using large language models. CoRR **abs/2305.07766** (2023). https://doi.org/10.48550/arXiv.2305.07766, https://doi.org/10.48550/arXiv.2305.07766
7. Czechowski, K., et al.: Subgoal search for complex reasoning tasks. In: Advances in Neural Information Processing Systems, vol. 34, pp. 624–638 (2021)
8. Donnarumma, F., Maisto, D., Pezzulo, G.: Problem solving as probabilistic inference with subgoaling: explaining human successes and pitfalls in the tower of hanoi. PLoS Comput. Biol. **12**(4), e1004864 (2016)
9. Gill, P.E., Murray, W., Saunders, M.A.: SNOPT: an SQP algorithm for large-scale constrained optimization. SIAM Rev. **47**(1), 99–131 (2005). https://doi.org/10.1137/S0036144504446096
10. Gurobi Optimization, Inc.: Gurobi optimizer reference manual (2012). http://www.gurobi.com
11. Kapoor, P., Balakrishnan, A., Deshmukh, J.V.: Model-based reinforcement learning from signal temporal logic specifications. arXiv preprint arXiv:2011.04950 (2020)
12. Kurtz, V., Lin, H.: Mixed-integer programming for signal temporal logic with fewer binary variables. IEEE Control Syst. Lett. **6**, 2635–2640 (2022)
13. Leahy, K., Mann, M., Vasile, C.I.: Rewrite-based decomposition of signal temporal logic specifications. In: Rozier, K.Y., Chaudhuri, S. (eds.) NFM 2023. LNCS, pp. 224–240. Springer, Cham (2023). https://doi.org/10.1007/978-3-031-33170-1_14
14. Leung, K., Aréchiga, N., Pavone, M.: Backpropagation through signal temporal logic specifications: Infusing logical structure into gradient-based methods. Int. J. Robot. Res. 02783649221082115 (2023)
15. Lindemann, L., Dimarogonas, D.V.: Control barrier functions for signal temporal logic tasks. IEEE Control Syst. Lett. **3**, 96–101 (2019). https://api.semanticscholar.org/CorpusID:50767137
16. Maler, O., Nickovic, D.: Monitoring temporal properties of continuous signals. In: FORMATS/FTRTFT (2004). https://api.semanticscholar.org/CorpusID:15642684
17. Menghi, C., Tsigkanos, C., Pelliccione, P., Ghezzi, C., Berger, T.: Specification patterns for robotic missions. IEEE Trans. Softw. Eng. **47**(10), 2208–2224 (2021). https://doi.org/10.1109/TSE.2019.2945329
18. Nair, S., Finn, C.: Hierarchical foresight: self-supervised learning of long-horizon tasks via visual subgoal generation. ArXiv **abs/1909.05829** (2019). https://api.semanticscholar.org/CorpusID:202565422
19. Pnueli, A.: The temporal logic of programs. In: 18th Annual Symposium on Foundations of Computer Science (sfcs 1977), pp. 46–57 (1977). https://doi.org/10.1109/SFCS.1977.32

20. Raman, V., Donzé, A., Maasoumy, M., Murray, R.M., Sangiovanni-Vincentelli, A., Seshia, S.A.: Model predictive control with signal temporal logic specifications. In: 53rd IEEE Conference on Decision and Control, pp. 81–87 (2014). https://doi.org/10.1109/CDC.2014.7039363
21. Sadraddini, S., Belta, C.: Formal synthesis of control strategies for positive monotone systems. IEEE Trans. Autom. Control **64**(2), 480–495 (2019). https://doi.org/10.1109/TAC.2018.2814631
22. Sun, D., Chen, J., Mitra, S., Fan, C.: Multi-agent motion planning from signal temporal logic specifications. IEEE Robot. Autom. Lett. **PP**, 1–1 (2022). https://api.semanticscholar.org/CorpusID:245986629
23. Tedrake, R., the Drake Development Team: drake: model-based design and verification for robotics (2019). https://drake.mit.edu
24. Yu, X., Wang, C., Yuan, D., Li, S., Yin, X.: Model predictive control for signal temporal logic specifications with time interval decomposition (2022)

Formal Methods for Software Engineering

Structuring Formal Methods into the Undergraduate Computer Science Curriculum

Sarnath Ramnath[1] (✉) and Stephen Walk[2]

[1] Department of Computer Science and Information Technology, St Cloud State University, St Cloud, MN 56301, USA
sarnath@stcloudstate.edu

[2] Department of Mathematics and Statistics, St Cloud State University, St Cloud, MN 56301, USA

Abstract. There is an urgent need to emphasize and integrate Formal Methods into the undergraduate curriculum in Computer Science in the United States. We are entering an age defined by a highly interconnected, ubiquitous computing environment, with a large AI component. Knowing the precise capability of our systems is particularly vital to safeguard safety-critical and mission-critical applications. In such an environment, the lack of a well-structured exposure to formal methods is a serious shortcoming in our computing curricula. We examine the curricular, pedagogical, and organizational challenges involved in bringing Formal Methods into the mainstream of computing disciplines, note efforts made to address the challenges, and suggest further initiatives to help address them.

Keywords: Computer Science · Formal Methods · Software Engineering · Curriculum Development · Teaching and Learning

1 Introduction

The relationship between mathematical foundations and programming skills has a long history in the Computer Science curriculum. The typical Computer Science program started out as an extension to mathematics, developed into a separate entity for which a strong mathematical foundation early in the program was still considered essential, and became one where a single Discrete Math course is now the only prerequisite for most Computer Science courses. This change has been accompanied by a shift in the approach taken towards programming: away from mathematical and logical foundations, and towards example and intuition. The admission requirement has also moved from completion of Calculus, Discrete Math, and a semester of programming, to one where students "directly declare" the major and complete two semesters of programming before they take Discrete Math. The requirement of a second course in Discrete Math, dealing exclusively with logic, axioms, and inference, has all but disappeared.

Although the dropped math courses were seen as losing their relevance and becoming hoops for students to jump through, we now face new challenges that require us to

N. Benz et al. (Eds.): NFM 2024, LNCS 14627, pp. 399–405, 2024.
https://doi.org/10.1007/978-3-031-60698-4_24

reassess our priorities. Specifically, we are now dealing with a highly inter-connected, ubiquitous computing environment, with a large AI component. Knowing precisely what our systems can and cannot do has become more important, and this awareness is particularly vital for safety-critical and mission-critical applications. Formal methods for verifying code are more important now than ever before. High personnel costs have often been cited as a reason for not embracing formal methods; this indicates that we need to improve the way we train our workforce and change the prevailing view of formal methods within our academic institutions.

In this article we discuss the challenge of structuring Formal Methods into the Computer Science curriculum and make some suggestions. The next section discusses relevant background: efforts that have been made over the years to introduce these concepts into the courses at various levels, the pedagogical challenges and approaches, and some experiences and observations. Section 3 suggests possible initiatives to be undertaken, and Sect. 4 concludes the paper.

2 The Current Situation

To get a better understanding, it is useful to examine the existing situation in the field of formal methods from a few different viewpoints.

2.1 Developing Coursework and Pedagogy

The teaching of formal methods does not appear to get enough emphasis in the large mass of computer science programs [23, 25]. Several reasons have been identified for this: limited number of university programs in computer science, formal methods being perceived as a "difficult" topic, lack of research-and-development investment, and lack of sufficiently trained engineers to design and build safety critical systems [1]. The perception that formal methods are all about "writing proofs" [3] relegates it to the "theoretical" side of computer science.

There appears to be considerable variation in the prerequisites and the set of topics across courses in formal methods [2], which points to a lack of consensus about such courses. Further, the considerable amount of time spent in these courses on sets and logic is an indicator that discrete math as widely taught is insufficient.

2.2 The Mathematics Connection in Computer Science Program

The area of formal methods "... bridges the gap between mathematics and computer science" and fosters "mathematical reasoning skills and problem-solving abilities" [4]. New programmers must connect program execution to proof. This connection is "...best made by the use of coordinated tools and examples that appear in both introductory programming and discrete mathematics" [4]. This would require that math syllabi emphasize more of axiomatic systems and proofs.

2.3 Pedagogical Challenges and Approaches

For the most part, our challenges stem from prevailing attitudes: perception that formal methods are a "fringe" subject, belief that all proof-writing is difficult, and a preference for "writing quasi-correct programs and testing them" over "thinking about and planning" code. Fortunately, some of the educational and pedagogical innovations listed below can help us reach this goal.

1. *Working with Threshold Concepts.* Threshold concepts, and approaches for integrating them into curricula, are now well understood [5, 6]. There is evidence to suggest that the ability to grasp the framework of a proof structure is a threshold concept [7], and grasping the significance of formal methods and mastering the techniques of formal methods mirror the same challenges.
2. *Using Different Kinds of Activities at Different Levels.* Using different strategies at different levels of learning [9] can be effective in the teaching of formal methods [1].
3. *Employing the Whole-Part-Whole Approach.* The whole-part-whole approach [11] has been particularly effective with adult learners, as documented in [12, 13].
4. *Strategies that Promote Enduring Learning.* Engaging students in retrieval of previously learned information, and promoting deep understanding through self-explanation, can help with retention, organization, and integration of knowledge [10].

2.4 Experiences and Observations

Some experiments in the literature provide observations about students' reasoning with respect to their own programs, investigating, for example, students' ability to connect code with assertions [14] and to explain the structure and execution of their small programs after they had submitted them to a programming exercise [15]. Lack of such ability is related, we believe, to students' tendency to jump straight into coding without crafting a reasonable design. In a second-semester programming course at our institution, for example, when assigning students to translate a given design (a flowchart) into code and repeatedly noting that code must follow design, we are not surprised if a significant fraction of the students still attempts to bypass the given design and write code from the functional requirements. We need to wean students away from this habit of writing code directly, based on intuition and (limited) experience, and to help them replace it with the habits of planning and design; this needs to happen early in students' academic lives.

A few other researchers [16–19] have reported on their attempts to integrate and assimilate formal methods into undergraduate programs. They have been effective to varying degrees and provide valuable insight for any program that seeks to place greater emphasis on formal methods. Nonetheless, there remains a need for a structured approach that has broad institutional recognition and can be replicated across programs with measurable results.

As mentioned earlier, there is a need to see math and computer science courses as synergetic curricular subjects. The authors of [4] and [19] have described their experiences with tools and content to strengthen this connection, We have attempted to address the matter at our institution by developing a sophomore/junior level math class, in which topics of mathematics and computer science are intermixed and students in both programs are told up front that they will see how the two disciplines contribute significantly to each other. Various topics are explored in tandem: Issues like computer numeration and pitfalls of floating-point arithmetic are a prelude to the constructions of the familiar number systems from the natural numbers. Comparisons and contrasts are emphasized between declarations of variables in programming and in proof-writing, with approaches for keeping track of assumptions in a proof likened to those for keeping track of the depths of loops in programs. The consideration of axiom systems for predicate calculus is compared with the programming of a computer, with proper axioms being seen as macros to load. The parallel experiences help both populations of students see the interconnection between the disciplines.

3 Possible Initiatives (Recommendations)

Recognizing the central importance of formal methods will clearly involve a culture-shift in the computing curriculum. We propose some initiatives to be considered as part of a broader discussion toward this goal.

3.1 A Framework for the Undergraduate Curriculum

We see two vital aspects to a curricular framework: a culture that recognizes and emphasizes the role of mathematics in computer science, and a computer science curriculum that explicitly builds an appreciation for and proficiency in formal methods. These are in line with the suggestions from [16, 22, 23], but perhaps wider in scope. Such a framework also has the potential to address several of the concerns highlighted in a recent survey of experts in the area of formal methods [27].

The role of mathematics can be addressed by the following:

1. *Promoting mathematical thinking and reasoning.* Students should develop an appreciation of proofs and be able to craft and comprehend abstract proofs.
2. *Forging strong connections between math and Computer Science.* In addition to stressing the importance of mathematics in computer science, we need a shared use of formalisms and notation, and the use of common technological tools.

The computer science curriculum presents several opportunities for introducing and building on the concepts and use of formal methods:

1. *CS1 and Data Structures.* Students are exposed to assertions, invariants and the use of models in the course of defining and solving problems.
2. *Logic circuit design.* Sequential circuit design provides a great opportunity for students to model requirements as finite state machines.
3. *Concepts of programming languages.* This course can emphasize language semantics, especially axiomatic semantics, and introduce the Java Modelling Language.
4. *Computing Ethics.* Special emphasis could be placed on the need to ensure correctness of code.

5. *Object-oriented software construction.* A focus on modelling and examining the Liskov Substitution Principle [8] could set the stage for later courses on formal methods.
6. *Software Engineering courses.* Software Analysis courses can include formal specification methods and Software Quality courses can include formal validation.
7. *Course dedicated to Formal Verification and Validation.* A course built around a project-based learning model could replace a course like Theory of Computation.

3.2 Special Recognition for Higher Standards

Since such a change in culture will require a high degree of commitment from both the programs and the students, some distinction would likely have to be conferred upon participants. These distinctions could be conferred in two ways:

1. *Recognizing programs that provide the necessary structure.* These would be in line with program recognitions as suggested in [24]. Effective teaching of formal methods will require tailoring curricular materials and monitoring student learning outcomes.
2. *Recognizing students who meet the higher standards.* We suspect that a significant fraction of graduating students will not have mastered the use of formal methods at the appropriate level. Requiring graduating students to earn specific badges and certificates can help to address this issue.

3.3 Exerting Influence Through Prominent Bodies

Bodies that play a significant role in creating the culture will have to be a part of the solution. Association for Computing Machinery (ACM) code of ethics [20] exhorts computing professionals to "Recognize and take special care of systems that become integrated into the infrastructure of society". The National Institute of Standards and Technology (NIST) standards for secure software development [21] describe the software development life cycle as a "…formal or informal methodology for designing software…". Clauses such as these need to be rephrased to convey the higher level of reliability obtained by using formal methods and stress the importance of using formal methods wherever possible. Efforts like [26] can play a part in this.

4 Conclusions

In this paper we have attempted to capture some of the dilemmas that those in academia face in their attempts to equip software engineers who are ready to join teams working on safety-critical and mission-critical systems. Based on the literature and our experiences, we see a connection between preparing these students and shaping their abilities for and attitude towards proofs and theorems. Further, we have suggested some initiatives that we believe will be critical to success in this endeavour.

The effort needs to start with the curriculum. We cannot expect graduates to become experts in program verification as professionals if they never encountered the ideas as students. The more we engage students with proofs, counterexamples, and axiomatic systems and semantics, the more their eyes will be open to the possibility of unexpected cases and unintended consequences of something as seemingly cut-and-dried as a computer program. Ideally, they will come to see that the unexpected can happen if possibilities are not considered carefully and rigorously—and come to see themselves as professionals responsible for checking for such possibilities.

Effecting such a culture change is a formidable undertaking and will require a lot of effort. Our objective in writing this paper is to place this issue before this forum of researchers and educators and contribute to momentum in the desired direction. Formulating a plan of action will clearly be a larger exercise involving the larger community of professionals who see value in such an initiative.

References

1. Cerone, A., Lermer, K.R.: Adapting to different types of target audience in teaching formal methods. In: Cerone, A., Roggenbach, M. (eds.) FMFun 2019. CCIS, vol. 1301, pp. 106–123. Springer, Cham (2021). https://doi.org/10.1007/978-3-030-71374-4_5
2. What I've Learned About Formal Methods In Half a Year (2023). https://jakob.space/blog/what-ive-learned-about-formal-methods.html
3. Make Formal Verification and Provably Correct Software Practical and Mainstream. Comments posted in May 2022. https://news.ycombinator.com/item?id=31543953
4. Wonnacott, D.G., Osera, P.M.: A bridge anchored on both sides: formal deduction in introductory CS, and code proofs in discrete math. arXiv preprint arXiv:1907.04134 (2019)
5. Meyer, J., Land, R.: Threshold concepts and troublesome knowledge: linkages to ways of thinking and practising within the disciplines. ETL Project Occasional Report 4 (2003). http://www.ed.ac.uk/etl/docs/ETLreport4.pdf
6. Fouberg, E.H.: 5 ways to integrate threshold concepts into your classroom. The Wiley Network (2019). https://www.wiley.com/network/latest-content/5-ways-to-integrate-threshold-concepts-into-your-classroom
7. Easdown, D.: Teaching proofs in mathematics. In: 1st Joint International Meeting between the American Mathematical Society and the New Zealand Mathematical Society (2007). http://at.yorku.ca/c/a/t/m/51
8. Ramnath, S., Dathan, B.: Crossing learning thresholds progressively via active learning. In Proceedings of the 2022 ACM SIGPLAN International Symposium on SPLASH-E (SPLASH-E 2022). Association for Computing Machinery, New York, NY, USA, pp. 14–23 (2022). https://doi.org/10.1145/3563767.3568128
9. HIGH IMPACT TEACHING STRATEGIES. https://www.education.vic.gov.au/Documents/school/teachers/management/highimpactteachingstrat.pdf
10. Help Students Retain, Organize and Integrate Knowledge https://tll.mit.edu/teaching-resources/how-to-teach/help-students-retain-organize-and-integrate-knowledge/
11. Knowles, M.S., Holton, E.F. III, Swanson, R.A.: The Adult Learner, Sixth Edition: The Definitive Classic in Adult Education and Human Resource Development, Taylor and Francis, seventh edition (2011)
12. Ramnath, S., Dathan, B.: Evolving an integrated curriculum for object-oriented analysis and design. SIGCSE Bull. **40**(1), 337–341 2008. https://doi.org/10.1145/1352322.1352252
13. Ramnath, S., Hoover, J.H.: Enhancing engagement by blending rigor and relevance. In Proceedings of the 47th ACM Technical Symposium on Computing Science Education (SIGCSE '16). Association for Computing Machinery, New York, NY, USA, pp. 108–113 (2016). https://doi.org/10.1145/2839509.2844554A.A, Author, "Online Article Title," Periodical Title, vol. Volume, no. Issue, pp.-pp., Publication Year. Retrieved from URL 2016
14. Blankenship, S.: Learning to reason about code with assertions: an exploration with two student populations (2022). https://tigerprints.clemson.edu/all_theses/3950/

15. Lehtinen, T., Lukkarinen, A., Haaranen, L.: Students struggle to explain their own program code. In Proceedings of the 26th ACM Conference on Innovation and Technology in Computer Science Education V 1, pp. 206–212 (2021). https://arxiv.org/pdf/2104.06710.pdf
16. Skevoulis, S., Makarov, V.: Integrating formal methods tools into undergraduate computer science curriculum. In: Proceedings. Frontiers in Education. 36th Annual Conference, San Diego, CA, USA, pp. 1–6 (2006). https://doi.org/10.1109/FIE.2006.322570
17. Sebern, M., Welch, H.: Formal methods in the undergraduate software engineering curriculum. In: 2008 Annual Conference & Exposition (2008). peer.asee.org
18. Zamansky, A., Farchi, E.: Exploring the role of logic and formal methods in information systems education. In: Bianculli, D., Calinescu, R., Rumpe, B. (eds.) SEFM 2015. LNCS, vol. 9509, pp. 68–74. Springer, Heidelberg (2015). https://doi.org/10.1007/978-3-662-49224-6_7
19. Alabi, O., Vu, A., Osera, P.M.: Snowflake: supporting programming and proofs. In: Proceedings of the 54th ACM Technical Symposium on Computer Science Education V. 2, p. 1398 (2022)
20. The ACM Code of Ethics. https://www.acm.org/code-of-ethics
21. Souppaya, M., Scarfone, K., Dodson, D.: NIST Special Publication 800–218 Secure Software Development Framework (SSDF) Version 1.1: Recommendations for Mitigating the Risk of Software Vulnerabilities
22. Pepper, P.: Distributed teaching of formal methods. In: Dean, C.N., Boute, R.T. (eds.) TFM 2004. LNCS, vol. 3294, pp. 140–152. Springer, Heidelberg (2004). https://doi.org/10.1007/978-3-540-30472-2_9
23. da Silva Junior, A., da Costa Cavalheiro, S.A., Foss, L., da Silva, J.V.:Formal specification in basic education: what does it take? In: 2023 IEEE Frontiers in Education Conference (FIE), College Station, TX, USA, pp. 1–9 (2023). https://doi.org/10.1109/FIE58773.2023.10343074
24. National Centers of Academic Excellence in Cybersecurity. https://www.nsa.gov/Academics/Centers-of-Academic-Excellence/
25. Cerone, A., et al.: Rooting formal methods within higher education curricula for computer science and software engineering — a white paper —. In: Cerone, A., Roggenbach, M. (eds.) FMFun 2019. CCIS, vol. 1301, pp. 1–26. Springer, Cham (2021). https://doi.org/10.1007/978-3-030-71374-4_1
26. Ter Beek, M H., Broy, M., Dongol, B., Sekerinski, E.: The role of formal methods in computer science education. https://csed.acm.org/wp-content/uploads/2023/11/Formal-Methods-Nov-2023-1.pdf
27. Garavel, H., Beek, M.H.T., Pol, JVd.: The 2020 expert survey on formal methods. In: ter Beek, M.H., Ničković, D. (eds.) FMICS 2020. LNCS, vol. 12327, pp. 3–69. Springer, Cham (2020). https://doi.org/10.1007/978-3-030-58298-2_1

Integrated Contract-Based Unit and System Testing for Component-Based Systems

John Hatcliff[1](✉), Jason Belt[1], Robby[1], and David Hardin[2]

[1] Kansas State University, Manhattan, KS 66506, USA
hatcliff@ksu.edu
[2] Collins Aerospace, Cedar Rapids, IA, USA

Abstract. This paper presents a system testing framework for development of AADL-based systems using the HAMR model-driven development framework. A key theme of the framework is the integration of unit testing and program verification based on formal contracts that are synchronized between models and code. HAMR's scheduling framework is extended to enable test scripting aligned with AADL's standardized run-time services (RTS) and real-time task structures. Libraries of state observers and injectors aligned with the AADL RTS are auto-generated, enabling system property tests to observe system state and force the state to contain certain values. Executable versions of component contracts are automatically checked during system tests. A randomized property-based testing approach is used to generate vectors of input values for subsystem ports, helping to achieve coverage with reduced developer effort. A server-based architecture automatically distributes system tests in a continuous integration environment and accumulates and correlates coverage information. Together with HAMR's ability to generate system deployments on the verified seL4 micro-kernel, these capabilities provide another step towards the community's long-term objectives of practical model-based development that integrates formal models, specifications, and rigorously-assured application and infrastructure code at many different levels of abstraction.

1 Introduction

Model-based development continues to be pursued within the formal methods community as a means to abstract and organize complexity in critical systems. In our vision for model-based development, formal methods are aligned through layers of abstraction (models, application code, platform execution model semantics). Formal and semi-formal methods are included at strategic points during system development. These emphasize low barriers-to-entry and incremental "tightening up" of assurance as development unfolds.

This work is supported in part by U.S. Defense Advanced Research Projects Agency (DARPA).

N. Benz et al. (Eds.): NFM 2024, LNCS 14627, pp. 406–426, 2024.
https://doi.org/10.1007/978-3-031-60698-4_25

The Collins Aerospace tool chain developed for the DARPA Cyber-Assured Systems Engineering (CASE) program was designed to support the principles above [1,2]. A thesis of the approach is that the cyber-resiliency of systems could be improved by leveraging model-based development and the strong spatial and temporal separation provided by the seL4 verified micro-kernel [15]. Systems on CASE were modeled using component-based architectures specified in AADL (Architecture Analysis and Design Language), which also indicated the desired kernel-enforced partitioning (e.g., AADL process components indicated partition boundaries and connections between process components were specified as cross-partition communication). Key properties were formally specified and verified using component contract technology.

The HAMR (High Assurance Modeling and Rapid Engineering for embedded systems) tool chain [10] developed by the authors and engineers from Adventium Labs (subsequently acquired by Galois) provided multi-platform multi-language code generation that served as one of the foundational integrating technologies of the CASE program. Given an AADL model, HAMR generates AADL compliant run-time services (RTS) for real-time threading and port communication, and APIs that provide application developers with a consistent view of threading and port communication independent of the particular programming language or backend platform. To create deployments for seL4, HAMR generates [1] seL4 kernel partitioning configurations for the seL4 CAmKES framework as well as infrastructure for mapping AADL run-time libraries for threading and communication into CAmKES/seL4 primitives. Based on approaches used on certain Collins Aerospace product platforms, deterministic mono-processor based system executions were achieved using static scheduling of seL4 partitions.

We've also built a family of engineer-friendly assurance capabilities to support the development paradigm above. Our approach emphasizes a tight integration of model-level and code-level verification, integration of automated property-based testing and SMT-based formal verification, and strong alignment with the AADL's standard's presentation of semantic notions and its run-time service library. A formal semantics of the AADL run-time services for thread behavior and port communication was developed [10] and then significantly expanded and mechanized in the Isabelle theorem prover [7]. HAMR automatically translates AADL models and port/thread state information into this representation. We developed the GUMBO contract language [13] for model-level component behavioral specifications that are also translated to code-level contracts in HAMR-generated Slang [25] code. This enables the Logika verifier for Slang to verify that component application code conforms to code contracts; conformance to model-level component contracts follows as a corollary. We developed a property-based testing framework [11] that translates GUMBO contracts into executable predicates that are incorporated into auto-generated unit test oracles. These can be deployed on a scalable server-based randomizing testing infrastructure – enabling smooth integration of automated unit testing and SMT-based code verification against the same GUMBO contracts.

In this paper, we describe a new system testing framework that integrates with both the capabilities above as well and also the development workflows emphasized in our industry teams.

- We enhance the scheduling infrastructure used previously with Collins Aerospace to support test-scriptable control of scheduling – enabling system testers to control the system execution through certain trace segments of interest.
- We provide a library of state *observers* and *injectors* aligned with the AADL RTS – enabling system tests to both *observe* the system state and *force* port and thread states to certain values, e.g., for fault-injection.
- We integrate the GUMBO-derived executable component contracts in a framework that enables them to be automatically checked during system testing – equipping engineers to develop formal specifications that support both unit, integration, and system testing.
- We extended our server-based architecture for unit tests to support automated distribution of system tests in a continuous integration framework.
- We extend HAMR with a state logging mechanism that enables states/traces from system tests to be logged – enabling, e.g., segments of system tests (e.g., the input port values for a particular component) to be replayed as unit tests, which makes it easier for engineers to isolate and debug fault behaviors.
- We evaluate the above capabilities on a collection of examples.

Both tools and examples are publicly available [8].

2 Background

AADL: SAE International standard AS5506C defines the AADL core language for expressing the structure of embedded real-time systems via definitions of software and hardware components, their interfaces, and their communication. AADL provides a precise, tool-independent, and standardized modeling vocabulary of common embedded software and hardware elements using a component-based approach [6,14]. The AADL standard also describes its RTS – a collection of run-time libraries that provide key aspects of threading and communication behavior. A major subset of the RTS has been formalized and a reference implementation has been developed [12], and we have designed our contract language and associated translation to code-level contracts with these definitions in mind.

HAMR: HAMR generates code from AADL models for multiple execution platforms [10]. This includes generating threading, port communication, and scheduling infrastructure code that conforms to AADL RTS semantics as well as application code skeletons that engineers fill in to complete the behavior of the system. For the JVM platform, HAMR generates code in Slang – a high-integrity subset of Scala, which can be integrated with support code written in Scala and Java. Mixed Slang/Scala-based HAMR systems can also be translated to JavaScript (e.g., for simulation and prototyping) and run in a web browser or on the NodeJS platform. HAMR generates C infrastructure and application skeletons when targeting Linux and the seL4 micro-kernel. Slang can be transpiled to C, and HAMR factors its C code through a Slang-based "reference implementation" of the AADL RTS and application code skeletons. Using the Logika verification framework for Slang, Slang code can be verified with a high-degree of automation. This provides a basis for developing high-assurance AADL-based systems using Slang directly or via translation of Slang to C (without garbage collection runtime overhead). C code transpiled from Slang can be compiled using standard C compilers, as well as the CompCert Verified C compiler [20]. In addition, a Slang to Rust translation is currently under development to provide to engineers a safer alternative system language to develop HAMR components.

HAMR Workflows: Given HAMR's support for multiple languages, a number of workflows are possible. In this paper, we emphasize coding thread component application logic in Slang, testing and verifying the application code against model contracts using the GUMBO-based technologies referenced in Sect. 1, and then constructing system tests for Slang-based application code using the framework presented in this paper. In general, system requirements are realized as testable system properties, as well as decomposed to component-level contracts. The above activities are carried out on a JVM-based deployment, so precise timing properties and other aspects associated interfacing with hardware are not accounted for. Nevertheless, a very high degree of functional correctness can be addressed. The Slang-based implementation can be transpiled to C (or Rust later) and deployed on Linux and seL4, and final timing and end-to-end software/hardware issue can be addressed then.

In the DARPA CASE program, C workflows were emphasized due to industry engineer familiarity with C. In final system deployments, HAMR was used to generate C component APIs, and component application logic was implemented directly in C. Slang-based infrastructure code was transpiled to C as part of the build process without developers being aware that Slang was involved. This approach was used by Collins Aerospace engineers to develop experimental versions of the mission control software for the Boeing's CH-47F Chinook military helicopter platform [2]. Nevertheless, the Slang-based workflow described above played a valuable role in system design and prototyping. Often initial system examples were prototyped by the Collins research engineers in Slang, enabling vetting of system message types, prototyping of component functionality. The GUMBO contract-based unit testing/verification and system testing capabilities were in their infant stages on the CASE program, and experience indicated the need for easy-to-use auto-generated infrastructure. This led to the significant development effort for a comprehensive set of contract-based testing and verification capabilities that we build on in this paper.

Although the capabilities presented in this paper emphasize Slang-based development on a JVM platform, the framework's use of HAMR's APIs for the AADL run time should allow the framework to be adapted to C-centric workflows. This will be facilitated by the fact that almost all of the testing infrastructure code is written in Slang which can be transpiled to C and used behind the scenes in C-based workflows.

3 System Testing Framework Overview

HAMR implements a library of threading concepts and RTS for port communication described in the AADL standard and subsequently formalized via an operational semantics in [7,12]. This provides an abstraction layer that helps organize code generation concepts and aids in assuring code generation. A new backend for a different platform is added to HAMR by providing an implementation of the library for the target platform. Support for a new programming language is added by providing an API mapping in the new language to the library APIs. Thus, our design approach for our system testing framework is to avoid references to specific platform or language features, but instead have the framework reference features from the AADL model (e.g., component ports) and the abstraction layer – including making observations on the abstraction notions of port state and thread state (e.g., as formalized in [7,12]) and controlling behavior exploration by advancing execution in increments associated with AADL-standardized notions of thread dispatching.

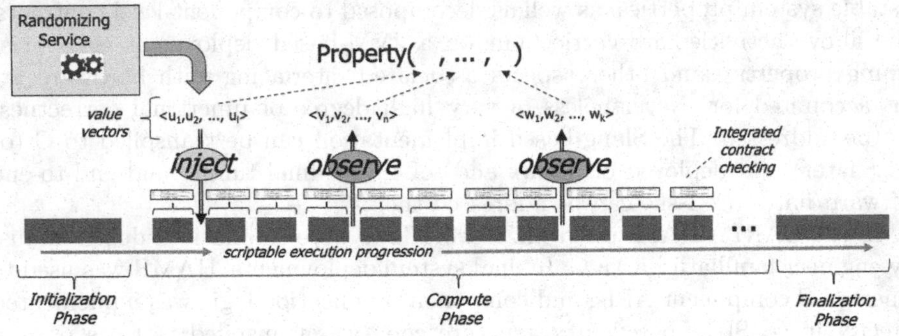

Fig. 1. HAMR System Testing Framework Concepts

Figure 1 presents the primary concepts of the framework. HAMR's infrastructure for static scheduling is extended with APIs that enable the advancing of execution to be controlled programmatically from test scripts – enabling the test engineer to move the system forward through primary phases of AADL run-time execution (e.g., the Initialization) or to step n scheduling slots, or m complete scheduling cycles (hyper-periods), etc. The scheduling control is aligned with the abstract concepts presented in the AADL standard, e.g., each schedule slot step involves a single execution of the AADL run-time service for dispatching a thread component and the dispatch executes the standard-specified thread *compute entry point*. This adherence to the abstract steps in the AADL computational model enables us to preserve the semantics of system properties and testing across deployments on different platforms and languages supported by the HAMR backends. The framework also provides support for making observations about a portion of the system's state. The engineer can declare different observations, where an observation specification includes a named set of ports whose queues/values are to be acquired in a "snapshot". A common example is the set of all output ports for a particular subsystem. For each such declaration, HAMR generates infrastructure for representing a vector of port values along with infrastructure for acquiring an observation vector. Interspersed with execution-stepping commands in the test script are calls to acquire observation vectors for possibly multiply-declared observation types. After all relevant observations have been acquired, code in the test script passes accumulated vectors to a boolean function representing a specific system property. In addition to system properties, the framework can be set to automatically check thread component pre- and post-conditions auto-generated from AADL-level GUMBO contracts.

Injections can also be declared using port set declarations similar to those for observations. A common example is the set of all input ports for a particular subsystem, or a set of ports communicating sensor values acquired from the system environment. In addition to auto-generating value vector types and infrastructure code to set ports to values from a vector, HAMR produces infrastructure code to generate a randomized vector, subject to engineer-configured constraints (e.g., range constraints on scalars). In the test script, these vectors can be acquired/pushed to the associated port set – giving the engineer the ability to force executions to states that are relevant for the property and to control the coverage associated with the tests. This facility enables engineers to flexibly control a variety of inputs to the system (or subsystem), and in many cases alleviates the need to create special-purpose stubs/mocks that generate values flowing into the unit under test.

Test scripts can be run directly in an IDE (in this work, we use the IntelliJ IDE support for Slang) to support interactive development. To provide scalability and to support a continuous integration process, HAMR auto-generates infrastructure for deploying tests in a distributed fashion (e.g., using Jenkins). This infrastructure serializes randomized vectors (supporting easy replay of failing system tests), and uses JaCoCo to provide integrated coverage reports.

4 Example

We illustrate the HAMR system testing framework using the Isolette example from the US Federal Aviation Administration (FAA) Requirements Engineering Management Handbook (REMH) [19]. An Isolette is an infant incubator (medical device), and the REMH presentation focuses on a heat (infant warming) control subsystem and a safety monitoring subsystem. The REMH uses the example to illustrate best practices in requirements engineering for critical embedded systems, and presents detailed requirements at multiple levels of abstraction.

We constructed an AADL model from Isolette design information in the REMH, and used HAMR to develop Slang implementations of the two subsystems. The architecture (directed by the REMH description) emphasizes periodic threads and data ports. The control system and the safety monitoring system include three periodic threads each. An additional periodic thread is used to implement/simulate the operator interface. Slang extensions were used to simulate the temperature sensor and heater components. HAMR generates the JVM deployment of the system (Scala and Java are used to develop the simulated hardware elements and the GUI for the operator interface). There are 11 thread components, 49 component ports, and 27 connections between the ports, with 10612 non-comment/space source lines of Slang/Scala code (NCSLOC) in the infrastructure code and 184 NCSLOC in the application logic. HAMR can also translate the Slang-based application and AADL RTS code for this example (with the exception of the GUI for the operator interface) to C and deploy the final system to Linux and seL4.

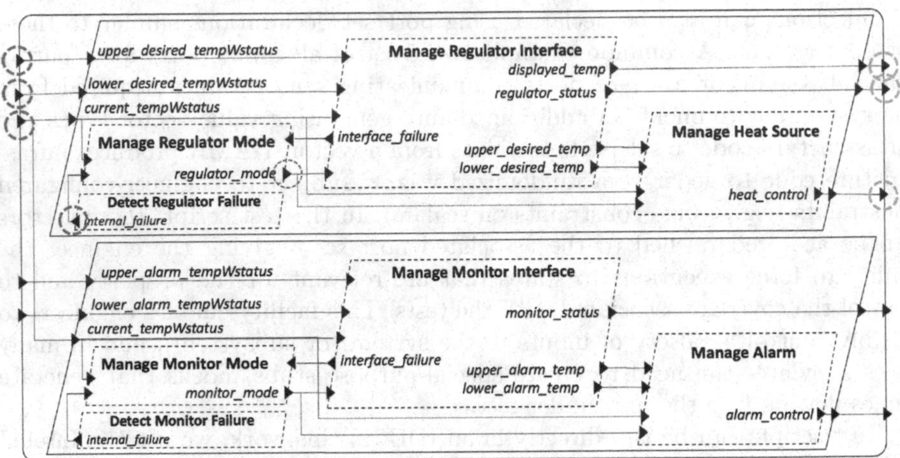

Fig. 2. Isolette - AADL Graphical View of Regulate and Monitor Subsystems

Figure 2 presents the AADL graphical view of the thread components in the Regulate (controller) and Monitor (safety) subsystems.[1]

```
thread Manage_Heat_Source
  features
    current_tempWstatus: in data port TempWstatus.impl;
    lower_desired_temp: in data port Temp.impl;
    upper_desired_temp: in data port Temp.impl;
    regulator_mode: in data port Regulator_Mode;
    heat_control: out data port On_Off;
  properties
    Dispatch_Protocol => Periodic;
    Period => 1000ms;
  annex GUMBO {**
    state
      lastCmd: On_Off;

    initialize
      guarantee REQ_MHS_1 "If the Regulator Mode is
        |INIT, the Heat Control shall be set to Off":
        heat_control == On_Off.Off
          & lastCmd == heat_control;
```

[1] The circle annotations indicate port sets to be declared for injections and observations – to be discussed later.

```
20
21       compute
22         assume lower_is_less_than_upper_temp:
23           lower_desired_temp.value < upper_desired_temp.value;
24         guarantee lastCmd
25           "Set lastCmd to value of output port":
26           lastCmd == heat_control;
27
28         cases
29           case REQ_MHS_1
30             "If the Regulator Mode is INIT, the Heat
31               |Control shall be set to Off.":
32             assume regulator_mode == Regulator_Mode.Init_Regulator_Mode;
33             guarantee heat_control == On_Off.Off;
34           case REQ_MHS_2
35             "If the Regulator Mode is NORMAL and the
36               |Current Temperature is less than the
37               |Lower Desired Temperature, the Heat
38               |Control shall be set to On.":
39             assume regulator_mode == Regulator_Mode.Normal_Regulator_Mode
40               & current_tempWstatus.value < lower_desired_temp.value;
41             guarantee heat_control == On_Off.Onn;
42           case REQ_MHS_3
43             "If the Regulator Mode is NORMAL and the
44               |Current Temperature is greater than
45               |the Upper Desired Temperature, the Heat
46               |Control shall be set to Off.":
47             assume regulator_mode == Regulator_Mode.Normal_Regulator_Mode
48               & current_tempWstatus.value > upper_desired_temp.value;
49               guarantee heat_control == On_Off.Off;
50
51           -- ** remaining two cases omitted **
52     **};
53   end Manage_Heat_Source;
```

Listing 1.1. Manage Heat Source (MHS) AADL

Listing 1.1 provides the AADL textual definition of the Manage Heat Source (MHS) thread interface, including component ports (lines 2–7) and thread properties (lines 8–10). Using AADL's annex mechanism, lines 11–52 provide excerpts of the GUMBO behavioral contract for the component.[2]

```
def timeTriggered(api: Manage_Heat_Source_impl_Operational_Api): Unit = {
  // --------  Auto-generated contract (excerpts) -----------
  Contract(
    Requires(
      // BEGIN COMPUTE REQUIRES timeTriggered
        // assume lower_is_less_than_upper_temp
        api.lower_desired_temp.value < api.upper_desired_temp.value
      // END COMPUTE REQUIRES timeTriggered ),
    Modifies(api,lastCmd),
    Ensures(
      // BEGIN COMPUTE ENSURES timeTriggered
        // guarantee lastCmd
        //   Set lastCmd to value of output port
        lastCmd == api.heat_control,
        // (...other aspect elided...)
        // case REQ_MHS_2
        //   If the Regulator Mode is NORMAL and the
        //   Current Temperature is less than the
```

[2] See [11,13] for a presentation of the full contract and its translation to both a declarative Slang contract as well as executable boolean functions that form oracles for unit testing.

```
19         //   Lower Desired Temperature, the Heat
20         //   Control shall be set to On.
21         (api.regulator_mode == Regulator_Mode.Normal_Regulator_Mode &
22            api.current_tempWstatus.value < api.lower_desired_temp.value)
23              -->: (api.heat_control == On_Off.Onn),
24         // (...other aspects elided)
25       // END COMPUTE ENSURES timeTriggered
26       ))
27   // --------  Developer-supplied application code ----------
28   val lower = api.get_lower_desired_temp().get
29   val upper = api.get_upper_desired_temp().get
30   val regulator_mode = api.get_regulator_mode().get
31   val currentTemp = api.get_current_tempWstatus().get
32
33   var currentCmd = lastCmd
34   regulator_mode match {
35     case Regulator_Mode.Init_Regulator_Mode =>
36       currentCmd = On_Off.Off
37     case Regulator_Mode.Normal_Regulator_Mode =>
38       if (currentTemp.value > upper.value) {
39         currentCmd = On_Off.Off
40       } else if (currentTemp.value < lower.value) {
41         currentCmd = On_Off.Onn }
42     case Regulator_Mode.Failed_Regulator_Mode =>
43       currentCmd = On_Off.Off }
44   api.put_heat_control(currentCmd)
45   lastCmd = currentCmd }
```

One of the significant design aspects of the GUMBO framework involves the combining the many different forms of model-level contracts (including data invariants, integration constraints, entry point contracts, etc.) into code-level contracts appropriate for a code verification or testing tool. In the listing above, lines 3–26 show excerpts of the HAMR auto-generated code-level contract for the Slang MHS thread compute entry point method (named `timeTriggered()`). The general `assume` clause in the GUMBO `compute` block (Listing 1.1, line 22) is translated to a pre-condition in the code-level `Requires(..)` clause (line 7), and the general `guarantee` clause (Listing 1.1, line 24) is translated to a post-condition in the code-level `Ensures(..)` clause (lines 14).

```
object StaticSchedulerCust {
  val maxExecutionTime: Z = 20 // platform clock ticks
  // staticSchedule represents the component dispatch order
  val staticSchedule: DScheduleSpec = DScheduleSpec(0, 0, DSchedule(ISZ(
    Schedule.Slot(0, maxExecutionTime),
    Schedule.Slot(1, maxExecutionTime),
    Schedule.Slot(2, maxExecutionTime),
    Schedule.Slot(3, maxExecutionTime),
    Schedule.Slot(4, maxExecutionTime),
    Schedule.Slot(5, maxExecutionTime),
    // ...(entries 6..10 for monitoring subsystem omitted)
  )))
  val domainToBridgeIdMap: ISZ[art.Art.BridgeId] = {
    ISZ(
      /* domain 0 */ Arch.operator_interface_oip_oit.id,
      /* domain 1 */ Arch.temperature_sensor_cpi_thermostat.id,
      /* domain 2 */ Arch.regulate_temperature_detect_regulator_failure.id,
      /* domain 3 */ Arch.regulate_temperature_manage_regulator_interface.id,
      /* domain 4 */ Arch.regulate_temperature_manage_regulator_mode.id,
      /* domain 5 */ Arch.regulate_temperature_manage_heat_source.id,
      // ... (entries for monitoring subsystem omitted)...
    )
```

```
}
val threadNickNames: Map[String, art.Art.BridgeId] = Map(
  ISZ(
    ...
    "RegMHS" ~> Arch.regulate_temperature_manage_heat_source.id,
    "RegMRM" ~> Arch.regulate_temperature_manage_regulator_mode.id,
    "RegMRI" ~> Arch.regulate_temperature_manage_regulator_interface.id,
    ...
    "HS" ~> Arch.heat_source_cpi_heat_controller.id, )
```

Listing 4 shows excerpts of Slang declarations that specify the static schedule for the system. The structure of these data types was adopted on the DARPA CASE project to enable HAMR to generate a static system schedule utilizing the seL4 domain scheduler. Each entry in `staticSchedule` specifies a schedule slot and includes the domain number (corresponding to the seL4 specified kernel partition) that will be executed during a time slice that will last `maxExecutionTime` platform clock ticks. `domainToBridgeIdMap` associates a scheduling domain to the system identifier of a specific AADL thread component. `threadNickNames` allows developers to specify simple string identifiers that can be used to uniquely refer to a thread id in both HAMR visualizations and logging reports as well as in schedule scripting that we introduce later. The resulting schedule executes operator interface and temperature sensor threads, the four threads from Regulate subsystem, the four threads from the Monitor subsystem, and finally the heat source actuation thread. AADL scheduling tools such as FASTAR [5] can be used to derive a static schedule from timing constraints specified in the system model using standardized AADL properties. Alternatively, developers can provide the data structures above by adapting defaults generated by HAMR.

5 System Test Scripting Framework

5.1 Observations and Injections

System properties are expressed as predicates on vectors of values (snapshots) of selected system features such as ports (indicating *what* is observed) that are acquired at a particular point in execution as defined in the test script (indicating *when* the observation is made). To support the observables described in Sect. 3, the framework enables the engineer to specify a set of ports whose values can be acquired in a single snapshot. For testing properties of the Regulate subsystem in Fig. 2, the initial reaction might be to just observe the subsystem inputs and outputs as present on the outer rounded rectangle. However, the natural language requirements in the original document are conditioned on the subsystem mode (organizing requirements by mode is a common approach) and (for a few requirements) also reference the results of internal hardware error detection performed by Detect Regulator Failure (DRF). Therefore, the mode, as computed Manage Regulator Mode (MRM), and the internal failure status, as computed by DRF, need to be observed as well. The static schedule indicates that the components will be executed in the following order: DRF, Manage Regulator Interface (MRI), MRM, and Manage Heat Source (MHS). This gives a "feed forward" design – moving the conceptual inputs forward to the computation of the output heat control signal.

Due to the implementation of component partition communication in seL4 shared memory slots, the semantics of AADL communication used on the Collins DARPA adopts AADL's `immediate` communication policy in which the outputs produced by a component are immediately propagated to consumer input ports before the next component in the schedule is dispatched.[3] Therefore, it is not necessarily the case that "inputs" of interest can be acquired in a single snapshot (i.e., at a single point in time). However, we will see in Sect. 5.3 that there is a single point in the schedule where a snapshot can be taken of the conceptual inputs marked in dashed red circles in Fig. 2. Based on that port set, HAMR produces the following type declaration for observation vectors for those ports.

```
@datatype class In_Obs_Vector(
    val lowerDesiredTempWStatus: TempWstatus_impl,
    val upperDesiredTempWStatus: TempWstatus_impl,
    val currentTempWStatus: TempWstatus_impl,
    val mode: Regulator_Mode.Type,
    val internalFailure: Failure_Flag_impl)
```

The field types are derived from port types declared in the AADL model using the AADL Data Modeling Annex. An accompanying function is generated to retrieve values from the underlying port representation to populate the vector. This is also more difficult than one would expect because AADL runtime state is strongly aligned with the structure of AADL's *instance model* in which aggregating component types like `system` and `process` are unfolded to get a flattened version of the system containing only thread component instances. Thus, the ports appearing on the subsystem rounded rectangle boundary are "conceptual" (depending on the representation of layout), and generating the observation function needs to trace down and refer to the appropriate thread port physical manifestations of the conceptual subsystem ports.

An observation for output values of heat control, regulator status, and displayed temperature is also defined. A similar process is followed for injections. For the example subsystem, it turns out that we want to inject values into the same port set indicated above, so the vector data types coincide.

5.2 Properties

Properties are currently specified programmatically as boolean functions on observation vectors.[4] The code below realizes the following requirement: "When

[3] Contrast this with AADL's `delayed` communication in which communication is delayed until some temporal boundary, giving the system a Lustre-like synchronous semantics in which all the components can be viewed as advancing in one step.

[4] With the infrastructure presented in this paper in place, some higher-level (more declarative) specification forms based on some form of temporal logic patterns (e.g., [22]) can be incorporated relatively easily because the infrastructure can already produce a stream of observations that can be monitored by an automata representing the temporal logic specification.

in Normal mode and when there are no error conditions, if the current temperature is less than the lower desired temperature, then the heat control shall be activated". The notion of "error conditions" is realized with a helper predicate, which examines internal failure value along with validity status fields on the current temperature, upper/lower desired temperatures.

```
def sysProp_NormalModeHeatOff(
        in_obs:   In_Obs_Vector,
        out_obs: Out_Obs_Vector): B = {
  val triggerCondition = (!RegulatorErrorCondition(in_obs)
     & in_obs.mode == Regulator_Mode.Normal_Regulator_Mode
     & in_obs.currentTempWStatus.value >
          inputs_container.upperDesiredTempWStatus.value)
  val desiredCondition = (out_obs.heat_control == On_Off.Off)
  return (triggerCondition ->: desiredCondition)
}
```

Understanding the temporal notions of the informal requirement is a bit subtle. With AADL's immediate communication, the components do not move forward together in a single conceptual step. So one needs to interpret the requirement stating that if the trigger conditions hold true at point in the schedule immediately before MRI, MRM, and MHS begin their execution (as reflected in the `in_obs` snapshot), then the desired condition will hold at the end of the schedule cycle (reflected in the `out_obs` snapshot). The length of the schedule slots can be analyzed in a separate step to provide a bound on the latency between the acquisition of inputs from the environment the actuation of the heat control.

5.3 Controlled Trace Exploration

The HAMR launcher interface has multiple implementations for launching and executing a HAMR system. We added a new option for this work to provide the *Explorer* framework described here (which is used for simulation, debugging, and testing). The *Explorer* maintains a scheduling state that includes the total number of hyperperiods that have been executed along with the index of the next schedule slot to be executed.

The following commands can be given within an *Explorer* to move execution forward in a controlled way. Sstep(n) advances execution n slots in the schedule (wrapping if necessary). Hstep(n) advances n hyperperiods (schedule cycles) – stopping at the conclusion of the last slot in the schedule on the nth cycle. RunToThread(id) advances through the schedule (wrapping if necessary) until the thread with nickname id is the next to be executed. RunToSlot(n) advances (wrapping if necessary) until the slot with index n is next to be executed. RunToHP(n) advances (wrapping if necessary) until beginning of the nth hyperperiod is reached.

The code below illustrates how the commands above are used in scripts that generate system traces and inject/observe at appropriate points in the schedule.

```
def Regulator_1HP_script_schema(
     in_inj: In_Obs_Vector,
     prop: (In_Obs_Vector, Out_Obs_Vector => B ): B = {
   // Advance past AADL run-time initialization phase
```

```
    Art.initializePhase(scheduler)
    // Advance two schedule cycles
    compute(ISZ(Hstep(2)))
    // Advance up to RegMRI schedule slot
    compute(ISZ(RunToThread("RegMRI")))
    // Inject vector of
    In_Obs_Inject(in_inj)
    // run to end of current hyper-period
    compute(ISZ(Hstep(1)))
    // observe subsystem output
    val out_obs = Out_Obs_Observe()
    // gracefully take system down
    Art.finalizePhase(scheduler)
    // evaluate property on observations
    return prop(in_inj, out_obs)
}
```

This script is schematic in that is parameterized by a property `prop` that references the conceptual subsystem pre-state (`In_Obs_Vector`) and post-state (`In_Obs_Vector`). Almost all of the requirements (16 of 19) for the Regulate subsystem can be tested with this pattern. The script is also parameterized by an injection vector used to force the pre-state port values to specific values (which will be randomly generated by the broader framework). This yields a notion of randomized property-based testing for system tests.

The script causes the run-time to execute the standard-defined *initialization phase* – executing the *initialize entry point* for all threads. In the subsequent *compute phase*, the schedule is advanced two full hyperperiods (this is chosen somewhat arbitrarily to allow aspects of the system state to stabilize) and then run up to the slot for the MRI thread component. At this point, the values from the randomized vector are injected to set the conceptual input state for the subsystem, then execution is advanced to the end of the schedule cycle. At this point, the state of the output ports is collected in `out_obs` and then passed to the property for evaluation.

5.4 Test Run Configuration

Given the artifacts above, a collection of test runs is specified by a list of run configurations. Each configuration has the following structure.

$$(\textit{scriptschema}, \textit{property}, \textit{randomizationprofile}, \textit{randomvectorfilter})$$

The first two items are identifiers for a explorer script schema and a system property as illustrated in Sects. 5.3 and 5.2 above. The framework will run the schema for the given property while generating random values for injection according to the randomization profile. The profile includes configuration information for random value generators for each port data type appearing in the injection vector type(s) associated with the script. Following a common approach in property-based testing, the framework includes libraries of value generators implementing different randomization strategy for each type. The SlangCheck framework [11], automatically generates generator libraries for each base type and developer-defined port type declared in the AADL model (defined using the AADL Data

Modeling Annex). When producing the system testing framework, HAMR automatically generates a vector generator that will be called to produce the vector of random port values. The SlangCheck framework includes configurable range-delimited generators for all base types. We use this facility to easily configure generators to produce values with the numeric ranges specified in the Isolette requirements document. The profile concept enables the developer to assign a name to a specific selection of generator features. The random vector filter is an optional capability that allows the test engineer to easily specify a filter that can establish constraints across the entire randomized vector.

The test configurations can be run within the IDE or launched by a Jenkins-based framework for distributed processing as described in the following section.

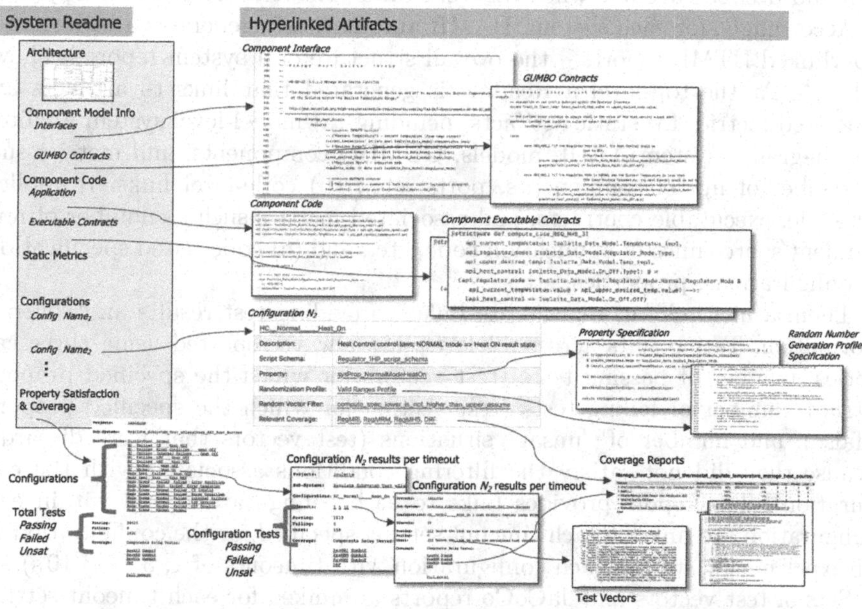

Fig. 3. Overview of Auto-Generated Test Report Structure

6 Auto-generated Test Reports

Significant effort was devoted to building an automated report generation infrastructure to convey the results of distributed testing. The design of the reports was influenced by two goals: (1) provide information that allows developers to understand the results and navigate to supporting evidence, and (2) provide information beyond what a developer would be interested in to help us understand the effectiveness of our proposed techniques.

For the first goal, we want developers to be able to quickly determine if tests are failing and then to be able to replay individual failing tests with the IDE.

When tests are passing, we want them to understand the confidence that should be placed in the tests. Confidence is potentially impacted by several factors including the coverage of application code, the coverage of executable contracts, the number of "effective" tests (i.e., test vectors that were able to pass through the filtering conditions associated with the random number generation). For each of these notions, we want developers to be able to draw conclusions about what happens globally (across all subsystems, components, configurations, and properties) and for specific situations (e.g., effective tests and coverage for a particular configuration/property).

For the second goal, we additionally want to understand the effectiveness of the framework under different time out settings for test vector generation – helping us understand issues such as the run-time necessary to generate effective tests and desired coverage when different randomization profiles were applied.

Accordingly, for each system, HAMR automatically generates a collection of hyperlinked HTML reports – the overall structure of a system report is shown in Fig. 3. At the top-level a Readme is generated that links to artifacts and associated metrics for static artifacts including (a) model-level system architecture diagrams, system AADL models, GUMBO components, and metrics such as number of model components, ports, etc., (b) code-level links to application code, executable contracts, and associated metrics such as number of non-comment source lines of application code, etc., and (c) code-based specifications of configurations, properties, etc.

Then, a hierarchy of reports are linked providing test results and coverage information. Test results across all levels are always reported using three categories: number of passing tests (test vectors for which the specified property is true), number of failing tests (test vectors for which the specified property is false), and number of "unsat" situations (test vectors that were discarded because they did not satisfy the filtering conditions associated with the configuration). The report provides links to each configuration, and within each configuration are links to each timeout setting specified for the configuration (in our experiments, we ran each configuration with timeouts of 1, 5, and 10 s).

Sets of test vectors and JaCoCo reports are linked for each timeout setting. JaCoCo reports are also linked for each configuration (summarizing coverage) across all the timeouts and for each component. The reports show coverage achieved on application code both numerically (e.g., in terms of lines/branches covered) and visually (e.g., showing colored markup of source code lines). This type of coverage information is produced for specific configurations and timeouts as well as globally (e.g., coverage across all configurations and properties).

The reports for the examples in this paper are available at [8].

7 Experience Report

We describe our experience in applying the system testing infrastructure in end-to-end development for several systems.

For the Isolette system (metrics given in Sect. 4), we specified 16 properties for Regulate subsystem and 15 properties for the Monitor subsystem. These properties were checked against randomized vectors of values for all subsystem input ports along with mode and internal failure internal state values.

Temperature Control: This is a "hello world" example used in our HAMR tutorials that includes 4 thread components, 9 thread component ports, and 5 connections between thread ports, with 6410 non-comment/space source lines of Slang/Scala code (NCSLOC) in the infrastructure code and 97 NCSLOC in the application logic. We specified 5 properties for the system, checked against randomized temperature values.

Nuclear Reactor Safety Subsystem: The HARDENS system artifacts [9] were originally developed on a Galois project that aimed to demonstrate end-to-end model-based development technologies and formal methods for the US Nuclear Regulatory Commission. The artifacts included requirements developed according to a rigorous methodology, SysMLv2 system models, application logic written in Galois' Cryptol domain-specific language, and executables derived from the Cryptol tooling (as well as many other artifacts such as assurance cases not relevant to this paper). From these artifacts, we considered the *actuation logic subsystem* (trip signal voting logic) and developed a corresponding AADL model (the Galois SysMLv2 modeling and our AADL model are structurally very similar), contracts in GUMBO, and component implementations in Slang. System deployments where developed for the JVM, Linux, and seL4 microkernel. In this subsystem, there are 15 thread components, 76 thread component ports, and 38 connections between thread ports, with 8847 non-comment/space source lines of Slang/Scala code (NCSLOC) in the infrastructure code and 156 NCSLOC in the application logic. We specified the complete behavior of the actuation system using 11 properties tested using randomized vectors of values for the entire 26 boolean trip signal input ports for the subsystem. One of the properties was a refinement check against a purely functional specification of the entire subsystem voting logic. In this case, the functional specification reflecting the composite reactor trip logic was represented as a side-effect-free boolean function and the function served as oracle that specified the desired relationship between input trip signals at the start of a scheduling and output actuation signals at the end of the frame. No extensions to the base framework were necessary to support this capability.

Experience: The significant amount of auto-generated infrastructure customized to features of the AADL model made activities like adding new injections and observations quite easy. Typically, once input injections and output observations were specified for a subsystem (Sect. 5.1) and an execution script constructed to support property checking of those observations (Sect. 5.3), a new property could be added in a few minutes (e.g., typically less than 10 lines of code for the Isolette properties), and these could be immediately evaluated automatically with hundreds of tests from the randomizing framework. In the Isolette example, a single script encompassing a single scheduling frame for each subsystem was sufficient to support all but 2–3 properties (the remaining properties needed a separate schema because the temporal distance between triggering actions and response actions spanned two scheduling frames). For HARDENS, only one script was needed.

We were interested in understanding if the framework can give high degrees of coverage of the application code in a relatively short time (for interactive use in development) and if tests can be run in a distributed fashion that allows the number of random tests that will be run to be easily scaled. To support this, we developed an HTML-based coverage reporting tool that is able to give precise information about application code coverage for each property (e.g., coverage achieved across all randomized tests for a property). Moreover, data can be combined across all properties/tests to assess the complete coverage. We ran experiments on a simple server configuration of three 8-core Linux Xeon 3.2 GHz 32 GB memory used to generate test vectors and a 8-core M1 Mac Mini with 16 GB memory to execute tests.

To determine effectiveness for different "developer wait times", we ran the automated testing infrastructure for each property using timeouts of 1, 5, and 10 s. Detailed reports (linked from the README files for each system in our examples repository [8]) are provided to the user in the form of passing/failing tests and code coverage. Tests can fail due to violation of system properties or due to contract violations (there are no failing tests in the current state of the repository). These reports also break down tests into those "candidate" test vectors generated according to the randomization profile and the subset of those vectors that were able to satisfy specified filter condition (described in Sect. 5.4) to achieve an "effective test".

For instance, for the Isolette Regulate subsystem property used earlier in the paper 73, 400, 834 effective tests were executed on the server architecture with timeouts of 1, 5, 10 s, respectively. For a HARDENS system property related to temperature trips, 81, 398, and 854 effective tests were executed on the server architecture with timeouts of 1, 5, 10 s, respectively. The number of tests for all other properties is very similar to these examples. Typically, we were able to achieve very high percentage of coverage within the 5 s time out. 100% branch coverage was achieved for the HARDENS system, and for the Isolette all by a tiny number of branches were originally covered, and the remainder can be covered by easily designed custom randomizing profiles that focused value generation of tight ranges of values. Of course, more experience with a variety of systems is needed for a confident assessment.

Because these code bases had been treated extensively before with component contract unit testing and verification, most of the issues that we encountered were related to properties being improperly specified. We did uncover a few integration bugs. In the HARDENS example, an early system test uncovered that a source port was connected to the wrong target port in the AADL model. In another instance in the Isolette, we found that the preconditions on a component contract were not being satisfied. There were several cases where incomplete coverage led us to design additional randomizing profiles for a particular property to drive execution down specific paths.

Needs: It was sometimes hard to tell if properties containing implifications were being satisfied trivially because their "triggering conditions" (antecedents) were never true. What we wished for the most was a tool for collecting detailed coverage information about the boolean subexpressions in each property (similar to MCDC coverage reporting for the property expressions) with special awareness of the implication structure of the property. In addition, when debugging properties on system traces, we lack the ability to easily observe the values in each port in the system and the values of each injection and observation. We have begun prototyping a GUI that enables these other visualizations of the system state.

8 Related Work

There is not a lot of prior work on AADL-related testing. The work that exists tends to focus on test case generation or test design using model-level transition systems. Dong et al. [4] apply Markov chains for testing state machine descriptions in AADL models, Yang [27] generates test cases for achieving branch coverage of behavioral models expressed using AADL's Behavioral Annex (inspired by Extended Finite State Machines); [21]is a similar work that uses an interface automaton formalization of the annex. These works do not connect at all with the underlying semantics of AADL as realized in the AADL run-time services, nor do these connect with executable code or data types beyond simple scalars. Sun et al. [26] use adaptive random testing techniques to generate test vectors for timing properties of AADL flow specifications that have distributions related to common failure patterns. The TASTE analysis and code generation framework for AADL [24] strongly connects to code and real system deployments. It provides a Python-based scripting capability for advancing system execution and querying component state – this is similar in spirit to our test scripting framework described in Sect. 5.3. However, it does not seem to provide support for observations/vector generation, injection of values, aggregate retrieval of observation data, nor facilities for randomized property based testing, and contract checking.

Recent unpublished work describes an industrial framework called Automated Test and Re-Test (ATRT) [16] that enhances AADL modeling and code generation via Ocarina [18] to support system testing and run-time monitoring of system properties based on system events and state changes gathered through telemetry. This has ideas similar to our notion of observers with properties based on observations. A difference is that ATRT seems to be focused more on scalable run-time monitoring instead of the controlled and scriptable execution of (randomized) traces emphasized in our work.

Our work on the GUMBO contract language was inspired by previous work on AADL contract languages AGREE [3] and BLESS [17]. A difference in emphasis is that AGREE and BLESS focus on verification with respect to Lustre-based or state-machine based behaviors, which can be contrasted with GUMBO's emphasis on integrating formal verification and testing with strong connections to conventional source code aligned with AADL threading and run-time services.

NASA's Copilot tool [22] emphasizes observations of system executions, but is more focused on run-time monitoring (it generates C-based monitors) rather than system testing via controlled and randomized generation of execution traces. NASA's FRET framework has been integrated [23] as a layer on top of Copilot to provide a temporal-logic-based formal specification of requirements that reference observed system state and events. Perez et al. showed how FRET/Copilot-monitored systems can be tested by using the QuickCheck property-based testing framework to generate test vectors. The overall spirit of this framework has similarities to our framework – the novelty of our work lies its strong ties to the AADL-support model of computation, generation of observers/injectors for AADL typed component ports, integrated contract checking and the test reporting/distribution framework.

9 Conclusion

We have presented what we believe is a pragmatic and scalable approach to system testing of AADL/HAMR-based systems. Combining this framework with GUMBO-based technologies for unit-level testing and verification of code to contracts gives engineers a suite of formal methods capabilities for assurance. We plan to develop the property coverage and visualization tools described in Sect. 7. We have also developed a SysMLv2 front end for HAMR, and in upcoming DoD projects we will be recasting our assurance framework for SysMLv2 and extending the Slang-based testing and verification capabilities to Rust.

References

1. Belt, J., et al.: Model-driven development for the seL4 microkernel using the HAMR framework. J. Syst. Archit. **134**, 102789 (2022)
2. Cofer, D.D., et al.: Cyberassured systems engineering at scale. IEEE Secur. Priv. **20**(3), 52–64 (2022)
3. Cofer, D.D., Gacek, A., Miller, S.P., Whalen, M.W., LaValley, B., Sha, L.: Compositional verification of architectural models. In: Goodloe, A.E., Person, S. (eds.) NASA Formal Methods. Lecture Notes in Computer Science, vol. 7226, pp. 126–140. Springer, Berlin (2012). https://doi.org/10.1007/978-3-642-28891-3_13
4. Dong, Y.W., Wang, G., Zhao, H.B.: A model-based testing for AADL model of embedded software. In: 2009 Ninth International Conference on Quality Software, pp. 185–190 (2009)
5. Edman, R., Shackleton, H., Shackleton, J., Smith, T., Vestal, S.: A framework for compositional timing analysis of embedded computer systems. In: IEEE International Conference on Embedded Software and Systems (2015)
6. Feiler, P.H., Gluch, D.P.: Model-Based Engineering with AADL: An Introduction to the SAE Architecture Analysis & Design Language. Addison-Wesley, Boston (2013)
7. Hallerstede, S., Hatcliff, J.: A mechanized semantics for component-based systems in the HAMR AADL runtime. In: Camara, J., Jongmans, S.S. (eds.) Formal Aspects of Component Software. Lecture Notes in Computer Science, vol. 14485, pp. 45–64. Springer, Cham (2023). https://doi.org/10.1007/978-3-031-52183-6_3

8. HAMR system testing case studies repository (2023). https://github.com/santoslab/hamr-system-testing-case-studies
9. HARDENS: high assurance rigorous digital engineering for nuclear safety (artifacts repository). https://github.com/GaloisInc/HARDENS
10. Hatcliff, J., Belt, J., Robby, Carpenter, T.: HAMR: an AADL multi-platform code generation toolset. In: Margaria, T., Steffen, B. (eds.) Leveraging Applications of Formal Methods, Verification and Validation. Lecture Notes in Computer Science(), vol. 13036, pp. 274–295. Springer, Cham (2021). https://doi.org/10.1007/978-3-030-89159-6_18
11. Hatcliff, J., Belt, J., Robby, Legg, J., Stewart, D., Carpenter, T.: Automated property-based testing from AADL component contracts. In: Cimatti, A., Titolo, L. (eds.) Formal Methods for Industrial Critical Systems. Lecture Notes in Computer Science, vol. 14290, pp. 131–150. Springer, Cham (2023). https://doi.org/10.1007/978-3-031-43681-9_8
12. Hatcliff, J., Hugues, J., Stewart, D., Wrage, L.: Formalization of the AADL runtime services. In: Margaria, T., Steffen, B. (eds.) Leveraging Applications of Formal Methods, Verification and Validation. Software Engineering. Lecture Notes in Computer Science, vol. 13702. Springer, Cham (2022). https://doi.org/10.1007/978-3-031-19756-7_7
13. Hatcliff, J., Stewart, D., Belt, J., Robby, Schwerdfeger, A.: An AADL contract language supporting integrated model- and code-level verification. In: Proceedings of the 2022 ACM Workshop on High Integrity Language Technology (2022)
14. Hugues, J., Wrage, L., Hatcliff, J., Stewart, D.: Mechanization of a large DSML: an experiment with AADL and Coq. In: 20th ACM-IEEE International Conference on Formal Methods and Models for System Design, MEMOCODE 2022, Shanghai, China, October 13-14, 2022, pp. 1–9. IEEE (2022)
15. Klein, G., et al.: seL4: formal verification of an OS kernel. In: Proceedings of the ACM SIGOPS 22nd Symposium on Operating Systems Principles, pp. 207–220 (2009)
16. Kline, S., Hudak, J., O'Neill, A.: Automated test and re-test for AADL (SBIR project between Innovative Defense Technologies and the Software Engineering Institute) (2022). https://resources.sei.cmu.edu/library/asset-view.cfm?assetid=651952
17. Larson, B., Chalin, P., Hatcliff, J.: BLESS: formal specification and verification of behaviors for embedded systems with software. In: Brat, G., Rungta, N., Venet, A. (eds.) NASA Formal Methods. Lecture Notes in Computer Science, vol. 7871, pp. 276–290. Springer, Berlin (2013). https://doi.org/10.1007/978-3-642-38088-4_19
18. Lasnier, G., Zalila, B., Pautet, L., Hugues, J.: Ocarina: an environment for AADL models analysis and automatic code generation for high integrity applications. In: Kordon, F., Kermarrec, Y. (eds.) Reliable Software Technologies - Ada-Europe 2009. Lecture Notes in Computer Science, vol. 5570, pp. 237–250. Springer, Berlin (2009). https://doi.org/10.1007/978-3-642-01924-1_17
19. Lempia, D., Miller, S.: DOT/FAA/AR-08/32. Requirements engineering management handbook, Federal Aviation Administration (2009)
20. Leroy, X., Blazy, S., Kästner, D., Schommer, B., Pister, M., Ferdinand, C.: CompCert-a formally verified optimizing compiler. In: ERTS 2016: Embedded Real Time Software and Systems, 8th European Congress (2016)
21. Ma, C., Li, Y., Dong, Y., Liu, Y.: Automatic generation of systematic test cases using AADL for embedded software. Int. J. Fut. Comput. Commun. **1**(2), 106–110 (2012)

22. Perez, I., Dedden, F., Goodloe, A.: Copilot 3. Technical Report 20200003164, NASA (2020). https://ntrs.nasa.gov/api/citations/20200003164/downloads/20200003164.pdf
23. Perez, I., Mavridou, A., Pressburger, T., Goodloe, A., Giannakopoulou, D.: Integrating FRET with Copilot: Automated Translation of Natural Language Requirements to Runtime Monitors. Technical Report 20220000049, NASA (2022)
24. Perrotin, M., Conquet, E., Delange, J., Schiele, A., Tsiodras, T.: Taste: a real-time software engineering tool-chain overview, status, and future. In: Ober, I., Ober, I. (eds.) SDL 2011: Integrating System and Software Modeling. Lecture Notes in Computer Science, vol. 7083, pp. 26–37. Springer, Berlin (2012). https://doi.org/10.1007/978-3-642-25264-8_4
25. Robby, Hatcliff, J.: Slang: The Sireum programming language. In: International Symposium on Leveraging Applications of Formal Methods, pp. 253–273 (2021)
26. Sun, B., Dong, Y., Ye, H.: On enhancing adaptive random testing for AADL model. In: 2012 9th International Conference on Ubiquitous Intelligence and Computing and 9th International Conference on Autonomic and Trusted Computing, pp. 455–461. IEEE (2012)
27. Yang, Y.L., Qian, H.B., Li, Y.Z.: Test case automatic generation research based on AADL behavior annex. In: Deng, H., Miao, D., Lei, J., Wang, F.L. (eds.) Artif. Intell. Comput. Intell., pp. 137–145. Springer, Berlin Heidelberg (2011)

Verifying PLC Programs via Monitors: Extending the Integration of FRET and PLCverif

Xaver Fink[1(✉)], Anastasia Mavridou[2], Andreas Katis[2], and Borja Fernández Adiego[1]

[1] European Organization for Nuclear Research (CERN), Geneva, Switzerland
{xaver.eugen.fink,borja.fernandez.adiego}@cern.ch

[2] KBR at NASA Ames Research Center, Moffett Field, CA, USA
{anastasia.mavridou,andreas.katis}@nasa.gov

Abstract. Verification of Programmable Logic Controller (PLC) programs requires reasoning about propositions qualified in terms of time. CERN's PLCverif, an open-source tool for the analysis of safety-critical PLC systems, uses Linear Temporal Logic (LTL) for the specification of properties. Until now, PLCverif depended on third-party tools that accept LTL specifications to perform verification. However, our experience with industrial PLC programs shows that, to overcome analysis limitations, a wide range of techniques are needed to successfully verify complex properties. In this paper, we extend PLCverif to enable PLC program verification of pure-past LTL (PLTL) safety properties with assertion-based verification tools. To this end, we take an algorithm from the runtime-monitoring domain, apply it to bounded model checking of PLC programs, and implement it in PLCverif. We extend the integration of NASA's Formal Requirements Elicitation Tool (FRET) into PLCverif to use PLTL properties generated with FRET. In addition, we leverage the program structure induced by the PLC scan-cycle for a state-space reduction. Finally, we expose the algorithm to a real-world case study of critical systems at CERN.

1 Introduction

Programmable Logic Controllers (PLCs) are heavily used in industrial control systems, even in safety-critical industrial installations, where a failure of the control system may have catastrophic consequences. To minimize risks, functional safety standards like IEC 61508 and IEC 61511 recommend the use of

N. Benz et al. (Eds.): NFM 2024, LNCS 14627, pp. 427–435, 2024.
https://doi.org/10.1007/978-3-031-60698-4_26

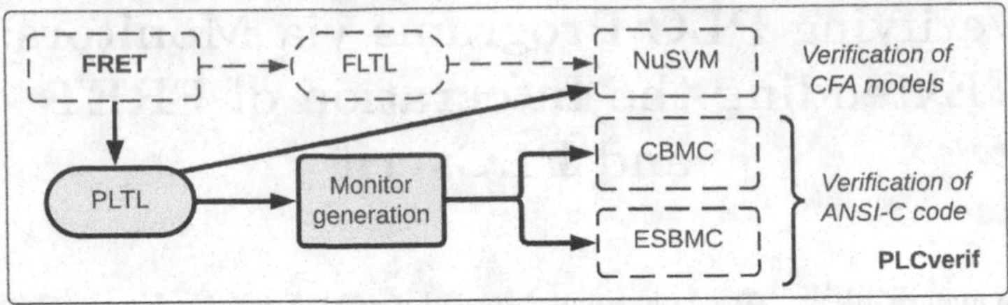

Fig. 1. PLCverif-FRET updated workflow.

formal methods to verify the correct behaviour of safety-critical PLC programs against formally specified *safety properties*. To this end, the PLCverif tool[1], actively developed at CERN, provides a platform for automated verification of PLC code against property specifications, utilizing various third-party verification backends. A critical part of the verification process in PLCverif is the specification of properties. Currently, this can be done either in the form of *boolean assertions* directly in the program code, or *patterns* (i.e., premade LTL templates), or *structured natural language* through the integration with NASA's FRET[2], a formal requirement authoring tool that can express a variety of pure past-time and pure future-time *LTL* formulas [1].

Case studies on industrial programs have shown that ensembles of verification tools enable a greatly improved verification coverage [3,8]. Notably, cutting-edge commercial tools are known to employ a wide variety of verification methods [2]. Employing a diverse portfolio of tools comes with its challenges though, especially with regards to supporting different specification languages. For instance, state-of-the-art formal verification tools for ANSI C programs focus on the support of code assertions and a limited set of LTL properties [3]. Thus, very often such tools are incompatible with properties expressed using the full expressibility of LTL. Related work has focused on bridging this gap, via means of generating assertions from LTL specifications, in the form of *monitors* [6,7].

In this paper, we leverage the monitoring work by Havelund & Roşu [7] to enable the verification of safety PLTL properties on infinite-loop PLC programs. For this, we transform PLTL into ordered monitor assignments over which a Boolean assertion is equivalent to the evaluation of the property on finite traces of the program. The property can then be verified by, the integrated in PLCverif, CBMC and esbmc[3] assertion-based verification tools.

Figure 1 shows the workflow between the FRET and PLCverif tools. The first workflow (FRET to NuSMV[4]), presented in our prior work [1], supports the verification of pure-future LTL (FLTL) properties on control flow automaton (CFA) models generated from PLC code. However, this presents limitations since NuSMV does not natively support the verification of properties over explicit time (only time-steps). To overcome this limitation and also support verification of

[1] PLCverif is publicly available under https://gitlab.com/plcverif-oss.

[2] FRET is publicly available under https://github.com/NASA-SW-VnV/fret.

[3] https://www.cprover.org/cbmc/, http://www.esbmc.org.

[4] https://nuxmv.fbk.eu.

ANSI-C code against LTL properties, the second workflow (bold continuous lines in Fig. 1) represents the contributions of this work, which can be summarized as follows: (1) an extension of [7] with bounded temporal operations and an interpretation of the algorithm for assertion-based Bounded Model Checking (BMC) on PLC programs; (2) an implementation of the algorithm in the open source tool PLCverif, as well as an extension of the existing FRET integration; and (3) a case study of applying the workflow to safety-critical projects at CERN.

2 Preliminaries: PLC Verification and Specification

PLC Program Verification with PLCverif. PLCs are standardized robust industrial systems, performing computations in a well-defined cyclic structure known as *scan cycle*. The scan cycle consists of several phases, but for the purpose of program verification only three are relevant: (1) read and store sensor values, (2) execute the main PLC program and (3) send the calculated values to the actuators. This cycle is repeated continuously until the PLC is stopped. Most PLC safety properties are verified at the end of the scan cycle, since it is the most critical point in the system's execution. PLCverif models the three phases with a *control flow automaton* (CFA), with the end of the scan cycle being represented as a location in the CFA, called *EoC*.

PLC Program Specification with FRET. In this work, we use and extend the PLCverif-FRET integration [1] to allow users to author requirements using the structured natural language of FRET, called FRETISH, which circumvents the need for expertise on writing temporal logic specifications. Once a requirement is written in FRETISH, FRET generates equivalent PLTL and FLTL formulas.

The FRETISH language provides a rich set of features to express temporal and functional constraints. The requirements presented later in this paper exercise the following subset[5]: 1) `condition` is a Boolean expression that either a) Upon keyword: triggers the `response` to occur at the time the expression's value becomes true, or is true at the beginning of the execution trace, or b) Whenever keyword: triggers the `response` to occur every time the expression's value is true 2) `component` is the system component that the requirement is levied upon, 3) `timing` specifies when the response shall happen, and 4) `response` is the Boolean expression that the component's behavior must satisfy.

We also use the `persisted(n, p)` special predicate offered by FRET that describes the persistence of a condition. Here `p` is any Boolean expression, which may include temporal predicates itself. The predicate `persisted` means that `p` has held true for the previous `n` time points, as well as the current time point.

3 Generating Monitors for PLTL Properties

Figure 2 shows the BMC pipeline workflow implemented for this work. The original PLCverif-FRET integration only considered FLTL formulas. As part of this

[5] We exclude FRET's scope field [5] as it is not used in this paper.

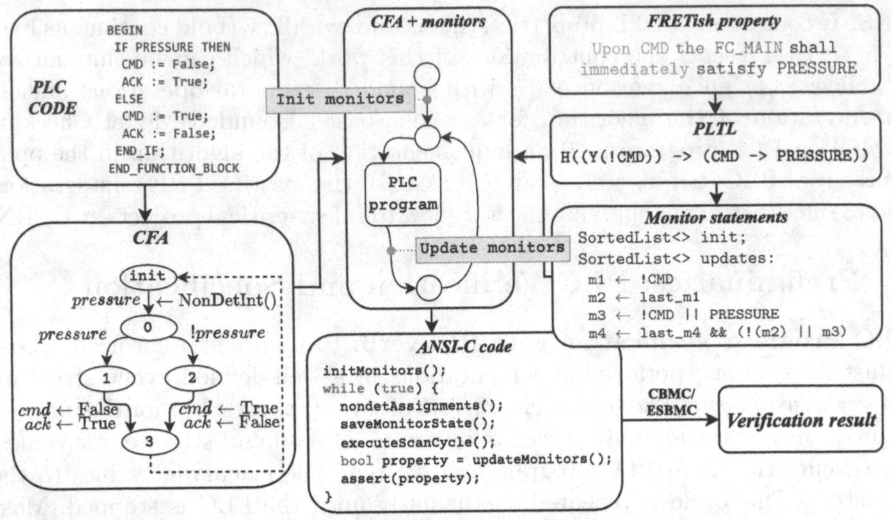

Fig. 2. Verification Pipeline in PLCverif via Monitor Generation.

work, we implemented the appropriate means in PLCverif to retrieve the PLTL variant of a given FRET requirement. For the next step in the pipeline, the generation of monitor statements, we implemented the monitor synthesis algorithm by Havelund & Roşu [7].

The algorithm reduces the verification problem of PLTL to a Boolean query over runtime monitors. Essentially, for each finite unrolling of the model, the acceptance of a PLTL formula only depends on the current and previous variable state, allowing a simple recursive computation procedure.

We chose this algorithm (opposed to other LTL-to-Büchi approaches e.g., [6]) due to its simplicity for implementation and extension to specifics of the PLC-domain. This also extends to the evaluation of the monitors during runtime. For the algorithm by Havelund & Roşu this becomes a simple boolean query which is natively supported by BMC tools for ANSI C programs; monitoring alternatives such as Büchi automata require a more complex decision procedure based on infinite-state visits which was out-of-scope for this study.

In its original version, the algorithm does not provide the capability of monitoring metric properties, such as *"upon a, after two seconds b should hold"*. This is a key requirement for verifying PLC programs that include timer modules. Additionally, while the monitors are trivial to compute, they can add significant overhead to the verification task. Let n be the number of temporal operators in the PLTL formula, and m the number of variable state updates in the model. The algorithm by Havelund and Roşu adds $2 \cdot n$ boolean variables as monitors for the state change between cycles $\{t; t-1\}$, and $2 \cdot n \cdot m$ variable assignments to update the monitor variables after each variable value change. To tackle these problems, we propose two modifications of the algorithm.

Extending the Algorithm to Metric PLTL. To model PLC Timers, we extend the algorithm by Havelund & Roşu with recursive procedures for computing bounded temporal operations by utilizing Integer counters. As an example, the PLTL *"bounded historically"* operation intuitively corresponds to the FRET predicate `persisted(n, p)` with its semantics given by:

$\mathbf{H}[0,n]\,\varphi$ is true at time t if φ holds in all previous time steps $t-n \leq t' \leq t$.

The satisfaction relation can be calculated on the fly via a recursive definition:

$$timer_{n,\varphi} : Trace \rightarrow \mathbb{N}, \pi_i \mapsto \begin{cases} \max(timer_{n,\varphi}(\pi_{i-1}) - 1, 0), & \text{if } \pi_i \models \varphi \\ n, & \text{otherwise} \end{cases}$$

$$\pi_i \models \mathrm{H}[0,n]\,\varphi \text{ iff } \pi_i \models \neg(timer_{n,\varphi}(\pi_i) > 0).$$

Upon violation of φ by trace π_i, a counter variable is activated, blocking the property for n steps. Other metric PLTL operators are similarly derived.

Restricting the value-range of the counters to known regions and the caching of previously computed values improves efficiency.

Overall, this algorithm allows for an elegant implementation and extension to our use case, while staying within the scope of this case study.

Abstracting Over the Scan Cycle. We perform an abstraction over the scan cycle to tackle the high number of added variable assignments by the monitor generation. Instead of updating the monitors after each individual variable-update, the whole cycle is treated as one system-state update-function. This means, that the monitor variables are only updated once at the end of each cycle. Note, that this abstraction requires consideration while formulating the LTL requirements. To give an example, Y φ *("phi holds at the previous state")* on the abstracted state-model, is equivalent to *"φ holds at the end of the previous cycle"* on the original model.

Intuitively, this makes reasoning over cycle-internal properties impossible. To motivate the abstraction withstanding this limitation, consider that almost all PLC safety properties are evaluated at the end of the cycle as explained in Sect. 2. The abstraction reduces the number of added variable assignments from $2 \cdot n \cdot m$ to $2 \cdot n$.

Remark 1. The execution time of the program inside of the scan cycle is bounded by design. This means that if the scan cycle time exceeds the limit, a system failure would stop the PLC and any such program would not pass into production systems. This results in the abstraction having a nice interpretation under BMC of PLC programs. Since only the outermost scan cycle loop has to be unrolled, each unrolling represents a true-prefix of all possible program execution traces.

4 Case Study

This new workflow has been applied to two critical PLC programs at CERN. Table 1 shows the FRETISH requirements and their equivalent PLTL formulas generated by FRET for both PLC programs. Due to their temporal operators all properties were only directly verifiable via NuSMV until now.

ELISA Safety Program. ELISA (**E**xperimental **LI**near accelerator for **S**urface **A**nalysis) is a proton accelerator that will allow CERN visitors to observe a particle beam with their naked eyes and apply Ion Beam Analyses in different fields. The ELISA safety PLC program is in charge of protecting the CERN visitors and the expensive accelerator equipment from the risks related to the high voltage and radio frequency power needed to produce the particle beam. As part of the PLC program design phase, fifteen functional safety requirements were formalized. The verification revealed bugs in the original design (subsequently fixed), as well as inaccuracies in the requirement formalization. For this paper we selected one violated, one satisfied, and one timed property:

- **[EL1]**: a state change for the `RF_CMD` output should only occur when the correct input (`RF_PRESSURE_SWSt`) is given. This requirement was violated due to an incomplete functional safety specification. According to the risk analysis of the ELISA experiment, the proton beam can reduce the levels of O_2 and increase the levels of O_3 in the confined space of the experiment. A software failure related to this requirement could have serious safety implications for the CERN personnel and visitors.
- **[EL2]**: if the operator requests grounding (`OP_RQ`) while no safety condition is triggered (`PS_FarSt` and `VAC_PT06St`), the power supplies should remain ungrounded (`GND_CMD`). This requirement holds.
- **[EL3]**: the system is allowed to be grounded (`!GND_CMD`) only if both power supplies were off (`!EX_CMD` and `!FO_CMD`) for at least t milliseconds. We verified the property for $t \in \{500, 2000, 3000\}$, assuming 100 ms of cycle time. The property holds for the first two cases and a violation is expected for $t = 3000$, as the PLC code TON timer is set to trigger after 2 s.

The UNICOS OnOff Library. The OnOff PLC program is part of the CERN-made UNICOS framework[6] for the development of industrial control applications. This program was analyzed in a previous study by Ádám et al. [1]. It is used in hundreds of industrial installations, which means that a program failure may have enormous economical impact. We present two properties extracted from the functional documentation of the OnOff object. The properties were chosen as they were found to be violated due to correct, yet undocumented, edge case behavior, which until now was only verifiable via NuSMV.

- **[OnOff1]**: while in Manual operation mode (`MMoSt`), a request to move to the Automatic operation mode (`AuAuMoR`) arrives, the OnOff shall be in Automatic operation mode (`AuMoSt`) at the next cycle.
- **[OnOff2]**: if an interlock (`FuStopI`) triggers, the OnOff output (`OutOnOV`) should be in the fail-safe position (`PFsPosOn`) until the interlock is acknowledged (`AuAlAck` or `MAlAckR`).

[6] UNICOS website https://unicos.web.cern.ch.

Table 1. ELISA and UNICOS OnOff requirements in FRETISH and PLTL.

<table>
<tr><th>Req</th><th>FRETish & PLTL</th></tr>
<tr><td>[EL1]</td><td>Upon RF_CMD the FC_MAIN shall immediately satisfy RF_PRESSURE_SWSt
(H ((RF_CMD and (Z (!RF_CMD))) --> RF_PRESSURE_SWSt))</td></tr>
<tr><td>[EL2]</td><td>Upon (OP_RQ & PS_FarSt & VAC_PT06St) the FC_MAIN shall immediately satisfy (GND_CMD)
H ((((OP_RQ and PS_FarSt) and VAC_PT06St) and (Z (!(OP_RQ and PS_FarSt and VAC_PT06St)))) --> GND_CMD)</td></tr>
<tr><td>[EL3]</td><td>Whenever !GND_CMD & !OP_RQ the FC_MAIN shall immediately satisfy persisted(⟨t⟩,!EX_CMD & !FO_CMD)
H (((!GND_CMD) and (!OP_RQ)) --> (H[0,⟨t⟩] ((!EX_CMD) and (!FO_CMD))))</td></tr>
<tr><td>[OnOff1]</td><td>Whenever MMoSt & AuAuMoR the OnOff shall at the next timepoint satisfy AuMoSt
(H ((Y (MMoSt and AuAuMoR)) --> (AuMoSt or (!(Y (TRUE))))))</td></tr>
<tr><td>[OnOff2]</td><td>Upon FuStopI the OnOff shall until (AuAlAck | MAlAckR) satisfy (PFsPosOn -> OutOnOV)
(H ((H (!FuStopI)) or ([(!(AuAlAck or MAlAckR)) S ((!(AuAlAck or MAlAckR)) and (FuStopI and ((Y (!FuStopI)) or (!(Y (TRUE))))))] --> (PFsPosOn --> OutOnOV))))</td></tr>
</table>

Results. Table 2 shows the benchmark results of our monitoring-based technique together with the CBMC/esbmc assertion-based verification tools against the native PLTL verification with NuSMV. The BMC runs were performed with an incrementally increasing unwinding limit; this is natively supported by esbmc and NuSMV, and was implemented via a wrapper-script for CBMC. A time limit of one hour was set for the verification experiments and all the experiments were run on a Lenovo X1 Carbon (7th Gen) with an Intel i5 8365U processor and 16 GB RAM, running on Windows 11. Note, that BDD and k-induction based algorithms are sound and complete. Thus, timeouts of these algorithms on properties with known counterexamples are failures (e.g. [EL1] with the NuSMV BDD algorithm), as the tool failed to find the (existing) counterexample within the time limit (represented as `TO` in Table 2). Conversely, BMC is known to be sound but only complete up to a specified loop-unrolling limit. For benchmarks it is common to utilize unlimited incremental loop-unrolling until either a counterexample is found or the execution times out. Thus, a timeout on properties that are known to be correct should be interpreted as *"correct up to unrolling x"*. Alternatively, the reachability diameter of a program can be computed which acts as an upper bound for the unrolling-limit with which BMC is sound and complete [4].

Two main conclusions can be extracted from Table 2: (1) Overall, our approach shows better results than NuSMV on the OnOff program (a larger program than ELISA), and competitive results on ELISA. We encountered a false-positive

Table 2. Verification results ($\top$: *"property holds"*, $\top^-(n)$: *"holds up to n-th unrolling"*, $-$: *"unknown"*, $\bot$: *"counterexample"*) and time (in seconds) for the ELISA and UNICOS OnOff case studies. [TO]: "timeout"; [$\times$]: "cannot be verified".

		ELISA										**UNICOS OnOff**			
						EL3									
		EL1		*EL2*		$t = 500$		$t = 2000$		$t = 3000$		*OnOff1*		*OnOff2*	
Tool		time	result	time	result	time	result	time	result	time	result	time	result	time	result
CBMC	BMC	3.34	$\bot$	TO	$\top^-(206)$	TO	$\top^-(209)$	TO	$\top^-(194)$	4.74	$\bot$	7.03	$\bot$	25.95	$\bot$
esbmc	k-Ind	1.47	$\bot$	1.42	$\top$	2.23	$\top$	5.64	$\top$	7.74	$\bot$	4.18	$\top$	4.57	$\bot$
	BMC	1.62	$\bot$	TO	$\top^-(810)$	TO	$\top^-(258)$	TO	$\top^-(186)$	5.62	$\bot$	2.78	$\bot$	3.21	$\bot$
NuSMV	BDD	TO	$-$	0.91	$\top$	$\times$		$\times$		$\times$		4.37	$\bot$	TO	$-$
	BMC	1.20	$\bot$	TO	$\top^-(155)$	$\times$		$\times$		$\times$		7.44	$\bot$	42.83	$\bot$

in the k-induction run of esbmc for the [`OnOff1`] property, confirmed by the ESBMC developers[7]. This reinforces the necessity for a portfolio of verification algorithms. (2) Verification of properties using explicit time units (e.g. seconds) is now possible in PLCverif, shown by the fact that some [`EL3`] variants are provable with CBMC/ESBMC, using our monitor-based approach.

5 Conclusion

We presented an implemented extension of the PLCverif-FRET workflow to enable assertion-based verification of PLC programs via monitors of PLTL formulas. Algorithmic adaptations of the monitor generation algorithm to the PLC domain allow the efficient verification of metric PLTL properties. The new workflow was applied to critical PLC programs at CERN and showed that leveraging heterogeneous verification techniques provides stronger analysis capabilities. In the future, we plan to extend this work to finite-trace FLTL monitors.

References

1. Ádám, Z., et al.: From natural language requirements to the verification of programmable logic controllers: integrating FRET into PLCverif. In: Rozier, K.Y., Chaudhuri, S. (eds.) NASA Formal Methods, pp. 353–360. Springer Nature Switzerland, Cham (2023). https://doi.org/10.1007/978-3-031-33170-1_21
2. Afzal, M., et al.: VeriAbs : verification by abstraction and test generation. In: 2019 34th IEEE/ACM International Conference on Automated Software Engineering (ASE), pp. 1138–1141 (2019). https://doi.org/10.1109/ASE.2019.00121
3. Beyer, D.: Progress on software verification: SV-COMP 2022. In: Fisman, D., Rosu, G. (eds.) Tools and Algorithms for the Construction and Analysis of Systems. Lecture Notes in Computer Science, vol. 13244, pp. 375–402. Springer, Cham (2022). https://doi.org/10.1007/978-3-030-99527-0_20

[7] https://github.com/esbmc/esbmc/issues/1735.

4. Biere, A., Cimatti, A., Clarke, E.M., Strichman, O., Zhu, Y.: Bounded model checking. Handb. Satisfiability **185**(99), 457–481 (2009)
5. Giannakopoulou, D., Pressburger, T., Mavridou, A., Schumann, J.: Automated formalization of structured natural language requirements. Inf. Softw. Technol. **137**, 106590 (2021). https://doi.org/10.1016/j.infsof.2021.106590, https://www.sciencedirect.com/science/article/pii/S0950584921000707
6. Havelund, K., Peled, D.: Runtime verification: from propositional to first-order temporal logic. In: Colombo, C., Leucker, M. (eds.) Runtime Verification. Lecture Notes in Computer Science(), vol. 11237, pp. 90–112. Springer, Cham (2018). https://doi.org/10.1007/978-3-030-03769-7_7
7. Havelund, K., Roşu, G.: Synthesizing monitors for safety properties. In: Katoen, J.P., Stevens, P. (eds.) Tools and Algorithms for the Construction and Analysis of Systems. Lecture Notes in Computer Science, vol. 2280, pp. 342–356. Springer, Berlin (2002). https://doi.org/10.1007/3-540-46002-0_24
8. Westhofen, L., Berger, P., Katoen, J.P.: Benchmarking software model checkers on automotive code. In: Lee, R., Jha, S., Mavridou, A., Giannakopoulou, D. (eds.) NASA Formal Methods. LNCS, vol. 12229, pp. 133–150. Springer, Cham (2020). https://doi.org/10.1007/978-3-030-55754-6_8

Author Index

N. Benz et al. (Eds.): NFM 2024, LNCS 14627, pp. 437–438, 2024.
https://doi.org/10.1007/978-3-031-60698-4

Printed in the United States
by Baker & Taylor Publisher Services

Printed in the United States
by Baker & Taylor Publisher Services